8th Workshop on Innovative Use of NLP for Building Educational Applications 2013

Atlanta, Georgia, USA
13 June 2013

ISBN: 978-1-62993-001-5

Printed from e-media with permission by:

Curran Associates, Inc.
57 Morehouse Lane
Red Hook, NY 12571

Some format issues inherent in the e-media version may also appear in this print version.

Printed by Curran Associates, Inc. (2013)

Association for Computational Linguistics
209 N. Eighth Street
Stroudsburg, Pennsylvania 18360

Phone: 1-570-476-8006
Fax: 1-570-476-0860

acl@aclweb.org

Additional copies of this publication are available from:

Curran Associates, Inc.
57 Morehouse Lane
Red Hook, NY 12571 USA
Phone: 845-758-0400
Fax: 845-758-2634
Email: curran@proceedings.com
Web: www.proceedings.com

Preface

Research focusing on natural language processing (NLP) applications for education has continued to progress using innovative statistical and rule-based NLP methods, or most commonly, a combination of the two. NLP-based educational applications continue to develop in order to serve the learning and assessment needs of students, teachers, schools, and testing organizations, often guided by educational policy and learner needs.

The practical need for language-analysis capabilities has been further motivated by increased requirements for state and national assessments, and a growing population of foreign and second language learners. In the United States, the need for applications for language analysis is emphasized by the Common Core State Standards Initiative (Standards), now adopted by 46 States: (http://www.corestandards.org/). The Standards describe what K-12 students should be learning with regard to Reading, Writing, Speaking, Listening, Language, and Media and Technology, and have clear alignments with NLP research and potential applications. Motivated by the Common Core State Standards Initiative, the use of NLP in educational contexts took two major steps forward. First, outside of the computational linguistics community, the Hewlett Foundation reached out to both the public and private sectors and sponsored two competitions: one on automated essay scoring (Automated Student Assessment Prize: ASAP, Phase 1), and a second on short-answer scoring (Phase 2). The motivation driving these competitions was to engage the larger scientific community to harness the collective knowledge toward the development of new ideas and methods. In April 2013, a New York Times article by John Markoff discussed automated essay scoring use by EdX, one of the two competing Massive Online Educational Course (MOOC) companies. Within the computational linguistics community, a breakthrough for educational applications is a new Shared Task co-located with the BEA workshop, NLI-2013, in which the task involves identifying the native language (L1) of a writer based solely on a sample of their writing. Independent of the BEA workshop, there were two additional shared task competitions: the CoNLL Shared Task on Grammatical Error Correction, and a SemEval Shared Task on Student Response Analysis. NAACL and ACL each hosted other education-centered workshops, including the Workshop on Using NLP to Improve Text Accessibility at NAACL, and the 2nd Workshop on Predicting and Improving Text Readability for Target Reader Populations at ACL. Further, a new book, The Handbook of Automated Essay Evaluation (2013) (Eds., Mark Shermis and Jill Burstein) reports on the state-of-the-art in the field, and a Special Issue of the International Journal of Applied Linguistics, Current research in readability and text simplification (forthcoming) (Eds. Thomas François and Delphine Bernhard) calls for new work. The competitions, the recent deployment of automated essay grading in MOOCs, the education-related workshops, and are evidence of the high visibility of Educational Applications in NLP.

As a community, we continue to improve existing capabilities and to identify and generate innovative ways to use NLP in applications for writing, reading, speaking, critical thinking, curriculum development, and assessment. Steady growth in the development of NLP-based applications for education has prompted an increased number of workshops, typically focusing on one specific subfield. In this workshop, we present papers from these subfields: tools for automated scoring of text and speech, dialogue and intelligent tutoring, use of corpora, grammatical error detection, and native language identification. Consistent with 2012, the workshop made an attempt to focus on contributions that could be described in core educational problem spaces, including: development of curriculum and assessment (e.g., applications that help teachers develop reading materials), delivery of curriculum and assessments (e.g., applications where the student receives instruction and interacts with the system), and reporting of assessment outcomes (e.g., automated essay scoring). This workshop is the eighth in a series, specifically related to "Building NLP Applications for Education", that began at NAACL/HLT 2003 (Edmonton), and continued at ACL 2005 (Ann Arbor), ACL/HLT 2008 (Columbus), NAACL/HLT 2009 (Boulder), NAACL/HLT 2010 (Los Angeles), ACL/HLT 2011 (Portland), NAACL/HLT 2012 (Montreal), and now, NAACL/HLT 2013 (Atlanta). This year, the workshop is co-located with the NLI-2013 (Native Language Identification Shared Task) – another indication of how this field is developing.

We received 25 submissions and accepted nine papers as oral presentations and six as poster presentation plus an oral presentation of the summary report for the NLI Shared Task. All of the papers appear in these proceedings. Each paper was reviewed by three members of the Program Committee who were most appropriate for each paper. We continue to have a very strong policy to deal with conflicts of interest. First, we made a concerted effort to not assign papers to reviewers to evaluate if the paper had an author from their institution. Second, with respect to the organizing committee, authors of papers where there was a conflict of interest recused themselves from the discussion.

This workshop offers an opportunity to present and publish work that is highly relevant to NAACL/HLT, but is also highly specialized, and so this workshop is often a more appropriate venue for such work. The Poster session offers more breadth in terms of topics related to NLP and education, and maintains the original concept of a workshop. We believe that the workshop framework designed to introduce work in progress and new ideas needs to be revived, and we hope that we have achieved this with the breadth and variety of research accepted for this workshop. The total number of acceptances represents a 60% acceptance rate across oral and poster presentations.

While the field is growing, we do recognize that there is a core group of institutions and researchers who work in this area. With a higher acceptance rate, we were able to include papers from a wider variety of topics and institutions. The papers accepted to this workshop were selected on the basis of several factors, including the relevance to a core educational problem space, the novelty of the approach or domain, and the strength of the research. The accepted papers fall under several main themes:

Automatic Writing Assessment Measures: Four papers focus on writing assessment and feedback. Östling et al. describe work into automatic scoring of Swedish essays and Andersen et al. describe a system which provides automatic on English learners' writing. Vajjala and Loo describe work into proficiency classification of Estonian language learners, and Madnani et al. describe work into the automatic scoring of a summarization task designed to measure reading comphrension in young students.

Assessing Speech: Four papers focus on different methods of assessing spoken the language of different populations of non-native speakers of English (Xie and Chen; Evanini et al.; Zechner and Wang; Chen).

Grammatical Error Correction: Two papers describe work into the creation of an error-annotated corpus of learner English (Dahlmeier et al.) and the automatic detection of hyphens in learner English (Cahill et al.).

Other Learning Assistance Research: Finally, we have several papers on other topics which use NLP to develop educational applications. Topics include intelligent tutoring (Dzikovska et al.), use of machine translation metrics to rate student translations (Michaud and McCoy), semantic analysis of interactive learner sentences (Levi and Dickinson), dependency annotation in learner writing (Ragheb and Dickinson) and the use of linguistic error codes for identifying neurodevelopmental disorders (Morley et al.).

This year, we are excited to host the first Shared Task in Native Language Identification (http://www.nlisharedtask2013.org/). The task involves automatically predicting the native language of a English language learner based solely on their essay. 29 teams competed and 24 teams submitted descriptions of their submitted systems. These papers are found in these proceedings and are presented as posters in conjunction with the BEA7 poster session. A summary report of the shared task (Tetreault et al.) is also found in the proceedings.

We wish to thank everyone who showed interest and submitted a paper, all of the authors for their contributions, the members of the Program Committee for their thoughtful reviews, and everyone who attended this workshop. The eighth edition of the BEA workshop is notable one as this is the first year that the workshop has sponsors. We would like to thank our four sponsors: Appen Butler-Hill, CTB/McGraw-Hill, Educational Testing Service, and PacificMetrics, whose contributions allowed us to subsidize students at the workshop dinner, and make workshop t-shirts! In addition, we would like to thank Joya Tetreault for creating the t-shirt design.

Joel Tetreault, Nuance Communications, Inc.
Jill Burstein, Educational Testing Service
Claudia Leacock, CTB/McGraw-Hill

Organizers:

Joel Tetreault, Nuance Communications, Inc.
Jill Burstein, Educational Testing Service
Claudia Leacock, CTB McGraw-Hill

Program Committee:

Andrea Abel, EURAC, Italy
Sumit Basu, Microsoft Research, USA
Lee Becker, Avaya Labs, USA
Beata Beigman Klebanov, Educational Testing Service, USA
Delphine Bernhard, Universite de Strasbourg, France
Jared Bernstein, Pearson, USA
Kristy Boyer, North Carolina State University, USA
Chris Brew, Educational Testing Service, USA
Ted Briscoe, University of Cambridge, UK
Chris Brockett, Microsoft, USA
Aoife Cahill, Educational Testing Service, USA
Martin Chodorow, Hunter College, CUNY, USA
Mark Core, USC Institute for Creative Technologies, USA
Daniel Dahlmeier, National University of Singapore, Singapore
Markus Dickinson, Indiana University, USA
Bill Dolan, Microsoft, USA
Myrosia Dzikovska, University of Edinburgh, UK
Keelan Evanini, Educational Testing Service, USA
Michael Flor, Educational Testing Service, USA
Peter Foltz, Pearson Knowledge Technologies, USA
Jennifer Foster, Dublin City University, Ireland
Horacio Franco, SRI, USA
Michael Gamon, Microsoft, USA
Caroline Gasperin, SwiftKey, UK
Kallirroi Georgila, USC Institute for Creative Technologies, USA
Iryna Gurevych, University of Darmstadt, Germany
Kadri Hacioglu, Rosetta Stone, USA
Na-Rae Han, University of Pittsburgh, USA
Trude Heift, Simon Frasier University, Canada
Michael Heilman, Educational Testing Service, USA
Derrick Higgins, Educational Testing Service, USA
Ross Israel, Indiana University, USA
Heng Ji, Queens College, USA
Pamela Jordan, University of Pittsburgh, USA
Ola Knutsson, Stockholm University, Sweden

Mamoru Komachi, Nara Institute of Science and Technology, Japan
John Lee, City University of Hong Kong, China
Jackson Liscombe, Nuance Communications Inc., USA
Diane Litman, University of Pittsburgh, USA
Annie Louis, University of Pennsylvania, USA
Xiaofei Lu, Penn State University, USA
Nitin Madnani, Educational Testing Service, USA
Montse Maritxalar, University of the Basque Country, Spain
James Martin, University of Colorado, USA
Aurélien Max, LIMSI-CNRS, France
Detmar Meurers, University of Tübingen, Germany
Lisa Michaud, Merrimack College, USA
Michael Mohler, University of North Texas, USA
Smaranda Muresan, Rutgers University, USA
Ani Nenkova, University of Pennsylvania, USA
Hwee Tou Ng, National University of Singapore, Singapore
Rodney Nielsen, University of North Texas, USA
Ted Pedersen, University of Minnesota, USA
Bryan Pellom, Rosetta Stone, USA
Heather Pon-Barry, Arizona State University, USA
Patti Price, PPRICE Speech and Language Technology, USA
Andrew Rosenberg, Queens College, CUNY, USA
Mihai Rotaru, TextKernel, The Netherlands
Dan Roth, UIUC, USA
Alla Rozovskaya, UIUC, USA
Izhak Shafran, Oregon Health and Science University, USA
Serge Sharoff, University of Leeds, UK
Richard Sproat, Google, USA
Svetlana Stenchikova, Columbia University, USA
Helmer Strik, Radboud University Nijmegen, The Netherlands
Joseph Tepperman, Rosetta Stone, USA
Nai-Lung Tsao, National Central University, Taiwan
Elena Volodina, University of Gothenburg, Sweden
Monica Ward, Dublin City University, Ireland
Pete Whitelock, Oxford University Press, UK
David Wible, National Central University, Taiwan
Peter Wood, University of Saskatchewan in Saskatoon, Canada
Klaus Zechner, Educational Testing Service, USA
Torsten Zesch, University of Darmstadt, Germany

Table of Contents

Conference Program

Thursday, June 13, 2013

8:45–9:00 Load Presentations

9:00–9:15 Opening Remarks

9:15–9:40 *The Utility of Manual and Automatic Linguistic Error Codes for Identifying Neurodevelopmental Disorders*
Eric Morley, Brian Roark and Jan van Santen

9:40–10:05 *Shallow Semantic Analysis of Interactive Learner Sentences*
Levi King and Markus Dickinson

10:05–10:30 *Building a Large Annotated Corpus of Learner English: The NUS Corpus of Learner English*
Daniel Dahlmeier, Hwee Tou Ng and Siew Mei Wu

10:30–11:00 Break

11:00–11:25 *Developing and testing a self-assessment and tutoring system*
Øistein E. Andersen, Helen Yannakoudakis, Fiona Barker and Tim Parish

11:25–11:45 *Automated Essay Scoring for Swedish*
Robert Östling, André Smolentzov, Björn Tyrefors Hinnerich and Erik Höglin

11:45–12:10 *A Report on the First Native Language Identification Shared Task*
Joel Tetreault, Daniel Blanchard and Aoife Cahill

12:10–1:50 Lunch

1:50–2:40 BEA8 Poster Session A

Applying Unsupervised Learning To Support Vector Space Model Based Speaking Assessment
Lei Chen

Role of Morpho-Syntactic Features in Estonian Proficiency Classification
Sowmya Vajjala and Kaidi Loo

Thursday, June 13, 2013 (continued)

Automated Content Scoring of Spoken Responses in an Assessment for Teachers of English
Klaus Zechner and Xinhao Wang

1:50–2:40 NLI 2013 Poster Session A

Experimental Results on the Native Language Identification Shared Task
Amjad Abu-Jbara, Rahul Jha, Eric Morley and Dragomir Radev

VTEX System Description for the NLI 2013 Shared Task
Vidas Daudaravicius

Feature Space Selection and Combination for Native Language Identification
Cyril Goutte, Serge Léger and Marine Carpuat

Discriminating Non-Native English with 350 Words
John Henderson, Guido Zarrella, Craig Pfeifer and John D. Burger

Maximizing Classification Accuracy in Native Language Identification
Scott Jarvis, Yves Bestgen and Steve Pepper

Recognizing English Learners' Native Language from Their Writings
Baoli LI

NLI Shared Task 2013: MQ Submission
Shervin Malmasi, Sze-Meng Jojo Wong and Mark Dras

NAIST at the NLI 2013 Shared Task
Tomoya Mizumoto, Yuta Hayashibe, Keisuke Sakaguchi, Mamoru Komachi and Yuji Matsumoto

Cognate and Misspelling Features for Natural Language Identification
Garrett Nicolai, Bradley Hauer, Mohammad Salameh, Lei Yao and Grzegorz Kondrak

Exploring Syntactic Representations for Native Language Identification
Ben Swanson

Simple Yet Powerful Native Language Identification on TOEFL11
Ching-Yi Wu, Po-Hsiang Lai, Yang Liu and Vincent Ng

Thursday, June 13, 2013 (continued)

2:40–3:30 BEA8 Poster Session B

Prompt-based Content Scoring for Automated Spoken Language Assessment
Keelan Evanini, Shasha Xie and Klaus Zechner

Automated Scoring of a Summary-Writing Task Designed to Measure Reading Comprehension
Nitin Madnani, Jill Burstein, John Sabatini and Tenaha O'Reilly

Inter-annotator Agreement for Dependency Annotation of Learner Language
Marwa Ragheb and Markus Dickinson

2:40–3:30 NLI 2013 Poster Session B

Native Language Identification with PPM
Victoria Bobicev

Using Other Learner Corpora in the 2013 NLI Shared Task
Julian Brooke and Graeme Hirst

Combining Shallow and Linguistically Motivated Features in Native Language Identification
Serhiy Bykh, Sowmya Vajjala, Julia Krivanek and Detmar Meurers

Linguistic Profiling based on General–purpose Features and Native Language Identification
Andrea Cimino, Felice Dell'Orletta, Giulia Venturi and Simonetta Montemagni

Improving Native Language Identification with TF-IDF Weighting
Binyam Gebrekidan Gebre, Marcos Zampieri, Peter Wittenburg and Tom Heskes

Native Language Identification: a Simple n-gram Based Approach
Binod Gyawali, Gabriela Ramirez and Thamar Solorio

Feature Engineering in the NLI Shared Task 2013: Charles University Submission Report
Barbora Hladka, Martin Holub and Vincent Kriz

Native Language Identification: A Key N-gram Category Approach
Kristopher Kyle, Scott Crossley, Jianmin Dai and Danielle McNamara

Thursday, June 13, 2013 (continued)

	Using N-gram and Word Network Features for Native Language Identification Shibamouli Lahiri and Rada Mihalcea
	LIMSI's participation to the 2013 shared task on Native Language Identification Thomas Lavergne, Gabriel Illouz, Aurélien Max and Ryo Nagata
	Native Language Identification using large scale lexical features André Lynum
	The Story of the Characters, the DNA and the Native Language Marius Popescu and Radu Tudor Ionescu
	Identifying the L1 of non-native writers: the CMU-Haifa system Yulia Tsvetkov, Naama Twitto, Nathan Schneider, Noam Ordan, Manaal Faruqui, Victor Chahuneau, Shuly Wintner and Chris Dyer
3:30–4:00	Break
4:00–4:20	*Evaluating Unsupervised Language Model Adaptation Methods for Speaking Assessment* Shasha Xie and Lei Chen
4:20–4:40	*Improving interpretation robustness in a tutorial dialogue system* Myroslava Dzikovska, Elaine Farrow and Johanna Moore
4:40–5:00	*Detecting Missing Hyphens in Learner Text* Aoife Cahill, Martin Chodorow, Susanne Wolff and Nitin Madnani
5:00–5:20	*Applying Machine Translation Metrics to Student-Written Translations* Lisa Michaud and Patricia Ann McCoy
5:20–5:30	Closing Remarks

The Utility of Manual and Automatic Linguistic Error Codes for Identifying Neurodevelopmental Disorders*

Eric Morley, Brian Roark and Jan van Santen
Center for Spoken Language Understanding, Oregon Health & Science University
morleye@gmail.com, roarkbr@gmail.com, vansantj@ohsu.edu

Abstract

We investigate the utility of linguistic features for automatically differentiating between children with varying combinations of two potentially comorbid neurodevelopmental disorders: autism spectrum disorder and specific language impairment. We find that certain manual codes for linguistic errors are useful for distinguishing between diagnostic groups. We investigate the relationship between coding detail and diagnostic classification performance, and find that a simple coding scheme is of high diagnostic utility. We propose a simple method to automate the pared down coding scheme, and find that these automatic codes are of diagnostic utility.

1 Introduction

In Autism Spectrum Disorders (ASD), language impairments are common, but not universal (American Psychiatric Association, 2000). Whether these language impairments are distinct from those in Specific Language Impairment (SLI) is an unresolved issue (Williams et al., 2008; Kjelgaard and Tager-Flusberg, 2001). Accurate and detailed characterization of these impairments is important not only for resolving this issue, but also for diagnostic practice and remediation.

Language ability is typically assessed with structured instruments ("tests") that elicit brief, easy to score, responses to a sequence of items. For example, the CELF-4 includes nineteen multi-item subtests with tasks such as object naming, word definition, reciting the days of the week, or repeating sentences (Semel et al., 2003). Researchers are beginning to discuss the limits of structured instruments in terms of which language impairments they tap into and how well they do so, and are advocating the potential benefits of *language sample analysis* – analyzing natural language samples – to complement structured assessment, specifically for language assessment in ASD where pragmatic and social communication issues are paramount yet are hard to assess in a conventional test format (e.g. Tager-Flusberg et al. 2009). However, language sample analysis faces two labor-intensive steps: transcription and detailed coding of the transcripts.

To illustrate the latter, consider the Systematic Analysis of Language Transcripts (SALT) (Miller and Chapman, 1985; Miller et al., 2011), which is the de-facto standard choice by clinicians looking to code elicited language samples. SALT comprises a scheme for coding transcripts of recorded speech, together with software that tallies these codes, computes scores describing utterance length and error counts, and compares these scores with normative samples. SALT codes indicate bound morphemes, edits (which are referred to in the clinical literature as 'mazes'), and several types of errors in transcripts of natural language, e.g., omitted or inappropriate words.

Although this has not been formally documented, our experience with SALT coding has shown that the codes vary in terms of: 1) difficulty of manual coding – e.g., relatively subtle pragmatic errors versus overgeneralization or marking bound morphemes;

*This research was supported in part by NIH NIDCD award R01DC012033 and NSF award #0826654. Any opinions, findings, conclusions or recommendations expressed in this publication are those of the authors and do not reflect the views of the NIH or NSF. Thanks to Emily Prud'hommeaux for useful discussion on this topic and help with the data.

2) utility for identifying particular disorders; and 3) difficulty of automating the code. This raises an important question: Is there a combination of codes that jointly discriminate well between relevant diagnostic groups, and at the same time are either easy to code manually or can in principle be automated? This paper explores, first, how well the various manual SALT codes classify certain diagnostic groups; and, second, whether we can automate manual codes that are of diagnostic utility. Our goal is limited: it is not the automation of all SALT codes, but the automation of those that in combination are of high diagnostic utility. Automating all SALT codes is substantially more challenging; yet, we note that even when some of these codes do not aid in classifying groups, they nevertheless may be of importance for developing remediation strategies for individual children. We are particularly interested in the impact of Autism in addition to language impairments for the utility of particular SALT codes.

The diagnostic groups are carefully chosen to be pairwise matched either on language abilities or on autism symptomatology, thus enabling a precise, "surgical" determination of the degrees to which SALT codes reflect language-specific vs. autism-specific factors. Specifically, the groups include children with ASD with language impairment (ALI); ASD with no language impairment (ALN); SLI alone; and typically developing (TD), which is strictly defined to exclude any neurodevelopmental disorder. The TD and ALN groups, as well as the ALI and SLI groups, are matched on language and overall cognitive abilities, while the ALN and ALI groups are matched on autism symptomatology but not on language and overall cognitive abilities; all groups are matched on chronological age.

Regarding our algorithmic approach, we note that automatic detection of relatively subtle errors may be exceedingly difficult, but perhaps such subtle errors are less critical for diagnosis than more obvious ones. Most prior work in grammaticality detection in spoken language has focused on specialized detectors (e.g., Caines and Buttery 2010; Hassanali and Liu 2011), such as mis-use of particular verb constructions rather than coarser detectors for the presence of diverse classes of errors. We demonstrate that these specialized error detectors can break down when confronted with real world dialogue, and that in general, the features in these detectors restricts their utility in detecting other sorts of errors.

We implement a detector to automatically extract coarse SALT codes from an uncoded transcript. This detector only depends upon part of speech tags, as opposed to the parse features that are often used in grammaticality detectors. In most cases, these automatically extracted codes enable us to distinguish between diagnostic groups more effectively than do features that can be extracted trivially from an uncoded transcript.

As far as we know, researchers have not previously considered the utility of grammatical error codes to identify ASD or SLI. Prudhommeaux and Rouhizadeh (2012), however, found that automatically extracted pragmatic features are useful for identifying children with ASD, among children both with and without SLI. Gabani et al. (2009) found that features derived from language models are useful for distinguishing between children with and without a language impairment, both in monolingual English speakers, and in children who are bilingual in English and Spanish.

Improving the characterization of a child's language impairments is a prerequisite to developing a sound plan for language training and education for that child. This paper presents a step in the direction of effective automated analysis of linguistic samples that can provide useful information even in the face of comorbid disorders such as ASD and SLI.

2 Systematic Analysis of Language Transcripts

Here we give an overview of what SALT requires of transcriptions, and of SALT coding. The approach has been in wide use for nearly 30 years (Miller and Chapman, 1985), and now also exists as a software package[1] providing transcription and coding support along with tools for aggregating statistics for manual codes over the annotated corpora and comparing with age norms. The SALT software is not the focus of this investigation, so we do not discuss it further.

2.1 Basic Transcription

We apply the automated methods to what will be called *basic transcripts*. Key for this concept is that, first, these transcripts do not require linguistic expertise and thus can be performed by standard transcription services; and, second, that – as we shall

[1] `http://www.saltsoftware.com/`

see – useful features can be automatically computed from them.

Following the SALT guidelines, a basic transcript should indicate: the speaker of each utterance, partial words (or stuttering), overlapping speech, unintelligible words, and non-speech sounds. It should be verbatim, regardless of whether a child's utterance contains neologisms (novel words) or grammatical errors (for example 'I goed' should be written as such).

A somewhat subtle issue is that SALT prescribes that the basic transcript be broken into *communication units* (which in this paper will be synonymous with *utterance*). Communication units are defined as "a main clause with all its dependent clauses" (Miller et al., 2011). One reason for defining utterance boundaries with communication units, rather than turns or sentences, is that in addition to this being standard practice in language sample analysis, doing so does not reward children for making long, but rather simple statements, nor does it penalize children for being interrupted. To illustrate the first point, the utterance "I like apples, and bananas, and pears, and oranges, and grapes." is one sentence long, but has five communication units (one at each comma). If the sentence were used as the basic unit, the utterance would indicate the same level complexity as the obviously more intricate "for the past three years we have lived in an apartment". In the basic transcript, each communication unit should be terminated by one of the following punctuation marks: '?' if it is a question, '^' if the speaker was interrupted, '>' if the speaker abandoned the utterance, and '.' in all other cases. Thus, the above example would be transcribed as "C: I like apples. ...C: and grapes."

2.2 Markup

There are three broad categories of SALT codes: indicators of 1) certain bound morphemes, 2) *edits* (discussed below), and 3) errors.

Morphology The following inflectional suffixes must be coded according to the SALT guidelines: plural -s (/S), possessive -'s (/Z), possessive plural -s' (/S/Z), past tense -ed (/ED), 3rd person singular -s (/3S), progressive -ing (/ING). The following clitics must also be delimited with a '/', provided the resulting root is unmodified in the surface form: n't, 't, 'd, 're, 's, 've. Since these morphemes are only indicated if the root is unmodified in the surface form, "won't" will remain unsegmented because 'wo' is not the root; "can't" will be segmented "can/'T" and "don't" will be segmented "do/N'T", so as to preserve their respective roots. Nominal or verbal forms with any of the preceding suffixes or clitics are written as the base form with the code appended, for example *hitting → hit/ING*, *bases → base/S*.

Edits Edits consist of filler words such as 'like', 'um' and 'uh', false starts, and revisions. There may be multiple edits in a single utterance, as well as multiple adjacent edits. Edits are indicated by parentheses, for example: "(And they like) and she (like) faint/3S." Note that in the SALT manual, and the language sample analysis literature, edits are referred to as *mazes*. We use the term *edit* here because this is the more widely used term for this phenomenon in natural language processing.

Error codes The exact set of error codes used depends upon the clinician's needs and the errors of interest. Here we consider several key errors outlined in the SALT manual. These error codes and examples are shown in Table 1. Some of these codes describe precise classes of errors, for example [EO] or [OW], but others do not. For example, [EW] can describe using the wrong verb, tense, preposition or pronoun (in terms of case, person or gender), as well as other errors. Note that [EU] (and [EC]) error codes can occur in grammatical utterances. The [EU] code marks utterances that are ungrammatical for reasons not captured by the other error codes, for example severe problems with word order, or utter-

Table 1: SALT error codes and examples

Code	Meaning	Example	Count in Corpus
[EC]	Inappropriate response	Did you help yourself stop? Mom[EC].	9
[EO]	Overgeneralization	Yeah, cuz I almost saw/ED[EO] one.	229
[EW]	Error word	I play/ED of[EW] the cat.	1,456
[EU]	Utterance-level error	You can see it very hard because it/'S under my hair[EU].	532
[EX]	Extraneous word	Would you like to be[EX] fall down?	322
[OM]	Omitted morpheme	The cat eat[OM] fish.	881
[OW]	Omitted word	He [OW] going now.	770

ances which are simply nonsensical, as in Table 1.

3 Evaluation of Manual Codes

In this section we use features extracted from SALT-coded transcripts for classification. We consider two different types of features: baseline features, which are easily derived from a basic transcript; and features derived from SALT codes. We investigate these features to determine which SALT codes are most worth automating for classification.

3.1 Data

Our data is a collection of 144 transcripts of the Autism Diagnostic Observation Schedule (ADOS), which is a semi-structured task that includes an examiner and a child (Lord et al., 2002). *Semi-structured* means that the examiner carries out a sequence of rigorously specified activities, but her prompts and questions are not scripted verbatim for all of them. Detailed guidelines exist for scoring the ADOS, but these are not considered in the current paper. All transcripts have been manually coded with SALT codes, described in Table 1.

Subjects ranged in age between 4 and 8 years and were required to be intelligible, to have a full-scale IQ of greater than 70, and to have a mean length of utterance (MLU) of at least 3. Diagnoses of ASD and of SLI followed standard procedures, and were based on clinical consensus in accordance to diagnostic criteria outlined in the DSM-IV (American Psychiatric Association, 2000). Furthermore, ASD diagnosis required ADOS and Social Communication Questionnaire scores (SCQ) (Berument et al., 1999) to meet conventional thresholds. Diagnosis of SLI required a CELF Core Language Score of at least 1 standard deviation below the mean, in addition to exclusion of ASD.

Children were partitioned into pairs of groups matched on certain key measures. Table 2 shows these pairs and what they were matched on. The individuals were selected from the initial pool of all participants using the algorithm proposed by van Santen et al. (2010), in which, for a given pair of groups, children are iteratively removed from each group until there is no significant difference (at $p < 0.02$) on any measure on which we want the pair to be matched. We combined some groups into composite groups: ASD (ALI and ALN), nASD (SLI and TD), LN ('language normal': ALN and TD), and LI ('language impaired': ALI and SLI).

Group 1		Group 2		
Group	N	Group	N	Matched on
ALI	25	ALN	21	Age, ADOS, SCQ
ALI	24	SLI	19	Age, NVIQ, VIQ
ALN	25	TD	27	Age, NVIQ, VIQ
ASD	48	nASD	61	Age
LN	61	LI	39	Age
SLI	15	TD	38	Age

Table 2: Matched measures for paired groups (ADOS = ADOS score, NVIQ = non-verbal IQ, VIQ = verbal IQ)

3.2 Features

The term "feature" will be used to refer to instances of various classes of SALT codes as well as to instances of other events that can be trivially extracted from the basic transcripts but do not involve SALT codes (e.g, the ratio of 'uh' to 'um'). We distinguish between five levels of features, enumerated in Table 3, that vary in the number and complexity of codes required. This ranges from the baseline features that require no manual codes to SALT-5 features that require full SALT coding. We consider two normalized variants of each feature: one normalized by the number of utterances spoken by the child, and the other normalized by the number of words spoken by the child (except for TKCT). The ratios OCRAT and UMUHRAT are never normalized. Each feature level includes all features on lower levels. Finally, to make our investigation into feature combinations more tractable, we do not consider combining two different normalizations of the same feature.

3.3 Classification

We perform six classification tasks in our investigation, according to the paired groups in Table 2: ALI/ALN; ALI/SLI; ALN/TD; ASD/nASD; LN/LI; and SLI/TD. We extract various features from the ADOS transcripts, and then classify the children in a leave-pair-out (LPO) schema (Cortes et al., 2007) using the scikit logistic regression classifier with default parameters (Pedregosa et al., 2011). For LPO analysis, we iterate over all possible pairs that contain one positive and one negative instance (i.e. children with different diagnoses), training on all other instances, and testing on that pair. We count a trial as a success if the classifier assigns a higher probability of being positive to the positive instance than to the negative instance. We then divide the number of successes by the number of pairs to get an unbiased estimate of the area under the receiver operating curve (AUC) (Airola et al., 2011). AUC is

Group	Feature	Description
Baseline	CEOLP	# of times examiner speaks while child is talking
	ECOLP	# of times child speaks while examiner is talking
	INCCT	Incomplete word count
	OCRAT	Ratio of open- to closed-class words
	TKCT	Token count
	TPCT	Type count
	UMUHRAT	Ratio of 'uh' to 'um'
	UINTCT	Unintelligible word count
SALT-1	All baseline features +	
	MPCT	Morpheme count
	EDITCT	Edit count
SALT-2	All SALT-1 features +	
	NERRUTT	Number of utterances with any SALT error codes
SALT-3	All SALT-2 features +	
	ERRCT	Count of SALT error codes
SALT-4	All SALT-3 features +	
	UTLERRCT	Count of utterance level errors (EC / EU)
	WDLERRCT	Count of word level errors (all other error codes)
SALT-5	All SALT-4 features +	
	XCT	Count of individual error codes (X=EC, EO, ...; see Table 1)

Table 3: Features by Level

the probability that the classifier will assign a higher score to a randomly chosen positive example than to a randomly chosen negative example.

3.4 Determining Relevant Features

We use a t-test based criterion as a simple way to determine which features to investigate for each classification task. For a given classification task, we perform a t-test for independent samples on each feature under both normalization schemes (if appropriate). We retain a feature for investigation if that feature is significantly different between the two groups at the $\alpha = 0.10$ level. If a particular feature varies significantly between groups under both normalization schemes, we retain the version that has the larger T-statistic. For the sake of brevity, we do not report all of the features that varied between groups here, but this data is available upon request from the authors.

3.5 Initial Feature Ablation

We perform feature ablation to see which features are most useful for performing each classification task. Figure 1 shows the maximum performance (in terms of AUC) over all subsets of features at each feature level (on the x-axis) on each of the six diagnostic classification tasks. Missing values for a particular level of features for any comparison indicate that no features in that level that passed the t-test based criterion for the two groups being compared.

Figure 1 illustrates two important points. First, classification difficulty depends heavily on the pair that is being compared. For example, the AUC for ALI/SLI is at most 0.723 (SALT-5), while the AUC for SLI/TD reaches 0.982 (SALT-5). This is not surprising, as some pairs, most notably SLI/TD, differ widely in coarse measures of language ability (such as non-verbal IQ), while other pairs, including ALI/SLI, do not. Second, in many of the tasks, SALT-derived features are of high utility, but the biggest gain in classification performance comes with SALT-2, which is a count of the number of sentences containing any SALT error code. In fact, for all but one classification task (ASD/nASD), the AUC achieved with SALT-2 is at least 96% of the maximum AUC. Furthermore, the best feature set using SALT-2 features for most of these tasks is either the NERRUTT feature alone, or in the case of ALI/SLI, NERRUTT and TPCT. These results lead us to conclude that the most important SALT-derived feature to code is NERRUTT.

Perhaps surprisingly, Figure 1 also shows that for ALN/TD and SLI/TD, performance at SALT-1 is lower than the baseline. There are two reasons for this, which we explain in turn: 1) the SALT-1 feature set must include a feature that is less useful than those in the optimal baseline feature set, and 2) the classifier will not ignore this feature. MPCT must be included in SALT-1 for both pairs, because the only

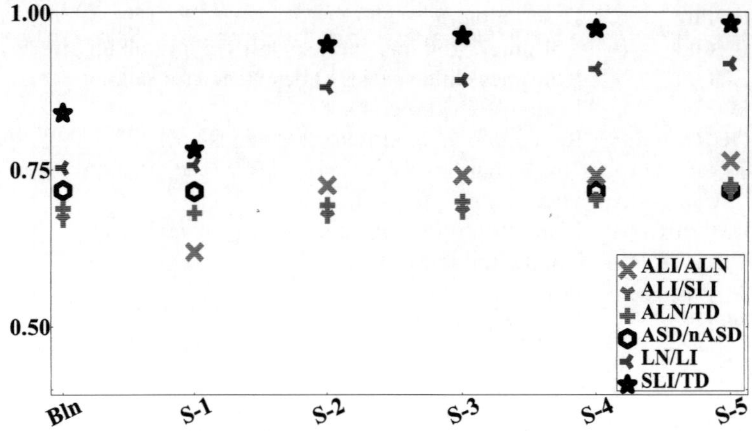

Figure 1: Maximum classification performance (AUC) at different feature levels (Bln=Baseline, S-N=SALT-N)

other SALT-1 feature, EDITCT, does not vary significantly between either ALN/TD or SLI/TD. Furthermore, MPCT is highly correlated with TKCT, yet TKCT is not in the best baseline feature set for either of these pairs. Therefore, the SALT-1 feature set is required to include a feature that is less useful than the most useful ones in the baseline set, which results in lower performance. Once MPCT is included in the SALT-1 feature set, the logistic regression classifier will not ignore it by assigning it a zero coefficient. This is because MPCT distinguishes between groups, and because the classifier is trained at each round of LPO classification to maximize the likelihood of the training data, rather than the AUC estimate provided by LPO classification.

3.6 Counting Specific Error Codes

The single feature in SALT-2, NERRUTT, counts how many utterances spoken by the child contain at least one SALT error code. Some of these heterogenous errors, for example overgeneralization errors ([EO]), should be straightforward to identify automatically. Automatically identifying others, for example utterances that are inappropriate in context ([EC]), would be more difficult. Therefore, before automating the extraction of NERRUTT, we should see which errors most need to be identified, and which can safely be ignored. To do this, we repeat our LPO classification procedure on various tasks using SALT-2 features.

We perform the following procedure to identify the most diagnostically informative errors: for each subset s of SALT error codes, 1) compute the feature NERRUTTSUBSET by counting the number of utterances that contain any of the errors in s; then 2) perform the LPO diagnostic classification task using NERRUTTSUBSET as the only feature. The results of this experiment are in Table 4. The '% Max' column shows classification performance when a particular subset of error codes were counted, relative to the maximum performance yielded by any subset of error codes for that particular task. We exclude the ALN/TD and ASD/nASD tasks from this experiment because NERRUTT does not improve performance on these tasks. This is perhaps unsurprising, because SALT codes were designed to be diagnostic of SLI, not ASD.

We find that in all tasks, ignoring certain error codes raises performance. These results also show that it is not necessary, and indeed not ideal, to identify utterances containing any SALT code. Identifying utterances that contain any of the following three codes is sufficient to achieve at least 97% of the maximum AUC enabled by counting any subset of SALT codes: [EW], [OM], [OW]. For clarity, NERRUTTMOD is the count of utterances that contain any of those three SALT codes.

Table 4: AUC from Counting Subsets of Errors

Classification	Errors Counted	AUC	% Max
ALI/ALN	EW, OM	0.762	100
	EW, OM, OW	0.739	97
	all	0.724	93
ALI/SLI	EW, OM	0.715	100
	EW, OM, OW	0.704	98
	all	0.676	95
LN/LI	EW, OM, OW	0.901	100
	all	0.881	98
SLI/TD	OM, OW	0.984	100
	EW, OM, OW	0.970	99
	all	0.951	97

3.7 Robustness of NERRUTTMOD feature to noise: a simulation experiment

We will consider two general ways of automatically extractingNERRUTTMOD. The first way is to build a detector to identify utterances that contain at least one relevant error. The second way is to make detectors for the each relevant error, then combine the output of these detectors. It is unlikely that any error detector will perform perfectly. Prior to investigation of automation strategies, we would like to get an idea of how much such errors will affect diagnostic classification performance. To this end, we investigate how well we can perform the diagnostic classification tasks when noise is deliberately introduced into the NERRUTTMOD values via simulation.

We consider two scenarios. In the first, we assume a single error detector will be used to extract NERRUTTMOD. We take each manually coded utterance, then randomly change whether or not that sentence is counted as having an error to simulate different precision and recall levels of the automated NERRUTTMOD extractor. We repeat this procedure 100 times for each classification task, and then examine the mean AUC over all trials. In the second scenario, we assume a detector for each error code that counts a sentence as having an error any time one of the detectors fires. We randomly corrupt the detection of each error code considered in NERRUTTMOD in turn to simulate different precision and recall levels of each individual error detector. We assume perfect detection of all errors not being randomly corrupted. Again, we repeat this procedure 100 times for each classification task, and consider the mean AUC over all trials.

In both experiments, and in all classification tasks, we find that the NERRUTTMOD feature is extremely robust to noise. For example, finding the NERRUTTMOD feature with a single detector with a precision/recall of 0.1/0.3 enables SLI/TD classification with an average AUC of 0.975, as compared to the maximum AUC of 0.984, enabled by a perfect detector. When we use a cascaded detector to corrupt each of the two errors counted in NERRUTTMOD for classifying SLI/TD, so long as one error is detected perfectly, the other error only needs to be detected with precision and recall of 0.1 to enable a classification AUC within 0.02 of the maximum.

The extreme robustness of this feature may appear surprising, but it is easily explained by the data. The mean value of NERRUTTMOD for the SLI group is 7.8 times the mean value of this feature for the TD group. So long as there is a correlation between the true value of NERRUTTMOD and the estimated value, as we have assumed in this experiment, then the estimated value is bound to be of utility in classification. This bodes well for the utility of automation, even for a difficult task of discovering some of the relatively subtle errors coded in SALT.

4 Automatic Feature Extraction

4.1 Evaluating Hassanali and Liu's System

Hassanali and Liu developed two grammaticality detectors that they used to identify ungrammatical utterances in transcriptions of speech from children both with and without language impairments (Hassanali and Liu, 2011). They tested their grammaticality detectors on the Paradise corpus, which consists of conversations with children elicited during an investigation of *otitis media*, a hearing disorder. They present both a rule-based and a statistical grammaticality detector. Both detectors consist of sub-detectors for the errors shown in Table 5. The rule-based and statistical detectors perform well, with the statistical detector outperforming the rule-based one (F1=0.967 vs. 0.929). The statistical detector, however, requires each error identified by any of the sub-detectors to be manually identified in the training data.

We reimplement both the rule based and statistical detectors proposed by Hassanali and Liu, and apply it to our data, with three modifications. The first two are minor: 1) we substitute the Charniak-Johnson reranking parser (2005) for Charniak's original parser (Charniak, 2000), and 2) we use the scikit multinomial naive bayes classifier (Pedregosa et al., 2011) instead of the one in WEKA (Hall et al., 2009). The third difference is that we use these detectors to identify SALT error codes rather than the errors these classifiers were originally built to detect. The mapping of the original errors to SALT error codes is given in Table 5. To clarify, if we are training the 'Missing Verb' detector, then any utterance with an [OW] code is taken to be a positive example. This issue does not present itself with the rule-based detector because it is not trained. Note that the two verb agreement features may correspond to either [EW] or [OM] SALT codes. For example, 'you does' would be [EW] because of the otiose 3rd per-

Error	SALT code
Misuse of -ing participle	[EW]
Missing copulae	[OW]
Missing verb	[OW]
Subject-auxilliary agreement	[EW]
Subject-verb agreement	[EW]/[OM]
Missing infinitive 'to'	[OW]

Table 5: Error detectors proposed by Hassanali and Liu

son singular suffix, while 'he do' would be an [OM] because it is missing that same suffix.

Hassanali and Liu's error detectors perform poorly on our data. Table 6 reports the performance of their detectors detecting utterances with various error codes. Five of the six statistical error detectors that Hassanali and Liu proposed are unable to identify any of the errors in our data. The'misuse of -ing participle' detector, however, is an exception, and its performance detecting the analogous error code [EW], using 10-fold cross validation is, shown in Table 6. To detect the two pairs of error codes, [EW][OM] and [OM][OW], and all three relevant error codes ([EW][OM][OW]), we use the appropriate rule based detectors. For example, to detect utterances with either [EW] or [OM] errors, we pool the detectors for the analogous error codes: 'misuse of -ing participle', 'subject-auxilliary agreement', and 'subject-verb agreement'.

There are three factors that may explain the poor performance observed with most of Hassanali and Liu's error detectors when used with our data. The first is that the three SALT codes we try to detect ([EW], [OM], and [OW]) capture a wider variety of errors than the six in Hassanali and Liu's system. This could account for the low recall. Second, there are many utterances in our data that Hassanali and Liu's system would label an error, but which are not marked with any SALT error codes. For example, if the examiner asks the child what she is doing, 'eating spaghetti' is a faultless response, even though it is missing both the subject and auxiliary verb. Such utterances may account for the low precision. Finally, most of Hassanali and Liu's sub-detectors depend upon features describing the presence or absence of specific structures in the parses of the input. The exception to this is the statistical 'misuse of -ing participle' detector, which uses part of speech (POS) tag bigrams and skip bigrams as features. It should come as no surprise then that the 'misuse of -ing participle' is the most robust of these detectors. Indeed,

System	Codes Detected	P	R	F1
Hassanali & Liu	[EW]†	0.074	0.218	0.110
	[EW][OM]*	0.049	0.277	0.083
	[OM][OW]*	0.028	0.191	0.049
	All three*	0.066	0.354	0.111
POS-tag feature-based classifier	[EW]	0.074	0.218	0.110
	[OM]	0.070	0.191	0.103
	[OW]	0.064	0.210	0.099
	[EW][OM]	0.102	0.269	0.148
	[OM][OW]	0.102	0.269	0.148
	All three	0.127	0.308	0.180

Table 6: Performance on automatic detection of utterances with certain error codes using Hassanali and Liu's detectors, and general POS-tag-feature-based classifier. † = 'misuse of -ing participle', statistical; * = rule-based

in what follows, we make use of general POS-tag features (tag n-gram and skip n-grams) as they do in this detector, for a general purpose detector not targeted specifically at this particular construction, but rather to detect the presence of arbitrary given sets of error tags.

4.2 Automatic SALT error code detection

We compare three types of automatic error code detectors: 1) *individual* error code detectors; 2) *pair* detectors, each of which detects a pair of error codes included in NERRUTTMOD, following Table 4; and 3) a *generic* detector that identifies any utterance containing any of the following SALT codes: [EW], [OM], or [OW]. We investigate four different features, all of which are easily derived from the basic transcript: bigrams and skip bigrams of words, and POS tags. We use POS tags extracted from the output of the Charniak-Johnson reranking parser (2005) (also used in our reimplementation of Hassanali and Liu's detectors) for simplicity. We use the Bernoulli Naive Bayes classifier in scikit with the default settings (Pedregosa et al., 2011).

We find that the word features do not aid classification in any condition, and that using both bigrams and skip bigrams of POS tags improves on using either alone. We report the performance of the three types of error detectors in Table 6. These results are from 10-fold cross-validation using POS tag bigrams and skip bigrams as features. Note that the general POS-tag-feature-based classifier uses the same features as Hassanali and Liu's statistical 'misuse of -ing participle' detector, which is why the performance for detecting [EW] error codes alone

	Manual features		Automatic extraction SALT-2 features			
	Baseline	SALT-2	Baseline θ		Optimized θ	
Diagnoses	AUC	AUC	θ	AUC	θ	AUC
ALI/ALN	0.619†	0.723	0.5	0.611	0.94	0.676
ALI/SLI	0.562	0.686	0.5	0.632	0.99	0.671
LN/LI	0.755	0.881	0.5	0.801	0.50	0.801
SLI/TD	0.840	0.951	0.5	0.805	0.99	0.840

† SALT-1; no significantly different baseline features

Table 7: Diagnostic classification AUC using automatically extracted NERRUTTMOD

is identical between the two systems.

The generic error detector yields higher performance than either the individual or pair error detectors. Coding training data for the generic detector is simpler than doing so for the others because it only involves a single round of binary coding.

4.3 Diagnostic Classification

We repeat the LPO diagnostic classification tasks using the automatically extracted NERRUTTMOD feature. We recompute NERRUTTMOD for each speaker at each iteration, training on all data except for the two speakers in the test pair, and the speaker whose NERRUTTMOD feature we are predicting. The results from this task are shown in Table 7.

As can be seen in Table 7, diagnostic classification performance using the automatically extracted the NERRUTTMOD feature is markedly lower than when we extracted this feature from manual codes. However, raising the probability threshold θ at which utterances are counted as containing an error from its default value of 0.5, improves diagnostic classification performance for all but one pair (LN/LI). This is because increasing the probability threshold at which we count an utterance as having an error improves in NERRUTTMOD detection. For example, in the ALI/SLI group, using the default $\theta = 0.5$, and a leave-one-out scenario, we can automatically extract NERRUTTMOD with a precision/recall score of 0.19/0.47. When we increase θ to 0.99, the precision and recall become 0.23/0.24. Even though there is a massive drop in recall, the improvement in precision is able to boost diagnostic classification performance.

In all but one pair (SLI/TD), the automatically extracted NERRUTTMOD feature improves classification over the baseline, even though the NERRUTTMOD extractor performs poorly in terms of intrinsic evaluation, with an F1 score of 0.180. These results are in line with the experiments performing diagnostic classification with an artificially noisy NERRUTTMOD feature (see Section 3.7). These results also demonstrate that the automatically extracted values of NERRUTTMOD are sufficiently correlated with the true values of this feature to be of some diagnostic utility.

5 Conclusions

We have found that the SALT codes provide useful information for distinguishing between certain diagnostic groups, but not all of them. Specifically, and not surprisingly given SALT's focus on language disorders and not generally on atypical language use characteristic of ASD, adding SALT-derived features to baseline features added little to ASD/nASD, ALI/SLI, or ALN/TD classification accuracy, but added substantially to SLI/TD, ALI/ALN, and LN/LI classification accuracy. Furthermore, we found that a simplified coding schema is almost as useful as the complete one for differentiating between these groups. Finally, we have proposed a simple method to automatically extract a variant of the most useful SALT-derived feature, NERRUTTMOD, which is a count of sentences that contain any of three types of errors (omitted morphemes or words, and generic word-level errors). Although this feature's utility degrades when extracted automatically, it still has considerable discriminative value.

In future work, we will investigate the utility of more sophisticated features for extracting NERRUTTMOD and other SALT-derived features. We will also investigate the utility of other linguistic features, for example parse structure, for the diagnostic classification task. Finally, we will also consider whether we can perform the diagnostic classification task more effectively using cascaded binary classifiers (for example language impaired vs. language normal), as opposed to having a classifier for every diagnostic pair.

References

Antti Airola, Tapio Pahikkala, Willem Waegeman, Bernard De Baets, and Tapio Salakoski. 2011. An experimental comparison of cross-validation techniques for estimating the area under the roc curve. *Computational Statistics & Data Analysis*, 55(4):1828–1844.

American Psychiatric Association. 2000. *DSM-IV-TR: Diagnostic and Statistical Manual of Mental Disorders.* American Psychiatric Publishing, Washington, DC, 4th edition.

Sibel Kazak Berument, Michael Rutter, Catherine Lord, Andrew Pickles, and Anthony Bailey. 1999. Autism screening questionnaire: diagnostic validity. *The British Journal of Psychiatry*, 175(5):444–451.

Andrew Caines and Paula Buttery. 2010. You talking to me?: A predictive model for zero auxiliary constructions. In *Proceedings of the 2010 Workshop on NLP and Linguistics: Finding the Common Ground*, pages 43–51. Association for Computational Linguistics.

Eugene Charniak and Mark Johnson. 2005. Coarse-to-fine n-best parsing and maxent discriminative reranking. In *Proceedings of the 43rd Annual Meeting on Association for Computational Linguistics*, pages 173–180. Association for Computational Linguistics.

Eugene Charniak. 2000. A maximum-entropy-inspired parser. In *Proceedings of the 1st North American chapter of the Association for Computational Linguistics conference*, pages 132–139. Morgan Kaufmann Publishers Inc.

Corinna Cortes, Mehryar Mohri, and Ashish Rastogi. 2007. An alternative ranking problem for search engines. In *Proceedings of WEA-2007, LNCS 4525*, pages 1–21. Springer-Verlag.

Keyur Gabani, Melissa Sherman, Thamar Solorio, Yang Liu, Lisa M Bedore, and Elizabeth D Pena. 2009. A corpus-based approach for the prediction of language impairment in monolingual english and spanish-english bilingual children. In *Proceedings of Human Language Technologies: The 2009 Annual Conference of the North American Chapter of the Association for Computational Linguistics*, pages 46–55. Association for Computational Linguistics.

M. Hall, E. Frank, G. Holmes, B. Pfahringer, P. Reutemann, and I.H. Witten. 2009. The weka data mining software: an update. *ACM SIGKDD Explorations Newsletter*, 11(1):10–18.

K. Hassanali and Y. Liu. 2011. Measuring language development in early childhood education: a case study of grammar checking in child language transcripts. In *Proceedings of the 6th Workshop on Innovative Use of NLP for Building Educational Applications*, pages 87–95. Association for Computational Linguistics.

Margaret M Kjelgaard and Helen Tager-Flusberg. 2001. An investigation of language impairment in autism: Implications for genetic subgroups. *Language and cognitive processes*, 16(2-3):287–308.

Catherine Lord, Michael Rutter, PC DiLavore, and Susan Risi. 2002. *Autism diagnostic observation schedule: ADOS.* Western Psychological Services.

J. Miller and R. Chapman. 1985. Systematic analysis of language transcripts. *Madison, WI: Language Analysis Laboratory.*

Jon F. Miller, Karen Andriacchi, and Ann Nockerts. 2011. *Assessing language production using SALT software: A Clinician's Guide to Language Sample Analysis.* SALT Software, LLC.

F. Pedregosa, G. Varoquaux, A. Gramfort, V. Michel, B. Thirion, O. Grisel, M. Blondel, P. Prettenhofer, R. Weiss, V. Dubourg, J. Vanderplas, A. Passos, D. Cournapeau, M. Brucher, M. Perrot, and E. Duchesnay. 2011. Scikit-learn: Machine learning in Python. *Journal of Machine Learning Research*, 12:2825–2830.

Emily Prudhommeaux and Masoud Rouhizadeh. 2012. Automatic detection of pragmatic deficits in children with autism. In *Proceedings of the 3rd Workshop on Child, Computer and Interaction (WOCCI 2012).*

Eleanor Messing Semel, Elisabeth Hemmersam Wiig, and Wayne Secord. 2003. *Clinical evaluation of language fundamentals.* The Psychological Corporation, A Harcourt Assessment Company, Toronto, Canada, fourth edition.

Helen Tager-Flusberg, Sally Rogers, Judith Cooper, Rebecca Landa, Catherine Lord, Rhea Paul, Mabel Rice, Carol Stoel-Gammon, Amy Wetherby, and Paul Yoder. 2009. Defining spoken language benchmarks and selecting measures of expressive language development for young children with autism spectrum disorders. *Journal of Speech, Language and Hearing Research*, 52(3):643.

Jan PH van Santen, Emily T Prud'hommeaux, Lois M Black, and Margaret Mitchell. 2010. Computational prosodic markers for autism. *Autism*, 14(3):215–236.

David Williams, Nicola Botting, and Jill Boucher. 2008. Language in autism and specific language impairment: Where are the links? *Psychological Bulletin*, 134(6):944.

Shallow Semantic Analysis of Interactive Learner Sentences

Levi King
Indiana University
Bloomington, IN USA
levikinq@indiana.edu

Markus Dickinson
Indiana University
Bloomington, IN USA
md7@indiana.edu

Abstract

Focusing on applications for analyzing learner language which evaluate semantic appropriateness and accuracy, we collect data from a task which models some aspects of interaction, namely a picture description task (PDT). We parse responses to the PDT into dependency graphs with an an off-the-shelf parser, then use a decision tree to classify sentences into syntactic types and extract the logical subject, verb, and object, finding 92% accuracy in such extraction. The specific goal in this paper is to examine the challenges involved in extracting these simple semantic representations from interactive learner sentences.

1 Motivation

While there is much current work on analyzing learner language, it usually focuses on grammatical error detection and correction (e.g., Dale et al., 2012) and less on semantic analysis. At the same time, Intelligent Computer-Assisted Language Learning (ICALL) and Intelligent Language Tutoring (ILT) systems (e.g., Heift and Schulze, 2007; Meurers, 2012) also tend to focus more on grammatical feedback. An exception to this rule is *Herr Komissar*, an ILT for German learners that includes rather robust content analysis and sentence generation (DeSmedt, 1995), but this involves a great deal of hand-built tools and does not connect to modern NLP. Some work addresses content assessment for short answer tasks (Meurers et al., 2011), but this is still far from naturalistic, more conversational interactions (though, see Petersen, 2010).

Our overarching goal is to facilitate ILTs and language assessment tools that maximize free interaction, building as much as possible from existing NLP resources. While that goal is in the distant future, the more immediate goal in this paper is to pinpoint the precise challenges which interactive learner sentences present to constructing semantic analyses, even when greatly constrained. We approximate this by collecting data from a task which models some aspects of interaction, namely a picture description task (PDT), parsing it with an off-the-shelf parser, extracting semantic forms, and noting the challenges throughout.

The focus towards interaction is in accord with contemporary theory and research in Second Language Acquisition (SLA) and best practices in second language instruction, which emphasize the limiting of explicit grammar instruction and feedback in favor of an approach that subtly integrates the teaching of form with conversation and task-based learning (Celce-Murcia, 1991, 2002; Larsen-Freeman, 2002). Indeed, Ellis (2006) states, "a traditional approach to teaching grammar based on explicit explanations and drill-like practice is unlikely to result in the acquisition of the implicit knowledge needed for fluent and accurate communication." For our purposes, this means shifting the primary task of an ICALL application from analyzing grammar to evaluating semantic appropriateness and accuracy.

The data for error detection work is ideal for developing systems which provide feedback on essays, but not necessarily for more interactive communication. Thus, our first step is to collect data similar to what we envision processing in something like an

ILT game, data which—as far as we know—does not exist. While we desire relatively free production, there are still constraints; for games, for example, this comes in the form of contextual knowledge (pictures, rules, previous interactions). To get a handle on variability under a set of known constraints and to systematically monitor deviations from target meanings, we select a PDT as a constrained task that still promotes interactive communication. Collecting and analyzing this data is our first major contribution, as described in section 3.

Once we have the data, we can begin to extract semantic forms, and our second major contribution is to outline successes and pitfalls in obtaining shallow semantic forms in interactive learner data, as described in section 4, working from existing tools. Although we observe a lot of grammatical variation, we will demonstrate in section 5 how careful selection of output representations (e.g., the treatment of prepositions) from an off-the-shelf parser and a handful of syntax-to-semantics rules allow us to derive accurate semantic forms for most types of transitive verb constructions in our data. At the same time, we will discuss the difficulties in defining a true gold standard of meanings for such a task. This work paves the way for increasing the range of constructions and further exploring the space between free and constrained productions (see also the discussion in Amaral and Meurers, 2011).

2 Related Work

In terms of our overarching goals of developing an interactive ILT, a number of systems exist (e.g., TAGARELA (Amaral et al., 2011), e-Tutor (Heift and Nicholson, 2001)), but few focus on matching semantic forms. *Herr Komissar* (DeSmedt (1995)) is one counter-example; in this game, learners take on the role of a detective tasked with interviewing suspects and witnesses. The system relies largely on a custom-built database of verb classes and related lexical items. Likewise, Petersen (2010) designed a system to provide feedback on questions in English, extracting meanings from the Collins parser (Collins, 1999). Our work is is in the spirit of his, though our starting point is to collect data of the type of task we aim to analyze, thereby pinpointing how one should begin to build a system.

The basic semantic analysis in this paper parallels work on content assessment (e.g., ETS's c-rater system (Leacock and Chodorow, 2003)). Different from our task, these systems are mostly focused on essay and short answer scoring, though many focus on semantic analysis under restricted conditions. As one example, Meurers et al. (2011) evaluate English language learners' short answers to reading comprehension questions, constrained by the topic at hand. Their approach performs multiple levels of annotation on the reading prompt, including dependency parsing and lexical analysis from WordNet (Fellbaum, 1998), then attempts to align elements of the sentence with those of the (similarly annotated) reading prompt, the question, and target answers to determine whether a response is adequate or what it might be missing. Our scenario is based on images, not text, but our future processing will most likely need to include similar elements, e.g., determining lexical relations from WordNet.

3 Data Collection

The data involved in this study shares much in common with other investigations into semantic analysis of descriptions of images and video, such as the Microsoft Research Video Description Corpus (MSRvid; Chen and Dolan (2011)) and the SemEval-2012 Semantic Textual Similarity (STS) task utilizing MSRvid as training data for assigning similarity scores to pairs of sentences (Agirre et al., 2012). However, because our approach requires both native speaker (NS) and non-native speaker (NNS) responses and necessitates constraining both the form and content of responses, we assembled our own small corpus of NS and NNS responses to a PDT. Research in SLA often relies on the ability of task design to induce particular linguistic behavior (Skehan et al., 1998), and the PDT should induce more interactive behavior. Moreover, the use of the PDT as a reliable language research tool is well-established in areas of study ranging from SLA to Alzheimer's disease (Ellis, 2000; Forbes-McKay and Venneri, 2005).

The NNSs were intermediate and upper-level adult English learners in an intensive English as a Second Language program at Indiana University. We rely on visual stimuli here for a number of reasons. Firstly, computer games tend to be highly visual, so collecting responses to visual prompts is in keeping with the nature of our desired ILT. Secondly, by using images, the information the response should contain is limited to the information contained in the image. Relatedly, particularly simple images should restrict elicited responses to a tight range of expected contents. For this initial experiment, we chose or developed each of the visual stimuli because it presents an event that we believe to be transitive in nature and likely to elicit responses with an unambiguous subject, verb and object, thereby restricting form in addition to content. Finally, this format allows us to investigate pure interlanguage without the influence of verbal prompts and shows learner language in a functional context, modeling real language use.

Response (L1)
He is droning his wife pitcher. (Arabic)
The artist is drawing a pretty women. (Chinese)
The artist is painting a portrait of a lady. (English)
The painter is painting a woman's paint. (Spanish)

Figure 1: Example item and responses

The PDT consists of 10 items (8 line drawings and 2 photographs) intended to elicit a single sentence each; an example is given in Figure 1. Participants were asked to view the image and describe the action, and care was taken to explain to participants that either past or present tense (and simple or progressive aspect) was acceptable. Responses were typed by the participants themselves (without automatic spell checking). To date, we have collected responses from 53 informants (14 NSs, 39 NNSs), for a total of 530 sentences. The distribution of first languages (L1s) is as follows: 14 English, 16 Arabic, 7 Chinese, 2 Japanese, 4 Korean, 1 Kurdish, 1 Polish, 2 Portuguese, and 6 Spanish.

4 Method

We parse a sentence into a dependency representation (section 4.1) and then extract a simple semantic form from this parse (section 4.2), to compare to gold standard semantic forms.

4.1 Obtaining a syntactic form

We start analysis with a dependency parse. Because dependency parsing focuses on labeling dependency relations, rather than constituents or phrase structure, it easily finds the subject, verb and object of a sentence, which can then map to a semantic form (Kübler et al., 2009). Our approach must eventually account for other relations, such as negation and adverbial modification, but at this point, since we focus on transitive verbs, we take an naïve approach in which subject, verb and object are considered sufficient for deciding whether or not a response accurately describes the visual prompt.

We use the Stanford Parser for this task, trained on the Penn Treebank (de Marneffe et al., 2006; Klein and Manning, 2003).[1] Using the parser's options, we set the output to be Stanford typed dependencies, a set of labels for dependency relations. The Stanford parser has a variety of options to choose from for the specific parser ouput, e.g., how one wishes to treat prepositions (de Marneffe and Manning, 2012). We use the `CCPropagatedDependencies / CCprocessed` option to accomplish two things:[2] 1) omit prepositions and conjunctions from the sentence text and instead add the word to the dependency label between content words; and 2) propagate relations across any conjunctions. These decisions are important to consider for any semantically-informed processing of learner language.

[1] `http://nlp.stanford.edu/software/lex-parser.shtml`

[2] `http://nlp.stanford.edu/software/dependencies_manual.pdf`

To see the impetus for removing prepositions, consider the learner response (1), where the preposition *with* is relatively unimportant to collecting the meaning. Additionally, learners often omit, insert, or otherwise use the wrong preposition (Chodorow et al., 2007). The default parser would present a `prep` relation between *played* and *with*, obscuring what the object is; with the options set as above, however, the dependency representation folds the preposition into the label (`prep_with`), instead of keeping it in the parsed string, as shown in Figure 2.

(1) The boy played with a ball.

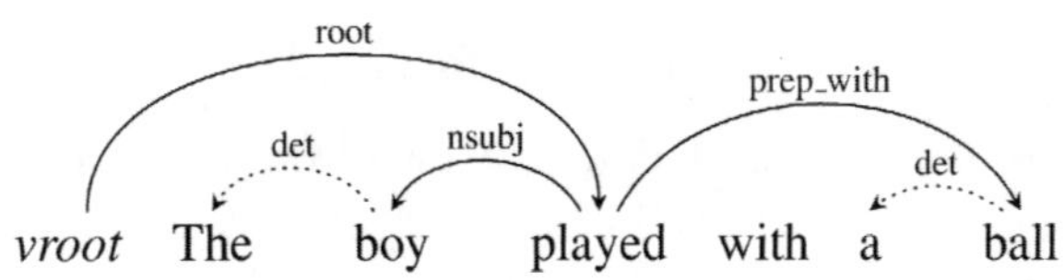

Figure 2: The dependency parse of (1)

This is a very lenient approach to prepositions, as prepositions certainly carry semantic meaning—e.g., *the boy played in a ball* means something quite different than what (1) means. However, because we ultimately compare the meaning to an expected semantic form (e.g., *play(boy,ball)*), it is easier to give the benefit of the doubt. In the future, one may want to consider using a semantic role labeler (e.g., SENNA (Collobert et al., 2011)).

As for propagating relations across conjunctions, this ensures that each main verb connects to its arguments, as needed for a semantic form. For example, in (2), the default parser returns the relation between the first verb of the conjunction structure, *setting* and its subject, *man*, but not between *reading* and *man*. The options we select, however, return an `nsubj` relation between *setting* and *man* and also between *reading* and *man* (similarly for the object, *paper*).

(2) The man is setting and reading the paper.

In addition to these options, many dependency relations are irrelevant for the next step of obtaining a semantic form. For example, we can essentially ignore determiner (`det`) relations between a noun and its determiner, allowing for variability in how a learner produces or does not produce determiners.

4.2 Obtaining a semantic form

4.2.1 Sentence types

We categorized the sentences in the corpus into 12 types, shown in Table 1. We established these types because each type corresponds to a basic sentence structure and thus has consistent syntactic features, leading to predictable patterns in the dependency parses. We discuss the distribution of sentence types in section 5.1.

4.2.2 Rules for sentence types

A sentence type indicates that the logical (i.e., semantic) subject, verb, and object can be found in a particular place in the parse, e.g., under a particular dependency label. For example, for simple transitive sentences of type A, the words labeled `nsubj`, `root`, and `dobj` exactly pinpoint the information we require. Thus, the patterns for extracting semantic information—in the form of *verb(subj,obj)* triples—reference particular Stanford typed dependency labels, part-of-speech (POS) tags, and interactions with word indices.

More complicated sentences or those containing common learner errors (e.g., omission of the copula *be*) require slightly more complicated extraction rules, but, since we examine only transitive verbs at this juncture, these still boil down to identifying the sentence type and extracting the appropriate triple. We do this by arranging a small set of binary features into a decision tree to determine the sentence type, as shown in Figure 3.

To illustrate this process, consider (3). We pass this sentence through the parser to obtain the dependency parse shown in Figure 4. The parsed sentence then moves to the decision tree shown in Figure 3. At the top of the tree, the sentence is checked for an `expl` (expletive) label; having none, it moves rightward to the `nsubjpass` (noun subject, passive) node. Because we find an `nsubjpass` label, the sentence moves leftward to the `agent` node. This label is also found, thereby reaching a terminal node and being labeled as a type F2 sentence.

(3) A bird is shot by a man.

With the sentence now typed as F2, we apply specific F2 extraction rules. The logical subject is taken from under the `agent` label, the verb from

Type	Description	Example	NS	NNS
A	Simple declarative transitive	The boy is kicking the ball.	117	286
B	Simple + preposition	The boy played with a ball.	5	23
C	Missing tensed verb	Girl driving bicycle.	10	44
D	Missing tensed verb + preposition	Boy playing with a ball.	0	1
E	Intransitive (No object)	A woman is cycling.	2	21
F1	Passive	An apple is being cut.	4	2
F2	Passive with agent	A bird is shot by a man.	0	6
Ax	Existential version of A or C	There is a boy kicking a ball.	0	0
Bx	Existential version of B or D	There was a boy playing with a ball.	0	0
Ex	Existential version of E	There is a woman cycling.	0	0
F1x	Existential version of F1	There is an apple being cut.	0	1
F2x	Existential version of F2	There is a bird being shot by a man.	0	0
Z	All other forms	The man is trying to hunt a bird.	2	6

Table 1: Sentence type examples, with distributions of types for native speakers (NS) and non-native speakers (NNS)

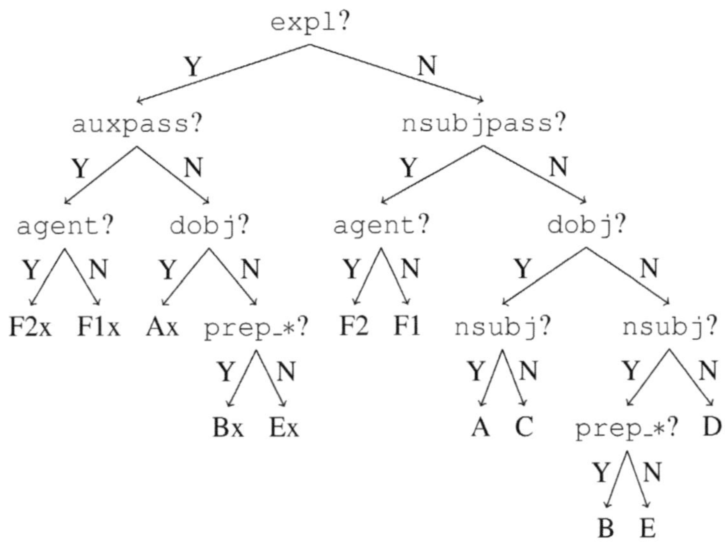

Figure 3: Decision tree for determining sentence type and extracting semantic information

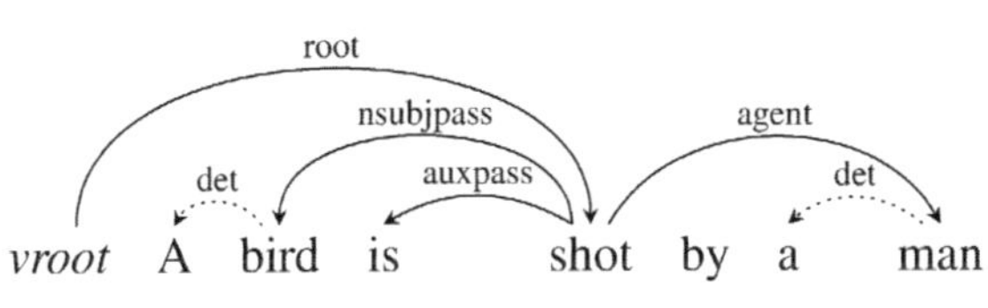

Figure 4: The dependency parse of (3)

root, and the logical object from nsubjpass, to obtain *shot(man,bird)*, which can be lemmatized to *shoot(man,bird)*. Very little effort goes into this process: the parser is pre-built; the decision tree is small; and the extraction rules are minimal.

We are able to use little effort in part due to the constraints in the pictures. For figure 1, for example, *the artist*, *the man in the beret*, and *the man* are all acceptable subjects, whereas if there were multiple men in the picture, *the man* would not be specific enough. In future work, we expect to relax such constraints on image contents by including rules to handle relative clauses, adjectives and other modifiers in order to distinguish between references to similar elements, e.g., *a man shooting a bird* vs. *a man reading the newspaper*.

5 Evaluation

To evaluate this work, we need to address two major questions. First, how accurately do we extract semantic information from potentially innovative sentences (section 5.2)? Due to the simple structures of the sentences (section 5.1), we find high accuracy with our simple system. Secondly, how many semantic forms does one need in order to capture the variability in meaning in learner sentences (section 5.3)? We operationalize this second question by asking how well the set of native speaker semantic forms models a gold standard, with the intuition that a language is defined by native speaker usage, so their answers can serve as targets. As we will see, this is a naïve view.

5.1 Basic distribution of sentences

Before a more thorough analysis, we look at the distribution of sentence types, shown in Table 1, broken down between native speakers (NSs) and non-native speakers (NNSs). A few sentence types clearly dominate here: if one looks only at simple declaratives, with or without a main verb (types A and C), one accounts for 90.7% of the NS forms and 84.6% of the NNS ones, slightly less. Adding prepositional forms (types B and D) brings the total to 94.3% and 90.8%, respectively. Although there will always be variability and novel forms (cf. type Z), this shows that, for situations with basic transitive actions, developing a system (by hand) for a few sentence types is manageable. More broadly, we see that clear and simple images nicely constrain the task to the point where shallow processing is feasible.

5.2 Semantic extraction

For the purpose of evaluating our extraction system, we define two major classes of errors. The first are *triple errors*, responses for which our system fails to extract one or more of the desired subject, verb, or object, based on the sentence at hand and without regard to the target content. Second are *content errors*, responses for which our system extracts the desired subject, verb and object, but the resulting triple does not accurately describe the image (i.e., is an error of the participant's). We are of course concerned with reducing the triple errors. Examples are in Table 2.

Triple errors are subcategorized as *speaker*, *parser*, or *extraction* errors, based on the earliest part of the process that led to the error. Speaker errors typically involve misspellings in the original sentence, leading to an incorrect POS tag and parse. Parser errors involve a correct sentence parsed incorrectly or in such a way as to indicate a different meaning from the one intended; an example is given in Figure 5. Extraction errors involve a failure of the extraction script to find one or more of the desired subject, verb or object in a correct sentence. These typically involve more complex sentence structures such as conjoined or embedded clauses.

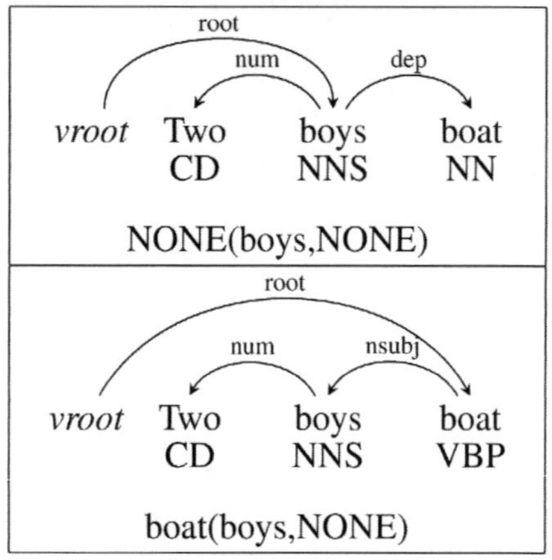

Figure 5: A parser error leading to a triple error (top), and the desired parse and triple (bottom).

As shown in table 2, we obtain 92.3% accuracy on extraction for NNS data and roughly the same for NS data, 92.9%. However, many of the errors for NNSs involve misspellings, while for NSs a higher percentage of the extraction errors stem only from our hand-written extractor, due to native speakers using more complex structures. For a system interacting with learners, spelling errors are thus more of a priority (cf. Hovermale, 2008).

Content errors are subcategorized as *spelling* or *meaning* errors. Spelling errors involve one or more of the extracted subject, verb or object being misspelled severely enough that the intended spelling cannot be discerned. A spelling error here is unlike those included in *speaker* errors above in that it does not result in downstream errors and is a well-

		Error type	Example Sentence	Triple	Count (%)
Triple error	NNS	Speaker	A man swipped leaves.	leaves(swipped,man)	16 (4.1%)
		Parser	Two boys boat.	NONE(boys,NONE)	5 (1.3%)
		Extraction	A man is gathering lots of leafs.	gathering(man,lots)	9 (2.3%)
		Total (390)			**30 (7.7%)**
	NS	Speaker	*(None)*		0 (0%)
		Parser	An old man raking leaves on a path.	leaves(man,path)	2 (1.4%)
		Extraction	A man has shot a bird that is falling from the sky.	shot(bird,sky)	8 (5.7%)
		Total (140)			**10 (7.1%)**
Content error	NNS	Spelling	The artiest is drawing a portret.	drawing(artiest,portret)	36 (9.2%)
		Meaning	The woman is making her laundry.	making(woman,laundry)	23 (5.9%)
		Total (390)			**59 (15.1%)**
	NS	Spelling	*(None)*		0 (0%)
		Meaning	A picture is being taken of a girl on a bike.	taken(NONE,picture)	3 (2.1%)
		Total (140)			**3 (2.1%)**

Table 2: Triple errors and content errors by subcategory, with error rates reported (e.g., 7.7% error = 92.3% accuracy)

formed triple except for a misspelled target word. Meaning errors involve an inaccurate word within the triple. This includes misspellings that result in a real but unintended word (e.g., *shout(man,bird)* instead of *shoot(man,bird)*).

The goal of a system is to identify the 15.1% of NNS sentences which are content errors, in order to provide feedback. Currently, the 7.7% triple errors would also be grouped into this set, showing the need for further extraction improvements. Also notable is that three content errors were encountered among the NS responses. All three were meaning errors involving some meta-description of the image prompt rather than a direct description of the image contents, e.g., *A picture is being taken of a girl on a bike* vs. *A girl is riding a bike.*

5.3 Semantic coverage

Given a fairly accurate extraction system, as reported above, we now turn to evaluating how well a gold standard represents unseen data, in terms of semantic matching. To measure coverage, we take the intuition that a language is defined by native speaker usage, so their answers can serve as targets, and use NS triples as our gold standard. The set of NS responses was manually arbitrated to remove any unacceptable triples (both *triple* and *content* errors), and the remaining set of lemmatized triples was taken as a gold standard set for each item.

Similarly, with the focus on coverage, the NNS triples were amended to remove any triple errors. From the remaining NNS triples, we call an appropriate NNS triple found in the gold standard set a **true positive (TP)** (i.e., a correct match), and an appropriate NNS triple *not found* in the gold standard set a **false negative (FN)** (i.e., an incorrect non-match), as shown in Table 4. We adopt standard terminology here (TP, FN), but note that we are investigating what *should be* in the gold standard, making these false negatives and not false positives. To address the question of how many (NS) sentences we need to obtain good coverage, we define **coverage** (=recall) as *TP/(TP+FN)*, and report, in Table 3, 23.5% coverage for unique triple types and 50.8% coverage for triple tokens.

		NNS +	NNS −
NS	Y	TP	FP
	N	FN	TN

Table 4: Contingency table comparing presence of NS forms (Y/N) with correctness (+/−) of NNS forms

We define an inappropriate NNS triple (i.e., a content error) *not found* in the gold standard set as a **true**

Item	NS	NNS	TP	TN	FN	Coverage Ty.	Coverage Tok.	Accuracy Ty.	Accuracy Tok.
1	5	14	3	2	9	3/12	23/38	5/14	25/39
2	6	14	3	5	6	3/9	15/28	8/14	20/32
3	6	19	5	7	7	5/12	23/30	12/19	30/36
4	4	8	2	2	4	2/6	32/37	4/8	34/39
5	4	24	1	8	15	1/16	3/25	9/24	11/33
6	8	22	3	5	14	3/17	16/31	8/22	21/36
7	7	23	5	4	14	5/19	14/35	9/23	18/39
8	6	23	5	6	11	5/16	10/30	11/22	17/36
9	7	33	3	12	18	3/21	3/23	15/33	15/35
10	5	21	2	13	6	2/8	14/24	15/21	27/35
Total	58	201	32	64	104	32/136 23.5%	153/301 50.8%	96/200 48.0%	218/360 60.6%

Table 3: Matching of semantic triples: *NS*/*NNS*: number of unique triples for NSs/NNSs. Comparing NNS types to NS triples, *TP*: number of true positives (types); *TN*: number of true negatives; *FN*: number of false negatives. *Coverage* for *Ty*pes and *Tok*ens = $\frac{TP}{TP+FN}$; *Accuracy* for *Ty*pes and *Tok*ens = $\frac{TP+TN}{TP+TN+FN}$

negative (TN) (i.e., a correct non-match). **Accuracy** based on this gold standard—assuming perfect extraction—is defined as *(TP+TN)/(TP+TN+FN)*.[3] We report 48.0% accuracy for types and 60.6% accuracy for tokens.

The immediate lesson here is: NS data alone may not make a sufficient gold standard, in that many correct NNS answers are not counted as correct. However, there are a couple of issues to consider here.

First, we require exact matching of triples. If maximizing coverage is desired, extracting individual subjects, verbs and objects from NS triples and recombining them into the various possible *verb(subj,obj)* combinations would lead to a sizable improvement. An example of triples distribution and coverage for a single item, along with this recombination approach is presented in Table 5.

It should be noted, however, that automating this recombination without lexical knowledge could lead to the presence of unwanted triples in the gold standard set. Consider, for example, *do(woman,shirt)*—an incorrect triple derived from the correct NS triples, *wash(woman,shirt)* and *do(woman,laundry)*. In addition to handling pro-

Type	NNS	NS	Coverage
cut(woman,apple)	*5*	*0*	*(5)*
cut(someone,apple)	4	2	4
cut(somebody,apple)	3	0	
cut(she,apple)	3	0	
slice(someone,apple)	2	5	2
cut(person,apple)	2	1	2
cut(NONE,apple)	*2*	*0*	*(2)*
slice(woman,apple)	1	1	1
slice(person,apple)	1	1	1
slice(man,apple)	1	0	
cut(person,fruit)	1	0	
cut(people,apple)	1	0	
cut(man,apple)	1	0	
cut(knife,apple)	1	0	
chop(woman,apple)	1	0	
chop(person,apple)	1	0	
slice(NONE,apple)	0	2	
Total	30	12	10 *(17)*

Table 5: Distribution of valid tokens across types for a single PDT item. Types in italics do not occur in the NS sample, but could be inferred to expand coverage by recombining elements of NS types that do occur.

nouns (e.g., *cut(she,apple)*) and lexical relations (e.g., *apple* as a type of *fruit*), one approach might be

[3] Accuracy is typically defined as (TP+TN)/(TP+TN+FN+FP), but false positives (FPs) are cases where an incorrect learner response was in the gold standard, and we have already removed such cases (i.e., FP=0).

to prompt NSs to give multiple alternative descriptions of each PDT item.

A second issue to consider is that, even when only examining cases where the meaning is literally correct, NNSs produce a wider range of forms to describe the prompts than NSs. For example, for a picture showing what NSs overwhelmingly described as a *raking* action, many NNSs referred to a man *cleaning* an area. Literally, this may be true, but it is not native-like. This behavior is somewhat expected, given that learners are encouraged to use words they know to compensate for gaps in their vocabularies (Agustín Llach, 2010). This also parallels the observation in SLA research that while second language learners may attain native-like grammar, their ability to use pragmatically native-like language is often much lower (Bardovi-Harlig and Dörnyei, 1998). The answer to what counts as a correct meaning will most likely lie in the purpose of an application, reflecting whether one is developing native-ness or whether the facts of a situation are expressed correctly. In other words, rather than rejecting all non-native-like responses, an ILT may need to consider whether a sentence is native-like or non-native-like as well as whether it is semantically appropriate.

6 Summary and Outlook

We have begun the process of examining appropriate ways to analyze the semantics of language learner constructions for interactive situations by describing data collected for a picture description task. We parsed this data using an off-the-shelf parser with settings geared towards obtaining appropriate semantic forms, wrote a small set of semantic extraction rules, and obtained 92–93% extraction accuracy. This shows promise at using images to constrain the syntactic form of a "free" learner text and thus be able to use pre-built software. At the same time, we discussed how learners give responses which are literally correct, but are non-native-like. These results can help guide the development of ILTs which aim to process the meaning of interactive statements: there is much to be gained with a small amount of computational effort, but much work needs to go into delineating a proper set of gold standard forms.

There are several ways to take this work. First, given the preponderance of spelling errors in NNS data and its effect on downstream processing, the effect of automatic spelling correction must be taken into account. Secondly, we only investigated transitive verbs, and much needs to be done to investigate interactions with other types of constructions, including the definition of more elaborate semantic forms (Hahn and Meurers, 2012). Finally, to better model ILTs and the interactions found in activities and games, one can begin by modeling more complex visual prompts. By using video description tasks or story retell tasks, we can elicit more complex narrative responses. This would allow us to investigate the possibility of extending our current approach to tasks that involve greater learner interaction.

Acknowledgments

We would like to thank the task participants, David Stringer for assistance in developing the task, Kathleen Bardovi-Harlig, Marlin Howard and Jayson Deese for recruitment help, and Ross Israel for evaluation discussion. For their helpful feedback, we would also like to thank the three anonymous reviewers and the attendees of the Indiana University Linguistics Department Graduate Student Conference.

References

Eneko Agirre, Mona Diab, Daniel Cer, and Aitor Gonzalez-Agirre. 2012. Semeval-2012 task 6: a pilot on semantic textual similarity. In *Proceedings of the First Joint Conference on Lexical and Computational Semantics - Volume 1: Proceedings of the main conference and the shared task, and Volume 2: Proceedings of the Sixth International Workshop on Semantic Evaluation*, SemEval '12, pages 385–393. Association for Computational Linguistics, Stroudsburg, PA, USA.

Maria Pilar Agustín Llach. 2010. Lexical gap-filling mechanisms in foreign language writing. *System*, 38(4):529 – 538.

Luiz Amaral and Detmar Meurers. 2011. On using intelligent computer-assisted language learning in real-life foreign language teaching and learning. *ReCALL*, 23(1):4–24.

Luiz Amaral, Detmar Meurers, and Ramon Ziai. 2011. Analyzing learner language: Towards a flexible NLP architecture for intelligent language tutors. *Computer Assisted Language Learning*, 24(1):1–16.

Kathleen Bardovi-Harlig and Zoltán Dörnyei. 1998. Do language learners recognize pragmatic violations? Pragmatic versus grammatical awareness in instructed L2 learning. *TESOL Quarterly*, 32(2):233–259.

Marianne Celce-Murcia. 1991. Grammar pedagogy in second and foreign language teaching. *TESOL Quarterly*, 25:459–480.

Marianne Celce-Murcia. 2002. Why it makes sense to teach grammar through context and through discourse. In Eli Hinkel and Sandra Fotos, editors, *New perspectives on grammar teaching in second language classrooms*, pages 119–134. Lawrence Erlbaum, Mahwah, NJ.

David L. Chen and William B. Dolan. 2011. Collecting highly parallel data for paraphrase evaluation. In *Proceedings of the 49th Annual Meeting of the Association for Computational Linguistics (ACL-2011)*. Portland, OR.

Martin Chodorow, Joel Tetreault, and Na-Rae Han. 2007. Detection of grammatical errors involving prepositions. In *Proceedings of the 4th ACL-SIGSEM Workshop on Prepositions*, pages 25–30. Prague.

Michael Collins. 1999. *Head-Driven Statistical Models for Natural Language Parsing*. Ph.D. thesis, University of Pennsylvania, Philadelphia, PA.

Ronan Collobert, Jason Weston, Léon Bottou, Michael Karlen, Koray Kavukcuoglu, and Pavel Kuksa. 2011. Natural language processing (almost) from scratch. *Journal of Machine Learning Research (JMLR)*, 12:2461–2505.

Robert Dale, Ilya Anisimoff, and George Narroway. 2012. HOO 2012: A report on the preposition and determiner error correction shared task. In *Proceedings of the Seventh Workshop on Building Educational Applications Using NLP*, pages 54–62. Montréal.

Marie-Catherine de Marneffe, Bill MacCartney, and Christopher D. Manning. 2006. Generating typed dependency parses from phrase structure parses. In *Proceedings of LREC 2006*. Genoa, Italy.

Marie-Catherine de Marneffe and Christopher D. Manning. 2012. *Stanford typed dependencies manual*. Originally published in September 2008; Revised for Stanford Parser v. 2.0.4 in November 2012.

William DeSmedt. 1995. Herr Kommissar: An ICALL conversation simulator for intermediate german. In V. Holland, J. Kaplan, and M. Sams, editors, *Intelligent Language Tutors. Theory Shaping Technology*, pages 153–174. Lawrence Erlbaum Associates, Inc., New Jersey.

Rod Ellis. 2000. Task-based research and language pedagogy. *Language teaching research*, 4(3):193–220.

Rod Ellis. 2006. Current issues in the teaching of grammar: An SLA perspective. *TESOL Quarterly*, 40:83–107.

Christiane Fellbaum, editor. 1998. *WordNet: An Electronic Lexical Database*. The MIT Press, Cambridge, MA.

Katrina Forbes-McKay and Annalena Venneri. 2005. Detecting subtle spontaneous language decline in early Alzheimer's disease with a picture description task. *Neurological sciences*, 26(4):243–254.

Michael Hahn and Detmar Meurers. 2012. Evaluating the meaning of answers to reading comprehension questions: A semantics-based approach. In *Proceedings of the 7th Workshop on Innovative Use of NLP for Building Educational Applications (BEA7)*, pages 326–336. Association for Computational Linguistics, Montreal, Canada.

Trude Heift and Devlan Nicholson. 2001. Web delivery of adaptive and interactive language tutoring. *International Journal of Artificial Intelligence in Education*, 12(4):310–325.

Trude Heift and Mathias Schulze. 2007. *Errors and Intelligence in Computer-Assisted Language Learning: Parsers and Pedagogues*. Routledge.

DJ Hovermale. 2008. Scale: Spelling correction adapted for learners of English. Pre-CALICO Workshop on "Automatic Analysis of Learner

Language: Bridging Foreign Language Teaching Needs and NLP Possibilities". March 18-19, 2008. San Francisco, CA.

Dan Klein and Christopher D. Manning. 2003. Accurate unlexicalized parsing. In *Proceedings of ACL-03*. Sapporo, Japan.

Sandra Kübler, Ryan McDonald, and Joakim Nivre. 2009. *Dependency Parsing*. Morgan & Claypool Publishers.

Diane Larsen-Freeman. 2002. Teaching grammar. In Diane Celce-Murcia, editor, *Teaching English as a second or foreign language*, pages 251–266. Heinle & Heinle, Boston, third edition.

Claudia Leacock and Martin Chodorow. 2003. C-rater: Automated scoring of short-answer questions. *Computers and Humanities*, pages 389–405.

Detmar Meurers. 2012. Natural language processing and language learning. In Carol A. Chapelle, editor, *Encyclopedia of Applied Linguistics*. Blackwell. to appear.

Detmar Meurers, Ramon Ziai, Niels Ott, and Stacey Bailey. 2011. Integrating parallel analysis modules to evaluate the meaning of answers to reading comprehension questions. *Special Issue on Free-text Automatic Evaluation. International Journal of Continuing Engineering Education and Life-Long Learning (IJCEELL)*, 21(4):355–369.

Kenneth A. Petersen. 2010. *Implicit Corrective Feedback in Computer-Guided Interaction: Does Mode Matter?* Ph.D. thesis, Georgetown University, Washington, DC.

Peter Skehan, Pauline Foster, and Uta Mehnert. 1998. Assessing and using tasks. In Willy Renandya and George Jacobs, editors, *Learners and language learning*, pages 227–248. Seameo Regional Language Centre.

Building a Large Annotated Corpus of Learner English: The NUS Corpus of Learner English

Daniel Dahlmeier[1,2] and **Hwee Tou Ng**[2,3] and **Siew Mei Wu**[4]
[1]SAP Technology and Innovation Platform, SAP Singapore
d.dahlmeier@sap.com
[2]NUS Graduate School for Integrative Sciences and Engineering
[3]Department of Computer Science, National University of Singapore
{danielhe,nght}@comp.nus.edu.sg
[4]Centre for English Language Communication, National University of Singapore
elcwusm@nus.edu.sg

Abstract

We describe the NUS Corpus of Learner English (NUCLE), a large, fully annotated corpus of learner English that is freely available for research purposes. The goal of the corpus is to provide a large data resource for the development and evaluation of grammatical error correction systems. Although NUCLE has been available for almost two years, there has been no reference paper that describes the corpus in detail. In this paper, we address this need. We describe the annotation schema and the data collection and annotation process of NUCLE. Most importantly, we report on an unpublished study of annotator agreement for grammatical error correction. Finally, we present statistics on the distribution of grammatical errors in the NUCLE corpus.

1 Introduction

Grammatical error correction for language learners has recently attracted increasing interest in the natural language processing (NLP) community. Grammatical error correction has the potential to create commercially viable software tools for the large number of students around the world who are studying a foreign language, in particular the large number of students of English as a Foreign Language (EFL).

The success of statistical methods in NLP over the last two decades can largely be attributed to advances in machine learning and the availability of large, annotated corpora that can be used to train and evaluate statistical models for various NLP tasks. The biggest obstacle for grammatical error correction has been that until recently, there was no large, annotated corpus of learner text that could have served as a standard resource for empirical approaches to grammatical error correction (Leacock et al., 2010). The existing annotated learner corpora were all either too small or proprietary and not available to the research community. That is why we decided to create the NUS Corpus of Learner English (NUCLE), a large, annotated corpus of learner texts that is freely available for research purposes. The corpus was built in collaboration with the Centre for English Language Communication (CELC) at NUS. NUCLE consists of about 1,400 student essays from undergraduate university students at NUS with a total of over one million words which are completely annotated with error tags and corrections. All annotations and corrections have been performed by professional English instructors. To the best of our knowledge, NUCLE is the first annotated learner corpus of this size that is freely available for research purposes. However, although the NUCLE corpus has been available for almost two years now, there has been no reference paper that describes the details of the corpus. That makes it harder for other researchers to start working with the NUCLE corpus. In this paper, we address this need by giving a detailed description of the NUCLE corpus, including a description of the annotation schema, the data collection and annotation process, and various statistics on the distribution of grammatical errors in the corpus. Most importantly, we report on an unpublished study of annotator agreement for grammatical error correction that was conducted prior to creating

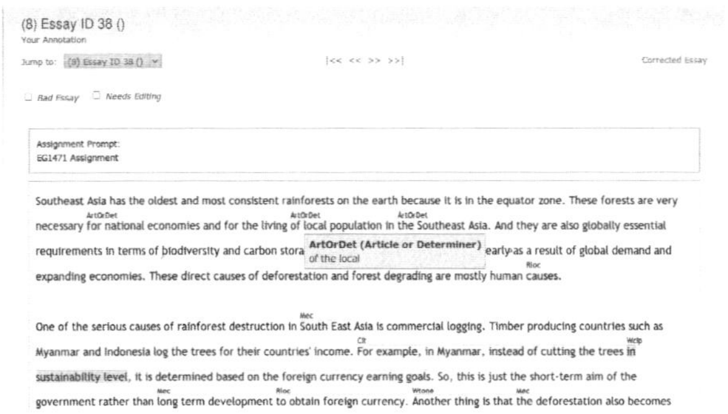

Figure 1: The WAMP annotation interface

the NUCLE corpus. The study gives some insights regarding the difficulty of the annotation task.

The remainder of this paper is organized as follows. The next section explains the annotation schema that was used for labeling grammatical errors. Section 3 reports the results of the inter-annotator agreement study. Section 4 describes the data collection and annotation process. Section 5 contains the error statistics. Section 6 gives the related work, and Section 7 concludes the paper.

2 Annotation Schema

Before starting the corpus creation, we had to develop a set of annotation guidelines. This was done in a pilot study before the actual corpus was created. Three instructors from CELC participated in the pilot study. The instructors annotated a small set of student essays that had been collected by CELC previously. The annotation was performed using an in-house, online annotation tool, called Writing, Annotation, and Marking Platform (WAMP), that was developed by the NUS NLP group specially for creating the NUCLE corpus. The annotation tool allows the annotators to work over the Internet using a web browser. Figure 1 shows a screen shot of the WAMP interface. Annotators can browse through a batch of essays that has been assigned to them and perform the following tasks:

- **Select** arbitrary, contiguous text spans using the cursor to identify grammatical errors.
- **Classify** errors by choosing an error tag from a drop-down menu.
- **Correct** errors by typing the correction into a text box.
- **Comment** to give additional explanations if necessary.

We wanted to impose as few constraints as possible on the annotators and to give them an experience that would closely resemble their usual marking using pen and paper. Therefore, the WAMP annotation tool allows annotators to select arbitrary text spans, including overlapping text spans.

After some annotation trials, we decided to use a tag set which had been developed by CELC in a previous study. Some minor modifications were made to the original tag set based on the feedback of the annotators. The result of the pilot study was a tag set of 27 error categories which are grouped into 13 categories. The tag set is listed in Table 1. It is important to note that our annotation schema not only labels each grammatical error with an error category, but also requires an annotator to provide a suitable correction for the error as well. The annotators were asked to provide a correction that would fix the grammatical error if the selected text span containing the grammatical error is replaced with the correction. If multiple alternative text spans could be selected, the annotators were asked to select the minimal text span so that minimal changes were made to arrive at the corrected text.

We chose to use the tag set in Table 1 since this tag set was developed and used in a previous study at CELC and was found to be a suitable tag set. Furthermore, the tag set offers a reasonable compromise in terms of its complexity. With 27 error categories, it is sufficiently fine-grained to enable meaningful statistics for different error categories, yet not as complex as other tag sets that are much larger in size.

3 Annotator Agreement

How reliably can human annotators agree on whether a word or sentence is grammatically correct? The pilot annotation project gave us the opportunity to investigate this question in a quantitative analysis. Annotator agreement is also a measure for how difficult a task is and serves as a test of whether humans can reliable perform the annotation task with the given tag set. During the pilot study, we randomly sampled 100 essays for measuring annotator agreement. These essays are part of the pilot

Error Tag	Error Category	Description / Example
Verbs		
Vt	Verb Tense	A university **[had conducted — conducted]** the survey last year.
Vm	Verb modal	No one **[will — would]** bother to consider a natural balance.
V0	Missing verb	This **[may — may be]** due to a traditional notion that boys would be the main labor force in a farm family.
Vform	Verb form	Will the child blame the parents after he **[growing — grows]** up?
Subject-verb agreement		
SVA	Subject-verb-agreement	The boy **[play — plays]** soccer.
Articles/determiners		
ArtOrDet	Article or Determiner	From the ethical aspect, sex selection technology should not be used in **[non-medical — a non-medical]** situation.
Nouns		
Nn	Noun Number	Sex selection should therefore be used for medical **[reason — reasons]** and nothing else.
Npos	Noun possessive	The education of **[mother's — mothers]** is a significant factor in reducing son preference.
Pronouns		
Pform	Pronoun form	90% of couples seek treatment for family balancing reasons and 80% of **[those — them]** want girls.
Pref	Pronoun reference	Moreover, children may find it hard to communicate with **[his/her — their]** parents.
Word choice		
Wcip	Wrong collocation/idiom/preposition	Singapore, for example, has invested heavily **[on — in]** the establishment of Biopolis
Wa	Acronyms	Using acronyms without explaining what they stand for.
Wform	Word form	Sex-selection may also result in **[addition — additional]** stress for the family.
Wtone	Tone	**[Isn't it — Is it not]** what you always dreamed for?
Sentence Structure		
Srun	Runons, comma splice	**[Do spare some thought and time, we can make a difference! — Do spare some thought and time. We can make a difference!]** (Should be split into two sentences)
Smod	Dangling modifier	**[Faced — When we are faced]** with the unprecedented energy crisis, finding an alternative energy resource has naturally become the top priority issue.
Spar	Parallelism	The use of sex selection would prevent rather than **[contributing — contribute]** to a distorted sex ratio.
Sfrag	Fragment	Although he is a student from the Arts faculty.
Ssub	Subordinate clause	It is the wrong mindset of people that boys are more superior than girls **[should — that should]** be corrected.

Table 1: NUCLE error categories. Grammatical errors in the examples are printed in bold face in the form **[<mistake>— <correction>]**.

Error Tag	Error Category	Description / Example
Word Order		
WOinc	Incorrect sentence form	Why can **[not we — we not]** choose more intelligent and beautiful babies?
WOadv	Adverb/adjective position	It is similar to the murder of many valuable lives **[only based — based only]** on the couple's own wish.
Transitions		
Trans	Link words/phrases	In the process of selecting the gender of the child, ethical problems arise **[where — because]** many innocent lives of unborn fetuses are taken away.
Mechanics		
Mec	Punctuation, capitalization, spelling, typos	The **[affect — effect]** of that policy has yet to be felt.
Redundancy		
Rloc	Local redundancy	Currently, abortion is available to end a life only **[because of — because]** the fetus or embryo has the wrong sex.
Citation		
Cit	Citation	Poor citation practice.
Others		
Others	Other errors	Any error that does not fit into any other category, but can still be corrected.
Um	Unclear meaning	The quality of the passage is so poor that it cannot be corrected.

Table 1: NUCLE error categories (continued)

data set and are not included in the official NUCLE corpus. The essays were then annotated by our three annotators in a way that each essay was annotated independently by two annotators. Four essays had to be discarded as they were of very poor quality and did not allow for any meaningful correction. This left us with 96 essays with double annotation.

Comparing two sets of annotation is complicated by the fact that the set of annotations that corrects an input text to a corrected output text is ambiguous (Dahlmeier and Ng, 2012). In other words, it is possible that two different sets of annotations produce the same correction. For example, one annotator could choose to select a whole phrase as one error, while the other annotator selects each word individually. Our annotation guidelines ask annotators to select the minimum span that is necessary to correct the error, but we do not enforce any hard constraints and different annotators can have a different perception of where an error starts or ends.

An especially difficult case is the annotation of omission errors, for example missing articles. Selecting a range of whitespace characters is difficult for annotators, especially if the annotation tool is web-based (as whitespace is variable in web pages). We asked annotators to select the previous or next word and include them into the suggested correction. To change *conduct survey* to *conduct **a** survey*, the annotator could change *conduct* to *conduct a*, or change *survey* to *a survey*. If we only compare the exact text spans selected by the annotators when measuring agreement, these different ways to select the context could easily cause us to conclude that the annotators disagree when they in fact agree on the corrected phrase. This would lead to an underestimation of annotator agreement. To address this problem, we perform a simple text span normalization. First, we "grow" the selected context to align with whitespace boundaries. For example, if an annotator just selected the last character *e* of the word *use* and provided *ed* as a correction, we grow this annotation so that the whole word *use* is selected and *used* is the correction. Second, we tokenize the text and "trim" the context by removing tokens at the start and end that are identical in the original and the correction. Finally, the annotations are "projected" onto the individual tokens they span, i.e., an annotation that spans a phrase of multiple to-

Source	:	This phenomenon opposes the real .
Annotator A	:	This phenomenon opposes (the $\rightarrow \epsilon$ (ArtOrDet)) (real $\rightarrow$ reality (Wform)) .
Annotator B	:	This phenomenon opposes the (real $\rightarrow$ reality (Wform)) .

Table 2: Example of a sentence from the annotator agreement study with annotations from two different annotators.

kens is broken up into multiple token-level annotations. We align the tokens in the original text span and the tokenized correction string using minimum edit distance. Now, we can compare two annotations in a more meaningful way at the token level. Table 2 shows a tokenized example sentence from the annotator agreement study with annotations from two different annotators. Annotator A and B agree that the first three words *This, phenomenon*, and *opposes* and the final period are correct and do not need any correction. The annotators also agree that the word *real* is part of a word form (Wform) error and should be replaced with *reality*. However, they disagree with respect to the article *the*: annotator A believes there is an article error (ArtOrDet) and that the article has to be deleted while annotator B believes that the article is acceptable in this position.

The example shows that annotator agreement can be measured with respect to three different criteria: whether there is an error, what type of error it is, and how the error should be corrected. Accordingly, we analyze annotator agreement under three different conditions:

- **Identification** Agreement of tagged tokens regardless of error category or correction.
- **Classification** Agreement of error category, given identification.
- **Exact** Agreement of error category and correction, given identification.

In the identification task, we are interested to see how well annotators agree on whether something is a grammatical error or not. In the example above, annotators A and B agree on 5 out of 6 tokens and disagree on one token (*the*). That results in an identification agreement of $5/6 = 83\%$. In the classification task, we investigate how well annotators agree on the type of error, given that both have tagged the token as an error. In the example, the classification agreement is 100% as both annotator A and B tagged the word *real* as a word form (Wform) error. Finally, for the exact task, annotators are considered to agree if they agree on the error category and the correction given that they both have tagged the token as an error. In the example, the exact agreement is 100% as both annotators give the same error category Wform and the same correction *reality* for the word *real*. We use the popular Cohen's Kappa coefficient (Cohen, 1960) to measure annotator agreement between annotators. Cohen's Kappa is defined as

$$\kappa = \frac{Pr(a) - Pr(e)}{1 - Pr(e)} \tag{1}$$

where $Pr(a)$ is the probability of agreement and $Pr(e)$ is the probability of chance agreement. We can estimate $Pr(a)$ and $Pr(e)$ from the double annotated essays through maximum likelihood estimation. For two annotators A and B, the probability of agreement is

$$Pr(a) = \frac{\text{\#agreed tokens}}{\text{\#total tokens}} \tag{2}$$

where the number of agreed tokens is counted as described above, and the total number of tokens is the total token count of the subset of jointly annotated documents. The probability of chance agreement is computed as

$$\begin{aligned} Pr(e) &= Pr(A=1, B=1) + Pr(A=0, B=0) \\ &= Pr(A=1) \times Pr(B=1) \\ &\quad + Pr(A=0) \times Pr(B=0) \end{aligned}$$

where $Pr(A = 1)$ and $Pr(A = 0)$ symbolize the events of annotator A tagging a token as "error" or "no error" respectively. We make use of the fact that both annotators perform the task independently. $Pr(A = 1)$ and $Pr(A = 0)$ can be computed through maximum likelihood estimation.

$$\begin{aligned} Pr(A=1) &= \frac{\text{\# annotated tokens of annotator A}}{\text{\# total tokens}} \\ Pr(A=0) &= \frac{\text{\# unannotated tokens of annotator A}}{\text{\# total tokens}} \end{aligned}$$

Annotators	Kappa-iden	Kappa-class	Kappa-exact
A – B	0.4775	0.6206	0.5313
A – C	0.3627	0.5352	0.4956
B – C	0.3230	0.4894	0.4246
Average	0.3877	0.5484	0.4838

Table 3: Cohen's Kappa for annotator agreement.

The probabilities $Pr(B = 1)$ and $Pr(B = 0)$ are computed analogously. The chance agreement for this task is quite high, as the number of un-annotated tokens is much higher than the number of annotated tokens. Cohen's Kappa coefficients for the three annotators and the average Kappa coefficient are listed in Table 3. We observe that the Kappa scores are relatively low and that there is a substantial amount of variability in the Kappa coefficients; annotator A and B show a higher agreement with each other than they do with annotator C. According to Landis and Koch (1977), Kappa scores between 0.21 and 0.40 are considered fair, and scores between 0.41 and 0.60 are considered moderate. The average Kappa score for identification can therefore only be considered fair and the Kappa scores for classification and exact agreement are moderate. Thus, an interesting result of the pilot study was that annotators find it harder to agree on whether a word is grammatically correct than agreeing on the type of error or how it should be corrected. The annotator agreement study shows that grammatical error correction, especially grammatical error identification, is a difficult problem.

Our findings support previous research on annotator agreement that has shown that grammatical error correction is a challenging task (Tetreault and Chodorow, 2008; Lee et al., 2009). Tetreault and Chodorow (2008) report a Kappa score of 0.63 which in their words "shows the difficulty of this task and also show how two highly trained raters can produce very different judgments." An interesting related work is (Lee et al., 2009) which investigates the annotation of article and noun number errors. The annotation is performed with either a single sentence context only or the five preceding sentences. The agreement between annotators increases when more context is given, from a Kappa score of 0.55 to a Kappa score of 0.60. Madnani *et al.* (2011) and Tetreault *et al.* (2010) propose crowdsourcing to overcome the problem of annotator variability.

4 Data Collection and Annotation

The main data collection for the NUCLE corpus took place between August and December 2009. We collected a total of 2,249 student essays from 6 English courses at CELC. The courses are designed for students who need language support for their academic studies. The essays were written as course assignments on a wide range of topics, like technology innovation or health care. Some example question prompts are shown in Table 4. All students are at a similar academic level, as they are all undergraduate students at NUS. Students would typically have to write two essay assignments during a course. The length of each essay was supposed to be around 500 words, although most essays were longer than the required length. From this data set, a team of 10 CELC English instructors annotated 1,414 essays with over 1.2 million words between October 2009 and April 2010. Due to budget constraints, we were unfortunately not able to perform double annotations for the main corpus. Annotators were allowed to label an error multiple times if the error could be assigned to more than one error tag, although we observed that annotators did not make much use of this option. Minimal post-processing was done after the annotation process. Annotators were asked to review some corrections that appeared to contain annotation mistakes, for example redundancy errors that did not remove the annotated word. The final results of the annotation exercise were a total of 46,597 error tags. The essays and the annotations were released as the NUCLE corpus through the NUS Enterprise R2M portal in June 2011. The link to the corpus can be found on the NUS NLP group's website[1].

5 NUCLE Corpus Statistics

This section provides basic statistics about the NUCLE corpus and the collected annotations. These statistics already reveal some interesting insights about the nature of grammatical errors in learner text. In particular, we are interested in the following questions: how frequent are errors in the NUCLE corpus and what are the most frequent error

[1] `www.comp.nus.edu.sg/~nlp/corpora.html`

"Public spending on the aged should be limited so that money can be diverted to other areas of the country's development." Do you agree?
Surveillance technology such as RFID (radio-frequency identification) should not be used to track people (e.g., human implants and RFID tags on people or products). Do you agree? Support your argument with concrete examples.
Choose a concept or prototype currently in research and development and not widely available in the market. Present an argument on how the design can be improved to enhance safety. Remember to consider influential factors such as cost or performance when you summarize and rebut opposing views. You will need to include very recently published sources in your references.

Table 4: Example question prompts from the NUCLE corpus.

NUS Corpus of Learner English	
Documents	1,414
Sentences	59,871
Word tokens	1,220,257
Word types	30,492
Error annotations	46,597
# of sentences per document	42.34
# of word tokens per document	862.98
# of word tokens per sentence	20.38
# of error annotations per document	32.95
# of error annotations per 100 word tokens	3.82

Table 5: Overview of the NUCLE corpus

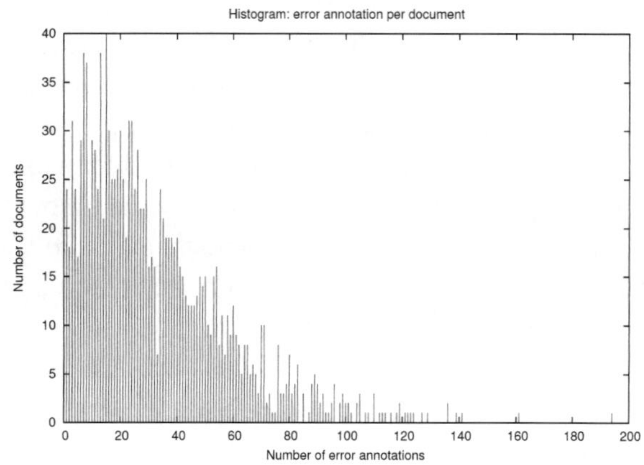

Figure 2: Histogram of error annotations per document in NUCLE.

categories? The basic statistics of the NUCLE corpus are shown in Table 5. In these statistics, we treat multiple alternative annotations for the same error as separate errors, although it could be argued that these should be merged into a single error with multiple alternative corrections. Fortunately, only about 1% of the errors are labeled with more than one annotation. We can see that grammatical errors are very *sparse*, even in learner text. In the NUCLE corpus, there are 46,597 annotated errors for 1,220,257 word tokens. That makes an error density of 3.82 errors per hundred words. In other words, most of the word tokens in the corpus are grammatically correct. This shows that the students whose essays were used for the corpus already have a relative high proficiency of English. When we look at the distribution of errors across documents, we can make another interesting observation. Figure 2 shows a histogram of the number of error annotations per document. The distribution appears non-Gaussian and is heavily skewed to the left with most documents having less than 30 errors while some documents have significantly more errors than the average document. That means that although grammatical errors are rare *in general*, there are also documents with many error annotations. 32 documents have more than 100 error annotations and the highest number of error annotations in a document is 194. The mode, i.e., the most frequent value in the histogram, is 15 which is to the left of the average of 32.95. A similar pattern can be observed when we look at the distribution of errors per sentence. Figure 3 shows a histogram of the number of error annotations per sentence in the NUCLE corpus. For this histogram, only the error annotations which start and end within sentence boundaries are considered (this accounts for 98.6% of all error annotations). Sentence boundaries are determined automatically using the NLTK Punkt sentence splitter[2]. The histogram shows that 57.64% of all sentences have zero errors, 20.48% have exactly one error, and 10.66% have exactly two errors, and 11.21% of all sentences have more than two errors. Although the frequency decreases quickly for higher error counts, the highest observed number of error annotations for a sentence is 28.

[2] `nltk.org`

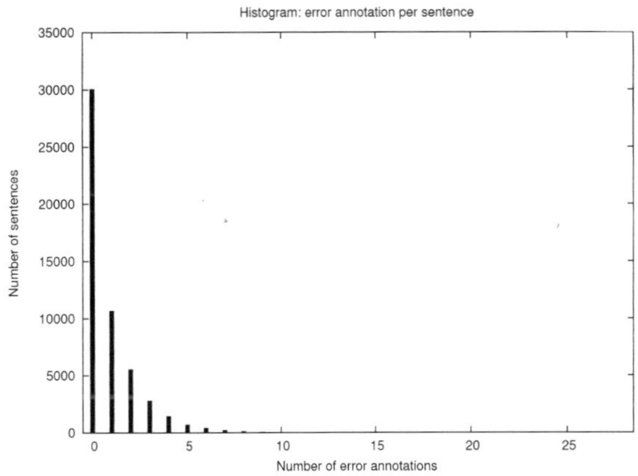

Figure 3: Histogram of error annotations per sentence in NUCLE.

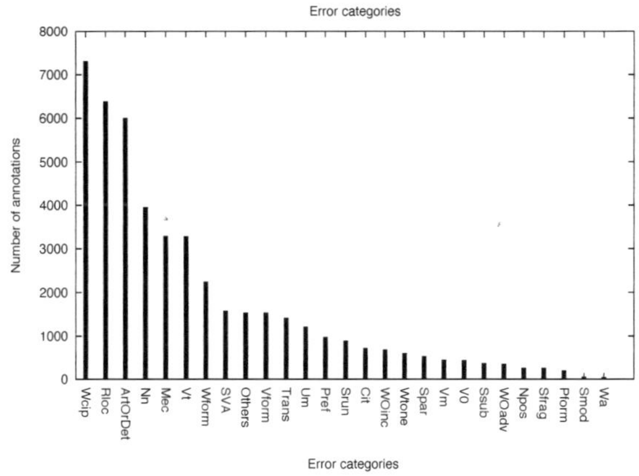

Figure 4: Error categories histogram for the NUCLE corpus.

The skewed distribution of errors in the NUCLE corpus is an interesting observation. A possible explanation for the long tail of the distribution could be a "rich-get-richer" type of dynamics: if a learner has made a lot of mistakes in her essay so far, the chance of her making more errors in the remainder of the essay increases, for example because she makes systematic errors which are likely to be repeated. Explaining the cognitive processes that produce the observed error distribution is beyond the scope of this paper, but it would certainly be an interesting question to investigate.

So far, we have only been concerned with how many errors learners make overall. But it is also important to understand what types of errors language learners make. Error categories that appear more frequently should be addressed with higher priority when creating an automatic error correction system. Figure 4 shows a histogram of error categories. Again, we can observe a skewed distribution with a few error categories being very frequent and many error categories being comparatively infrequent. The top five error categories are wrong collocation/idiom/preposition (Wcip) with 7,312 instances or 15.69% of all annotations, local redundancies (Rloc) (6,390 instances, 13.71%), article or determiner (ArtOrDet) (6,004 instances, 12.88%), noun number (Nn) (3,955 instances, 8.49%), and mechanics (Mec) (3,290 instances, 7.06%). These top five error categories account for 57.83% of all error annotations. The next 5 categories are verb tense (Vt) (3,288 instances, 7.06%) word form (Wform) (2,241 instances, 4.81%), subject-verb agreement (SVA) (1,578 instances, 3.38%), other errors that could not be grouped into any of the error categories (1,532 instances, 3.29%), and Verb form (Vform) (1,531, 3.29%). Together, the top 10 error categories account for 79.66% of all annotated errors. A manual inspection showed that a large percentage of the local redundancy errors involve articles that are deemed redundant by the annotator and should be deleted. These errors could also be considered article or determiner errors. For the Wcip errors, we observed that most Wcip errors are preposition errors. This confirms that articles and prepositions are the two most frequent error categories for EFL learners (Leacock et al., 2010).

6 Related Work

In this section, we compare NUCLE with other learner corpora. While there were almost no annotated learner corpora available for research purposes until recently, non-annotated learner corpora have been available for a while. Two examples are the International Corpus of Learner English (ICLE) (Granger et al., 2002) and the Chinese Learner English Corpus (Gui and Yang., 2003)[3]. Rozovskaya and Roth (2010) annotated a portion of each of these two learner corpora with error categories and corrections. However, with 63,000 words, the annotated data is small compared to NUCLE.

[3]The Chinese Learner English Corpus contains annotations for error types but does not include corrections for the errors.

The Cambridge Learner Corpus (CLC) (Nicholls, 2003) is possibly the largest annotated English learner corpus. Unfortunately, to our knowledge, the corpus is not freely available for research purposes. A subset of the CLC was released in 2011 by Yannakoudakis *et al.* (2011). The released data set contains short essays written by students taking the First Certificate in English (FCE) examination. The data set was also used in the recent HOO 2012 shared task on preposition and determiner correction (Dale et al., 2012). Comparing the essays in the FCE data set and NUCLE, we observe that the essays in the FCE data set are shorter than the essays in NUCLE and show a higher density of grammatical errors. One reason for the higher number of errors (in particular spelling errors) is most likely that the FCE data was not collected from take-home assignments where students have the chance to spell check their writing before submission. But it could also mean that the essays in FCE are from students with a lower proficiency in English compared to NUCLE. With regards to the annotation schema, the CLC annotations include both the type of error (missing, unnecessary, replacement, form) and the part of speech. As a result, the CLC tag set is large with 88 different error categories, far more than the 27 error categories in NUCLE.

Finally, the HOO 2011 shared task (Dale and Kilgarriff, 2011) released an annotated corpus of fragments from academic papers written by non-native speakers and published in a conference or workshop of the Association for Computational Linguistics. The corpus uses the annotation schema from the CLC. Comparing the data set with NUCLE, the HOO 2011 data set is much smaller (about 20,000 words for training and testing, respectively) and represents a specific writing genre (NLP papers). The NUCLE corpus is much larger and covers a broader range of topics.

7 Conclusion

We have presented the NUS Corpus of Learner English (NUCLE), a large, annotated corpus of learner English. The corpus contains over one million words which are completely annotated with grammatical errors and corrections. The NUCLE corpus is freely available for research purposes. We have also reported an inter-annotator agreement study for grammatical error correction. The study shows that grammatical error correction is a difficult task, even for humans. The error statistics from the NUCLE corpus show that learner errors are generally sparse and have a long-tail distribution.

Acknowledgments

This research is supported by the Singapore National Research Foundation under its International Research Centre @ Singapore Funding Initiative and administered by the IDM Programme Office.

References

J. Cohen. 1960. A coefficient of agreement for nominal scales. *Educational and Psychological Measurement*, 20(1):37–46.

D. Dahlmeier and H.T. Ng. 2012. Better evaluation for grammatical error correction. In *Proceedings of HLT-NAACL*, pages 568–572.

R. Dale and A. Kilgarriff. 2011. Helping Our Own: The HOO 2011 pilot shared task. In *Proceedings of the Generation Challenges Session at the 13th European Workshop on Natural Language Generation*, pages 242–249.

R. Dale, I. Anisimoff, and G. Narroway. 2012. HOO 2012: A report on the preposition and determiner error correction shared task. In *Proceedings of the Seventh Workshop on Innovative Use of NLP for Building Educational Applications*, pages 54–62.

S. Granger, F. Dagneaux, E. Meunier, and M. Paquot. 2002. *The International Corpus of Learner English*. Presses Universitaires de Louvain, Louvain-la-Neuve, Belgium.

S. Gui and H. Yang. 2003. *Zhongguo Xuexizhe Yingyu Yuliaohu (Chinese Learner English Corpus)*. Shanghai Waiyu Jiaoyu Chubanshe. In Chinese.

J.R. Landis and G.G Koch. 1977. The measurement of observer agreement for categorical data. *Biometrics*, 33(1):159–174.

C. Leacock, M. Chodorow, M. Gamon, and J. Tetreault. 2010. *Automated Grammatical Error Detection for Language Learners*. Morgan & Claypool Publishers.

J. Lee, J. Tetreault, and M. Chodorow. 2009. Human evaluation of article and noun number usage: Influences of context and construction variability. In *Proceedings of the Linguistic Annotation Workshop III (LAW3)*, pages 60–63.

N. Madnani, J. Tetreault, M. Chodorow, and R. Rozovskaya. 2011. They can help: using crowdsourcing to improve the evaluation of grammatical error detection systems. In *Proceedings of ACL:HLT*, pages 508–513.

D. Nicholls. 2003. The Cambridge learner corpus: Error coding and analysis for lexicography and ELT. In *Proceedings of the Corpus Linguistics 2003 Conference*, pages 572–581.

A. Rozovskaya and D. Roth. 2010. Annotating ESL errors: Challenges and rewards. In *Proceedings of the Fifth Workshop on Innovative Use of NLP for Building Educational Applications*, pages 28–36.

J. Tetreault and M. Chodorow. 2008. Native judgments of non-native usage: Experiments in preposition error detection. In *Proceedings of the Workshop on Human Judgements in Computational Linguistics*, pages 24–32.

J. Tetreault, E. Filatova, and M. Chodorow. 2010. Rethinking grammatical error annotation and evaluation with the Amazon Mechanical Turk. In *Proceedings of the Fifth Workshop on Innovative Use of NLP for Building Educational Applications*, pages 45–48.

H. Yannakoudakis, T. Briscoe, and B. Medlock. 2011. A new dataset and method for automatically grading ESOL texts. In *Proceedings of ACL:HLT*, pages 180–189.

Developing and testing a self-assessment and tutoring system

Øistein E. Andersen
iLexIR
Streets, 62 Hills Road
Cambridge, CB2 1LA
and@ilexir.co.uk

Helen Yannakoudakis
Cambridge English
1 Hills Road
Cambridge, CB1 2EU
yannakoudakis.h@cambridgeenglish.org

Fiona Barker
Cambridge English
1 Hills Road
Cambridge, CB1 2EU
barker.f@cambridgeenglish.org

Tim Parish
iLexIR
Streets, 62 Hills Road
Cambridge, CB2 1LA
tim@ilexir.co.uk

Abstract

Automated feedback on writing may be a useful complement to teacher comments in the process of learning a foreign language. This paper presents a self-assessment and tutoring system which combines an holistic score with detection and correction of frequent errors and furthermore provides a qualitative assessment of each individual sentence, thus making the language learner aware of potentially problematic areas rather than providing a panacea. The system has been tested by learners in a range of educational institutions, and their feedback has guided its development.

1 Introduction

Learning to write a foreign language well requires a considerable amount of practice and appropriate feedback. Good teachers are essential, but their time is limited. As recently shown in a study by Wang et al. (in press) conducted amongst first-year students of English at a Taiwanese university, automated writing evaluation can lead to increased learner autonomy and higher writing accuracy. In this paper, we investigate the merits of a self-assessment and tutoring (SAT) system specifically aimed at intermediate learners of English, at around B2 level in the Common European Framework of Reference for Languages (CEFR) (Council of Europe, 2001). There are a large number of students at this level, and they should have sufficient knowledge of the language to benefit from the system whilst at the same time committing errors which can be identified reliably.

The system provides automated feedback on learners' writing at three different levels of granularity: an overall assessment of their proficiency, a score for each individual sentence, highlighting well-written passages as well as ones requiring more work, and specific comments on local issues including spelling and word choice.

Computer-based writing tools have been around for a long time, with Criterion (Burstein et al., 2003, which also provides a number of features for teachers) and ESL Assistant (Gamon et al., 2009, not currently available) aimed specifically at second-language learners, but the idea of indicating the relative quality of different parts of a text (sentences in our case) has, to the best of our knowledge, not been implemented previously. This kind of non-specific feedback does not provide a precise diagnosis or immediate cure, but might have the advantage of fostering learning.

In addition to describing the SAT system itself, we present a series of three trials in which learners of English in a number of educational contexts used the system as a tool to work on written responses to specific tasks and improve their writing skills.

2 System

The SAT system is made available to students learning English as a Web service to which they can sign up with a code ('class key') provided by their teacher. Once they have filled in a short demographic questionnaire, the users can respond to one, two, three or more writing tasks. The students can save their work at any time and ask the system to assess the current version of their text, which will

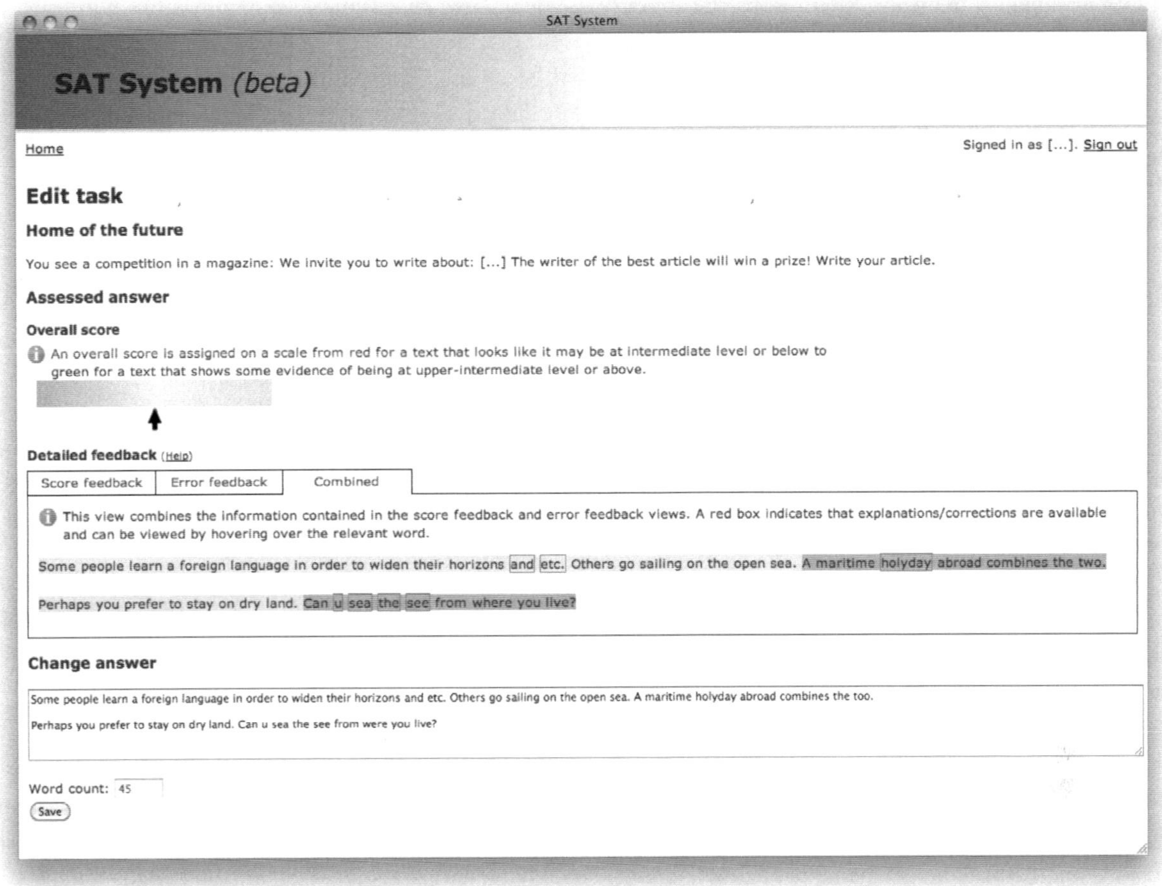

Figure 1: SAT system screen where students can see the automated feedback and revise their piece of writing. The 'score feedback' and 'error feedback' views are shown in Figures 2 and 3.

give feedback as shown in Figure 1 and described in more detail in the following subsections. Assessment times are currently around 15sec, which facilitates incremental and exploratory editing of a text to improve it, giving the students the ability to try out different ways of correcting a problematic turn of phrase. The teacher can see which students have signed up and look at the last saved version of their responses. Finally, the students are asked to answer a few questions about their experience with the system.

2.1 Text assessment

The SAT system provides an overall assessment of someone's proficiency by automatically analysing and scoring the text as a whole. There is a large body of literature with regard to automated text scoring systems (Page, 1968; Rudner and Liang, 2002; Attali and Burstein, 2006; Briscoe et al., 2010). Existing systems, overviews of which have been published in various studies (Dikli, 2006; Williamson, 2009; Shermis and Hamner, 2012), involve a large range of techniques, such as discriminative and generative machine learning, clustering algorithms and vectorial semantics, as well as syntactic parsers.

We approach automated text assessment as a supervised machine learning problem, which enables us to take advantage of existing annotated data. We use the publically-available First Certificate in English (FCE) dataset of upper-intermediate learner English (Yannakoudakis et al., 2011) and focus on assessing general linguistic competence. Systems that measure English competence directly are easier and faster to deploy, since they are more likely to be re-usable and generalise better across different genres than topic-specific ones, which are not immediately usable when new tasks are added, since the model cannot be applied until a substantial amount of manually annotated responses have been collected for a specific prompt.

Following previous research, we employ discriminative ranking, which has been shown to achieve state-of-the-art results on the task of assessing free-text writing competence (Yannakoudakis et al., 2011). The underlying idea is that high-scoring texts (or 'scripts') should receive a higher rank than low-scoring ones. We train a linear ranking perceptron (Bös and Opper, 1998) on features derived from previous work (namely, lexical and grammatical properties of text) and compare it to our previous model (Yannakoudakis et al., 2011), which is trained using ranking Support Vector Machines (Joachims, 2002). Our new perceptron model achieves 0.740 and 0.765 Pearson product-moment (r) and Spearman's rank correlation coefficient (ρ) respectively between the gold and predicted scores; this is comparable to our previous SVM model, which achieves 0.741 and 0.773, and the differences are not significant.

In order to provide scoring feedback[1] based on the predictions of our model, we use visual presentations. Visualisation techniques allow us to go beyond the mere display of a number, can stimulate the learners' visual perceptions, and, when used appropriately, information can be displayed in an intuitive and easily interpretable way. Furthermore, aesthetics in computer-based interfaces have been shown to have an effect on the users. For example, Ben-Bassat et al. (2006) have found an interdependence between perceived aesthetics and usability in questionnaire-based assessments, and have shown that users' preferences are not necessarily based only upon performance; aesthetics also play a role.

More specifically, we assign an overall score on a scale from red for a text that looks like it may be at intermediate level or below to green for a text that shows some evidence of being at upper-intermediate level (the level assessed by the FCE exam) or above (*i.e.,* advanced). This is illustrated in Figure 1 below the *Overall score* section, where an arrow is used to indicate the level of text quality on a colour gradient defined by the two extreme points, red and green. A text with the highest score possible would indicate that the learner has potentially shown evidence of being at a level higher than that assessed by FCE, the latter, of course, being dependent on the extent to which higher-order linguistic skills are elicited by the prompts. On the contrary, a very low score indicates poor linguistic abilities corresponding to a lower level.

Although exams that encompass the full range of language proficiency exhibited at different stages of learning are hard to design, the FCE exam, benchmarked at the B2 level and reserving some of its score range for performances beneath and beyond, allows us to roughly estimate someone's proficiency as being far below, just below, around or above an upper intermediate level. The task of predicting attainment levels has recently started to receive attention (Dickinson et al., 2012; Hawkins and Filipović, 2012).

2.2 Sentence evaluation

The second component of the SAT system automatically assesses and scores the quality of individual sentences, independently of their context. The challenge of assessing intra-sentential quality lies in the limited linguistic evidence that can be extracted automatically from relatively short sentences for them to be assessed reliably, in addition to the difficulty in acquiring annotated data, since rating a response sentence by sentence is not something examiners typically do and would therefore require an additional and expensive manual annotation effort.

Previous work has primarily focused on automatic content scoring of short answers, ranging from a few words to a few sentences (Pulman and Sukkarieh, 2005; Attali et al., 2008; Mohler et al., 2011; Ziai et al., 2012). On the other hand, scoring of individual sentences with respect to their linguistic quality, specifically in learner texts, has received considerably less attention. Higgins et al. (2004) devised guidelines for the manual annotation of sentences in learner texts, and evaluated a rule-based approach that classifies sentences with respect to clarity of expression based on grammar, mechanics and word usage errors; however, their system performs binary classification, whereas we are focusing on scoring sentences. Writing instruction tools, such as Criterion (Burstein et al., 2003), give advice on stylistic

[1]Note that ranks can be transformed to scores through linear regression, while correlation remains unaltered as it is invariant to linear transformations.

and organisational issues and automatically detect a variety of errors in the text, though they do not explicitly allow for an overall evaluation of sentences with respect to various writing aspects. The latter, used in combination with an error feedback component (see Section 2.3), can be a useful instrument informing learners about the severity of their mistakes; for example, although sentences may contain some errors, they may still maintain a certain level of acceptability that does not impede communication. Moreover, indicating problematic regions may be better from a pedagogic point of view than detecting and correcting all errors identified in the text.

To date, there is no publically available annotated dataset consisting of sentences marked with a score representing their linguistic quality. Manual annotation is typically expensive and time-consuming, and a certain amount of annotator training is generally required. Instead, we exploit already available annotated data – scores and error annotation in the FCE dataset – and evaluate various approaches, two of which are: a) to use the script-level model (see Section 2.1) to predict sentence quality scores, and b) to use the script-level score divided by the total number of (manually annotated) errors in a sentence as pseudo-gold labels to train a sentence-level model.

As the models above are expected to contain a certain amount of noise, it is imperative that we identify evaluation measures that are indicative of our application – that is, assign higher scores to high-quality sentences compared to low-quality ones – and not only depend on the labels they have been trained on. More specifically, we use correlation with pseudo-gold scores (r_g and ρ_g; not applicable to the script-level model), correlation with the script-level scores by first averaging predicted sentence-level scores (r_s and ρ_s), correlation with error counts (r_e and ρ_e), average precision (AP) and pairwise accuracy. AP is a measure used in information retrieval to evaluate systems that return a ranked list of documents. Herein, sentences are ranked by their predicted scores, precision is calculated at each correct sentence (that is, containing no errors), and averaged over all correct sentences (in other words, we treat sentences with no errors as the 'relevant documents'). Pairwise accuracy is calculated based on the number of times the corrected sentence (available through the error annotation in the FCE dataset) is ranked higher than the original one written by the candidate, ignoring sentences without errors. Correlation with error counts, average precision and pairwise accuracy are particularly important as they reflect more directly the extent to which good and bad sentences are discriminated. Again, in both cases, we employ a linear ranking perceptron.

We conducted a series of experiments on a separate development set to evaluate the performance of features beyond the ones used in the script-level model. The final results, reported in Table 1, are calculated on the FCE test set (Yannakoudakis et al., 2011).

Our best configuration is model b, which achieves the highest results according to most evaluation measures with a feature space consisting of 1) error counts identified through the absence of word trigrams in a large background corpus, 2) phrase-structure rules, 3) presence of frequent errors, as well as the number of words defining an error, as described in Section 2.3, 4) the presence of main verbs, nouns, adjectives, subordinating conjuctions and adverbs, 5) affixes and 6) the presence of clausal subjects and modifiers. The texts were parsed using RASP (Briscoe et al., 2006).

Model a, the script-level model, does not work as well at the sentence level. However, it does perform better when evaluated against script-level scores (r_s and ρ_s), and this is expected given that it is trained directly on gold script-level scores. On the other hand, this evaluation measure is not as indicative of good performance in our application as the others, as it does not take into account the varying quality of individual sentences within a script.

Training the script-level model with different feature sets (including those utilised in the sentence-level model) did not yield an improvement in performance (the results are omitted due to space restrictions). Additional experiments were conducted to investigate the effect of training the sentence-level model with different pseudo-gold labels (*e.g.*, additive/subtractive pseudo-gold scores rather than divisive/multiplicative), but the results are not reported here as the difference in performance was not substantial.

Table 1 shows that better performance can be achieved with our pseudo-gold labels, used to train a model at the sentence level, rather than gold la-

	Model a	Model b
r_g	—	0.550
ρ_g	—	0.646
r_s	0.572	0.385
ρ_s	0.578	0.301
r_e	–0.111	–0.750
ρ_e	–0.078	–0.702
AP	0.393	0.747
Pairwise		
Correct	0.608	0.703
Incorrect	0.359	0.204

Table 1: Results on the FCE test set for the script-level model (a) and our model (b).

bels at the script level. To evaluate this further, we trained a sentence-level model using the script-level scores as labels (that is, sentences within the same script are all assigned the same label/score). However, this did not improve performance (again, the results are omitted due to space restrictions). We also point out that the best-performing feature space (described above) is based on text properties that are more likely to be present in relatively short sentences (*e.g.,* the presence of main verbs), compared to those used for script-level models in previous work (Yannakoudakis et al., 2011), such as word and part-of-speech bigrams and trigrams, which may be too sparse for a sentence-level model.

Analogously to what we did to present the overall score, we developed a sentence score feedback view to indicate the general quality of the sentences, as given by our best model, by highlighting each of them with a background colour ranging from green for a well-written sentence, via yellow and orange for a sentence which the system thinks is acceptable, to dark orange and red for a sentence which may have a few problems. Figure 2 shows how the SAT system evaluates and colour-codes a few authentic student-written sentences containing errors, as well as their corrected counterparts based on the error-coding in the FCE test set. Overall, the system correctly identifies correct and incorrect versions of each sentence, attributing a higher score (greener colour) to the corrected sentence in each pair.

2.3 Word-level feedback

Basic spelling checkers have been around since the 1970s and grammar checkers since the 1980s (Kukich, 1992), but misleading 'corrections' may be bewildering (Galletta et al., 2005), and the systems do not always focus on the kinds of error frequently committed, even less so in the case of learners as was pointed out early on by Liou (1992), who tested commercial grammar checkers on and developed a system for detecting common errors in Taiwanese learners' writing.

For word-level feedback within the SAT system, we have implemented a method similar to one we have used earlier in the context of pre-annotation of learner corpora (Andersen, 2011). To ensure high precision and good coverage of local errors typically committed by learners, error rules are generated from the Cambridge Learner Corpus (CLC) (Nicholls, 2003) to detect word unigrams, bigrams and trigrams which have been annotated as incorrect at least five times and at least ninety per cent of the times they occur. This way, rules can be extracted from the existing error annotation in the corpus, obviating the need for manually constructed mal-rules, although the rules obtained by the two different methods may to some extent be complementary. In addition to corpus-derived rules, many classes of incorrect but plausible derivational and inflectional morphology are detected by means of rules derived from a machine-readable dictionary. Many mistakes are still not detected, but precision has been found to be more important in terms of learning effect (Nagata and Nakatani, 2010), and errors missed by this module will often give lower sentence scores.

Figure 3 illustrates some types of error detected by the system. The feedback text is generated from a small number of templates corresponding to different categories of error marked up in the CLC.

We are currently working on extending this part of the system with more general rules in addition to word n-grams, *e.g.,* part-of-speech tags and grammatical relations, in order to detect more errors without loss in precision.

3 Trials

After the SAT system had been developed, a series of trials were set up in order to test the online sys-

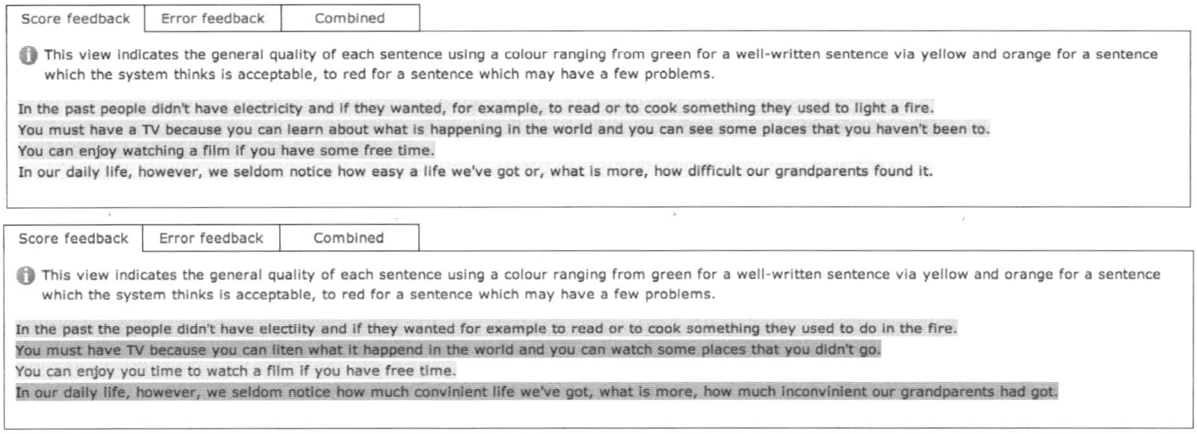

Figure 2: Examples of correct sentences (top) and incorrect ones (bottom) colour-coded by the SAT system.

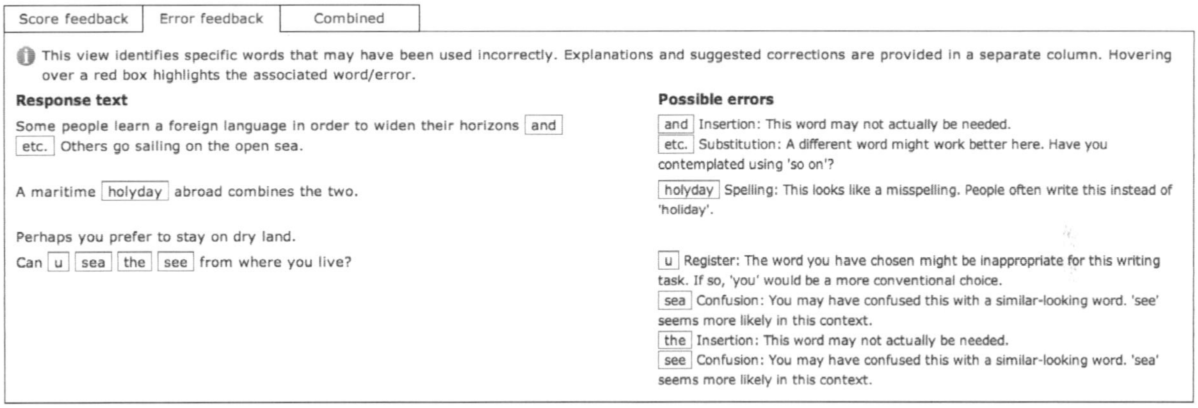

Figure 3: The *error feedback* view identifies specific words that may have been used incorrectly. Explanations and suggested corrections are provided in a separate column. The system actually proposes two different corrections for *and etc.*, namely *etc.* and *and so on*; the user will have to choose one or the other. The confusion between the verb *see* and the noun *sea* is identified, but the *the* is not actually unnecessary; in this case, the system has been led astray by the surrounding errors.

tem and to collect feedback from language learners and their teachers in a variety of contexts. Three trials were undertaken in November 2012, December 2012 and in March 2013, with changes made to the system between each pair of trials.

English Profile Network member institutions were contacted who had access to language learners and who had previously participated in data collection for the English Profile Programme[2]. Teachers at universities, secondary schools and private language schools signed up for two or more trials so that their learners could use and provide feedback on several iterations of the SAT system. Certificates of participation were offered to encourage involvement in the trials.

Ten institutions were involved from nine countries, namely Belgium, the Czech Republic, France, Lithuania, Poland, Romania, Russia, Slovakia and Spain. Eight universities, one secondary school and one private language school were represented, including specialist and generalist institutions of educational sciences, agricultural science, veterinary medicine and foreign languages. Each trial had between 4 and 8 institutions taking part, and each institution participated in two or three trials with many students undertaking more than one trial.

All students who took part in the trials, over 450

[2]See *www.englishprofile.org*

in total, were expected to be at or above the upper-intermediate (CEFR B2) level as this was the level at which the SAT system was designed to function.

Three initial sets of tasks were developed for the planned system trials, each set consisting of three short written prompts which asked the users to write on a specified topic for a particular purpose, for example:

> *Daily life*
>
> *Your English class is going to make a short video about daily life in your town. Write a report for your teacher, suggesting which activities should be filmed, and why.*

Tasks were based on retired questions from an international proficiency test at B2 level of the CEFR. Each task was given a short name which was shown in the SAT system in order for the users to select the most interesting or relevant task for themselves.

A short set of instructions was produced for both teachers and students which was emailed to the main contact in each institution and passed on to their colleagues, teachers and students who were interested in taking part in the trial.

The trials operated as follows:

- The main institutional contact receives an invitation to participate in the trials.
- Interested institutions receive instructions and confirm the number of class keys required (sign-up codes for the system).
- Main contact and teachers at each institution log in and work through the system as if they are a language learner, by completing a demographic questionnaire, writing 1–3 tasks which are assessed by the system, and finally completing a short user satisfaction questionnaire.
- Students work through the SAT system either with the support of their teacher in class or remotely.

3.1 SAT system usage

During Trial 1, on the busiest day there were 155 submissions and the highest number of users on a single day was 32. These figures indicate that all users were submitting their work for assessment more than once, which suggests that the system is being used in an iterative fashion as envisaged. During Trial 2, the busiest day saw more than twice as many submissions as during the first trial (442), and the most people online on any one day almost doubled to 62. Across both trials we collected around 3000 submissions in total, including revisions; the average number of revisions for a submitted piece of writing is 3.2 with the highest figure being 54 revisions (see Table 2 for details). This suggests that some users write their first response, then make changes to one word or phrase at a time, resulting in such a large number of revisions. When more than one revision has been submitted, the score given by the system to the last revision is higher than that given to the initial revision in over 80% of the cases. Current changes to the system allowing system administrators to check on intermediate versions of submitted texts are underway.

Revisions	Count
1	292
2	272
3	142
4	78
5	50
6	28
7	15
8	25
9	11
10	14
11–15	21
16–20	6
20–	5

Table 2: Number of revisions per task response.

3.2 Feedback

In addition to looking at the writing submitted by users of the system, there was both numerical and written feedback available to the system developers. This was used to suggest changes to the system at subsequent trials.

As can be seen from Table 3, user satisfaction scores were generally high and increased from Trial 1 to Trial 2. In the first pilot, the written feedback from instructors was generally positive whilst

	Trial 1	Trial 2
Using the SAT system helps me to write better in English.	3.80	3.92
I find the SAT system useful for understanding my mistakes.	3.74	3.96
I think the sentence colouring is useful.	3.74	4.15
I think the word-level information [error feedback] is useful.	3.86	4.12
The SAT system is easy to use.	4.45	4.49
The feedback on my writing is clear.	3.80	3.93
If you have used the SAT system before, has it improved since the last time?		3.86

Table 3: Average feedback scores on a scale from 1 (strongly disagree) to 5 (strongly agree).

the learner feedback was mixed, especially when it comes to sentence evaluation:

> *In summary, I liked this system, because the sentence colouring suggests me to think about my writing style, mistakes, what I should improve, change. This system is not like a teacher, who checks all our errors, but makes us develop our critical thinking, which is the most important for writing especially. [...]*
>
> *It's okay the way of colouring system, the problem is that it doesn't tell you specifically what's wrong with constructions so you have think what you failed.*

The fact that the system provides almost immediate feedback has been appreciated:

> *I like that the paragraphs which I wrote assesed so quickly. ... Secondly, I really like that student can correct his text till it gets ideal.*

Users have also made suggestions for improvements, which have been essential for deciding which parts of the system should be developed further.

3.3 System changes

As a result of feedback and the team's extensive use of the system, after each trial changes were made both to the on-screen experience and behind the scenes. After Trial 1, the system was amended to enable users to see paragraph breaks in the corrected version (which before had not been shown in the assessed view of the text). There was also a new error view with permanently visible explanations and examples and an additional question on the feedback questionnaire which asked whether users felt the system had improved since the previous time they used it. Behind the scenes, the server was upgraded to cope with anticipated demand and code was written so that administrators could review statistics on usage.

Words	Count
0– 99	540
100–199	1,294
200–299	928
300–399	201
400–499	67
500–999	26
1,000–	36

Table 4: Number of words per submission.

At the time of writing the third SAT system trial was underway. In the first two trials the total number of words collected was over 600,000 with an average response length of around 1100 characters or 200 words. Encouragingly, there were many longer responses including twelve over 1080 words in length and the longest written to date is 1773 words. These figures indicate that the system is not restrictive, but encourages and inspires students to write. Table 4 gives an overview of the script length distribution.

Following two successful trials, the third trial aimed to involve new and existing users and to provide more detailed teacher feedback.

4 Conclusions

In this paper, we described a tool that provides feedback to learners of English at three different levels of granularity: an overall assessment of their proficiency, assessment of individual sentences, and diagnostic feedback on local issues including spelling and word choice. We argued that the use of visualisation techniques is important, as they allow us to go beyond the mere display of a number, can stimulate the learners' visual perceptions, and can display information in an intuitive and easily interpretable way. The usefulness and usability of the tool as a whole, as well as of its components, was confirmed through questionnaire-based evaluations, where, for example, the perceived usefulness of the sentence colouring received an average of 4.15 on a 5-point scale.

The first component of the SAT system, script-level assessment, uses a machine learner to predict a score for a text and roughly estimate someone's proficiency level based on lexical and grammatical features. The second component allows for an automatic evaluation of the linguistic quality of individual sentences. We proposed a method for generating sentence-level scores, which we use for training our model. Using this method, we were able to learn what features can be used to evaluate linguistic quality of (relatively short) sentences. Indicating problematic regions via highlighting of sentences may be better from a pedagogic point of view than detecting and correcting all errors identified in the text. The third component automatically provides diagnostic feedback on local errors with high precision on the basis of a few templates, without relying on manually crafted rules.

The trials undertaken so far have improved the functionality of the system in regard to what is on offer to teachers and their students, but they have also provided the basis for further research and development to enhance the system's functionality and design and move towards wider deployment. We plan to continue improving the methodologies used for providing feedback to learners, as well as adding further functionality, such as L1-specific feedback. Another logical next step would be to continue towards lower levels of granularity, moving from the sentence as the unit of assessment to clauses and phrases, which may be particularly beneficial for more advanced language users who write longer and more complex sentences.

Acknowledgements

Special thanks to Ted Briscoe and Marek Rei, as well as to the anonymous reviewers, for their valuable contributions at various stages.

References

Øistein E. Andersen. 2011. Semi-automatic ESOL error annotation. *English Profile Journal*, 2.

Yigal Attali and Jill Burstein. 2006. Automated essay scoring with e-Rater v.2.0. *Journal of Technology, Learning, and Assessment*, 4(3):1–30.

Yigal Attali, Don Powers, Marshall Freedman, Marissa Harrison, and Susan Obetz. 2008. Automated Scoring of short-answer open-ended GRE subject test items. Technical Report 04, ETS.

Tamar Ben-Bassat, Joachim Meyer, and Noam Tractinsky. 2006. Economic and subjective measures of the perceived value of aesthetics and usability. *ACM Transactions on Computer-Human Interaction*, 13(2):210–234.

Siegfried Bös and Manfred Opper. 1998. Dynamics of batch training in a perceptron. *Journal of Physics A: Mathematical and General*, 31(21):4835–4850.

Ted Briscoe, John Carroll, and Rebecca Watson. 2006. The second release of the RASP system. In *ACL-Coling'06 Interactive Presentation Session*, pages 77–80.

Ted Briscoe, Ben Medlock, and Øistein E. Andersen. 2010. Automated assessment of ESOL free text examinations. Technical Report UCAM-CL-TR-790, University of Cambridge, Computer Laboratory.

Jill Burstein, Martin Chodorow, and Claudia Leacock. 2003. Criterion: Online essay evaluation: An application for automated evaluation of student essays. In *Proceedings of the fifteenth annual conference on innovative applications of artificial intelligence*, pages 3–10.

Council of Europe. 2001. *Common European Framework of Reference for Languages: Learning, Teaching, Assessment*. Cambridge University Press.

Markus Dickinson, Sandra Kübler, and Anthony Meyer. 2012. Predicting learner levels for online exercises of Hebrew. In *Proceedings of the Seventh Workshop on Innovative Use of NLP for Building Educational Applications*, pages 95–104. Association for Computational Linguistics.

Semire Dikli. 2006. An overview of automated scoring of essays. *Journal of Technology, Learning, and Assessment*, 5(1).

Dennis F. Galletta, Alexandra Durcikova, Andrea Everard, and Brian M. Jones. 2005. Does spell-checking software need a warning label? *Communications of the ACM*, 48(7):82–86.

Michael Gamon, Claudia Leacock, Chris Brockett, William B Dolan, Jianfeng Gao, Dmitriy Belenko, and

Alexandre Klementiev. 2009. Using statistical techniques and web search to correct ESL errors. *Calico Journal*, 26(3):491–511.

John A. Hawkins and Luna Filipović. 2012. *Criterial Features in L2 English: Specifying the Reference Levels of the Common European Framework.* English Profile Studies. Cambridge University Press.

Derrick Higgins, Jill Burstein, Daniel Marcu, and Claudia Gentile. 2004. Evaluating multiple aspects of coherence in student essays. In *Proceedings of the Human Language Technology Conference of the North American Chapter of the Association for Computational Linguistics*.

Thorsten Joachims. 2002. Optimizing search engines using clickthrough data. In *Proceedings of the ACM Conference on Knowledge Discovery and Data Mining*, pages 133–142.

Karen Kukich. 1992. Techniques for automatically correcting words in text. *ACM Computing Surveys*, 24(4):377–439.

Hsien-Chin Liou. 1992. An automatic text-analysis project for EFL writing revision. *System: The International Journal of Educational Technology and Language Learning Systems*, 20(4):481–492.

Michael A.G. Mohler, Razvan Bunescu, and Rada Mihalcea. 2011. Learning to grade short answer questions using semantic similarity measures and dependency graph alignments. In *Proceedings of the 49th Annual Meeting of the Association for Computational Linguistics: Human Language Technologies*.

Ryo Nagata and Kazuhide Nakatani. 2010. Evaluating performance of grammatical error detection to maximize learning effect. In *Proceedings of the 23rd International Conference on Computational Linguistics: Posters*, COLING '10, pages 894–900, Stroudsburg, PA, USA. Association for Computational Linguistics.

Diane Nicholls. 2003. The Cambridge Learner Corpus: Error coding and analysis for lexicography and ELT. In Dawn Archer, Paul Rayson, Andrew Wilson, and Tony McEnery, editors, *Proceedings of the Corpus Linguistics conference*, volume 16 of *Technical Papers*, pages 572–581. University Centre For Computer Corpus Research on Lanugage, Lancaster University, Lancaster.

Ellis B. Page. 1968. The use of the computer in analyzing student essays. *International Review of Education*, 14(2):210–225.

Stephen G. Pulman and Jana Z. Sukkarieh. 2005. Automatic short answer marking. In *Proceedings of the second workshop on Building Educational Applications Using natural language processing*, pages 9–16.

Lawrence M. Rudner and Tahung Liang. 2002. Automated essay scoring using Bayes' theorem. *The Journal of Technology, Learning and Assessment*, 1(2):3–21.

Mark D. Shermis and Ben Hamner. 2012. Contrasting state-of-the-art automated scoring of essays: analysis. Technical report, The University of Akron and Kaggle.

Ying-Jian Wang, Hui-Fang Shang, and Paul Briody. In press. Exploring the impact of using automated writing evaluation in English as a foreign language university students' writing. *Computer Assisted Language Learning*.

David M. Williamson. 2009. A framework for implementing automated scoring. In *Proceedings of the Annual Meeting of the American Educational Research Association and the National Council on Measurement in Education*, San Diego, CA.

Helen Yannakoudakis, Ted Briscoe, and Ben Medlock. 2011. A new dataset and method for automatically grading ESOL texts. In *Proceedings of the 49th Annual Meeting of the Association for Computational Linguistics: Human Language Technologies*.

Ramon Ziai, Niels Ott, and Detmar Meurers. 2012. Short answer assessment: Establishing links between research strands. In *Proceedings of the workshop on Building Educational Applications Using natural language processing*, pages 190–200.

Automated Essay Scoring for Swedish

Robert Östling
Department of Linguistics
Stockholm University
SE-106 91 Stockholm
robert@ling.su.se

Andre Smolentzov
Department of Linguistics
Stockholm University
SE-106 91 Stockholm
asmolentzov@gmail.com

Björn Tyrefors Hinnerich
Department of Economics
Stockholm University
SE-106 91 Stockholm
bjorn.hinnerich@ne.su.se

Erik Höglin
National Institute of Economic Research
Kungsgatan 12-14
103 62 Stockholm
erik.hoglin@konj.se

Abstract

We present the first system developed for automated grading of high school essays written in Swedish. The system uses standard text quality indicators and is able to compare vocabulary and grammar to large reference corpora of blog posts and newspaper articles. The system is evaluated on a corpus of 1 702 essays, each graded independently by the student's own teacher and also in a blind re-grading process by another teacher. We show that our system's performance is fair, given the low agreement between the two human graders, and furthermore show how it could improve efficiency in a practical setting where one seeks to identify incorrectly graded essays.

1 Introduction

Automated Essay Scoring (AES) is the field of automatically assigning grades to student essays (Shermis and Burstein, 2003; Dikli, 2006).

Previous work on AES has primarily focused on English texts, and to the best of our knowledge no AES system for Swedish essays has been published. We exploit some peculiarities of the Swedish language, such as its compounding nature, to design new features for classification. We also use constructions in the shape of *hybrid n-grams* (Tsao and Wible, 2009) extracted from large corpora in the classification.

Earlier results from this work have been presented in the B.A. thesis of Smolentzov (2013), where further details can be found. Source code, a trained model as well as an on-line version of our tool are available from the website of the Department of Linguistics.[1] Due to legal restrictions, we are currently unable to publish the corpus of essays used for training the model and in our evaluation. While this is very regrettable, there are so far no suitable training corpora available for Swedish that are publicly available. We hope in the future to be able to produce an anonymized version of the corpus, to be shared with other researchers.

2 Data

We use a corpus of essays from the essay writing part of the Swedish high school national exams in Swedish.[2] These were collected using random sampling by Hinnerich et al. (2011), who had them digitized, anonymized, and re-graded by high school teachers experienced with grading the national exams. The essays were originally graded by the student's own teacher. In total, 1 702 essays have all the information we require: digitized text and the two grades. The size of the corpus is 1 116 819 tokens, or an average of 656 per essay. The essays have been automatically annotated with lemma and part of speech (PoS) information using Stagger (Östling, 2012).

There are four grades: IG (fail), G (pass), VG (pass with distinction) and MVG (excellent). Hinnerich et al. (2011) found that the agreement between the two human graders is rather low, and in the set of essays used in this study only 780 (45.8%) of the 1 702 essays received the same grade by both

[1] http://www.ling.su.se/aes

[2] Course *Svenska B*, fall 2005/spring 2006.

		Teacher				
		IG	G	VG	MVG	Sum
Blind grader	IG	74	147	50	5	276
	G	68	437	293	55	853
	VG	12	136	223	75	446
	MVG	1	25	55	46	127
	Sum	155	745	621	181	1 702

Table 1: Confusion matrix for the grades assigned by the students' own teachers, and during the blind re-grading process. In total, 780 essays (45.8%) are assigned the same grade. Linear weighted $\kappa = 0.276$

graders. In 148 cases (8.7%), the grade difference was more than one step.

In Table 1, we can clearly see that the blind graders' grades are generally lower. The disagreement is also more severe for the grades at the extremes of the scale.

It is important to note that the grading guidelines for the national exams do not focus exclusively on the quality of the language used, but rather on the ability of the student to produce a coherent and convincing argument, understanding and relating to other texts, or describing personal experiences. Some work has been carried out using high-level features in automated essay scoring. Miltsakaki and Kukich (2004) use some manual annotation to explore the role of coherence, and Attali and Burstein (2005) automatically analyze the overall structure of essays. Others take the contents of essays into account (Landauer et al., 2003), which is suitable for essay questions in non-language subjects.

We will, however, focus on form rather than content. One important reason for this is that our corpus of essays is spread out over 19 different topics (in several cases with as few as 20–30 essays each), where the type of text expected can vary considerably between topics.

3 Methods

We use a supervised machine learning approach, based on a Linear Discriminant Analysis classifier in the implementation of Pedregosa et al. (2011). Each essay is represented by a *feature vector*, whose contents we will describe in some detail in the following sections.

It is important to note that we are using *correlations* between grade and different features of the text, but the relationship between these features and the qualities of the essay on which the grade should be based may be complex. As a cautionary tale, we could mention that vocabulary related to cell phones was found to correlate strongly with essay grade. It turned out that poor students showed a strong preference for one of the given essay topics, which happened to center around cell phones. In the field of AES, it is particularly important to keep in mind that *correlation does not imply causation*.

3.1 Simple features

We use a number of features that may be directly measured from the text. These are presented below, roughly in decreasing order of correlation with essay grade. Most of the features have been discussed in previous literature on AES (Attali and Burstein, 2005), and specifically in the context of Swedish high school essays by Hultman and Westman (1977). Some further features that did not contribute much to grading accuracy were tried, but will be omitted from this discussion.

Text length Since the essays are composed in a classroom setting with a fixed amount of time allotted (five hours), a student's fluency in writing is directly mirrored in the length of an essay, which becomes the feature that most strongly correlates with grade. While one might want to exclude the length from consideration in the grading process, it is important to keep this correlation in mind since other measures may correlate with length, and therefore indirectly correlate with essay grade without contributing any new information.

Average word length The average number of letters per word also correlates with grade but only weakly with the length (in words). It does however correlate strongly with the distribution of parts of speech, primarily pronouns (which tend to be short) and nouns (which tend to be long, particularly since Swedish is a compounding language).

OVIX lexical diversity measure OVIX (Hultman, 1994) was in fact developed for the very purpose of analyzing lexical diversity in Swedish high school essays, and has been found to correlate strongly with grade in this setting. At the same time, the measure is mostly independent of text length.

$$OVIX = \log n_{tokens} / \left(2 - \frac{\log n_{types}}{\log n_{tokens}}\right)$$

Part of speech distribution The relative frequencies of different parts of speech also correlate with essay grade, although more weakly so than the related measure of average word length.

3.2 Corpus-induced features

While the size our corpus of graded student essays is in the order of one million words, much larger amounts of Swedish text are available from different sources, such as opinion pieces, news articles, and blog posts. Due to the large amounts of text available, from tens of millions to several billions of words depending on the source, we can extract reliable statistics even about relatively rare language phenomena.

By comparing student essays to statistics gathered from different text types, we obtain new variables that often correlate strongly with essay grades.

PoS tag cross-entropy The average cross-entropy per token from a PoS trigram model (with simple additive smoothing) is used to model the similarity on a syntactic level. This includes both elements of style (e.g. frequent use of passive constructions) and mechanics (e.g. agreement errors). We use a corpus of news texts[3] to train the model.

Vocabulary cross-entropy With word frequency statistics from two different text sources, we compute the average cross-entropy per token given a unigram model, and use the difference between these values for the two models to indicate which type of text the present essay is most similar to. In our experiments, the two text sources are of equal size and consist of the news texts mentioned above, and a corpus of blog posts.

Hybrid n-gram cross-entropy We can generalize the vocabulary cross-entropy measure described above by using *hybrid n-grams* (Tsao and Wible, 2009) rather than single words. This allows for some patterns that are neither entirely grammatical nor entirely lexical to be used, complementing the two previous approaches. The same news and blog corpora as above are used.

[3]The corpus consists of ca 200 million words, crawled from the WWW editions of Dagens Nyheter and Svenska Dagbladet.

3.3 Language error features

Spelling errors We implemented a simple spell checker, using the SALDO lexicon (Borin and Forsberg, 2009) and statistics from a corpus of news text. On average, a misspelling was detected in 0.63% of all word tokens, or about four misspellings per essay. Manual inspection showed that the spell checker made some errors, so it is reasonable to assume that results could be improved somewhat using a more accurate tool.

Split compound errors Swedish is a compounding language, with noun compounding particularly frequent. It is a fairly common error among inexperienced writers to separate the segments of a compound word. We use word uni- and bigram statistics from a corpus of news texts to find instances of these errors in the essays. Only 0.10% of word tokens are found to be incorrectly split, or less than one instance per essay on average. As expected, there is a (weak) negative correlation between split compound frequency and grade, which seems to be due to a small number of poor essays with many such errors.

3.4 Evaluation measures

The simplest measure of overlap between two graders (either among humans, or between human(s) and machine) is the percentage of essays on which they agree about the grade. However, in our setting this is not so informative because there is a high chance of graders assigning the same grade by chance, and this probability varies between different pairs of graders.

This makes comparisons difficult, so we instead use Cohen's kappa value (Cohen, 1968), linearly weighted according to the numeric values of grades used by the Swedish school system: IG corresponds to 0 points, G to 10, VG to 15, and MVG to 20. A kappa value of 1 would indicate perfect agreement, while 0 would mean random agreement. The

Feature	Correlation
$n_{tokens}^{0.25}$	0.535
n_{tokens}	0.502
hybrid n-gram cross-entropy	0.363
vocabulary cross-entropy	0.361
average word length	0.307
OVIX	0.304
n_{long}/n_{tokens}	0.284
spelling errors	-0.257
PoS cross-entropy	0.216
split compound errors	-0.208

Table 2: Correlation between grade (average of two graders) and features. Interactions between features are not taken into account. Only features with Pearson coefficient $\rho > 0.2$ are included, all are highly significant.

		Computer				
		IG	G	VG	MVG	Sum
Human avg.	IG	107	176	6	0	289
	G	61	752	110	11	934
	VG	2	225	189	17	433
	MVG	0	9	27	10	46
	Sum	170	1 162	332	38	1 702

Table 3: Confusion matrix for the grades assigned by the system, and the average (rounded down) of the two human graders. In total, 1 058 essays (62.2%) are assigned the same grade, $\kappa = 0.399$.

weighted kappa value is computed as:

$$\kappa = 1 - \frac{\sum_{i,j} w_{ij} O_{ij}}{\sum_{i,j} w_{ij} E_{ij}}$$

where O_{ij} is the number of times annotator 1 assigned grade i and annotator 2 assigned grade j, while E_{ij} is the *expected* number of times for the same event, given that both annotators randomly assign grades according to a multinomial distribution. w_{ij} is the difference in score between grades i and j, according to the above.

4 Results

4.1 Feature-grade correlations

First, we look at the correlations between the human-assigned grades and individual features. Since a linear machine learning algorithm is used, we use the Pearson coefficient to measure linear dependence. Spearman's rank correlation coefficient gives similar results.

From Table 2 we can see that only ten of the features show a correlation above 0.2. There were statistically significant (but weak) correlations below this threshold, e.g. the ratios of different parts of speech, where the strongest correlations were $\rho = -0.192$ (pronouns) and $\rho = 0.177$ (prepositions).

4.2 Automated grading

Table 3 shows the performance of our system, using the leave-one-out evaluation method on all 1 702 essays, i.e. evaluating each essay using a model trained on all the other 1 701 essays. We see that the computer's grades are biased towards the most common grade (G, pass), but that overall accuracy is quite high (62.2%, $\kappa = 0.399$) compared to 58.4% ($\kappa = 0.249$) when using only the strongest feature (4th root of essay length), 54.9% when assigning the most common grade to all essays, or the 45.8% ($\kappa = 0.276$) agreement between the two human graders.

It is also encouraging to see that only 28 essays (1.6%) receive a grade by the computer that differs more than one step from the human-assigned grade. The corresponding figure is 148 essays (8.7%) between the two humans.

When training and evaluating using only the grades of the blind grader, the agreement between computer and human was 57.6% ($\kappa = 0.369$), and only 53.6% ($\kappa = 0.345$) using the grades of the student's teacher. Both these figures are below the 62.2% ($\kappa = 0.399$) obtained when using the average grade, and the explanation closest at hand is that the features we model (partially) represent or correlate with the actual grading criteria of the exam.

Since the teachers are affected by various sources of bias (Hinnerich et al., 2011), a weaker correlation (mirrored by a lower κ) to any kind of "objective" measure would be expected. Similarly, using the average of two graders should decrease the large individual variance due to the difficult and partially subjective nature of the task, leading to a stronger correlation with relevant features of the text.

4.3 Re-grading

In 148 cases (8.7%) of our 1 702 essays, the grade assigned in the blind re-grading process differs by more than one step from the original grade, and we performed an experiment to see how efficiently these *highly deviant* grades could be identified. This scenario could arise within an organization responsible for evaluating the consistency in grading a national exam, where resources are insufficient for re-grading *all* essays manually. Given a training corpus of graded essays, our system could then be used to select candidates among the larger set of essays for further manual re-grading.

In other to evaluate the usefulness of this method, we let the system re-grade all essays based on the blind grades of all other essays (leave-one-out). In the cases where the system's grade differs by more than one step from the teacher's grade, we check whether the difference between the system's grade and that of the blind grader is less than between the two human graders. It turns out that we can correctly identify 43 (29.1%) of the 148 cases in this way, with only 91 essays (5.3% of the total) considered.

In a scenario where we have a large amount of essays but only the resources to manually re-grade a fraction of them, we can thus increase the ratio of highly deviant grades found from 8.7% (148/1702, by randomly choosing essays to re-grade) to 47% (43/91, by only re-grading those identified by our system).

5 Conclusions and future work

We have presented a system for automatic grading of Swedish high school essays. While its accuracy is not high enough to be used in grading high-stakes exams, we have demonstrated its usefulness in a practical setting of finding instances of incorrect grading (as identified by humans). Novel aspects include features based on constructions induced using unsupervised methods, and on (language-specific) compounding errors.

It would be interesting to apply some of our methods to other languages and other data sets, for instance of second language learners. Since our system is quite general, all that would be needed to adapt it to another domain is a training corpus of graded essays. Adapting to another language would in addition require a PoS tagger and suitable unlabeled text corpora.

Acknowledgments

We would like to thank the anonymous reviewers for their useful comments.

References

Yigal Attali and Jill Burstein. 2005. Automated essay scoring with e-rater® v.2.0. Technical report, Educational Testing Services.

Lars Borin and Markus Forsberg. 2009. All in the family: A comparison of SALDO and WordNet. In *Proceedings of the Nodalida 2009 Workshop on WordNets and other Lexical Semantic Resources – between Lexical Semantics, Lexicography, Terminology and Formal Ontologies*, Odense.

Jacob Cohen. 1968. Weighted kappa: Nominal scale agreement provision for scaled disagreement or partial credit. *Psychological Bulletin*, 70:213–220.

Semire Dikli. 2006. An overview of automated scoring of essays. *Journal of Technology, Learning, and Assessment*, 5.

Björn Tyrefors Hinnerich, Erik Höglin, and Magnus Johannesson. 2011. Are boys discriminated in swedish high schools? *Economics of Education Review*, 30:682–690.

Tor G. Hultman and Margareta Westman. 1977. *Gymnasistsvenska*. LiberLäromedel.

Tor G. Hultman. 1994. Hur gick det med ovix? In *Språkbruk, grammatik och språkförändring. En festskrift till Ulf Teleman*, pages 55–64. Lund University.

Thomas K. Landauer, Darrell Laham, and Peter Foltz. 2003. Automatic essay assessment. *Assessment in Education*, 10:295–308.

E. Miltsakaki and K. Kukich. 2004. Evaluation of text coherence for electronic essay scoring systems. *Natural Language Engineering*, 10:25–55.

Robert Östling. 2012. Stagger: A modern POS tagger for Swedish. In *Proceedings of the Swedish Language Technology Conference (SLTC)*.

F. Pedregosa, G. Varoquaux, A. Gramfort, V. Michel, B. Thirion, O. Grisel, M. Blondel, P. Prettenhofer, R. Weiss, V. Dubourg, J. Vanderplas, A. Passos, D. Cournapeau, M. Brucher, M. Perrot, and E. Duchesnay. 2011. Scikit-learn: Machine learning in Python. *Journal of Machine Learning Research*, 12:2825–2830.

M.D. Shermis and J. Burstein, editors. 2003. *Automated Essay Scoring: A Cross Disciplinary Perspective*. L. Erlbaum Associates.

André Smolentzov. 2013. *Automated Essay Scoring: Scoring Essays in Swedish.* Bachelor's thesis, Department of Linguistics, Stockholm University.

Nai-Lung Tsao and David Wible. 2009. A method for unsupervised broad-coverage lexical error detection and correction. In *Proceedings of the Fourth Workshop on Innovative Use of NLP for Building Educational Applications*, EdAppsNLP '09, pages 51–54, Stroudsburg, PA, USA. Association for Computational Linguistics.

A Report on the First Native Language Identification Shared Task

Joel Tetreault*, **Daniel Blanchard**† **and Aoife Cahill**†

* Nuance Communications, Inc., 1198 E. Arques Ave, Sunnyvale, CA 94085, USA
Joel.Tetreault@nuance.com
† Educational Testing Service, 660 Rosedale Road, Princeton, NJ 08541, USA
{dblanchard, acahill}@ets.org

Abstract

Native Language Identification, or NLI, is the task of automatically classifying the L1 of a writer based solely on his or her essay written in another language. This problem area has seen a spike in interest in recent years as it can have an impact on educational applications tailored towards non-native speakers of a language, as well as authorship profiling. While there has been a growing body of work in NLI, it has been difficult to compare methodologies because of the different approaches to pre-processing the data, different sets of languages identified, and different splits of the data used. In this shared task, the first ever for Native Language Identification, we sought to address the above issues by providing a large corpus designed specifically for NLI, in addition to providing an environment for systems to be directly compared. In this paper, we report the results of the shared task. A total of 29 teams from around the world competed across three different sub-tasks.

1 Introduction

One quickly growing subfield in NLP is the task of identifying the native language (L1) of a writer based solely on a sample of their writing in another language. The task is framed as a classification problem where the set of L1s is known *a priori*. Most work has focused on identifying the native language of writers learning English as a second language. To date this topic has motivated several papers and research projects.

Native Language Identification (NLI) can be useful for a number of applications. NLI can be used in educational settings to provide more targeted feedback to language learners about their errors. It is well known that speakers of different languages make different kinds of errors when learning a language (Swan and Smith, 2001). A writing tutor system which can detect the native language of the learner will be able to tailor the feedback about the error and contrast it with common properties of the learner's language. In addition, native language is often used as a feature that goes into authorship profiling (Estival et al., 2007), which is frequently used in forensic linguistics.

Despite the growing interest in this field, development has been encumbered by two issues. First is the issue of data. Evaluating an NLI system requires a corpus containing texts in a language other than the native language of the writer. Because of a scarcity of such corpora, most work has used the International Corpus of Learner English (ICLEv2) (Granger et al., 2009) for training and evaluation since it contains several hundred essays written by college-level English language learners. However, this corpus is quite small for training and testing statistical systems which makes it difficult to tell whether the systems that are developed can scale well to larger data sets or to different domains.

Since the ICLE corpus was not designed with the task of NLI in mind, the usability of the corpus for this task is further compromised by idiosyncrasies in the data such as topic bias (as shown by Brooke and Hirst (2011)) and the occurrence of characters which only appear in essays written by speakers of certain languages (Tetreault et al., 2012). As a result, it is hard to draw conclusions about which features actually perform best. The second issue is that there has been little consistency in the field in the use of cross-validation, the number of L1s, and which L1s are used. As a result, comparing one approach to another has been extremely difficult.

The first Shared Task in Native Language Identification is intended to better unify this community and help the field progress. The Shared Task addresses the two deficiencies above by first using a new corpus (TOEFL11, discussed in Section 3) that is larger than the ICLE and designed specifically for the task of NLI and second, by providing a common set of L1s and evaluation standards that everyone will use for this competition, thus facilitating direct comparison of approaches. In this report we describe the methods most participants used, the data they evaluated their systems on, the three sub-tasks involved, the results achieved by the different teams, and some suggestions and ideas about what we can do for the next iteration of the NLI shared task.

In the following section, we provide a summary of the prior work in Native Language Identification. Next, in Section 3 we describe the TOEFL11 corpus used for training, development and testing in this shared task. Section 4 describes the three sub-tasks of the NLI Shared Task as well as a review of the timeline. Section 5 lists the 29 teams that participated in the shared task, and introduce abbreviations that will be used throughout this paper. Sections 6 and 7 describe the results of the shared task and a separate post shared task evaluation where we asked teams to evaluate their system using cross-validation on a combination of the training and development data. In Section 8 we provide a high-level view of the common features and machine learning methods teams tended to use. Finally, we offer conclusions and ideas for future instantiations of the shared task in Section 9.

2 Related Work

In this section, we provide an overview of some of the common approaches used for NLI prior to this shared task. While a comprehensive review is outside the scope of this paper, we have compiled a bibliography of related work in the field. It can be downloaded from the NLI Shared Task website.[1]

To date, nearly all approaches have treated the task of NLI as a supervised classification problem where statistical models are trained on data from the different L1s. The work of Koppel et al. (2005) was the first in the field and they explored a multitude of features, many of which are employed in several of the systems in the shared tasks. These features included character and POS n-grams, content and function words, as well as spelling and grammatical errors (since language learners have tendencies to make certain errors based on their L1 (Swan and Smith, 2001)). An SVM model was trained on these features extracted from a subsection of the ICLE corpus consisting of 5 L1s.

N-gram features (word, character and POS) have figured prominently in prior work. Not only are they easy to compute, but they can be quite predictive. However, there are many variations on the features. Past reseach efforts have explored different n-gram windows (though most tend to focus on unigrams and bigrams), different thresholds for how many n-grams to include as well as whether to encode the feature as binary (presence or absence of the particular n-gram) or as a normalized count.

The inclusion of syntactic features has been a focus in recent work. Wong and Dras (2011) explored the use of production rules from two parsers and Swanson and Charniak (2012) explored the use of Tree Substitution Grammars (TSGs). Tetreault et al. (2012) also investigated the use of TSGs as well as dependency features extracted from the Stanford parser.

Other approaches to NLI have included the use of Latent Dirichlet Analysis to cluster features (Wong et al., 2011), adaptor grammars (Wong et al., 2012), and language models (Tetreault et al., 2012). Additionally, there has been research into the effects of training and testing on different corpora (Brooke and Hirst, 2011).

Much of the aforementioned work takes the perspective of optimizing for the task of Native Language Identification, that is, what is the best way of modeling the problem to get the highest system accuracy? The problem of Native Language Identifica-

[1]http://nlisharedtask2013.org/bibliography-of-related-work-in-nli

tion is also of interest to researchers in Second Language Acquisition where they seek to explain syntactic transfer in learner language (Jarvis and Crossley, 2012).

3 Data

The dataset for the task was the new TOEFL11 corpus (Blanchard et al., 2013). TOEFL11 consists of essays written during a high-stakes college-entrance test, the Test of English as a Foreign Language (TOEFL®). The corpus contains 1,100 essays per language sampled as evenly as possible from 8 prompts (i.e., topics) along with score levels (low/medium/high) for each essay. The 11 native languages covered by our corpus are: Arabic (ARA), Chinese (CHI), French (FRE), German (GER), Hindi (HIN), Italian (ITA), Japanese (JAP), Korean (KOR), Spanish (SPA), Telugu (TEL), and Turkish (TUR).

The TOEFL11 corpus was designed specifically to support the task of native language identification. Because all of the essays were collected through ETS's operational test delivery system for the TOEFL® test, the encoding and storage of all texts in the corpus is consistent. Furthermore, the sampling of essays was designed to ensure approximately equal representation of native languages across topics, insofar as this was possible.

For the shared task, the corpus was split into three sets: training (TOEFL11-TRAIN), development (TOEFL11-DEV), and test (TOEFL11-TEST). The train corpus consisted of 900 essays per L1, the development set consisted of 100 essays per L1, and the test set consisted of another 100 essays per L1. Although the overall TOEFL11 corpus was sampled as evenly as possible with regard to language and prompts, the distribution for each language is not exactly the same in the training, development and test sets (see Tables 1a, 1b, and 1c). In fact, the distribution is much closer between the training and test sets, as there are several languages for which there are no essays for a given prompt in the development set, whereas there are none in the training set, and only one, Italian, for the test set.

It should be noted that in the first instantiation of the corpus, presented in Tetreault et al. (2012), we used TOEFL11 to denote the body of data consisting of TOEFL11-TRAIN and TOEFL11-DEV. However, in this shared task, we added 1,100 sentences for a test set and thus use the term TOEFL11 to now denote the corpus consisting of the TRAIN, DEV and TEST sets. We expect the corpus to be released through the the Linguistic Data Consortium in 2013.

4 NLI Shared Task Description

The shared task consisted of three sub-tasks. For each task, the test set was TOEFL11-TEST and only the type of training data varied from task to task.

- **Closed-Training**: The first and main task was the 11-way classification task using only the TOEFL11-TRAIN and optionally TOEFL11-DEV for training.
- **Open-Training-1**: The second task allowed the use of any amount or type of training data (as is done by Brooke and Hirst (2011)) *excluding* any data from the TOEFL11, but still evaluated on TOEFL11-TEST.
- **Open-Training-2**: The third task allowed the use of TOEFL11-TRAIN and TOEFL11-DEV combined with any other additional data. This most closely reflects a real-world scenario.

Additionally, each team could submit up to 5 different systems per task. This allowed a team to experiment with different variations of their core system.

The training data was released on January 14, with the development data and evaluation script released almost one month later on February 12. The train and dev data contained an index file with the L1 for each essay in those sets. The previously unseen and unlabeled test data was released on March 11 and teams had 8 days to submit their system predictions. The predictions for each system were encoded in a CSV file, where each line contained the file ID of a file in TOEFL11-TEST and the corresponding L1 prediction made by the system. Each CSV file was emailed to the NLI organizers and then evaluated against the gold standard.

5 Teams

In total, 29 teams competed in the shared task competition, with 24 teams electing to write papers describing their system(s). The list of participating

Lang.	P1	P2	P3	P4	P5	P6	P7	P8
ARA	113	113	113	112	112	113	112	112
CHI	113	113	113	112	112	113	112	112
FRE	128	128	76	127	127	60	127	127
GER	125	125	125	125	125	26	125	124
HIN	132	132	132	71	132	38	132	131
ITA	142	70	122	141	141	12	141	131
JAP	108	114	113	113	113	113	113	113
KOR	113	113	113	112	112	113	112	112
SPA	124	120	38	124	123	124	124	123
TEL	139	139	139	41	139	26	139	138
TUR	132	132	72	132	132	37	132	131
Total	1369	1299	1156	1210	1368	775	1369	1354

(a) Training Set

Lang.	P1	P2	P3	P4	P5	P6	P7	P8
ARA	12	13	13	13	14	7	14	14
CHI	14	14	0	15	15	14	13	15
FRE	17	18	0	14	19	0	13	19
GER	15	15	16	10	13	0	15	16
HIN	16	17	17	0	17	0	16	17
ITA	18	0	0	30	31	0	21	0
JAP	0	14	15	14	15	14	14	14
KOR	15	8	15	2	13	15	16	16
SPA	7	0	0	21	7	21	21	23
TEL	16	17	17	0	17	0	16	17
TUR	22	4	0	22	7	0	22	23
Total	152	120	93	141	168	71	181	174

(b) Dev Set

Lang.	P1	P2	P3	P4	P5	P6	P7	P8
ARA	13	11	12	14	10	13	12	15
CHI	13	14	13	13	7	14	14	12
FRE	13	14	11	15	14	8	11	14
GER	15	14	16	16	12	2	12	13
HIN	13	13	14	15	7	15	10	13
ITA	13	19	16	16	15	0	11	10
JAP	8	14	12	11	10	15	14	16
KOR	12	12	8	14	12	14	13	15
SPA	10	13	16	14	4	12	15	16
TEL	10	10	11	14	13	15	11	16
TUR	15	9	18	16	8	6	13	15
Total	135	143	147	158	112	114	136	155

(c) Test Set

Table 1: Number of essays per language per prompt in each data set

teams, along with their abbreviations, can be found in Table 2.

6 Shared Task Results

This section summarizes the results of the shared task. For each sub-task, we have tables listing the

Team Name	Abbreviation
Bobicev	BOB
Chonger	CHO
CMU-Haifa	HAI
Cologne-Nijmegen	CN
CoRAL Lab @ UAB	COR
CUNI (Charles University)	CUN
cywu	CYW
dartmouth	DAR
eurac	EUR
HAUTCS	HAU
ItaliaNLP	ITA
Jarvis	JAR
kyle, crossley, dai, mcnamara	KYL
LIMSI	LIM
LTRC IIIT Hyderabad	HYD
Michigan	MIC
MITRE "Carnie"	CAR
MQ	MQ
NAIST	NAI
NRC	NRC
Oslo NLI	OSL
Toronto	TOR
Tuebingen	TUE
Ualberta	UAB
UKP	UKP
Unibuc	BUC
UNT	UNT
UTD	UTD
VTEX	VTX

Table 2: Participating Teams and Team Abbreviations

top submission for each team and its performance by overall accuracy and by L1.[2]

Table 3 shows results for the Closed sub-task where teams developed systems that were trained solely on TOEFL11-TRAIN and TOEFL11-DEV. This was the most popular sub-task with 29 teams competing and 116 submissions in total for the sub-task. Most teams opted to submit 4 or 5 runs.

The Open sub-tasks had far fewer submissions. Table 4 shows results for the Open-1 sub-task where teams could train systems using any training data *excluding* TOEFL11-TRAIN and TOEFL11-DEV. Three teams competed in this sub-task for a total of 13 submissions. Table 5 shows the results for the third sub-task "Open-2". Four teams competed in this task for a total of 15 submissions.

The challenge for those competing in the Open tasks was finding enough non-TOEFL11 data for each L1 to train a classifier. External corpora commonly used in the competition included the:

- **ICLE**: which covered all L1s except for Arabic, Hindi and Telugu;
- **FCE: First Certificate in English Corpus** (Yannakoudakis et al., 2011): a collection of essay written for an English assessment exam, which covered all L1s except for Arabic, Hindi and Telugu
- **ICNALE: International Corpus Network of Asian Learners of English** (Ishikawa, 2011): a collection of essays written by Chinese, Japanese and Korean learners of English along with 7 other L1s with Asian backgrounds.
- **Lang8: http://www.lang8.com**: a social networking service where users write in the language they are learning, and get corrections from users who are native speakers of that language. Shared Task participants such as NAI and TOR scraped the website for all writng samples from English language learners. All of the L1s in the shared task are represented on the site, though the Asian L1s dominate.

The most challenging L1s to find data for seemed to be Hindi and Telugu. TUE used essays written by Pakastani students in the ICNALE corpus to substitute for Hindi. For Telugu, they scraped material from bilingual blogs (English-Telugu) as well as other material for the web. TOR created corpora for Telugu and Hindi by scraping news articles, tweets which were geolocated in the Hindi and Telugu speaking areas, and translations of Hindi and Telugu blogs using Google Translate.

We caution directly comparing the results of the Closed sub-task to the Open ones. In the Open-1 sub-task most teams had smaller training sets than used in the Closed competition which automatically puts them at a disadvantage, and in some cases there

[2]For those interested in the results of all submissions, please contact the authors.

			L1 F-Score										
Team Name	Run	Overall Acc.	ARA	CHI	FRE	GER	HIN	ITA	JPN	KOR	SPA	TEL	TUR
JAR	2	0.836	0.785	0.856	0.860	0.893	0.775	0.905	0.854	0.813	0.798	0.802	0.854
OSL	2	0.834	0.816	0.850	0.874	0.912	0.792	0.873	0.828	0.806	0.783	0.792	0.840
BUC	5	0.827	0.840	0.866	0.853	0.931	0.736	0.873	0.851	0.812	0.779	0.760	0.796
CAR	2	0.826	0.859	0.847	0.810	0.921	0.762	0.877	0.825	0.827	0.768	0.802	0.790
TUE	1	0.822	0.810	0.853	0.806	0.897	0.768	0.883	0.842	0.776	0.772	0.824	0.812
NRC	4	0.818	0.804	0.845	0.848	0.916	0.745	0.903	0.818	0.790	0.788	0.755	0.790
HAI	1	0.815	0.804	0.842	0.835	0.903	0.759	0.845	0.825	0.806	0.776	0.789	0.784
CN	2	0.814	0.778	0.845	0.848	0.882	0.744	0.857	0.812	0.779	0.787	0.784	0.827
NAI	1	0.811	0.814	0.829	0.828	0.876	0.755	0.864	0.806	0.789	0.757	0.793	0.802
UTD	2	0.809	0.778	0.846	0.832	0.892	0.731	0.866	0.846	0.819	0.715	0.784	0.784
UAB	3	0.803	0.820	0.804	0.822	0.905	0.724	0.850	0.811	0.736	0.777	0.792	0.786
TOR	1	0.802	0.754	0.827	0.827	0.878	0.722	0.850	0.820	0.808	0.747	0.784	0.798
MQ	4	0.801	0.800	0.828	0.789	0.885	0.738	0.863	0.826	0.780	0.703	0.782	0.802
CYW	1	0.797	0.769	0.839	0.782	0.833	0.755	0.842	0.815	0.770	0.741	0.828	0.788
DAR	2	0.781	0.761	0.806	0.812	0.870	0.706	0.846	0.788	0.776	0.730	0.723	0.767
ITA	1	0.779	0.738	0.775	0.832	0.873	0.711	0.860	0.788	0.742	0.708	0.762	0.780
CHO	1	0.775	0.764	0.835	0.798	0.888	0.721	0.816	0.783	0.670	0.688	0.786	0.758
HAU	1	0.773	0.731	0.820	0.806	0.897	0.686	0.830	0.832	0.763	0.703	0.702	0.736
LIM	4	0.756	0.737	0.760	0.788	0.886	0.654	0.808	0.775	0.756	0.712	0.701	0.745
COR	5	0.748	0.704	0.806	0.783	0.898	0.670	0.738	0.794	0.739	0.616	0.730	0.741
HYD	1	0.744	0.680	0.778	0.748	0.839	0.693	0.788	0.781	0.735	0.613	0.770	0.754
CUN	1	0.725	0.696	0.743	0.737	0.830	0.714	0.838	0.676	0.670	0.680	0.697	0.684
UNT	3	0.645	0.667	0.682	0.635	0.746	0.558	0.687	0.676	0.620	0.539	0.667	0.609
BOB	4	0.625	0.513	0.684	0.638	0.751	0.612	0.706	0.647	0.549	0.495	0.621	0.608
KYL	1	0.590	0.589	0.603	0.643	0.634	0.554	0.663	0.627	0.569	0.450	0.649	0.507
UKP	2	0.583	0.592	0.560	0.624	0.653	0.558	0.616	0.631	0.565	0.456	0.656	0.489
MIC	3	0.430	0.419	0.386	0.411	0.519	0.407	0.488	0.422	0.384	0.400	0.500	0.396
EUR	1	0.386	0.500	0.390	0.277	0.379	0.487	0.522	0.441	0.352	0.281	0.438	0.261
VTX	5	0.319	0.367	0.298	0.179	0.297	0.159	0.435	0.340	0.370	0.201	0.410	0.230

Table 3: Results for closed task

			L1 F-Score										
Team Name	Run	Overall Acc.	ARA	CHI	FRE	GER	HIN	ITA	JPN	KOR	SPA	TEL	TUR
TOR	5	0.565	0.410	0.776	0.692	0.754	0.277	0.680	0.660	0.650	0.653	0.190	0.468
TUE	2	0.385	0.114	0.502	0.420	0.430	0.167	0.611	0.485	0.348	0.385	0.236	0.314
NAI	2	0.356	0.329	0.450	0.331	0.423	0.066	0.511	0.426	0.481	0.314	0.000	0.207

Table 4: Results for open-1 task

			L1 F-Score										
Team Name	Run	Overall Acc.	ARA	CHI	FRE	GER	HIN	ITA	JPN	KOR	SPA	TEL	TUR
TUE	1	0.835	0.798	0.876	0.844	0.883	0.777	0.883	0.836	0.794	0.846	0.826	0.818
TOR	4	0.816	0.770	0.861	0.840	0.900	0.704	0.860	0.834	0.800	0.816	0.804	0.790
HYD	1	0.741	0.677	0.782	0.755	0.829	0.693	0.784	0.777	0.728	0.613	0.766	0.744
NAI	3	0.703	0.676	0.695	0.708	0.846	0.618	0.830	0.677	0.610	0.663	0.726	0.688

Table 5: Results for open-2 task

was a mismatch in the genre of corpora (for example, tweets by Telugu speakers are different in composition than essays written by Telugu speakers). TUE and TOR were the only two teams to participate in all three sub-tasks, and their Open-2 systems outperformed their respective best systems in the Closed and Open-1 sub-tasks. This suggests, unsurprisingly, that adding more data can benefit NLI, though quality and genre of data are also important factors.

7 Cross Validation Results

Upon completion of the competition, we asked the participants to perform 10-fold cross-validation on a data set consisting of the union of TOEFL11-TRAIN and TOEFL11-DEV. This was the same set of data used in the first work to use any of the TOEFL11 data (Tetreault et al., 2012), and would allow another point of comparison for future NLI work. For direct comparison with Tetreault et al. (2012), we provided the exact folds used in that work.

The results of the 10-fold cross-validation are shown in Table 6. Two teams had systems that performed at 84.5 or better, which is just slightly higher than the best team performance on the TOEFL11-TEST data. In general, systems that performed well in the main competition also performed similarly (in terms of performance and ranking) in the cross-validation experiment. Please note that we report results as they are reported in the respective papers, rounding to just one decimal place where possible.

Team	**Accuracy**
CN	84.6
JAR	84.5
OSL	83.9
BUC	82.6
MQ	82.5
TUE	82.4
CAR	82.2
NAI	82.1
Tetreault et al. (2012)	80.9
HAU	79.9
LIM	75.9
CUN	74.2
UNT	63.8
MIC	63

Table 6: Results for 10-fold cross-validation on TOEFL11-TRAIN + TOEFL11-DEV

8 Discussion of Approaches

With so many teams competing in the shared task competition, we investigated whether there were any commonalities in learning methods or features between the teams. In this section, we provide a coarse grained summary of the common machine learning methods teams employed as well as some of the common features. Our summary is based on the information provided in the 24 team reports.

While there are many machine learning algorithms to choose from, the overwhelming majority of teams used Support Vector Machines. This may not be surprising given that most prior work has also used SVMs. Tetreault et al. (2012) showed that one could achieve even higher performance on the NLI task using ensemble methods for combining classifiers. Four teams also experimented with different ways of using ensemble methods. Three teams used Maximum Entropy methods for their modeling. Finally, there were a few other teams that tried different methods such as Discriminant Function Analysis and K-Nearest Neighbors. Possibly the most distinct method employed was that of string kernels by the BUC team (who placed third in the closed competition). This method only used character level features. A summary of the machine learning methods is shown in Table 7.

A summary of the common features used across teams is shown in Table 8. It should be noted that the table does not detail the nuanced differences in how the features are realized. For example, in the case of n-grams, some teams used only the top k most frequently n-grams while others used all of the n-grams available. If interested in more information about the particulars of a system and its feature, we recommend reading the team's summary report.

The most common features were word, character and POS n-gram features. Most teams used n-grams ranging from unigrams to trigrams, in line with prior literature. However several teams used higher-order n-grams. In fact, four of the top five teams (JAR, OSL, CAR, TUE) generally used at least 4-grams,

Machine Learning	Teams
SVM	CN, UNT, MQ, JAR, TOR, ITA, CUN, TUE, COR, NRC, HAU, MIC, CAR
MaxEnt / logistic regression	LIM, HAI, CAR
Ensemble	MQ, ITA, NRC, CAR
Discriminant Function Analysis	KYL
String Kernels / LRD	BUC
PPM	BOB
k-NN	VTX

Table 7: Machine Learning algorithms used in Shared Task

and some, such as OSL and JAR, went as high 7 and 9 respectively in terms of character n-grams.

Syntactic features, which were first evaluated in Wong and Dras (2011) and Swanson and Charniak (2012) were used by six teams in the competition, with most using dependency parses in different ways. Interestingly, while Wong and Dras (2011) showed some of the highest performance scores on the ICLE corpus using parse features, only two of the six teams which used them placed in the top ten in the Closed sub-task.

Spelling features were championed by Koppel et al. (2005) and in subsequent NLI work, however only three teams in the competition used them.

There were several novel features that teams tried. For example, several teams tried skip n-grams, as well as length of words, sentences and documents; LIM experimented with machine translation; CUN had different features based on the relative frequencies of the POS and lemma of a word; HAI tried several new features based on passives and context function; and the TUE team tried a battery of syntactic features as well as text complexity measures.

9 Summary

We consider the first edition of the shared task a success as we had 29 teams competing, which we consider a large number for any shared task. Also of note is that the task brought together researchers not only from the Computational Linguistics community, but also those from other linguistics fields such as Second Language Acquisition.

We were also delighted to see many teams build on prior work but also try novel approaches. It is our hope that finally having an evaluation on a common data set will allow researchers to learn from each other on what works well and what does not, and thus the field can progress more rapidly. The evaluation scripts are publicly available and we expect that the data will become available through the Linguistic Data Consortium in 2013.

For future editions of the NLI shared task, we think it would be interesting to expand the scope of NLI from identifying the L1 of student essays to be able to identify the L1 of any piece of writing. The ICLE and TOEFL11 corpora are both collections of academic writing and thus it may be the case that certain features or methodologies generalize better to other writing genres and domains. For those interested in robust NLI approaches, please refer to the TOR team shared task report as well as Brooke and Hirst (2012).

In addition, since the TOEFL11 data contains proficiency level one could include an evaluation by proficiency level as language learners make different types of errors and may even have stylistic differences in their writing as their proficiency progresses.

Finally, while this may be in the periphery of the scope of an NLI shared task, one interesting evaluation is to see how well human raters can fare on this task. This would of course involve knowledgeable language instructors who have years of experience in teaching students from different L1s. Our thinking is that NLI might be one task where computers would outperform human annotators.

Acknowledgments

We would like to thank Derrick Higgins and members of Educational Testing Service for assisting us in making the TOEFL11 essays available for this shared task. We would also like to thank Patrick Houghton for assisting the shared task organizers.

Feature	Type	Teams
Word N-Grams	1	CN, UNT, JAR, TOR, KYL, ITA, CUN, BOB, OSL, TUE, UAB, CYW, NAI, NRC, MIC, CAR
	2	CN, UNT, JAR, TOR, KYL, ITA, CUN, BOB, OSL, TUE, COR, UAB, CYW, NAI, NRC, HAU, MIC, CAR
	3	UNT, MQ, JAR, KYL, CUN, COR, HAU, MIC, CAR
	4	JAR, KYL, CAR
	5	CAR
POS N-grams	1	CN, UNT, JAR, TOR, ITA, LIM, CUN, BOB, TUE, HAI, CAR
	2	CN, UNT, JAR, TOR, ITA, LIM, CUN, BOB, TUE, COR, HAI, NAI, NRC, MIC, CAR
	3	CN, UNT, JAR, TOR, LIM, CUN, TUE, COR, HAI, NAI, NRC, CAR
	4	CN, JAR, TUE, HAI, NRC, CAR
	5	TUE, CAR
Character N-Grams	1	CN, UNT, MQ, JAR, TOR, LIM, BOB, OSL, HAI, CAR
	2	CN, UNT, MQ, JAR, TOR, ITA, LIM, BOB, OSL, COR, HAI, NAI, HAU, MIC, CAR
	3	CN, UNT, MQ, JAR, TOR, LIM, BOB, OSL, VTX, COR, HAI, NAI, NRC, HAU, MIC, CAR
	4	CN, JAR, LIM, BOB, OSL, HAI, HAU, MIC, CAR
	5	CN, JAR, BOB, OSL, HAU, CAR
	6	CN, JAR, OSL,
	7	JAR, OSL
	8-9	JAR
Function N-Grams		MQ, UAB
Syntactic Features	Dependencies	MQ, TOR, ITA, TUE, NAI, NRC
	TSG	MQ, TOR, NAI,
	CF Productions	TOR,
	Adaptor Grammars	MQ
Spelling Features		LIM,CN, HAI

Table 8: Common Features used in Shared Task

In addition, thanks goes to the BEA8 Organizers (Joel Tetreault, Jill Burstein and Claudia Leacock) for hosting the shared task with their workshop. Finally, we would like to thank all the teams for participating in this first shared task and making it a success. Their feedback, patience and enthusiasm made organizing this shared task a great experience.

References

Daniel Blanchard, Joel Tetreault, Derrick Higgins, Aoife Cahill, and Martin Chodorow. 2013. TOEFL11: A Corpus of Non-Native English. Technical report, Educational Testing Service.

Julian Brooke and Graeme Hirst. 2011. Native language detection with 'cheap' learner corpora. In *Conference of Learner Corpus Research (LCR2011)*, Louvain-la-Neuve, Belgium. Presses universitaires de Louvain.

Julian Brooke and Graeme Hirst. 2012. Robust, Lexicalized Native Language Identification. In *Proceedings of COLING 2012*, pages 391–408, Mumbai, India, December. The COLING 2012 Organizing Committee.

Dominique Estival, Tanja Gaustad, Son Bao Pham, Will Radford, and Ben Hutchinson. 2007. Author profiling for English emails. In *Proceedings of the 10th Conference of the Pacific Association for Computational Linguistics*, pages 263–272, Melbourne, Australia.

Sylviane Granger, Estelle Dagneaux, and Fanny Meunier. 2009. *The International Corpus of Learner English: Handbook and CD-ROM, version 2*. Presses Universitaires de Louvain, Louvain-la-Neuve, Belgium.

Shin'ichiro Ishikawa. 2011. A New Horizon in Learner Corpus Studies: The Aim of the ICNALE Projects. In G. Weir, S. Ishikawa, and K. Poonpon, editors, *Cor-*

pora and Language Technologies in Teaching, Learning and Research. University of Strathclyde Publishing.

Scott Jarvis and Scott Crossley, editors. 2012. *Approaching Language Transfer Through Text Classification: Explorations in the Detection-based Approach*, volume 64. Multilingual Matters Limited, Bristol, UK.

Moshe Koppel, Jonathan Schler, and Kfir Zigdon. 2005. Determining an author's native language by mining a text for errors. In *Proceedings of the eleventh ACM SIGKDD international conference on Knowledge discovery in data mining*, pages 624–628, Chicago, IL. ACM.

Michael Swan and Bernard Smith, editors. 2001. *Learner English: A teacher's guide to interference and other problems*. Cambridge University Press, 2 edition.

Benjamin Swanson and Eugene Charniak. 2012. Native Language Detection with Tree Substitution Grammars. In *Proceedings of the 50th Annual Meeting of the Association for Computational Linguistics (Volume 2: Short Papers)*, pages 193–197, Jeju Island, Korea, July. Association for Computational Linguistics.

Joel Tetreault, Daniel Blanchard, Aoife Cahill, and Martin Chodorow. 2012. Native tongues, lost and found: Resources and empirical evaluations in native language identification. In *Proceedings of COLING 2012*, pages 2585–2602, Mumbai, India, December. The COLING 2012 Organizing Committee.

Sze-Meng Jojo Wong and Mark Dras. 2011. Exploiting Parse Structures for Native Language Identification. In *Proceedings of the 2011 Conference on Empirical Methods in Natural Language Processing*, pages 1600–1610, Edinburgh, Scotland, UK., July. Association for Computational Linguistics.

Sze-Meng Jojo Wong, Mark Dras, and Mark Johnson. 2011. Topic Modeling for Native Language Identification. In *Proceedings of the Australasian Language Technology Association Workshop 2011*, pages 115–124, Canberra, Australia, December.

Sze-Meng Jojo Wong, Mark Dras, and Mark Johnson. 2012. Exploring Adaptor Grammars for Native Language Identification. In *Proceedings of the 2012 Joint Conference on Empirical Methods in Natural Language Processing and Computational Natural Language Learning*, pages 699–709, Jeju Island, Korea, July. Association for Computational Linguistics.

Helen Yannakoudakis, Ted Briscoe, and Ben Medlock. 2011. A New Dataset and Method for Automatically Grading ESOL Texts. In *Proceedings of the 49th Annual Meeting of the Association for Computational Linguistics: Human Language Technologies*, pages 180–189, Portland, Oregon, USA, June. Association for Computational Linguistics.

Applying Unsupervised Learning To Support Vector Space Model Based Speaking Assessment

Lei Chen
Educational Testing Service
600 Rosedale Rd
Princeton, NJ
LChen@ets.org

Abstract

Vector Space Models (VSM) have been widely used in the language assessment field to provide measurements of students' vocabulary choices and content relevancy. However, training reference vectors (RV) in a VSM requires a time-consuming and costly human scoring process. To address this limitation, we applied unsupervised learning methods to reduce or even eliminate the human scoring step required for training RVs. Our experiments conducted on data from a non-native English speaking test suggest that the unsupervised topic clustering is better at selecting responses to train RVs than random selection. In addition, we conducted an experiment to totally eliminate the need of human scoring. Instead of using human rated scores to train RVs, we used used the machine-predicted scores from an automated speaking assessment system for training RVs. We obtained VSM-derived features that show promisingly high correlations to human-holistic scores, indicating that the costly human scoring process can be eliminated.

Index Terms: Vector Space Model (VSM), speech assessment, unsupervised learning, document clustering

1 Introduction

A Vector Space Model (VSM) is a simple, yet effective, method to measure similarities between documents or utterances, which has been utilized in the educational testing field. For example, VSM has been applied to detect students' off-topic essays (Higgins et al., 2006) and to automatically score essays (Attali and Burstein, 2004).

The following three steps are required to use VSM for automated assessment: (1) a collection of responses are selected from each score category to construct reference vectors (RV); (2) for an input response under scoring, the same vectorization method used for constructing RVs is applied to compute an input vector (IV); (3) similarities between this IV and the RVs for all score categories are computed as features reflecting vocabulary usage and content relevancy, including a widely used feature, the cosine similarity between the IV and the RV for the highest score category.

Clearly, the quality of VSM-derived features depends on the proper training of RVs. In language assessment, we tend to use a large number of manually scored responses to build RVs for each testing question (called *item* in the assessment field). However, this raises an issue: the requirement of manual scoring of these responses by human raters. Also, for large-scale assessments administrated globally, a high number of items are typically administered to both ensure the assessment security and support the large volume of test-takers. To address this challenge of application of VSM, we will describe our solutions based on applying unsupervised learning methods in this paper.

The rest of the paper is organized as follows: Section 2 reviews the related previous research; Section 3 describes the English assessment, the data used in our experiments, and the Automatic Speech Recognition (ASR) system used; Section 4 reports the three experiments we conducted; and Section 5 discusses our findings and plans for future research.

2 Previous Work

Attali and Burstein (2004) used the VSM method to measure non-native English writers' vocabulary choices when scoring their essays by comparing the words contained in an student's response to the words found in a sample of essays from each score category. One belief behind this methodology is that good essays will resemble each other in terms of the word choice. In particular, two VSM-derived features were used, including the maximum cosine similarity and cosine similarity to the top score category. Higgins et al. (2006) applied the VSM technology to detect students' off-topic essays whereby the word-based IV from a student's essay was compared to an RV built from a collection of on-topic essays. When the difference was larger than a pre-defined threshold, the essay was marked as off-topic. Zechner and Xi (2008) applied VSM as a content relevancy measurement to score non-native English speaking responses. Recently, Xie et al. (2012) explored the VSM technology on automated speech scoring. Using a superior ASR to the one used in (Zechner and Xi, 2008), they found that the VSM-derived features had moderately high correlations with human proficiency scores.

Dimension reduction, a critical step in applying VSM, removes the noises and minor details in word-based vectors and keeps a concise semantic structure. Latent Semantic Analysis (LSA) (Deerwester et al., 1990) and Latent Dirichlet Allocation (LDA) (Blei et al., 2003) are two widely used dimension-reduction methods. Kakkonen et al. (2005) systematically investigated the dimension reduction methods used in the VSM methods for essay grading. Their experiments showed that LSA slightly out-performs LDA.

Compared to supervised learning, unsupervised learning can skip the time-consuming and costly manual labeling process and has been widely used in many machine-learning tasks. Both LSA and LDA have been utilized in unsupervised document clustering (Hofmann, 2001) to automatically separate a collection of documents into several sets without any human intervention. Co-training is a type of semi-supervised learning method (Blum and Mitchell, 1998), consisting of two classifiers trained from independent sets of features to predict the same labels. It uses automatically predicted labels from one classifier to train the other classifier.

3 Data

The data used in our experiments were collected from the speaking section of Test Of English as a Foreign Language (TOEFL®), an English speaking test used to evaluate students' basic English-speaking skills for use in academic institutions that use English as their primary teaching language. Our data contains the speech responses for a total of 24 test items. For each item, both the stimulus material and question were presented to test-takers followed by a short amount of preparation time. The test-takers were then given up to 60 seconds to provide their spoken responses. These responses were scored by using carefully developed rating rubrics by a group of experienced human raters. The scoring rubrics covered a comprehensive list of different aspects of speaking ability, such as pronunciation, prosody, vocabulary, content organization, etc. A 4-point holistic scoring scale was used where the score of 4 marks the most advanced English speakers in the TOEFL® test. Table 1 summarizes the responses across these 24 items, including $mean$, sd, and sample size (n) of the total number of responses and the number of responses per each score level.

	Overall	$SC1$	$SC2$	$SC3$	$SC4$
$mean$	1969.63	81.88	701.96	963.46	222.33
sd	12.92	30.02	62.36	67.24	37.79
n	47271	1965	16847	23123	5336

Table 1: Summary statistics of the number of total responses and the number of responses per each score level measured in $mean$, sd, and sample size n across 24 items

The transcriptions of these spoken responses were obtained by running a state-of-the-art non-native ASR system. This ASR system uses a cross-word tri-phone acoustic model (AM) and n-gram language models (LMs) that were trained on approximately 800 hours of spoken data and the corresponding transcriptions. When being evaluated on an held-out data set transcribed by humans from the same test, a 33.0% word error rate was obtained.

4 Experiments

The three experiments described below shared the same procedure: (1) for each item, available responses were divided into two sets - a set for training RVs and a set for evaluating the VSM-derived features; (2) RVs were trained by using different response selection methods investigated in this paper; (3) the trained RVs were used to compute the VSM-derived features; and (4) Pearson correlation coefficients (rs) between the VSM-derived features and human-holistic scores were computed to measure these features' predictive abilities in speech scoring. This experimental procedure was conducted on all 24 items and was repeated in 10 iterations by using varied training/evaluation-splitting plans and the averages of these results across the items and iterations are reported. Note that we removed some common function words, such as *a*, *the*, etc., and some noise words from ASR outputs, such as *uh* and *um*, when applying the VSM method and always used LSA dimension reduction. We used the Gensim (Řehůřek and Sojka, 2010) Python package to implement the VSM-related computations in this paper. Also, in this paper, we focused on one VSM-derived feature $cos4$, the cosine distance between an IV to the RV representing the highest-score category (4) for TOEFL® test.

4.1 Data size for training RVs

In previous studies, researchers typically used a large number of responses to construct RVs. For example, Zechner and Xi (2008) used $1,000$ responses while Xie et al. (2012) increased the RV training data to $2,000$ responses for each item. We ask, is it possible to use fewer responses so that we would not be forced to manually score so many responses? To answer this question, we have investigated the relationship between the size of the RV training data and $cos4$'s predictive ability.

For each item, we first randomly selected $1,800$ responses as the RV training data and used the remaining responses as the evaluation set. We then gradually reduced the RV training set to $1,000$, 500, 200, and even 50 responses and trained a series of RVs. On the evaluation set, using these trained RVs, we extracted $cos4$ VSM feature and calculated the r_{cos4} for human-holistic scores. Table 2 reports the average r_{cos4}, which will de denoted as $\overline{r_{cos4}}$ thereafter, for the different-sized RV training sets. Table 2 shows that $\overline{r_{cos4}}$ continuously increases with the increase of the dataset size for training RVs. However, it is worth noting that using just 50 responses to train RVs still provides a reasonably high $\overline{r_{cos4}}$ (0.383). Between the two $size_{RV}$ conditions: 200 vs. 1800, $\overline{r_{cos4}}$ did not show a statistically significant increase based on a t-test ($p = 0.314$).

$size_{RV}$	50	200	500	1000	1800
$\overline{r_{cos4}}$	0.383	0.428	0.435	0.439	0.440

Table 2: $\overline{r_{cos4}}$, a measurement of VSM features' scoring performance, from different RV training data sizes

4.2 Using document clustering for training RVs

In the experiment described in section 4.1, we found that using even a limited number of human-scored responses can provide useful VSM features with a reasonably high r to human-holistic scores. If we can intelligently select such a small-sized dataset, we think that the VSM-derived features will show further improved predicting power. Armed with this idea, we proposed a solution to use unsupervised document clustering technology to find the responses for training RVs.

In particular, for each item, of the $1,800$ responses used for training the RVs, we run an LDA document-clustering process to split all of responses into K clusters. Then, for each cluster, we randomly selected M responses. Therefore, we selected $K \times M$ responses for human scoring and for training the RVs. Note that $K \times M$ can be much smaller than the original dataset size ($n = 1800$). We believed that comprehensive coverage of all of the latent topics would produce a better VSM that, in turn, would provide more effective VSM-derived features for scoring.

In our experiment, based upon a pilot study, we decided to use $K = 10$ and $M = 5$ to control the total scoring demand to be 50 responses per item. Compared to the $\overline{r_{cos4}}$ value obtained from randomly selecting 50 responses for training RVs (0.383 in Table 2), the response selection based on the document clustering improved the $\overline{r_{cos4}}$ to be 0.411. Furthermore, a t-test showed that such an increase in $\overline{r_{cos4}}$ is statistically significant ($p < 0.05$).

4.3 Using machine predicted scores for training RVs

Many of the previous automated speaking scoring systems focused on the features measuring fluency, pronunciation, and prosody (Witt, 1999; Franco et al., 2010; Bernstein et al., 2010; Chen et al., 2009). The scores predicted by these systems show promisingly high correlations with human rated scores. In order to eliminate the time-consuming and costly human scoring step required by applications of VSM, we considered using the scores automatically scored by algorithms (AS) instead of the scores rated by humans (HS).

In our experiment, we used a set of speech features following (Chen et al., 2009) for automated speech scoring. To estimate AS, a five-fold cross-validation was applied on the entire dataset. For each fold, a linear regression model was trained from 80% of responses by using their HS and was used to predict regression results on the remaining 20% of responses. The continuous scores produced by the regression model were rounded to the four discrete score levels (1 to 4) to serve as AS. Between the obtained AS and HS, a Pearson r 0.56 was observed.

Using the predicted scores, we re-ran our VSM feature experiment by using the $1,800$ responses to train the RVs. When the dataset sizes for training the RVs was at $1,800$, we found that the $\overline{r_{cos4}}$ was 0.410 when using machine-predicted scores. Although it was lower than the $\overline{r_{cos4}}$ value obtained by using human-rated scores (0.440), a feature with such correlational magnitude is still useful for building an automatic scoring model.

4.4 A summary of experiments

	HS_{1800}	HS_{50}	$HS_{cluster50}$	AS_{1800}
$\overline{r_{cos4}}$	0.440	0.383	0.411	0.410

Table 3: A summary of $\overline{r_{cos4}}$ using different RV training sizes, unsupervised-response clustering, and automated-predicted scores

Table 3 summarizes the three experiments described above. HS_{1800} refers to using $1,800$ responses with human scores (HS) to train RVs for each item. HS_{50} refers to using only 50 responses with human rated scores. $HS_{cluster50}$ refers to using 50 responses that were selected to cover 10 latent topics detected by using an LDA unsupervised topic clustering method. Compared to HS_{50}, we find that the unsupervised topic clustering method helped to improve $\overline{r_{cos4}}$. AS_{1800} refers to using $1,800$ responses with automatically predicted scores (AS) to train RVs for each item. Compared to HS_{1800}, AS_{1800} that avoids using a time-consuming and costly human scoring process, shows a reasonably high $\overline{r_{cos4}}$.

5 Conclusions and Future Work

Vector Space Models (VSMs) have been widely used in essay and speech assessment tasks to provide vocabulary usage and content relevance measurements. However, applying VSM on the assessments with many items requires a lot of work by human raters. To make the application of VSM in assessments more economical and efficient, we propose the use of unsupervised learning methods to reduce and even eliminate the time-consuming and costly human-scoring process. First, we found that it was possible to just use hundreds rather than thousands of responses to train RVs when applying VSM. In our experiments with TOEFL® data, we found that using a minimum 200 responses to train RVs for each item, was not statistically significantly different from using $1,800$ responses. Next, we used an LDA document-clustering method to identify latent topics from all of the items and used the topic information to select responses for training RVs. Our experiments clearly suggest that such a method of selection provides more effective VSM features than random selection. Finally, we used the scores predicted by an automated speech scoring system that mostly uses fluency and pronunciation features to replace human-rated scores in building the VSM. Our experiments suggest that the features derived from such a VSM that can be constructed without the need of human scoring show promisingly high correlations to human-holistic scores.

This research can be extended in several new directions. First, we will apply the proposed methods on other language assessment tasks, such as on long (written) essays, to fully test that the proposed methods are universally helpful. Second, we are considering doing the third experiment in more iterations – adding the VSM-derived features into the automated scoring model so that more accurate machine-predicted scores can be used for building further improved VSM.

References

Y. Attali and J. Burstein. 2004. Automated essay scoring with e-rater v.2.0. In *Presented at the Annual Meeting of the International Association for Educational Assessment*.

J. Bernstein, A. Van Moere, and J. Cheng. 2010. Validating automated speaking tests. *Language Testing*, 27(3):355.

David M. Blei, Andrew Y. Ng, and Michael I. Jordan. 2003. Latent dirichlet allocation. *the Journal of machine Learning research*, 3:993–1022.

Avrim Blum and Tom Mitchell. 1998. Combining labeled and unlabeled data with co-training. In *Proceedings of the eleventh annual conference on Computational learning theory*, page 92100.

L. Chen, K. Zechner, and X Xi. 2009. Improved pronunciation features for construct-driven assessment of non-native spontaneous speech. In *NAACL-HLT*.

Scott Deerwester, Susan T. Dumais, George W. Furnas, Thomas K. Landauer, and Richard Harshman. 1990. Indexing by latent semantic analysis. *Journal of the American society for information science*, 41(6):391407.

H. Franco, H. Bratt, R. Rossier, V. Rao Gadde, E. Shriberg, V. Abrash, and K. Precoda. 2010. EduSpeak: a speech recognition and pronunciation scoring toolkit for computer-aided language learning applications. *Language Testing*, 27(3):401.

D. Higgins, J. Burstein, and Y. Attali. 2006. Identifying off-topic student essays without topic-specific training data. *Natural Language Engineering*, 12.

Thomas Hofmann. 2001. Unsupervised learning by probabilistic latent semantic analysis. *Machine Learning*, 42(1):177–196.

Tuomo Kakkonen, Niko Myller, Erkki Sutinen, and Jari Timonen. 2005. Comparison of dimension reduction methods for automated essay grading. *Natural Language Engineering*, 1:1–16.

Radim Řehůřek and Petr Sojka. 2010. Software Framework for Topic Modelling with Large Corpora. In *Proceedings of the LREC 2010 Workshop on New Challenges for NLP Frameworks*, pages 45–50, Valletta, Malta, May. ELRA.

S. M. Witt. 1999. *Use of Speech Recognition in Computer-assisted Language Learning*. Ph.D. thesis, University of Cambridge.

S. Xie, K. Evanini, and K. Zechner. 2012. Exploring content features for automated speech scoring. *Proceedings of the NAACL-HLT, Montreal, July*.

Klaus Zechner and Xiaoming Xi. 2008. Towards automatic scoring of a test of spoken language with heterogeneous task types. In *Proceedings of the Third Workshop on Innovative Use of NLP for Building Educational Applications*, pages 98–106. Association for Computational Linguistics.

Role of Morpho-Syntactic Features in Estonian Proficiency Classification

Sowmya Vajjala
Seminar für Sprachwissenschaft
Universität Tübingen
sowmya@sfs.uni-tuebingen.de

Kaidi Lõo
Seminar für Sprachwissenschaft
Universität Tübingen
kaidi.loo@student.uni-tuebingen.de

Abstract

We developed an approach to predict the proficiency level of Estonian language learners based on the CEFR guidelines. We performed learner classification by studying morpho-syntactic variation and lexical richness in texts produced by learners of Estonian as a second language. We show that our features which exploit the rich morphology of Estonian by focusing on the nominal case and verbal mood are useful predictors for this task. We also show that re-formulating the classification problem as a multi-stage cascaded classification improves the classification accuracy. Finally, we also studied the effect of training data size on classification accuracy and found that more training data is beneficial in only some of the cases.

1 Introduction and Motivation

Every year, language learners across the world learn various languages and take tests that measure their proficiency level. The Estonian language proficiency examination[1] in particular is usually taken by the immigrant population for citizenship and/or employment needs in Estonia. Assessing learner texts to classify them into relevant proficiency levels is usually done by human evaluators and is often a time consuming process. An approach to automate this process would complement the human annotators and reduce the overall effort in evaluating learner texts for their proficiency. Investigating features that follow any sort of trend across the various proficiency levels among learners is a first step in building such automatic proficiency classification systems. This is the main motivation for our research.

Several factors might play a role in determining a learner's proficiency in a given language. Since we study the learner corpus of Estonian, a morphologically complex language with an elaborate declension and conjugation system, we hypothesized that studying the role of morpho-syntactic features would be a good starting point to perform proficiency classification. We used the Estonian Interlanguage Corpus (EIC)[2], a publicly accessible corpus of written texts produced by learners of Estonian as a second language, for this purpose. All the texts were annotated with a proficiency level that is based on the Common European Framework of Reference for Languages Council of Europe (CEFR). We constructed various proficiency classification models based on this corpus by using features motivated primarily by the morphological complexity of Estonian and found that true to our hypothesis, they turn out to be good predictors of the proficiency level.

We also studied the effect of breaking up the main classification task into sub-tasks and cascading them. We show that this approach increases the overall accuracy of proficiency classification. In addition, we studied the effect of training data size and found that it does not have a significant impact in most of the classification tasks we performed. To summarize, we studied the task of proficiency classification for Estonian by studying both the aspects feature engineering and model construction.

[1] http://www.ekk.edu.ee/

[2] http://evkk.tlu.ee/wwwdata/what_is_evk

The rest of this paper is organized as follows: Section 2 briefly surveys related work and explains the context of our research. Section 3 describes our corpus and the experimental setup. Section 4 describes our feature set. Section 5 describes our experiments and results. Section 6 concludes the paper with a discussion on results and directions for future work.

2 Related Work

With the availability of computer based learner corpora, research focusing on studying the criterial features that correlate with proficiency levels began to emerge. A wide body of research exists on studying the syntactic complexity of texts produced by learners across different proficiency levels, their lexical richness and the errors they make (e.g., Lu, 2012; Vyatkina, 2012; Tono, 2000) . Learner data from both longitudinal and cross sectional studies was analyzed to understand the linguistic patterns among learners of different proficiency levels, in Second Language Acquisition (SLA) research.

Automatic proficiency assessment of learner texts is another active area of related research, which plays an important role in language testing. Automated systems are now being used both for evaluation of language learners and for offering feedback on their language proficiency (e.g., Williamson, 2009; Burstein et al., 2003). Forms of text used for assessment include mathematical responses, short answers, essays and spoken responses among others (Williamson et al., 2010). Standardized tests like GRE and GMAT too use such systems to complement human scorers while evaluating student essays automatically (Burstein, 2003; Rudner et al., 2005). Zhang (2008) discusses proficiency classification for the Examination for the Certificate of Proficiency in English (ECPE) in detail, by comparing procedures based on four types of measurement models. The problem of automatic student classification i.e., making inferences about a student's skill level by using some form of data about them is an active area of research in Educational data mining (e.g., Desmarais and Baker, 2012; Baker 2010).

But, automatic approaches for classifying language learners into standardized proficiency levels (e.g., the European CEFR levels[3], Common Core Standards[4]) is a relatively new area of interest.

Supnithi et al. (2003) used a dataset consisting of audio transcripts by Japanese learners of English to build a proficiency classification model with a feature set that modeled vocabulary, grammatical accuracy and fluency. This dataset had 10 levels of proficiency. Hasan and Khaing (2008) performed proficiency classification with the same dataset using error rate and fluency features. Dickinson et al. (2012) developed a system for classifying Hebrew learners into five proficiency levels, using features that focus on the nature of errors in a corpus of scrambled sentence exercise questions.

Proficiency Classification so far has been predominantly focused on the correlation of error-rate with proficiency. Although error-rate is a strong indicator of a learner's proficiency in a language, considering other factors like lexical indices or syntactic and morphological complexity would help in providing multiple views about the same data. Providing a non-error driven model, Crossley et al. (2011) studied the impact of various lexical indices in predicting the learner proficiency level. Using a corpus of 100 writing samples by L2 learners of English classified in to three levels (beginner, intermediate, advanced), they built a classification system that analyses language proficiency using the Coh-metrix[5] lexical indices.

Most of the research about the distinguishing factors among learners of various proficiency levels has focused on English. However, issues like morphological variation, which may not be strong predictors of learner proficiency in English, could be useful in proficiency classification of other languages. Hence, in this paper, we study the texts produced by the learners of a morphologically rich and complex language, Estonian and show that morphology can be a good predictor for learner proficiency classification.

We build our classification models using the Estonian Interlanguage Corpus (EIC), which contains texts produced by learners of Estonian as a second language. We modeled our approach based on the features motivated by the morphological complexity of Estonian. To our knowledge, this is the first

[3]http://www.coe.int/t/dg4/linguistic/Cadre1_en.asp

[4]http://www.corestandards.org/

[5]http://cohmetrix.memphis.edu

work that studies the role of morphology based features for proficiency classification in general and in Estonian in particular.

3 Corpus and Experimental Setup

3.1 Corpus

The Estonian Interlanguage Corpus (EIC)[6] was created by the Talinn University. It is a collection of written texts produced by learners of Estonian as a second language. Most of the learners were native speakers of Russian. The corpus consists mainly of short essays, answers to questions, translations and personal letters. The texts are annotated with error types and incorrect forms. The corpus also provides information about the learner's age, gender, education and about other languages known to the learner. Descriptive statistics about the corpus are available on their website[7]. The corpus contains around 8000 documents (two million words), most of which are texts from the Estonian language proficiency examination. The length of the texts varies in general between 50 and 1000 words (Eslon, 2007).

Information about the learner's level of competence is based on the CEFR guidelines[8] and is decided by human annotator judgement. Until late 2008, Estonian language proficiency was tested by conducting proficiency exams at three levels - the lowest level A, the medium level B and the highest level C. Later, the CEFR standards were adapted, dividing the development of language proficiency into six levels (A1, A2, B1, B2, C1, C2). A1 indicates a basic proficiency and C2 indicates a mastery.

For our current work, we use a sub-corpus consisting of 2000 texts that can be accessibly through the EIC. These texts are spread across three broad levels A, B, C instead of the more fine grained six levels and contain all kinds of texts including short answers. Although these texts also have an annotated version containing information about error-types and corrections, since our aim in this paper is to study the effect of morpho-syntactic features, we considered the raw texts produced by the learners as they were, without looking at the error annotations. Table 1 shows a summary of the entire corpus that was made available.

We prepared a test set consisting of 50 documents from each category, picked randomly. This test set was not used to train any of the classifiers we used in this paper. Further, to avoid a training bias towards any class, we used equal number of instances from all classes during all our binary and three-class training processes.

Proficiency Level	#Docs	Avg. #tokens
A-level	807	182.9
B-level	876	260.3
C-level	307	431.8

Table 1: The EIC Corpus

3.2 Pre-processing

All the texts in our corpus were POS-tagged with the TreeTagger[9] and the tagged output was then used to extract the required features. The TreeTagger (Schmid, 1994) is a probabilistic part of speech tagger, which contains parameter files to tag Estonian data. The tag set was derived from the Tartu Morphologically Disambiguated Corpus tag set[10]. As mentioned earlier, we do not use the error annotation information for these learner texts, in this paper.

4 Features

Our choice of features were primarily motivated by the nature of the morphology of Estonian.

4.1 The Estonian Language

The Estonian language has about one million native speakers. It belongs to the Finnic branch of Uralic languages and is known for it's complex morphology. It is both an agglutinative and a flectional (fusional) language. Some of the prominent features of Estonian language include:

- 14 productive nominal cases

[6] http://evkk.tlu.ee/

[7] http://evkk.tlu.ee/statistics.html

[8] http://en.wikipedia.org/wiki/Common_European_Framework_of_Reference_for_Languages

[9] http://www.ims.uni-stuttgart.de/projekte/corplex/TreeTagger/

[10] http://www.cl.ut.ee/korpused/morfkorpus/

- no grammatical gender (either of nouns or personal pronouns) and no articles (either definite or indefinite)
- the verbal system lacks a morphological future tense (the present tense is used instead)
- relatively free word order (relations between words are expressed by case endings)
- extensive compound word formation
- impersonal voice (specific to the Finnic languages and similar to passive voice. The verb is conjugated in "fourth person", who is never mentioned)
- Most of the inflected words in Estonian have two distinctive parts: the stem and the formative. For example, *raamatutele* (book, plural, allative) consists of the stem *raamatu* and the formative *tele*, which in turn consists of plural marker *te* and allative case marker *le* (Erelt et al., 2007, p. 203).
- Unlike most of other Finnic languages, Estonian also has flective features, i.e., the same morpheme may have different shapes in different word forms. For example, the stem *jalg* ("foot", singular, nominative) may appear as *jala* (singular, genitive) or *jalga* (singular, partitive) and plural marker may appear as *d*, *de*, *te* or *i* or merged with the stem as in *jalad* (plural, nominative), *jalgade* (plural, genitive) and *jalgu* (plural, partitive) (Erelt et al., 2007, p. 203).

As many of these characteristics are morphological in nature, we hypothesized that this morphological complexity of Estonian may play a role in the process of language learning and hence may be a useful predictor for proficiency classification. Hence, we built our feature set primarily focusing on the morphological properties of the learner texts. Apart from these features, we also included other features based on the Parts of Speech and lexical variation.

4.2 Morphological Features

In Estonian, as in other Finnic languages, nominals (nouns, adjectives, numerals and pronouns) and verbs are inflected for number and case. Estonian nominals are inflected in 14 different cases. Three of the nominal cases are grammatical cases, i.e., nominative, genitive and partitive. They fulfill mainly a syntactic purpose and have a very general grammatical meaning. All the other cases are semantic cases, and they have a more concrete meaning than grammatical cases, which often can be explained by means of adverbs or adpositions (Erelt et al., 2007, p. 241). We considered the proportion of nouns and adjectives tagged with various cases per document and included them as our declension features. The cases we considered in this paper are: nominative, genitive, partitive, illative, inessive, elative, allative, adessive, ablative, translative, terminative, essive, abessive, comitative and short singular illative, i.e., aditive case.

The verb in Estonian has finite forms that occur as predicates and auxiliary components of complex predicates and non-finite forms. Finite forms are inflected for mood, tense, voice, aspect, person and number. The verb has altogether five moods: the indicative, conditional, imperative, quotative and jussive. It has two simple tenses: the present and the past, two voices: personal and impersonal, affirmation and negation. Non-finite forms behave differently. Participles are inflected for voice and tense, present participles also for case and number, and supines for voice and case. There is one infinitive and one gerund, which can be explained as the inessive case form of the infinitve (Erelt, 2003, p. 52). In this paper, we considered the proportion of verbs belonging to various tense, mood, voice, number and person categories as our features.[11].

4.3 POS features

We included the various degrees of comparison of adjectives and the proportion of words belonging to various parts of speech among our features. This group of features also included the proportion of adpositions (=prepositions+postpositions) along with the proportion of prepositions and postpositions separately. We also included the proportion of coordinating conjunctions and subordinating conjunctions along with that of all conjunctions.

[11]Examples of various forms of declension and conjugation can be found in the Estonian morphology guide at: `http://lpcs.math.msu.su/~pentus/etmorf.htm`

4.4 Lexical Variation features

Lexical variation, also called lexical range indicates the range of vocabulary displayed in a learner's language use. We implemented the measures of lexical variation that are used in the English SLA research to measure the lexical richness of the learners of English as a second language (Lu, 2012). These included the noun variation, verb variation, adjective variation and verb variation which indicated the ratio of the words with the respective parts of speech to the total number of lexical words (instead of all words).

4.5 Text Length Feature

Since text length is one of the most commonly used measures of learner proficiency and also because of the variation in average text length across the proficiency levels (Table1), we included the number of word tokens per document as a feature.

4.6 Most Predictive Features

Apart from these individual feature groups, we also performed a feature selection, to identify the most predictive ones among all our features. We used the Correlation based Feature Subset (CFS) selection method in WEKA for this purpose. CFS chooses a feature subset considering the correlation and the degree of redundancy between the features. Table 2 consists of a list of the most predictive and non-redundant features after ranking all the selected features based on their Information Gain. This list consisted of five verb morphology based features followed by three nominal declension features.

Feature	Group
Nominative case	NounMorph
Impersonal	VerbMorph
Personal	VerbMorph
Num. words	TextLength
Present tense	VerbMorph
2nd person verbs	VerbMorph
Prepositions	POS
Allative case	NounMorph
Imperatives	VerbMorph
Translative case	NounMorph

Table 2: 10 Most Predictive, Non-redundant Features

It is interesting to note that several characteristics that are prominent in Estonian (cf. Section 4.1) figured among this list of most predictive features. *Nominative* being the top predictor can be explained due to the difference in (the number of) cases between Estonian and other languages. For example (Eslon, 2011) found in her corpus study based on the same corpus that the learners frequently use nominative case instead of genitive and partitive case. So, it is to be expected that the usage of the nominative case changes as the proficiency increases. *Impersonal* and *personal* voice are distinctive features in Estonian and other Finnic languages, as they are different from the active and passive voice that typically exist in other languages (Erelt, 2003). This may make them difficult to master for language learners, making them one of the top predictors for proficiency. Further, Estonian has more postpositions than prepositions. Hence, one could that the use of prepositions will be replaced by postpositions as the language acquisition progresses (Ehala, 1994).

5 Experiments and Results

We first studied the effect of the individual feature groups as well as their combination for a three class classification of Estonian learners into A, B and C classes. We also studied the impact of a stacking ensemble on the overall classification accuracy and found out that it did not result in a significant improvement on the test set. Hence, we further investigated the problem as a collection of multi-stage two-class cascades instead of a single stage three class classification. For all our classification experiments, we used the WEKA (Hall et al., 2009) toolkit. We report the overall classification accuracy as our evaluation metric.

5.1 Three Class-Classification

We first considered the learner classification as a single step, three class classification problem. Since 50 documents from each category were separated as a held-out test set (cf. Section 3.1), we built our three-class models with 250 texts per category as our training set to ensure that there is a balanced distribution between classes. We trained multiple classification models considering the individual feature groups and the most predictive feature group. Table 3 shows the classification accuracy of various feature groups, reported using the Sequential Minimal Optimization (SMO) implementation in WEKA (Platt, 1998).

Features	10-Fold CV	Test set
Random baseline	33.33%	33.33%
Noun Morph.	56.64%	52%
Verb Morph	57.55%	58%
POS	52.99%	47.33%
Lex. Variation	43.36%	47.33%
Text Length	33.72%	34%
All Features	**62.45%**	59.33%
Noun+Verb Morph	**61.45%**	58%
Top10 features (Table 2)	57.34%	56.58%

Table 3: Estonian Learner Proficiency Classification with various Feature groups

Although the classification accuracies overall are not very high, it can be seen from the results that the morphological variation does play a key role in proficiency classification of Estonian. While the verbal morphology features performed best as an individual feature sub group, the addition of lexical variation and POS features to the morphological features added very little to the overall classification accuracy.

Text length turned out to be the most predictive single feature among the top features. It can be seen from Table 3 that this feature alone resulted in a classification accuracy of 34%, which is just above the random baseline (33.33%). But the fact that the C level in general contained a higher number of essays and translations compared to other categories of text like letters and short answers (than the A and B levels), thereby resulting in longer texts in general, may have resulted text length being the single most predictive feature. The Top-10 features also performed on par with the individual morphological feature subgroups.

5.1.1 Ensemble Model

Since ensemble models are known to obtain a better performance than their constituent models, we compared the performance of a stacking ensemble against its individual constituent models. We trained three classification models on the entire feature set, using the same train-test sets as explained before and trained an ensemble model with three classifiers. We used the StackingC implementation of WEKA (Seewald, 2002) to combine the models, with a linear regression model as our meta classifier. Table 4 shows the classification accuracies for the individual classifiers as well as the ensemble on a 10-fold CV of the training set and on the held out test set. The ensemble did not result in any significant improvement (<1%) compared to the best model amongst the three of its individual components (SMO). The ensemble's performance on the test set was poor compared to the best classification model.

Classifier	10-Fold CV	Test set
SMO	62.45%	59.33%
Logistic Regression	59.37%	52%
Decision Tree	57.29%	52.33%
Stacked Ensemble	**63.28%**	57.33%

Table 4: Proficiency Classification With an Ensemble

5.2 Classification Through Two-Class Cascades

Since combining the classifiers as a stacking ensemble did not work, we turned to reformulating our problem as a cascade of two-class classifiers. Cascade generalization is the process of sequentially using a set of small classifiers to perform an overall classification task. Gama and Brazdil (2000) showed that a cascade can outperform other ensemble methods like stacking or boosting. Kaynak and Alpaydin (2000) proposed a method to sequentially cascade classifiers and showed that this improves the accuracy without increasing the computational complexity and cost. Although the creation of our classifier cascades in this paper is not the same as any of the above mentioned research, their conclusion that cascading subsets of classifiers to build an overall classifier can possibly result in a better accuracy was the main motivation for this experiment.

The SMO implementation in WEKA also considers multi-class classification as a combination of pairwise binary classifications. But, in our subsequent experiments, we combine our two-class classifiers as a multi-stage cascade rather than a multi-expert stacking ensemble. For these experiments, we first built the various binary classifiers that were later used to construct the cascades. We chose our combinations both by using a One vs All (OvA) as well as a One vs One (OvO) strategy. Thus, six binary classifiers were created, namely:

- (A, B) classifier
- (B, C) classifier
- (C, A) classifier
- (A and Not A) classifier
- (B and Not B) classifier
- (C and Not C) classifier

In all the cases, our training data consisted of equal number of instances per class. In the cases of the last three classifiers, the training data for NotA, NotB and NotC categories consisted of instances from both the classes that were included in the respective "Not-" classes. The data from the held-out test set was not included in any of these binary classification experiments. The training data size for each classifier has a different size depending on the classes involved. In all cases, the number of training samples per category is equal to the number of documents belonging to the category with the least number of documents. Hence, in cases involving the C-class (ABC, AC, BC, CnotC), we trained the classifiers with 250 documents per category. In all the other cases (AB, AnotA, BnotB), we trained the classifiers with 750 documents per category. Table 5 summarizes the training data size and the classification accuracies using 10-fold cross validation. All the models were trained using the SMO algorithm.

Classifer	Training data size	Accuracy
A,B	750 per cat	70.8%
B,C	250 per cat	74.59%
A,C	250 per cat	85.93%
A,NotA	750 per cat	74.20%
B,NotB	750 per cat	60.04%
C,NotC	250 per cat	79.69%

Table 5: Binary Classifications of Estonian Learners

This binary classification shows that there is a clear trend among the features across the proficiency levels. In the case of a pair-wise classification between classes, the highest classification accuracy was achieved for the binary classifier that considered the A and C classes. Although the classification accuracies of the binary classifiers (A,B) and (B,C) are considerably higher than the overall three class classification accuracy (Table 3), they are very low compared to that of the binary classifier (A,C). The confusion between the three classes is the highest when it involves the middle class, B. This confirmed the ordinal nature of proficiency classification. In the second set of binary classifiers, again, the classifier with a poor performance turned out to be (B,NotB).

To take advantage of the fact that the two-class classification is much more accurate than the three-class classification, we studied three class classification by building multi-stage classifier cascades using the above binary classifiers. Based on the output of the first stage (which is the most accurate classifier), we feed the test instance to one of the remaining classifiers to get the final prediction.

5.2.1 Cascade-1

For the first cascade, we considered the pairwise binary classifiers that used a One vs One (OvO) strategy from Table 5. We constructed a classifier cascade as follows: For each test instance,

- Classify the instance using the classifier (A,C).
- If A, re-classify the instance using the classifier (A,B).
- if C, re-classify the instance using the classifier (B,C).

5.2.2 Cascade-2

For the second cascade, we considered the second set of binary classifiers from Table 5, which use a One vs All (OvA) strategy. The cascade is constructed as follows: For each test instance,

- Classify the instance using the classifier (C,NotC).
- If C, classify the instance as C.
- Else, re-classify the instance using the classifier (A,notA).

The choice of these particular combinations of cascades was motivated by two factors:

- To understand the performance of OvO and OvA binary classifier cascades independently
- To start with the classifier that has the highest accuracy as the first stage.

Table 6 compares the performance on the test set of the cascaded classifiers against the normal 3-class classifier and a classifier ensemble. Compared to a normal three-class classifier, the cascaded approach showed more than 5% improvement in the classification accuracy using both the cascades. Compared to Cascade-1, Cascade-2 performed even better with a 66.66% classification accuracy on the test set. Since binary classification for certain pairs seemed to be possible with higher accuracy than the three-class classification, reformulating three class classification as a cascade of binary classifications may result in a better classification accuracy. This was the initial motivation for the choice of cascade classification. Our results clearly showed that it was a fruitful experiment.

Classifer	**Accuracy**
Cascade-1	**64.66%**
Cascade-2	**66.66%**
3-class,without cascade	59.33%
3-class ensemble	57.33%

Table 6: Comparison of Cascade classification

The cascades need more exploration though. Also, although the morphological features turned out to be useful predictors of proficiency classification, the classification accuracies are still not very high. Two possible explanations could be that our features are good but not sufficient or that the training data was insufficient.

It is clear from our various classification experiments that the morphological features are good predictors of proficiency levels. But, surely, there is much more to language proficiency than morphological complexity. So, exploring more features will be the natural next step to improve the overall classification accuracy. However, to gain some more insights at this level, we studied the effect of training data sizes on the various classification tasks we performed.

5.3 Effect of Training Sample Size

We took all the seven different classification models we used in the earlier experiments and studied the impact of gradually increasing the training data size on classification accuracy. For this purpose,we trained all the classifiers with the complete feature set using the SMO algorithm. The classifiers studied include the three class ABC classifier and the binary classifiers AB, BC, AC, AnotA, BnotB and CnotC. Table 7 summarizes the effect of splitting the respective training sets into various train-test splits, on the classification accuracies.

classifier	**50-50**	**60-40**	**70-30**	**80-20**
ABC	56.73%	60.05%	61.76%	62.76%
AB	71.07%	71.3%	71.2%	72.04%
BC	71.33%	72.35%	71.73%	74.86%
AC	86.31%	84.95%	84.15%	85.55%
AnotA	75.39%	75.20%	76.65%	75.82%
BnotB	59.05%	57.95%	56.91%	58.08%
CnotC	77.34%	77.56%	77.27%	76.52%

Table 7: Effect of training size on classification accuracy

As the table shows, training data size had an impact only on some of the classification tasks. For the three class classification, training set size had a clear effect. Although our corpus had a large number of texts from A and B compared to C (Table 1), since we used balanced training sets to train all models, the three-class model had relatively fewer number of documents per category (250) compared to, say, the AB classifier (750 per category). Reduction of this small training set further by 50% decreased the three class classification accuracy from 62.76% (when 80% of the data was used for training) to 56.73%. So, in this case, training data size had an effect.

However, an interesting observation is that this small training sample size (250 documents per category) did not have any impact on the classification performance of the classifier (A,C). This classifier consistently performed at a higher level compared to all the other classifiers even when the training data was only 50% (125 documents per category). Although it is possible that the length of the document played a role here, there was little difference in the performance ($< 1\%$) even after removing the text length feature. This indicates a strong differentiation between the texts of the language learners of levels A and C, in terms of the features we used.

In case of the other classification tasks, only the (B,C) classifier showed some effect of the training data on its overall classification accuracy. While there might be other reasons that we did not notice yet, it is possible that the inter class overlap between (A,B) is more compared to the overlap between (B,C) at least in terms of the features we considered. Also, the fact that the B-level lies in between A and C could also have contributed to the fact that more training data has little effect on classifiers involving data from all the three classes (AnotA, BnotB, CnotC).

6 Conclusion and Discussion

In this paper, we discussed the task of classifying learner texts into standardized proficiency levels based on the texts produced by learners of Estonian as a second language. We used the publicly accessible Estonian Interlanguage Corpus (EIC) and modeled our classifiers by considering the morpho-syntactic variation as our primary feature group. We hypothesized that the morphology may play an important role in detecting the proficiency levels as Estonian is a morphologically rich and complex language.

For building our classifiers, we experimented with various methods such as three class classifiers, an ensemble model and multi-stage cascades. Our experiments showed that the multi-stage cascades improved the classification accuracy compared to the other approaches. Our experiments also showed a clear trend across the proficiency levels. There was little classification overlap between the beginner (A) and the advanced (C) level texts but a strong overlap of both these levels with the intermediate (B) level.

We can conclude from our experiments that the morphological features can indeed play an important role in the proficiency classification of Estonian. Although the classification accuracies we achieved (60-65%) have a long way to go in terms of a real-world grading application, we believe that this is a good starting point to explore the role of morphology in proficiency classification of Estonian in particular and other morphologically rich languages in general.

As a part of our future work, we intend to investigate the role of morphology in Estonian proficiency classification further. We also want to compare the proficiency levels across various genres of texts in the corpus (e.g, essays, personal and official letters, translations etc.). Another interesting dimension we want to explore further is the distribution of specific kinds of morphological phenomena (e.g., case markers) that exist in Estonian but not in the learner's native language, across the different proficiency levels. It would also be interesting to apply insights from the theories of second language acquisition research and study their utility for proficiency classification. Apart from morphology, we also intend to study the impact of other features such as lexical sophistication, error rate, syntactic complexity and discourse coherence. Finally, on the model construction side, we plan to investigate and understand the working of cascaded classifiers better in this context.

Acknowledgments

We thank Dr Pille Eslon from the Talinn University for sharing the corpus with us. We also thank Serhiy Bykh, Dr Detmar Meurers and the three anonymous reviewers for their feedback on the paper. This research is partially funded by the European Commission's 7th Framework Program under grant agreement number 238405 (CLARA)[12]

References

R.S.J.d. Baker. 2010. Mining data for student models. In *Advances in Intelligent Tutoring Systems*, pages 323–338. Springer.

Jill Burstein, Martin Chodorow, and Claudia Leacock. 2003. Criterion: Online essay evaluation: An application for automated evaluation of student essays. In *Proceedings of the Fifteenth Annual Conference on Innovative Applications of Artificial Intelligence (IAAI-03)*, pages 3–10, Acapulco, Mexico, August.

Jill Burstein, 2003. *The e-rater Scoring Engine: Automated Essay Scoring with Natural Language Processing*, chapter 7, pages 107–115. Lawrence Erlbaum Associates, Inc.

[12] http://clara.uib.no

Scott A. Crossley, Tom Salsbury, and Danielle S. McNamara. 2011. Predicting the proficiency level of language learners using lexical indices. In *Language Testing*.

M.C. Desmarais and R.S.J.d. Baker. 2012. A review of recent advances in learner and skill modeling in intelligent learning environments. In *User Modeling and User-Adapted Interaction, 22(1-2)*.

Markus Dickinson, Sandra Kübler, and Anthony Meyer. 2012. Predicting learner levels for online exercises of Hebrew. In *Proceedings of the Seventh Workshop on Building Educational Applications Using NLP*, pages 95–104, Montréal, Canada, June. Association for Computational Linguistics.

Martin Ehala. 1994. Russian influence and the change in progress in the Estonian adpositional system. In *Linguistica Uralica, 3*, pages 177–193.

M. Erelt, T. Erelt, and K. Ross. 2007. *Eesti keele käsiraamat*. Eesti Keele Sihtasutus.

M. Erelt. 2003. *Estonian language*. Linguistica Uralica. Estonian Academy Publishers.

Pille Eslon. 2007. Õppijakeelekorpused ja keeleõp. In *Tallinna Ülikooli keelekorpuste optimaalsus, töötlemine ja kasutamine*, pages 87–120.

Pille Eslon. 2011. Millest räägivad eesti keele käändeadendused? lähivõrdlusi. In *Lähivertailuja, 21*, pages 45–64.

Joao Gama and Pavel Brazdil. 2000. Cascade generalization.

Mark Hall, Eibe Frank, Geoffrey Holmes, Bernhard Pfahringer, Peter Reutemann, and Ian H. Witten. 2009. The WEKA data mining software: An update. In *The SIGKDD Explorations*, volume 11, pages 10–18.

Md Maruf Hasan and Hnin Oo Khaing. 2008. Learner corpus and its application to automatic level checking using machine learning algorithms. In *Proceedings of ECTI-CON*.

C. Kaynak and E. Alpaydin. 2000. Multistage cascading of multiple classifiers: One mans noise is another man's data. In *Proceedings of the 17th International Conference on Machine Learning (ICML)*.

Xiaofei Lu. 2012. The relationship of lexical richness to the quality of esl learners' oral narratives. *The Modern Languages Journal*.

John C. Platt. 1998. Sequential minimal optimization: A fast algorithm for training support vector machines. Technical Report MSR-TR-98-14, Microsoft Research.

Lawrence Rudner, Veronica Garcia, and Catherine Welch. 2005. An evaluation of intellimetric^{TM} essay scoring system using responses to gmat awa prompts. Technical report, Graduate Management Admission Council (GMAC).

Helmut Schmid. 1994. Probabilistic part-of-speech tagging using decision trees. In *Proceedings of the International Conference on New Methods in Language Processing*, pages 44–49, Manchester, UK.

A.K. Seewald. 2002. How to make stacking better and faster while also taking care of an unknown weakness. In *In the proceedings of the Nineteenth International Conference on Machine Learning*, pages 554–561.

Thepchai Supnithi, Kiyotaka Uchimoto, Toyomi Saiga, Emi Izumi, Sornlertlamvanich Virach, and Hitoshi Isahara. 2003. Automatic proficiency level checking based on sst corpus. In *In Proceedings of RANLP*.

Yukio Tono. 2000. A corpus-based analysis of interlanguage development: analysing pos tag sequences of EFL learner corpora. In *PALC'99: Practical Applications in Language Corpora*, pages 323–340.

Nina Vyatkina. 2012. The development of second language writing complexity in groups and individuals: A longitudinal learner corpus study. *The Modern Language Journal*. to appear.

David M. Williamson, Randy Elliot Bennett, Stephen Lazer, Jared Bernstein, Peter W. Foltz, Thomas K. Landauer, David P. Rubin, Walter D. Way, and Kevin Sweeney. 2010. Automated scoring for the assessment of common core standards. White Paper.

David M. Williamson. 2009. A framework for implementing automated scoring. In *The annual meeting of the American Educational Research Association (AERA) and the National Council on Measurement in Education (NCME)*.

Bo Zhang. 2008. Investigating proficiency classification for the examination for the certificate of proficiency in english (ecpe). In *Spaan Fellow Working Papers in Second or Foreign Language Assessment*.

Automated Content Scoring of Spoken Responses in an Assessment for Teachers of English

Klaus Zechner, Xinhao Wang
Educational Testing Service
660 Rosedale Road
Princeton, NJ 08541, USA
kzechner@ets.org, xwang002@ets.org

Abstract

This paper presents and evaluates approaches to automatically score the content correctness of spoken responses in a new language test for teachers of English as a foreign language who are non-native speakers of English. Most existing tests of English spoken proficiency elicit responses that are either very constrained (e.g., reading a passage aloud) or are of a predominantly spontaneous nature (e.g., stating an opinion on an issue). However, the assessment discussed in this paper focuses on essential speaking skills that English teachers need in order to be effective communicators in their classrooms and elicits mostly responses that fall in between these extremes and are moderately predictable. In order to automatically score the content accuracy of these spoken responses, we propose three categories of robust features, inspired from flexible text matching, *n*-grams, as well as string edit distance metrics. The experimental results indicate that even based on speech recognizer output, most of the feature correlations with human expert rater scores are in the range of $r = 0.4$ to $r = 0.5$, and further, that a scoring model for predicting human rater proficiency scores that includes our content features can significantly outperform a baseline without these features ($r = 0.56$ vs. $r = 0.33$).

1 Introduction

With the increased need for instruction of international learners of English as a foreign language (EFL), there is a concomitant rise in demand to assess the language competence of English teachers who are non-native speakers of English. This situation arises because it is neither possible nor affordable for countries where English is not spoken as a native language to employ only or even mostly native speakers of English as EFL teachers. Moreover, as the language of instruction increasingly becomes English in most classrooms, teachers' competence in the productive language modality of speaking becomes substantially more important than in the past. In order to meet this demand for assessing the English language proficiency of teachers of English, a new test, English Teachers Language Assessment (ETLA), was developed recently and piloted in 2012. The test comprises items for all four main language modalities: reading, listening, writing and speaking.

While reading and listening items use a multiple-choice paradigm, test items for speaking and writing elicit open responses. For cost and efficiency reasons, we aim to employ automated scoring of written and spoken responses in this test. This paper is concerned in particular with the conceptualization, implementation and evaluation of features that can assess one aspect of English speaking proficiency: the content correctness of a test taker's response. Our automated speech scoring system, SpeechRater[SM] (Zechner et al., 2009), also has features addressing other aspects of speaking proficiency, such as fluency or pronunciation, but the details of these features will not be discussed as part of this paper.

The speaking items in ETLA range in complexity from reading a text passage aloud to more challenging tasks requiring multi-sentence responses related to typical teaching situations. The items, therefore, elicit speech in which predictability ranges from high (e.g., reading aloud) to medium (e.g., open responses based on teaching material).

While approaches to capture the content of mostly predictable speech have been widely used in the past (see, e.g., Alwan et al., 2007; Franco et al., 2010), this is not the case for responses that exhibit considerable variation but are still much shorter and more constrained than spontaneous items from other language tests, such as TOEFL iBT®.

Therefore, the goal of the study reported in this paper is to conceptualize, implement and evaluate features that can address the subset of ETLA speaking items where responses are not strongly predictable but are still fairly short and constrained by the context of the item stimulus and prompt.[1] One important aspect of any features used for content scoring is that they have to be robust with respect to speech recognition errors. Robustness is necessary because we are using an automatic speech recognition (ASR) system as a front end, and the average word error rate of the system is around 27% for moderately predictable item responses.

To illustrate what an ETLA speaking item may look like, we provide a relatively simple example here. Suppose the test taker (i.e., an English language teacher) is asked to request that the class open their textbooks on page 55. We could see a range of responses, from "perfect" (score level 3, e.g., "Please open your textbooks on page 55." or "Please open your textbooks and turn to page 55."), to "good" (score level 2, e.g., "Please open the books on the page 55.") and to "poor" (score level 1, e.g., "Open book page 55."). Again, note that for this paper we are not interested in potential issues with fluency, such as long pauses or speaking rate, nor with pronunciation or prosody. We just look at the content of the test takers' responses, either in idealized form by means of a human transcription of what a test taker actually said, or in a realistic operational scenario, where we look at the output of an ASR system. In both cases, we consider the sequence of words only (i.e., a textual representation of the test takers' spoken responses).

In order to investigate the effectiveness of candidate content features in a short-term development cycle before a larger amount of pilot data would be available, we first conducted a small scale in-house data collection effort focusing on the moderately predictable spoken items in ETLA. Based on the analysis of this mini-corpus, several different categories of promising features were selected for potential operational use and then evaluated on the pilot data.

The paper is organized as follows: Section 2 provides an overview on related work; Section 3 describes the in-house data set, the pilot data and the ASR system; the developed features are presented in Section 4; Section 5 presents our experiments; we then discuss our findings in Section 6 and we conclude the paper in Section 7.

2 Related Work

Related to the automated assessment of writing free-text, research to date has concentrated mainly on two tasks: (1) scoring of short answers (Mitchell et al., 2002; Leacock and Chodorow, 2003; Mohler and Mihalcea, 2009) and (2) scoring of essays (Foltz et al., 1999; Kanejiya et al., 2003; Attali and Burstein, 2006). For example, Leacock and Chodorow (2003) built an automated scoring system, c-rater™, to evaluate the short constructed or free-text responses, where the concepts given in test items were modeled, and the presence of these expected concepts in students' answers would be detected.

As for the evaluation of free-text essays, Attali and Burstein (2006) used a selected set of meaningful features to measure different constructed aspects of writing essays, such as grammar, usage, mechanics, style, organization, development, lexical complexity and prompt-specific vocabulary usage. In addition, the Intelligent Essay Assessor (Foltz et al., 1999) used Latent Semantic Analysis (LSA) to score students' answers by comparing them to domain-representative texts. Since LSA is based on the bag-of-words model, researchers have also tried to expand it by introducing additional information, such as part-of-speech (POS) tags (Kanejiya et al., 2003).

In addition, research efforts have also been made to evaluate the content relatedness and correctness for spoken responses. For example, Xie et al. (2012) used LSA and Pairwise Mutual Information approaches to evaluate the content correctness of unrestricted spontaneous spoken responses. Moreover, Chen and Zechner (2011) explored fea-

[1] A test item is a basic element of a test, consisting of stimulus material, such as text and/or visuals, and a prompt (test question) that elicits a response from the test taker.

tures related to grammatical complexity in an automated speech scoring system.

In order to address the moderately predictable speaking test items in the new ETLA, this paper presents several different types of features to score the content correctness of the elicited spoken responses. Following a series of experiments and comparisons, seven features from three content feature categories are selected and evaluated.

3 Data Sets and ASR System

This study conducts experiments and evaluations based on two different data sets: (1) a small scale in-house data collection effort, which was used for the design and development of content features; and (2) a larger-scale pilot data collection, which was used to further evaluate the features selected according to the in-house data and to build scoring models for the prediction of human proficiency scores.

3.1 In-house Data Collection

Twenty-two items from ETLA with moderately predictable responses were selected for the in-house data collection.[2] Firstly, 1,053 text responses in total for all three score levels (3 = high proficiency, 2 = medium proficiency, 1 = low proficiency) were drafted and collected by human experts. In order to simulate the operational scenario with an ASR system in place, a subset of responses was recorded by a small set of predominantly non-native speakers of English. For each test item, four responses were randomly selected from each score level, which resulted in 22 × 3 × 4 = 264 responses for voice recording. The remainder of 789 text responses comprised the set for feature development and training. In addition, about two thirds of the 264 text responses were randomly double-recorded by a second speaker, resulting in a speech corpus with 444 spoken responses in total, used as the evaluation set. Furthermore, all these spoken responses were manually transcribed to accommodate the errors introduced by reading, such as insertions of various speech disfluencies.

[2] We decided to focus our efforts only on the moderately predictable items since scoring of highly predictable item types has been extensively studied in previous research already.

3.2 Pilot Data Collection

This study uses data from a 2012 pilot administration of the ETLA assessment. In particular, we focus on 14 moderately predictable items from the pilot, covering 2,308 test takers. In order to build the automatic speech recognizer and the scoring models, the pilot data were partitioned into five different subsets without any speaker and response overlaps. The first three data partitions were used for training, development and evaluation of the speech recognition system (hereafter, "asrTrain", "asrDev" and "asrEval"), which included spoken responses from both the moderately and highly predictable items. The asrTrain partition was further used to develop and train the content features described below. The remaining two partitions were used for training and evaluation of scoring models that predicted item scores based on a set of features (hereafter, "smTrain" and "smEval"), where only the spoken responses from 14 moderately predictable items from one pilot form were included.

The detailed partition information is listed in Table 1. All these spoken responses have been manually transcribed and scored with holistic scores from 1 to 3 by trained human expert raters. For the smTrain and smEval partitions, there were 6,367 responses receiving double annotation, and the inter-rater correlation was 0.73. Furthermore, the average length of responses from smTrain and smEval sets was 10.5 words, and the corresponding vocabulary size was 855 (not including partial words).

Partitions	# Speakers	# Responses
asrTrain	1,658	27,604
asrDev	25	700
asrEval	25	700
smTrain	300	3,452
smEval	300	3,466

Table 1. Number of speakers and number of responses included within each data partition.

3.3 System Architecture

Our automated speech scoring system, SpeechRater (Zechner et al., 2009), consists of an ASR system described below which generates a word hypothesis for every response by a test taker, including information about timing, energy and pitch, and other information from the input audio file. Next, the feature computation modules take the outputs of the ASR system and compute a set of features, related to fluency, pronunciation, prosody, as well as content, the focus of this paper. Finally, a scoring model (linear regression model) is trained based on the smTrain set to predict scores and then evaluated on unseen data (smEval set).

3.4 ASR System

In this study, a state-of-the-art gender-independent Hidden Markov Model speech recognition system trained on about 800 hours of non-native speech is taken as the baseline recognizer, and its language model (LM) is then further adapted using the transcriptions from the asrTrain data partition. The language model adaptation weights are tuned on the asrDev set, and the resulting word error rate (WER) on the asrEval set (with both moderately and highly predictable responses) is 11.7%, and its WER on the subset of 264 moderately predictable responses is 19.7%. This speech recognizer is further evaluated on both smTrain and smEval sets as shown in Table 2, only including moderately predictable responses.

Partition	WER (%)
smTrain	26.7
smEval	26.9

Table 2. Word error rates (WER) of the speech recognizer on smTrain and smEval[3] data sets.

4 Content Features

Following a careful inspection and analysis of the collected in-house data (described in Section 3.1 above), several different categories of content features were designed and developed. The initial data analysis showed that features need to be able to capture very narrow ranges of expressions with minor variations, but also should be able to capture something like the "overall accuracy" of expression, where local word sequences or phrases should conform to the expectations of the item design without requiring that a response follows a confined pattern in its entirety. For the former situation, features like regular expression matches seem appropriate to be a good match, whereas for the latter, more flexible approaches such as n-gram models or string edit distance metrics may be more appropriate. We list and describe our proposed content features in the following section.

A. Flexible String Matching Metrics

AI. Regular Expressions

Since many responses in ETLA are expected to follow certain patterns, it is intuitive to construct limited regular expressions (RegEx) to match gold standard responses for candidates with high proficiency score levels. Accordingly, one type of regular expression related features, *re_match*, can be extracted to detect whether the test response can be matched by any of the pre-built regular expressions. This feature can obtain the values of 0 (does not match), 1 (partially matches) and 2 (exactly matches). Here, a partial match indicates that a RegEx can be matched within a test response that also has other spoken material, which is useful when the speaker repeats or corrects the answer multiple times in a single item response, and the compiled RegEx can still be used to match parts of the test response.

This content feature has the advantage of high precision, as it can precisely examine the content correctness of the test responses. Thus, the RegEx should be compiled to match all the example responses at the highest score level 3 from the training set. For some test items with relatively short and fixed answer patterns, this feature is quite useful; however, it is very time-consuming and difficult to manually build regular expressions for items with longer and more flexible expressions. Meanwhile, the mechanism of exact matching can make this feature fail in very small variations of expression. Especially when applying this feature on ASR output, it is difficult to successfully match some content-correct responses that have disfluencies or recognition errors.

Therefore, in order to improve the robustness of RegEx, another regular expression related feature is proposed. In general, for each item in ETLA, some pieces of specific expressions are required in a test response to represent its content correctness. Accordingly, we can segment the reference responses into several fragments and identify some pieces as key fragments. For example, when looking at the reference response "Please open your

[3] The calculation of WER is based on only the recognized outputs with more than one word. Thus, the number of actually recognized responses is less than that in Table 1, i.e., 3,264 responses for smTrain and 3,255 responses for smEval.

text books and turn to page 55." two key fragments can be extracted with "Please open your text books" and "turn to page 55." We group versions of these key fragments from the training corpus together and construct regular expressions to match each group. Afterwards, a feature can be defined to count how many key fragments can be matched by a test response, namely *num_fragments*.

AII. Keyword Detection

For moderately predictable items on ETLA, keyword lists can be extracted from the stimulus material and the item prompt, containing the words that need to be included in a test response by test takers. Then a feature, *num_keywords,* can be used to examine how many keywords appear in a test response, which can be further normalized by the number of predefined keywords for each item, i.e., *percent_keywords*. In addition, as some keywords may be a phrase with multiple words, such as "page 55," we can split all the keywords into single words and get another sub-keywords list. Then two corresponding features can be extracted as *num_sub_keywords* and *percent_sub_keywords*.

B. *N*-grams

BI. Word *N*-grams

The word *n*-gram model is introduced here to capture the similarity of word usage between the test and the reference responses. Based on the collected training samples, trigrams are trained using the text responses from the highest score level 3. Then, the LM can be used to score a test response, and the resulting probability can be taken as feature, called *lm_3*.

BII. POS Similarity

This feature measures the syntactic complexity of test responses based on the distribution of POS tags. First, all the responses from the training data set are assigned with POS tag sequences via an automatic POS tagger. Then, a POS vector according to each score level can be obtained by gathering the POS unigram, bigram or trigram statistics from the same score level.

Given a test response, its corresponding POS sequence can be determined by the same POS tagger, and the cosine similarities between the test POS *n*-gram vector and the POS vectors from three different score levels can be calculated as *pos_1*, *pos_2* and *pos_3*, where *pos_3* is used as a feature in our experiments below. Furthermore, by comparing these three cosine similarities, the score category with the highest similarity can be extracted as another feature, i.e., *pos_score*.

BIII. Machine Translation Evaluation Metric (BLEU)

BLEU (Papineni et al., 2002) is one of the most popular metrics for automatic evaluation of machine translation, where the score is calculated based on the modified *n*-gram precision. In this study, the BLEU score is introduced to evaluate the content quality of a test response, where three different gold standard reference corpora are extracted from the training set according to each score level. Similar to the edit distance and WER features described below, three BLEU scores are calculated by comparing them with reference responses from each score level (i.e., *bleu_1*, *bleu_2* and *bleu_3*). We decide to use the following two features for our experiments below: *bleu_3* and *bleu_score,* the score level which receives the maximum BLEU score.

C. String Edit Distance Metrics

CI. String Edit Distance

As the edit distance is an effective string metric for measuring the amount of difference between two word sequences, including insertions, deletions and substitutions, we use it to capture the sequence distance between the test and reference responses.

Given a test response, we can separately calculate the edit distance by comparing it with training responses from each score level. Afterwards, the minimum edit distance from each score level can be extracted as *ed_1*, *ed_2* and *ed_3*, where *ed_3* is selected as feature for our experiments. Furthermore, by comparing these three edit distances, the score category with the minimum value is taken as another feature, *ed_score*.

CII. Word Error Rate (WER)

By dividing the edit distance by the length of the reference response, we obtain the word error rate (WER) metrics, commonly used in speech recognition, and two additional features, *wer_3* and *wer_score*, similarly as above, can be calculated.

Compared to the above category of *n*-gram related features, which capture the *n*-gram fragment matching between the test and reference samples, the category of edit distance features try to find the most similar reference sample to the test sample at the whole-response level.

Finally, all the proposed features are implemented and then examined based on both the ideal human transcription and the realistic ASR output. The speech recognizer used with the small in-house data is the same as the ASR system described in Section 3.4, but its language model is adapted with the much smaller set of 789 training text responses. The WER of this system is 17.8%, evaluated on 444 spoken responses.

In addition, in order to increase the robustness of the extracted features, a preprocessing stage is introduced to remove all the disfluencies from the ASR output, such as filler words, recognized partial words and repeated words. Afterwards, each feature is evaluated on both the transcription and the ASR output of the 444 collected spoken responses, and its corresponding Pearson correlation coefficient with human scores is presented in Table 3.

Based on overall correlation, inter-correlation analyses, as well as on construct[4] considerations, seven content features from three categories are selected and will be evaluated on a larger scale on ETLA pilot data in the next section: *re_match (A1)*, *num_fragments (A2)*, *percent_sub_keywords (A3)*, *bleu_3 (B1)*, *ed_score (C1)*, *wer_3 (C2)* and *wer_score (C3)*.

5 Experiments and Results

This section first describes experiments related to the performance of the seven selected content features on a larger corpus from an ETLA pilot administration (described above in Section 3.2). Then, a similar analysis is conducted based on human rater analytic content scores on a subset of this data. Finally, the selected content features are combined with other features related to pronunciation, prosody and fluency to build a scoring model for the prediction of human scores.

[4] A construct is the set of knowledge, skills and abilities measured by a test. The term "construct considerations" in the context of feature selection refers to the process of ensuring that the selected feature set obtains a high coverage of all aspects of the relevant construct.

	Feature	Trans	ASR
A	re_match	0.789	***0.537***
	num_fragments	0.629	***0.523***
	num_keywords	0.269	0.254
	percent_keywords	0.419	0.375
	num_sub_keywords	0.249	0.239
	percent_sub_keywords	0.482	***0.417***
B	lm_3	0.482	0.461
	pos_3	0.270	0.270
	pos_score	0.315	0.339
	bleu_3	0.531	***0.458***
	bleu_score	0.144	0.194
C	ed_3	-0.362	-0.337
	ed_score	0.642	***0.614***
	wer_3	-0.573	***-0.513***
	wer_score	0.585	***0.557***

Table 3. Pearson correlation coefficients (r) of content features with human holistic scores.

5.1 Feature Evaluation on Pilot Data

In the following experiments, we use the asrTrain set to train the content features. Then these features are examined on the smTrain and smEval data sets. In order to extract the edit distance, WER- and BLEU-related features for each item, three text reference corpora according to different score levels, are needed. Duplicate reference responses with the same content are removed within each score level.

Furthermore, we improve two RegEx features using the reference responses from the highest score level 3 in the asrTrain set. (1) Since the previously obtained *re_match* feature based on the in-house data may not be able to match multiple content-correct responses in the pilot data, we need to augment the set of RegEx for this feature based on correct responses from score level 3 in the asrTrain set. (2) Since the maximum number of candidate fragments varies across different ETLA items, the *num_fragments* feature values are not comparable across items. Therefore, we redesign this feature by assigning a list of manually selected keywords for each fragment. During feature extraction, we count the number of distinct keywords associated with all the matched fragments and divide this number by the number of predefined keywords for each item (as in AII. Keyword Detection), which results in another feature: *perc_fragment_kw (A2)*.

Based on the ASR output of smTrain and smEval data sets, seven content features are extracted and their Pearson correlation coefficients with the holistic human scores are calculated and shown in Table 4.

Feature	smTrain (*r*)		smEval (*r*)	
	Trans	ASR	Trans	ASR
A1	0.53	0.415	0.534	0.441
A2	0.576	0.458	0.583	0.48
A3	0.42	0.286	0.419	0.297
B1	0.597	0.478	0.564	0.452
C1	0.535	0.412	0.52	0.39
C2	-0.588	-0.469	-0.564	-0.446
C3	0.554	0.433	0.51	0.428

Table 4. Pearson correlation coefficients between content features and human holistic scores, based on both the transcription and the ASR output of smTrain and smEval.[5] Features include A1 (*re_match*), A2 (*perc_fragment_kw*), A3 (*percent_sub_keywords*), B1 (*bleu_3*), C1 (*ed_score*), C2 (*wer_3*) and C3 (*wer_score*)

5.2 Evaluations Using Human Rater Analytic Content Scores

In addition to the human rating of all spoken responses of the ETLA pilot data set with holistic scores that take into account both the dimensions of "delivery" (fluency, pronunciation, prosody) and "content," a subset of the data was further scored by human expert raters in these two dimensions separately, resulting in so-called analytic scores for delivery and content. The inter-correlation for content analytic scores was 0.79.

1,410 responses from the smTrain set and 1,402 responses from the smEval set received such analytic content scores. On this subset, table 5 shows the Pearson correlation coefficients between the content features and the analytic content scores, as well as the holistic scores, for comparison.

5.3 Scoring Model Comparison

We further examine these content features by introducing them in a scoring model to predict human rater holistic proficiency scores, using smTrain for training of the models and smEval for their evaluation. The baseline system employs 14 features related to the construct dimension of delivery, such as pronunciation, prosody and fluency.

[5] The evaluation is conducted on recognition output with more than one word. In addition, due to technical problems, such as high background noise, some responses are non-scorable for human raters, and these responses are removed from the evaluation sets. Finally, there are 3176 responses included in smTrain, and 3084 responses in smEval.

Feature	smTrain (*r*)			
	Holistic		Content	
	Trans	ASR	Trans	ASR
A1	0.529	0.415	0.563	0.434
A2	0.564	0.46	0.646	0.525
A3	0.422	0.283	0.452	0.277
B1	0.6	0.499	0.654	0.504
C1	0.527	0.43	0.555	0.46
C2	-0.588	-0.473	-0.627	-0.488
C3	0.542	0.434	0.563	0.462
Feature	**smEval (*r*)**			
	Holistic		**Content**	
	Trans	**ASR**	**Trans**	**ASR**
A1	0.525	0.424	0.538	0.436
A2	0.579	0.472	0.621	0.512
A3	0.423	0.308	0.454	0.321
B1	0.563	0.442	0.606	0.471
C1	0.521	0.4	0.539	0.422
C2	-0.543	-0.42	-0.584	-0.457
C3	0.514	0.417	0.529	0.439

Table 5. Pearson correlation coefficients between content features and human analytic content scores as well as human holistic scores.

Furthermore, an extended scoring model is built by adding the selected seven content features to the model. Table 6 provides the comparison between these two scoring models, reporting both quadratic weighted kappa and Pearson correlation coefficients between automatically predicted scores and human holistic scores on the smEval data set.

Scoring Model	Kappa	*r*
Baseline (Delivery only)	0.30	0.33
Extended (Delivery+Content)	0.53	0.56

Table 6. Scoring model comparison: quadratic weighted kappa and Pearson correlation coefficients between predicted scores (unrounded) and human holistic scores.

6 Discussion

The goal of this paper was to conceptualize, implement and evaluate features that can determine the content correctness of spoken item responses in an English language test for teachers of English who are not native speakers of English.

Based on observations from a small in-house data collection, where human test developers and content experts created example responses to 22 test items for three different score levels, we decided to implement a range of features that can capture the content correctness of test takers' responses in varying degree of precision. Our features belong to three classes: features related to fixed expressions, with potential small variations, such as regular expressions or keywords; features based on *n*-grams of words or POS tags, including the BLEU metrics frequently used for evaluations of machine translation output; and features related to measures of string edit distance, including the WER metrics commonly used in speech recognition evaluations.

It should be noted that we use the term "content" in a fairly broad way in this paper, namely, everything in a spoken response that is not related to lower-level aspects of speech production such as fluency or pronunciation. Since the scoring rubrics for ETLA place a high emphasis both on the grammatical accuracy, as well as on the correct content (in a more narrow sense), this situation is reflected by our choice of features that focus both on elements traditionally associated with content (such as matching of keywords), as well as on elements more related to correct grammatical expressions (e.g., sequences of POS tags).

Our initial evaluations on the small in-house data collection showed that most of these features correlate well with human expert scores, both when using transcribed speech as well as when using ASR output. The absolute correlations for human transcriptions of speech range from r = 0.144 (*bleu_score*) to r = 0.789 (*re_match*), and for ASR output from r = 0.194 (*bleu_score*) to r = 0.614 (*ed_score*). The relative drop in correlation between these two conditions varies across features, but is generally around 5%-15%, with *re_match* having a much larger performance drop from r = 0.789 for transcribed speech to r = 0.537 for ASR output (32% relative decrease in performance).[6]

From this initial set of 15 features, we selected seven features based on feature performance, inter-correlation analyses (i.e., avoiding features that have a high inter-correlation and measure a similar aspect of content), and considerations of construct, i.e., which features are representing content in a way that is consistent with what human experts would consider important in determining the content correctness of a response. This subset of seven features includes three features each from the classes of flexible string matching and string edit distance, and one feature (*bleu_3*) from the *n*-gram class.

When evaluating these seven features on a larger data set, the smTrain and smEval sets of the 2012 ETLA pilot data, we find absolute correlations between features and human holistic scores ranging from r = 0.286 to r = 0.480 for ASR output, and from r = 0.419 to r = 0.597 for transcriptions. The relative decrease in correlation between transcriptions and ASR outputs ranges from 16% to 32% in these data sets (smTrain and smEval). The magnitude of content feature correlations observed in this study is similar to that of features related to fluency and pronunciation computed on spontaneous speech, as reported in Zechner et al. (2009). In fact, due to the brevity of the moderately predictable responses in ETLA, features related to fluency and pronunciation achieve correlations of less than 0.3 on this data set, making content features crucial for the assessment of speech here.

When comparing the six content features that are identical between the original feature set of 15 features (in-house data collection) and the final feature set, we observe a relative drop in feature correlation between the in-house data set and the smEval pilot data set between 1% (*blue_3*) and 36% (*ed_score*), with an average decrease of 20%. This performance decrease can be explained by (1) the more challenging data set of the pilot, as indicated, e.g., by a much higher word error rate of the ASR system (27% vs. 18%); and (2) the fact that the in-house data collection was much more constrained in terms of test taker response variation compared to the real-world pilot data.

Since a subset of the ETLA responses was also scored analytically by human raters, we could further compare the feature correlations between holistic vs. analytic content scores (Section 5.2). We find that on smEval, for all features, absolute correlations increase on human analytic content scores compared to human holistic scores. Although these differences are rather small (0.01 to 0.04), this is an indicator that our features are measuring what they are supposed to measure, since the holistic scores also take other dimensions of speech, such as fluency and pronunciation, into account.

[6] The correlation of one feature, *pos_3*, remained unchanged between the two conditions, and two features, *pos_score* and *bleu_score*, showed higher correlations for ASR output than for human transcriptions.

7 Conclusion and Future Work

This paper presented a study whose aim was to conceptualize, implement and evaluate features to measure the content correctness of test takers' responses in a new assessment for EFL teachers whose native language is not English.

We implemented and evaluated an initial set of 15 content features from three feature classes: flexible string matching, *n*-grams and string edit distance metrics. A subset of these features was then evaluated on a 2012 ETLA pilot administration, and we found correlations between features and human holistic scores in the range of $r = 0.29$ to $r = 0.48$ on ASR output. Correlations increased when comparing features with human analytic content scores.

Finally, we compared a baseline regression scoring model for prediction of human holistic scores without any content features to an extended model using seven content features and found that the model correlation substantially improved from $r = 0.33$ (baseline) to $r = 0.56$ (extended model).

Future work will include devising strategies on how to obtain RegEx features more quickly in a semi-automated way in order to reduce human labor. Further, we plan more in-depth analysis of the feature performance across different test items and item types which potentially could lead to further improvements and refinements of our content features.

References

Abeer Alwan, Yijian Bai, Matt Black, Larry Casey, Matteo Gerosa, Margaret Heritage, Markus Iseli, Barbara Jones, Abe Kazemzadeh, Sungbok Lee, Shrikanth Narayanan, Patti Price, Joseph Tepperman and Shizhen Wang. 2007. A system for technology based assessment of language and literacy in young children: the role of multiple information sources. *Proceedings of IEEE International Workshop on Multimedia Signal Processing*, 26-30.

Yigal Attali and Jill Burstein. 2006. Automated essay scoring with e-rater® V.2.0. *Journal of Technology, Learning, and Assessment*, 4(3): 159-174.

Miao Chen and Klaus Zechner. 2011. Computing and evaluating syntactic complexity features for automated scoring of spontaneous non-native speech. *Proceedings of ACL*, 722-731.

Peter W. Foltz, Darrell Laham and Thomas K. Landauer. 1999. The intelligent essay assessor: Applications to educational technology. *Interactive Multimedia Electronic Journal of Computer-Enhanced Learning*, 1(2).

Horacio Franco, Harry Bratt, Romain Rossier, Venkata Rao Gadde, Elizabeth Shriberg, Victor Abrash and Kristin Precoda. 2010. EduSpeak®: A speech recognition and pronunciation scoring toolkit for computer-aided language learning applications. *Language Testing*, 27(3): 401-418.

Dharmendra Kanejiya, Arun Kumary and Surendra Prasad. 2003. Automatic evaluation of students' answers using syntactically enhanced LSA. *Proceedings of Workshop on Building Educational Applications Using Natural Language Processing*, 53-60.

Claudia Leacock and Martin Chodorow. 2003. C-rater: Automated scoring of short-answer questions. *Computers and Humanities*,37: 389–405.

Tom Mitchell, Terry Russell, Peter Broomhead and Nicola Aldridge. 2002. Towards robust computerised marking of free-text responses. *Proceedings of International Computer Assisted Assessment Conference*, 233-249.

Michael Mohler and Rada Mihalcea. 2009. Text-to-text semantic similarity for automatic short answer grading. *Proceedings of EACL*, 567-575.

Kishore Papineni, Salim Roukos, Todd Ward and Wei-Jing Zhu. 2002. BLEU: A method for automatic evaluation of machine translation. *Proceedings of ACL*, 311-318.

Shasha Xie, Keelan Evanini and Klaus Zechner. 2012. Exploring content features for automated speech scoring. *Proceedings of NAACL-HLT*, 103-111.

Klaus Zechner, Derrick Higgins, Xiaoming Xi and David M. Williamson. 2009. Automatic scoring of non-mative spontaneous speech in tests of spoken English. *Speech Communication*, 51: 883-895.

Experimental Results on the Native Language Identification Shared Task

Amjad Abu-Jbara, Rahul Jha, Eric Morley, Dragomir Radev
Department of EECS
University of Michigan
Ann Arbor, MI, USA
[amjbara, rahuljha, eamorley, radev]@umich.edu

Abstract

We present a system for automatically identifying the native language of a writer. We experiment with a large set of features and train them on a corpus of 9,900 essays written in English by speakers of 11 different languages. our system achieved an accuracy of 43% on the test data, improved to 63% with improved feature normalization. In this paper, we present the features used in our system, describe our experiments and provide an analysis of our results.

1 Introduction

The task of Native Language Identification (NLI) is the task of identifying the native language of a writer or a speaker by analyzing their writing in English. Previous work in this area shows that there are several linguistic cues that can be used to do such identification. Based on their native language, different speakers tend to make different kinds of errors pertaining to spelling, punctuation, and grammar (Garfield, 1964; Wong and Dras, 2009; Kochmar, 2011). We describe the complete set of features we considered in Section 4. We evaluate different combinations of these features, and different ways of normalizing them in Section 5.

There are many possible applications for an NLI system, as noted by Kochmar (2011): finding the origins of anonymous text; error correction in various tasks including speech recognition, part-of-speech tagging, and parsing; and in the field of second language acquisition for identifying learner difficulties. We are most interested in statistical approaches to this problem because it may point towards fruitful avenues of research in language and sound transfer, which are how people apply knowledge of their native language, and its phonology and orthography, respectively, to a second language. For example, Tsur and Rappoport (2007) found that character bigrams are quite useful for NLI, which led them to suggest that second language learners' word choice may in part be driven by their native languages. Analysis of such language and sound translation patterns might be useful in understanding the process of language acquisition in humans.

2 Previous Work

The work presented in this paper was done as part of the NLI shared task (Tetreault et al., 2013), which is the first time this problem has been the subject of a shared task. However, several researchers have investigated NLI and similar problems. Authorship attribution, a related problem, has been well studied in the literature, starting from the seminal work on disputed Federalist Papers by Mosteller and Wallace (1964). The goal of authorship attribution is to assign a text to one author from a candidate set of authors. This technique has many applications, and has recently been used to investigate terrorist communication (Abbasi and Chen, 2005) and digital crime (Chaski, 2005). The goal of NLI somewhat similar to authorship attribution, in that NLI attempts to distinguish between candidate communities of people who share a common cultural and linguistic background, while authorship attribution distinguishes between candidate individuals.

In the earliest treatment of this problem, Koppel et al. (2005) used stylistic text features to identify the native language of an author. They used features based on function words, character n-grams and errors and idiosyncrasies such as spelling errors and non-standard syntactic constructions. They experimented on a dataset with essays written by non-native English speakers from five countries, Russia, Czech Republic, Bulgaria, France and Spain, with 258 instances from each dataset. They trained a multi-class SVM model using the above features and reported 10-fold cross validation accuracy of 80.2%.

Tsur and Rappoport (2007) studied the problem of NLI with a focus on *language transfer*, i.e. how a seaker's native language affects the way in which they acquire a second language, an important area in Second Language Acquisition research. Their feature analysis showed that character bigrams alone can lead to a classification accuracy of about 66% in a 5-class task. They concluded that the choice of words people make when writing in a second language is highly influenced by the phonology of their native language.

Wong and Dras (2009) studied syntactic errors derived from contrastive analysis as features for NLI. They used the five languages from Koppel et al. (2008) along with Chinese and Japanese, but did not find an improvement in classification accuracy by adding error features based on contrastive analysis. Later, Wong and Dras (2011) studied a more general set of syntactic features and showed that adding these features improved the accuracy significantly. They also investigated classification models based on LDA (Wong et al., 2011), but did not find them to be useful overall. They did, however, notice that some of the topics were capturing information that would be useful for identifying particular native languages. They also proposed the use of adaptor grammars (Johnson et al., 2007), which are a generalization of probabilistic context-free grammars, to capture collocational pairings. In a later paper, Wong et al. explored the use of adapter grammars in detail (Wong et al., 2012) and showed that an extension of adaptor grammars to discover collocations beyond lexical words can produce features useful for the NLI task.

3 Dataset

The experiments for this paper were performed using the TOEFL11 dataset (Blanchard et al., 2013) provided as part of the shared task. The dataset contains essays written in English from native speakers of 11 languages (Arabic, Chinese, French, German, Hindi, Italian, Japanese, Korean, Spanish, Telugu, and Turkish). The corpus contains 12,099 essays per language sampled evenly from 8 prompts or topics. This dataset was designed specifically to support the task of NLI and addresses some of the shortcomings of earlier datasets used for research in this area. Specifically, the dataset has been carefully selected in order to maintain consistency in topic distributions, character encodings and annotations across the essays from different native languages. The data was split into three data sets: a training set comprising 9,900 essays, a development set comprising 1,100 essays, and a test set comprising 1,100 essays.

4 Approach

We addressed the problem as a supervised, multi-class classification task. We trained a Support Vector Machine (SVM) classifier on a set of lexical, syntactic and dependency features extracted from the training data. We computed the minimum and maximum values for each of the features and normalized the values by the range (max - min). Here we describe the features in turn.

Character and Word N-grams Tsur and Rappoport (2007) found that character bigrams were useful for NLI, and they suggested that this may be due to the writer's native language influencing their choice of words. To reflect this, we compute features using both characters and word N-grams. For characters, we consider 2,3 and 4-grams, with padding characters at the beginning and end of each sentence. The features are generated over the entire training data, i.e., every n-gram occurring in the training data is used as a feature. Similarly, we create features with 1,2 and 3-grams of words. Each word n-gram is used as a separate feature. We explore both binary features for each character or word n-gram, as well as normalized count features.

Part-Of-Speech N-grams Several investigations, for example those conducted by Kochmar (2011) and Wong and Dras (2011), have found that part-of-speech tags can be useful for NLI. Therefore we include part-of-speech (POS) n-grams as features. We parse the sentences with the Stanford Parser (Klein and Manning, 2003) and extract the POS tags. We use binary features describing the presence or absence of POS bigrams in a document, as well as numerical features describing their relative frequency in a document.

Function Words Koppel et al. (2005) found that function words can help identify someone's native language. To this end, we include a categorical feature for the presence of function words that are included in list of 321 function words.

Use of punctuation Based on our experience with speakers of native languages, as well as Kochmar's (2011) observations of written English produced by Germanic and Romance language speakers, we suspect that speakers of different native languages use punctuation in different ways, presumably based on the punctuation patterns in their native language. For example, comma placement differs between German and English, and neither Chinese nor Japanese requires a full stop at the end of every sentence. To capture these kinds of patterns, we create two features for each essay: the number of punctuation marks used per sentence, and the number of punctuation marks used per word.

Number of Unique Stems Speakers of different native languages might differ in the amount of vocabulary they use when communicating in English. We capture this by counting the number of unique stems in each essay and using this as an additional feature. The hypothesis here is that depending on the similarity of the native language with English, the presence of common words, and other cultural cues, people with different native language might have access to different amounts of vocabulary.

Misuse of Articles We count instances in which the number of an article is inconsistent with the associated noun. To do so, we fist identify all the *det* dependency relations in the essay. We then compute the ratio of *det* relations between 'a' or 'an' and a plural noun (NNS), to all *det* relations. We also count the ratio of *det* relations between 'a' or 'an' and an uncountable noun, to all *det* relations. We do this using a list of 288 uncountable nouns.[1]

Capitalization The writing systems of some languages in the data set, for example Telugu, do not include capitalization. Furthermore, other languages may use capitalization quite differently from English, for example German, in which all nouns are capitalized, and French, in which nationalities are not. Character capitalization mistakes may be common in the text written by the speakers of such languages. We compute the ratio of words with at least two letters that are written in all caps to identify excessive capitalization. We also count the relative frequency of capitalized words that appear in the middle of a sentence that are not tagged as proper nouns by the part of speech tagger.

Tense and Aspect Frequency Verbal tense and aspect systems vary widely between languages. English has obligatory tense (past, present, future) and

[1] http://www.englishclub.com/vocabulary/nouns-uncountable-list.htm

aspect (imperfect, perfect, progressive) marking on verbs. Other languages, for example French, may require verbs to be marked for tense, but not aspect. Still other languages, for example Chinese, may use adverbials and temporal phrases to communicate temporal and aspectual information. To attempt to capture some of the ways learners of English may be influenced by their native language's system of tense and aspect, we compute two features. First, we compute the relative frequency of each tense and aspect in the article from the counts of each verb POS tags (ex. VB, VBD, VBG). We also compute the percentage of sentences that contain verbs of different tenses or aspect, again using the verb POS tags.

Missing Punctuation We compute the relative frequency of sentences that include an introductory phrase (e.g. however, furthermore, moreover) that is not followed by a comma. We also count the relative frequency of sentences that start with a subordinating conjunction (e.g. sentences starting with if, after, before, when, even though, etc.), but do not contain a comma.

Average Number of Syllables We count the number of syllables per word and the ratio of words with three or more syllables. To count the number of syllables in a word, we used a perl module that estimates the number of syllables by applying a set of hand-crafted rules.[2].

Arc Length We calculate several features pertaining to dependency arc length and direction. We parse each sentence separately, using the Stanford Dependency Parser, and then compute a single value for each of these features for each document. First, we simply compute the percentage of arcs that point left or right (PCTARCL, PCTARCR). We also compute the minumum, maximum, and mean dependency arc length, ignoring arc direction. We also compute similar features for typed dependencies: the minimum, maximum, and mean dependency arc length for each typed dependency; and the percentage of arcs for each typed dependency that go to the left or right.

Downtoners and Intensifiers We compute three features to describe the use of downtoners, and three for intensifiers in each document. First, we count the number of downtoners or intensifiers in a given document.[3] We normalize this count by the number of tokens, types, and sentences in the document to yield the three features capturing the use of downtoners or intensifiers.

Production Rules We compute a set of features to describe the relative frequency of production rules in a given document. First, we parse each sentence using the Stanford Parser, using the default English PCFG (Klein and Manning, 2003). We then count all non-terminal production rules in a given document, and report the relative frequency of each production rule in that document.

Subject Agreement We count the number of sentences in which there appears to be a mistake in subject agreement. To do this, we first identify *nsubj* and *nsubjpass* dependency relationships. Of these dependencies, we count ones meeting the following criteria as mistakes: a third person singular present tense verb with a nominal that is not third person singular, and a third person singular subject with a present tense verb not marked as third person singular. We then normalize the count of errors by the total number of nsubj and nsubj pass dependencies in the document, and the number of sentences in the document to produce two features.

Words per Sentence We compute both the number of tokens per line and the number of types per

[2]http://search.cpan.org/dist/Lingua-EN-Syllable/Syllable.pm

[3]The words we count as downtoners are: 'almost', 'alot', 'a lot', 'barely', 'a bit', 'fairly', 'hardly', 'just', 'kind of', 'least', 'less', 'merely', 'mildly', 'nearly', 'only', 'partially', 'partly', 'practically', 'rather', 'scarcely', 'sort of', 'slightly', and 'somewhat'. The intensifiers are: 'a good deal', 'a great deal', 'absolutely', 'altogether', 'completely','enormously', 'entirely', 'extremely', 'fully', 'greatly', 'highly', 'intensely', 'more', 'most', 'perfectly', 'quite', 'really', 'so', 'strongly', 'super', 'thoroughly', 'too', 'totally', 'utterly', and 'very'.

line.

Topic Scores We construct an unsupervised topic model for all of the documents using Mallet (McCallum, 2002) with 100 topics, dirichlet hyperparameter reestimation every 10 rounds, and all other options set to default values. We then use the topic weights as features.

Passive Constructions We count the number of times an author uses passive constructions by counting the number of *nsubjpass* dependencies in each document. We normalize this count in two ways to produce two different features: dividing by the number of sentences, and dividing by the total number of nsubj and nsubjpass dependencies.

5 Experiments and Results

We used weka (Hall et al., 2009) and libsvm (Chang and Lin, 2011) to run the experiments. The classification was done using an SVM classifier. We experimented with different SVM kernels and different values for the cost parameter. The best performance was achieved with a linear kernel and $cost = 0.001$. We trained the model using the combination of the training and the development sets. We submitted the output of the system to the NLI shared task workshop. Our system achieved 43.3% accuracy. Table 1 shows the confusion matrix and the precision, recall, and F-measure for each language. After the NLI submission deadline, we noticed that we our system was not handling the normalization of the features properly which resulted in the poor performance. After fixing the problem, our system achieved 63% accuracy on both test data and 10-fold cross validation on the entire data.

6 Analysis

We did feature analysis on the training and development data sets using the Chi-squared test. Our feature analysis shows that the most important features for the classifier were topic models, character n-grams of all orders, word unigrams and bigrams, POS bigrams, capitalization features, function words, production rules, and arc length. These results are consistent with those presented in previous work done on this task.

Looking at the confusion matrix in Figure 1, we see that Korean and Japanese were the most commonly confused pair of languages. Hindi and Telugu, two languages from the Indian subcontinent, were also often confused. To analyze this further, we did another experiment by training just a binary classifier on Korean and Japanese using the exact same feature set as earlier. We achieved a 10-fold cross validation accuracy of 83.3% on this classification task. Thus, given just these two languages, we were able to obtain high classification accuracy. This suggests that a potentially fruitful strategy for NLI systems might be to fuse often-confused pairs, such as Korean/Japanese and Hindi/Telugu, into singleton classes for the initial run, and then run a second classifier to do a more fine grained classification within these higher level classes.

When doing feature analysis for these two languages, we found that the character bigrams representing the country names were some of the top features used for classification. For example "Kor" occurred as a trigram frequently in essays from native language speakers of Korean. Based on this, we designed a small experiment where we created features corresponding to the country name associated with each native language, e.g., "Korea", "China", "India", "France", etc. For Arabic, we used a list of 22 countries where Arabic is spoken. Just using this feature, we obtained a 10-fold cross validation accuracy of 21.3% on the development set. This suggests that in certain genres, one may be able to leverage information conveying geographical and demographic attributes for NLI.

7 Conclusion

In this paper, we presented a supervised system for the task of Native Language Identification. We describe and motivate several features for this task and report results of supervised classification using these features on a test data set consisting of 11 lan-

	ARA	CHI	FRE	GER	HIN	ITA	JPN	KOR	SPA	TEL	TUR	Precision	Recall	F-measure
ARA	41	7	8	3	6	2	3	5	10	7	8	44.6%	41.0%	42.7%
CHI	6	38	5	2	2	8	15	8	3	3	10	40.0%	38.0%	39.0%
FRE	8	6	43	8	1	14	2	4	6	1	7	39.1%	43.0%	41.0%
GER	3	3	10	49	4	9	1	7	6	0	8	54.4%	49.0%	51.6%
HIN	5	2	6	9	34	0	3	1	3	32	5	47.9%	34.0%	39.8%
ITA	5	3	10	5	1	52	2	1	17	0	4	46.0%	52.0%	48.8%
JPN	3	11	0	1	1	3	49	26	1	1	4	37.4%	49.0%	42.4%
KOR	2	6	6	1	1	2	35	40	1	1	5	38.1%	40.0%	39.0%
SPA	4	6	14	1	1	17	6	2	38	0	11	40.9%	38.0%	39.4%
TEL	9	7	3	4	18	2	2	2	2	48	3	51.1%	48.0%	49.5%
TUR	6	6	5	7	2	4	13	9	6	1	41	38.7%	41.0%	39.8%
Accuracy = 43.0%														

Table 1: The results of our original submission to the NLI shared task on the test set. These results reflect the performance of the system that does not normalize the features properly

guages provided as part of the NLI shared task. We found that our classifier often confused two pairs of languages that are spoken near one another, but are linguistically unrelated: Hindi/Telugu and Korean/Japanese. We found that we could obtain high classification accuracy on these two pairs of languages using a binary classifier trained on just these pairs. During our feature analysis, we also found that certain features that happened to convey geographical and demographic information were also informative for this task.

References

Ahmed Abbasi and Hsinchun Chen. 2005. Applying authorship analysis to extremist-group web forum messages. *IEEE Intelligent Systems*, 20(5):67–75, September.

Daniel Blanchard, Joel Tetreault, Derrick Higgins, Aoife Cahill, and Martin Chodorow. 2013. TOEFL11: A Corpus of Non-Native English. Technical report, Educational Testing Service.

Chih-Chung Chang and Chih-Jen Lin. 2011. LIBSVM: A library for support vector machines. *ACM Transactions on Intelligent Systems and Technology*, 2:27:1–27:27.

Carole E. Chaski. 2005. Who's at the keyboard: Authorship attribution in digital evidence investigations. *International Journal of Digital Evidence*, 4:2005.

Eugene Garfield. 1964. Can citation indexing be automated?

Mark Hall, Eibe Frank, Geoffrey Holmes, Bernhard Pfahringer, Peter Reutemann, and Ian H. Witten. 2009. The weka data mining software: an update. *SIGKDD Explor. Newsl.*, 11(1):10–18.

Mark Johnson, Thomas L. Griffiths, and Sharon Goldwater. 2007. Adaptor grammars: A framework for specifying compositional nonparametric bayesian models. *Advances in neural information processing systems*, 19:641.

Dan Klein and Christopher D Manning. 2003. Accurate unlexicalized parsing. In *Proceedings of the 41st Annual Meeting on Association for Computational Linguistics-Volume 1*, pages 423–430. Association for Computational Linguistics.

Ekaterina Kochmar. 2011. *Identification of a Writer's Native Langauge by Error Analysis*. Ph.D. thesis.

Moshe Koppel, Jonathan Schler, and Kfir Zigdon. 2005. Determining an author's native language by mining a text for errors. In *Proceedings of the eleventh ACM SIGKDD international conference on Knowledge discovery in data mining*, pages 624–628, Chicago, IL. ACM.

Moshe Koppel, Jonathan Schler, and Shlomo Argamon. 2008. Computational methods in authorship attribution. *Journal of the American Society for information Science and Technology*, 60(1):9–26.

Andrew Kachites McCallum. 2002. Mallet: A machine learning for language toolkit. http://mallet.cs.umass.edu.

Frederick Mosteller and David L. Wallace. 1964. *Inference and Disputed Authorship: The Federalist Papers*. Addison-Wesley, Reading, Mass.

Joel Tetreault, Daniel Blanchard, and Aoife Cahill. 2013. A report on the first native language identification shared task. In *Proceedings of the Eighth Workshop on Innovative Use of NLP for Building Educational Applications*, Atlanta, GA, USA, June. Association for Computational Linguistics.

Oren Tsur and Ari Rappoport. 2007. Using classifier features for studying the effect of native language on the choice of written second language words. In *Proceedings of the Workshop on Cognitive Aspects of Computational Language Acquisition*, CACLA '07, pages 9–16, Stroudsburg, PA, USA. Association for Computational Linguistics.

Sze-Meng Jojo Wong and Mark Dras. 2009. Contrastive Analysis and Native Language Identification. In *Proceedings of the Australasian Language Technology Association Workshop 2009*, pages 53–61, Sydney, Australia, December.

Sze-Meng Jojo Wong and Mark Dras. 2011. Exploiting Parse Structures for Native Language Identification. In *Proceedings of the 2011 Conference on Empirical Methods in Natural Language Processing*, pages 1600–1610, Edinburgh, Scotland, UK., July. Association for Computational Linguistics.

Sze-Meng Jojo Wong, Mark Dras, and Mark Johnson. 2011. Topic Modeling for Native Language Identification. In *Proceedings of the Australasian Language Technology Association Workshop 2011*, pages 115–124, Canberra, Australia, December.

Sze-Meng Jojo Wong, Mark Dras, and Mark Johnson. 2012. Exploring Adaptor Grammars for Native Language Identification. In *Proceedings of the 2012 Joint Conference on Empirical Methods in Natural Language Processing and Computational Natural Language Learning*, pages 699–709, Jeju Island, Korea, July. Association for Computational Linguistics.

VTEX System Description for the NLI 2013 Shared Task

Vidas Daudaravičius
VTEX
Akademijos 2a
Vilnius, Lithuania
vidas.daudaravicius@vtex.lt

Abstract

This paper describes the system developed for the NLI 2013 Shared Task, requiring to identify a writer's native language by some text written in English. I explore the given manually annotated data using word features such as the length, endings and character trigrams. Furthermore, I employ k-NN classification. Modified TFIDF is used to generate a stop-word list automatically. The distance between two documents is calculated combining n-grams of word lengths and endings, and character trigrams.

1 Introduction

Native Language Identification (NLI) is the task of identifying the first spoken language (L1) of a person based on the person's written text in another language. As a natural language processing (NLP) task, it is properly categorized as text classification, and standard approaches like support vector machines (SVM) are successfully applied to it. Koppel et al. (2005) trained SVM models with a set of stylistic features, including Part of Speech (POS) and character n-grams (sequences), function words, and spelling error types, achieving 80% accuracy in a 5-language task. Tsur and Rappoport (2007) focused on character n-grams. Wong and Dras (2011) showed that syntactic patterns, derived by a parser, are more effective than other stylistic features. The Cambridge Learner Corpus has been used recently by Kochmar (2011), who concluded that character n-grams are the most promising features. Brooke and Hirst (2012) investigated function words, character n-grams, POS n-grams, POS/function n-grams, CFG productions, dependencies, word n-grams.

A notable problem in the recent NLI research is a clear interaction between native languages and topics in the corpora. The solution in the mentioned work was to avoid lexical features that might carry topical information.

2 Data

The NLI 2013 Shared Task uses the TOEFL11 corpus (Blanchard et al., 2013) which was designed specifically for the task of native language identification. The corpus contains 12 100 English essays from the TOEFL (**T**est of **E**nglish as a **F**oreign **L**anguage) that were collected through ETS (Educational Testing Service) operational test delivery system. TOEFL11 contains eleven native languages: Arabic, Chinese, French, German, Hindi, Italian, Japanese, Korean, Spanish, Telugu, and Turkish. The sampling of essays ensures approximately equal representation of native languages across eight topics, labeled as prompts. The corpus contains more than 1000 essays for each L1 language. Each essay is labelled with an English language proficiency level – high, medium, or low – given by human assessment specialists. The essays are usually 300 to 400 words long. The corpus is split into training, development and test data (9900, 1100 and 1100, respectively). The corpus contains plain text files and the index for these

File name	Prompt	Native language	Language proficiency
1000025.txt	P2	CHI	high
100021.txt	P1	ARA	low
1000235.txt	P8	TEL	medium
1000276.txt	P4	TEL	high
1000392.txt	P3	JPN	medium
1000599.txt	P6	CHI	medium
1000617.txt	P4	GER	high
1000719.txt	P1	HIN	high
100082.txt	P2	TUR	medium

Table 1: The sample of the training data index.

files. Sample of this index is shown in Table 1.

3 *N*end transformation

The training and the development corpora contain a lot of spelling errors and no POS tagging is provided. For instance, a sentence from the training corpus *"Acachely I write abawet may communitie and who the people support youg people"*. Therefore I needed to find features which encode the information about native language of a writer in a more generalized way. Also, my primary interest was to build a system which does not utilize any language processing tool, such as part of speech or syntactic trees, and topic-related information, such as full words. The reason for that is to have the possibility to apply the same techniques for the texts written in other languages than English in the future. Thus, I choose to use the word length as the number of characters together with the last n characters of that word. Words in the essays were transformed into tokens using five kinds of transformations:

0end – takes the pure length of a word (for example, *make* $\mapsto$ *4*);

1end – adds to the length of a word the last character (*make* $\mapsto$ *4e*);

2end – adds to the length of a word the last two characters (*make* $\mapsto$ *4ke*);

3end – adds to the length of a word the last three characters (*make* $\mapsto$ *4ake*);

4end – adds to the length of a word the last four characters (*make* $\mapsto$ *4make*).

For instance, the sentence "*Difference makes a lot of opportunities .*" is translated to:

0end:	10	5	1	3	2	13	1
1end:	10e	5s	1a	3t	2f	13s	1.
2end:	10ce	5es	1a	3ot	2of	13es	1.
3end:	10nce	5kes	1a	3lot	2of	13ies	1.
4end:	10ence	5akes	1a	3lot	2of	13ties	1.

4 *N*-gram features

The VTEX NLI 2013 system is based on n-gram features. There are no strict rules for how long n-grams should be. Frequently used n-grams are unigrams, bigrams and trigrams as in Brooke and Hirst (2012; Wong and Dras (2011). The training NLI 2013 corpus is large enough to build higher-order n-grams of $n$end tokens. I use unigrams, bigrams, trigrams, quad-grams and five-grams based on $n$end tokens. Some examples of these n-grams are shown below:

0end					
1-gram:	3				
2-gram:	1	3			
3-gram:	1	10	6		
4-gram:	1	5	3	3	
5-gram:	1	3	3	3	7
3end					
1-gram:	7ess				
2-gram:	2to	7ess			
3-gram:	4est	2to	7ess		
4-gram:	3but	3not	3for	7ess	
5-gram:	3try	5eir	4est	2to	7ess

Beside n-grams of $n$ends, the character n-grams are of interest also. Kochmar (2011) noted that character n-grams provide promissing features for NLI task. Therefore, I tried to use character trigrams also. For instance, from the sentence "*Difference makes a lot of opportunities .*" the following trigrams were generated:

Dif iff ffe fer ere ren enc nce ce e m
* ma mak ake kes es s a a a l lo lot*
ot t o of of f o op opp ppo por ort
rtu tun uni nit iti tie ies es s .

Whitespace is included in character trigrams and denotes the beginning or the end of a word.

5 CTFIDF for weigthing features

The most widely used technique for weighting items in a list is Term-Frequency–Inverse-Document-Frequency, known as TF–IDF. Daudaravicius (2012) shows that the small change of TF–IDF allows to the generation of stop-word lists automatically. For the NLI 2013 Shared Task I use *Conditional TF–IDF*:

$$\mathrm{CTFIDF}(x) = \mathrm{TF}(x) \cdot \ln \frac{\mathrm{D_{max}} - \mathrm{d}(x) + 1}{4 \cdot \mathrm{d}(x) + 1},$$

where $\mathrm{TF}(x)$ is the frequency of the item x in the training corpus, $\mathrm{d}(x)$ is the number of documents in the training corpus where the item x appears, known as *document frequency*, $\mathrm{D_{max}}$ is the maximum of document frequency of any item in the training corpus.

The idea of my Conditional TF–IDF is as follows: if a term occures in less than $\mathrm{D_{max}}/4$ documents then this term is considered a normal term, and the term is considered as *stop-word* if it occures in more than $\mathrm{D_{max}}/4$ documents. The range of TF-IDF is between 0 and positive infinity. The range of CTFIDF is from minus infinity to zero for items that are considered stop-words. And the range of CTFIDF is from zero to infinity for the rest of the items.

For instance, the $\mathrm{D_{max}}$ for the different n-gram length and different Nend transformations is presented in Table 2. The example list of 4end ungrams with positive and negative CTFIDFs are shown in Tables 4 and 3, respectively.

It is important to note that I count $\mathrm{D_{max}}$ and $\mathrm{d}(x)$ for each training language separately; i.e., when I measure the distance between a document and the document in the training data, I use $\mathrm{D_{max}}$ and $\mathrm{d}(x)$ of the language which the training document denotes.

	The number of n-grams				
	1	2	3	4	5
0end	900	899	834	444	168
1end	900	759	358	320	148
2end	899	581	354	319	148
3end	899	572	320	303	148
4end	899	572	320	303	148

Table 2: The maximum of the document frequency in the training corpus.

token	ctfidf	token	ctfidf	token	ctfidf
5earn	0.00	4Most	1.16	10ents	2.51
7ally	0.04	7lity	1.20	4your	2.59
10sion	0.10	2Of	1.22	7arly	2.59
7ieve	0.10	6ance	1.22	6eple	2.64
5hing	0.12	6mous	1.22	7tory	2.71
10ence	0.12	5hier	1.24	8tics	2.94
9tion	0.15	3Now	1.25	9gers	3.00
2us	0.22	5eing	1.27	4cool	3.07
6rson	0.23	12tion	1.30	3Let	3.13
7hout	0.29	2He	1.30	4rule	3.29
3may	0.30	4ways	1.41	5imes	3.52
3say	0.31	6hers	1.43	3job	3.53
3see	0.34	5reat	1.45	13ties	3.60
3try	0.35	9rent	1.53	8cial	3.68
3did	0.36	3him	1.55	5eals	3.81
2”	0.42	5ower	1.61	6lent	3.81
2“	0.44	12ties	1.65	4lose	3.95
2he	0.46	3You	1.68	8naly	4.13
4hard	0.52	11lity	1.74	6skes	4.34
7pany	0.58	4cost	1.76	7cted	4.34
5akes	0.60	5ince	1.78	7test	4.34
4kind	0.68	6ills	1.82	6alth	4.36
7blem	0.70	5isks	1.82	5eall	4.60
5ever	0.71	5oney	1.89	9dent	4.73
4been	0.74	6rget	2.07	7cess	4.75
4same	0.81	5ired	2.10	7kers	5.36
8king	0.86	9nies	2.11	9ters	5.46
6king	0.93	4ever	2.15	2D.	5.52
5ften	0.96	6ates	2.15	5neof	5.52
6urse	0.97	3his	2.22	8idnt	5.52
7ling	0.97	10ered	2.24	8klin	5.52
4Even	0.98	4love	2.24	9velt	5.52
8ible	0.99	6ited	2.24	10sful	6.62
4used	1.02	9ties	2.27	4four	7.62
10tely	1.07	4earn	2.30	3oil	8.05
4best	1.09	6llow	2.30	9cans	8.26
7ught	1.10	9ated	2.37	4jobs	8.96
4easy	1.12	3got	2.42	3FDR	11.04
4Then	1.12	8ngly	1.13		

Table 3: The list of 4end unigrams with positive CTFIDFs of one document from the training corpus.

token	ctfidf	token	ctfidf	token	ctfidf
1.	-224.19	3but	-3.48	3lot	-0.92
1,	-127.63	5bout	-2.58	2we	-0.88
2to	-69.62	3get	-2.57	5hich	-0.85
2of	-56.92	7mple	-2.54	9ment	-0.84
3the	-45.09	2by	-2.39	3who	-0.84
3and	-27.25	4from	-2.26	3The	-0.81
2is	-24.79	4they	-2.18	4them	-0.79
1a	-23.19	3can	-2.12	3one	-0.77
6ople	-22.78	4will	-2.11	4only	-0.75
3not	-22.31	3all	-1.83	4much	-0.70
3are	-18.11	2If	-1.72	4what	-0.68
3for	-15.82	2at	-1.63	4also	-0.64
4that	-14.39	2In	-1.50	4want	-0.57
2do	-13.16	6ings	-1.38	6cond	-0.56
2it	-12.50	5irst	-1.35	9tant	-0.43
4have	-11.53	3For	-1.33	3how	-0.35
4with	-9.39	5gree	-1.33	3new	-0.31
1I	-8.72	3you	-1.31	6ould	-0.31
7ause	-7.73	2so	-1.30	4need	-0.20
2in	-6.40	4time	-1.15	5oing	-0.15
5heir	-6.23	3was	-1.08	4take	-0.11
2be	-5.44	7ever	-0.98	2So	-0.10
4many	-5.40	5ther	-0.95	6ally	-0.09
2as	-5.06	4make	-0.93	3But	-0.08
5here	-3.92	5hink	-3.64		

Table 4: The list of 4end unigrams with negative CTFIDFs of the same document as in Fig. 3.

6 Distance between documents

Cosine distance is a widely used technique to measure the distance between two feature vectors. It is calculated as follows:

$$\cos(X,Y) = \frac{\sum_i (X_i Y_i)}{\sqrt{\sum_i X_i^2} + \sqrt{\sum_i Y_i^2}}.$$

CTFIDF allows the splitting of feature vectors into the list of "informative" items and the list of functional items. For the NLI 2013 Shared task, I combine two cosine distances of negative and positive CTFIDFs as follows:

$$\cos'(X,Y) = \frac{2\cos(X',Y') + \cos(X'',Y'')}{3},$$

where

$$X' = \text{filter}_{\geq 0} X, \qquad Y' = \text{filter}_{\geq 0} Y,$$
$$X'' = \text{abs}(\text{filter}_{<0} X), \quad Y'' = \text{abs}(\text{filter}_{<0} Y),$$

so X' and Y' contain features with positive CTFIDF, while X'' and Y'' contain features with negative CTFIDF.

The $\cos'$ combines two cosine distances giving the weight for cosine of positive CTFIDFs equal to 2 and for the negative CTFIDFs equal to 1. I have also tested combinations of 1 to 0, 0 to 1, 1 to 1, and 1 to 2. But these combinations did not achieve better results. Therefore, for all submitted system results I used the same combination of 2 to 1.

I utilize 26 feature vectors and obtain 26 combined cosine distances for each document: one for character trigrams and other 25 for token n-grams of diverse word transformations. Each combined cosine distance has an assigned weight to get the final distance between two documents. The distance between two documents X and Y is calculated as follows:

$$\text{dist}(X,Y) = \frac{\sum_i w_i \cos'(X_i, Y_i)}{\sum_i w_i} \in [0,1],$$

where w_i is the weight of ith feature vector.

The most difficult task was to find the best combination of these 26 weights. For the NLI 2013 Shared Task I have used the combinations shown in Table 5. The n-gram weights in most cases are diagonal with the highest value at the 0end unigram and the lowest at the 4end five-gram. In the beggining I tested the opposite combination, but this led to worse results. Also, the influence of character trigrams on the results was high. The first and second combinations in Table 5 differ in the use of five-grams and 4end transformations, while the leverage of character trigrams were kept the same. The final official results show that richer features improve results. Also, I found that the higher leverage is for character trigrams over n-grams the better the results are. But, the results of character trigrams only resulted in lower performance. It is a long way to find the optimal combination of the weights.

	Token n-gram				
	1	2	3	4	5
1-closed					
Character trigrams					64
0end	7	6	5	4	0
1end	6	5	4	3	0
2end	5	4	3	2	0
3end	4	3	2	1	0
4end	0	0	0	0	0
2-closed					
Character trigrams					125
0end	9	8	7	6	5
1end	8	7	6	5	4
2end	7	6	5	4	3
3end	6	5	4	3	2
4end	5	4	3	2	1
3-closed					
Character trigrams					25
0end	1	1	1	1	1
1end	1	1	1	1	1
2end	1	1	1	1	1
3end	1	1	1	1	1
4end	1	1	1	1	1
4-closed					
Character trigrams					225
0end	17	15	13	11	9
1end	15	13	11	9	7
2end	13	11	9	7	5
3end	11	9	7	5	3
4end	9	7	5	3	1
5-closed					
Character trigrams					550
0end	17	15	13	11	9
1end	15	13	11	9	7
2end	13	11	9	7	5
3end	11	9	7	5	3
4end	9	7	5	3	1

Table 5: Weights of the NLI 2013 different submissions.

7 Assigning native language to a text

I used the k-NN technique to assign native language to a text. I counted the distances between the test document and all training documents, and take some amount of closest documents for each language. To reduce the influnce of outliers, I dropped off the n closest documents and only then take some amount from the rest. At first, I remove the 10 top documents from each language, and then kept the 20 closest documents for each language. In total, I obtained 220 documents and ranked them by distance. Then, I employed voting for the closest 20 documents. A winner language is assigned to a document as the native language. This technique was used for VTEX-closed-(1, 2 and 3) system submitions. For the VTEX-closed-(4 and 5) I used another number for outliers and the top closest ones: the 50 closest documents for each language were dropped off, the remianing 25 for each language were kept, and, finally, the closest 25 documents are used for the voting of native language.

8 Results

My primary interest in participating in the NLI 2013 Shared Task was to investigate new features that were not used earlier, and what the value of each feature in the identification of a writer's native language is. The results of five submitted systems are shown in Tables 6 and 7. The best submitted system had 31.9 percent accuracy. This result was the worst of all participating teams. At the time of writing this report, I tested new combinations of outliers and tops, "stop-words" and significant items, $n$end n-grams and character trigram weights. New settings improved my best submitted system accuracy from 31.9 to 63.9 percent. This result was achieved with the following settings. I took the last 50 percent of closest documents for each language. I set to use only stop-words and to exclude significant items, i.e., items with only negative CTFIDF. Finaly, I set n-gram weights accordingly: 84 for character trigrams, and for $n$end 1,1,1,1,1, 1,3,3,3,1, 1,3,5,3,1, 1,3,3,3,1, 1,1,1,1,1. This result shows that 2end and 3end transformation trigrams have the highest impact on the results. Nevertheless, all tested transformations help to improve the results. In conclusion, I investigated the influence of features, such as character trigrams and Nend n-grams, to the identification of writer's native language and found them very informative.

Results for VTEX-closed-1

	ARA	CHI	FRE	GER	HIN	ITA	JPN	KOR	SPA	TEL	TUR	Precision	Recall	F-measure
ARA	**30**	5	2	5	5	11	12	6	10	13	1	26.3%	30.0%	28.0%
CHI	4	**20**	2	5	5	6	21	20	5	9	3	24.1%	20.0%	21.9%
FRE	6	8	**9**	13	3	14	14	9	8	10	6	28.1%	9.0%	13.6%
GER	6	4	5	**30**	7	13	4	1	7	20	3	35.3%	30.0%	32.4%
HIN	15	5	0	7	**17**	5	6	5	3	31	6	23.0%	17.0%	19.5%
ITA	7	2	4	3	4	**47**	9	3	4	15	2	34.8%	47.0%	40.0%
JPN	4	5	1	4	5	7	**44**	12	4	14	0	25.3%	44.0%	32.1%
KOR	2	8	1	3	2	9	35	**27**	3	9	1	26.0%	27.0%	26.5%
SPA	13	10	4	3	5	15	13	8	**12**	13	4	19.0%	12.0%	14.7%
TEL	13	8	0	1	13	4	2	1	4	**52**	2	26.3%	52.0%	34.9%
TUR	14	8	4	11	8	4	14	12	3	12	**10**	26.3%	10.0%	14.5%

Accuracy = 27.1%

Results for VTEX-closed-2

	ARA	CHI	FRE	GER	HIN	ITA	JPN	KOR	SPA	TEL	TUR	Precision	Recall	F-measure
ARA	**31**	5	1	3	5	11	13	6	8	15	2	26.5%	31.0%	28.6%
CHI	6	**23**	1	4	6	5	21	15	6	10	3	27.7%	23.0%	25.1%
FRE	5	8	**7**	12	7	15	12	10	6	10	8	25.9%	7.0%	11.0%
GER	7	4	4	**28**	9	12	6	1	6	20	3	35.0%	28.0%	31.1%
HIN	13	5	2	6	**17**	4	6	5	4	30	8	20.2%	17.0%	18.5%
ITA	7	2	4	3	4	**47**	9	3	4	15	2	35.1%	47.0%	40.2%
JPN	4	7	0	5	6	7	**36**	16	3	15	1	22.0%	36.0%	27.3%
KOR	3	7	1	3	2	9	34	**26**	4	9	2	25.7%	26.0%	25.9%
SPA	15	7	3	5	6	17	10	7	**10**	15	5	16.4%	10.0%	12.4%
TEL	13	6	1	0	15	2	2	1	6	**52**	2	25.5%	52.0%	34.2%
TUR	13	9	3	11	7	5	15	11	4	13	**9**	20.0%	9.0%	12.4%

Accuracy = 26.0%

Results for VTEX-closed-3

	ARA	CHI	FRE	GER	HIN	ITA	JPN	KOR	SPA	TEL	TUR	Precision	Recall	F-measure
ARA	**27**	6	1	5	6	11	11	7	11	13	2	25.2%	27.0%	26.1%
CHI	6	**22**	2	6	8	2	21	14	5	12	2	27.2%	22.0%	24.3%
FRE	6	8	**6**	12	8	14	15	7	5	10	9	17.1%	6.0%	8.9%
GER	7	4	6	**24**	9	13	1	2	7	22	5	27.3%	24.0%	25.5%
HIN	15	4	2	7	**17**	4	6	3	5	30	7	19.5%	17.0%	18.2%
ITA	7	0	6	3	4	**45**	8	5	4	16	2	34.1%	45.0%	38.8%
JPN	4	9	0	5	6	8	**32**	15	4	16	1	21.2%	32.0%	25.5%
KOR	2	6	1	5	2	9	31	**26**	4	12	2	27.7%	26.0%	26.8%
SPA	15	7	4	6	8	16	7	6	**11**	14	6	15.3%	11.0%	12.8%
TEL	10	6	2	0	13	5	2	1	10	**50**	1	23.9%	50.0%	32.4%
TUR	8	9	5	15	6	5	17	8	6	14	**7**	15.9%	7.0%	9.7%

Accuracy = 24.3%

Table 6: The results for closed-task VTEX systems.

Results for VTEX-closed-4

	ARA	CHI	FRE	GER	HIN	ITA	JPN	KOR	SPA	TEL	TUR	Precision	Recall	F-measure
ARA	**21**	5	1	6	4	14	15	6	14	12	2	30.4%	21.0%	24.9%
CHI	2	**22**	2	5	5	5	24	18	7	7	3	26.2%	22.0%	23.9%
FRE	4	9	**8**	13	3	14	16	9	6	12	6	22.2%	8.0%	11.8%
GER	5	4	8	**25**	8	13	5	2	6	19	5	28.7%	25.0%	26.7%
HIN	7	7	1	7	**15**	5	7	7	4	31	9	22.1%	15.0%	17.9%
ITA	2	3	3	4	2	**48**	12	3	4	16	3	33.8%	48.0%	39.7%
JPN	1	5	1	5	4	8	**42**	17	4	13	0	21.8%	42.0%	28.7%
KOR	1	6	1	2	1	7	36	**33**	2	10	1	30.0%	33.0%	31.4%
SPA	9	11	5	6	4	18	14	5	**10**	14	4	15.9%	10.0%	12.3%
TEL	8	5	3	1	15	5	2	1	4	**53**	3	27.0%	53.0%	35.8%
TUR	9	7	3	13	7	5	20	9	2	9	**16**	30.8%	16.0%	21.1%

Accuracy = 26.6%

Results for VTEX-closed-5

	ARA	CHI	FRE	GER	HIN	ITA	JPN	KOR	SPA	TEL	TUR	Precision	Recall	F-measure
ARA	**40**	7	0	2	2	14	10	4	7	11	3	33.9%	40.0%	36.7%
CHI	6	**32**	4	0	4	4	21	16	4	8	1	27.8%	32.0%	29.8%
FRE	5	13	**13**	9	2	15	14	8	6	12	3	28.9%	13.0%	17.9%
GER	10	5	8	**22**	2	13	7	3	8	16	6	45.8%	22.0%	29.7%
HIN	12	9	4	5	**11**	5	6	6	4	30	8	28.9%	11.0%	15.9%
ITA	3	5	6	2	1	**54**	7	4	5	11	2	36.5%	54.0%	43.5%
JPN	2	6	0	3	1	8	**48**	16	3	12	1	26.4%	48.0%	34.0%
KOR	1	12	1	0	2	6	29	**39**	2	7	1	35.1%	39.0%	37.0%
SPA	12	9	5	1	3	20	14	5	**16**	12	3	27.1%	16.0%	20.1%
TEL	14	6	0	0	8	5	2	0	3	**59**	3	31.4%	59.0%	41.0%
TUR	13	11	4	4	2	4	24	10	1	10	**17**	35.4%	17.0%	23.0%

Accuracy = 31.9%

Table 7: The results for closed-task VTEX systems.

References

Blanchard D., Tetreault J. and Cahill A. 2013. Summary Report on the First Shared Task on Native Language Identification. *In Proceedings of the Eighth Workshop on Building Educational Applications Using NLP*, Association for Computational Linguistics, Atlanta, GA, USA

Brooke, J. and Hirst, G. 2012. Robust, Lexicalized Native Language Identification. *In Proceedings of COLING 2012*, Mumbai, India, 391–408.

Daudaravicius, V. 2012. Collocation segmentation for text chunking. *PhD thesis, Vytautas Magnus University*.

Kochmar, E. 2011. Identification of a Writer's Native Language by Error Analysis. *Master's thesis, University of Cambridge*.

Koppel M., Schler J. and Zigdon, K. 2005. Determining an author's native language by mining a text for errors. *In Proceedings of the 11th ACM SIGKDD International Conference on Knowledge Discovery in Data Mining (KDD '05)*, 624-628.

Tsur, O. and Rappoport, A. 2007. Using classifier features for studying the effect of native language on the choice of written second language words. *In Proceedings of the Workshop on Cognitive Aspects of Computational Language Acquisition (CACLA'07)*, 9-16.

Wong, S.J. and Dras, M. 2011. Exploiting parse structures for native language identification. *In Proceedings of the Conference on Empirical Methods in Natural Language Processing*, 1600-1610.

Feature Space Selection and Combination for Native Language Identification

Cyril Goutte
National Research Council
1200 Montreal Rd,
Ottawa, ON K1A 0R6
Cyril.Goutte@nrc.ca

Serge Léger
National Research Council
100, des Aboiteaux St.,
Moncton, NB E1A 7R1
Serge.Leger@nrc.ca

Marine Carpuat
National Research Council
1200 Montreal Rd,
Ottawa, ON K1A 0R6
Marine.Carpuat@nrc.ca

Abstract

We decribe the submissions made by the National Research Council Canada to the Native Language Identification (NLI) shared task. Our submissions rely on a Support Vector Machine classifier, various feature spaces using a variety of lexical, spelling, and syntactic features, and on a simple model combination strategy relying on a majority vote between classifiers. Somewhat surprisingly, a classifier relying on purely lexical features performed very well and proved difficult to outperform significantly using various combinations of feature spaces. However, the combination of multiple predictors allowed to exploit their different strengths and provided a significant boost in performance.

1 Introduction

We describe the National Research Council Canada's submissions to the Native Language Identification 2013 shared task (Tetreault et al., 2013). Our submissions rely on fairly straightforward statistical modelling techniques, applied to various feature spaces representing lexical and syntactic information. Our most successful submission was actually a combination of models trained on different sets of feature spaces using a simple majority vote.

Much of the work on Natural Language Processing is motivated by the desire to have machines that can help or replace humans on language-related tasks. Many tasks such as topic or genre classification, entity extraction, disambiguation, are fairly straightforward for humans to complete. Machines typically trade-off some performance for ease of application and reduced cost. Equally fascinating are tasks that seem non-trivial to humans, but on which machines, through appropriate statistical analysis, discover regularities and dependencies that are far from obvious to humans. Examples may include categorizing text by author gender (Koppel et al., 2003) or detecting whether a text is an original or a translation (Baroni and Bernardini, 2006). This is one motivation for addressing the problem of identifying the native language of an author in this shared task.

In the following section, we describe various aspects of the models and features we used on this task. In section 3, we describe our experimental settings and summarize the results we obtained. We discuss and conclude in section 4.

2 Modelling

Our submissions rely on straightforward statistical classifiers trained on various combinations of features and feature spaces. We first describe the classifier we used, then give the list of features that we have been combining. Our best performing submission used a combination of the three systems we submitted in a majority vote, which we also describe at the end of this section.

2.1 Classification Model

We decided to use a straightforward and state-of-the-art statistical classifier, in order to focus our attention on the combination of features and models rather than on the design of the classifier.

We used freely available implementations of Support Vector Machines (SVM) provided in SVM-light (Joachims, 1999) and SVM-perf (Joachims, 2006). SVM performance may be influenced by at least two important factors: the choice of the kernel and the trade-off parameter "C". In our experiments, we did not observe any gain from using either polynomial or RBF kernels. All results below are therefore obtained with linear models. Similarly, we investigated the optimization of parameter "C" on a held-out validation set, but found out that the resulting performance was not consistently significantly better than that provided by the default value. As a consequence our results were obtained using the SVM-light default.

One important issue in this shared task was to handle multiple classes (the 11 languages). There are essentially two easy approaches to handle single label, multiclass classification with binary SVM: one-versus-all and one-versus-one. We adopted the one-versus-all setting, combined with a calibration step. We first trained 11 classifiers using the documents for each language in turn as "positive" examples, and the documents for the remaining 10 languages as negative examples. The output score for each class-specific SVM model was then mapped into a probability using isotonic regression with the pair-adjacent violators (PAV) algorithm (Zadrozny and Elkan, 2002). A test document is then assigned to the class with the highest probability.

2.2 Feature Space Extraction

We extracted the following features from the documents provided for the shared task.

Character ngrams: We index trigrams of characters within each word (Koppel et al., 2005). The beginning and end of a word are treated as special character. For example, the word "at" will produce two trigrams: " at" and "at ". These features allow us to capture for example typical spelling variants. In a language with weak morphology such as English, they may also be able to capture patterns of usage of, e.g. suffixes, which provides a low-cost proxy for syntactic information.

Word ngrams: We index unigrams and bigrams of words within each sentence. For bigrams, the beginning and end of a sentence are treated as special tokens. Note that we do not apply any stoplist filtering. As a consequence, function words, an often-used feature (Koppel et al., 2005; Brooke and Hirst, 2012), are naturally included in the unigram feature space.

Spelling features: Misspelled words are identified using GNU Aspell V0.60.4[1] and indexed with their counts. Some parser artifacts such as "n't" are removed from the final mispelled word index. Although misspellings may seem to provide clues as to the author's native language, we did not find these features to be useful in any of our experiments. Note however, that misspelled words will also appear in the unigram feature space.

Part-of-speech ngrams: The texts were tagged with the Stanford tagger v. 3.0[2] using the largest and best (bidirectional) model. Note that the language in a couple of documents was so poor that the tagger was unable to complete, and we reverted to a slightly weaker (left three words) model for those. After tagging, we indexed all ngrams of part-of-speech tags, with $n = 2, 3, 4, 5$. We experimented with the choice of n and found out that $n > 2$ did not bring any significant difference in performance.

Syntactic dependencies: We ran the Stanford Parser v2.0.0 on all essays, and use the typed dependency output to generate features. Our goal is to capture phenomena such as preposition selection which might be influenced by the native language of the writer. In order to reduce sparsity, each observed dependency is used to generate three features: one feature for the full lexicalized dependency relation; one feature for the head (which generalizes over all observed modifiers); one feature for the modifier (which generalizes over all possible heads). For instance, in the sentence "they participate to one 's appearance", the parser extracts the following dependency: "prep$_{to}$(participate,appearance)". It yields three features "prep$_{to}$(participate,appearance)", "prep$_{to}$(participate,X)" and "prep$_{to}$(X,appearance)". We experimented with all three feature types, but the systems used for the

[1] `http://aspell.net`

[2] `http://nlp.stanford.edu/software/tagger.shtml`

official evaluation results only used the last two (head and modifier features.) Note that while these features can capture long distance dependencies in theory, they significantly overlap with word ngram features in practice.

For each feature space, we used a choice of two weighting schemes inspired by SMART (Manning et al., 2008):

ltc: log of the feature count, combined with the log inverse document frequency (idf), with a cosine normalization;

nnc: straight feature count, no idf, with cosine normalization.

Normalization is important with SVM classifiers as they are not scale invariant and tend to be sensitive to large variations in the scale of features.

2.3 Voting Combination

Investigating the differences in predictions made by different models, it became apparent that there were significant differences between systems that displayed similar performance. For example, our first two submissions, which perform within 0.2% of each other on the test data, disagree on almost 20% of the examples.

This suggests that there is potentially a lot of information to gain by combining systems trained on different feature spaces. An attempt to directly combine the predictions of different systems into a new predictive score proved unsuccessful and failed to provide a significant gain over the systems used in the combination.

A more successful combination was obtained using a simple majority vote. Our method relies on simply looking at the classes predicted by an ensemble of classifier for a given document. The prediction for the ensemble will be the most predicted class, breaking possible ties according to the overall scores of the component models: for example, for an ensemble of only 2 models, the decision in the case of a tie will be that of the best model.

3 Experiments

We describe the experimental setting that we used to prepare our submissions, and the final performance we obtained on the shared task (Tetreault et al., 2013).

3.1 Experimental Setting

In order to test the performance of various choices of feature spaces and their combination, we set up a cross-validation experimental setting. We originally sampled 9 equal sized disjoint folds of 1100 documents each from the training data. We used stratified sampling across the languages and the prompts. This made sure that the folds respected the uniform distribution across languages, as well as the distribution across prompts, which was slightly uneven for some languages. These 9 folds were later augmented with a 10th fold containing the development data released during the evaluation.

All systems were evaluated by computing the accuracy (or equivalently the micro-averaged F-score) on the cross-validated predictions.

3.2 Experimental Results

We submitted four systems to the shared task evaluation:

1. BOW2^{ltc}+CHAR3^{ltc}: Uses counts of word bigrams and character trigrams, both weighted independently with the ltc weighting scheme (tf-idf with cosine normalization);

2. BOW2^{ltc}+DEP^{ltc}: Uses counts of word bigrams and syntactic dependencies, both weighted independently with the ltc weighting scheme;

3. BOW2^{ltc}+CHAR3^{ltc}+POS2^{nnc}: Same as system #1, adding counts of bigrams of part-of-speech tags, independently cosine-normalized;

4. 3-system vote: Combination of the three submissions using majority vote.

The purpose of submission #1 was to check the performance that we could get using only surface form information (words and spelling). As shown on Table 1, it reached an average test accuracy of 79.5%, which places it in the middle of the pack over all submissions. For us, it establishes a baseline of what is achievable without any additional syntactic information provided by either taggers or parsers.

Model	#	Acc(%)
BOW2^{ltc}+CHAR3^{ltc}	1	79.27
BOW2^{ltc}+DEP^{ltc}	2	79.55
BOW2^{ltc}+CHAR3^{ltc}+POS2^{nnc}	3	78.82
3-system vote	4	81.82
10-system vote	-	84.00

Table 1: The four systems submitted by NRC, plus a more extensive voting combination. System 1 uses only surface information. Systems 2 and 3 use two types of syntactic information and system #4 uses a majority vote among the three previous submissions. The last (unsubmitted) uses a majority vote among ten systems.

Our submissions #2 and #3 were meant to check the effect of adding syntactic features to basic lexical information. We evaluated various combinations of feature spaces using cross-validation performance and found out that these two combinations seemed to bring a small boost in performance. Unfortunately, as shown on Table 1, this did not reflect on the actual test results. The test performance of submission #2 was a mere 0.2% higher than our baseline, when we expected +0.6% from the cross-validation estimate. The test performance for submission #3 was 0.5% *below* that of the baseline, whereas we expected a small increase.

Submission #4 was our majority voting submission. Due to lack of time, we could not generate test predictions for all the systems that we wanted to include in the combination. As a consequence, we performed a majority voting over just the 3 previous submissions. Despite this, the majority voting proved remarkaby effective, yielding a 2.5% performance boost over our baseline, and a 2.3% increase over our best single system.

In order to further test the potential of the majority vote, we later applied it to the 10 best systems in a pool generated from various combinations of feature spaces (*10-system vote* in Table 1). That (unsubmitted) combination outperformed our official submissions by another 2.2% accuracy, and in fact outperformed the best system in the official evaluation results by a small (and very likely not significant) margin.

In comparison with submissions from other groups, our top submission was 1.8% below the top performing system (Table 2). According to the results of significance tests released by the organizers, the difference is slightly below the traditional threshold of statistical significance (0.05).

Model	Accuracy(%)	p-value
Jarvis	83.6	0.082
Oslo NLI	83.4	0.1
Unibuc	82.7	0.361
MITRE-Carnie	82.6	0.448
Tuebingen	82.2	0.715
NRC	**81.8**	
CMU-Haifa	81.5	0.807
Cologne-Nijmegen	81.4	0.665
NAIST	81.1	0.472
UTD	80.9	0.401
UAlberta	80.3	0.194
Toronto	80.2	0.167
MQ	80.1	0.097

Table 2: Resulting accuracy scores and significance vs. NRC top submission (3-system vote).

4 Discussion and Conclusion

Our results suggest that on the shared task, a combination of features relying only on word and character ngrams provided a strong baseline. Our best system ended up being a combination of models trained on various sets of lexical and syntactic features, using a simple majority vote. Our submission #4 combined only our three other submissions, but we later experimented with a larger pool of models. Table 3 shows that the best performance is obtained using the top 10 models, and many of the combinations are competitive with the best performance achieved during the evaluation. Our cross-validation estimate was also maximized for 10 models, with as estimated accuracy of 83.23%. It is interesting that adding some of the weaker models does not seem to hurt the voting combination very much.

One obvious limitation of this study is that it was applied to a well defined and circumscribed setting. There is definitely no guarantee on the performance that may be obtained on a different corpus of documents.

Another limitation is that although the resulting performance of our models seems encouraging, it is not obvious that we have learned particularly useful clues about what differentiates the English written by authors with different native languages. This is of course a side effect of a format where systems compete on a specific performance metric, which encourages using large, well-regularized models which optimize the relevant metric, at the expense of sparser models focusing on a few markers that may be more easily understandable.

During the workshop, we plan to show more complete results using the majority vote strategy, involving a wider array of base models.

Rank	Model score	Vote score	Feature set
1	79.55	79.55	BOW2+DEP
2	79.36	79.55	BOW1+DEP
3	79.27	82.18	BOW2+CHAR3
4	79.00	82.27	BOW1+DEPL
5	78.91	82.91	BOW2+CHAR3+POS3
6	78.82	83.18	BOW2+CHAR3+POS2
7	78.73	83.45	BOW2+DEPL
8	78.36	83.55	BOW2
9	77.09	**83.82**	BOW1+POS3
10	76.82	**84.00**	BOW2+POS2
11	76.55	**83.64**	BOW2+POS3
12	76.55	**83.82**	BOW1+POS2
13	75.27	83.55	BOW1
14	74.36	**83.73**	BOW1+CHAR3
15	74.27	**83.73**	DEP
16	66.91	**83.91**	DEPL
17	64.18	**83.82**	CHAR3
18	51.64	**83.82**	POS3
19	49.64	83.36	POS2

Table 3: Majority vote among the top-N models. BOWn=word ngrams; CHAR3=char trigrams; POSn=POS ngrams; DEP/DEPL=syntactic dependecies.

References

M. Baroni and S. Bernardini. 2006. A new approach to the study of translationese: Machine-learning the difference between original and translated text. *Literary and Linguistic Computing*, 21(3):259–274.

Julian Brooke and Graeme Hirst. 2012. Robust, lexicalized native language identification. In *Proceedings of COLING 2012*.

T. Joachims. 1999. Making large-scale SVM learning practical. In *Advances in Kernel Methods - Support Vector Learning*.

T. Joachims. 2006. Training linear SVMs in linear time. In *Proceedings of the ACM Conference on Knowledge Discovery and Data Mining (KDD)*.

M. Koppel, S. Argamon, and A. R. Shimoni. 2003. Automatically categorizing written texts by author gender. *Literary and Linguistic Computing*, 17:401–412.

M. Koppel, J. Schler, and K. Zigdon. 2005. Determining an authors native language by mining a text for errors. In *Proceedings of the 11th ACM SIGKDD International Conference on Knowledge Discovery in Data Mining (KDD 05)*, pages 624–628, Chicago, Ilinois, USA.

Christopher D. Manning, Prabhakar Raghavan, and Hinrich Schtze. 2008. Document and query weighting schemes. In *Introduction to Information Retrieval*. Cambridge University Press.

Joel Tetreault, Daniel Blanchard, and Aoife Cahill. 2013. A report on the first native language identification shared task. In *Proceedings of the Eighth Workshop on Innovative Use of NLP for Building Educational Applications*, Atlanta, GA, USA, June. Association for Computational Linguistics.

B. Zadrozny and C. Elkan. 2002. Transforming classifier scores into accurate multiclass probability estimates. In *Proceedings of the Eighth International Conference on Knowledge Discovery and Data Mining (KDD'02)*.

Discriminating Non-Native English with 350 Words

John Henderson, Guido Zarrella, Craig Pfeifer and **John D. Burger**
The MITRE Corporation
202 Burlington Road
Bedford, MA 01730-1420, USA
{jhndrsn,jzarrella,cpfeifer,john}@mitre.org

Abstract

This paper describes MITRE's participation in the native language identification (NLI) task at BEA-8. Our best effort performed at an accuracy of 82.6% in the eleven-way NLI task, placing it in a statistical tie with the best performing systems. We describe the variety of machine learning approaches that we explored, including Winnow, language modeling, logistic regression and maximum-entropy models. Our primary features were word and character n-grams. We also describe several ensemble methods that we employed for combining these base systems.

1 Introduction

Investigations into the effect of authors' latent attributes on language use have a long history in linguistics (Labov, 1972; Biber and Finegan, 1993). The rapid growth of social media has sparked increased interest in automatically identifying author attributes such as gender and age (Schler et al., 2006; Burger and Henderson, 2006; Argamon et al., 2007; Mukherjee and Liu, 2010; Rao et al., 2010). There is also a long history of computational aids for language pedagogy, both for first- and second-language acquisition. In particular, automated native language identification (NLI) is a useful aid to second language learning. This is our first foray into NLI, although we have recently described experiments aimed at identifying the gender of unknown Twitter authors (Burger et al., 2011). We performed well using only character and word n-grams as evidence. In the present work, we apply that same approach to NLI, and combine it with several other baseline classifiers.

In the remainder of this paper, we describe our high-performing system for identifying the native language of English writers. We explore a varied set of learning algorithms and present two ensemble methods used to produce a better system than any of the individuals. In Section 2 we describe the data and task in detail as well as the evaluation metric. In Section 3 we discuss details of the particular system configuration that scored best for us. We describe our experiments in Section 4, including our exploration of several different classifier types and parametrizations. In Section 5 we present and analyze performance results, and inspect some of the features that were useful in discrimination. Finally in Section 6 we summarize our findings, and describe possible extensions to the work.

2 Task, data and evaluation

Native Language Identification was a shared task organized as part of the *Eighth Workshop on Innovative Use of NLP for Building Educational Applications*, 2013. The task was to identify an author's native language based on an English essay.

The data provided consisted of a set of 12,100 Test of English as a Foreign Language (TOEFL) examinations contributed by the Educational Testing Service (Blanchard et al., to appear). These were English essays written by native speakers of Arabic, Chinese, French, German, Hindi, Italian, Japanese, Korean, Spanish, Telugu, and Turkish. A set of 1000 essays for each language was identified as training data, along with 100 per language for development, and another 100 per language for a final test set. The mean length of an essay is 348 words.

The primary evaluation metric for shared task submissions was simple accuracy: the fraction of the test essays for which the correct native language was identified. A baseline accuracy would thus be about 9% (one out of eleven). Results were also reported in terms of F-measure on a per-language basis. F-measure is a harmonic mean of precision and recall: $F = \frac{2PR}{P+R}$. For the evaluation, the precision denominator was the number of items labeled with a particular language by the system and the recall denominator was the number of items marked with a particular language in the reference set.

The training, development, and test sets all had balanced distributions across the native languages, so error rates and accuracy did not favor any particular language in any set.

3 System overview

The systems we used to generate results for the NLI competition were all machine-learning-based, with no handwritten rules or features. The final submitted systems were ensembles built from the outputs and confidence scores of independent eleven-way multinomial classifiers.

3.1 Features

The features used to build these systems were language-independent and were generated using the same infrastructure designed for the experiments described in Burger et al. (2011).

We incorporated a variety of binary features into our systems, each of which was hashed into a 64-bit numeric representation using MurmurHash3 (Appleby, 2011). The bulk of our features were case-sensitive word- and character-based n-grams, in which a feature was turned "on" if its sequence of words or characters appeared at least once in the text of an essay. We also added binary features describing surface characteristics of the text such as average word length and word count. Features were separated into tracks such that the word unigram "i" and the character unigram "i" would each generate a distinct feature.

Part of speech tag n-grams were added to the feature set after reviewing performance results in Brooke and Hirst (2012). We used the Stanford log-linear part of speech tagger described in Toutanova et al. (2003), with the english-left3words-distsim.tagger pretrained model and the Penn Treebank tagset. The tagger was run on each essay and outputs were incorporated as sequence features with n-grams up to length 5.

3.2 Classifiers

Carnie[1] is a MITRE-developed linear classifier that implements the Winnow2 algorithm of Carvalho and Cohen (2006), generalized for multinomial classification. Carnie was developed to perform classification of short, noisy texts with many training examples. It maintains one weight per feature per output class, and performs multiplicative updates that reinforce weights corresponding to the correct class while penalizing weights associated with the top-scoring incorrect class. The learner is mistake-driven and performs an update of size ϵ after an error or when the ratio of weight masses of the correct and top incorrect classes is below $1 + \delta$. It iterates over the training data, cooling its updates after each iteration. For the purposes of these experiments, an input to Carnie was the text of a single TOEFL essay, and the output was the highest scoring class and several related scores.

SRI's Language Modeling Toolkit (SRILM) is a toolkit for sequence modeling that continues to be relevant after more than a decade of development (Stolcke, 2002). It can be used to both build models of sequence likelihoods and to evaluate likelihoods of previously unseen sequences. Building a multinomial text classifier with a language model toolkit involves building one model for each target class and choosing the label whose model gives the highest probability.

Many smoothing methods are implemented by SRILM, along with a variety of n-gram filtering techniques. The out-of-the-box default configuration produces trigram models with Good-Turing smoothing. It worked well for this competition. Using open vocabulary models (`-unk`), turning off sentence boundary insertion (`-no-sos -no-eos`) and treating each essay as one sentence

[1] It is named for entertainers who guess personal characteristics of carnival goers.

worked best in our development environment.

LIBLINEAR is a popular open source library for classification of large, sparse data. We experimented with several of their standard Support Vector Machine and logistic regression configurations (Fan et al., 2008). We selected multiclass ℓ_2-regularized logistic regression with the dual-form solver and default parameters. Inputs to the model were binary features generated from a single TOEFL essay. Features for this model were generated by Carnie. The model provided probability estimates for each candidate output class (L1) for each essay, which were then combined with the outputs of Carnie and SRILM in an ensemble to produce a single prediction.

3.3 Ensembles

The classifiers described above were selected for inclusion as components in a larger ensemble on the basis of their performance and the observation that errors committed by these systems were not highly correlated. We used the entirety of our training data for construction of each component system, leaving scant data available for estimating parameters of ensembles. This scenario led us to choose naive Bayes to combine the outputs of the original components.

Given $h_1, \ldots, h_k$ hypothesis labels from k different systems, one approximates the conditional likelihood of the reference label $P(R|H_1 \ldots H_k)$ using the Bayes transform and the development set estimates of $P(H_i|R)$. One investigates all possible labels to decode $r^* = \mathrm{argmax}_r\, P(r) \prod_i P(h_i|r)$. The class balance in every set we operated on made the prior $P(r)$ irrelevant for maximization and simplified many of the denominators along the way. This is a typical formulation of naive Bayes.

Confidence All of our component systems produce scores as well as a predicted label. Carnie produces (non-probability) scores for all of the candidate labels, SRILM produces log-probabilities and perplexities, and LIBLINEAR produces $P(h|r)$, the likelihood of each of the possible labels. We experimented with several transformations of those scores to best use them to predict correctness of their hypothesis. There were several graphical models we could use for folding these scores into the Bayes ensemble, and we chose a simple, discretized $P(H, S|R)$. We evenly partitioned and relabeled our system outputs according to their scores (S), and used those partition labels in the Bayes ensemble. Thus when a particular reference label was scored in the ensemble during decoding, both its prediction and score contributed to the label in the naive Bayes table lookup.

3.4 Best configuration

We submitted five systems with a variety of configurations. One of our systems was our individual Carnie system on its own for calibration. The other four were ensembles.

The best system we submitted was a Bayes ensemble of the Carnie, SRILM, and LIBLINEAR components each trained on the train+development sets. Carnie was trained for twelve iterations with $\epsilon = 0.03$, $\delta = 0.05$, and a cooling rate of 0.1. SRILM models were trained for open vocabulary and the default trigram, Good-Turing setting. Logistic regression from LIBLINEAR was run with ℓ_2 regularization and using the dual form solver.

Parameters for the Bayes model were collected from the development set when the components were trained only on the training set. A grid search was performed over likely candidates for λ, the Dirichlet parameter, and ρ, the number of score-based partitions, resulting in $\lambda = 0.03125$ and $\rho = 2$. The grid search was performed with the component models trained only on the training set and using 10-fold cross validation on the development set.

4 Experiments

In all experiments described below, systems were trained initially on the 9900 training examples alone, with the 1100 item development set held back to allow for hyperparameter estimation. When preparing our final test set submissions, the development set was folded into the training data, and all models were re-trained on this new dataset containing 11000 items.

4.1 Baselines

How hard is the NLI task? Simple baselines often give us a quick glimpse into what matters in a NLP task. In Figure 1, we give accuracy results on ten different baselines we trained on the training

Baseline	Accuracy(%)
random	9.1
char length	9.6
SRILM(letter unigram)	10.8
word length	12.0
proficiency	14.9
SRILM(letter bigram)	15.1
JS(vowels)	20.6
JS(consonants)	33.8
JS(vowels+consonants)	34.1
JS(bag-of-words)	52.5

Figure 1: Simple baseline development set scores.

set and evaluated on the development set. Predictions based on simple character and word lengths show only slight gains over random. Using the high/medium/low proficiency score that accompanied the data similarly gives a tiny amount of information over baseline (14.9%). We ignored those ratings elsewhere in our work, to focus on the core task of prediction based on essay content.

We collected some simple distributions of vowel and consonant clusters and used them for prediction, scoring with Jensen-Shannon divergence. JS divergence is a symmetrized form of KL divergence to alleviate the mathematical problem involved with missing observations. It has behaved well in the context of language processing applications (Lee, 1999). The score progression from consonant clusters, to vowel clusters, to words suggests that there is NLI information scattered at various levels of surface features.

4.2 Varied Carnie configurations

Carnie's out-of-the-box configuration is one that has been optimized for application to micro-blogs and other ungrammatical short texts. While our hypothesis was that this configuration would be well suited to analysis of English TOEFL essays, we investigated a number of possible techniques to help Carnie adapt to the new domain.

We began by performing a grid search to select model hyperparameters that enabled our standard configuration to generalize well from the training dataset to the development dataset. These values of ϵ, δ, and cooling rate were then applied to various new feature configurations.

The standard configuration included binary features for word unigrams and bigrams, character n-grams of sizes 1 to 5, and surface features. We experimented here with word trigrams, character 6-grams, and lowercased character n-grams of sizes 1 to 6. We also added skip bigrams, which were ordered word pairs in which 1 to 6 intervening words were omitted. We incorporated part of speech tags in a number of ways, including POS n-grams of lengths 1 to 5, POS k-skip bigrams with k ranging from 1 to 6, and POS n-grams in which closed-class POS tags were replaced with the actual content word used. We also measured the impact of using frequency-weighted features.

Our standard approach with Carnie is to perform multinomial classification using one model trained on all the data simultaneously. We experimented with other ways of framing the NLI problem, such as building eleven binary classifiers, each of which was trained on all of the data but with the sole task of accepting or rejecting a single candidate L1. We also partitioned the training data to build 55 binary classifiers for all possible pairs of L1s. These binary classifiers were then combined via a voting mechanism to select a single winner. This allowed us to apply focused efforts to improve discrimination in language pairs which Carnie found challenging, such as Hindi-Telugu or Japanese-Korean. To this end, we collected a substantial amount of additional out-of-domain training data from the websites lang8.com (70,000 entries) and gohackers.com (40,000 entries). Although we did not use this data in our final submission, we performed experiments to measure the value of this new data in the TOEFL11 domain with no adaptation, with feature filtering to limit training features to items observed in the test sets, and with "frustratingly easy" domain adaptation, EasyAdapt, described in Daumé and Marcu (2007).

4.3 Varied SRILM configurations

SRILM offers a number of parameters for experimentation. We hill-climbed on the training/development split to select a good configuration. We experimented with n-gram lengths from 1-5 (bag of words through word 5-grams), using the tokenization given by the NLI organizers. We tried the lighter weight smoothing techniques offered by

System	Confidence	MRD
Carnie	$s(h_1)/s(h_2)$	343
	$s(h_1)/\sum_i s(h_i)$	268
	$s(h_1) - s(h_2)$	72
SRILM	$\log p(h_1)/\log p(h_2)$	315.7
	$\log p(h_1) - \log p(h_2)$	315.3
	$ppl1(h_1)/ppl1(h_2)$	315.12
	$ppl1(h_1) - ppl1(h_2)$	260
	$ppl1$	77
	$\log p(h_1)$	40
MaxEnt (JCarafe)	$\sum_i p(h_i) \log p(h_i)$	385.7
	$p(h_1)$	383.15
	$\log p(h_1)$	383.15
	$p(h_1)/p(h_2)$	373.75
	$\log p(h_1)/\log p(h_2)$	379.8
LIBLINEAR	$\sum_i p(h_i) \log p(h_i)$	379.8

Figure 2: Confidence candidates measured in Mean Rank Difference between correct and incorrect labels.

SRILM including Good-Turing, Witten-Bell, Ristad's natural discounting, both modified and original Kneser-Ney. We built both closed vocabulary and open vocabulary language models and with special symbols added for sentence boundaries.

4.4 Component confidence experiments

Our components generate scores, but those scores were not always scaled in the same way. Winnow (in Carnie) is a margin-based, mistake-driven learner generating scores which are interpretable only as sums of weights. SRILM produces $\log p(d_j|h_i)$, but renormalizing those (with priors) into estimates of $p(h_i|d_j)$ is unreliable because the different submodels are not connected with smoothing. Logistic regression produces a distribution for $p(h_i|d_j)$. We aimed to express these notions of confidence in a way that was common to all systems. We did this by relabeling system hypotheses after sorting by confidence, but not all metrics were equally good at this sorting.

We performed an ad hoc assessment of several candidate scoring functions. Our goal was to find functions that best separated correct answers from incorrect answers in a sorted ranking. We ran several candidates on our development set and measured the difference between the mean rank of correct answers and the mean rank of incorrect answers. Figure 2 displays the results. In each case h_1 was the best hypothesis generated by the system and h_2 is second best. $p(\cdot)$ indicates probabilities, $s(\cdot)$ indicates non-probability scores. We chose those functions with the highest values.

4.5 Simple models for combination

In this work, we focused our ensembles only on the output of our individual components, ignoring the features from the original data that they attempt to model. The base systems are all trained to minimize errors, and did not appear to have any particular preferential capabilities. Thus we rely on them entirely for the primary processing and focus on their outputs.

In our naive Bayes formulation, the random variables produced by the component systems (H) need not take on values directly comparable with the reference labels to be predicted (R). We experimented with folding in several one-shot systems that produced labels in $\{L, \bar{L}\}$, for particular native language groups, but none of these proved to be good complements for the components described above.

To cope with decode-time configurations of H that hadn't been seen during estimation, we used a Dirichlet prior on R in this ensemble. A single parameter, λ, was introduced. Thus our estimates for $P(h_i|r)$ were based on smoothed counts: $\frac{c(h_i,r)+\lambda}{c(r)+\lambda|R|}$. The search for λ was performed using cross-validation on the development set.

Assignment In many prediction settings, we know that our evaluation data consists of examples drawn from a particular allocation of candidate classes. One can take advantage of this in a probabilistic setting by doing a global search for the maximum likelihood assignment of the test documents to the L1 languages under the constraint that each L1 language must have a particular occupancy by the documents – in this case, an even split. More generally, once we have $p(h_i|d_j)$ for each candidate language h_i and document d_j, we can find an assignment $A = \{(i,j) : \alpha_{i,j} = 1\}$ that maximizes the likelihood $P(H|D) = \prod_{(i,j)\in A} p(h_i|d_j) = \prod_{i,j} p(h_i|d_j)^{\alpha_{i,j}}$ under the constraints that $\sum_i \alpha_{i,j} = |D|/|H|$ and $\sum_j \alpha_{i,j} = 1$. The first constraint says that each language should get an even allocation of documents assigned to it and the second constraint says that each document should be assigned to only one language. This reduces to a maximum weight matching on $\sum_{i,j} \alpha_{i,j} \log p(h_i|d_j)$. This problem is directly convertible into a max flow problem or a linear program. It can be solved with methods such as the Hungarian algorithm, Ford-Fulkerson, or linear programming. In our case, we used `LPSOLVE`[2] to find this global maximum. This looks at first glance like an integer programming problem, but one can relax the constraints into inequalities and still be guaranteed that the solution will end up with all $\alpha_{i,j}$ landing on either zero or one in the right amounts. We applied this assignment combination as a post-processing step to the probabilities generated in the naive Bayes ensemble and also to the raw LIBLINEAR outputs. The hope in doing this is that the optimizer will move the less likely assignments around appropriately while preserving the assignments where it has more confidence. We observed mixed results on our development set and submitted two systems using this ensemble technique.

4.6 Other components explored

LIBLINEAR provides an implementation of a linear SVM as well as a logistic regression package. We experimented with various combinations of ℓ_1- and ℓ_2 -loss SVMs, with both ℓ_1 and ℓ_2-regularization, but in the end opted to use the ℓ_2-regularized logistic regression due to slightly superior performance and the ease with which we could extract eleven values of $P(H)$ for inclusion in our ensemble.

Another component that was tested in development of our ensemble systems was a maximum entropy classifier. This particular effort used the implementation from JCarafe,[3] which uses L-BFGS for optimization.

We approached the NLI task as document classification, following a typical JCarafe recipe (Gibson et al., 2007). The class of the document is the native language of the author. Each document was treated as a bag of words, and several classes of features were extracted: token n-gram frequency, character n-gram frequency, part of speech n-gram frequency. The feature mix that produced the best score was token bigrams and trigrams, character trigrams and POS trigrams. A feature frequency threshold of 5 was used to curb the number of features.

[2]`http://lpsolve.sourceforge.net`

[3]`https://github.com/wellner/jcarafe`

L1	Mean F		Our Best F	
GER	1	0.776	1	0.921
ITA	2	0.757	2	0.88
CHI	3	0.723	4	0.85
JPN	4	0.708	5	0.837
FRE	5	0.701	7	0.818
TEL	6	0.667	3	0.802
KOR	7	0.665	6	0.827
TUR	8	0.656	8	0.81
ARA	9	0.65	3	0.872
SPA	10	0.631	10	0.768
HIN	11	0.606	11	0.762

Figure 3: L1s by empirical prediction difficulty. Mean F incorporates all submissions by all competition teams.

5 Results

Our best performing ensemble was 82.6% accurate when scored on the competition test set, and was composed of Carnie, SRILM, and logistic regression, using naive Bayes to combine the subsystem outputs and confidence scores into a single prediction. The best performing subsystem during system development scored 79.3% on the test set in isolation, demonstrating once again the value of combining systems that make independent errors.

Certain L1s gave our systems more difficulty than others. Our best submitted F-measure scores ranged from 0.921 for German to 0.762 for Hindi. Figure 3 demonstrates that our systems' scores were highly correlated with average scores from all submissions by all teams ($R^2 = 0.84$). From this we infer that our performance differences between L1s may be explained by inherent difficulties in certain languages or by the selection of similar L1s as a part of the competition task, rather than quirks of our approach. Our submissions do appear to have a particular advantage on Arabic and Korean, relative to the field.

Figure 4 shows the overall performance of our submissions and subsystems on the development and test evaluation sets.

Our scores dropped 4 to 5% between development and test evaluations, representing significant overfit-

Configuration	dev %	test %
Components		
base Carnie	82.6	
+ trigrams	83.1	
+ POS tags	83.6	79.3
1v1 voted Carnie	79.4	
SRILM	77.1	
MaxEnt	77.7	
Linear SVM	81.9	
Logistic Regression	83.4	
assignment(LR)	82.4	
Ensembles		
bayes(Carnie,SRILM,LR)	87.3	82.6
assign(Carnie,SRILM,LR)	86.5	82.0
assign(Carnie,SRILM,MaxEnt)	86.4	82.3
bayes(Carnie,SRILM)	86.9	81.7

Figure 4: Results.

ting to the development set. The development set was used for model selection, ensemble parameterization, and eventually as additional training data for final submissions. Later tests showed that this final retraining actually reduced the Carnie score by 0.9%.

Figure 4 also shows the effect of various efforts to improve our baseline Carnie system. Adding part-of-speech n-grams and word trigrams as features improved the score on the development set by 1% in total. Meanwhile many of our experiments with new types of features yielded no gains. Lowercased character n-grams, skip bigrams and all non-vanilla formulations of part-of-speech tags provided no improvement and were discarded.

It was observed that all of our systems showed a strong preference for binary features over frequency-weighted inputs. In the case of the JCarafe classifier, switching to binary features yielded a 10% accuracy gain. Although JCarafe didn't provide a gain over the ensemble of Carnie, SRILM, and LIBLINEAR logistic regression, development set results indicated that JCarafe served capably as a replacement for LIBLINEAR in some ensembles.

We also measured the impact of using out-of-domain Japanese and Korean L1 data to train a pairwise JPN/KOR system. Only 78.5% of JPN and KOR texts were correctly identified in our eleven-way baseline system. We restricted train and evaluation data to only those two L1s and found our baseline technique was 86.5% accurate. When we added our out-of-domain data with no domain adaptation technique, that score dropped to 82.0%. Removing features that didn't appear in our test set only raised the score to 82.5%. However, the EasyAdapt technique (Daumé and Marcu, 2007) showed promise. By making an additional source-specific copy of each feature, we were able to raise the score to 88.5%. While this result was of limited applicability in our final submission, and was therefore not submitted to the open data competition task, we believe that this technique may prove useful in enabling cross-domain NLI system transfer.

Rank	L1	Score	Feature
14	GER	21.05	(for,example)
40	GER	15.95	(have,to)
55	HIN	14.80	(as,compared,to)
57	ITA	14.60	(I,think,that)
58	TEL	14.18	(and,also)
60	HIN	13.97	(as,compared)
79	TEL	12.82	(the,people)
96	TEL	12.14	(for,a)
101	ITA	11.83	(that,in)
116	ITA	10.94	(think,that)
119	GER	10.93	(has,to)
120	TEL	10.89	(with,the,statement)

Figure 5: Word n-gram features predicting particular L1.

Figure 5 provides a small sample of word-level features discovered by the Winnow classifier. The table shows the rank of each n-gram relative to all features, and the native language that the feature predicts. The weight assigned by the Winnow2 algorithm is not readily interpretable, although higher weights indicate a stronger association.

Similarly, the top character n-grams can be seen in Figure 7, along with manually selected examples of each. These features can be seen to mainly fall into several broad categories. There are mentions of the authors' home countries as in Korean, Italian and Turkey. There are also characteristic misspellings and infelicities such as personnaly, perhaps incorrectly modeled from the French *personnellement*.

It is worth noting that the weights (and thus the ranks) for the top character n-gram features are

System	Accuracy (%)	Errors
Carnie	80.4	2153
SRILM	74.5	2800
LIBLINEAR	80.8	2116
ensemble-assign	81.9	1990
ensemble-Bayes	82.2	1961

Figure 6: Training set cross-validation results.

higher than for the top word features, indicating that Winnow found the former to be more informative.

Finally, the top part-of-speech n-gram features are shown in Figure 8, again with manually selected examples. These features have similar weights to the character n-gram features and for the most part seem to represent ungrammatical constructions (e.g., the first feature indicates that a personal pronoun followed by an uninflected verb predicts Chinese). However, there are some perfectly grammatical items that are indicative of a particular native language (e.g., *as compared to* for Hindi). One possible explanation might be a dominant L2 pedagogy for that language.

5.1 Cross-validation results

The task organizers requested that the participants run a ten-fold cross validation on a particular split of the union of the training and development sets after the evaluation was over. Results of our leading component systems and ensemble systems are presented in Table 6. These are comparable with the TOEFL-11 column of Figure 3 in Tetreault et al. (2012).

6 Conclusion

In this paper, we have presented MITRE's participation in the native language identification task at BEA-8. Our best system was a naive Bayes ensemble combining component systems that used Winnow, language modeling and logistic regression approaches, all using relatively simple character and word n-gram features. This ensemble performed at an accuracy of 82.6% in the eleven-way NLI task, placing it in a statistical tie with the winning systems submitted by 29 teams. For individual native languages, our submission performed best among the participants on Arabic, as ranked by F-measure.

In addition to the three base systems in our best ensemble, we experimented with a maximum entropy classifier and an assignment-based ensemble method. We described a variety of experiments we performed to determine the best configurations and settings for the various systems. We also covered experiments aimed at using out-of-domain data for several native languages. In future work we will expand upon these, with the goal of applying domain adaptation approaches.

One concern with NLI as framed in this evaluation is the interaction between native language and essay topic. The distribution of topics was very similar in the various subcorpora, but in more natural settings this is unlikely to be the case, and there is a danger of overtraining on topic, to the detriment of language identification performance. This is especially problematic for a highly lexical approach such as ours. In future work, we intend to explore the extent of this effect, using topic-based splits of the corpus. Our initial experiments to remedy this problem are likely to involve domain adaptation approaches, such as Daumé and Marcu (2007).

As described above, we have had success using the Winnow-based system Carnie for other latent author attributes, such as gender. We would like to explore ensembles similar to those described here for these attributes as well.

The techniques described in this paper successfully identified an author's native language 82.6% of the time using a sample of text averaging less than 350 words in length. Future work could study the interaction of text length and NLI performance, including texts shorter than 140 characters in length.

Acknowledgments

This work was funded under the MITRE Innovation Program. Approved for Public Release; Distribution Unlimited: 13-1876.

References

Austin Appleby. 2011. MurmurHash, murmur3. `https://sites.google.com/site/murmurhash/`.

Shlomo Argamon, Moshe Koppel, James W. Pennebaker, and Jonathan Schler. 2007. Mining the blogosphere: Age, gender, and the varieties of self-expression. *First Monday*, 12(9), September.

Rank	L1	Score	Feature	Snippet
1	KOR	57.34	orea	first thing that Korean college students usually buy
2	GER	48.68	,_tha	the fact , that people have less moral values
3	SPA	23.65	omen	consequences related with the enviroment and the atmosphere
4	ARA	23.23	_alot	becouse you have alot of knowledge
6	TUR	22.84	s_abo	their searchings about the products
11	ITA	21.56	Ital	the Italian scholastic system
19	TEL	20.19	d_als	the whole system and also the concept
20	TUR	19.96	urk	in Turkey all young people go to the parties
21	CHI	19.51	Ta	Take school teachers for example
23	GER	19.34	_-_	constantly - or as mentioned before even exponentially - breaking
27	JPN	17.62	s_,_I	For those reasons , I think
32	FRE	16.90	ndeed	Indeed , facts are just applications of ideas
36	JPN	16.57	apan	been getting weaker these days in Japan .
37	FRE	16.57	onn	I personnaly prefer
38	GER	16.04	,_bec	would be great , because so everyone
41	SPA	15.92	esa	its not necesary to ask
47	HIN	15.23	in_i	the main idea and concept
53	ITA	14.93	act_	due to the fact that too much
74	ITA	13.00	,_in	academic subjects and , in the mean time
81	TEL	12.74	h_ou	cannot do with out a tour guide

Figure 7: Character n-gram features predicting particular L1.

Rank	L1	Score	Feature	Snippet
35	CHI	16.58	(PRP,VB)	What if he go and see
43	CHI	15.85	(NNS,POS)	products 's
45	SPA	15.41	(NNS,NNS)	companies universities
59	TEL	14.05	(RB,IN,VBG)	Usually in schooling
64	TEL	13.95	(DT,NNS,WDT)	the topics which
65	TUR	13.71	(IN,DT,IN)	after a while
66	TEL	13.69	(IN,VBG)	in telling
69	TUR	13.42	(VBG,DT,NNS)	learning the ways
70	HIN	13.39	(IN,VBN,TO)	as compared to
80	HIN	12.81	(FW)	[foreign word]

Figure 8: Part of Speech n-gram features predicting particular L1.

Douglas Biber and Edward Finegan, editors. 1993. *Sociolinguistic Perspectives on Register*. Oxford studies in sociolinguistics. Oxford University Press.

Daniel Blanchard, Joel Tetreault, Derrick Higgins, Aoife Cahill, and Martin Chodorow. to appear. TOEFL11: A Corpus of Non-Native English. Technical report, Educational Testing Service.

Julian Brooke and Graeme Hirst. 2012. Robust, Lexicalized Native Language Identification. In *Proceedings of COLING 2012*, pages 391–408, Mumbai, India, December.

John D. Burger and John C. Henderson. 2006. An exploration of observable features related to blogger age. In *Computational Approaches to Analyzing Weblogs: Papers from the 2006 AAAI Spring Symposium*. AAAI Press.

John D. Burger, John Henderson, George Kim, and Guido Zarrella. 2011. Discriminating gender on twitter. In *Proceedings of the 2011 Conference on Empirical Methods in Natural Language Processing*, pages 1301–1309, Edinburgh, Scotland, UK, July. Association for Computational Linguistics.

Vitor R. Carvalho and William W. Cohen. 2006. Single-pass online learning: performance, voting schemes and online feature selection. In *Proceedings of the 12th ACM SIGKDD International Conference on Knowledge Discovery and Data Mining*, KDD '06, pages 548–553, New York, NY, USA. ACM.

Hal Daumé and D Marcu. 2007. Frustratingly easy domain adaptation. In *Proceedings of the Association for Computational Linguistics*, volume 45, page 256.

Rong-En Fan, Kai-Wei Chang, Cho-Jui Hsieh, Xiang-Rui Wang, and Chih-Jen Lin. 2008. LIBLINEAR: A library for large linear classification. *Journal of Machine Learning Research*, 9:1871–1874.

John Gibson, Ben Wellner, and Susan Lubar. 2007. Adaptive web-page content identification. In *Proceedings of the 9th Annual ACM International Workshop on Web information and Data Management*, WIDM '07, pages 105–112, New York, NY, USA. ACM.

William Labov. 1972. *Sociolinguistic Patterns*. Conduct & Communication Series. University of Pennsylvania Press.

Lillian Lee. 1999. Measures of distributional similarity. In *Proceedings of the 37th Annual Meeting of the Association for Computational Linguistics*, ACL '99, pages 25–32, Stroudsburg, PA, USA. Association for Computational Linguistics.

Arjun Mukherjee and Bing Liu. 2010. Improving gender classification of blog authors. In *Proceedings of the 2010 Conference on Empirical Methods in Natural Language Processing*, Cambridge, MA, October. Association for Computational Linguistics.

Delip Rao, David Yarowsky, Abhishek Shreevats, and Manaswi Gupta. 2010. Classifying latent user attributes in Twitter. In *2nd International Workshop on Search and Mining User-Generated Content*. ACM.

Jonathan Schler, Moshe Koppel, Shlomo Argamon, and James Pennebaker. 2006. Effects of age and gender on blogging. In *Computational Approaches to Analyzing Weblogs: Papers from the 2006 AAAI Spring Symposium*. AAAI Press, March.

Andreas Stolcke. 2002. SRILM—an extensible language modeling toolkit. In *Proceedings of the International Conference on Spoken Language Processing*, volume 2, pages 901–904.

Joel Tetreault, Daniel Blanchard, Aoife Cahill, and Martin Chodorow. 2012. Native tongues, lost and found: Resources and empirical evaluations in native language identification. In *Proceedings of COLING 2012*, pages 2585–2602, Mumbai, India, December. The COLING 2012 Organizing Committee.

Kristina Toutanova, Dan Klein, Christopher D. Manning, and Yoram Singer. 2003. Feature-rich part-of-speech tagging with a cyclic dependency network. In *Proceedings of HLT-NAACL*, pages 252–259.

Maximizing Classification Accuracy in Native Language Identification

Scott Jarvis
Ohio University
Department of Linguistics
Athens, OH, USA
jarvis@ohio.edu

Yves Bestgen
Université catholique de Louvain
Centre for English Corpus Linguistics
Louvain-la-Neuve, Belgium
yves.bestgen@uclouvain.be

Steve Pepper
Department of Linguistic
Aesthetic and Literary Studies
University of Bergen, Norway
pepper.steve@gmail.com

Abstract

This paper reports our contribution to the 2013 NLI Shared Task. The purpose of the task was to train a machine-learning system to identify the native-language affiliations of 1,100 texts written in English by nonnative speakers as part of a high-stakes test of general academic English proficiency. We trained our system on the new TOEFL11 corpus, which includes 11,000 essays written by nonnative speakers from 11 native-language backgrounds. Our final system used an SVM classifier with over 400,000 unique features consisting of lexical and POS n-grams occurring in at least two texts in the training set. Our system identified the correct native-language affiliations of 83.6% of the texts in the test set. This was the highest classification accuracy achieved in the 2013 NLI Shared Task.

1 Introduction

The problem of automatically identifying a writer's or speaker's first language on the basis of features found in that person's language production is a relatively new but quickly expanding line of inquiry. It seems to have begun in 2001, but most of the studies published in this area have appeared in just the past two years. Although the practical applications of native-language identification (NLI) are numerous, most of the existing research seems to be motivated by one or the other of two types of questions: (1) questions about the nature and extent of native-language influence in nonnative speakers' speech or writing, and (2) questions about the maximum levels of NLI classification accuracy that are achievable, which includes questions about the technical details of the systems that achieve the best results. Our previous work in this area has been motivated primarily by the former (see the multiple studies in Jarvis and Crossley, 2012), but in the present study we conform to the goals of the 2013 NLI Shared Task (Tetreault et al., 2013) in a pursuit of the latter.

2 Related Work

The first published study to have performed an NLI analysis appears to have been Mayfield Tomokiyo and Jones (2001). The main goal of the study was to train a Naïve Bayes system to identify native versus nonnative speakers of English on the basis of the lexical and part-of-speech (POS) n-grams found in their speech. The nonnative speakers in the study included six Chinese speakers and 31 Japanese speakers, and as a secondary goal, the researchers trained the system to identify the nonnative speakers by their native language (L1) backgrounds. The highest NLI accuracy they achieved was 100%. They achieved this result using a model made up of a combination of lexical 1-grams and 2-grams in which nouns (and only nouns) were replaced with a POS identifier (=N).

As far as we are aware, an NLI accuracy of 100% has not been achieved since Mayfield Tomokiyo and Jones (2001), but the NLI tasks that researchers have engaged in since then have been a great deal more challenging than theirs. This is true primarily in the sense that no other NLI study we are aware of has had such a high baseline accuracy, which is the accuracy that would be achieved if all cases were classified as belonging to the largest group. Because 31 of the 37 participants in the Mayfield Tomokiyo and Jones study were Japanese speakers, the baseline accuracy was already 83.8%. To avoid such a bias and to provide a greater challenge to their systems, researchers in recent years have engaged in NLI tasks that have involved more equally balanced groups with a far larger number of L1s. Most of these studies have focused on the identification of the L1s of nonnative writers who produced the texts included in the International Corpus of Learner English (ICLE) (Granger et al., 2009).

NLI studies that have focused on the ICLE include but are not limited to, in chronological order, Koppel et al. (2005), Tsur and Rappoport (2007), Jarvis (2011), Bestgen et al. (2012), Jarvis and Paquot (2012), Bykh and Meuers (2012), and Tetreault et al. (2012). The highest NLI accuracy achieved in any of these studies was 90.1%, which was reported by Tetreault et al. (2012). The researchers in this study used a system involving the LIBLINEAR instantiation of Support Vector Machines (SVM) with the L1-regularized logistic regression solver and default parameters. The features in their model included character n-grams, function words, parts of speech, spelling errors and features of writing quality, such as grammatical errors, style markers, and so forth. They used specialized software to extract error counts, grammar fragments, and counts of basic dependencies. They also created language model perplexity scores that reflected the lexical 5-grams most representative of each L1 in the corpus. This combination of features is more comprehensive than that used in any other NLI study, but the authors reported that their success was not due simply to the combination of features, but also because of the ensemble classification method they used. The ensemble method involved the creation of separate classifier models for each category of features; the L1 affiliations of individual texts were later predicted by the combined probabilities produced by the different classifier models. The authors pointed out that combining all features into a single classifier gave them an NLI accuracy of only 82.6%, which is far short of the 90.1% they achieved through the ensemble method.

The number of L1s represented in the study by Tetreault et al. (2012) was seven, and it is noteworthy that they achieved a higher NLI accuracy than any of the previous NLI studies that had examined the same number (Bykh and Meurers, 2012) or even a smaller number of L1s in the ICLE (e.g., Koppel et al., 2005, Tsur and Rappoport, 2007; Bestgen et al., 2012). The only NLI studies we know of that have examined more than seven L1s in the ICLE are Jarvis (2011) and Jarvis and Paquot (2012). Both studies examined 12 L1s in the ICLE, and both used a combination of features that included only lexical n-grams (1-grams, 2-grams, 3-grams, and 4-grams). Jarvis (2011) compared 20 different NLI systems to determine which would provide the highest classification accuracy for this particular task, and he found that LDA performed best with an NLI accuracy of 53.6%. This is the system that was then adopted for the Jarvis and Paquot (2012) study. It is important to note that the primary goal for Jarvis and Paquot was not to maximize NLI accuracy per se, but rather to use NLI as a means for assisting in the identification of specific instances and types of lexical influence from learners' L1s in their English writing.

As noted by Bestgen et al. (2012), Jarvis and Paquot (2012), and Tetreault et al. (2012), there are certain disadvantages to using the ICLE for NLI research. One problem made especially clear by Bestgen et al. is that the language groups represented in the ICLE are not evenly balanced in terms of their levels of English proficiency. This creates an artificial sampling bias that allows an NLI system to distinguish between L1 groups on the basis of proficiency-related features without creating a classification model that accurately reflects the influences of the learners' language backgrounds. Another problem mentioned by these and other authors is that writing topics are not evenly distributed across the L1 groups in the ICLE. That is, learners from some L1 groups tended to write their essays in response to certain writing prompts, whereas learners from other L1 groups tended to write in response to other writing prompts. Tetreault et al. took extensive measures to remove as much of the topic bias as possible before running their analyses, but they also introduced a new corpus of nonnative English writing that is much larger and better balanced than the ICLE in terms of the distribution of topics across L1 groups. The new corpus is the TOEFL11, which will be described in detail in Section 3.

Prior to the 2013 NLI Shared Task, the only NLI study to have been conducted on the TOEFL11 corpus was Tetreault et al. (2012). As described earlier, they performed an NLI analysis on a subsample of the ICLE representing seven L1 backgrounds. They also used the same system (including an identical set of features) in an NLI analysis of the TOEFL11. The fact that the TOEFL11 is better balanced than the ICLE is advantageous in terms of the strength of the NLI classification model that it promotes, but this also makes the classification task itself more challenging because it gives the system fewer cues (i.e., fewer systematic differences across groups) to rely on. The fact that the TOEFL11 includes 11 L1s, as opposed to the seven L1s in the subsample of the ICLE the authors examined, also makes the NLI task more challenging. For these reasons, NLI accuracy is bound to be higher for the ICLE than for the TOEFL11. This is indeed what the authors found. The NLI accuracy they reported for the TOEFL11 was nearly 10% lower than for the ICLE (80.9% vs. 90.1%). Nevertheless, their result of 80.9% accuracy was still remarkable for a task involving 11 L1s. Tetreault et al. have thus set a very high benchmark for the 2013 NLI Shared Task.

3 Data

The present study tests the effectiveness of our own NLI system for identifying the L1s represented in the TOEFL11 (Blanchard et al., 2013). The TOEFL11 is a corpus of texts consisting of 11,000 essays written by nonnative English speakers as part of a high-stakes test of general proficiency in academic English. The essays were written by learners from the following 11 L1 backgrounds: Arabic, Chinese, French, German, Hindi, Italian, Japanese, Korean, Spanish, Telugu, and Turkish. The corpus is perfectly balanced in terms of its number of essays per L1 group (i.e., 1,000 per L1), and it is also fairly well balanced in relation to the topics written about. The essays in the TOEFL11 were written in response to any of eight different writing prompts, and all eight prompts are reflected in all 11 L1 groups. Within four of the L1 groups, all prompts are almost equally represented with a proportion of approximately 12.5% per prompt (i.e., 100% ÷ 8 prompts = 12.5%). In other groups, there is more variability. The Italian group shows the largest discrepancies, with one prompt representing only 1.2% of the essays, and another prompt representing 17.2% of the group's essays.

		English Proficiency		
L1		Low	Medium	High
ARABIC	Count	274	545	181
	%	27.4%	54.5%	18.1%
CHINESE	Count	90	662	248
	%	9.0%	66.2%	24.8%
FRENCH	Count	60	526	414
	%	6.0%	52.6%	41.4%
GERMAN	Count	14	371	615
	%	1.4%	37.1%	61.5%
HINDI	Count	25	399	576
	%	2.5%	39.9%	57.6%
ITALIAN	Count	145	569	286
	%	14.5%	56.9%	28.6%
JAPANESE	Count	207	617	176
	%	20.7%	61.7%	17.6%
KOREAN	Count	154	617	229
	%	15.4%	61.7%	22.9%
SPANISH	Count	73	502	425
	%	7.3%	50.2%	42.5%
TELUGU	Count	86	595	319
	%	8.6%	59.5%	31.9%
TURKISH	Count	73	561	366
	%	7.3%	56.1%	36.6%

Table 1: Distribution of English Proficiency Levels

The distribution of learners' proficiency levels (low, medium, high) is even more variable across groups. Ideally, 33% of each group would fall into each proficiency level, but Table 1 shows that the distribution of proficiency levels does not come close to this in any L1 group. The distribution is especially skewed in the case of the German speakers, where only 1.4% of the participants fall into the low proficiency category whereas 61.5% fall into the high proficiency category. In any case, in nine of the 11 groups, the bulk of participants falls into the medium proficiency category, and in seven of those nine groups, the proportion of high-proficiency learners is greater than the proportion of low-proficiency learners. Clearly, the TOEFL11 is not a perfectly balanced corpus, but it is much larger than the ICLE and involves fewer prompts, which are more evenly distributed across L1 groups. Another advantage of the TOEFL11 is that each text is associated with a proficiency level that has been determined by assessment experts using a consistent rating procedure for the entire corpus. This fact may allow researchers to isolate the effects of learners' proficiency levels and to adjust their systems accordingly.

The TOEFL11 data were distributed to the 2013 NLI Shared Task participants in three stages. The initial distribution was a training set consisting of 9,900 of the 11,000 texts in the TOEFL11. The training set was made up of 900 texts from each L1 group. Later, a development set was made available. This included the remaining 1,100 texts in the TOEFL11, with 100 texts per L1. Finally, a test set was also provided to the teams participating in the 2013 NLI Shared Task. The test set consisted of 1,100 texts representing the same 11 L1s that are found in the TOEFL11. The test set included information about the prompt that each text was written in response to, as well as information about the writer's proficiency level, but did not include information about the writer's L1.

4 System

Although our previous work has used NLI as a means toward exploring and identifying the effects of crosslinguistic influence in language learners' written production (see Jarvis and Crossley, 2012), in the present study we approached NLI exclusively as a classification task, in keeping with the goals of the NLI Shared Task (Tetreault et al. 2013). In order to maximize classification accuracy for the present study, we chose a system that would allow for the inclusion of thousands of features without violating statistical assumptions. Due to the unrestricted number of features it allows and the high levels of classification accuracy it has achieved in previous research, such as in the study by Tetreault et al. (2012), we chose to use linear Support Vector Machines (SVM) via the LIBLINEAR software package (Fan et al., 2008). The software allows the user to choose among the following types of solvers:

a: L2-regularized L1-loss SVM (dual)
b: L2-regularized L2-loss SVM (dual)
c: L2-regularized logistic regression (primal)
d: L1-regularized L2-loss SVM
e: L1-regularized logistic regression
f: L2-regularized L1-loss SVM (primal)
g: L2-regularized L2-loss SVM (primal)
h: Multi-class SVM by Crammer and Singer

Although Tetreault et al. (2012) used the Type e solver, we found Type b to be the most efficient in terms of both speed and accuracy. LIBLINEAR implements SVM via a multi-class classification strategy that juxtaposes each class (i.e., each L1) against all others. It also optimizes a cost parameter (Parameter C) using a grid search that relies on a crossvalidation criterion. The software iterates over multiple values of C until it arrives at an optimal value. Although LIBLINEAR has a built-in program for optimizing C, we used our own optimization program in order to have more flexibility in choosing values of C to test.

4.1 Features Used

The features we tried represented three broad categories: words, characters, and complex features. The word category included lexemes, lemmas, and POS tags, as well as n-grams consisting of lexemes, lemmas, and POS tags. Lexemes were defined as the observed forms of words, numbers, punctuation marks, and even symbols that were encountered in the TOEFL11. Lemmas were defined as the dictionary forms of lexemes, and we used the TreeTagger software package (Schmid, 1995) to automate the task of converting lexemes to lemmas. TreeTagger is unable to determine lemmas for rare words, misspelled words, and newly borrowed or coined words, and in such cases, it outputs "unknown" in place of a lemma. We also used TreeTagger to automate the identification of the parts of speech (POS) associated with individual words. TreeTagger can only estimate the POS for unknown words, and it is also not perfectly accurate in determining the correct POS for words that it does recognize. Nevertheless, Schmid (1995) found that its POS tagging accuracy tends to be between 96% and 98%, which we consider to be adequate for present purposes. We included in our system all 1-grams, 2-grams, 3-grams, and 4-grams of lexemes, lemmas, and POS tags that occurred in at least two texts in the training set.

Our character n-grams included all character n-grams from one character to nine characters in length that occurred in at least two texts in the training set. Finally, our complex features included nominalization suffixes (e.g., -tion, -ism), number of tokens per essay, number of types, number of sentences, number of characters, mean sentence length, mean length of lexemes, and a measure of lexical variety (i.e., type-token ratio).

5 Results

We applied the system described in the previous section to the TOEFL11 corpus. We did this in multiple stages, first by training the system on the original training set of 9,900 texts while using LIBLINEAR's built-in 5-fold crossvalidation. With the original training set, we tried multiple combinations of features in order to arrive at an optimal model. We found that our complex features contributed very little to any model we tested, and that we could achieve higher levels of NLI accuracy by excluding them altogether. We also found that models made up of optimal sets of lexical features gave us roughly the same levels of NLI accuracy as models made up of optimal sets of character n-grams. However, models made up of a combination of lexical features and character features together performed worse than models made up of just one or the other. Our best performing model, by a small margin, was a model consisting of 1-grams, 2-grams, and 3-grams involving lexemes, lemmas, and POS tags. The results of our comparison of multiple lexical models is shown in Table 2, with the best performing model represented as Model A.

Table 2 shows that Model A consists of all 1-gram, 2-gram, and 3-gram lexemes, lemmas, and POS tags that occur in at least two texts, using a log-entropy weighting schema and normalizing each text to unit length. It is noteworthy that normalizing each text vector, but also using a log-entropy weighting schema clearly improves the model accuracy. Normalizing each text vector as recommended by Fan et al. (2008), but also using a log-entropy weighting schema (Dumais, 1991; Bestgen, 2012) clearly improves the model accuracy. The total number of unique features in Model A is over 400,000. Our initial run of this model on the training set gave us a 5-fold cross-validated NLI accuracy of 82.53%.

We then attempted to determine whether these results could be replicated using other test materials. We first applied the best performing models displayed in Table 2 to the development set—using the development set as a test set—and achieved an NLI accuracy of over 86% for Model A, which remained the most accurate one.

Then we applied these models to our own test set built to be evenly balanced in terms of the stratification of both L1s and prompts. We built this test set because we discovered large differences when we compared the distribution of prompts across L1 groups in the official test set for the 2013

Model	Lexemes			Lemmas			Parts of Speech (POS tag)			Frequency cut-off	Weighting schema	Normalization (to 1 per text)	Accuracy (5-fold)
	1g	2g	3g	1g	2g	3g	1g	2g	3g				
A	x	x	x	x	x	x	x	x	x	≥2	LE	Yes	82.53
B	x	x	x	x	x	x	x	x	x	≥5	LE	Yes	82.52
C	x	x	x	x	x	x	x	x	x	≥10	LE	Yes	82.48
D	x	x	x	x	x	x	x	x	x	≥2	LE	No	80.46
E	x	x	x	x	x	x	x	x	x	≥2	Bin	Yes	79.13
F	x	x	x	x	x	x	x	x	x	≥2	LFreq	Yes	79.12
G	x	x		x	x		x	x		≥2	LE	Yes	82.49
H	x			x			x			≥2	LE	Yes	76.42
I	x	x	x	x	x	x				≥2	LE	Yes	82.09
J	x	x	x				x	x	x	≥2	LE	Yes	81.24
K				x	x	x	x	x	x	≥2	LE	Yes	80.92
L	x	x	x							≥2	LE	Yes	81.57
M				x	x	x				≥2	LE	Yes	81.02
N							x	x	x	≥2	LE	Yes	54.95

Weighting schema: LE = Log-Entropy, Bin = Binary, LFreq = log of the raw frequencies

Table 2: Feature Combinations

NLI Shared Task versus both the training set and development set. To build it, we combined the training set and development set into a single corpus (i.e., the full TOEFL11), and then divided the TOEFL11 into a double-stratified set of cells cross-tabulated by L1 and prompt. This resulted in 11 x 8 = 88 cells, and we randomly selected 10 texts per cell for the test set. This gave us a test set of 880 texts. We used the remaining 10,120 texts as a training set. However, the new division of training and test sets did not strongly modify our results, so we retained the previous Model A as our final model.

In preparation for the final task of identifying the L1 affiliations of the 1,100 texts included in the official test set for the 2013 NLI Shared Task, we used the entire TOEFL11 corpus of 11,000 texts as our training set—with the features in Model A—in order to select the final values for the cost parameter (C) of our SVM system. By means of a 10-fold crossvalidation (CV) procedure on this dataset, the C parameter was set to 3200.

The results of a 10-fold CV (using the fold splitting of Tetreault et al., 2012) of the system's performance with the TOEFL11 are shown in Table 3. The total number of texts per L1 group is consistently 1000, which makes the raw frequencies in the table directly interpretable as percentages. The lowest rate of accurate identification for any L1 in the 10-fold CV was 78.6%, and this was for Telugu. For all other L1s, the NLI accuracy rate exceeded 80%, and in the case of German, it reached 96.5%. The overall NLI accuracy for the 10-fold CV was 84.5%.

For the final stage of the analysis, we applied our system to the official test set in order to determine how well it can identify writers' L1s in texts it has not yet encountered. The results of the final analysis are shown in Table 4. The classification accuracy (or recall) for individual L1s in the final

	Predicted L1											
Actual L1	ARA	CHI	FRE	GER	HIN	ITA	JPN	KOR	SPA	TEL	TUR	Total
ARA	**802**	16	41	14	28	11	9	12	47	8	12	1000
CHI	6	**894**	5	6	15	2	20	31	7	3	11	1000
FRE	24	11	**856**	28	11	25	4	4	33	1	3	1000
GER	2	4	6	**965**	5	3	1	2	9	0	3	1000
HIN	10	6	1	7	**803**	0	1	1	11	155	5	1000
ITA	3	3	26	24	8	**890**	3	1	35	1	6	1000
JPN	10	29	3	11	3	0	**810**	108	9	4	13	1000
KOR	5	51	3	8	7	1	98	**802**	12	1	12	1000
SPA	20	9	40	24	10	65	5	5	**807**	5	10	1000
TEL	5	0	2	1	200	0	1	2	1	**786**	2	1000
TUR	22	11	16	20	18	5	7	14	17	5	**865**	1000

Accuracy = 84.5%

Table 3: 10-Fold Crossvalidation Results

	ARA	CHI	FRE	GER	HIN	ITA	JPN	KOR	SPA	TEL	TUR	Prec.	F
ARA	**75**	0	5	2	2	1	1	2	7	3	2	82.4	78.5
CHI	1	**89**	0	1	1	0	4	2	0	0	2	82.4	85.6
FRE	2	1	**86**	6	2	1	0	0	2	0	0	86.0	86.0
GER	0	0	1	**96**	0	0	0	0	2	0	1	83.5	89.3
HIN	1	0	0	0	**81**	0	0	0	4	13	1	74.3	77.5
ITA	0	1	3	4	0	**90**	0	0	2	0	0	90.9	90.5
JPN	2	3	0	1	1	2	**85**	3	2	0	1	85.9	85.4
KOR	0	10	1	0	1	0	8	**76**	1	2	1	87.4	81.3
SPA	4	0	4	2	3	3	0	1	**81**	0	2	78.6	79.8
TEL	1	1	0	1	18	0	0	0	0	**79**	0	81.4	80.2
TUR	5	3	0	2	0	2	1	3	2	0	**82**	89.1	85.4

Accuracy = 83.6%

Table 4: Final NLI Results

analysis ranges from 75% (Arabic) to 96% (German), and precision ranges from 74.3% (Hindi) to 90.9% (Italian). Our overall accuracy in identifying the L1s in the test set was 83.6%.

6 Conclusion

Our system turned out to be the most successful system in the 2013 NLI Shared Task. Our 10-fold crossvalidated accuracy of 84.5% is also higher than the result of 80.9% previously achieved by Tetreault et al. (2012) in their earlier NLI analysis of the TOEFL11. We find this to be both interesting and unexpected given that Tetreault et al. used more complex measures than we did, such as 5-gram language models, and they also used an ensemble method of classification. Accordingly, we interpret the success of our model as an indication that the most reliable L1 specificity in the TOEFL11 is to be found simply in the words, word forms, sequential word combinations, and sequential POS combinations that the nonnative writers produced. Tetreault et al. emphasized the usefulness of features that reflect L1-specific language models, but we believe that the multiple binary class comparisons that SVM makes might already take full advantage of L1 specificity as long as all of the relevant features are fed into the system.

As for the ensemble method of classification used by Tetreault et al., their results clearly indicate that this method enhanced their NLI accuracy not only for the TOEFL11, but also for three additional learner corpora, including the ICLE. Our own study did not compare our single-model system with the use of an ensemble method, but we are naturally curious about whether our own results could have been enhanced through the use of an ensemble method. As mentioned earlier, our preliminary attempts to construct a model based on character n-grams produced nearly as high levels of NLI accuracy as our final model involving lexical and POS n-grams. Although we found that combining lexical and character n-grams worsened our results, we believe that a fruitful avenue for future research would be to test whether an ensemble of separate models based on character versus lexical n-grams could improve classification accuracy. Importantly, however, a useful ensemble method generally needs to include more than two models unless it is based on probabilities rather than on the majority-vote method (cf. Jarvis, 2011; Tetreault et al., 2012).

Our original interest in NLI began with a curiosity about the evidence it can provide for the presence of crosslinguistic influence in nonnative speakers' speech and writing. We believe that NLI strongly supports investigations of L1 influence, but in the case of the present results, we do not believe that L1 influence is solely responsible for the 83.6% NLI accuracy our system has achieved. Other factors are certainly also at play, such as the educational systems and cultures that the nonnative speakers come from. Apparent effects of cultural and/or educational background can be seen in the misclassification results in Table 4. Note, for example, that when Hindi speakers are miscategorized, they are overwhelmingly identified as Telugu speakers and vice versa. Importantly, Hindi and Telugu are both languages of India, but they belong to separate language families. Thus, L1 influence appears to overlap with other background variables that, together, allow texts to be grouped reliably. To the extent that this is true, the term NLI might be somewhat misleading. Clearly, NLI research has the potential to contribute a great deal to the understanding of crosslinguistic influence, but it of course also needs to be combined with other types of evidence that demonstrate L1 influence (see Jarvis, 2012).

Acknowledgments

The authors wish to thank the organizers of the 2013 NLI Shared Task for putting together this valuable event and for promptly responding to all questions and concerns raised throughout the process. We also wish to acknowledge the support of the Belgian Fund for Scientific Research (F.R.S-FNRS); Yves Bestgen is a Research Associate with the F.R.S-FNRS. Additionally, we acknowledge the support of the University of Bergen's ASKeladden Project, which is funded by the Norwegian Research Council (NFR).

References

Yves Bestgen. 2012. DEFT2009 : essais d'optimisation d'une procédure de base pour la tâche 1. In Cyril Grouin and Dominic Forest (Eds.), *Expérimentations et évaluations en fouille de textes : un panorama des campagnes DEFT* (pp. 135–151). Hermes Lavoisier, Paris, France.

Yves Bestgen, Sylviane Granger, and Jennifer Thewissen. 2012. Error patterns and automatic L1 identification. In Scott Jarvis and Scott Crossley (Eds.), *Approaching Language Transfer through Text Classification: Explorations in the Detection-based Approach* (pp. 127–153). Multilingual Matters, Bristol, UK.

Daniel Blanchard, Joel Tetreault, Derrick Higgins, Aoife Cahill, and Martin Chodorow. 2013. *TOEFL11: A Corpus of Non-Native English*. Educational Testing Service, Princeton, NJ.

Serhiy Bykh and Detmar Meurers. 2012. Native language identification using recurring n-grams—Investigating abstraction and domain dependence. *Proceedings of COLING 2012: Technical Papers* (pp. 425-440).

Susan Dumais 1991. Improving the retrieval of information from external sources. *Journal Behavior Research Methods, Instruments, & Computers*, 23:229–236.

Rong-En Fan, Kai-Wei Chang, Cho-Jui Hsieh, Xiang-Rui Wang, and Chih-Jen Lin. 2008. LIBLINEAR: A library for large linear classification. *Journal of Machine Learning Research*, 9:1871–1874. (LIBLINEAR available at http://www.csie.ntu.edu.tw/~cjlin/liblinear).

Sylviane Granger, Estelle Dagneaux, and Fanny Meunier. 2009. *The International Corpus of Learner English: Handbook and CD-ROM, version 2*. Presses Universitaires de Louvain, Louvain-la-Neuve, Belgium.

Scott Jarvis. 2011. Data mining with learner corpora: Choosing classifiers for L1 detection. In Fanny Meunier, Sylvie De Cock, Gaëtanelle Gilquin, and Magali Paquot (Eds.), *A Taste for Corpora: In Honor of Sylviane Granger* (pp. 127–154). Benjamins, Amsterdam.

Scott Jarvis. 2012. The detection-based approach: An overview. In Scott Jarvis and Scott Crossley (Eds.), *Approaching Language Transfer through Text Classification: Explorations in the Detection-based Approach* (pp. 1–33). Multilingual Matters, Bristol, UK.

Scott Jarvis and Scott Crossley. 2012. *Approaching Language Transfer through Text Classification: Explorations in the Detection-based Approach*. Multilingual Matters, Bristol, UK.

Scott Jarvis and Magali Paquot. 2012. Exploring the role of n-grams in L1 identification. In Scott Jarvis and Scott Crossley (Eds.), *Approaching Language Transfer through Text Classification: Explorations in the Detection-based Approach* (pp. 71–105). Multilingual Matters, Bristol, UK.

Moshe Koppel, Jonathan Schler, and Kfir Zigdon. 2005. Automatically determining an anonymous author's native language. *ISI* (pp. 209–217).

Helmut Schmid. 1995. Improvements in part-of-speech tagging with an application to German. *Proceedings of the ACL SIGDAT-Workshop*. Dublin, Ireland.

Laura Mayfield Tomokiyo and Rosie Jones. 2001. You're not from 'round here, are you? Naïve Bayes detection of non-native utterance text. *Proceedings of the Second Meeting of the North American Chapter of the Association for Computational Lingusitics (NAACL '01)*. The Association for Computational Linguistics, Cambridge, MA.

Joel Tetreault, Daniel Blanchard, Aoife Cahill, and Martin Chodorow. 2012. Native tongues, lost and found: Resources and empirical evaluations in native language identification. *Proceedings of COLING 2012: Technical Papers* (pp. 2585–2602).

Joel Tetreault, Daniel Blanchard, and Aoife Cahill. 2013. Summary report on the first shared task on native language identification. *Proceedings of the Eight Workshop on Building Educational Applications Using NLP*. Association for Computational Linguistics, Atlanta, GA.

Oren Tsur and Ary Rappoport. 2007. Using classifier features for studying the effect of native language on the choice of written second language words. *Proceedings of the Workshop on Cognitive Aspects of Computational Language Acquisition* (pp. 9–16). Association for Computational Linguistics, Prague, Czech Republic.

Recognizing English Learners' Native Language from Their Writings

Baoli LI
Department of Computer Science
Henan University of Technology
1 Lotus Street, High & New Technology Industrial Development Zone
Zhengzhou, China, 450001
csblli@gmail.com

Abstract

Native Language Identification (NLI), which tries to identify the native language (L1) of a second language learner based on their writings, is helpful for advancing second language learning and authorship profiling in forensic linguistics. With the availability of relevant data resources, much work has been done to explore the native language of a foreign language learner. In this report, we present our system for the first shared task in Native Language Identification (NLI). We use a linear SVM classifier and explore features of words, word and character n-grams, style, and metadata. Our official system achieves accuracy of 0.773, which ranks it 18th among the 29 teams in the closed track.

1 Introduction

Native Language Identification (NLI) (Ahn, 2011; Kochmar, 2011), which tries to identify the native language (L1) of a second language learner based on their writings, is expected to be helpful for advancing second language learning and authorship profiling in forensic linguistics. With the availability of relevant data resources, much work has been done to explore the effective way to identify the native language of a foreign language learner (Koppel et al., 2005; Wong et al., 2011; Brooke and Hirst, 2012a, 2012b; Bykh and Meurers, 2012; Crossley and McNamara, 2012; Jarvis et al., 2012; Jarvis and Paquot, 2012; Tofighi et al., 2012; Torney et al. 2012).

To evaluate different techniques and approaches to Native Language Identification with the same setting, the first shared task in Native Language Identification (NLI) was organized by researchers from Nuance Communications and Educational Testing Service (Tetreault et al., 2013). A larger and more reliable data set, TOEFL11 (Blanchard et al., 2013), was used in this open evaluation.

This paper reports our NLI2013 shared task system that we built at the Department of Computer Science, Henan University of Technology, China. To be involved in this evaluation, we would like to obtain a more thorough knowledge of the research on native language identification and its state-of-the-art, as we may focus on authorship attribution (Koppel et al., 2008) problems in the near future.

The NLI2013 shared task is framed as a supervised text classification problem where the set of native languages (L1s), i.e. categories, is known, which includes Arabic, Chinese, French, German, Hindi, Italian, Japanese, Korean, Spanish, Telugu, and Turkish. A system is given a large part of the TOEFL11 dataset for training a detection model, and then makes predictions on the test writing samples.

Inspired by our experience of dealing with different text classification problems, we decide to employ a linear support vector machine (SVM) in our NLI2013 system. We plan to take this system as a starting point, and may explore other complex classifiers in the future. Although in-depth syntactic features may be helpful for this kind of tasks (Bergsma et al., 2012; Wong and Dras, 2011; Swanson and Charniak, 2012; Wong et al., 2012), we decide to explore the effectiveness of the traditional word and character features, as well as style features, in our system. We would like to verify on the first open available large dataset whether these traditional features work and how good they are.

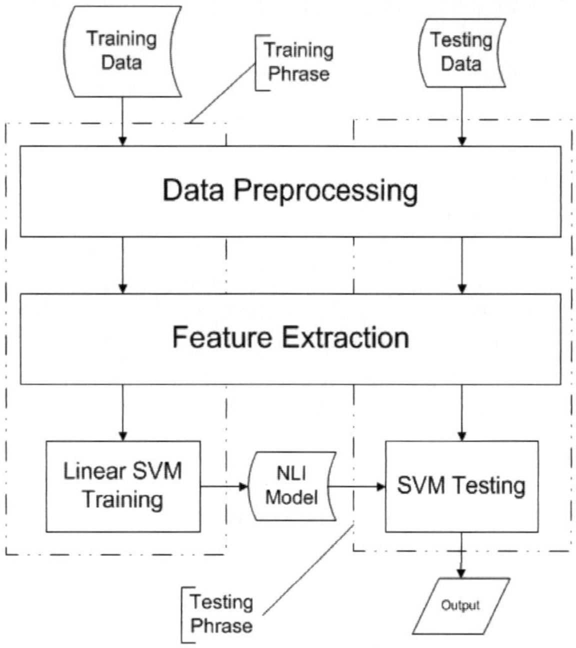

Figure 1. System Architecture.

We submitted four runs with different feature sets. The run with all the features achieved the best accuracy of 0.773, which ranks our system 18th among the 29 systems in the closed track.

In the rest of this paper we describe the detail of our system and analyze the results. Section 2 gives the overview of our system, while Section 3 discusses the various features in-depth. We present our experiments and discussions in Section 4, and conclude in Section 5.

2 System Description

Figure 1 gives the architecture of our NLI2013 system, which takes machine learning framework. At the training stage, annotated data is first processed through preprocessing and feature extraction, then fed to the classifier learning module, and we can finally obtain a NLI model. At the testing stage, each test sample goes through the same preprocessing and feature extraction modules, and is assigned a category with the learned NLI model.

Data Preprocessing: this module aims at transforming the original data into a suitable format for the system, e.g. inserting the category information into the individual writing sample and attaching metadata to essays.

Feature Extraction: this module tries to obtain all the useful features from the original data. We considered features like: word, word n-gram, character n-gram, style, and available metadata.

Linear SVM training and testing: these two modules are the key components. The training module takes the transformed digitalized vectors as input, and train an effective NLI model, where the testing module just applies the learned model on the testing data. As linear support vector machines (SVM) achieves quite good performance on a lot of text classification problems, we use this general machine learning algorithm in our NLI2013 system. The excellent SVM implementation, Libsvm (Chang and Lin, 2011), was incorporated in our system and TFIDF is used to derive the feature values in vectors. Then, we turn to focus on what features are effective for native language identification. We explore words, word n-grams, character n-grams, style, and metadata features in the system.

3 Features

In this section, we explain what kind of features we used in our NLI2013 system.

3.1 Word and Word n-gram

The initial feature set is words or tokens in the dataset. As the dataset is tokenized and sentence/paragraph split, we simply use space to delimit the text and get individual tokens. We remove rare features that appear only once in the training dataset. Words or tokens are transformed to lowercase.

Word n-grams are combined by consecutive words or tokens. They are expecting to capture some syntactic characteristics of writing samples. Two special tokens, "BOS" and "EOS", which indicate "Beginning" and "Ending", are attached at the two ends of a sentence. We considered word 2-grams and word 3-grams in our system.

3.2 Character n-gram

We assume sub-word features like prefix and suffix are useful for detecting the learners' native languages. To simplify the process rather than employing a complex morphological analyzer, we consider character n-grams as another important feature set. The n-grams are extracted from each sentence by regarding the whole sentence as a large word / string and replacing the delimited symbol (i.e. white space) with a special uppercase character 'S'. As what we did in getting word n-grams, we attached two special character "B" and "E" at the two ends of a sentence. Character 2-grams, 3-grams, 4-grams, and 5-grams are used in our system.

3.3 Style

We would like to explore whether the traditional style features are helpful for this task as those features are widely used in authorship attribution. We include the following style features:

- __PARA__: a paragraph in an essay;
- __SENT__: a sentence in an essay;
- PARASENTLEN=NN: a paragraph of NN sentences long;
- SENTWDLEN=NN: a sentence of 4*NN words long;
- WDCL=NN: a word of NN characters long;

3.4 Other

As the TOEFL11 dataset includes two metadata for each essay, English language proficiency level (high, medium, or low) and Prompt ID, we include them as additional features in our system.

4 Experiments and Results

4.1 Dataset

The dataset of the NLI2013 shared task contains 12,100 English essays from the Test of English as a Foreign Language (TOEFL). Educational Testing Service (ETS) published the dataset through the LDC with the motivation to create a larger and more reliable data set for researchers to conduct Native Language Identification experiments on. This dataset, henceforth TOEFL11, comprises 11 native languages (L1s) with 1,000 essays per language. The 11 covered native languages are: Arabic, Chinese, French, German, Hindi, Italian, Japanese, Korean, Spanish, Telugu, and Turkish. In addition, each essay in the TOEFL11 is marked with an English language proficiency level (high, medium, or low) based on the judgments of human assessment specialists. The essays are usually 300 to 400 words long. 9,900 essays of this set are chosen as the training data, 1,100 are for development and the rest 1,100 as test data.

Runs	HAUTCS-1	HAUTCS-2	HAUTCS-3	HAUTCS-4
Accuracy	**0.773**	**0.758**	**0.76**	**0.756**
ARA	0.731[1]	0.703	0.703	0.71
CHI	0.82	0.794	0.794	0.782
FRE	0.806	0.788	0.786	0.783
GER	**0.897**	**0.899**	**0.899**	**0.867**
HIN	*0.686*	0.688	0.694	0.707
ITA	0.83	0.84	0.844	0.844
JPN	0.832	0.792	0.798	0.81
KOR	0.763	0.764	0.768	0.727
SPA	0.703	*0.651*	*0.651*	*0.65*
TEL	0.702	0.702	0.702	0.751
TUR	0.736	0.715	0.716	0.698

Table 1. Official results of our system.

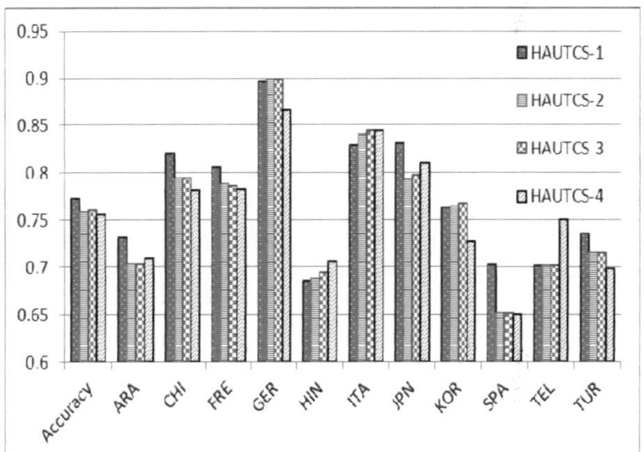

Figure 2. Performance of our official runs.

4.2 Official Results

Accuracy, which measures the percentage of how many essays are correctly detected, is used as the main evaluation metric in the NLI2013 shared task.

Table 1 gives the official results of our system on the evaluation data. We submitted four runs with different feature sets:

HAUTCS-1: all the features, which include words, word 2-grams, word 3-grams, **character 2-grams, character 3-grams, character 4-grams,**

[1] This number, as well as others in the cells from this row to the bottom, is value of F-1 measure for each language.

character 5-grams, style, and other metadata features;

HAUTCS-2: uses words, word 2-grams, word 3-grams, **style**, and other metadata features;

HAUTCS-3: uses words, **word 2-grams, word 3-grams**, and other metadata features;

HAUTCS-4: uses words or tokens and other metadata features.

For the runs HAUTCS-2, HAUTCS-3, and HAUTCS-4, we combined the development and training data for learning the identification model, where for the HAUTCS-1, it's a pity that we forgot to include the development data for training the model.

Our best run (HAUTCS-1) achieved the overall accuracy (0.773). The system performs best on the German category, but poorest on the Hindi category, as can be easily seen on figure 2.

Analyzing the four runs' performance showing on figure 2, we observe: word features are quite effective for Telugu and Hindi categories, but not powerful enough for others; word n-grams are helpful for languages Chinese, French, German, Korean, and Turkish, but useless for others; Style features only boost a little for French; Character n-grams work for Arabic, Chinese, French, Japanese, Spanish, and Turkish; Spanish category prefers character n-grams, where Telugu category likes word features. As different features have different effects on different languages, a better NLI system is expected to use different features for different languages.

After the evaluation, we experimented with the same setting as the HAUTCS-1 run, but included both training and development data for learning the NLI model. We got accuracy 0.781 on the new released test data, which has the same format with paragraph split as the training and development data.

As we include style features like how many paragraphs in an essay, the old test data, which removed the paragraph delimiters (i.e. single blank lines), may be not good for our trained model. Therefore, we did experiments with the new test data. Unfortunately, the accuracy 0.772 is a little poorer than that we obtained with the old test data. It seems that the simple style features are not effective in this task. As shown in table 1, HAUTCS-2 performs poorer than HAUTCS-3, which helps us derive the same conclusion.

4.3 Additional Experiments

We did 10-fold cross validation on the training and development data with the same setting as the HAUTCS-1 run. The data splitting is given by the organizers. Accuracies of the 10 runs are show in table 2. The overall accuracy 0.799 is better than that on the test data.

Fold	**1**	**2**	**3**	**4**	**5**
Accuracy	0.802	0.795	0.81	0.791	0.79
Fold	**6**	**7**	**8**	**9**	**10**
Accuracy	0.805	0.789	0.803	0.798	0.805

Table 2. Results of 10-fold cross validation on the training and development data.

To check how metadata features work, we did another run HAUTCS-5, which uses only words as features. This run got the same overall accuracy 0.756 on the old test data as HAUTCS-4 did, which demonstrates that those metadata features may not provide much useful information for native language identification.

5 Conclusion and Future Work

In this paper, we report our system for the NLI2013 shared task, which automatically detecting the native language of a foreign English learner from her/his writing sample. The system was built on a machine learning framework with traditional features including words, word n-grams, character n-grams, and writing styles. Character n-grams are simple but quite effective.

We plan to explore syntactic features in the future, and other machine learning algorithms, e.g. ECOC (Li and Vogel, 2010), also deserve further experiments. As we discussed in section 4, we are also interested in designing a framework to use different features for different categories.

Acknowledgments

This work was supported by the Henan Provincial Research Program on Fundamental and Cutting-Edge Technologies (No. 112300410007), and the High-level Talent Foundation of Henan University of Technology (No. 2012BS027). Experiments were performed on the Amazon Elastic Compute Cloud.

References

Ahn, C. S. 2011. Automatically Detecting Authors' Native Language. Master's thesis, Naval Postgraduate School, Monterey, CA.

Bergsma, S., Post, M., and Yarowsky, D. 2012. Stylometric analysis of scientific articles. In Proceedings of the 2012 Conference of the North American Chapter of the Association for Computational Linguistics: Human Language Technologies, pages 327–337, Montréal, Canada. Association for Computational Linguistics.

Blanchard, D., Tetreault, J., Higgins, D., Cahill, A., and Chodorow, M. 2013. TOEFL11: A Corpus of Non-Native English. Technical report, Educational Testing Service.

Brooke, J. and Hirst, G. 2012a. Measuring interlanguage: Native language identification with l1-influence metrics. In Calzolari, N., Choukri, K., Declerck, T., Dogan, M. U., Maegaard, B., Mariani, J., Odijk, J., and Piperidis, S., editors, Proceedings of the Eighth International Conference on Language Resources and Evaluation (LREC-2012), pages 779–784, Istanbul, Turkey

Brooke, J. and Hirst, G. 2012b. Robust, Lexicalized Native Language Identification. In Proceedings of COLING 2012, pages 391-408, Mumbai, India.

Bykh, S. and Meurers, D. 2012. Native Language Identification using Recurring n-grams - Investigating Abstraction and Domain Dependence. In Proceedings of COLING 2012, pages 425-440, Mumbai, India.

Chang, C.-C. and Lin C.-J. 2011. LIBSVM : a library for support vector machines. ACM Transactions on Intelligent Systems and Technology, 2:3:27:1-27.

Crossley, S. A. and McNamara, D. 2012. Detecting the First Language of Second Language Writers Using Automated Indices of Cohesion, Lexical Sophistication, Syntactic Complexity and Conceptual Knowledge. In Jarvis, S. and Crossley, S. A., editors, Approaching Language Transfer through Text Classification, pages 106-126. Multilingual Matters.

Jarvis, S., Castañeda-Jiménez, G., and Nielsen, R. 2012. Detecting L2 Writers' L1s on the Basis of Their Lexical Styles. In Jarvis, S. and Crossley, S. A., editors, Approaching Language Transfer through Text Classification, pages 34-70. Multilingual Matters.

Jarvis, S. and Paquot, M. 2012. Exploring the Role of n-Grams in L1 Identification. In Jarvis, S. and Crossley, S. A., editors, Approaching Language Transfer through Text Classification, pages 71-105. Multilingual Matters.

Kochmar, E. 2011. Identification of a writer's native language by error analysis. Master's thesis, University of Cambridge.

Koppel, M., Schler, J., and Zigdon, K. 2005. Determining an author's native language by mining a text for errors. In Proceedings of the eleventh ACM SIGKDD international conference on Knowledge discovery in data mining, pages 624–628, Chicago, IL. ACM.

Koppel, M., Schler, J., and Argamon, S. 2008. Computational methods in authorship attribution. Journal of the American Society for information Science and Technology, 60(1):9–26.

Li, B., and Vogel, C. 2010. Improving Multiclass Text Classification with Error-Correcting Output Coding and Sub-class Partitions. In Proceedings of the 23rd Canadian Conference on Artificial Intelligence, pages 4-15, Ottawa, Canada.

Swanson, B. and Charniak, E. 2012. Native language detection with tree substitution grammars. In Proceedings of the 50th Annual Meeting of the Association for Computational Linguistics (Volume 2: Short Papers), pages 193–197, Jeju Island, Korea.

Tetreault, J., Blanchard, D., and Cahill, A. 2013. A report on the first native language identification shared task. In Proceedings of the Eighth Workshop on Innovative Use of NLP for Building Educational Applications. Atlanta, GA, USA.

Tofighi, P.; Köse, C.; and Rouka, L. 2012. Author's native language identification from web-based texts. International Journal of Computer and Communication Engineering. 1(1):47-50

Torney, R.; Vamplew, P.; and Yearwood, J. 2012. Using psycholinguistic features for profiling first language of authors. Journal of the American Society for Information Science and Technology. 63(6):1256-1269.

Wong, S.-M. J. and Dras, M. 2011. Exploiting Parse Structures for Native Language Identification. In Proceedings of the 2011 Conference on Empirical Methods in Natural Language Processing, pages 1600–1610, Edinburgh, Scotland, UK.

Wong, S.-M. J., Dras, M., and Johnson, M. 2012. Exploring Adaptor Grammars for Native Language Identification. In Proceedings of the 2012 Joint Conference on Empirical Methods in Natural Language Processing and Computational Natural Language Learning, pages 699–709, Jeju Island, Korea.

NLI Shared Task 2013: MQ Submission

Shervin Malmasi **Sze-Meng Jojo Wong** **Mark Dras**
Centre for Language Technology
Macquarie University
Sydney, Australia
{shervin.malmasi,sze.wong,mark.dras}@mq.edu.au

Abstract

Our submission for this NLI shared task used for the most part standard features found in recent work. Our focus was instead on two other aspects of our system: at a high level, on possible ways of constructing ensembles of multiple classifiers; and at a low level, on the granularity of part-of-speech tags used as features. We found that the choice of ensemble combination method did not lead to much difference in results, although exploiting the varying behaviours of linear versus logistic regression SVM classifiers could be promising in future work; but part-of-speech tagsets showed noticeable differences.

We also note that the overall architecture, with its feature set and ensemble approach, had an accuracy of 83.1% on the test set when trained on both the training data and development data supplied, close to the best result of the task. This suggests that basically throwing together all the features of previous work will achieve roughly the state of the art.

1 Introduction

Among the efflorescence of work on Native Language Identification (NLI) noted by the shared task organisers, there are two trends in recent work in particular that we considered in building our submission. The first is the proposal and use of new features that might have relevance to NLI: for example, Wong and Dras (2011), motivated by the Contrastive Analysis Hypothesis (Lado, 1957) from the field of Second Language Acquisition, introduced syntactic structure as a feature; Swanson and Charniak (2012) introduced more complex Tree Substitution (TSG) structures, learned by Bayesian inference; and Bykh and Meurers (2012) used recurring n-grams, inspired by the variation n-gram approach to corpus error annotation detection (Dickinson and Meurers, 2003). Starting from the features introduced in these papers and others, then, other recent papers have compiled a comprehensive collection of features based on the earlier work — Tetreault et al. (2012) is an example, combining and analysing most of the features used in previous work. Given the timeframe of the shared task, there seemed to be not much mileage in trying new features that were likely to be more peripheral to the task.

A second trend, most apparent in 2012, was the examination of other corpora besides the International Corpus of Learner English used in earlier work, and in particular the use of cross-corpus evaluation (Brooke and Hirst, 2012; Tetreault et al., 2012) to avoid topic bias in determining native language. Possible topic bias had been a reason for avoiding a full range of n-grams, in particular those containing content words (Koppel et al., 2009); the development of new corpora and the analysis of the effect of topic bias mitigated this. The consequent use of a full range of n-grams further reinforced the view that novel features were unlikely to be a major source of interesting results.

We therefore concentrated on two areas: the use of classifier ensembles, and the choice of part-of-speech tags. With classifier ensembles, Tetreault et al. (2012) noted that these were highly useful in their system; but while that paper had extensive feature descriptions, it did not discuss in detail the approach to its ensembles. We therefore decided to examine a range of possible ensemble architectures. With part-of-speech tags, most work has used the Penn Treebank tagset, including those based on syntactic structure. Kochmar (2011) on the other hand used the CLAWS tagset,[1] which is much richer and more oriented to linguistic analysis than the Penn Treebank one. Given the much larger size of the TOEFL11 corpus used for this shared task than the corpora used for much earlier work, data sparsity could be less of an issue, and the tagset a viable one for future work.

The description of our submission is therefore in three parts. In §2 we present the system description, with a focus on the ensemble architectures we investigated; in §3 we list the features we used, which are basically those of much of the previous work; in §4 we present results of some of the variants we tried, particularly with respect to ensembles and tagsets; and in §5 we discuss some of the interesting characteristics of the data we noted during the shared task.

2 System Design

Our overall approach in terms of features and classifiers used is a fairly standard one. One difference from most approaches, but inspired by Tetreault et al. (2012), is that we train multiple classifiers over subsets of the features, over different feature representations, and over different regularisation approaches; we then combine them in ensembles (Dietterich, 2000).

2.1 SVM Ensemble Construction

To construct our ensemble, we train individual classifiers on a single feature type (e.g. PoS n-grams), using a specific feature value representation and classifier. We utilise a parallel ensemble structure where the classifiers are run on the input texts independently and their results are then fused into the final output using a combiner.

Additionally, we also experiment with bagging (bootstrap aggregating), a commonly used method for ensemble generation (Breiman, 1996) to generate multiple ensembles per feature type.

[1] http://ucrel.lancs.ac.uk/claws/

For our classifier, we use SVMs, specifically the LIBLINEAR SVM software package (Fan et al., 2008),[2] which is well-suited to text classification tasks with large numbers of features and large numbers of documents. LIBLINEAR provides both logistic regression and linear SVMs; we experiment with both. In general, the linear classifier performs better, but it only provides the decision output. The logistic regression classifier on the other hand gives probability estimates, which are required by most of our combination methods (§2.3). We therefore mostly use the logistic regression classifiers.

2.2 L1- and L2-regularized SVM Classifiers

In our preliminary experiments we noted that some feature types performed better with L1-regularization and others with L2. In this work we generate classifiers using both methods and evaluate their individual and combined performance.

2.3 Classifier Combination Methods

We experiment with the following decision combination methods, which have been discussed in the machine learning literature. Polikar (2006) provides an exposition of these rules and methods.

Plurality vote: Each classifier votes for a single class label, the label with the highest number of votes wins. Ties are broken arbitrarily.

Sum: All probability estimates are added together and the label with the highest sum is picked.

Average: The mean of all scores for each class is calculated and the label with the highest average probability is chosen.

Median: Each label's estimates are sorted and the median value is selected as the final score for that label. The label with the highest value is picked.

Product: For each class label, all of the probability estimates are multiplied together to create the label's final estimate. The label with the highest estimate is selected. A single low score can have a big effect on the outcome.

Highest Confidence: In this simple method, the class label that receives the vote with the largest degree of confidence is selected as the final output.

[2] Available at http://www.csie.ntu.edu.tw/~cjlin/liblinear/

Borda Count: The confidence estimates are converted to ranks and the final label selected using the Borda count algorithm (Ho et al., 1994). In this combination approach, broadly speaking points are assigned to ranks, and these tallied for the overall weight.

With the exception of the plurality vote, all of these can be weighted. In our ensembles we also experiment with weighting the output of each classifier using its individual accuracy on the training data as an indication of our degree of confidence in it.

2.4 Feature Representation

Most NLI studies have used two types of feature representations: binary (presence or absence of a feature in a text) and normalized frequencies. Although binary feature values have been used in some studies (e.g. Wong and Dras (2011)), most have used frequency-based values.

In the course of our experiments we have observed that the effect of the feature representation varies with the feature type, size of the feature space and the learning algorithm itself. In our current system, then, we generate two classifiers for each feature type, one trained with frequency-based values (raw counts scaled using the L2-norm) and the other with binary. Our experiments assess both their individual and joint performance.

2.5 Proficiency-level Based Classification

To utilise the proficiency level information provided in the TOEFL11 corpus (texts are marked as either low, medium or high proficiency), we also investigate classifiers that are trained using only texts from specific proficiencies.

Tetreault et al. (2012) established that the classification accuracy of their system varied across proficiency levels, with high proficiency texts being the hardest to classify. This is most likely due to the fact that writers at differing skill levels commit distinct types of errors at different rates (Ortega, 2009, for example). If learners of different backgrounds commit these errors with different distributions, these patterns could be used by a learner to further improve classification accuracy. We will use these features in one of our experiments to investigate the effectiveness of such proficiency-level based classifiers for NLI.

3 Features

We roughly divide out feature types into lexical, part-of-speech and syntactic. In all of the feature types below, we perform no feature selection.

3.1 Lexical Features

As all previous work, we use function words as features. In addition, given the attempts to control for topic bias in the TOEFL11 corpus, we also make use of various lexical features which have been previously avoided by researchers due to the reported topic bias (Brooke and Hirst, 2011) in other NLI corpora such as the ICLE corpus.

Function Words In contrast to content words, function words do not have any meaning themselves, but rather can be seen as indicating the grammatical relations between other words. Examples include articles, determiners, conjunctions and auxiliary verbs. They have been widely used in studies of authorship attribution as well as NLI and established to be informative for these tasks. We use the list of 398 common English function words from Wong and Dras (2011). We also tested smaller sets, but observed that the larger sets achieve higher accuracy.

Function Word n-grams We devised and tested a new feature that attempts to capture patterns of function word use at the sentence level. We define function word *n*-grams as a type of word *n*-gram where content words are skipped: they are thus a specific subtype of skip-gram discussed by Guthrie et al. (2006). For example, the sentence *We should all start taking the bus* would be reduced to *we should all the*, from which we would extract the n-grams.

Character n-grams Tsur and Rappoport (2007) demonstrated that character *n*-grams are a useful feature for NLI. These *n*-grams can be considered as a sub-word feature and their effectiveness is hypothesized to be a result of phoneme transfer from the writer's L1. They can also capture orthographic conventions of a language. Accordingly, we limit our *n*-grams to a maximum size of 3 as longer sequences would correspond to short words and not phonemes or syllables.

Word n-grams There has been a shift towards the use of word-based features in several recent studies (Brooke and Hirst, 2012; Bykh and Meurers, 2012;

Tetreault et al., 2012), with new corpora come into use for NLI and researchers exploring and addressing the issues relating to topic bias that previously prevented their use. Lexical choice is considered to be a prime feature for studying language transfer effects, and researchers have found word n-grams to be one of the strongest features for NLI. Tetreault et al. (2012) expanded on this by integrating 5-gram language models into their system. While we did not replicate this, we made use of word trigrams.

3.2 POS n-grams

Most studies have found that POS tag n-grams are a very useful feature for NLI (Koppel et al., 2005; Bykh and Meurers, 2012, for example). The tagset provided by the Penn TreeBank is the most widely used in these experiments, with tagging performed by the Stanford Tagger (Toutanova et al., 2003).

We investigate the effect of tagset granularity on classification accuracy by comparing the classification accuracy of texts tagged with the PTB tagset against those annotated by the RASP Tagger (Briscoe et al., 2006). The PTB POS tagset contains 36 unique tags, while the RASP system uses a subset of the CLAWS2 tagset, consisting of 150 tags.

This is a significant size difference and we hypothesize that a larger tagset could provide richer levels of syntactically meaningful info which is more fine-grained in distinction between syntactic categories and contains more morpho-syntactic information such as gender, number, person, case and tense. For example, while the PTB tagset has four tags for pronouns (`PRP, PRP$, WP, WP$`), the CLAWS tagset provides over 20 pronoun tags (`PPHO1, PPIS1, PPX2, PPY`, etc.) distinguishing between person, number and grammatical role. Consequently, these tags could help better capture error patterns to be used for classification.

3.3 Syntactic Features

Adaptor grammar collocations Drawing on Wong et al. (2012), we also utilise an adaptor grammar to discover arbitrary lengths of n-gram collocations for the TOEFL11 corpus. We explore both the pure part-of-speech (POS) n-grams as well as the more promising mixtures of POS and function words. Following a similar experimental setup as per Wong et al. (2012), we derive two adaptor grammars where each is associated with a different set of vocabulary: either pure POS or the mixture of POS and function words. We use the grammar proposed by Johnson (2010) for capturing topical collocations as presented below:

$$\begin{array}{ll}
Sentence \rightarrow Doc_j & j \in 1, \ldots, m \\
Doc_j \rightarrow _j & j \in 1, \ldots, m \\
Doc_j \rightarrow Doc_j\ Topic_i & i \in 1, \ldots, t; \\
 & j \in 1, \ldots, m \\
\underline{Topic_i} \rightarrow Words & i \in 1, \ldots, t \\
Words \rightarrow Word & \\
Words \rightarrow Words\ Word & \\
Word \rightarrow w & w \in V_{pos}; \\
 & w \in V_{pos+fw}
\end{array}$$

As per Wong et al. (2012), V_{pos} contains 119 distinct POS tags based on the Brown tagset and V_{pos+fw} is extended with 398 function words used in Wong and Dras (2011). The number of topics t is set to 50 (instead of 25 as per Wong et al. (2012)) given that the TOEFL corpus is larger than the ICLE corpus. The inference algorithm for the adaptor grammars are based on the Markov Chain Monte Carlo technique made available by Johnson (2010).[3]

Tree Subtitution Grammar fragments In relation to the context-free grammar (CFG) rules explored in the previous NLI work of Wong and Dras (2011), Tree Substitution Grammar (TSG) fragments have been proposed by Swanson and Charniak (2012) as another form of syntactic features for NLI classification tasks. Here, as an approximation to deploying the Bayesian approach to induce a TSG (Post and Gildea, 2009; Swanson and Charniak, 2012), we first parse each of the essays in the TOEFL training corpus with the Stanford Parser (version 2.0.4) (Klein and Manning, 2003) to obtain the parse trees. We then extract the TSG fragments from the parse trees using the TSG system made available by Post and Gildea (2009).[4]

Stanford dependencies In Tetreault et al. (2012), Stanford dependencies were investigated as yet another form of syntactic features. We follow a similar approach: for each essay in the training corpus, we extract all the basic (rather than

[3] `http://web.science.mq.edu.au/~mjohnson/Software.htm`

[4] `https://github.com/mjpost/dptsg`

the collapsed) dependencies returned by the Stanford Parser (de Marneffe et al., 2006). Similarly, we generate all the variations for each of the dependencies (grammatical relations) by substituting each lemma with its corresponding PoS tag. For instance, a grammatical relation of `det(knowledge, the)` yields the following variations: `det(NN, the)`, `det(knowledge, DT)`, and `det(NN, DT)`.

4 Experiments and Results

We report our results using 10-fold cross-validation on the combined training and development sets, as well as by training a model using the training and development data and running it on the test set.

We note that for our submission, we trained only on the training data; the results here thus differ from the official ones.

4.1 Individual Feature Results and Analysis

We ran the classifiers generated for each feature type to assess their performance. The results are summarized in Table 1: the Train + Dev Set results were for the system when trained on the training and development data with 10 fold cross-validation, and the Test Set results for the system trained on the training and development data combined.

Character n-grams are an informative feature and our results are very similar to those reported by previous researchers (Tsur and Rappoport, 2007). In particular, it should be noted that the use of punctuation is a very powerful feature for distinguishing languages. Romance language speakers were most likely to use more punctuation symbols (colons, semicolons, ellipsis, parenthesis, etc.) and at higher rates. Chinese, Japanese and Korean speakers were far less likely to use punctuation.

The performance for word n-grams, TSG fragments and Stanford Dependencies is very strong and comparable to previously reported research. For the adaptor grammar n-grams, the mixed POS/function word version yielded best results and was included in the ensemble.

4.2 POS-based Classification and Tagset Size

To compare the tagsets we trained individual classifiers for n-grams of size 1–4 using both tagsets and tested them. The results are shown in Table 2 and

Feature	Train + Dev Set	Test Set
Chance Baseline	9.1	9.1
Character unigram	33.99	34.70
Character bigram	51.64	49.80
Character trigram	66.43	66.70
RASP POS unigram	43.76	45.10
RASP POS bigram	58.93	61.60
RASP POS trigram	59.39	62.70
Function word unigram	51.38	54.00
Function word bigram	59.73	63.00
Word unigram	74.61	75.50
Word bigram	74.46	76.00
Word trigram	63.60	65.00
TSG Fragments	72.16	72.70
Stanford Dependencies	73.78	75.90
Adaptor Grammar POS/FW n-grams	69.76	70.00

Table 1: Classification results for our individual features.

N	PTB	RASP
1	34.03	43.76
2	48.85	58.93
3	51.06	**59.39**
4	49.85	52.81

Table 2: Classification accuracy results for POS n-grams of size N using both the PTB and RASP tagset. The larger RASP tagset performed significantly better for all N.

N	Accuracy
1	51.38
2	**59.73**
3	52.14

Table 3: Classification results for Function Word n-grams of size N. Our proposed Function Word bigram and trigram features outperform the commonly used unigrams.

Ensemble	Train + Dev Set	Test Set
Complete Ensemble	81.50	81.60
Only binary values	**82.46**	**83.10**
Only freq values	65.28	67.20
L1-regularized solver only	80.33	81.10
L2-regularized solver only	81.42	81.10
Bin, L1-regularized only	81.57	82.00
Bin, L2-regularized only	82.00	82.50

Table 4: Classification results for our ensembles, best result in column in bold (binary values with L1- and L2-regularized solvers).

show that the RASP tagged data provided better performance in all cases. While it is possible that these differences could be attributed to other factors such as tagging accuracy, we do not believe this to be the case as the Stanford Tagger is known for its high accuracy (97%). These differences are quite clear; this finding also has implications for other syntactic features that make use of POS tags, such as Adaptor Grammars, Stanford Dependencies and Tree Substitution Grammars.

4.3 Function Word n-grams

The classification results using our proposed Function Word n-gram feature are shown in Table 3. They show that function word skip-grams are more informative than the simple function word counts that have been previously used.

4.4 Ensemble Results

Table 4 shows the results from our ensembles. The feature types included in the ensemble are those whose results are listed individually in Table 1. (So, for example, we only use the RASP-tagged PoS n-grams, not the Penn Treebank ones.) The complete ensemble consists of four classifiers per feature type: L1-/L2-regularized versions with both binary and freq. values.

Bagging Our experiments with bagging did not find any improvements in accuracy, even with larger numbers of bootstrap samples (50 or more). Bagging is said to be more suitable for unstable classifiers which have greater variability in their performance and are more susceptible to noise in the training data (Breiman, 1996). In our experiments with individual feature types we have found the classifiers to be quite stable in their performance, across different folds and training set sizes. This is one potential reason why bagging did not yield significant improvements.

Combiner Methods Of the methods outlined in §2.3 we found the sum and weighted sum combiners to be the best performing, but the weighted results did not improve accuracy in general over their unweighted counterparts. Our results are reported using the unweighted sum combiner. A detailed comparison of the results for the combiners has been omitted here due to time constraints; the differences across all combination methods was roughly 1–2%. Any new approach to ensemble combination methods would consequently want to be radically different to expect a notable improvement in performance.

As noted at the start of this section, results here are for the system trained on training and development data. The best result on the test set (83.1%) is almost 4% higher than our submission result, and close to the highest result achieved (83.6%).

Binary & Frequency-Based Feature Values Our results are consistent with those of Brooke and Hirst (2012), who conclude that there is a preference for binary feature values instead of frequency-based ones. Including both types in the ensemble did not improve results.

However, in other experiments on the TOEFL11 corpus we have also observed that use of frequency information often leads to significantly better results when using a linear SVM classifier: in fact, the linear classifier is better on all frequency feature types, and also on some of the binary feature types. We present results in Table 5 comparing the two. An approach using the linear SVM that provides an associated probability score — perhaps through bagging — allowing it to be combined with the methods described in §2.3 could then perhaps boost results. All these results were from a system using the training data with 10 fold cross-validation.

Combining Regularisation Approaches Results show that combining the L1- and L2-regularized classifiers in the ensemble provided a small in-

Feature	L2-norm scaled counts		Binary	
	linear	log. regr.	linear	log. regr.
Char unigram	**31.60**	26.23	25.68	26.36
Char bigram	**51.59**	41.81	41.20	45.11
Char trigram	**65.78**	54.97	58.30	61.76
RASP POS bigram	**60.38**	54.00	50.31	54.56
RASP POS trigram	**58.75**	53.92	55.93	58.58
Function word unigram	**51.38**	45.09	46.67	47.13
Function word bigram	**58.95**	53.22	54.97	58.53
Word unigram	70.33	55.60	69.40	**72.00**
Word bigram	73.90	54.25	73.65	**74.93**
Word trigram	63.78	52.46	64.78	**64.94**

Table 5: Classification results for our individual features.

crease in accuracy. Ensembles with either the L1 or L2-regularized solver have lower accuracy than the combined methods (row 2).

4.5 Proficiency-level Based Classification

Table 6 shows our results for training models with texts of a given proficiency level and the accuracy on the test set. The numbers show that in general texts should be classified with a learner trained with texts of a similar proficiency. They also show that not all texts in a proficiency level are of uniform quality as some levels perform better with data from the closest neighbouring levels (e.g. Medium texts perform best with data from all proficiencies), suggesting that the three levels form a larger proficiency continuum where users may fall in the higher or lower ends of a level. A larger scale with more than three levels could help address this.

Train	Test	Acc.	Train	Test	Acc.
Low	Low	52.2	All	Med	**86.8**
Med	Low	72.1	M + H	Med	85.3
High	Low	40.3	L + M	Med	83.8
All	Low	75.2	Low	High	16.1
L + M	Low	**76.0**	Med	High	68.1
Low	Med	40.7	High	High	65.7
Med	Med	83.6	M + H	High	74.7
High	Med	62.1	All	High	**75.2**

Table 6: Results for classifying the test set documents using classifiers trained with a specific proficiency level. Each level's best result in bold.

5 Discussion

5.1 Unused Experimental Features

We also experimented with some other feature types that were not included in the final system.

CCG SuperTag *n*-grams In order to introduce additional rich syntactic information into our system, we investigated the use CCG SuperTags as feature for NLI classification. We used the C&C CCG Parser and SuperTagger (Curran et al., 2007) to extract SuperTag *n*-grams from the corpus, which were then used as features to construct classifiers. The best results were achieved by using *n*-grams of size 2–4, which achieved classification rates of around 44%. However, adding these features to our ensemble did not improve the overall system accuracy. We believe that this is because when coupled with the other syntactic features in the system, the information provided by the SuperTags is redundant, and thus they were excluded from our final ensemble.

Hapax Legomena and Dis Legomena The special word categories *Hapax Legomena* and *Dis legomena* refer to words that appear only once and twice, respectively, in a complete text. In practice, these features are a subset of our Word Unigram feature, where *Hapax Legomena* correspond to unigrams with an occurrence count of 1 and *Hapax dis legomena* are unigrams with a count of 2.

In our experimental results we found that *Hapax Legomena* alone provides an accuracy of 61%. Combining the two features together yields an accuracy of 67%. This is an interesting finding as both of these features alone provide an accuracy close to the whole set of word unigrams.

5.2 Corpus Representativeness

We conducted a brief analysis of our extracted features, looking at the most predictive ones according to their Information Gain. Although we did not find any obvious indicators of topic bias, we noted some other issues of potential concern.

Chinese, Japanese and Korean speakers make excessive use of phrases such as *However*, *First of all* and *Secondly*. At first glance, the usage rate of these phrases seems unnaturally high (more than 50% of Korean texts had a sentence beginning with *However*). This could perhaps be a cohort effect relating to those individually attempting this particular TOEFL exam, rather than an L1 effect: it would be useful to know how much variability there is in terms of where candidates come from.

It was also noticed that many writers mention the name of their country in their texts, and this could potentially create a high correlation between those words and the language class label, leading perhaps to an artificial boosting of results. For example, the words *India*, *Turkey*, *Japan*, *Korea* and *Germany* appear with high frequency in the texts of their corresponding L1 speakers — hundreds of times, in fact, in contrast to frequencies in the single figures for speakers of other L1s. These might also be an artefact of the type of text, rather than related to the L1 as such.

5.3 Hindi vs. Telugu

We single out here this language pair because of the high level of confusion between the two classes. Looking at the results obtained by other teams, we observe that this language pair provided the worst classification accuracy for almost all teams. No system was able to achieve an accuracy of 80% for Hindi (something many achieved for other languages). In analysing the actual and predicted classes for all documents classified as Hindi and Telugu by our system, we find that generally all of the actual Hindi and Telugu texts (96% and 99%, respectively) are within the set. Our classifier is clearly having difficulty discriminating between these two specific classes.

Given this, we posit that the confounding influence may have more to do with the particular style of English that is spoken and taught within the country, rather than the specific L1 itself. Consulting other research about SLA differences in multilingual countries could shed further light on this.

Analysing highly informative features provides some clues about the influence of a common culture or national identity: in our classifier, the words *India*, *Indian* and *Hindu* were highly predictive of both Hindi and Telugu texts, but no other languages. In addition, there were terms that were not geographically- or culturally-specific that were strongly associated with both Hindi and Telugu: these included *hence*, *thus*, and *etc*, and a much higher rate of use of male pronouns. It has been observed in a number of places (Sanyal, 2007, for example) that the English spoken across India still retains characteristics of the English that was spoken during the time of the Raj and the East India Company that have disappeared from other varities of English, so that it can sound more formal to other speakers, or retain traces of an archaic business correspondence style; the features just noted would fit that pattern. The effect is likely to occur regardless of the L1.

Looking at individual language pairs in this way could lead to incremental improvement in the overall classification accuracy of NLI systems.

References

Leo Breiman. 1996. Bagging predictors. In *Machine Learning*, pages 123–140.

Ted Briscoe, John Carroll, and Rebecca Watson. 2006. The second release of the rasp system. In *Proceedings of the COLING/ACL on Interactive presentation sessions*, COLING-ACL '06, pages 77–80, Stroudsburg, PA, USA. Association for Computational Linguistics.

Julian Brooke and Graeme Hirst. 2011. Native language detection with 'cheap' learner corpora. In *Conference of Learner Corpus Research (LCR2011)*, Louvain-la-Neuve, Belgium. Presses universitaires de Louvain.

Julian Brooke and Graeme Hirst. 2012. Robust, Lexicalized Native Language Identification. In *Proceedings of COLING 2012*, pages 391–408, Mumbai, India, December. The COLING 2012 Organizing Committee.

Serhiy Bykh and Detmar Meurers. 2012. Native Language Identification using Recurring n-grams – Investigating Abstraction and Domain Dependence. In *Proceedings of COLING 2012*, pages 425–440, Mumbai, India, December. The COLING 2012 Organizing Committee.

James Curran, Stephen Clark, and Johan Bos. 2007. Linguistically motivated large-scale nlp with c&c and boxer. In *Proceedings of the 45th Annual Meeting of the Association for Computational Linguistics Companion Volume Proceedings of the Demo and Poster Sessions*, pages 33–36, Prague, Czech Republic, June. Association for Computational Linguistics.

Marie-Catherine de Marneffe, Bill Maccartney, and Christopher D. Manning. 2006. Generating typed dependency parses from phrase structure parses. In *Proceedings of the Fifth International Conference on Language Resources and Evaluation (LREC'06)*, pages 449–454, Genoa, Italy.

Markus Dickinson and W. Detmar Meurers. 2003. Detecting errors in part-of-speech annotation. In *Proceedings of the 10th Conference of the European Chapter of the Association for Computational Linguistics (EACL-03)*, pages 107–114, Budapest, Hungary.

Thomas G Dietterich. 2000. Ensemble methods in machine learning. In *Multiple classifier systems*, pages 1–15. Springer.

Rong-En Fan, Kai-Wei Chang, Cho-Jui Hsieh, Xiang-Rui Wang, and Chih-Jen Lin. 2008. LIBLINEAR: A library for large linear classification. *Journal of Machine Learning Research*, 9:1871–1874.

David Guthrie, Ben Allison, Wei Liu, Louise Guthrie, and Yorick Wilks. 2006. A Close Look at Skip-gram Modelling. In *Proceedings of the Fifth International Conference on Language Resources and Evaluation (LREC 2006)*, pages 1222–1225, Genoa, Italy.

Tin Kam Ho, Jonathan J. Hull, and Sargur N. Srihari. 1994. Decision combination in multiple classifier systems. *Pattern Analysis and Machine Intelligence, IEEE Transactions on*, 16(1):66–75.

Mark Johnson. 2010. Pcfgs, topic models, adaptor grammars and learning topical collocations and the structure of proper names. In *Proceedings of the 48th Annual Meeting of the Association for Computational Linguistics*, pages 1148–1157, Uppsala, Sweden, July. Association for Computational Linguistics.

Dan Klein and Christopher D. Manning. 2003. Accurate unlexicalized parsing. In *Proceedings of the 41st Annual Meeting on Association for Computational Linguistics - Volume 1*, ACL '03, pages 423–430, Sapporo, Japan. Association for Computational Linguistics.

Ekaterina Kochmar. 2011. Identification of a writer's native language by error analysis. Master's thesis, University of Cambridge.

Moshe Koppel, Jonathan Schler, and Kfir Zigdon. 2005. Automatically determining an anonymous author's native language. *Intelligence and Security Informatics*, pages 41–76.

Moshe Koppel, Jonathan Schler, and Shlomo Argamon. 2009. Computational Methods in Authorship Attribution. *Journal of the American Society for Information Science and Technology*, 60(1):9–26.

Robert Lado. 1957. *Linguistics Across Cultures: Applied Linguistics for Language Teachers*. University of Michigan Press, Ann Arbor, MI, US.

Lourdes Ortega. 2009. *Understanding Second Language Acquisition*. Hodder Education, Oxford, UK.

Robi Polikar. 2006. Ensemble based systems in decision making. *Circuits and Systems Magazine, IEEE*, 6(3):21–45.

Matt Post and Daniel Gildea. 2009. Bayesian learning of a tree substitution grammar. In *Proceedings of the ACL-IJCNLP 2009 Conference Short Papers*, ACLShort '09, pages 45–48, Suntec, Singapore. Association for Computational Linguistics.

Jyoti Sanyal. 2007. *Indlish: The Book for Every English-Speaking Indian*. Viva Books Private Limited.

Benjamin Swanson and Eugene Charniak. 2012. Native Language Detection with Tree Substitution Grammars. In *Proceedings of the 50th Annual Meeting of the Association for Computational Linguistics (Volume 2: Short Papers)*, pages 193–197, Jeju Island, Korea, July. Association for Computational Linguistics.

Joel Tetreault, Daniel Blanchard, Aoife Cahill, and Martin Chodorow. 2012. Native tongues, lost and found: Resources and empirical evaluations in native language identification. In *Proceedings of COLING 2012*, pages 2585–2602, Mumbai, India, December. The COLING 2012 Organizing Committee.

Kristina Toutanova, Dan Klein, Christopher D. Manning, and Yoram Singer. 2003. Feature-rich part-of-speech tagging with a cyclic dependency network. In *IN PROCEEDINGS OF HLT-NAACL*, pages 252–259.

Oren Tsur and Ari Rappoport. 2007. Using Classifier Features for Studying the Effect of Native Language on the Choice of Written Second Language Words. In *Proceedings of the Workshop on Cognitive Aspects of Computational Language Acquisition*, pages 9–16,

Prague, Czech Republic, June. Association for Computational Linguistics.

Sze-Meng Jojo Wong and Mark Dras. 2011. Exploiting Parse Structures for Native Language Identification. In *Proceedings of the 2011 Conference on Empirical Methods in Natural Language Processing*, pages 1600–1610, Edinburgh, Scotland, UK., July. Association for Computational Linguistics.

Sze-Meng Jojo Wong, Mark Dras, and Mark Johnson. 2012. Exploring Adaptor Grammars for Native Language Identification. In *Proceedings of the 2012 Joint Conference on Empirical Methods in Natural Language Processing and Computational Natural Language Learning*, pages 699–709, Jeju Island, Korea, July. Association for Computational Linguistics.

NAIST at the NLI 2013 Shared Task

Tomoya Mizumoto, Yuta Hayashibe
Keisuke Sakaguchi, Mamoru Komachi, Yuji Matsumoto
Graduate School of Information Science
Nara Institute of Science and Technology
8916-5, Takayama, Ikoma, Nara 630-0192, Japan
{ tomoya-m, yuta-h, keisuke-sa, komachi, matsu }@is.naist.jp

Abstract

This paper describes the Nara Institute of Science and Technology (NAIST) native language identification (NLI) system in the NLI 2013 Shared Task. We apply feature selection using a measure based on frequency for the closed track and try Capping and Sampling data methods for the open tracks. Our system ranked ninth in the closed track, third in open track 1 and fourth in open track 2.

1 Introduction

There have been many studies using English as a second language (ESL) learner corpora. For example, automatic grammatical error detection and correction is one of the most active research areas in this field. More recently, attention has been paid to native language identification (NLI) (Brooke and Hirst, 2012; Bykh and Meurers, 2012; Brooke and Hirst, 2011; Wong and Dras, 2011; Wong et al., 2011). Native language identification is the task of identifying the ESL learner's L1 given a learner's essay.

The NLI Shared Task 2013 (Tetreault et al., 2013) is the first shared task on NLI using the common dataset "TOEFL-11" (Blanchard et al., 2013; Tetreault et al., 2012). TOEFL-11 consists of essays written by learners of 11 native languages (Arabic, Chinese, French, German, Hindi, Italian, Japanese, Koran, Spanish, Telugu, Turkish), and it contains 1,100 essays for each native language. In addition, the essay topics are balanced, and the number of topics is 8.

In the closed track, we tackle feature selection for increasing accuracy. We use a feature selection method based on the frequency of each feature (e.g., document frequency, TF-IDF).

In the open tracks, to address the problem of imbalanced data, we tried two approaches: **Capping** and **Sampling** data in order to balance the size of training data.

In this paper, we describe our system and experimental results. Section 2 describes the features we used in the system for NLI. Section 3 and Section 4 describe the systems for closed track and open track in NLI Shared Task 2013. Section 5 describes the results for NLI Shared Task 2013. Section 6 describes the experimental result for 10-fold cross validation on the data set used by Tetreault et al. (2012).

2 Features used in all tracks

In this section, we describe the features in our systems. We formulate NLI as a multiclass classification task. Following previous work, we use LIBLINEAR [2] for the classification tool and tune the C parameter using grid-search.

We select the features based on previous work (Brooke and Hirst, 2012; Tetreault et al., 2012). All features used are binary. We treated the features as shown in Table 1. The example of features in Table 1 shows the case whose input is "I think not a really difficult question".

We use a special symbol for the beginning and end of sentence (or word) for bigrams and trigrams. For surface forms, we lowercased all words. POS, POS-function and dependency features are extracted

[1]http://www.lextek.com/manuals/onix/stopwords1.html
[2]http://www.csie.ntu.edu.tw/~cjlin/liblinear/

Name	Description	Example	
Word N-gram (N=1,2)	Surface form of the word.	N=1 N=2	i, think, not BOS i, i think
POS N-gram (N=2,3)	POS tags of the word.	N=2 N=3	BOS PRP, PRP VBP BOS PRP VBP, PRP VBP RB
Character N-gram (N=2,3)		N=2 N=3	^ t, t h, hi, in, nk, k$ ^ t h, t h i
POS-function N-gram (N=2,3)	We use surface form for words in stop word list [1], otherwise we use POS form.	N=2 N=3	RB difficult, difficult NN RB difficult NN
Dependency	the surface and relation name the surface and the dependend token's surface the surface, relation name and the dependend token's surface		(i, nsubj) (think, i) (nsubj, i, think)
Tree substitution grammer	Fragments of TSG		(PRP_UNK-INITC-KNOWNLC) (VB_think) (NP_RB_DT_ADJP_NN) (JJ_UNK-LC)

Table 1: All features for native language identification.

using the Stanford Parser 2.0.2 [3].

We use tree substitution grammars as features. TSGs are generalized context-free grammars (CFGs) that allow nonterminals to re-write to tree fragments. The fragments reflect both syntactic and surface structures of a given sentence more efficiently than using several CFG rules. In practice, efficient Bayesian approaches have been proposed in prior work (Post and Gildea, 2009). In terms of the application of TSG to NLI task, (Swanson and Charniak, 2012) have shown a promising result. Post (2011) also uses TSG to judge grammaticality of a sentence written by language learners. With these previous findings in mind, we also extract TSG rules. We use the training settings and public software from Post (2011)[4], obtaining 21,020 unique TSG fragments from the training dataset of the TOEFL-11 corpus.

3 Closed Track

In this section, we describe our system for the closed track. We use the tools and features described in Section 2.

In our system, feature selection is performed using a measure based on frequency. Although Tsur and Rappoport (2007) used TF-IDF, they use it to decrease the influence of topic bias rather than for increasing accuracy. Brooke and Hirst (2012) used document frequency for feature selection, however it does not affect accuracy.

We use the native language frequency (hereafter we refer to this as NLF). NLF is the number of native languages a feature appears in. Thus, NLF takes values from 1 to 11. Figure 1 shows an example of NLF. The word bigram feature "in Japan" appears only in essays of which the learners' native language is Japanese, therefore the NLF is 1.

The assumption behind using this feature is that a feature which appears in all native languages affects NLI less, while a feature which appears in few native language affects NLI more. The features whose NLFs are 11 include e.g. "there are", "PRP VBP" and "a JJ NN". Table 2 shows some examples of the features appearing in only 1 native language in the TOEFL-11 corpus. The features include place-name or company name such as "tokyo", "korea", "samsung", which are certainly specific for some native language.

[3]http://nlp.stanford.edu/software/lex-parser.shtml
[4]https://github.com/mjpost/post2011judging

Native Language		
Chinese	Japanese	Korean
carry more	this : NN	samsung
i hus become	of tokyo	of korea
JJ whole and	when i worked	debatable whether
striking conclusion	usuful	NN VBG whether
traffic tools	oppotunity for	in thesedays

Table 2: Example of feature appearing in 1 native language for Chinese, Japanese and Korean

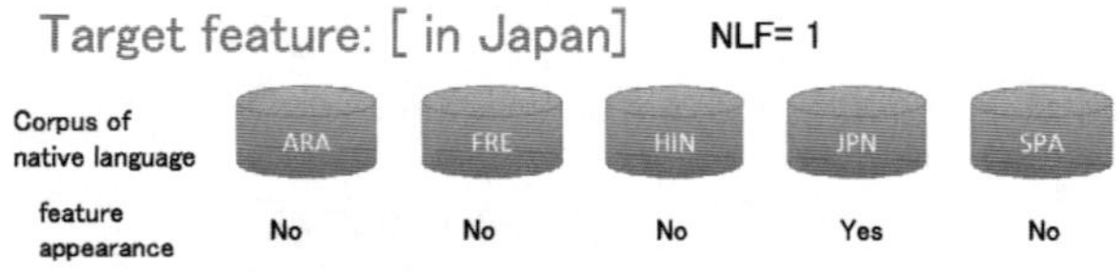

Figure 1: Example of native language frequency

Native Language	# of articles
Japanese	258,320
Mandarin	48,364
Korean	31,188
Spanish	5,106
Italian	2,589
Arabic	1,549
French	1,168
German	832
Turkish	504
Hindi	223
Telugu	19

Table 3: Distribution of native languages in Lang-8 corpus

4 Open tracks

4.1 Lang-8 corpus

For the open tracks, we used Lang-8 as a source to create a learner corpus tagged with the native languages of learners. Lang-8 is a language learning social networking service. [5] Users write articles in their non-native languages and native speakers correct them. We used all English articles written through the end of 2012. We removed all sentences which contain non-ASCII characters. [6]

Almost all users register their native language on the site. We regard users' registered native language as the gold label for each article. We split the learner corpus extracted from Lang-8 into sub-corpora by the native languages. The numbers of articles in all corpora are summarized in Table 3. Unfortunately, some sub-corpora are too small to train the model. For example, the Telugu corpus has only 19 articles.

In order to balance the size of the training data, we tried two approaches: **Capping** and **Sampling**. We confirmed in preliminary experiments that the model with these approaches work better than the model with the original sized data.

Capping

In this approach, we limit the size of a sub-corpus for training to N articles. For a sub-corpus which contains over N articles, we randomly extract articles up to N. We set $N = 5000$ and adapt this approach for Run 1 and Run 3 in the open tracks.

Sampling

In this approach, we equalize the size of all sub-corpora. For corpora which contain less than N articles, we randomly copy articles until their size becomes N. We set $N = 5000$ and adapt this approach for Run 2 and Run 4 in the open tracks.

4.2 Models

We compared two approaches with baseline features and all features.

The models in Run 1 and Run 3 were trained with the data created by the Capping approach, and the models in Run 2 and Run 4[7] were trained by the Sampling approach.

We used only word N-grams ($N = 1, 2$) as baseline features. As extra features we used the following features.

[5] http://lang-8.com/

[6] Some users also add translation in their native languages for correctors' reference.

[7] We did not have time to train the model for Run 4 in the open 1 track.

- POS N-grams ($N = 2, 3$)
- dependency
- character N-grams ($N = 2, 3$)

In open track 2, we also add the TOEFL-11 dataset to the training data for all runs.

5 Result for NLI shared Task 2013

Table 4 shows the results of our systems for NLI Shared Task. Chance accuracy is 0.09. All results outperform random guessing.

5.1 Closed track

In the closed track, we submitted 5 runs. Run 1 is the system using only word 1,2-grams features. Run 2 is the system using all features with NLF feature selection (1 < NLF < 11). Run 3 is the system using word 1,2-grams and POS 2,3-grams features. Run 4 is the system using word 1,2-grams, POS 2,3-grams, character 2,3-grams and dependency features without parameter tuning. Run 5 is the system using word 1,2-grams without parameter tuning. The method using the feature selection method we proposed achieved the best performance of our systems.

5.2 Open tracks

Comparison of the two data balancing approaches

In open track 1, the method of "Sampling" outperforms that of "Capping" (Run 2 > Run 1). This means even duplicated training data can improve the performance.

On the other hand, in open track 2, "Capping" works better than "Sampling" (Run 1 > Run 2 and Run 3 > Run 4). In the first place, the models trained with both Lang-8 data and TOEFL data do not perform better than ones trained with only TOEFL data. This means the less Lang-8 data we use, the better performance we obtain.

Comparison on two feature sets

In open track 1, adding extra features seems to have a bad influence because the result of Run 3 is worse than that of Run 1. This may be because Lang-8 data is out of domain of the test corpus (TOEFL).

	Closed	Open 1	Open 2
Run	Accuracy	Accuracy	Accuracy
1	0.811	0.337	0.699
2	*0.817	0.356	0.661
3	0.808	0.285	0.703
4	0.771	-	0.665
5	0.783	-	-

Table 4: Result for systems which submitted in NLI 2013 *We re-evaluated the Run2 because we submitted the Run1 with the same output as Run2.

In open track 2, adding extra features makes the performance better (Run 3 > Run 1, Run 4 > Run 2). In-domain TOEFL data seem to be effective for training with extra features. In order to improve the result with extra features in open track 2, domain adaptation may be effective.

6 Experiment and Result for 10 fold Cross-Validation

We conducted an experiment using 10-fold cross validation on the data set used by Tetreault et al. (2012). Table 5 shows the results for different feature set. The table consists of 3 blocks; the first block is results of the system using 1 feature, the second block is the result of the system using word 1,2-grams feature and another feature, and the third block is the result of the system using word 1,2-grams and more features.

In the first block results, the system using the word 1,2-grams feature achieved 0.8075. It is the highest accuracy in the first block, and third highest accuracy in the results of Table 5. From the second block of results, adding an extra feature does not improve accuracy, however in the third block the systems in (14) and (15) outperform the system using only word 1,2-grams.

Table 6 shows the results of using feature selection by NLF. The table consists of 3 blocks; the first block is the results of the system using features whose NLF is smaller than N (N = 11, 10, 9, 8), the second block is the results of the system using features whose NLF is greater than N (N = 1, 2, 3, 4), and the third block is the results of the system using features whose NLF is smaller than 11 and greater than N (N = 1, 2, 3, 4).

The best accuracy is achieved by excluding fea-

	Feature	Accuracy
(1)	Word 1,2-gram	0.8075
(2)	POS 2,3-gram	0.5555
(3)	POS,Function 2,3-gram	0.7080
(4)	Chracter 2,3-gram	0.6678
(5)	Dependency	0.7236
(6)	Tree substitution grammar	0.6455
(7)	1 + 2	0.7825
(8)	1 + 3	0.7913
(9)	1 + 4	0.7953
(10)	1 + 5	0.8020
(11)	1 + 6	0.7999
(12)	1 + 2 + 3	0.7849
(13)	1 + 2 + 3 + 4	0.8000
(14)	1 + 2 + 3 + 4 + 5	**0.8097**
(15)	ALL	0.8088

Table 5: 10-fold cross validation results for each feature

tures whose NLF is 1 or 11. While the results of the first block and the second block are intuitive, the results of the third block are not (looking at the second block of Table 6, excluding features whose NLF is greater than N (1, 2, 3, 4) reduces accuracy). One possible explanation is that features whose NLF is 1 includes features that rarely appear in the training corpus.

	Accuracy
NLF < 11	0.8176
NLF < 10	0.8157
NLF < 9	0.8123
NLF < 8	0.8098
1 < NLF	0.8062
2 < NLF	0.8062
3 < NLF	0.8057
4 < NLF	0.8053
1 < NLF < 11	**0.8209**
2 < NLF < 11	0.8206
3 < NLF < 11	0.8201
4 < NLF < 11	0.8195

Table 6: 10-fold cross validation results using feature selection by NLF. (feature selection is not applied to word N-grams features.)

7 Conclusion

In this paper, we described our systems for the NLI Shared Task 2013. We tried feature selection using native language frequency for the closed track and Capping and the Sampling data to balance the size of training data for the open tracks. The feature selection we proposed improves the performance for NLI. The system using our feature selection achieved 0.817 on the test data of NLI Shared Task and 0.821 using 10-fold cross validation. While the Sampling system outperformed Capping system for open track 1, the Capping system outperformed Sampling system in open track 2 (because it reduced the amount of out of domain data).

References

Daniel Blanchard, Joel Tetreault, Derrick Higgins, Aoife Cahill, and Martin Chodorow. 2013. Toefl11: A corpus of non-native english. Technical report, Educational Testing Service.

Julian Brooke and Graeme Hirst. 2011. Native language detection with 'cheap' learner corpora. In *Proceedings of LCR 2011*.

Julian Brooke and Graeme Hirst. 2012. Robust, lexicalized native language identification. In *Proceedings of COLING 2012*, pages 391–408.

Serhiy Bykh and Detmar Meurers. 2012. Native language identification using recurring n-grams – investigating abstraction and domain dependence. In *Proceedings of COLING 2012*, pages 425–440.

Matt Post and Daniel Gildea. 2009. Bayesian Learning of a Tree Substitution Grammar. In *Proceedings of the ACL-IJCNLP 2009*, pages 45–48.

Matt Post. 2011. Judging Grammaticality with Tree Substitution Grammar Derivations. In *Proceedings of ACL 2011*, pages 217–222.

Ben Swanson and Eugene Charniak. 2012. Native Language Detection with Tree Substitution Grammars. In *Proceedings of ACL 2012*, pages 193–197.

Joel Tetreault, Daniel Blanchard, Aoife Cahill, and Martin Chodorow. 2012. Native tongues, lost and found: Resources and empirical evaluations in native language identification. In *Proceedings of COLING 2012*, pages 2585–2602.

Joel Tetreault, Daniel Blanchard, and Aoife Cahill. 2013. A report on the first native language identification shared task. In *Proceedings of the Eighth Workshop on Building Educational Applications Using NLP*.

Oren Tsur and Ari Rappoport. 2007. Using classifier features for studying the effect of native language on the choice of written second language words. In *Proceedings of CACLA*, pages 9–16.

Sze-Meng Jojo Wong and Mark Dras. 2011. Exploiting parse structures for native language identification. In *Proceedings of EMNLP 2011*, pages 1600–1610.

Sze-Meng Jojo Wong, Mark Dras, and Mark Johnson. 2011. Topic modeling for native language identification. In *Proceedings of the Australasian Language Technology Association Workshop 2011*, pages 115–124.

Cognate and Misspelling Features for Natural Language Identification

Garrett Nicolai, Bradley Hauer, Mohammad Salameh, Lei Yao, Grzegorz Kondrak
Department of Computing Science
University of Alberta
Edmonton, AB, Canada
{nicolai,bmhauer,msalameh,lyao1,gkondrak}@ualberta.ca

Abstract

We apply Support Vector Machines to differentiate between 11 native languages in the 2013 Native Language Identification Shared Task. We expand a set of common language identification features to include cognate interference and spelling mistakes. Our best results are obtained with a classifier which includes both the cognate and the misspelling features, as well as word unigrams, word bigrams, character bigrams, and syntax production rules.

1 Introduction

As the world becomes more inter-connected, an increasing number of people devote effort to learning one of the languages that are dominant in the global community. English, in particular, is studied in many countries across the globe. The goal is often related to increasing one's chances to obtain employment and succeed professionally. The language of work-place communication is often not a speaker's native language (L1) but their second language (L2). Speakers and writers of the same L1 can sometimes be identified by similar L2 errors. The weak Contrastive Analysis Hypothesis (Jarvis and Crossley, 2012) suggests that these errors may be a result of L1 causing linguistic interference; that is, common tendencies of a speaker's L1 are superimposed onto their L2. Native Language Identification, or NLI, is an attempt to exploit these errors in order to identify the L1 of the speaker from texts written in L2.

Our group at the University of Alberta was unfamiliar with the NLI research prior to the announcement of a shared task (Tetreault et al., 2013). However, we saw it as an opportunity to apply our expertise in character-level NLP to a new task. Our goal was to propose novel features, and to combine them with other features that have been previously shown to work well for language identification.

In the end, we managed to define two feature sets that are based on spelling errors made by L2 writers. Cognate features relate a spelling mistake to cognate interference with the writer's L1. Misspelling features identify common mistakes that may be indicative of the writer's L1. Both feature sets are meant to exploit the Contrastive Analysis Hypothesis, and benefit from the writer's L1 influence on their L2 writing.

2 Related Work

Koppel et al. (2005b) approach the NLI task using Support Vector Machines (SVMs). They experiment with features such as function-word unigrams, rare part-of-speech bigrams, character bigrams, and spelling and syntax errors. They report 80% accuracy across 5 languages. We further investigate the role of word unigrams and spelling errors in native language identification. We consider not only function words, but also content words, as well as word bigrams. We also process spell-checking errors with a text aligner to find common spelling errors among writers with the same L1.

Tsur and Rappoport (2007) also use SVMs on the NLI task, but limit their feature set to character bigrams. They report 65% accuracy on 5 languages, and hypothesize that the choice of words when writing in L2 is strongly affected by the phonology of their L1. We also consider character bigrams in our feature set, but combine them with a number of other features.

Wong and Dras (2011) opt for a maximum entropy classifier, and focus more on syntax errors than lexical errors. They find that syntax tree production rules help their classifier in a seven language classification task. They only consider non-lexicalized rules, and rules with function words. In contrast, we consider both lexicalized and non-lexicalized production rules, and we include content words.

Bergsma et al. (2012) consider the NLI task as a sub-task of the authorship attribution task. They focus on the following three questions: (1) whether the native language of the writer of a paper is English, (2) what is the gender of the writer, and (3) whether a paper is a conference or workshop paper. The authors conclude that syntax aids the native language classification task, further motivating our decision to use part-of-speech n-grams and production rules as features for our classifier. Furthermore, the authors suggest normalizing text to reduce sparsity, and implement several meta-features that they claim aid the classification.

3 Classifier

Following Koppel et al. (2005b) and others, we perform classification with SVMs. We chose the SVM-Multiclass package, a version of the SVM-light package(Joachims, 1999) specifically modified for multi-class classification problems. We use a linear kernel, and two hyperparameters that were tuned on the development set: the c soft-margin regularization parameter, which measures the tradeoff between training error and the size of the margin, and ϵ, which is used as a stopping criterion for the SVM. C was tuned to a value of 5000, and epsilon to a value of 0.1.

4 Features

As features for our SVM, we used a combination of features common in the literature and new features developed specifically for this task. The features are listed in the following section.

4.1 Word n-grams

Following previous work, we use word n-grams as the primary feature set. We normalize the text before selecting n-grams using the method of Bergsma et al. (2012). In particular, all digits are replaced with a representative '0' character; for example, '22' and '97' are both represented as '00'. However, unlike Koppel et al. (2005b), we incorporate word bigrams in addition to word unigrams, and utilize both function words and content words.

4.1.1 Function Words

Using a list of 295 common function words, we reduce each document to a vector of values representing their presence or absence in a document. All other tokens in the document are ignored. When constructing vectors of bigrams, any word that is not on the list of function words is converted to a placeholder token. Thus, most of our function-word bigrams consist of a single function word preceded or followed by a placeholder token.

4.1.2 Content Words

Other than the normalization mentioned in Section 4.1, all tokens in the documents are allowed as possible word unigrams. No spelling correction is used for reducing the number of word n-grams. Furthermore, we consider all token unigrams that occur in the training data, regardless of their frequency.

An early concern with token bigrams was that they were both large in number, and sparse. In an attempt to reduce the number of bigrams, we conducted experiments on the development set with different numbers of bigrams that exhibited the highest information gain. It was found that using all combinations of word bigrams improved predictive accuracy the most, and did not lead to a significant cost to the SVM. Thus, for experiments on the test set, all token bigrams that were encountered in the training set were used as features.

4.2 Character n-grams

Following Tetreault et al. (2012), we utilize all character bigrams that occur in the training data, rather than only the most frequent ones. However, where the literature uses either binary indicators or relative frequency of bigrams as features, we use a modified form of the relative frequency in our classifier.

In a pre-processing step, we calculate the average frequency of each character bigram across all training documents. Then, during feature extraction, we again determine the relative frequency of each character bigram across documents. We then use binary features to indicate if the frequency of a bigram is higher than the average frequency. Experiments conducted on the development set showed that although this modified frequency was out-performed by the original relative frequency on its own, our method performed better when further features were incorporated into the classifier.

4.3 Part-of-speech n-grams

All documents are tagged with POS tags using the Stanford parser (Klein and Manning, 2003), From the documents in the training data, a list of all POS bigrams was generated, and documents were represented by binary indicators of the presence or absence of a bigram in the document. As with character bigrams, we did not simply use the most common bigrams, but rather considered all bigrams that appeared in the training data.

4.4 Syntax Production Rules

After generating syntactic parse trees with the Stanford Parser. we extract all possible production rules from each document, including lexicalized rules. The features are binary; if a production rule occurs in an essay, its value is set to 1, and 0 otherwise. For each language, we use information gain for feature selection to select the most informative production rules as suggested by Wong and Dras (2011). Experiments on the development set indicated that the information gain is superior to raw frequency for the purpose of syntax feature selection. Since the accuracy increased as we added more production rules, the feature set for final testing includes all production rules encountered in the training set. The majority of the rules are of the form *POS* $\Rightarrow$ *terminal*. We hypothesized that most of the information contained in these rules may be already captured by the word unigram features. However, experiments on the development set suggested that the lexicalized rules contain information that is not captured by the unigrams, as they led to an increase in predictive accuracy.

4.5 Spelling Errors

Koppel et al. (2005a) suggested spelling errors could be helpful as writers might be affected by the spelling convention in their native languages. Moreover, spelling errors also reflect the pronunciation characteristics of the writers' native languages. They identified 8 types of spelling errors and collected the statistics of each error type as their features. Unlike their approach, we focus on the specific spelling errors made by the writers because 8 types may be insufficient to distinguish the spelling characteristics of writers from 11 different languages. We extract the spelling error features from character-level alignments between the misspelled word and the intended word. For example, if the word *abstract* is identified as the intended spelling of a misspelling *abustruct*, the character alignments are as follows:

a	bu	s	t	ru	ct
|	|	|	|	|	|
a	b	s	t	ra	ct

Only the alignments of the misspelled parts, i.e. *(bu,b)* and *(ru,ra)* in this case, are used as features. The spell-checker we use is *aspe*ll[1], and the character-level alignments are generated by *m2m-aligner* (Jiampojamarn et al., 2007).

4.6 Cognate Interference

Cognates are words that share their linguistic origin. For example, English *become* and German *bekommen* have evolved from the same word in a common ancestor language. Other cognates are words that have been transfered between languages; for example, English *system* comes from the Greek word $\sigma\upsilon\sigma\tau\eta\mu\alpha$ via Latin and French. On average, pairs of cognates exhibit higher orthographic similarity than unrelated translation pairs (Kondrak, 2013).

Cognate interference may cause an L1-speaker to use a cognate word instead of a correct English translation (for example, *become* instead of *get*). Another instance of cognate interference is misspelling of an English word under the influence of the L1 spelling (Table 1).

We aim to detect cognate interference by identifying the cases where the cognate word is closer to

[1]http://aspell.net

Misspelling	Intended	Cognate
developped	*developed*	*developpé (Fre)*
exemple	*example*	*exemple (Fre)*
organisation	*organization*	*organisation (Ger)*
conzentrated	*concentrated*	*konzentrierte (Ger)*
comercial	*commercial*	*comercial (Spa)*
sistem	*system*	*sistema (Spa)*

Table 1: Examples of cognate interference in the data.

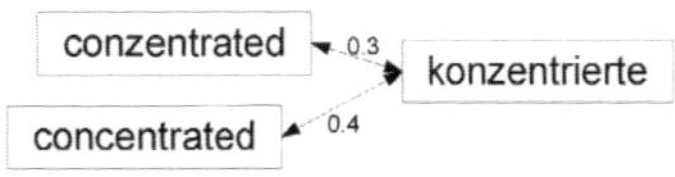

Figure 1: A cognate word influencing the spelling.

the misspelling than to the intended word (Figure 1). We define one feature to represent each language L, for which we could find a downloadable bilingual English-L dictionary. We use the following algorithm:

1. For each misspelled English word m found in a document, identify the most likely intended word e using a spell-checking program.

2. For each language L:

   (a) Look up the translation f of the intended word e in language L.

   (b) Compute the orthographic edit distance D between the words.

   (c) If $D(e, f) < t$ then f is assumed to be a cognate of e.

   (d) If f is a cognate and $D(m, f) < D(e, f)$ then we consider it as a clue that $L = L1$.

We use a simple method of computing orthographic distance with threshold $t = 0.58$ defined as the baseline method by Bergsma and Kondrak (2007). However, more accurate methods of cognate identification discussed in that paper could also be used.

Misspellings can betray cognate interference even if the misspelled word has no direct cognate in language L1. For example, a Spanish speaker might spell the word *quick* as *cuick* because of the existence of numerous cognates such as *question/cuestión*. Our misspelling features can detect such phenomena at the character level; in this case, *qu:cu* corresponds to an individual misspelling feature.

4.7 Meta-features

We included a number of document-specific *meta-features* as suggested by Bergsma et al. (2012): the average number of words per sentence, the average word length, as well as the total number of characters, words, and sentences in a document. We reasoned that writers from certain linguistic backgrounds may prefer many short sentences, while other writers may prefer fewer but longer sentences. Similarly, a particular linguistic background may influence the preference for shorter or longer words.

5 Results

The dataset used for experiments was the TOEFL11 Non-Native English Corpus (Blanchard et al., 2013). The dataset was split into three smaller datasets: the Training set, consisting of 9900 essays evenly distributed across 9 languages, the Development set, which contained a further 1100 essays, and the Test set, which also contained 1100 essays. As the data had a staggered release, we used the data differently. We further split the Training set, with a split of 80% for training, and 10% for development and testing. We then used the Development set as a held-out test set. For held-out testing, the classifier was trained on all data in the Training set, and for final testing, the classifier was trained on all data in both the Training and Development sets.

We used four different combinations of features for our task submissions. The results are shown in Table 2. We include the following accuracy values: (1) the results that we obtained on the Development set before the Test data release, (2) the official Test set results provided by the organizers (Tetreault et al., 2013), (3) the actual Test set results, and (4) the mean cross-validation results (for submissions 1 and 3). The difference between the official and the actual Test set results is attributed to two mistakes in our submissions. In submission 1, the feature lists used for training and testing did not match. In submissions 3 and 4, only non-lexicalized syntax production rules were used, whereas our intention was to use all of them.

No.	Features	Dev	Org	Test	CV
1	Base	82.0	61.2	80.4	58.2
2	– cont. words	67.4	68.7	68.7	–
3	+ char	81.4	80.3	81.7	58.5
4	+ char + meta	81.2	80.0	80.8	–

Table 2: Accuracy of our submissions.

All four submissions used the following base combination of features:

- word unigrams
- word bigrams
- error alignments
- syntax production rules
- word-level cognate interference features

In addition, submission 3 includes character bigrams, while submission 4 includes both character bigrams and meta-features. In submission 2, only function words are used, with the exclusion of content words.

Our best submission, which achieves 81.73% accuracy on the Test set, includes all features discussed in Section 4 except POS bigrams. Early tests indicated that any gains obtained with POS bigrams were absorbed by the production rules, so they were excluded form the final experiments. Character bigrams help on the Test set but not on the Development set. The meta-features decrease accuracy on both sets. Finally, the content words dramatically improve accuracy. The reason we included a submission which did not use content words is that it is a common practice in previous work. In our analysis of the data, we found content words that were highly indicative of the language of the writer. Particularly, words and phrases which contained the speaker's home country were useful in predicting the language. It should be noted that this correspondence may be dependent upon the prompt given to the writer. Furthermore, it may lead to false positives for L1 speakers who live in multi-lingual countries.

5.1 Confusion Matrix

We present the confusion matrix for our best submission in Table 5.1. The highest number of incorrect classifications are between languages that are either linguistically or culturally related (Jarvis and Crossley, 2012). For example, Korean is often misclassified as Japanese or Chinese. The two languages are not linguistically related to Korean, but both have historically had cultural ties with Korean. Likewise, while Hindi and Telugu are not related linguistically, they are both spoken in the same geographic area, and speakers are likely to have contact with each other.

	A	C	F	G	H	I	J	K	S	T	Tu
ARA	83	0	0	0	2	2	2	1	4	5	1
CHI	1	81	2	0	1	0	8	6	1	0	0
FRE	6	0	82	2	1	3	0	0	1	0	5
GER	1	0	0	90	1	1	1	0	2	0	4
HIN	1	2	2	0	76	1	0	0	0	16	2
ITA	1	1	0	1	0	89	1	0	5	1	1
JPN	2	1	1	1	0	1	86	6	0	0	2
KOR	1	8	0	0	0	0	11	78	0	1	1
SPA	2	2	7	0	3	5	0	2	75	0	4
TEL	2	0	0	2	15	0	0	0	1	80	0
TUR	4	3	2	1	0	1	1	5	2	2	79

Table 3: Confusion Matrix for our best classifier.

Features	Test
Full system	81.7
w/o error alignments	81.3
w/o word unigrams	81.1
w/o cognate features	81.0
w/o production rules	80.6
w/o character bigrams	80.4
w/o word bigrams	76.7

Table 4: Accuracy of various feature combinations.

5.2 Ablation Study

Table 4 shows the results of an ablation experiment on our best-performing submission. The word bigrams contribute the most to the classification; their removal increases the relative error rate by 27%. The word unigrams contribute much less., This is unsurprising, as much of the information contained in the word unigrams is also contained in the bigrams. The remaining features are also useful. In particular, our cognate interference features, despite applying to only 4 of 11 languages, reduce errors by about 4%.

6 Conclusions and Future Work

We have described the system that we have developed for the NLI 2013 Shared Task. The system combines features that are prevalent in the literature with our own novel character-level spelling features and word cognate interference features. Most of the features that we experimented with appear to increase the overall accuracy, which contradicts the view that simple bag-of-words usually perform better than more complex feature sets (Sebastiani, 2002).

Our cognate features can be expanded by including languages that do not use the Latin script, such as Russian and Greek, as demonstrated by Bergsma and Kondrak (2007). We utilized bilingual dictionaries representing only four of the eleven languages in this task[2]; yet our cognate interference features still improved classifier accuracy. With more resources and with better methods of cognate identification, the cognate features have the potential to further contribute to native language identification.

Our error-alignment features can likewise be further investigated in the future. Currently, after analyzing texts with a spell-checker, we automatically accept the first suggestion as the correct one. In many cases, this leads to faulty corrections, and misleading alignments. By using context sensitive spell-checking, we can choose better corrections, and obtain information which improves classification.

This shared task was a wonderful introduction to Native Language Identification, and an excellent learning experience for members of our group,

References

Shane Bergsma and Grzegorz Kondrak. 2007. Alignment-based discriminative string similarity. In *Proceedings of the 45th Annual Meeting of the Association for Computational Linguistics*, pages 656–663.

Shane Bergsma, Matt Post, and David Yarowsky. 2012. Stylometric analysis of scientific articles. In *Proceedings of the 2012 Conference of the North American Chapter of the Association for Computational Linguistics: Human Language Technologies*, pages 327–337, Montréal, Canada.

Daniel Blanchard, Joel Tetreault, Derrick Higgins, Aoife Cahill, and Martin Chodorow. 2013. TOEFL11: A Corpus of Non-Native English. Technical report, Educational Testing Service.

Scott Jarvis and Scott Crossley, editors. 2012. *Approaching Language Transfer Through Text Classification: Explorations in the Detection-based Approach*, volume 64. Multilingual Matters Limited, Bristol, UK.

Sittichai Jiampojamarn, Grzegorz Kondrak, and Tarek Sherif. 2007. Applying many-to-many alignments and HMMs to letter-to-phoneme conversion. In *Proceedings of NAACL-HLT*, pages 372–379.

Thorsten Joachims. 1999. Making large-scale support vector machine learning practical. In *Advances in kernel methods*, pages 169–184. MIT Press.

Dan Klein and Christopher D. Manning. 2003. Accurate unlexicalized parsing. In *Proceedings of the 41st Annual Meeting on Association for Computational Linguistics-Volume 1*, pages 423–430.

Grzegorz Kondrak. 2013. Word similarity, cognation, and translational equivalence. To appear.

Moshe Koppel, Jonathan Schler, and Kfir Zigdon. 2005a. Automatically determining an anonymous author's native language. *Intelligence and Security Informatics*, pages 41–76.

Moshe Koppel, Jonathan Schler, and Kfir Zigdon. 2005b. Determining an author's native language by mining a text for errors. In *Proceedings of the eleventh ACM SIGKDD international conference on Knowledge discovery in data mining*, pages 624–628, Chicago, IL. ACM.

Fabrizio Sebastiani. 2002. Machine learning in automated text categorization. *ACM computing surveys (CSUR)*, 34(1):1–47.

Joel Tetreault, Daniel Blanchard, Aoife Cahill, and Martin Chodorow. 2012. Native tongues, lost and found: Resources and empirical evaluations in native language identification. In *Proceedings of COLING 2012*, pages 2585–2602, Mumbai, India.

Joel Tetreault, Daniel Blanchard, and Aoife Cahill. 2013. A report on the first native language identification shared task. In *Proceedings of the Eighth Workshop on Innovative Use of NLP for Building Educational Applications*, Atlanta, GA, USA.

Oren Tsur and Ari Rappoport. 2007. Using classifier features for studying the effect of native language on the choice of written second language words. In *Proceedings of the Workshop on Cognitive Aspects of Computational Language Acquisition*, pages 9–16, Prague, Czech Republic.

Sze-Meng Jojo Wong and Mark Dras. 2011. Exploiting parse structures for native language identification. In *Proceedings of the 2011 Conference on Empirical Methods in Natural Language Processing*, pages 1600–1610, Edinburgh, Scotland, UK.

[2]French, Spanish, German, and Italian.

Exploring Syntactic Representations for Native Language Identification

Ben Swanson
Brown University
Providence, RI
chonger@cs.brown.edu

Abstract

Tree Substitution Grammar rules form a large and expressive class of features capable of representing syntactic and lexical patterns that provide evidence of an author's native language. However, this class of features can be applied to any general constituent based model of grammar and previous work has done little to explore these options, relying primarily on the common Penn Treebank annotation standard. In this work we contrast the performance of syntactic features for Native Language Indentification using five different formalisms. The use of different formalisms captures complementary information from second language data, and can be used in combination to yield classification performance superior to any formalism taken on its own.

1 Introduction

Native Language Identification, the automatic determination of an author's native language (L1) from their writing in a second language (L2), follows a general trend of supervised classification using features extracted from text. These systems can be optimized by both classification algorithm selection and the integration of diverse feature sets, and in this work we focus on the latter.

Syntactic features have been shown to provide a strong discriminative signal of an author's native language (Wong and Dras, 2011; Swanson and Charniak, 2012), but little work has been done to explore the various options for representation of syntax of learner text. Many such representations exist, and are routinely employed to improve performance on the widely studied task of parsing the Penn Treebank. Furthermore, most techniques that prove widely successful at this task have publicly available implementations, making them very feasible options for NLI systems.

In this work we investigate the use of Tree Substitution Grammars as features for NLI, focusing on the implication of syntactic paradigm (constituent vs dependency grammar) and the addition of annotations that have proved useful in statistical parsing. A Tree Substitution Grammar (TSG) is an intuitive extension of the Context Free Grammar (CFG) that allows rewrite rules of arbitrary tree structure. Alternatively, a CFG can be seen as a TSG in which the rewrite rules obey the constraint that each is a tree structure of unit depth.

While a collection of parsed data can be potentially generated by a TSG that is exponential in the length of the text, recent techniques allow for the efficient induction of compact grammars (Cohn and Blunsom, 2010). At a high level, this technique employs the rich-get-richer dynamics of a Dirichlet Process to sample derivations for the trees in the training corpus: the more that a rule is used in other derivations, the more likely it is that we will choose it when sampling a derivation.

We follow previous work in stylometry with TSGs for the NLI in that we parse the entirety of the training data and use it to induce a compact TSG using the method described above.[1] We then use the

[1] An alternative method of note that we do not consider in this work is to induce TSG rules on hand-annotated data such as the Penn Treebank, as in Bergsma et al. (2012).

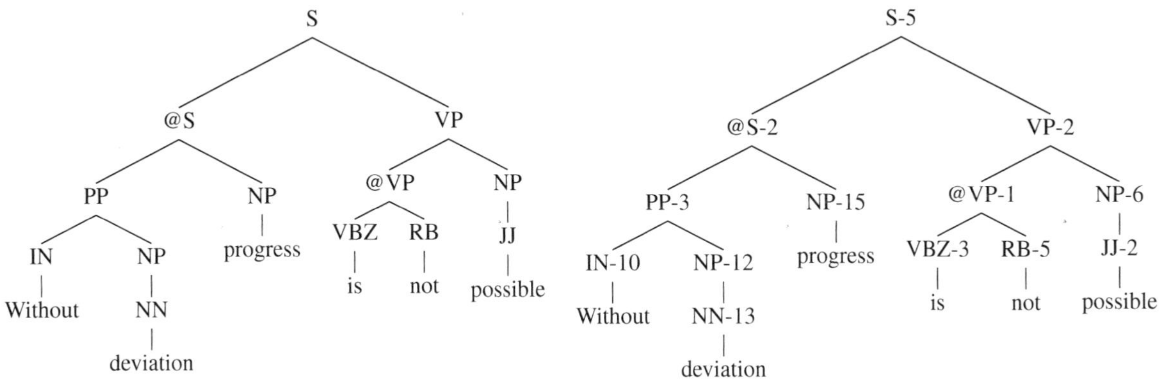

Figure 1: Sample parse trees produced by the Berkeley Parser. An example of what the tree might look like with split symbol annotations is shown on the right.

TSG rules as binary features for supervised classification such that the feature for a TSG rule is triggered on a document if that rule appears in the parse of some derivation of any of its sentences. This description purposefully treats the parsing of text as a black box whose input is plain text and whose output is any valid tree structure. Our work considers five alternatives for this black box, and evaluates the effect of this choice on the NLI Shared Task at the BEA Workshop of NAACL 2013 (Tetreault et al., 2013).

2 Syntactic Representations

We investigate five variations on the output of the parsing process. All five are easily produced by freely available Java software; two with the Berkeley Parser, two with the Stanford Parser, and one with a combination of both software packages.

2.1 Berkeley Constituent Parses

Our first representation reproduces previous work by using the output of the Berkeley Parser (Petrov et al., 2006), one of highest performing systems on the benchmark Penn Treebank task. The basic motivating principle involved is that the traditional nonterminal symbols used in Penn Treebank parsing are too coarse to satisfy the context free assumption of a CFG. To combat this, hierarchical latent annotations are induced that split a symbol into several subtypes, and a larger CFG is estimated on this set of split nonterminals. A sentence is parsed using this large CFG and each resulting symbol is mapped back to its original unsplit supertype to produce the final parse.

One important subtlety of the Berkeley Parser is its default binarization, which we leave intact in our downstream use of its parses. While binarization is normally motivated by the desired cubic complexity of parsing algorithms, it also benefits syntactic stylometry. Consider the nugget of wisdom from the great Frank Zappa shown on the left in Figure 1, in which artificially introduced binarization nodes are marked with the @ symbol.

The use of binarization allows us to capture patterns such as verb phrases that begin with "is not" independent of the following child constituents. The capabilities of TSG rules makes the use of binarization even more apt, as we can easily choose to recover the unbinarized pattern with a slightly larger fragment. This choice will be made in TSG induction based on the frequency with which the combination occurs, which intuitively aligns with our goal of choosing representative features.

The second form that we investigate is identical to the normal Berkeley Parser output, but with the split annotations used in parsing left intact, as shown the right of Figure 1. This parsed sentence shows how each nonterminal is annotated with a split category, and illustrates the potential advantages that this method affords. For example, consider the @VP node in the left-hand tree, whose subtree is generated with a CFG by first choosing to produce a VBZ and RB, and then by lexicalizing each independently. These two lexicalizations are not in fact independent, as can be seen by the combination of "is" with the RB "may", which is impossible although each are independently quite likely. Splitting the symbols as shown on the right allows us to create a special RB node that is most likely to produce "not" and VBZ node likely to produce "is". Their likely co-occurrence can then be modeled as shown by a rule with both specialized tags as children.

It is worth noting that this particular ability of split symbol grammars to coordinate lexical items is easily captured with the TSG rules that we induce on these parses, regardless of the presence of split symbols. The more orthogonal quality of these split grammars is their ability to categorize symbols that appear in similar syntactic situations. Consider that some adjectives are more likely to appear in "X is Y" sentences in the "Y" position, while some are more likely to be used directly to the left of nouns. A split symbol grammar handily captures this trait with a split POS tag, while a TSG cannot associate patterns containing different lexical items on its own.

2.2 Stanford Dependency Parses

The third and fourth syntactic models we employ are derived from dependency parses produced by the Stanford parser(Marneffe et al., 2006). In its standard form, a dependency parse is a directed tree in which each word except the special ROOT node has exactly one incoming edge and zero to many outgoing edges, where edges represent syntactic dependence. Arcs are labeled with the type of syntactic dependence that they indicate. Following convention, we represent each word in combination with its part of speech tag, as shown in the following example dependency parse.

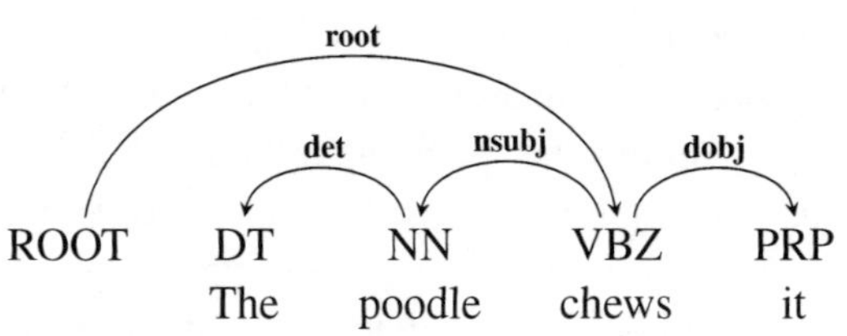

In order to apply the techniques of TSG induction to dependency parsed data, we implement a conversion from dependency tree to constituent form. The mechanics of this conversion are simple and illustrated in full by the following conversion of the dependency tree shown above, and are similar to transforms used in previous work in unsupervised dependency parsing(Carroll and Charniak, 1992).

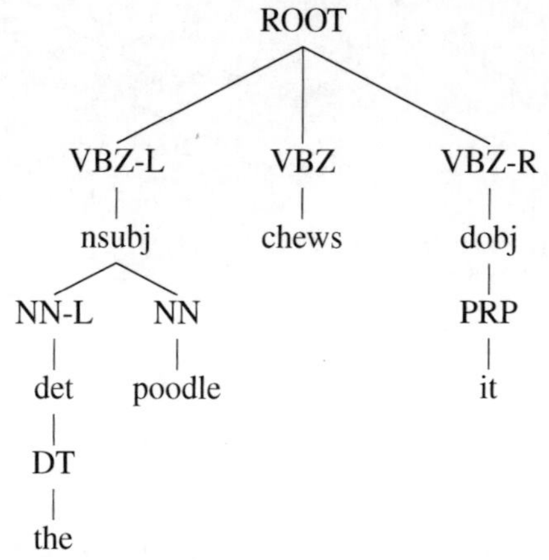

Note that it is always the case that the arc labels from the dependency parses are always produced by unary rules. This allows the simple removal of the nodes corresponding to arc labels, yielding our fourth syntactic model.

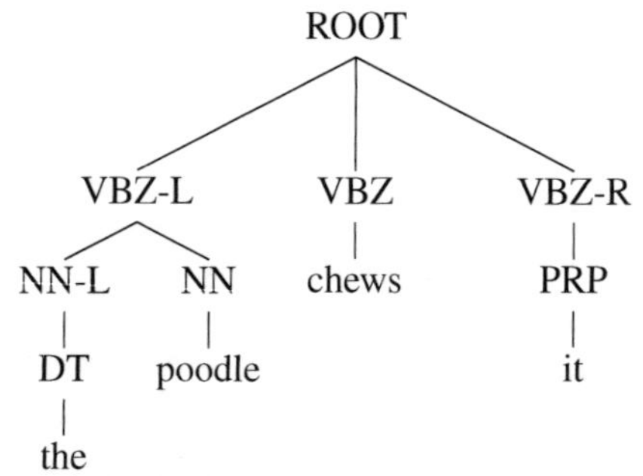

Those familiar with the Stanford Parser may be concerned that the dependency parses used here are determined by a deterministic transform of a constituent parse of Penn Treebank style, and then simply transformed back into constituent form. This is especially concerning when considering the second form in which arc labels have been removed; this form can be constructed directly from the Berkeley Parse form used above, and contains no additional information. Our motivation in the investigation of dependency parses is not that they offer new information, but that they are organized differently than constituent parses. When inducing a TSG, our ability to find a useful connections is impeded by physical distance between structures. In particular, in a dependency parse, the head of the subject and the verb are always contained in some TSG fragment made up of small number of CFG rules, five or four depending on the presence of arc labels. In constituent parses, the presence of modifying phrases can arbitrarily increase this distance.

2.3 Stanford Heuristic Annotations

Our final variation uses the annotations internal to the Stanford Penn Treebank parser, as presented in Klein and Manning (2003). These annotations are motivated in the same way as Berkeley Parser split states, but are deterministically applied to parse trees using linguistic motivations. Besides handling explicit tracking of binarization and parent annotation, several additional annotations are applied, such as the splitting of certain POS tags into useful categories and annotation of some nodes with their number of children or siblings.

For ease of implementation, we do not use the Stanford Parser itself to produce our trees, instead we used our results from the Berkeley Parser. The Stanford Parser annotations were then applied to these trees after binarization symbols were first collapsed. The following tree is an example of the actual annotations applied by this process, and includes a fair subset of the many annotation types that are used. The original symbol in each case is the leftmost string of capital letters in the resulting symbol strings shown.

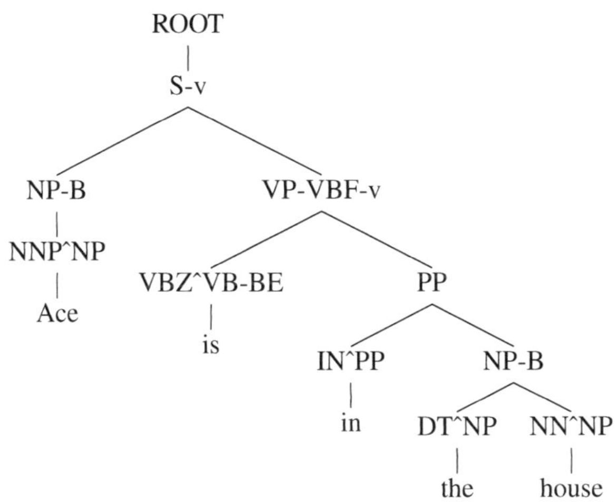

3 Experiments

We contrast the syntactic formalisms on the NLI shared task experimental setup for the NAACL 2013 BEA workshop. This new data set (Blanchard et al., 2013) consists of TOEFL essays drawn from speakers of 11 different L1 backgrounds. 9900 Essays were supplied as a training set, with an additional 1100 development set essays and 1100 test essays.

Previous work in NLI has relied heavily on the International Corpus of Learner English, but due to significant topic biases along L1 lines in this data set the explicit use of word tokens was frequently limited to a predetermined set of stopwords. With this in mind, the data set for the shared task was balanced across TOEFL essay prompts and proficiency levels. The result was that the participants in this task were not forced to limit the word tokens explicitly employed, with the hopes that mitigating factors had been minimized.

We prepared the data in the five forms described above and induced TSGs on each version of the parsed training set with the blocked sampling algorithm of Cohn and Blunsom (2010). The resulting rules were used as binary feature functions over documents indicating the presence of the rule in some derivation of sentence in that document. We used the Mallet implementation of a log-linear (MaxEnt) classifier with a zero mean Gaussian prior with variance .1 on the classifier's weights. Our results on the development set are shown in Figure 3.

While a range of performance is achieved, when we construct a classifier that simply averages the predictive distributions of all five methods we get better accuracy than any model on its own. We observed further evidence of the orthogonality of these methods by looking at pairs of formalisms and observing how many development set items were predicted correctly by one formalism and incorrectly by another. This was routinely around 10 percent of the development set in each direction for a given pair, implying that gains of up to at least 20 percent classification accuracy are possible with an expert system that approaches oracle selection of which formalism to use.

As our submission to the shared task, we used the Berkeley Parser output in isolation, the average of the five classifiers, and the weighted average of the classifiers using the optimal weights on the development set. The former two models use the development set as additional training data, which is one possible explanation of the slightly higher performance of the equally weighted average model. An-

	ARA	CHI	FRE	GER	HIN	ITA	JPN	KOR	SPA	TEL	TUR	P	R	F
ARA	76	2	4	1	2	2	2	1	4	3	3	76.8	76.0	76.4
CHI	2	86	0	1	1	0	4	4	1	0	1	81.1	86.0	83.5
FRE	2	1	77	3	2	6	2	1	5	1	0	82.8	77.0	79.8
GER	0	1	1	91	1	1	0	0	2	0	3	86.7	91.0	88.8
HIN	2	2	1	2	71	0	0	0	0	20	2	73.2	71.0	72.1
ITA	2	0	2	1	1	84	0	1	7	0	2	79.2	84.0	81.6
JPN	3	4	0	1	0	0	83	7	1	0	1	74.1	83.0	78.3
KOR	1	6	1	1	1	0	20	65	2	1	2	69.1	65.0	67.0
SPA	4	2	4	3	2	12	0	3	66	0	4	71.7	66.0	68.8
TEL	1	2	0	0	16	0	0	0	0	81	0	76.4	81.0	78.6
TUR	6	0	3	1	0	1	1	12	4	0	72	80.0	72.0	75.8

Figure 2: Confusion Matrix and per class results on the final test set evaluation using the evenly averaged model.

other explanation of note is that while the weight optimization was carried out with EM over the likelihood of the development set labels, this did not in correlate positively with classification accuracy; even as we optimized on the development set the accuracy in absolute classification of these items decreased slightly.

The confusion matrix for the evenly averaged model, our best performing system, is shown in Figure 2. The most frequently confused L1 pairs were Hindi and Telegu, Japanese and Korean, and Spanish and Italian. The similarity between Hindi and Telegu is particularly troubling, as they come from two completely different language families and their most obvious similarity is that they are both spoken primarily in India. This suggests that even though the TOEFL corpus has been balanced by topic that there is a strong geographical signal that is correlated with but not caused by native language.

	BP	BPS	DP	DPA	KM	AVG
Acc	74.5	69.3	72.4	73.5	73.5	77.3

Figure 3: The resulting classification accuracies on the development set for the various syntactic forms that we considered. The forms used are plain Berkeley Parses (BP), Berkeley Parses with split symbols (BPS), dependency parses (DP), dependency parses without arc labels (DPA), and the heuristic annotations from (Klein and Manning, 2003) (KM). When the predictive distributions of the five models are averaged (AVG), a higher accuracy is achieved.

	BP	AVG	AVG-EM
Acc	74.7	77.5	77.0

Figure 4: The classification accuracies obtained on the test data using the Berkeley parser output alone (BP), the arithmetic mean of all five predictive distributions (AVG) and the weighted mean using the optimal weights from the development set as determined with EM (AVG-EM)

4 Conclusion

In this work we open investigation of a generally unconsidered variable in syntactic stylometry: the actual syntactic formalism. We examine five potential candidates of which only one has been previously presented in the context of TSG features for NLI. These five formalisms cover both constituent and dependency grammars, and explore the possibility of split state annotations for constituent grammars and the inclusion of arc labels for dependency grammars. We find that the use of different grammar formalisms captures orthogonal information about an author's native language. Furthermore, the combination of different formalisms can be used to increase classification accuracy.

While our results are intriguing, they primarily serve as a proof of concept that syntactic stylometry can benefit from a range of representations and should not be taken as an exhaustive search for the best representations to use. Other syntactic forms exist, and even in our methods there are additional variables that can be adjusted.

One such variable is the number of splits used in

the Berkeley Parser when split states are included; the default number that we use in this work is 6, the optimal value for the parsing task, but this may be suboptimal as a representation for feature extraction. Binarization is another easily adjusted variable, with several available options in the literature. For example, binarization can be done that is aware of head attachment. Another option is to binarize more heavily, increasing the ability of TSG fragments to separate sister nodes and find frequent patterns.

Alternative syntactic forms not explored in this work are also available. These include well studied grammars such as Hierarchical Phrase Structure Grammars and Combinatory Categorial Grammars, and transforms that rearrange the tree such as the Left Corner Transform used in Roark and Johnson (1999). Furthermore, the use of the TSG as a feature extractor itself has the potential for extension to more powerful systems such as Tree Adjoining Grammars or Tree Insertion Grammars.

References

Shane Bergsma, Matt Post, and David Yarowsky. 2012. Stylometric Analysis of Scientific Articles. In *Proceedings of the 2012 Conference of the North American Chapter of the Association for Computational Linguistics: Human Language Technologies*, pages 327–337, Montréal, Canada, June. Association for Computational Linguistics.

Daniel Blanchard, Joel Tetreault, Derrick Higgins, Aoife Cahill, and Martin Chodorow. 2013. Toefl11: A corpus of non-native english. Technical report, Educational Testing Service.

Glenn Carroll and Eugene Charniak. 1992. Two experiments on learning probabilistic dependency grammars from corpora. Technical Report CS-92-16, Brown University, Providence, RI, USA.

Trevor Cohn and Phil Blunsom. 2010. Blocked inference in bayesian tree substitution grammars. In *ACL (Short Papers)*, pages 225–230.

Dan Klein and Christopher D. Manning. 2003. Accurate unlexicalized parsing. In *ACL*, pages 423–430.

Marie Catherine De Marneffe, Bill Maccartney, and Christopher D. Manning. 2006. Generating typed dependency parses from phrase structure parses. In *In Proc. Intl Conf. on Language Resources and Evaluation (LREC*, pages 449–454.

Slav Petrov, Leon Barrett, Romain Thibaux, and Dan Klein. 2006. Learning accurate, compact, and interpretable tree annotation. In *Proceedings of the 21st International Conference on Computational Linguistics and 44th Annual Meeting of the Association for Computational Linguistics*, pages 433–440, Sydney, Australia, July. Association for Computational Linguistics.

Brian Roark and Mark Johnson. 1999. Efficient probabilistic top-down and left-corner parsing. In *ACL*.

Benjamin Swanson and Eugene Charniak. 2012. Native Language Detection with Tree Substitution Grammars. In *Proceedings of the 50th Annual Meeting of the Association for Computational Linguistics (Volume 2: Short Papers)*, pages 193–197, Jeju Island, Korea, July. Association for Computational Linguistics.

Joel Tetreault, Daniel Blanchard, and Aoife Cahill. 2013. A report on the first native language identification shared task. In *Proceedings of the Eighth Workshop on Innovative Use of NLP for Building Educational Applications*, Atlanta, GA, USA, June. Association for Computational Linguistics.

Sze-Meng Jojo Wong and Mark Dras. 2011. Exploiting Parse Structures for Native Language Identification. In *Proceedings of the 2011 Conference on Empirical Methods in Natural Language Processing*, pages 1600–1610, Edinburgh, Scotland, UK., July. Association for Computational Linguistics.

Simple Yet Powerful Native Language Identification on TOEFL11

Ching-Yi Wu
University of Texas at Dallas
800 W Campbell Rd
Richardson, TX, USA
cxw120631@utdallas.edu

Po-Hsiang Lai
Emerging Technology Lab
Samsung R&D - Dallas
1301 Lookout Drive
Plano, TX, USA
s.lai@samsung.com

Yang Liu Vincent Ng
University of Texas at Dallas
800 W Campbell Rd
Richardson, TX, USA
yangl@hlt.utdallas.edu
vince@hlt.utdallas.edu

Abstract

Native language identification (NLI) is the task to determine the native language of the author based on an essay written in a second language. NLI is often treated as a classification problem. In this paper, we use the TOEFL11 data set which consists of more data, in terms of the amount of essays and languages, and less biased across prompts, i.e., topics, of essays. We demonstrate that even using word level n-grams as features, and support vector machine (SVM) as a classifier can yield nearly 80% accuracy. We observe that the accuracy of a binary-based word level n-gram representation (~80%) is much better than the performance of a frequency-based word level n-gram representation (~20%). Notably, comparable results can be achieved without removing punctuation marks, suggesting a very simple baseline system for NLI.

1 Introduction

Native language identification (NLI) is an emerging field in the natural language processing community and machine learning community (Koppel et al., 2005; Blanchard et al., 2013). It is a task to identify the native language (L1) of an author based on his/her texts written in a second language. The application of NLI can bring many benefits, such as providing a learner adaptive feedback of their writing errors based on the native language for educational purposes (Koppel et al., 2005; Blanchard et al., 2013).

NLI can be viewed as a classification problem. In a classification problem, a classifier is first trained using a set of training examples. Each training example is represented as a set of features, along with a class label. After a classifier is trained, the classifier is evaluated using a testing set (Murphy, 2012). Good data representation often yields a better classification performance (Murphy, 2012). Often time, the simpler representations might produce better performance. In this work, we demonstrate that a binary-based word level n-gram representation yields much better performance than a frequency-based word level n-gram representation. In addition, we observed that removing punctuation marks in an essay does not make too much difference in a classification performance.

The contributions of this paper are to demonstrate the usefulness of a binary-based word level n-gram representation, and a very simple baseline system without the need of removing punctuation marks and stop words.

This paper is organized as the following. In Section 2, we present related literatures. TOEFL11 data set is introduced in Section 3. In Section 4, our features and system design are described. The results are presented in Section 5, followed by conclusion in Section 6.

2 Related Work

The work by Koppel et al. (2005) is the first study to investigate native language identification. They use the International Corpus of Learner English (ICLE). They set up this task as a classification problem studied in machine learning community. They use three types of features: function words, character n-gram, errors and idiosyncrasies, e.g. spelling and grammatical errors. For errors and idiosyncrasies, they used Microsoft Office Word to detect those errors. Their features were evaluated on a subset of the ICLE corpus, including essays sampled from five native languages (Russian, Czech, Bulgarian, French and Spanish) with 10-fold cross validation. They achieve an accuracy of 80.2% by combining all of the features and using a support vector machine as the classification algorithm. In addition, Tsur and Rappoport (2007) show that using character n-gram only on the ICLE can yield an accuracy of 66%.

The work from Kochmar (2011) identifies an author's native language using error analysis. She suggests that writers with different native languages generate different grammatical error patterns. Instead of using ICLE, this work uses a different corpus, English learner essays from the Cambridge Learner Corpus. She uses SVM on manually annotated spelling and grammatical errors along with lexical features.

Most of the systems described in NLI literature reach good performance in predicting an author's native language, using character n-gram and part of speech n-gram as features (Blanchard et al., 2013). In recent years, various studies have started to look into complex features in order to improve the performance. Wong and Dras (2009) use contrastive analysis, a systematic analysis of structural similarities and differences in a pair of languages. A writer's native language influences the target language they aim to learn. They explore the impact of three English as Second Language (ESL) error types, subject-verb disagreement, noun-number disagreement and determiner errors, and use a subset of ICLE with 7 languages. However, although the determiner error feature seems useful, when it is combined with a baseline model of lexical features, the classification performance is not significantly improved (Wong and Dras, 2009).

Wong and Dras (2011) use complex features such as production rules from two parsers and reranking features into the classification framework, incorporating lexical features of Koppel et al. (2005). They achieve a classification performance of 81.71% on the 7-native-languages NLI, slightly better than 80.2% accuracy of the original Koppel et al. (2005).

Note that although the International Corpus of Learner English (ICLE) is used in most of the NLI studies, ICLE has been known to have fewer essays, and a skewed distribution toward topics of essays (Blanchard et al., 2013). In addition, even though there are 16 native languages in ICLE, as each language has different numbers of essays, most work often uses different subsets of 7 native languages, which makes comparison harder across different studies (Blanchard et al., 2013). The NLI shared task 2013 provides a new data set, namely the TOEFL11 (Blanchard et al., 2013), which addresses these issues. As previously discussed, complex features do not necessarily improve classification accuracy. In this work, we use TOEFL11 to investigate the classification performance using simple word n-gram based features.

3 Data

In this work, we use TOEFL11 as our corpus. TOEFL11 is a new data set for NLI (Blanchard et al., 2013). There are 11 native languages, including Arabic (ARA), Chinese (CHI), French (French), German (GER), Hindi (HIN), Italian (ITA), Japanese (JPN), Korean (KOR), Spanish (SPA), Telugu (TEL), and Turkish (TUR). Authors write essays based on 8 different topics in English. There are 1,100 essays for each language, and sampled from 8 different topics, i.e., prompts. Each essay is also annotated with an English proficiency level (low/medium/high) determined by assessment specialists. Among 12,100 essays, there are 9,900 essays in the training set, 1,100 essays in the development set, i.e., validation set in machine learning, and 1,100 essays in the testing set. In the training set and the development set, there are equal numbers of essays from each of the 11 native languages. By using TOEFL11, it makes our analysis less biased toward a specific topic of essays (Blanchard et al., 2013).

4 NIL System Design

In this section, we describe our NLI system, the features, and the classifier we use.

4.1 Data Preprocessing

Each essay is tokenized, and then capitalizations are removed. Note that we did not remove English stop words, which might be useful to discriminate the native language for a writer. For example, function words, which belong to stop words, such as '*the*', '*at*', '*which*', have been proven to be effective to distinguish native language for writers (Koppel et al., 2005). There are two settings: either punctuation marks are removed or kept. When punctuation marks are kept, they are viewed the same as word in constructing n-grams. For example, in the sentence "NLI is fun.", "fun ." is viewed as a bigram.

4.2 Features

In our system, word level n-grams are used to represent an essay. Previous studies have shown that word level n-grams are useful in determining the native language of a writer (Bykh and Meurers, 2012). One reasonable hypothesis is that non-native English writers with the same native languages tend to choose more similar words to express the same or similar concepts. In addition, the combination of a sequence of words might also be affected by the different native language of writers. Therefore, word n-gram is useful to distinguish the native language of a writer. Even though some previous studies have looked into using word level n-grams as features, how to use word level n-grams has not been explored too much yet on TOEFL11 corpus. To our knowledge, the most recent study by Blanchard et al. (2013) started to research the effect of different forms of word level n-gram representations.

There could be many ways to represent an essay by word level n-grams. One possible representation of an essay is to use the frequency of a specific word n-gram, i.e., the number of times a specific word n-gram appears in an essay divided by the number of times all word n-grams appear in an essay. In this representation, an essay is a vector whose elements are the frequency of different word n-grams in the essay. Another possible representation is to use binary representation, i.e., 1 indicates this word n-gram is in this essay, 0 indicates this word n-gram is not in this essay. One interesting question to ask is:

Which representation can be more informative to distinguish the native language of writers of essays?

Here we compare the performance of a frequency-based word level n-gram representation and a binary-based word level n-gram representation. We included all word level n-grams in the training set, without any frequency cutoff. For both binary-based and frequency-based representations, we run the experiments on the two settings: punctuation marks are either removed or kept.

In addition to word level n-grams, since TOEFL11 also consists of English proficiency levels evaluated by assessment experts, we also included it to test whether this feature might improve the classification performance. All of the features used in our system are summarized in Table 1. Besides each feature described above, we have also combined different features to test whether various combinations of features might improve the accuracy performance. Here, we simply aggregated different features, for example, all word level unigrams, combined with all word level bigrams.

4.3 Classifier

Previous literatures have used various methods such as Naïve Bayse, logistic regression and support vector machine on NLI problem. As it has been shown that when representing an essay in order to perform a classification task, it often results in an essay being represented in a very high dimensional space. Since support vector machine (SVM) is known to be adaptive when the feature dimension is high, we chose SVM as our classification algorithm. We also compared the results from Naïve Bayse for an experimental purpose and found that SVM is better. We use SVM-Light for our system (Joachims, 1999). We then train our SVM classifier on the training set (n=9900), and test the trained classifier on the testing set (n=1100).

5 Results and Discussions

5.1 Results

Table 1 and Table 2 show the accuracies on the testing set for the different feature sets, when punctuation marks are removed or kept respectively. As the results demonstrated, the accuracies of word level bigram are better than unigram using a binary-based representation. When combining word level unigram and bigram, the accuracy is improved in a binary-based representation. This is consistent when punctuations are either removed or kept. This observation is consistent with the existing NLI literatures: when combining word n-grams, it seems to improve the accuracy of the classifier, compared with a word n-gram alone. But we do not observe too much difference when punctuation marks are removed or kept, using both unigram and bigram. In fact, including punctuation marks lead to high accuracies in many scenarios, especially in unigram in a frequency-based representation, suggesting the usage of punctuation marks varies across native languages.

Features	Performance of Binary Word n-gram Representation	Performance of Freq. Word n-gram Representation
word unigram	70.91%	25.36%
word bigram	76.00%	17.64%
word unigram and word bigram	79.73%	23.36%

Table 1 Accuracy of Different Feature Sets, without Punctuation Marks

Features	Performance of Binary Word n-gram Representation	Performance of Freq. Word n-gram Representation
word unigram	70.18%	30.00%
word bigram	77.09%	18.73%
word unigram and word bigram	79.45%	28.73%

Table 2 Accuracy of Different Feature Sets, with Punctuation Marks

Table 3 shows the confusion matrix of classification performance, using unigram and bigram, in a binary-based representation when punctuation marks are removed. We observe that some of native languages, such as German, Italian, and Chinese, lead to better classification accuracy than for Korean, Spanish, and Arabic.

	ARA	CHI	FRE	GER	HIN	ITA	JPN	KOR	SPA	TEL	TUR	Precision	Recall	F-measure
ARA	**75**	1	5	3	1	3	1	1	3	4	3	78.9	75.0	76.9
CHI	3	**86**	0	0	1	0	5	4	0	0	1	81.9	86.0	83.9
FRE	1	1	**79**	7	3	4	2	0	1	0	2	77.5	79.0	78.2
GER	3	1	2	**87**	1	1	1	0	2	0	2	79.8	87.0	83.3
HIN	1	2	1	2	**77**	0	0	0	5	10	2	74.0	77.0	75.5
ITA	0	0	6	4	0	**85**	0	0	3	0	2	83.3	85.0	84.2
JPN	2	2	1	0	0	1	**86**	3	2	0	3	77.5	86.0	81.5
KOR	0	8	2	1	1	0	14	**72**	1	1	0	82.8	72.0	77.0
SPA	4	0	6	3	4	6	1	1	**70**	1	4	78.7	70.0	74.1
TEL	1	0	0	1	15	0	0	0	0	**82**	1	83.7	82.0	82.8
TUR	5	4	0	1	1	2	1	6	2	0	**78**	79.6	78.0	78.8

Average Performance: 79.7%. Precision, Recall, F-measures are in %.

Table 3 Confusion Matrix on Testing Set

5.2 Binary Based of Word N-Gram Representation

We observe that the accuracy of a binary-based word level n-gram representation in our system is significantly better than a frequency-based representation. This is similar to the result reported by Blanchard et al., (2013) in TOEFL11 corpus. The differences between their system and ours are that the system developed by Blanchard et al., (2013) used logistic regression with L1-regularzation, instead of SVM and they did not remove all punctuation marks and special characters.

This might imply that a frequency-based word n-gram representation do not capture the characteristics of the data. This might be because the data resides in a high dimension space, and the frequencies of word level n-grams would be skewed. In a future study, one might investigate a better representation form and other complex features that have a stronger interpretative power of the data.

5.3 Effects of Proficiency Level

In our results, we have included English proficiency level (low/medium/high) as a feature provided by assessment experts. However, we did not find a strong improvement in accuracies, for example, 79.13% using a binary-based word level n-grams when punctuation marks removed. We think this might be because only one feature will not dramatically change the accuracies. This may be due to the fact word n-grams have already contributed a large amount of features.

6 Conclusion

In this paper, we used a new data set, TOEFL11 to investigate NLI. In the most existing literatures, ICLE corpus was used. However, ICLE has fewer data and is known to be biased to topics of essays. The newly released corpus, TOEFL11 addresses these two drawbacks, which is useful for NLI community. Support vector machine (SVM) was used as a classifier in our system. We have demonstrated that a binary-based word level n-gram representation has resulted in a significantly better performance compared to a frequency-based n-gram representation. We observed that there is not much difference in classification accuracies when punctuation removed or kept, when combining both unigram and bigram. Interestingly, a frequency-based word unigram with punctuation marks outperforms than the case without punctuation marks, suggesting the potential of utilizing punctuation marks in NLI. In addition, English proficiency level has also been included in our feature set, but did not yield a significant improvement in accuracy. As most of the essays are represented in a high dimension space using word level n-grams, we are looking into feature selection to reduce dimensionality and how to represent those features in order to improve accuracy, as well as other features.

References

Blanchard, D., Tetreault, J., Higgins, D., Cahill, A., and Chodorow, M. 2013. *TOEFL11: A Corpus of Non-Native English.* Educational Testing Service.

Bykh, S. and Meurers, D. 2012. *Native Language Identification using Recurring n-grams - Investigating Abstraction and Domain Dependence.* In Proceedings of COLING 2012, 425-440, Mumbai, India. The COLING 2012 Organizing Committee.

Joachims, T. 1999. *Making large-Scale SVM Learning Practical.* Advances in Kernel Methods - Support Vector Learning, B. Schölkopf and C. Burges and A. Smola (ed.), MIT-Press.

Kochmar, E. 2011. *Identification of a writer's native language by error analysis.* Master's thesis, University of Cambridge.

Koppel, M., Schler, J., and Zigdon, K. 2005. *Automatically determining an anonymous author's native language.* In ISI, 209–217.

Murphy, K. P. 2012. Machine learning: a probabilistic perspective. MIT Press.

Tsur, O. and Rappoport, A. 2007. *Using classifier features for studying the effect of native language on the choice of written second language words.* In Proceedings of the Workshop on Cognitive Aspects of Computational Language Acquisition, 9–16, Prague, Czech Republic. Association for Computational Linguistics.

Wong, S.-M. J. and Dras, M. 2009. *Contrastive analysis and native language identification.* In Proceedings of the Australasian Language Technology Association Workshop 2009, 53–61, Sydney, Australia.

Wong, S.-M. J. and Dras, M. 2011. *Exploiting parse structures for native language identification.* In Proceedings of the 2011 Conference on Empirical Methods in Natural Language Processing, 1600–1610, Edinburgh, Scotland, UK. Association for Computational Linguistics.

Prompt-based Content Scoring for Automated Spoken Language Assessment

Keelan Evanini
Educational Testing Service
Princeton, NJ 08541, USA
kevanini@ets.org

Shasha Xie
Microsoft
Sunnyvale, CA 94089
shxie@microsoft.com

Klaus Zechner
Educational Testing Service
Princeton, NJ 08541, USA
kzechner@ets.org

Abstract

This paper investigates the use of prompt-based content features for the automated assessment of spontaneous speech in a spoken language proficiency assessment. The results show that single highest performing prompt-based content feature measures the number of unique lexical types that overlap with the listening materials and are not contained in either the reading materials or a sample response, with a correlation of $r = 0.450$ with holistic proficiency scores provided by humans. Furthermore, linear regression scoring models that combine the proposed prompt-based content features with additional spoken language proficiency features are shown to achieve competitive performance with scoring models using content features based on pre-scored responses.

1 Introduction

A spoken language proficiency assessment should provide information about how well the non-native speaker will be able to perform a wide range of tasks in the target language. Therefore, in order to provide a full evaluation of the non-native speaker's speaking proficiency, the assessment should include some tasks eliciting unscripted, spontaneous speech. This goal, however, is hard to achieve in the context of a spoken language assessment which employs automated scoring, due to the difficulties in developing accurate automatic speech recognition (ASR) technology for non-native speech and in extracting valid and reliable features. Because of this, most spoken language proficiency assessments which use automated scoring have focused on restricted speech, and have included tasks such as reading a word / sentence / paragraph out loud, answering single-word factual questions, etc. (Chandel et al., 2007; Bernstein et al., 2010).

In order to address this need, some automated spoken language assessment systems have also included tasks which elicit spontaneous speech. However, these systems have focused primarily on a non-native speaker's pronunciation, prosody, and fluency in their scoring models (Zechner et al., 2009), since these types of features are relatively robust to ASR errors. Some recent studies have investigated the use of features related to a spoken response's content, such as (Xie et al., 2012). However, the approach to content scoring taken in that study requires a large amount of responses for each prompt to be provided with human scores in order to train the content models. This approach is not practical for a large-scale, high-stakes assessment which regularly introduces many new prompts into the assessment–obtaining the required number of scored training responses for each prompt would be quite expensive and could lead to potential security concerns for the assessment. Therefore, it would be desirable to develop an approach to content scoring which does not require a large amount of actual responses to train the models. In this paper, we propose such a method which uses the stimulus materials for each prompt contained in the assessment to evaluate the content in a spoken response.

2 Related Work

There has been little prior work concerning automated content scoring for spontaneous spoken responses (a few recent studies include (Xie et al., 2012) and (Chen and Zechner, 2012)); however, several approaches have been investigated for written responses. A standard approach for extended written responses (e.g., essays) is to compare the content in a given essay to the content in essays that have been provided with scores by human raters using similarity methods such as Content Vector Analysis (Attali and Burstein, 2006) and Latent Semantic Analysis (Foltz et al., 1999). This method thus requires a relatively large set of pre-scored responses for each test question in order to train the content models. For shorter written responses (e.g., short answer questions targeting factual content) approaches have been developed that compare the similarity between the content in a given response and a model correct answer, and thus do not necessarily require the collection of pre-scored responses. These approaches range from fully unsupervised text-to-text similarity measures (Mohler and Mihalcea, 2009) to systems that incorporate hand-crafted patterns identifying specific key concepts (Sukkarieh et al., 2004; Mitchell et al., 2002).

For extended written responses, it is less practical to make comparisons with model responses, due to the greater length and variability of the responses. However, another approach that does not require pre-scored responses is possible for test questions that have prompts with substantial amounts of information that should be included in the answer. In these cases, the similarity between the response and the prompt materials can be calculated, with the hypothesis that higher scoring responses will incorporate certain prompt materials more than lower scoring responses. This approach was taken by (Gurevich and Deane, 2007) which demonstrated that lower proficiency non-native essay writers tend to use more content from the reading passage, which is visually accessible and thus easier to comprehend, than the listening passage. The current study investigates a similar approach for spoken responses.

3 Data

The data used in this study was drawn from TOEFL iBT, an international assessment of academic English proficiency for non-native speakers. For this study, we focus on a task from the assessment which elicits a 60 second spoken response from the test takers. In their response, the test takers are asked to use information provided in reading and listening stimulus materials to answer a question concerning specific details in the materials. The responses are then scored by expert human raters on a 4-point scale using a scoring rubric that takes into account the following three aspects of spoken English proficiency: delivery (e.g., pronunciation, prosody, fluency), language use (e.g., grammar, lexical choice), and topic development (e.g., content, discourse coherence). For this study, we used a total of 1189 responses provided by 299 unique speakers to four different prompts[1] (794 responses from 199 speakers were used for training and 395 responses from 100 speakers were used for evaluation).

4 Methodology

We investigated several variations of simple features that compare the lexical content of a spoken response to following three types of prompt materials: 1) *listening passage*: a recorded lecture or dialogue containing information relevant to the test question (the number of words contained in each of the four listening passages used in this study were 213, 223, 234, and 318), 2) *reading passage*: an article or essay containing additional information relevant to the test question (the number of words contained in the two reading passages were 94 and 111), and 3) *sample response*: a sample response provided by the test designers containing the main ideas expected in a model answer (the number of words contained in the four sample responses were 41, 74, 102, and 133).

The following types of features were investigated for each of the materials: 1) *stimulus_cosine*: the cosine similarity between the spoken response and the various materials, 2) *tokens/response*, *types/response*: the number of word tokens / types that occur in both the spoken response and each of

[1] Two out of the four tasks in this study had only listening materials; responses to these tasks are not included in the results for the features which require reading materials.

the materials, divided by the number of word tokens / types in the response,[2] and 3) *unique tokens*, *unique types*: the number of word tokens / types that occur in both the spoken response and one or two of the materials, but do not occur in the remaining material(s).

As a baseline, we also compare the proposed content features based on the prompt materials to content features based on collections of scored responses to the same prompts. This type of feature has been shown to be effective for content scoring both in non-native essays (Attali and Burstein, 2006) and spoken responses (Xie et al., 2012), and is computed by comparing the content in a test response to content models trained using responses from each of the score points. It is defined as follows:

- Sim_i: the similarity score between the words in the spoken response and a content model trained from responses receiving score i ($i \in 1, 2, 3, 4$ in this study)

The Sim_i features were trained on a corpus of 7820 scored responses (1955 for each of the four prompts), and we investigated two different methods for computing the similarity between the test responses and the content models: Content Vector Analysis using the cosine similarity metric (CVA) and Pointwise Mutual Information (PMI).

The spoken responses were processed using an HMM-based triphone ASR system trained on 800 hours of non-native speech (approximately 15% of the training data consisted of responses to the four test questions in this study), and the ASR hypotheses were used to compute the content features.[3]

5 Results

We first examine the performance of each of the individual features by calculating their correlations with the holistic English speaking proficiency scores provided by expert human raters. These results for the training partition are presented in Table 1.[4]

Feature Set	Feature	r
stimulus_cosine	listening	0.384
	reading	0.176
	sample	0.384
tokens/response	listening	0.022
	reading	0.096
	sample	0.121
types/response	listening	0.426
	reading	0.142
	sample	0.128
unique tokens	L'RS	0.116
	L'RS'	0.162
	LR'S	0.219
	LR'S'	0.337
unique types	L'RS	0.140
	L'RS'	0.166
	LR'S	0.259
	LR'S'	0.450
CVA	Sim_1	0.091
	Sim_2	0.186
	Sim_3	0.261
	Sim_4	0.311
PMI	Sim_1	0.191
	Sim_2	0.261
	Sim_3	0.320
	Sim_4	0.361

Table 1: Correlations of individual content features with holistic human scores on the training partition

As Table 1 shows, some of the individual content features based on the prompt materials obtain higher correlations with human scores than the baseline CVA and PMI features based on scored responses. Next, we investigated the overall contribution of the content features to a scoring model that takes into account features from various aspects of speaking proficiency. To show this, we built a baseline linear regression model to predict the human scores using 9 features from 4 different aspects of speaking

[2]Dividing the number of matching word tokens / types by the number of word tokens in the response factors out the overall length of the response from the calculation of the feature.

[3]Transcriptions were not available for the spoken responses used in this study, so the exact WER of the ASR system is unknown. However, the WER of the ASR system on a comparable set of spoken responses is 28%.

[4]For the *unique tokens* and *unique types* features, each row lists how the prompt materials were used in the similarity comparison as follows: R = reading, L = listening, S = sample, and ' indicates no lexical overlap between the spoken response and the material. For example, L'RS indicates content from the test response that overlapped with both the reading passage and sample response but was not contained in the listening material.

proficiency (fluency, pronunciation, prosody, and grammar) produced by SpeechRater, an automated speech scoring system (Zechner et al., 2009), as shown in Table 2.

Category	Features
Fluency	normalized number of silences > 0.15 sec, normalized number of silences > 0.495 sec, average chunk length, speaking rate, normalized number of disfluencies
Pronunciation	normalzied Acoustic Model score from forced alignment using a native speaker AM, average normalized phone duration differnce compared to a reference corpus
Prosody	mean deviation of distance between stressed syllables
Grammar	Language Model score

Table 2: Baseline speaking proficiency features used in the scoring model

In order to investigate the contribution of the various types of content features to the scoring model, linear regression models were built by adding the features from each of the feature sets in Table 1 to the baseline features. The models were trained using the 794 responses in the training set and evaluated on the 395 responses in the evaluation set. Table 3 presents the resulting correlations both for the individual responses (N=395) as well as the sum of all four responses from each speaker (N=97).[5]

As Table 3 shows, all of the scoring models using feature sets with the proposed content features based on the prompt materials outperform the baseline model. While none of the models incorporating features from a single feature set outperforms the baseline CVA model using features based on scored responses, a model incorporating all of the proposed prompt-based content features, *all prompt-based*, does outperform this baseline. Furthermore, a model incorporating all of the content features (both the proposed features and the baseline CVA / PMI features), *all content*, outperforms a model using only the baseline CVA and PMI features.[6]

[5]Three speakers were removed from the evaluation set for this analysis since they provided fewer than four responses.

Feature Set	response r	speaker r
Baseline	0.607	0.687
+ *types/response*	0.612	0.701
+ *tokens/response*	0.615	0.700
+ *unique tokens*	0.616	0.695
+ *stimulus_cosine*	0.630	0.716
+ *unique types*	0.658	0.761
+ CVA	0.665	0.762
+ all prompt-based	0.677	0.779
+ PMI	0.723	0.818
+ CVA and PMI	0.723	0.818
+ all content	0.742	0.838

Table 3: Performance of scoring models with the addition of content features

6 Discussion and Conclusion

This paper has demonstrated that the use of content scoring features based solely on the prompt stimulus materials and a sample response is a viable alternative to using features based on content models trained on large sets of pre-scored responses for the automated assessment of spoken language proficiency. Under this approach, automated scoring systems for large-scale spoken language assessments involving spontaneous speech can begin to address an area of spoken language proficiency (content appropriateness) which has mostly been neglected in systems that have been developed to date. Compared to an approach using pre-scored responses for training the content models, the proposed approach is much more cost effective and reduces the risk that test materials will be seen by test takers prior to the assessment; both of these attributes are crucial benefits for large-scale, high-stakes language assessments. Furthermore, the proposed prompt-based content features, when combined in a linear regression model with other speaking proficiency features, outperform a baseline set of CVA content features which use models trained on pre-scored responses,

[6]While the prompt-based content features do result in improvements, neither of these two differences are statistically significant at $\alpha = 0.05$ using the Hotelling-Williams Test, since both the magnitude of the increase and the size of the data set are relatively small.

and they add further improvement to a model incorporating the higher performing baseline with PMI content features.

The results in Table 1 indicate that the individual features based on overlapping lexical types (*types/response* and *unique types*) perform slightly better than the ones based on overlapping lexical tokens (*tokens/response* and *unique tokens*). This suggests that it is important for test takers to use a range of concepts that are contained in the stimulus materials in their responses. Similarly to the result from (Gurevich and Deane, 2007), Table 1 also shows that the features measuring overlap between the response and the listening materials typically perform better than the features measuring overlap between the response and the reading materials; the best individual feature, LR'S' for *unique types*, measures the amount of overlap with lexical types that are contained in the listening stimulus, but absent from the reading stimulus and sample response. This indicates that the use of content from the listening materials is a better differentiator among students of differing language proficiency levels than reading materials, likely because test takers generally have more difficulty understanding the content from listening materials.

Table 1 also shows the somewhat counterintuitive result that features based on no lexical overlap with the sample response produce higher correlations than features based on lexical overlap with the sample response, when there is lexical overlap with the listening materials and no overlap with the reading materials. That is, the LR'S' feature outperforms the LR'S feature for both the *unique types* and *unique tokens* features sets. However, as shown in Section 4, the sample responses varied widely in length (ranging from 41 to 133 words), and all were substantially shorter than the listening materials, which ranged from 213 to 318 words. Therefore, it is likely that many of the important lexical items from the sample response are also contained in the listening materials. Thus, the LR'S feature provided less information than the LR'S' feature.

The features used in this study are all based on simple lexical overlap statistics, and are thus trivial to implement. Future research will investigate more sophisticated methods of text-to-text similarity for prompt-based content scoring, such as those used in (Mohler and Mihalcea, 2009). Furthermore, future research will address the validity of the proposed features by ensuring that there are ways to filter out responses that are too similar to the stimulus materials, and thus indicate that the test taker simply repeated the source verbatim.

7 Acknowledgments

The authors would like to thank Yigal Attali for sharing his ideas about prompt-based content scoring.

References

Yigal Attali and Jill Burstein. 2006. Automated essay scoring with e-rater® V.2. *The Journal of Technology, Learning, and Assessment*, 4(3):3–30.

Jared Bernstein, Alistair Van Moere, and Jian Cheng. 2010. Validating automated speaking tests. *Language Testing*, 27(3):355–377.

Abhishek Chandel, Abhinav Parate, Maymon Madathingal, Himanshu Pant, Nitendra Rajput, Shajith Ikbal, Om Deshmuck, and Ashish Verma. 2007. Sensei: Spoken language assessment for call center agents. In *Proceedings of ASRU*.

Miao Chen and Klaus Zechner. 2012. Using an ontology for improved automated content scoring of spontaneous non-native speech. In *Proceedings of the 7th Workshop on Innovative Use of NLP for Building Educational Applications, NAACL-HLT*, Montréal, Canada. Association for Computational Linguistics.

Peter W. Foltz, Darrell Laham, and Thomas K. Landauer. 1999. The intelligent essay assessor: Applications to educational technology. *Interactive Multimedia Electronic Journal of Computer-Enhanced Learning*, 1(2).

Olga Gurevich and Paul Deane. 2007. Document similarity measures to distinguish native vs. non-native essay writers. In *Proceedings of NAACL HLT*, Rochester, NY.

Tom Mitchell, Terry Russell, Peter Broomhead, and Nicola Aldridge. 2002. Towards robust computerised marking of free-text responses. In *Proceedings of the 6th International Computer Assisted Assessment (CAA) Conference*, Loughborough.

Michael Mohler and Rada Mihalcea. 2009. Text-to-text semantic similarity for automatic short answer grading. In *Proceedings of the European Chapter of the Association for Computational Linguistics (EACL 2009)*, Athens, Greece.

Jana Sukkarieh, Stephen Pulman, and Nicholas Raikes. 2004. Auto-marking 2: An update on the UCLES-Oxford University research into using computational linguistics to score short, free text responses. In

International Association of Educational Assessment, Philadelphia.

Shasha Xie, Keelan Evanini, and Klaus Zechner. 2012. Exploring content features for automated speech scoring. In *Proceedings of the 2012 Conference of the North American Chapter of the Association for Computational Linguistics: Human Language Technologies*, pages 103–111, Montréal, Canada. Association for Computational Linguistics.

Klaus Zechner, Derrick Higgins, Xiaoming Xi, and David M. Williamson. 2009. Automatic scoring of non-native spontaneous speech in tests of spoken English. *Speech Communication*, 51(10):883–895.

Automated Scoring of a Summary Writing Task Designed to Measure Reading Comprehension

Nitin Madnani, Jill Burstein, John Sabatini and Tenaha O'Reilly

Educational Testing Service
660 Rosedale Road, Princeton, NJ 08541, USA
{nmadnani,jburstein,jsabatini,toreilly}@ets.org

Abstract

We introduce a cognitive framework for measuring reading comprehension that includes the use of novel summary writing tasks. We derive NLP features from the holistic rubric used to score the summaries written by students for such tasks and use them to design a preliminary, automated scoring system. Our results show that the automated approach performs well on summaries written by students for two different passages.

1 Introduction

In this paper, we present our preliminary work on automatic scoring of a summarization task that is designed to measure the reading comprehension skills of students from grades 6 through 9. We first introduce our underlying reading comprehension assessment framework (Sabatini and O'Reilly, In Press; Sabatini et al., In Press) that motivates the task of writing summaries as a key component of such assessments in §2. We then describe the summarization task in more detail in §3. In §4, we describe our approach to automatically scoring summaries written by students for this task and compare the results we obtain using our system to those obtained by human scoring. Finally, we conclude in §6 with a brief discussion and possible future work.

2 Reading for Understanding (RfU) Framework

We claim that to read for understanding, readers should acquire the knowledge, skills, strategies, and dispositions that will enable them to:

- learn and process the visual and typographical elements and conventions of printed texts and print world of literacy;
- learn and process the verbal elements of language including grammatical structures and word meanings;
- form coherent mental representations of texts, consistent with discourse, text structures, and genres of print;
- model and reason about conceptual content;
- model and reason about social content.

We also claim that the ability to form a coherent mental model of the text that is consistent with text discourse is a key element of skilled reading. This mental model should be concise but also reflect the most likely intended meaning of the source. We make this claim since acquiring this ability:

1. requires the reader to have knowledge of rhetorical text structures and genres;
2. requires the reader to model the propositional content of a text within that rhetorical frame, both from an author's or reader's perspective; and
3. is dependent on a skilled reader having acquired mental models for a wide variety of genres, each embodying specific strategies for modeling the meaning of the text sources to achieve reading goals.

In support of the framework, research has shown that the ability to form a coherent mental model is important for reading comprehension. Kintsch (1998) showed that it is a key aspect in the process of construction integration and essential to understanding the structure and organization of the text. Similarly, Gernsbacher (1997) considers mental models essential to structure mapping and in bridging and making knowledge-based inferences.

2.1 Assessing Mental Models

Given the importance of mental models for reading comprehension, the natural question is how does one assess whether a student has been able to build such models after reading a text. We believe that such an assessment must encompass asking a reader to (a) sample big ideas by asking them to describe the main idea or theme of a text, (b) find specific details in the text using locate/retrieve types of questions, and (c) bridging gaps between different points in the text using inference questions. Although these questions can be multiple-choice, existing research indicates that it is better to ask the reader to write a brief summary of the text instead. Yu (2003) states that a good summary can prove useful for assessment of reading comprehension since it contains the relevant important ideas, distinguishes accurate information from opinions, and reflects the structure of the text itself. More specifically, having readers write summaries is a promising solution since:

- there is considerable empirical support that it both measures and encourages reading comprehension and is an effective instructional strategy to help students improve reading skills (Armbruster et al., 1989; Bean and Steenwyk, 1984; Duke and Pearson, 2002; Friend, 2001; Hill, 1991; Theide and Anderson, 2003);
- it is a promising technique for engaging students in building mental models of text; and
- it aligns with our framework and cognitive theory described earlier in this section.

However, asking students to write summaries instead of answering multiple choice questions entails that the summaries must be scored. Asking human raters to score these summaries, however, can be time consuming as well as costly. A more cost-effective and efficient solution would be to use an automated scoring technique using machine learning and natural language processing. We describe such a technique in the subsequent sections.

Passage

During the Neolithic Age, humans developed agriculture-what we think of as farming. Agriculture meant that people stayed in one place to grow their crops. They stopped moving from place to place to follow herds of animals or to find new wild plants to eat. And because they were settling down, people built permanent shelters. The caves they had found and lived in before could be replaced by houses they built themselves.

To build their houses, the people of this Age often stacked mud bricks together to make rectangular or round buildings. At first, these houses had one big room. Gradually, they changed to include several rooms that could be used for different purposes. People dug pits for cooking inside the houses. They may have filled the pits with water and dropped in hot stones to boil it. You can think of these as the first kitchens.

The emergence of permanent shelters had a dramatic effect on humans. They gave people more protection from the weather and from wild animals. Along with the crops that provided more food than hunting and gathering, permanent housing allowed people to live together in larger communities.

Directions

Please write a summary. The first sentence of your summary should be about the whole passage. Then write 3 more sentences. Each sentence should be about one of the paragraphs.

Figure 1: An example passage for which students are asked to write a summary, and the summary-writing directions shown to the students.

3 Summary Writing Task

Before describing the automated scoring approach, we describe the details of the summary writing task itself. The summarization task is embedded within a larger reading comprehension assessment. As part of the assessment, students read each passage and answer a set of multiple choice questions and, in addition, write a summary for one of the passages. An example passage and the instructions can be seen in Figure 1. Note the structured format of summary that is asked for in the directions: the first sentence of the summary must be about the whole passage and the next three should correspond to each of the paragraphs in the passage. All summary tasks are structured similarly in that the first sentence should identify the "global concept" of the passage and the next three sentences should identify "local concepts" corresponding to main points of each subsequent paragraph.

Each summary written by a student is scored according to a holistic rubric, i.e., based on holistic criteria rather than criteria based on specific dimensions of summary writing. The scores are assigned on a 5-point scale which are defined as:

Grade 4: summary demonstrates excellent global understanding and understanding of all 3 local concepts from the passage; does not include verbatim text (3+ words) copied from the passage; contains no inaccuracies.

Grade 3: summary demonstrates good global understanding and demonstrates understanding of at least 2 local concepts; may or may not include some verbatim text, contains no more than 1 inaccuracy.

Grade 2: summary demonstrates moderate local understanding only (2-3 local concepts but no global); with or without verbatim text, contains no more than 1 inaccuracy; OR good global understanding only with no local concepts

Grade 1: summary demonstrates minimal local understanding (1 local concept only), with or without verbatim text; OR contains only verbatim text

Grade 0: summary is off topic, garbage, or demonstrates no understanding of the text; OR response is "I don't know" or "IDK".

Note that students had the passage in front of them when writing the summaries and were not penalized for poor spelling or grammar in their summaries. In the next section, we describe a system to automatically score these summaries.

4 Automated Scoring of Student Summaries

We used a machine learning approach to build an automated system for scoring summaries of the type described in §3. To train and test our system, we used summaries written by more than 2600 students from the 6th, 7th and 9th grades about two different passages. Specifically, there were a total of 2695 summaries – 1016 written about a passage describing the evolution of permanent housing through history (the passage shown in Figure 1) and 1679 written about a passage describing living conditions at the South Pole. The distribution of the grades for the students who wrote the summaries for each passage is shown in Table 1.

Passage	Grade	Count
South Pole	6	574
	7	521
	9	584
Perm. Housing	6	387
	7	305
	9	324

Table 1: The grade distribution of the students who wrote summaries for each of the two passages.

All summaries were also scored by an experienced human rater in accordance with the 5-point holistic rubric described previously. Figure 2 shows the distribution of the human scores for both sets of summaries.

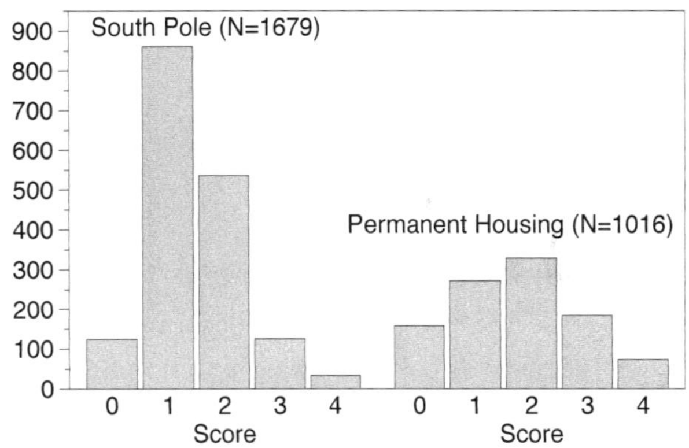

Figure 2: A histogram illustrating the human score distribution of the summaries written for the two passages.

Our approach to automatically scoring these summaries is driven by features based on the rubric. Specifically, we use the following features:

1. **BLEU**: BLEU (BiLingual Evaluation Understudy) (Papineni et al., 2002) is an automated metric used extensively in automatically scoring the output of machine translation systems.

It is a precision-based metric that computes n-gram overlap (n=1 . . . 4) between the summary (treated as a single sentence) against the passage (treated as a single sentence). We chose to use BLEU since it measures how many of the words and phrases are borrowed directly from the passage. Note that some amount of borrowing from the passage is essential for writing a good summary.

2. **ROUGE**: ROUGE (Recall-Oriented Understudy for Gisting Evaluation) (Lin and Hovy, 2003) is an automated metric used for scoring summaries produced by automated document summarization systems. It is a recall-based metric that measures the lexical and phrasal overlap between the summary under consideration and a set of "model" (or reference) summaries. We used a single model summary for the two passages by randomly selecting each from the set of student summaries assigned a score of 4 by the human rater.
3. **CopiedSumm**: Ratio of the sum of lengths of all 3-word (or longer) sequences that are copied from the passage to the length of the summary.
4. **CopiedPassage**: Same as CopiedSumm but with the denominator being the length of the passage.
5. **MaxCopy**: Length of the longest word sequence in the summary copied from the passage.
6. **FirstSent**: Number of passage sentences that the first sentence of the summary borrows 2-word (or longer) sequences from.
7. **Length**: Number of sentences in the summary.
8. **Coherence**: Token counts of commonly used discourse connector words in the summary.

ROUGE computes the similarity between the summary S under consideration and a high-scoring summary - a high value of this similarity indicates that S should also receive a high score. **CopiedSumm**, **CopiedPassage**, **BLEU**, and **MaxCopy** capture verbatim copying from the passage. **FirstSent** directly captures the "global understanding" concept for the first sentence, i.e., a large value for this feature means that the first sentence captures more of the passage as expected. **Length** captures the correspondence between the number of paragraphs in the passage and the number of sentences in the summary. Finally, **Coherence** captures how well the student is able to connect the different "local concepts" present in the passage. Note that:

- Although the rubric states that students not be penalized for spelling errors, we did not spell-correct the summaries before scoring them. We plan to do this for future experiments.
- The students were not explicitly told to refrain from verbatim copying since the summary-writing instructions indicated this implicitly ("*. . . about the whole passage*" and "*. . . about one of the paragraphs*"). However, for future experiments, we plan to include explicit instructions regarding copying.

All features were combined in a logistic regression classifier that output a prediction on the same 5-point scale as the holistic rubric. We trained a separate classifier for each of the two passage types.[1] The 5-fold cross-validation performance of this classifier on our data is shown in Table 2. We compute exact as well as adjacent agreement of our predictions against the human scores using the confusion matrices from the two classifiers. The exact agreement shows the rate at which the system and the human rater awarded the same score to a summary. Adjacent agreement shows the rate at which scores given by the system and the human rater were no more than one score point apart (e.g., the system assigned a score of 4 and the human rater assigned a score of 5 or 3). For holistic scoring using 5-point rubrics, typical exact agreement rates are in the same range as our scores (Burstein, 2012; Burstein et al., 2013). Therefore, our system performed reasonably well on the summary scoring task. For comparison, we also show the exact and adjacent agreement of the most-frequent-score baseline.

It is important to investigate whether the various features correlated in an expected manner with the score in order to ensure that the summary-writing construct is covered accurately. We examined the weights assigned to the various features in the classifier and found that this was indeed the case. As expected, the **CopiedSumm**, **CopiedPassage**, **BLEU**,

[1]We used the Weka Toolkit (Hall et al., 2009).

Method	Passage	Exact	Adjacent
Baseline	South Pole	.51	.90
	Perm. Housing	.32	.77
Logistic	South Pole	**.65**	**.97**
	Perm. Housing	**.52**	**.93**

Table 2: Exact and adjacent agreements of the most-frequent-score baseline and of the 5-fold cross-validation predictions from the logistic regression classifier, for both passages.

and **MaxCopy** features all correlate negatively with score, and **ROUGE**, **FirstSent** and **Coherence** correlate positively.

In addition to overall performance, we also examined which features were most useful to the classifier in predicting summary scores. Table 3 shows the various features ranked using the information-gain metric for both logistic regression models. These rankings show that the features performed consistently for both models.

South Pole	Perm. Housing
BLEU (.375)	BLEU (.450)
CopiedSumm (.290)	ROUGE (.400)
ROUGE (.264)	CopiedSumm (.347)
Length (.257)	Length (.340)
CopiedPassage (.246)	MaxCopy(.253)
MaxCopy (.231)	CopiedPassage (.206)
FirstSent (.120)	Coherence (.155)
Coherence (.103)	FirstSent (.058)

Table 3: Classifier features for both passages ranked by average merit values obtained using information-gain.

5 Related Work

There has been previous work on scoring summaries as part of the automated document summarization task (Nenkova and McKeown, 2011). In that task, automated systems produce summaries of multiple documents on the same topic and those machine-generated summaries are then scored by either human raters or by using automated metrics such as ROUGE. In our scenario, however, the summaries are produced by students—not automated systems—and the goal is to develop an automated system to assign scores to these human-generated summaries.

Although work on automatically scoring student essays (Burstein, 2012) and short answers (Leacock and Chodorow, 2003; Mohler et al., 2011) is marginally relevant to the work done here, we believe it is different in significant aspects based on the scoring rubric and on the basis of the underlying RfU framework. We believe that the work most directly related to ours is the Summary Street system (Franzke et al., 2005; Kintsch et al., 2007) which attempts to score summaries written for tasks not based on the RfU framework and uses latent semantic analysis (LSA) rather than a feature-based classification approach.

6 Conclusion & Future Work

We briefly introduced the Reading for Understanding cognitive framework and how it motivates the use of a summary writing task in a reading comprehension assessment. Our motivation is that such a task is theoretically suitable for capturing the ability of a reader to form coherent mental representations of the text being read. We then described a preliminary, feature-driven approach to scoring such summaries and showed that it performed quite well for scoring the summaries about two different passages. Obvious directions for future work include: (a) getting summaries double-scored to be able to compare system-human agreement against human-human agreement (b) examining whether a single model trained on all the data can perform as well as passage-specific models, and (c) using more sophisticated features such as TERp (Snover et al., 2010) which can capture and reward paraphrasing in addition to exact matches, and features that can better model the "local concepts" part of the scoring rubric.

Acknowledgments

The research reported here was supported by the Institute of Education Sciences, U.S. Department of Education, through Grant R305F100005 to the Educational Testing Service as part of the Reading for Understanding Research Initiative. The opinions expressed are those of the authors and do not represent views of the Institute or the U.S. Department of Education. We would also like to thank Kelly Bruce, Kietha Biggers and the Strategic Educational Research Partnership.

References

B. B. Armbruster, T. H. Anderson, and J. Ostertag. 1989. Teaching Text Structure to Improve Reading and Writing. *Educational Leadership*, 46:26–28.

T. W. Bean and F. L. Steenwyk. 1984. The Effect of Three Forms of Summarization Instruction on Sixth-graders' Summary Writing and Comprehension. *Journal of Reading Behavior*, 16(4):297–306.

J. Burstein, J. Tetreault, and N. Madnani. 2013. The E-rater Automated Essay Scoring System. In M.D. Shermis and J. Burstein, editors, *Handbook for Automated Essay Scoring*. Routledge.

J. Burstein. 2012. Automated Essay Scoring and Evaluation. In Carol Chapelle, editor, *The Encyclopedia of Applied Linguistics*. Wiley-Blackwell.

N. K. Duke and P. D. Pearson. 2002. Effective Practices for Developing Reading Comprehension. In A. E. Farstrup and S. J. Samuels, editors, *What Research has to Say about Reading Instruction*, pages 205–242. International Reading Association.

M. Franzke, E. Kintsch, D. Caccamise, N. Johnson, and S. Dooley. 2005. Summary Street: Computer support for comprehension and writing. *Journal of Educational Computing Research*, 33:53–80.

R. Friend. 2001. Effects of Strategy Instruction on Summary Writing of College Students. *Contemporary Educational Psychology*, 26(1):3–24.

M. A. Gernsbacher. 1997. Two Decades of Structure Building. *Discourse Processes*, 23:265–304.

P. Hall, E. Frank, G. Holmes, B. Pfahringer, P. Reutemann, and I. H. Witten. 2009. The WEKA Data Mining Software: An Update. *SIGKDD Explorations*, 11(1).

M. Hill. 1991. Writing Summaries Promotes Thinking and Learning Across the Curriculum – But Why are They So Difficult to Write? *Journal of Reading*, 34(7):536–639.

E. Kintsch, D. Caccamise, M. Franzke, N. Johnson, and S. Dooley. 2007. Summary Street: Computer-guided summary writing. In T. K. Landauer, D. S. McNamara, S. Dennis, and W. Kintsch, editors, *Handbook of latent semantic analysis*. Lawrence Erlbaum Associates Publishers.

W. Kintsch. 1998. *Comprehension: A Paradigm for Cognition*. Cambridge University Press.

C. Leacock and M. Chodorow. 2003. C-rater: Automated Scoring of Short-Answer Questions. *Computers and the Humanities*, 37(4):389–405.

C.-Y. Lin and E. H. Hovy. 2003. Automatic Evaluation of Summaries Using N-gram Co-occurrence Statistics. In *Proceedings of HLT-NAACL*, pages 71–78.

M. Mohler, R. Bunescu, and R. Mihalcea. 2011. Learning to Grade Short Answer Questions using Semantic Similarity Measures and Dependency Graph Alignments. In *Proceedings of ACL*, pages 752–762.

A. Nenkova and K. McKeown. 2011. Automatic Summarization. *Foundations and Trends in Information Retrieval*, 5(2–3):103–233.

K. Papineni, S. Roukos, T. Ward, and W. Zhu. 2002. BLEU: a Method for Automatic Evaluation of Machine Translation. In *Proceedings of ACL*, pages 311–318.

J. Sabatini and T. O'Reilly. In Press. Rationale For a New Generation of Reading Comprehension Assessments. In B. Miller, L. Cutting, and P. McCardle, editors, *Unraveling the Behavioral, Neurobiological, and Genetic Components of Reading Comprehension*. Brookes Publishing, Inc.

J. Sabatini, T. O'Reilly, and P. Deane. In Press. Preliminary Reading Literacy Assessment Framework: Foundation and Rationale for Assessment and System Design.

M. Snover, N. Madnani, B. Dorr, and R. Schwartz. 2010. TER-Plus: Paraphrase, Semantic, and Alignment Enhancements to Translation Edit Rate. *Machine Translation*, 23:117–127.

K. W. Theide and M. C. M. Anderson. 2003. Summarizing Can Improve Metacomprehension Accuracy. *Educational Psychology*, 28(2):129–160.

G. Yu. 2003. Reading for Summarization as Reading Comprehension Test Method: Promises and Problems. *Language Testing Update*, 32:44–47.

Inter-annotator Agreement for Dependency Annotation of Learner Language

Marwa Ragheb
Indiana University
Bloomington, IN USA
mragheb@indiana.edu

Markus Dickinson
Indiana University
Bloomington, IN USA
md7@indiana.edu

Abstract

This paper reports on a study of inter-annotator agreement (IAA) for a dependency annotation scheme designed for learner English. Reliably-annotated learner corpora are a necessary step for the development of POS tagging and parsing of learner language. In our study, three annotators marked several layers of annotation over different levels of learner texts, and they were able to obtain generally high agreement, especially after discussing the disagreements among themselves, without researcher intervention, illustrating the feasibility of the scheme. We pinpoint some of the problems in obtaining full agreement, including annotation scheme vagueness for certain learner innovations, interface design issues, and difficult syntactic constructions. In the process, we also develop ways to calculate agreements for sets of dependencies.

1 Introduction

Learner corpora have been essential for developing error correction systems and intelligent tutoring systems (e.g., Nagata et al., 2011; Rozovskaya and Roth, 2010). So far, error annotation has been the main focus, to the exclusion of corpora and annotation for more basic NLP development, despite the need for parse information for error detection (Tetreault et al., 2010), learner proficiency identification (Hawkins and Buttery, 2010), and acquisition research (Ragheb and Dickinson, 2011). Indeed, there is very little work on POS tagging (Thouësny, 2009; van Rooy and Schäfer, 2002; de Haan, 2000) or parsing (Rehbein et al., 2012; Krivanek and Meurers, 2011; Ott and Ziai, 2010) learner language, and, not coincidentally, there is a lack of annotated data and standards for these tasks. One issue is in knowing how to handle innovative learner forms: some map to a target form before annotating syntax (e.g., Hirschmann et al., 2010), while others propose directly annotating the text (e.g., Ragheb and Dickinson, 2011). We follow this latter strand and further our work towards a syntactically-annotated corpus of learner English by: a) presenting an annotation scheme for dependencies, integrated with other annotation layers, and b) testing the inter-annotator agreement for this scheme. Despite concerns that direct annotation of the linguistic properties of learners may not be feasible (e.g., Rosén and Smedt, 2010), we find that annotators have generally strong agreement, especially after adjudication, and the reasons for disagreement often have as much to do with the complexities of syntax or interface issues as they do with learner innovations.

Probing grammatical annotation can lead to advancements in research on POS tagging and syntactic parsing of learner language, for it shows what can be annotated reliably and what needs additional diagnostics. We specifically report on inter-annotator agreement (IAA) for the annotation scheme described in section 2, focusing on dependency annotation. There are numerous studies investigating inter-annotator agreement between coders for different types of grammatical annotation schemes, focusing on part-of-speech, syntactic, or semantic annotation (e.g., Passonneau et al., 2006; Babarczy et al., 2006; Civit et al., 2003). For learner language, a number of error annotation projects include measures of interannotator agreement, (see, e.g., Boyd, 2012; Lee et al., 2012; Rozovskaya and Roth, 2010; Tetreault and Chodorow, 2008; Bonaventura et al., 2000), but as far as we are aware, there have been no studies on IAA for grammatical annotation.

We have conducted an IAA study to investigate the quality and robustness of our annotation scheme, as reported in section 3. In section 4, we report quantitative results and a qualitative analysis of this study to tease apart disagreements due to inherent ambiguity or text difficulty from those due to the annotation scheme and/or the guidelines. The study has already reaped benefits by helping us to revise our annotation scheme and guidelines, and the insights gained here should be applicable for future development of other annotation schemes and to parsing studies.

On a final note, our dependency annotation allows for multiple heads for each token in the corpus, violating the so-called *single-head constraint* (Kübler et al., 2009). In the process of evaluating these dependencies (see section 4.1), we also make some minor contributions towards comparing sets of dependencies, moving beyond just F-measure (e.g., Cer et al., 2010) to account for partial agreements.

2 Annotation scheme

We present a sketch of the annotation scheme here, outlining the layers and the general motivation. Our general perspective is to annotate as closely as possible to what the learner wrote, marking grammatical properties even if the meaning of the sentence or clause is unclear within the particular grammatical analysis. For example, in the learner sentence (1), the verb *admit* clearly occurs in the form of an active verb, and is annotated as such, regardless of the (passive) meaning of the sentence (cf. *was admitted*). In this case, basing the annotation on syntactic evidence makes for a more straightforward task. Moreover, adhering to a syntactic analysis helps outline the grammatical properties of a learner's interlanguage and can thus assist in automatic tasks such as native language identification (e.g., Tetreault et al., 2012), and proficiency level determination (Yannakoudakis et al., 2011).

(1) When I admit to Korea University, I decide ...

Another part of the motivation for shying away from marking target forms and annotating the syntactic properties of those (cf., e.g., Rehbein et al., 2012) is that, for general essays from learners of many levels, the grammatical evidence can be understood even when the intended meaning is not. Consider (2): in the context of the learner's essay, the sentence probably means that this person guards their personal belongings very well because of prevalent theft in the city they are talking about.

(2) Now I take very hard my personal stuffs.

Annotating the syntax of a target form here could obscure the grammatical properties of the learner's production (e.g., pluralizing a mass noun). Encouraging annotators to focus on the syntactic properties and not intended meanings makes identifying the dependency relations in a sentence like this one easy.

Another aspect of our annotation scheme is that we do not directly annotate errors (except for lexical violations; see section 2.1). Annotators had access to an extensive manual detailing the annotation scheme, which will be made public soon.[1] A brief outline of the guidelines is in section 3.3.

2.1 Initial annotation layers

Using ideas developed for annotating learner language (Ragheb and Dickinson, 2012, 2011; Díaz-Negrillo et al., 2010; Dickinson and Ragheb, 2009), we annotate several layers before targeting dependencies: 1) lemmas (i.e., normalized forms), 2) morphological part-of-speech (POS), 3) distributional POS, and 4) lexical violations.

The idea for **lemma** annotation is to normalize a word to its dictionary form. In (3), for example, the misspelled *excersice* is normalized to the correctly-spelled *exercise* for the lemma annotation. We specify that only "reasonable" orthographic or phonetic changes are allowed; thus, for *prison*, it is lemma-annotated as *prison*, not *person*. In this case, the lemma annotation does not affect the rest of the annotation, as *prison* and *person* are both nouns, but for *no*, the entire analysis changes based on whether we annotate the lemma as *no* or *not*. Marking *no* makes the final tree more difficult, but fits with the principle of staying true to the form the learner has

[1]See: `http://cl.indiana.edu/~salle`

presented. As we will see in section 4.3, determining the lemma can pose challenges for building trees.

(3) After to start , I want to tell that this **excersice** is very important in the life , **no** only as a **prison** .

We annotate two POS layers, one capturing **morphological** evidence and one for **distributional**. For most words, the layers include the same information, but mismatches arise with non-canonical structures. For instance, in (3) the verb *(to) start* has a morphological POS of base form verb (VV0), but it appears in a context where some other verb form would better be licensed, e.g., a gerund. Since we do not want to overstate claims, we allow for underspecified POS tags and annotate the distributional POS simply as verb (VV). The use of two POS layers captures the mismatch between morphology and distribution without referencing a unified POS.

Finally, annotators can mark **lexical violations** when nothing else appears to capture a non-standard form. Specifically, lexical violations are for syntactically ungrammatical forms where the specific word choice seems to cause the ungrammaticality. In (4), for example, *about* should be marked as a lexical violation. Lexical violations were intended as a last resort, but as we will see in section 4.3, there was confusion about when to use lexical violations and when to use other annotations, e.g., POS mismatches.

(4) ... I agree **about** me that my country 's help and cooperation influenced . . .

2.2 Dependencies

While the initial annotation layers are used to build the syntactic annotation, the real focus of the annotation concerns dependencies. Using a set of 45 dependencies,[2] we mark two types of annotations here: 1) dependency relations rooted in the lemma and the morphological POS tag, and 2) subcategorization information, reflecting not necessarily what is in the tree, but what is required. Justification for a morphological, or morphosyntactic, layer of dependencies, along with a layer of subcategorization, is given in Ragheb and Dickinson (2012). Essentially, these two layers allow one to capture issues involving argument structure (e.g., missing argument), without having to make the kind of strong claims a layer of distributional dependencies would require. In (5), for example, *wondered* subcategorizes for a finite complement (COMP), but finds a non-finite complement (XCOMP), as the tree is based on the morphological forms (e.g., *to*).

(5) I wondered what success to be .

An example tree is shown in figure 1, where we can see a number of properties of our trees: a) we annotate many "raised" subjects, such as *I* being the subject (SUBJ) of both *would* and *like*, thereby allowing for multiple heads for a single token; b) we ignore semantic anomalies, such as the fact that *life* is the subject of *be (successful)*; and c) dependencies can be selected for, but not realized, as in the case of *career* subcategorizing for a determiner (DET).

3 Inter-annotator agreement study

3.1 Selection of annotation texts

From a learner corpus of written essays we have collected from students entering Indiana University, we chose a topic (*What Are Your Plans for Life?*) and randomly selected six essays, based on both learner proficiency (beginner, intermediate, advanced) and the native language of the speaker (L1).[3] From each essay, we selected the first paragraph and put the six paragraphs into two texts; each text contained, in order, one beginner, one intermediate, and one advanced paragraph. Text 1 contained 19 sentences (333 tokens), and Text 2 contained 22 sentences (271 tokens). Annotators were asked to annotate only these excerpts, but had access to the entire essays, if they wanted to view them.

While the total number of tokens is only 604, the depth of the annotation is quite significant, in that there are at least seven decisions to be made for every token: lemma, lexical violation, morphological POS, distributional POS, subcategorization, attachment, and dependency label, in addition to possible extra dependencies for a given word, i.e., a few thousand decisions. It is hard to quantify the effort, as some layers are automatically pre-annotated (see section 3.5) and some are used sparingly (lexical violations), but we estimate around 2000 new or changed annotations from each annotator.

[2] We use a label set adapted from Sagae et al. (2010).

[3] Korean, Spanish, Chinese, Arabic, Japanese, Hungarian.

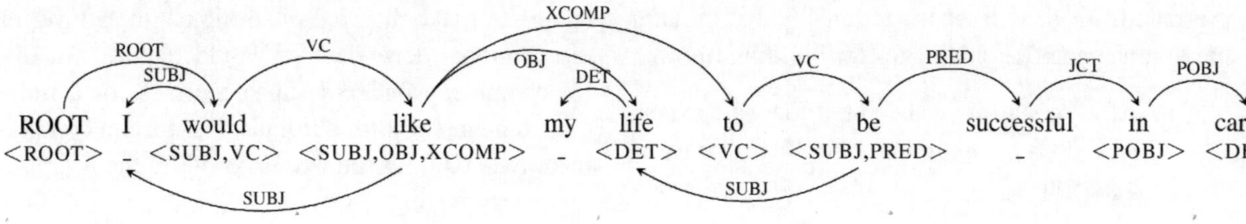

Figure 1: Morphosyntactic dependency tree with subcategorization information

3.2 Annotators

This study involved three annotators, who were undergraduate students at Indiana. They were native speakers of English and majors in Linguistics (2 juniors, 1 senior). Two had had a syntax course before the semester, and one was taking it concurrently. We trained them over the course of an academic semester (fall 2012), by means of weekly meetings to discuss relevant readings, familiarize them with the scheme, and give feedback about their annotation. The IAA study took place Nov. 9–Dec. 15.

Annotators were taking course credit for participating in this project. This being the case, they were encouraged to learn from the experience, and part of their training was to make notes of challenging cases and their decision-making process. This has provided significant depth in qualitatively analyzing the IAA outcomes (section 4.3).

3.3 Guidelines

At the start of the study, the annotators were given a set of guidelines (around 100 pages) to reference as they made decisions. These guidelines outline the general principles of the scheme (e.g., give the learner the benefit of the doubt), an overview of the annotation layers, and annotation examples for each layer. The guidelines refer to the label sets used for POS (Sampson, 1995) and dependencies (Sagae et al., 2010), but emphasize the properties of our scheme. Although the guidelines discuss general syntactic treatment (e.g., "attach high" in the case of attachment ambiguities), a considerable focus is on handling learner innovations, across different layers. While we cannot list every example of how learners innovate, we include instructions and examples that should generalize to other non-native constructions (e.g., when to underspecify a label). Examples of how to treat difficult syntactic constructions are also illustrated (e.g., coordination).

	Text 1				Text 2			
	Time	Avg.	Min.	Max.	Time	Avg.	Min.	Max.
A	224	11.8	3	25	151	6.9	2	21
B	280	14.7	4	30	170*	8.5	3	20
C	480	25.3	8	60	385	17.5	10	45

Table 1: Annotation time, in minutes, for phase 1 (*times for two sentences were not reported and are omitted)

3.4 Annotation task

Via oral and written instructions, the annotators were asked to independently annotate the two texts and take notes on difficult issues, in addition to marking how long they spent on each sentence. Times are reported in table 1 for the first phase, as described next. Longer sentences take more time (cf. Text 1 vs. Text 2), and annotator times vary, but, given the times of nearly 30–60 minutes per sentence at the start of the semester, these times seemed reasonable for the depth of annotation required.

The annotation task proceeded in phases. **Phase 1:** Text 1 was annotated over the course of one week, and Text 2 over the next week. **Phase 2:** After an hour-long meeting with annotators covering general annotation points that seemed to be problematic (e.g., lemma definitions), they were given another week to individually go over their annotations and make modifications. At the meeting, nothing about the scheme or guidelines was added, and no specific examples from the data being annotated were used (only ones from earlier in the semester). **Phase 3:** Each annotator received a document pointing out pairwise disagreements between annotators, in a simple textual format like (6). Each annotator was asked to use this document and make any changes where they thought that their analysis was not the best one, given the other two. This process took approximately a week. **Phase 4:** The annotators met (for three hours) and discussed remaining differences, to see whether they could reach a consensus. Each annotator fixed their own file based on the results of this discussion. At each point, we took a snapshot of the data, but at no point did we provide feedback to the annotators on their decisions.

(6) Sentence 2, word 1: relation ... JCT NJCT

3.5 Annotation interface

The annotation is done via the Brat rapid annotation tool (Stenetorp et al., 2012).[4] This online interface, shown in figure 2, allows an annotator to drag an arrow between words to create a dependency. Annotators were given automatically-derived POS tags from TnT (Brants, 2000), trained on the SUSANNE corpus (Sampson, 1995), but created the dependencies from scratch.[5] Subcategorizations, lemmas, and lexical violations are annotated within one of the POS layers; lemmas are noted by the blue shading, and the presence of other layers is noted by asterisks, an interface point discussed in section 4.2.3. Annotators liked the tool, but complained of its slowness.

4 Evaluation

4.1 Methods of comparison

For lemma and POS annotation, we can calculate basic agreement statistics, as there is one annotation for each token. But our primary focus is on subcategorization and dependency annotation, where there can be multiple elements (or none) for a given token.

For subcategorization, we treat elements as members of a set, as annotators were told that order was unimportant (e.g., <SUBJ,OBJ> = <OBJ,SUBJ>); we discuss metrics for this in section 4.1.1. For dependencies, we adapt standard parse evaluation (see Kübler et al., 2009, ch. 6). In brief, **unlabeled attachment agreement (UAA)** measures the number of attachments annotators agree upon for each token, disregarding the label, whereas **labeled attachment agreement (LAA)** requires both the attachment and labeling to be the same to count as an agreement. **Label only agreement (LOA)** ignores the head a token attaches to and only compares labels.

All three metrics (UAA, LAA, LOA) require calculations for *sets* of dependencies, described in sections 4.1.1 and 4.1.2. In figure 3, for instance, one annotator (accidentally) drew a JCT arrow in the wrong direction, resulting in two heads for *is*. For *is*, the annotator's set of dependencies is {(0,ROOT), (1,JCT)}, compared to another's of {(0,ROOT)}. We thus treat dependencies as sets of (head, label) pairs.

4.1.1 Metrics

For sets, we use two different calculations. First is **MASI** (Measuring Agreement on Set-valued Items, Passonneau et al., 2006), which assigns each comparison between sets a value between 0 and 1, assigning partial credit for partial set matches and allowing one to treat agreement on a per-token basis. We use a simplified form of MASI as follows: 1 = identical sets, $\frac{2}{3}$ = one set is a subset of the other, $\frac{1}{3}$ = the intersection of the sets is non-null, and so are the set differences, & 0 = disjoint sets.[6]

The second method is a global comparison method **(GCM)**, which counts all the elements in each annotator's sets in the whole file and counts up the total number of agreements. In the following subcategorization example over three tokens, there are two agreements, compared to four total elements used by A1 ($\text{GCM}_{A1} = \frac{2}{4}$) and compared to three elements used by A2 ($\text{GCM}_{A2} = \frac{2}{3}$). These metrics are essentially precision and recall, depending upon which annotator is seen as the "gold" (Kübler et al., 2009, ch. 6). For MASI scores, we have 0, 1, and $\frac{1}{3}$, respectively, giving $1\frac{1}{3}/3$, or 0.44.

- A1: {SUBJ}, A2: {}
- A1: {SUBJ}, A2: {SUBJ}
- A1: {SUBJ,PRED}, A2: {SUBJ,OBJ}

Since every word is annotated, the methods assign similar numbers for dependencies. Subcategorization gives different results, due to empty sets. If annotator 1 and annotator 2 both mark an empty set,

[4] http://brat.nlplab.org

[5] Annotators need to provide the dependency annotations since we lacked an appropriate L2 parser. It is a goal of this project to provide annotated data for parser development.

[6] Since our sets tend to be small (rarely bigger than two), we do not expect much change with a full MASI calculation.

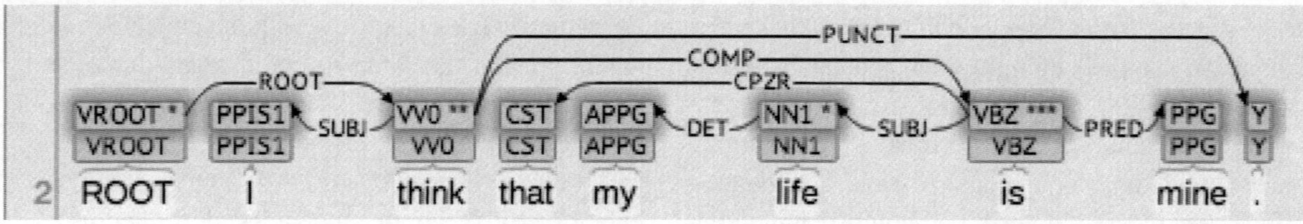

Figure 2: Example of the annotation interface

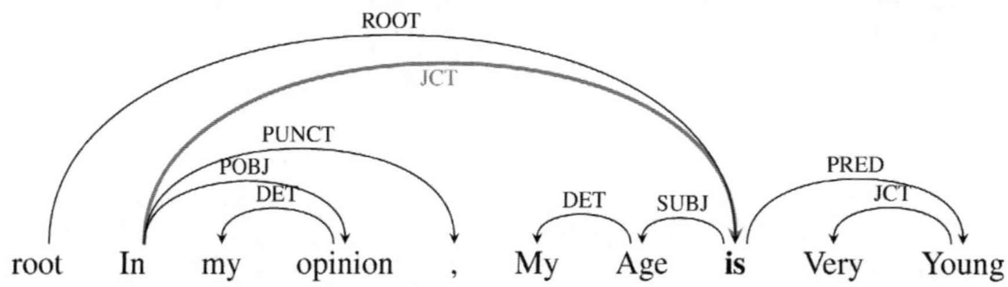

Figure 3: A mistaken arrow (JCT) leading to two dependencies for *is* ((0,ROOT),(1,JCT))

we count full agreement for MASI, i.e., a score of 1; for GCM, nothing gets added to the totals.

We could, of course, report various coefficients commonly used in IAA studies, such as kappa or alpha (see Artstein and Poesio, 2008), but, given the large number of classes and lack of predominant classes, chance agreement seems very small.

4.1.2 Dependency-specific issues

As a minor point: for dependencies, we calculate agreements for matches in only attachment or labeling. Consider (7), where there is one match only in attachment ((24,OBJ)-(24,JCT)), counting towards UAA, and one only in labeling ((24,SUBJ)-(22,SUBJ)) for LOA. Importantly, we have to ensure that (24,SUBJ) and (24,JCT) are not linked.

(7) A1: {(24,SUBJ), (24,OBJ)}
A2: {(22,SUBJ), (24,JCT)}

In general, we prioritize identical attachment over labeling, if a dependency could match in either. We wrote a short script to align attachment/label matches between two sets, but omit details here, due to space. We generally do not have large sets of dependencies to compare, but these technical decisions should allow for any situation in the future.

4.2 Results

4.2.1 Bird's-eye view

Table 2 presents an overview of pairwise agreements between annotators for all 604 tokens. Of the four phases of annotation, we report two: the files they annotated (and revised) independently (phase 2) and the final files after discussion of problematic cases (phase 4). Annotators reported feeling rushed during phase 1, so phase 2 numbers likely better indicate the ability to independently annotate, and phase 4 can help to investigate the reasons for lingering disagreements. The numbers for subcategorization and dependency (UAA, LAA) agreements are the MASI agreement rates.

A few observations are evident from these figures. First, for both POS_m (morphology) and POS_d (distribution), the high agreement rates reflect the fact that annotators made very few changes to the automatic pre-annotation, partly because such layers were not heavily emphasized. Lemmas were also pre-annotated, as identical to the surface form, but more changes were made here (decapitalization, affix-stripping, etc.). Comparing phases 2 and 4 shows an improvement in agreement, although agreement seems like it could be higher, given the simplicity of lemma information. We discuss lemmas, and associated lexical violations, more in sec-

Annotators	lemma		POS$_m$		POS$_d$		Subcat.		UAA		LAA	
	P2	P4	P2	P4	P2	P4	P2	P4	P2	P4	P2	P4
A, B	93.4	96.9	99.0	98.7	99.2	98.7	85.5	94.0	86.6	97.0	80.0	95.2
B, C	94.4	97.7	99.0	99.5	98.7	99.3	86.1	95.7	86.7	97.1	80.3	96.0
C, A	92.4	96.9	99.7	99.7	98.5	99.3	86.1	96.6	86.9	97.7	82.4	96.7

Table 2: Overview of agreement rates before & after discussion (phases 2 & 4)

tion 4.3.

Dependency-related annotations had no pre-annotation. While the starting value of agreement rates for these last three layers is not as high as for lemma and POS annotation, agreement rates around 80–85% still seem moderately high. More important is how much the agreement rates improved after discussion, achieving approximately 95% agreement. This was without any direct intervention from the researchers regarding how to annotate disagreements. We examine dependencies in section 4.2.2 and subcategorization in 4.2.3, breaking results down by text to see differences in difficulty.

4.2.2 Dependencies

We report MASI agreement rates for dependencies in tables 3 and 4 for Text 1 and Text 2, respectively.[7] Comparing the starting agreement values (e.g., 73.6% vs. 87.8% LAA for annotators A and B), it is clear that text difficulty had an enormous impact on annotator agreement. The clear difference in tokens per sentence (17.5 in Text 1 vs. 12.3 in Text 2; see section 3.1) contributed to the differences. The reported difficulty from annotators referred to more non-native properties present in the text, and, to a smaller extent, the presence of more complex syntactic structures. Though we take up some of these issues up again in section 4.3, an in-depth analysis of how text difficulty affects the annotation task is beyond the scope of this paper, and we leave it for future investigation.

Looking at the agreement rates for Text 1 in table 3, we can see that the initial rates of agreement for UAA and LOA are moderately high, indicating that annotator training and guideline descriptions were working moderately well. However, they are only 73% for LAA. Note, though, that this may be more related to issues of fatigue and hurry than of understanding of the guidelines: the numbers improve considerably by phase 4. The labeled attachment rates, for example, increase between 17 and 21 percent, to reach values around 95%.

Ann.	UAA		LAA		LOA	
	P2	P4	P2	P4	P2	P4
A, B	81.8	96.1	73.6	93.4	80.3	95.5
B, C	80.9	96.2	73.4	94.4	79.3	97.1
A,C	83.6	97.6	79.7	96.7	81.8	97.9

Table 3: MASI percentages for dependencies, Text 1

Ann.	UAA		LAA		LOA	
	P2	P4	P2	P4	P2	P4
A, B	92.6	98.1	87.8	97.4	89.3	97.8
B, C	93.8	98.3	88.7	97.9	90.2	98.6
A, C	90.9	97.9	85.7	96.8	87.6	97.9

Table 4: MASI percentages for dependencies, Text 2

For Text 2 in table 4, we notice again the higher phase 2 rates and the similar improvement in phase 4, with LAA around 97%. Encouragingly, despite the initially lower agreements for Text 1, annotators were able to achieve nearly the same level of agreement as for the "easier" text. This illustrates that annotators can learn the scheme, even for difficult sentences, though there may be a tradeoff between speed and accuracy.

4.2.3 Subcategorization

For subcategorization, we present both MASI and GCM percentage rates, as they give different emphases. Results are again broken down by text, in tables 5 and 6. As with dependencies, we see solid improvement from phase 2 to phase 4, and we see

[7] We only report MASI scores for dependencies, since the GCM scores are nearly the same. For example, for raters A & B, the GCM value for phase 4 is 96.15% with respect to either annotator vs. 96.10% for MASI.

generally higher agreement for Text 2.

Ann.	MASI		GCM_1		GCM_2	
	P2	P4	P2	P4	P2	P4
A,B	84.3	92.4	81.9	90.8	72.8	88.1
B,C	83.6	93.8	74.4	91.6	73.6	90.2
A,C	84.9	96.1	83.0	96.4	73.1	92.2

Table 5: Agreement rates for subcategorization, Text 1

Ann.	MASI		GCM_1		GCM_2	
	P2	P4	P2	P4	P2	P4
A,B	87.1	95.9	88.9	96.0	77.2	94.1
B,C	89.3	98.0	88.3	98.0	82.0	96.8
A,C	87.6	97.2	91.2	97.3	73.7	94.2

Table 6: Agreement rates for subcategorization, Text 2

The GCM numbers are much lower because of the way empty subcategorization values are handled—being counted towards agreement for MASI and not for GCM (see section 4.1.1). A further issue, though, is that one annotator often simply left out subcategorization annotation for a token. In table 6, for example, annotators A and C have vastly different GCM values for phase 2 (91.2% vs. 73.7%), due to annotator C annotating many more subcategorization labels. This is discussed more in section 4.3.2.

4.3 Qualitative differences

We highlight some of the important issues that stand out when we take a closer look at the nature of the disagreements in the final phase.

4.3.1 Text-related issues

As pointed out earlier regarding the differences between Text 1 and Text 2 (section 4.2.2), some disagreements are likely due to the nature of the text itself, both because of its non-native properties and because of the syntactic complexity. Starting with unique learner innovations leading to non-uniform treatment, several cases stemmed from not agreeing on the lemma, when a word looks non-English or does not fit the context. An example is *cares* in (8): although the guidelines should lead the annotators to choose *care* as the lemma, staying true to the learner form, one annotator chose to accommodate the context and changed the lemma to *case*. This relying too heavily on intended meaning and not enough on syntactic evidence—as the scheme is designed for—was a consistent problem.

(8) My majors are bankruptcy , corporate reorganizations . . . and arquisisiton **cares** .

For (8), the trees do not change because the different lemmas are of the same syntactic category, but more problematic are cases where the trees differ based on different readings. In the learner sentence (9), the non-agreement between *this* and *cause* led to a disagreement of *this* being a COORD of *and* vs. *this* being an APPOS (appositive) of *factors*. The annotator reported that the choice for this latter analysis came from treating *this* as *these*, again contrary to guidelines but consistent with one meaning.

(9) Sometimes animals are subjected to changed environmental factors during their developmental process and **this** cause FA .

Another great source of disagreement stems from the syntactic complexity of some of the structures, even if native-like, though this can be intertwined with non-native properties, as in (10). Although annotators eventually agreed on the annotation here, there was initial disagreement on the coordination structure of this sentence, questioning whether *to be* coordinates with *pursuing* or only with *to earn*, or whether *pursuing* coordinates only with *to earn* (the analysis they finally chose).

(10) My most important goals are **pursuing** the profession **to be** a top marketing manager and then **to earn** a lot of money to buy a beautiful house and a good car .

4.3.2 Task-related issues

Annotator disagreements stemmed not only from the text, but from other factors as well, such as aspects of the scheme that needed more clarification, some interface issues, and the fact that the guidelines though extensive, are still not comprehensive.

A few parts of the annotation scheme were confusing to annotators and likely need refinement. For example, if the form of a word was incorrect, we saw a lot of lexical violation annotation, even if it was only an issue of grammatical marking and POS (e.g., *did*/VVD instead of *done*/VVN), as opposed to a truly different word choice. We are currently tightening the annotation scheme and adding clarifications about lexical violations in our guidelines.

As another example, verb raising was often not marked (cf. figure 1), in spite of the scheme and guidelines requiring it. In their comments, annotators mentioned that it seemed "redundant" to them and that it caused arcs to cross, which they found "unappealing." One annotator commented that they did not have enough syntactic background to see why marking multiple subjects was necessary. We are thus considering a simpler treatment. Another option in the future is to hire annotators with more background in syntax.

The interface may be partly to blame for some disagreements, including subcategorizations which annotators often left unmarked (section 4.2.3) or only partly marked (e.g., leaving off a SUBJect for a verb which has been raised). There are a few reasons for this. First, marking subcategorization likely needed more emphasis in the training period, seeing as how it relates to complicated linguistic notions like distinguishing arguments and adjuncts. Secondly, the interface is an issue, as the subcategorization field is not directly visible, compared to the arcs drawn for dependencies; in figure 2, for instance, subcategorization can only be seen in the asterisks, which need to be clicked on to be seen and changed. Relatedly, because it is not always necessary, subcategorization may seem more optional and thus forgettable.

By the nature of being an in-progress project, the guidelines were necessarily not comprehensive. As one example, the TRANS(ition) label was only generally defined, leading to disagreements. As another, a slash could indicate coordination (*actor/actress*), and annotators differed on its POS labeling, as either CC (coordinating conjunction), or a PUNCT (punctuation). The different POS labels then led to vastly different dependency graphs. In spite of a lengthy section on how to handle coordination in the guidelines, it seems that an additional case needs to be added to the guidelines to cover when punctuation is used as a conjunction.

5 Conclusion and outlook

Developing reliable annotation schemes for learner language is an important step towards better POS tagging and parsing of learner corpora. We have described an inter-annotator agreement study that has helped shed light on several issues, such as the reliability of our annotation scheme, and has helped identify room for improvement. This study shows that it is possible to apply a multi-layered dependency annotation scheme to learner text with considerably good agreement rates between three trained annotators. In the future, we will of course be applying the (revised) annotation scheme to larger data sets, but we hope other grammatical annotation schemes can learn from our experience. In the shorter term, we are constructing a gold standard of the text files used here, to test annotation accuracy and whether any (or all) annotators had consistent difficulties. Another next step is to gather a larger pool of data and focus more on analyzing the effects of L1 and learner proficiency level on annotation. Finally, given that syntactic representations can assist in automating tasks such as developmental profiling of learners (e.g., Vyatkina, 2013), grammatical error detection (Tetreault et al., 2010), identification of native language (e.g., Tetreault et al., 2012), and proficiency level determination (Dickinson et al., 2012)—all of which impact NLP-based educational tools—one can explore the effect of specific syntactic decisions on such tasks, as a way to provide feedback on the annotation scheme.

Acknowledgments

We would like to thank the three annotators for their help with this experiment. We also thank the IU CL discussion group, as well as the three anonymous reviewers, for their feedback and comments.

References

Ron Artstein and Massimo Poesio. 2008. Inter-coder agreement for computational linguistics. *Computational Linguistics*, 34(4):555–596.

Anna Babarczy, John Carroll, and Geoffrey Sampson. 2006. Definitional, personal, and mechanical constraints on part of speech annotation performance. *Natural Language Engineering*, 12:77–90.

Patrizia Bonaventura, Peter Howarth, and Wolfgang Menzel. 2000. Phonetic annotation of a non-native speech corpus. In *Proceedings International Workshop on Integrating Speech Technology in the (Language) Learning and Assistive Interface, InStil*, pages 10–17.

Adriane Amelia Boyd. 2012. *Detecting and Diagnosing Grammatical Errors for Beginning Learners of German: From Learner Corpus Annotation to Constraint Satisfaction Problems*. Ph.D. thesis, Ohio State University.

Thorsten Brants. 2000. TnT – a statistical part-of-speech tagger. In *Proceedings of the Sixth Applied Natural Language Processing Conference (ANLP 2000)*, pages 224–231. Seattle, WA.

Daniel Cer, Marie-Catherine de Marneffe, Daniel Jurafsky, and Christopher D. Manning. 2010. Parsing to Stanford dependencies: Trade-offs between speed and accuracy. In *Proceedings of LREC-10*. Malta.

M. Civit, A. Ageno, B. Navarro, N. Bufí, and M. A. Martí. 2003. Qualitative and quantitative analysis of annotators' agreement in the development of Cast3LB. In *Proceedings of 2nd Workshop on Treebanks and Linguistics Theories (TLT-2003)*, pages 33–45.

Pieter de Haan. 2000. Tagging non-native English with the TOSCA-ICLE tagger. In Christian Mair and Markus Hundt, editors, *Corpus Linguistics and Linguistic Theory*, pages 69–79. Rodopi, Amsterdam.

Ana Díaz-Negrillo, Detmar Meurers, Salvador Valera, and Holger Wunsch. 2010. Towards interlanguage POS annotation for effective learner corpora in SLA and FLT. *Language Forum*, 36(1–2):139–154. Special Issue on New Trends in Language Teaching.

Markus Dickinson, Sandra Kübler, and Anthony Meyer. 2012. Predicting learner levels for online exercises of Hebrew. In *Proceedings of the Seventh Workshop on Building Educational Applications Using NLP*, pages 95–104. Association for Computational Linguistics, Montréal, Canada.

Markus Dickinson and Marwa Ragheb. 2009. Dependency annotation for learner corpora. In *Proceedings of the Eighth Workshop on Treebanks and Linguistic Theories (TLT-8)*, pages 59–70. Milan, Italy.

John A. Hawkins and Paula Buttery. 2010. Criterial features in learner corpora: Theory and illustrations. *English Profile Journal*, 1(1):1–23.

Hagen Hirschmann, Anke Lüdeling, Ines Rehbein, Marc Reznicek, and Amir Zeldes. 2010. Syntactic overuse and underuse: A study of a parsed learner corpus and its target hypothesis. Talk given at the Ninth Workshop on Treebanks and Linguistic Theory.

Julia Krivanek and Detmar Meurers. 2011. Comparing rule-based and data-driven dependency parsing of learner language. In *Proceedings of the Int. Conference on Dependency Linguistics (Depling 2011)*. Barcelona.

Sandra Kübler, Ryan McDonald, and Joakim Nivre. 2009. *Dependency Parsing*. Morgan & Claypool Publishers.

Sun-Hee Lee, Markus Dickinson, and Ross Israel. 2012. Developing learner corpus annotation for Korean particle errors. In *Proceedings of the Sixth Linguistic Annotation Workshop*, LAW VI '12, pages 129–133. Association for Computational Linguistics, Stroudsburg, PA, USA.

Ryo Nagata, Edward Whittaker, and Vera Sheinman. 2011. Creating a manually error-tagged and shallow-parsed learner corpus. In *Proceedings of the 49th Annual Meeting of the Association for Computational Linguistics: Human Language Technologies*, pages 1210–1219. Portland, OR.

Niels Ott and Ramon Ziai. 2010. Evaluating dependency parsing performance on German learner language. In *Proceedings of TLT-9*, volume 9, pages 175–186.

Rebecca Passonneau, Nizar Habash, and Owen Rambow. 2006. Inter-annotator agreement on a multilingual semantic annotation task. In *Proceedings of the Fifth International Conference on Language Resources and Evaluation (LREC)*, pages 1951–1956.

Marwa Ragheb and Markus Dickinson. 2011. Avoiding the comparative fallacy in the annotation of learner corpora. In *Selected Proceedings of the 2010 Second Language Research Forum: Re-*

considering SLA Research, Dimensions, and Directions, pages 114–124. Cascadilla Proceedings Project, Somerville, MA.

Marwa Ragheb and Markus Dickinson. 2012. Defining syntax for learner language annotation. In *Proceedings of the 24th International Conference on Computational Linguistics (Coling 2012), Poster Session*. Mumbai, India.

Ines Rehbein, Hagen Hirschmann, Anke Lüdeling, and Marc Reznicek. 2012. Better tags give better trees - or do they? *Linguistic Issues in Language Technology (LiLT)*, 7(10).

Victoria Rosén and Koenraad De Smedt. 2010. Syntactic annotation of learner corpora. In Hilde Johansen, Anne Golden, Jon Erik Hagen, and Ann-Kristin Helland, editors, *Systematisk, variert, men ikke tilfeldig. Antologi om norsk som andrespråk i anledning Kari Tenfjords 60-årsdag [Systematic, varied, but not arbitrary. Anthology about Norwegian as a second language on the occasion of Kari Tenfjord's 60th birthday]*, pages 120–132. Novus forlag, Oslo.

Alla Rozovskaya and Dan Roth. 2010. Annotating ESL errors: Challenges and rewards. In *Proceedings of the NAACL HLT 2010 Fifth Workshop on Innovative Use of NLP for Building Educational Applications*, pages 28–36. Los Angeles, California.

Kenji Sagae, Eric Davis, Alon Lavie, and Brian MacWhinney an Shuly Wintner. 2010. Morphosyntactic annotation of childes transcripts. *Journal of Child Language*, 37(3):705–729.

Geoffrey Sampson. 1995. *English for the Computer: The SUSANNE Corpus and Analytic Scheme*. Clarendon Press, Oxford.

Pontus Stenetorp, Sampo Pyysalo, Goran Topić, Tomoko Ohta, Sophia Ananiadou, and Jun'ichi Tsujii. 2012. brat: a web-based tool for nlp-assisted text annotation. In *Proceedings of the Demonstrations at the 13th Conference of the European Chapter of the Association for Computational Linguistics*, pages 102–107. Avignon, France.

Joel Tetreault, Daniel Blanchard, Aoife Cahill, and Martin Chodorow. 2012. Native tongues, lost and found: Resources and empirical evaluations in native language identification. In *Proceedings of COLING 2012*, pages 2585–2602. Mumbai, India.

Joel Tetreault and Martin Chodorow. 2008. Native judgments of non-native usage: experiments in preposition error detection. In *Proceedings of the Workshop on Human Judgements in Computational Linguistics*, HumanJudge '08, pages 24–32. Association for Computational Linguistics, Stroudsburg, PA, USA.

Joel Tetreault, Jennifer Foster, and Martin Chodorow. 2010. Using parse features for preposition selection and error detection. In *Proceedings of the ACL 2010 Conference Short Papers*, pages 353–358. Uppsala, Sweden.

Sylvie Thouësny. 2009. Increasing the reliability of a part-of-speech tagging tool for use with learner language. Presentation given at the Automatic Analysis of Learner Language (AALL'09) workshop on automatic analysis of learner language: from a better understanding of annotation needs to the development and standardization of annotation schemes.

Bertus van Rooy and Lande Schäfer. 2002. The effect of learner errors on POS tag errors during automatic POS tagging. *Southern African Linguistics and Applied Language Studies*, 20:325–335.

Nina Vyatkina. 2013. Specific syntactic complexity: Developmental profiling of individuals based on an annotated learner corpus. *The Modern Language Journal*, 97(S1):1–20.

Helen Yannakoudakis, Ted Briscoe, and Ben Medlock. 2011. A new dataset and method for automatically grading ESOL texts. In *Proceedings of the 49th Annual Meeting of the Association for Computational Linguistics: Human Language Technologies*, pages 180–189. Portland, OR.

Native Language Identification with PPM

Victoria Bobicev
Technical University of Moldova
168, Stefan Cel Mare bvd.
Chisinău, MD2004 Republic of Moldova
victoria_bobicev@rol.md

Abstract

This paper reports on our work in the NLI shared task 2013 on Native Language Identification. The task is to automatically detect the native language of the TOEFL essays authors in a set of given test documents in English. The task was solved by a system that used the PPM compression algorithm based on an n-gram statistical model. We submitted four runs; word-based PPMC algorithm with normalization and without, character-based PPMC algorithm with normalization and without. The worst result was obtained on training and testing data during the evaluation procedure using the character-based PPM method and normalization: accuracy = 31.9%; the best one was macroaverage F-measure = 0.708 with the word-based PPMC algorithm without normalization.

1 Introduction

With the emergence of user-generated web content, text author profiling is being increasingly studied by the NLP community. Various works describe experiments aiming to automatically discover hidden attributes of text which reveal author's gender, age, personality and others. While English remains one of the main global languages used for communication, interchange of information and ideas, English texts written by different language speakers differ considerably. This is yet another characteristic of the author that can be learned from a text. While a great number of works have presented investigations in this area there was no common ground to evaluate different techniques and approaches to Native Language Identification. NLI shared task 2013 on Native Language Identification provides a playground and a corpus for such an evaluation.

We participated in this shared task with the PPM compression algorithm based on a character-based and word-based n-gram statistical model.

2 Related work

The task of Native Language Identification is to automatically detect text's author's native language when having only English text written by this author. It is generally a sub-task of text classification or, more closely, text author profiling when various stylometric text features are used for certain author's characteristics (gender, age, education, cultural background, etc.) detection (Bergsma et al., 2012; Argamon et al., 2009).

This task is mostly solved by machine-learning algorithms, such as SVM (Witten and Frank, 2005). However, the algorithm itself is not the most influential choice for better performance but rather the set of features used for learning. This set can consist of character, word and PoS n-grams, functional words, punctuation, specific errors, syntactic structures, and others. Some works investigate the influence of thousands of features of very different types (Koppel et al., 2011; Abbasi and Chen, 2008). Extraction of all these features requires a substantial amount of text processing work. We, instead, concentrated on an easier method, namely, PPM, a statistical model used for text compression which almost needs no text preprocessing.

Several approaches that apply compression models to text classification have been presented in Eibe et al. (2000); Thaper (1996). The underlying idea of using compression methods for text classification was their ability to create a language model adapted to particular texts. It was hypothesized that this model captures individual features of the text being modelled. Theoretical background to this approach was given in Teahan and Harper (2001).

3 System description

Detection of the English text author's native language can be viewed as a type of classification task. Such tasks are solved using learning methods. There are different types of text classification. Authorship attribution, spam filtering, dialect identification are just several of the purposes of text categorization. It is natural that for different types of categorization different methods are pertinent. The most common type is the content-based categorization which classifies texts by their topic and requires the most common classification methods based on classical set of features. More specific methods are necessary in cases when classification criterions are not so obvious, for example, in the case of author identification.

In this paper the application of the PPM (Prediction by Partial Matching) model for automatic text classification is explored. Prediction by partial matching (PPM) is an adaptive finite-context method for text compression that is a back-off smoothing technique for finite-order Markov models (Bratko et al., 2006). It obtains all information from the original data, without feature engineering, is easy to implement and relatively fast. PPM produces a language model and can be used in a probabilistic text classifier.

PPM is based on conditional probabilities of the upcoming symbol given several previous symbols (Cleary and Witten, 1984). The PPM technique uses character context models to build an overall probability distribution for predicting upcoming characters in the text. A blending strategy for combining context predictions is to assign a weight to each context model, and then calculate the weighted sum of the probabilities:

$$P(x) = \sum_{i=1}^{m} \lambda_i p_i(x), \qquad (1)$$

where

λ_i and *pi* are weights and probabilities assigned to each order *i (i=1...m).*

For example, the probability of character ***'m'*** in context of the word ***'algorithm'*** is calculated as a sum of conditional probabilities dependent on different context lengths up to the limited maximal length:

$$P_{PPM}(\text{'}\mathbf{m}\text{'}) = \lambda_5 \cdot P(\text{'}\mathbf{m}\text{'} \mid \text{'}\mathbf{orith}\text{'}) + \lambda_4 \cdot P(\text{'}\mathbf{m}\text{'} \mid \text{'}\mathbf{rith}\text{'}) + \lambda_3 \cdot P(\text{'}\mathbf{m}\text{'} \mid \text{'}\mathbf{ith}\text{'}) + \lambda_2 \cdot P(\text{'}\mathbf{m}\text{'} \mid \text{'}\mathbf{th}\text{'}) + + \lambda_1 \cdot P(\text{'}\mathbf{m}\text{'} \mid \text{'}\mathbf{h}\text{'}) + + \lambda_0 \cdot P(\text{'}\mathbf{m}\text{'}) + + \lambda_{-1} \cdot P(\text{'esc'}), \qquad (2)$$

where

λ_i (i = 1...5) is the normalization weight;

5 - maximal length of the context;

P('esc') – 'escape' probability, the probability of an unknown character.

PPM is a special case of the general blending strategy. The *PPM* models use an escape mechanism to combine the predictions of all character contexts of length *m*, where *m* is the maximum model order; the order 0 model predicts symbols based on their unconditioned probabilities, the default order -1 model ensures that a finite probability (however small) is assigned to all possible symbols. The *PPM* escape mechanism is more practical to implement than weighted blending. There are several versions of the *PPM* algorithm depending on the way the escape probability is estimated. In our implementation, we used the escape method C (Bell et al., 1989), named PPMC. Treating a text as a string of characters, a character-based *PPM* avoids defining word boundaries; it deals with different types of documents in a uniform way. It can work with texts in any language and be applied to diverse types of classification; more details can be found in Bobicev (2007). Our utility function for text classification was cross-entropy of the test document:

$$H_d^{\,m} \; - = \sum_{i=1}^{n} p^m(x_i) \log p^m(x_i), \qquad (3)$$

where

n is the number of symbols in a text d,

$H_d^{\,m}$ – entropy of the text d obtained by model m,

$p^m(x_i)$ is a probability of a symbol x_i in the text *d*.

$H_d^{\,m}$ was estimated by the modelling part of the compression algorithm.

Usually, the cross-entropy is greater than the entropy, because the probabilities of symbols in diverse texts are different. The cross-entropy can be used as a measure for document similarity; the lower cross-entropy for two texts is, the more similar they are. Hence, if several statistical models had been created using documents that belong to different classes and cross-entropies are calculated for an unknown text on the basis of each model, the lowest value of cross-entropy will indicate the class of the unknown text. In this way cross-entropy is used for text classification.

On the training step, we created *PPM* models for each class of documents; on the testing step, we evaluated cross-entropy of previously unseen texts using models for each class. The lowest value of cross-entropy indicates the class of the unknown text.

The maximal length of a context equal to 5 in PPM model was proven to be optimal for text compression (Teahan, 1998). In other experiments, length of character n-grams used for text classification varied from 2 (Kukushkina et al., 2001) to 4 (Koppel et al., 2011) or a combination of several lengths (Keselj et al., 2003). Stamatatos (2009) pointed out that the best length of character n-grams depends on different conditions and varies for different texts. In all our experiments with character-based PPM model we used maximal length of a context equal to 5; thus our method is PPMC5.

The character-based *PPM* models were used for spam detection, source-based text classification and classification of multi-modal data streams that included texts. In Bratko et al. (2006), the character-based PPM models were used for spam detection. In this task there existed two classes only: spam and legitimate email (ham). The created models showed strong performance in the Text Retrieval Conference competition, indicating that data-compression models are well suited to the spam filtering problem. In Teahan (2000), a PPM-based text model and minimum cross-entropy as a text classifier were used for various tasks; one of them was an author detection task for the well known Federalist Papers. In Bobicev and Sokolova (2008), the PPM algorithm was applied to text categorization in two ways: on the basis of characters and on the basis of words. Character-based methods performed almost as well as SVM, the best method among several machine learning methods compared in Debole and Sebastiani (2004) for the Reuters-21578 corpus.

Usually, PPM models are character-based. However, word-based models were also used for various purposes. For example, if texts are classified by the contents, they are better characterized by words and word combinations than by fragments consisting of five letters. For some tasks words can be more indicative text features than character sequences. That's why we decided to use both character-based and word-based models for PPM text classification. In the case of word-based PPM, the context is only one word and an example for formula (1) looks like the following:

$$P_{PPM}(\text{'word}_i\text{'}) = \lambda_1 \cdot P(\text{'word}_i\text{'} \mid \text{'word}_{i-1}\text{'}) + \lambda_0 \cdot P(\text{'word}_i\text{'}) + \lambda_{-1} \cdot P(\text{'esc'}),$$

where

word_i is the current word;

word_{i-1} is the previous word.

This model is coded as PPMC1 because of the same C escape method and one length context used for probability estimation.

Training and testing data is distributed quite unevenly in many tasks, for example, in Reuters-21578 corpus. This imbalance drastically affected the results of the classification experiments; the classification was biased towards classes with a larger volume of data for training. Such imbalance class distribution problems were mentioned in Bobicev and Sokolova (2008), Stamatatos (2009), Narayanan et al. (2012). Considering the fact that unbalanced data affected classification results in such a substantial way we used a normalization procedure for balancing entropies of the statistical data models.

The first step of our algorithm was training. In the process of training, statistical models for each class of texts were created. This meant that probabilities of text elements were estimated. The next step after training was calculation of entropies of test documents on the basis of each class model. We obtained a matrix of entropies 'class statistical models x test documents'. The columns were entropies for the class statistical models and rows were entropies for a given test documents. After this step the normalization procedure was applied. The procedure consisted of several steps.

(1) Mean entropy for each class of texts was calculated on the base of the matrix;

(2) Each value in the matrix was divided by the mean entropy for this class. Thereby we obtained more balanced values and classification improved considerably.

Although the application of PPM model to the document classification is not new, PPM was never applied to the task of English text author's native language detection.

In order to evaluate the PPM classification method for English text author's native language identification a number of experiments were performed. The aim of the experiments was twofold:

- to evaluate the quality of PPM-based document classification;
- to compare letter-based and word-based PPM classification.

4 Evaluation

Three sets of experiments were carried out during the NLI shared task event. The first one was performed on the training and development data released in January. The second set consisted of evaluation runs on test data released in March and the results for these experiments were provided by the organizers. The third set was 10-fold cross-validation on training + development data requested by the organizers.

4.1 The First set of experiments

The first set of experiments was carried out on the first set of data released by the organizers: TOEFL essays written by 11 native languages speakers. 9,900 essays of this set were sequestered as the training data and 1,100 were for the development set. Thus, we trained our model on 900 files for each native language speakers, for each class. Next, we attributed classes to 1,100 development texts. We carried out four experiments. The first two were done on the basis of the character-based PPMC5 method with and without the normalization procedure described earlier. The second two experiments were done with the word-based PPMC1 method with and without the normalization. The Precision, Recall and F-measure for these four experiments are presented in Table 1. Tables 2 and 3 are confusion tables for the worst and for the best cases of the four experiments.

Model	**Microaverage F-score**	**Precision**	**Recall**	**Macroaverage F-score**
Character-based PPMC5 method without normalization	0.382	0.384	0.382	0.383
Character-based PPMC5 method with normalization	0.362	0.363	0.362	0.3625
Word-based PPMC1 method without normalization	**0.701**	**0.715**	**0.701**	**0.708**
Word-based PPMC1 method with normalization	0.687	0.702	0.687	0.695

Table 1. Results obtained on character-based and letter-based PPM models with and without normalization.

	ARA	CHI	FRE	GER	HIN	ITA	JPN	KOR	SPA	TEL	TUR
ARA	26	7	9	3	6	5	14	6	8	12	4
CHI	3	32	8	7	3	3	20	13	4	4	3
FRE	6	4	32	8	9	13	7	3	4	8	6
GER	1	6	10	36	3	10	8	7	6	5	8
HIN	2	3	4	5	36	7	6	3	1	29	4
ITA	5	3	16	6	2	45	1	4	10	4	4
JPN	3	14	2	3	2	6	49	13	5	1	2
KOR	2	6	5	5	2	3	21	42	1	8	5
SPA	3	4	8	8	3	19	13	5	25	9	3
TEL	1	5	0	4	18	2	4	4	0	60	2
TUR	5	9	9	9	8	5	17	11	3	9	15

Table 2. Confusion table for 1,100 development files for the first PPMC5 character-based experiment with normalization.

	ARA	CHI	FRE	GER	HIN	ITA	JPN	KOR	SPA	TEL	TUR
ARA	46	2	3	6	8	7	2	5	8	5	8
CHI	1	67	1	2	1	0	7	9	3	1	8
FRE	0	2	77	9	1	3	1	0	4	0	3
GER	0	0	3	90	1	2	0	0	2	0	2
HIN	0	0	1	2	69	0	0	0	2	26	0
ITA	1	1	6	3	0	82	0	0	3	0	4
JPN	1	7	1	5	0	0	65	15	1	1	4
KOR	1	3	0	2	0	0	20	67	2	1	4
SPA	1	1	7	10	2	9	1	1	62	0	6
TEL	0	0	0	0	31	0	0	1	0	68	0
TUR	0	0	2	7	7	0	2	0	2	2	78

Table 3. Confusion table for 1,100 development files for the first PPMC1 word-based experiment without normalization.

4.2 The second set of experiments

The second set of experiments was done on the 1,100 test files during the evaluation phase of the challenge. The results of these experiments were provided by the organizers. Again, we carried out four experiments: character-based PPMC5 method with and without normalization and word-based PPMC1 method with and without normalization. Confusion tables 4 and 5 presents the worst and the best results.
The overall accuracies for these experiments are:

Character-based PPMC5 method without normalization - 37.4%;

Character-based PPMC5 method with normalization - 31.9%;

Word-based PPMC1 method without normalization - 62.5%;

Word-based PPMC1 method with normalization - 62.2%.

	ARA	**CHI**	**FRE**	**GER**	**HIN**	**ITA**	**JPN**	**KOR**	**SPA**	**TEL**	**TUR**	**Precision**	**Recall**	**F-measure**
ARA	**7**	4	16	5	3	17	10	25	0	8	5	43.8%	7.0%	12.1%
CHI	1	**31**	8	5	1	9	19	23	0	2	1	38.8%	31.0%	34.4%
FRE	0	1	**55**	5	2	17	6	10	0	0	4	28.4%	55.0%	37.4%
GER	2	2	18	**33**	2	15	8	15	0	3	2	40.7%	33.0%	36.5%
HIN	0	6	20	9	**15**	7	15	14	0	11	3	36.6%	15.0%	21.3%
ITA	1	1	16	3	1	**58**	7	8	2	1	2	32.8%	58.0%	41.9%
JPN	0	2	7	0	0	8	**57**	24	1	0	1	29.2%	57.0%	38.6%
KOR	2	15	8	0	1	4	27	**37**	1	2	3	18.5%	37.0%	24.7%
SPA	0	8	21	9	1	18	19	14	**8**	1	1	66.7%	8.0%	14.3%
TEL	1	5	8	6	13	6	12	10	0	**35**	4	55.6%	35.0%	42.9%
TUR	2	5	17	6	2	18	15	20	0	0	**15**	36.6%	15.0%	21.3%

Table 4. Confusion table for 1,100 test files for the PPMC5 character-based experiment with normalization. The overall accuracy is 31.9%.

	ARA	CHI	FRE	GER	HIN	ITA	JPN	KOR	SPA	TEL	TUR	Precision	Recall	F-measure
ARA	**39**	2	7	9	6	1	3	1	14	7	11	75.0%	39.0%	51.3%
CHI	3	**65**	3	5	1	0	8	4	2	0	9	72.2%	65.0%	68.4%
FRE	1	0	**67**	10	1	11	1	0	4	0	5	60.9%	67.0%	63.8%
GER	0	0	4	**92**	1	0	0	0	2	0	1	63.4%	92.0%	75.1%
HIN	0	1	3	2	**64**	0	0	1	12	11	6	58.7%	64.0%	61.2%
ITA	1	1	10	10	0	**71**	0	0	4	0	3	70.3%	71.0%	70.6%
JPN	1	4	1	1	2	1	**66**	15	1	1	7	63.5%	66.0%	64.7%
KOR	2	9	3	2	3	0	22	**50**	2	0	7	61.0%	50.0%	54.9%
SPA	1	2	9	12	2	15	0	4	**51**	1	3	48.1%	51.0%	49.5%
TEL	1	3	0	0	27	0	1	0	8	**54**	6	73.0%	54.0%	62.1%
TUR	3	3	3	2	2	2	3	7	6	0	**69**	54.3%	69.0%	60.8%

Table 5. Confusion table for 1,100 test files for the PPMC1 word-based experiment without normalization. The overall accuracy is 62.5%.

Model	Microaverage F-score	Precision	Recall	Macroaverage F-score
Character-based PPMC5 method without normalization	0.366	0.368	0.366	0.367
Character-based PPMC5 method with normalization	0.353	0.366	0.353	0.359
Word-based PPMC1 method without normalization	**0.649**	**0.660**	**0.649**	**0.655**
Word-based PPMC1 method with normalization	0.640	0.652	0.640	0.640

Table 6. Results obtained on character-based and letter-based PPM models with and without normalization on the basis of training + development data.

	ARA	CHI	FRE	GER	HIN	ITA	JPN	KOR	SPA	TEL	TUR
ARA	22	7	13	1	1	11	18	10	7	6	4
CHI	1	29	7	2	1	8	22	22	2	2	4
FRE	6	4	40	8	4	9	10	7	7	2	3
GER	3	3	15	26	3	15	14	9	4	4	4
HIN	5	3	6	3	31	6	7	5	4	26	4
ITA	4	4	10	9	3	42	15	6	4	0	3
JPN	1	9	4	6	1	3	49	17	3	3	4
KOR	1	7	7	2	5	4	37	29	3	1	4
SPA	6	5	12	3	6	21	14	8	20	1	4
TEL	5	1	5	2	16	6	9	9	1	43	3
TUR	4	3	14	7	3	7	22	8	5	2	25

Table 7. Confusion table for the worst case in the third set of experiments; 10-fold cross-validation, fold 9, PPMC5 character-based, with normalization.

	ARA	CHI	FRE	GER	HIN	ITA	JPN	KOR	SPA	TEL	TUR
ARA	40	3	9	5	5	7	5	4	8	4	10
CHI	2	73	1	1	2	2	6	10	2	0	1
FRE	0	2	70	9	2	4	1	2	6	1	3
GER	0	0	2	87	3	1	0	1	5	0	1
HIN	1	0	2	3	69	0	0	1	3	15	6
ITA	0	1	11	10	3	72	1	0	2	0	0
JPN	0	6	0	1	2	2	68	16	3	0	2
KOR	1	5	3	1	3	0	16	63	5	0	3
SPA	2	1	8	4	4	5	1	6	65	0	4
TEL	1	1	0	1	25	0	1	1	2	66	2
TUR	1	1	3	4	6	1	0	0	10	1	73

Table 8. Confusion table for the best case in the third set of experiments; 10-fold cross-validation, fold 3, PPMC1 word-based, without normalization.

4.3 The third set of experiments

The third set of the experiments was done at the organizers' request on the basis of training + development data. 10-fold cross-validation was made on this data with exactly the same splitting used in Tetreault et al. (2012). The results of these experiments are presented in Table 6. Tables 7 and 8 are confusion tables for the worst and the best cases among all 10 folds and four experiments.

5 Conclusion

The task of identifying the native language of a writer based solely on a sample of their English writing is an exiting and intriguing task. It is a type of text classification task; however it requires task specific features. The PPM method presented in this paper uses two types of features: (1) character sequences of length from 5 characters and shorter, (2) words and bigrams of words. This method achieved lower results than methods which used carefully selected and adjusted feature sets. The advantage of this method is its relative simplicity of use and ability to work with any text.

Two interesting and surprising conclusions we have drawn from these experiments: (1) normalization did not improve the results for this data; (2) word-based method performed much better than character-based. In most previous experiments with PPM-based classification (Bobicev, 2007; Bobicev and Sokolova, 2008) we obtained inverse results: character-based methods were much better than word-based. The author recognition experiments showed the same, much better performance of character-based methods. The possible explanation is that the data for this experiment was cleaned and tokenized whereas the data in other experiments was much noisier which created problems for the word-based method.

The same was with normalization. The organizers prepared very well balanced data and there was no need of normalization which helped to gain another 20-25% of accuracy on other data.

References

Abbasi A. and Chen H. 2008. *Writeprints: A stylometric approach to identity-level identification and similarity detection in cyberspace*, ACM Trans. Inf. Syst., vol. 26, no. 2, pp. 7:1–7:29.

Argamon S., Koppel M., Pennebaker J. W., and Schler J. 2009. *Automatically profiling the author of an anonymous text*, Commun. ACM, vol. 52, no. 2, pp. 119–123.

Bell, T., Witten, I. and Cleary, J. 1989. *Modeling for text compression*, ACM Comput. Surv. 21(4):557–591.

Bergsma, S., Post, M., and Yarowsky, D. 2012. *Stylometric analysis of scientific articles*, 2012 Conference of the North American Chapter of the Association for Computational Linguistics: Human Language Technologies, pages 327–337, Montréal, Canada. Association for Computational Linguistics.

Bobicev, V. 2007. *Comparison of word-based and letter-based text classification*, RANLP'07, 76–80.

Bobicev V., Sokolova M. 2008. *An Effective and Robust Method for Short Text Classification*, Association for the Advancement of Artificial Intelligence (AAAI-2008), Cohn (ed), AAAI Press, Chicago, USA.

Bratko, A., Cormack, G. V., Filipic, B., Lynam, T. R., and Zupan, B. 2006. *Spam filtering using statistical data compression models*, Journal of Machine Learning Research 7:2673–2698.

Cleary, J., and Witten, I. 1984. *Data compression using adaptive coding and partial string matching*, IEEE Trans. Commun. 32(4):396–402.

Debole F. and Sebastiani F. 2004. *An Analysis of the Relative Hardness of Reuters-21578 Subsets*, Journal of the American Society for Information Science and Technology, vol. 56, pp. 971–974.

Eibe Frank, Chang Chui and Ian H. Witten. 2000. *Text categorisation using compression models*, DCC-00, IEEE Data Compression Conference.

Keselj V., Peng F., Cercone N., and Thomas C. 2003. *N-gram-based author profiles for authorship attribution*, PACLING '03, Halifax, pp. 255–264.

Koppel M., Schler J., and Argamon S. 2011. *Authorship attribution in the wild*, Lang Resources & Evaluation, vol. 45, no. 1, pp. 83–94.

Kukushkina O. V., Polikarpov A. A., and Khmelev D. V., 2001. *Using Literal and Grammatical Statistics for Authorship Attribution*, Probl. Inf. Transm., vol. 37, no. 2, pp. 172–184.

Narayanan A., Paskov H., Gong N. Z., Bethencourt J., Stefanov E., Shin E. C. R., and Song D. 2012. *On the Feasibility of Internet-Scale Author Identification*, in 2012 IEEE Symposium on Security and Privacy (SP), pp. 300 –314.

Stamatatos E. 2009. *A survey of modern authorship attribution methods*, J. Am. Soc. Inf. Sci. Technol., vol. 60, no. 3, pp. 538–556.

Teahan W. J. 1998. *Modelling English text*, PhD Thesis, University of Waikato, New Zealand.

Teahan W. J., McNab R., Wen Y., and Witten I. H. 2000. *A compression-based algorithm for Chinese word segmentation*, Comput. Linguist., vol. 26, no. 3, pp. 375–393.

Teahan W. J. and Harper D. J. 2001. *Using compression based language models for text categorization*, in J. Callan, B. Croft and J. Lafferty, editors, Workshop on Language Modeling and Information Retrieval, pages 83-88. ARDA, Carnegie Mellon University.

Tetreault J., Blanchard D., Cahill A., Chodorow M. 2012. *Native Tongues, Lost and Found*, Resources and Empirical Evaluations in Native Language Identification, COLING 2012.

Thaper N. 1996. *Using Compression For Source Based Classification Of Text*. Bachelor of Technology (Computer Science and Engineering), Indian Institute of Technology, Delhi, India.

Using Other Learner Corpora in the 2013 NLI Shared Task

Julian Brooke
Department of Computer Science
University of Toronto
jbrooke@cs.toronto.edu

Graeme Hirst
Department of Computer Science
University of Toronto
gh@cs.toronto.edu

Abstract

Our efforts in the 2013 NLI shared task focused on the potential benefits of external corpora. We show that including training data from multiple corpora is highly effective at robust, cross-corpus NLI (i.e. open-training task 1), particularly when some form of domain adaptation is also applied. This method can also be used to boost performance even when training data from the same corpus is available (i.e. open-training task 2). However, in the closed-training task, despite testing a number of new features, we did not see much improvement on a simple model based on earlier work.

1 Introduction

Our participation in the 2013 NLI shared task (Tetreault et al., 2013) follows on our recent work exploring cross-corpus evaluation, i.e. using distinct corpora for training and testing (Brooke and Hirst, 2011; Brooke and Hirst, 2012a; Brooke and Hirst, 2012b), an approach that is now becoming fairly standard alternative in relevant work (Bykh and Meurers, 2012; Tetreault et al., 2012; Swanson and Charniak, 2013). Our promotion of cross-corpus evaluation in NLI was partially motivated by serious issues with the most popular corpus for native language identification work up to now, the International Corpus of Learner English (Granger et al., 2009). The new TOEFL-11 (Blanchard et al., 2013) used for this NLI shared task addresses some of the problems with the ICLE (most glaringly, the fact that some topics in the ICLE appeared only in some L1 backgrounds), but, from the perspective of topic, proficiency, and particularly genre, it is necessarily limited in scope (perhaps even more so than the ICLE); in short, it addresses only a small portion of the space of learner texts. Our interest, then, continues to be in robust models for NLI that are not restricted to utility in a particular corpus, and in our participation in this task we have focused our efforts on the open-training tasks which allow the use of corpora beyond the TOEFL-11. Since participation in these tasks was low relative to the closed-training task, fewer papers will address them, making our emphasis here all the more relevant.

The models built for all of three of the tasks are extensions of the model used in our recent work (Brooke and Hirst, 2012b); we will discuss the aspects of this model common to all tasks in Section 2. Section 3 is a brief review of our methodology and results in the closed-training task, which was focused exclusively on testing features (both new and old); we found almost nothing that improved on our best feature set from previous work, and most features actually hurt performance. In Section 4, we discuss the corpora we used for the open-training tasks, some of which we collected and/or have not been applied to NLI before. Our approach to the open-training task 2 using these corpora is presented in Section 5. In Section 6, we discuss how we used domain adaption methods and our various external corpora to create the (winning) model for the open-training task 1, which did not permit usage of the TOEFL-11; we also present some post hoc testing (now that TOEFL-11 is no longer off limits). In Section 7 we offer conclusions.

2 Basic Model

In our recent work on cross-corpus NLI (Brooke and Hirst, 2012b), we tested a number of classifier and feature options, and most of our choices there are carried over to this work. In particular, we use the Liblinear SVM 1va (one versus all) classifier (Fan et al., 2008). Using the TOEFL-11 corpus, we briefly tested the other options explored in that paper (including SVM 1v1) as well as the logistic regression classifier included in Liblinear, and found that the SVM 1va classifier was still preferred (with our best feature set, see below), though the differences involved were marginal. Although small variations in the choice of C parameter within the SVM model did occasionally produce benefits (here and in our previous work), these were not consistent, whereas the default value of 1 showed consistently near optimal results. We used a binary feature representation, and then feature vectors were normalized to the unit circle. With respect to feature selection, our earlier work used a frequency cutoff of 5 for all features; we continue to use frequency cutoffs here; other common feature selection methods (e.g. use of information gain) were ineffective in our previous work, so we did not explore them in detail here.

With regards to the features themselves, our earlier work tested a fairly standard collection of distributional features, including function words, word n-grams (up to bigram), POS n-grams (up to trigram), character n-grams (up to trigram), dependencies, context-free productions, and 'mixed' POS/function n-grams (up to trigram), i.e. n-grams with all lexical words replaced with part of speech. Most of these had appeared in previous NLI work (Koppel et al., 2005; Wong and Dras, 2011; Wong et al., 2012), though until recently word n-grams had been avoided because of ICLE topic bias. Our best model used only two of these features, word n-grams and the mixed POS/function n-grams. This was our starting point for the present work. The Stanford parser (Klein and Manning, 2003) was used for POS tagging and parsing.

Obviously, the training set used varies throughout the paper, and other differences in specific models built for each task will be mentioned as they become relevant. For evaluation here, we primarily use the test set for NLI shared task, though we employ some other evaluation corpora, as appropriate. During the preparation for the shared task, we made our decisions regarding models for two tasks with TOEFL-11 training according to the results in two training/test sets (800 per language for training, 100 per language for testing) sampled from the released training data. Since our research was focused on cross-corpus evaluation, we never created mechanisms for cross-validation in our system, and in fact it creates practical difficulties for the open-training task 2, so we do not include cross-validated results here.

Table 1: Feature testing for closed-training task, previously investigated features; best result is in bold.

Feature Set	Accuracy (%)
Word+mixed	76.8
Word+mixed+characters	72.0
Word+mixed+POS	76.6
Word+mixed+productions	77.9
Word+mixed+dependencies	**78.9**
Word+mixed+dep+prod	78.4

3 Closed-training Task

Our approach to the closed-training task primarily involved feature testing. Table 1 contains the results of testing our previously investigated features from Brooke and Hirst (2012b) in the TOEFL-11, pivoted around the best set (word n-grams + mixed POS/Function n-grams) from that earlier work.

Some of the features we rejected in our previous work also underperform here, in particular character and POS n-grams. In fact, character n-grams had a much more negative effect on performance here than they had previously. Dependencies are clearly a useful feature in the TOEFL-11, this is fully consistent with out initial testing. CFG productions offer a small benefit on top of our base feature set, but are not useful when dependencies are also included, so we discarded them. Thus, our feature set going forward consists of word n-grams, mixed POS/function n-grams, and dependencies.

Next, we evaluate our feature frequency cutoff using this feature set (Table 2). We used the rather high cutoff of 5 (for all features) in the previous work because of our much larger training set. We looked at

Table 2: Feature frequency cutoff testing for closed-training task; best result is in bold.

Cutoff	Accuracy (%)
At least 5 occurrences	78.9
At least 3 occurrences	79.5
At least 2 occurrences	79.7
All features	**80.2**

Table 3: Feature testing for closed-training task, new features; best result is in bold.

Feature Set	Accuracy (%)
Best	**80.2**
Best+partial abstraction	79.7
Best+dependency chains	78.6
Best+wild card productions	78.8
Best+TSG fragments	78.1
Best+MRC lexicon	54.2

higher values there, but for this task we focused on testing lower values.

Lowering our frequency cutoff is indeed beneficial, and we got our best result in the test set when we had no feature selection at all. This was not consistent with our preparatory testing, which showed some benefit to removing hapax legomena, though the difference was marginal. However, we did include a run with this option in our final submission, and so this last result represents our best performance on the closed-training task.

We tested several other feature options that were added to our system for this task. Inspired by Bykh and Meurers (2012), we first considered *n*-grams (up to trigrams) where at least one lexical word is abstracted to its POS, and at least one isn't (partial abstraction). Since dependencies were found to be a positive feature, we tried adding dependency chains, which combine two dependencies, i.e. three lexical words linked by two grammatical relations. We tested productions with wild cards, e.g. S → NP VP * matches any sentence production which starts with NP VP. Tree Substitution grammar fragments have been shown to be superior to CFG productions (Swanson and Charniak, 2012); we used raw Tree Substitution Grammar (TSG) fragments for the TOEFL-11[1] and tested a subset of those fragments which involved at least two levels of the grammar (i.e. those not already covered by *n*-grams or CFG productions).

Our final feature option requires slightly more explanation. Crossley and McNamara (2012) report that metrics associated with word concreteness, imagability, meaningfulness, and familiarity are useful for NLI; the metrics they use are derived from the MRC Psycholinguistic database (Coltheart, 1980), which assign values for each dimension to individual words. We used the scores in the MRC to get an average score for each dimension for each text, further normalized to the range 0–1; texts with no words in the dictionaries were assigned the average across the training set.

Table 3 indicates that all of these new features were, to varying degrees, a drag on our model. The strongly negative effect of the MRC lexicons is particularly surprising. We speculate that this might might be due partially to problems with combining a large number of binary features with a small number of continuous metrics directly in a single SVM. A meta-classifier might solve this problem, but we did not explore meta-classification for features here.

Finally, since that information was available to us, we tested creating sub-models segregated by topic and proficiency. The topic-segregated model consisted of 8 SVMs, one for each topic; accuracy of this model was quite low, only 67.3%. The proficiency-segregated model used two groups, high and low/medium (there were few low texts, so we did not think they would be sufficient by themselves for a viable model). Results were higher, 74.9%, but still well below the best unsegregated model.

4 External Corpora

In this section we review corpora which will be used for the open-training tasks in the next two sections. Including the TOEFL-11, there are at least six publicly available multi-L1 learner text corpora for NLI, with many of these corpora becoming available relatively recently. Below, we introduce each corpus in detail; a summary of the number of tokens from each L1 background for each of the corpora is in Table 4.

[1]We thank Ben Swanson for letting us use his TSG fragments.

Table 4: Number of tokens (in thousands) in external learner corpora, by L1.

L1	Corpus				
	Lang-8 (new)	ICLE	FCE	ICCI	ICNALE
Japanese	11694k	227k	33k	232k	199k
Chinese	7044k	552k	30k	243k	366k
Korean	5174k	0k	37k	0k	151k
French	536k	256k	61k	0k	0k
Spanish	861k	225k	83k	49k	0k
Italian	450k	251k	31k	0k	0k
German	331k	258k	29k	91k	0k
Turkish	51k	222k	22k	0k	0k
Arabic	218k	0k	0k	0k	0k
Hindi	11k	0k	0k	0k	0k
Telugu	2k	0k	0k	0k	0k

Lang-8 Lang-8 is a website where language learners write journal entries in their L2 to be corrected by native speakers. We collected a large set of these entries, which we've shown to be useful for NLI (Brooke and Hirst, 2012b), despite the noisiness of the corpus (for instance, some entries directly mix L1 and L2). For this task we added more entries written since the first version was collected (58k on top of the existing 154k entries).[2] The corpus contains entries from all the L1 backgrounds in the TOEFL-11, though the amounts for Hindi and particularly Telugu are small. Since many of the entries are very short, as in our previous work we add entries of the same L1 together to reach a minimum size of 250 tokens.

ICLE Before 2011, nearly all work on NLI was done in the International Corpus of Learner English or ICLE (Granger et al., 2009), a collection of college student essays from 15 L1 backgrounds, 8 of which overlap with the 11 L1s in the TOEFL-11. Despite known issues that might cause problems (Brooke and Hirst, 2011), it is probably the closest match in terms of genre and writer proficiency to the TOEFL-11.

FCE What we call the FCE corpus is a small sample of the First Certificate in English portion of the Cambridge Learner Corpus, which was released for the purposes of essay scoring evaluation (Yannakoudakis et al., 2011); 16 different L1 backgrounds are represented, 9 of which overlap with the TOEFL-11. Each of the texts consists of two short answers in the form of a letter, a report, an article, or a short story. Relative to the other corpora, the actual amount of text in the FCE is small.

ICCI Like the ICLE and TOEFL-11, the International Corpus of Crosslinguistic Interlanguage (Tono et al., 2012) is also an essay corpus, though in contrast with other corpora it is focused on young learners, i.e. those in grade school. It includes both descriptive and argumentative essays on a number of topics. Only 4 of its L1s overlap with the TOEFL-11.

ICANLE The International Corpus Network of Asian Learners of English or ICANLE (Ishikawa, 2011) is a collection of essays from college students in 10 Asian countries; 3 of the L1s overlap with the TOEFL-11.[3] Even more so than the TOEFL-11, this corpus is strictly controlled for topic, it has only 2 topics (part-time jobs and smoking in restaurants).

One obvious problem with using the above corpora to classify L1s in the TOEFL-11 is the lack of Hindi and Telugu text, which we found were the two most easily confused L1s in the closed-

[2]We do not have permission to distribute the corpus directly; however, we can offer a list of URLs together with software which can be used to recreate the corpus.

[3]The ICANLE also contains 103K of Urdu text. Since Urdu and Hindi are mutually intelligible, this could be a good substitute for Hindi; we overlooked this possibility during our preparation for the task, unfortunately.

Table 5: Number of tokens (in thousands) in Indian corpora, by expected L1.

L1	Indian Corpus		
	News	Twitter	Blog
Hindi	996k	146k	2089k
Telugu	998k	133k	76k

training task. We explored a few methods to get data to fill this gap. First, we downloaded two collections of English language Indian news articles, one from a Hindi newspaper, the *Hindustan Times*, and one from a Telugu newspaper, the *Andhra Jyothy*.[4] Second, we extracted a collection of English tweets from the WORLD twitter corpus (Han et al., 2012) that were geolocated in the Hindi and Telugu speaking areas; as with the Lang-8, these were combined to create texts of at least 250 tokens.[5] Our third Indian corpus consists of translations (by Google Translate) of Hindi and Telugu blogs from the ICWSM 2009 Spinn3r Dataset (Burton et al., 2009), which we used in other work on using L1 text for NLI (Brooke and Hirst, 2012a). The number of tokens in each of these corpora are given in Table 5.

5 Open-training Task 2

Our approach to open-training task 2 is based on the assumption that in many ways it is a direct extension of the closed-training task. For example, we directly use the best feature set from that task, with no further testing. Based on the results in our initial testing, we used a feature frequency cutoff of 2 during our testing for open-training task 2; for consistency, we continue with that cutoff in this section.

We first attempted to integrate information from other corpora by using a meta-classifier, as was successfully used for features by Tetreault et al. (2012). Briefly, classifiers were trained on each major external corpus (including only the L1s in the TOEFL-11), and then tested on the TOEFL-11 training set; TOEFL-11 training was accomplished using 10-fold crossvalidation (by modifying the code for Liblinear crossvalidation to output margins). With the TOEFL-11 as the training set, the SVM margins from each 1va classifier (across all L1s and all corpora) were used as the feature input to the meta-classifier (also an SVM). In addition to Liblinear, we also outputted this meta-classification problem to WEKA format (Witten and Frank, 2005), and tested a number of other classifier options not available in Liblinear (e.g. Naïve Bayes, decision trees, random forests). In addition to (continuous) margins, we also tested using the classification directly. Ultimately, we came to the conclusion were that any use of a meta-classifer came with a cost (a minimum 2–3% drop in performance) that could not be fully overcome with the additional information from our external corpora. The result using SVM classifiers, margin features, and an SVM meta-classifier was 78.5%, well below the TOEFL-11–only baseline.

The other approach to using these external corpora is to add the data directly to the TOEFL-11 data and train a single classifier. This is very straightforward; really the only variable is which corpora will be included. However, we need to introduce, at this point, a domain-adaptation technique from our most recent work (Brooke and Hirst, 2012b), bias adaption, which we used to greatly improve the accuracy of cross-corpus classification. Without getting into the algorithmic details, bias adaption involves changing the bias (constant) factor of a model until the output of the model in some dataset is balanced across classes (or otherwise fits the expected distribution); it partially addresses skewed results due to differences between training and testing corpora. In the previous work, we used a separate development set, but here we rely on the test set itself; since the technique is unsupervised, we do not need to know the classes. Table 6 shows model performance after adding various corpora to the training set (TOEFL-11 is always included), with and without bias adaption (BA).

Many of the differences in Table 6 are modest, but there are are few points to be made. First, there is a small improvement using either the Lang-8 or the ICLE as additional data. The ICCI, on the other hand, has a clearly negative effect, perhaps be-

[4]As with the Lang-8, we cannot distribute the corpus directly but would be happy to provide URLs and scraping software for those would like to build it themselves.

[5]We extracted India regions 07 and 36 for Hindi, and 02 and 25 for Telegu; We can provide a list of tweet ids for reconstructing the corpus if desired. Our thanks to Bo Han and Paul Cook for helping us get these tweets.

Table 6: Corpus testing for open-training task; best result is in bold.

Training Set	Accuracy (%)	
	no BA	with BA
TOEFL-11 only	79.7	79.2
+Lang-8	79.5	**80.5**
+ICLE	80.2	80.2
+FCE	79.6	79.3
+ICCI	77.3	76.7
+ICANLE	79.7	79.3
+Lang-8+ICLE	80.4	80.4
+all but ICCI	80.0	80.4

cause of the age or proficiency of the contributors to that corpus. Bias adaption seems to help when the (messy and highly unbalanced) Lang-8 is involved (consistent with our previous work), but it does not seem useful applied to other corpora, at least not in this setting.

Our second adaptation technique involves training data selection, which has been used, for instance in cross-domain parsing (Plank and van Noord, 2011). The method used here is very simple: we count the number of times each word appears in a document in our test data, rank the texts in our training data according to the sum of counts (in the test data) each word that appears in a training texts, and throw away a certain numbers of low-ranked texts. For example, if a training text consists solely of the two words *I agree*[6] and *I* appears in 1053 texts in the test set, and *agree* appears in 325, then the value for that text is 1378. This method simultaneously penalizes short texts, those texts with low lexical diversity, and texts that do not use the same words as our test set. We use a fixed cutoff, r, which refers to the proportion of training data that is thrown away for each L1 (allowing this to work independent of L1 was not effective). We tested this on this method in tandem with bias adaption on two corpus sets: The TOEFL-11 and the Lang-8, and all corpora except the ICCI. The results are in Table 7. The number in italics is the best run that we submitted.

Again, it is difficult to come to any firm conclusions when the differences are this small, but

[6]This is not a made-up example; there is actually a text in the TOEFL-11 corpus like this.

Table 7: Training set selection testing for open-training task 2; best result is in bold, best submitted run is in italics.

Training Set	Accuracy (%)	
	no BA	with BA
TOEFL-11 only	79.7	79.2
+Lang-8	79.5	80.5
+Lang-8 $r = 0.1$	81.4	81.6
+Lang-8 $r = 0.2$	80.6	81.5
+Lang-8 $r = 0.3$	81.0	80.6
+all but ICCI	80.0	80.4
+all but ICCI $r = 0.1$	81.5	**82.5**
+all but ICCI $r = 0.2$	81.0	*81.6*
+all but ICCI $r = 0.3$	80.9	81.3

our best results involve all of the corpora (except the ICCI) and both adaptation techniques. Unfortunately, our initial testing suggested $r = 0.2$ was the better choice, so our official best result in this task (81.6%) is not the best result in this table. Performance clearly drops for $r > 0.2$. Nevertheless, nearly all the results in the table show clear improvement on our closed-training task model.

6 Open-training Task 1

The central challenge of open-training task 1 was that the TOEFL-11 was completely off-limits, even for testing. Therefore, a discussion of how we prepared for this task is very distinct from a post hoc analysis of the best method once we allowed ourselves access to the TOEFL-11; we separate the two here. We did use the feature set (and frequency cutoff) from the closed-training (and open-training 2) task; it was close enough to the feature set from our earlier work (using the Lang-8, ICLE, and FCE) that it did not seem like cheating to preserve it.

6.1 Method

Given our failure to create a meta-classifier in open-training task 2, we did not pursue that option here, focusing purely on adding corpora directly to a mixed training set. The central question was which corpora to add, and whether to use our domain-adaptation methods. Our experience with the ICCI in the open-training task 2 suggested that it might be worth leaving it (or perhaps other corpora) out, but

Table 8: ICLE testing for Open-training task 1; best result is in bold.

Training Set	Accuracy (%)	
	no BA	with BA
Lang-8	47.0	57.1
Lang-8+FCE	47.9	58.2
Lang-8+ICCI	46.4	54.8
Lang-8+ICNALE	46.9	57.5
Lang-8+ICNALE+FCE	47.7	**58.8**
Lang-8+ICNALE+FCE $r = 0.1$	46.6	58.2

Table 9: ICNALE testing for open-training task 1; best result is in bold.

Training Set	Accuracy	
	no BA	with BA
Lang-8	37.2	59.6
Lang-8+FCE	37.9	61.3
Lang-8+ICCI	35.7	61.4
Lang-8+ICLE	37.3	61.4
Lang-8+ICLE+FCE	37.6	61.7
Lang-8+ICLE+FCE $r = 0.1$	37.7	**61.9**

could we come to that conclusion independently?

Our approach involved considering each external corpus as a test set, and seeing which other corpora were useful when included in the training set; corpora which were consistently useful would be included in the final set. Our original exploration involved looking at all of the corpora (as test sets), but it was haphazard; here, we present results just with the ICLE and the ICANLE, which are arguably the two closest corpora to the TOEFL-11 in terms of proficiency and genre. For this, we used a different selection of L1s, 12 for the ICLE, 7 for the ICANLE; all of these languages appeared in at least the Lang-8, and 2 of them (Chinese and Japanese) appeared in all corpora. Both sets were balanced by L1. Again, we report results with and without bias adaption. The results for the ICLE are in Table 8.

The clearest result in Table 8 is the consistently positive effect of bias adaption, at least 10 percentage points, which is line with our previous work. Adding both ICLE and ICNALE to the Lang-8 corpus gave a small boost in performance, but the effect of the ICCI was once again negative, as was the effect of our training set selection.

The ICNALE results in Table 9 support many of the conclusions that we reached in the ICLE (and other sets like the FCE and ICCI, which are not included here but gave similar results); the effect of bias adaption is even more pronounced. Two differences: the slightly positive effect of training data selection and the positive effect of the ICCI, the latter of which we saw nowhere else. We speculate that this might be due to that fact that although the ICNALE is a college-level corpus, it is a corpus of Asian-language native speakers. Our theory is that Europeans are, on average, more proficient users of English (this is supported by, for instance, the testing from Granger et al. (2009)), and that therefore the European component of the low-proficiency ICCI actually interferes with using high proficiency as a way of distinguishing European L1s, a problem which would obviously not extend to an Asian-L1-only corpus. This is an interesting result, but we will not explore it further here. In any case, it would lead us to predict that including ICCI data would be a bad idea for TOEFL-11 testing.

Since we did not have any way to evaluate our Indian corpora (i.e. the news, twitter, and translated blogs from Section 4) without using the TOEFL-11, we instead took advantage of the option to submit multiple runs, submitting runs which use each of the corpora, and combining the blogs and news.

6.2 Post Hoc Analysis

With the TOEFL-11 data now visible to us, we first ask whether our specially collected Indian corpora can distinguish texts in the ICCI. The test set used in Table 10 contains only Hindi and Telugu texts. The results are quite modest (the guessing baseline is 50%), but suggest that all three corpora contain some information that distinguish Hindi and Telugu, particularly if bias adaption is used.

The results for a selection of models on the full set of TOEFL-11 languages is presented in Table 11. Since ours was the best-performing model in this task, we include results for both the TOEFL-11 training (including development set) and test set, to facilitate future comparison. Again, there is little doubt that bias adaption is of huge benefit, though in fact our results in the Lang-8 alone, without bias

Table 11: 11-language testing on TOEFL-11 sets for open-training task 1; best result is in bold, best submitted run is in italics.

Training Set	Accuracy (%)			
	TOEFL-11 test		TOEFL-11 training	
	no BA	with BA	no BA	with BA
Lang-8	39.5	53.2	37.2	48.2
Lang-8+ICCI	36.9	51.0	34.9	46.3
Lang-8+FCE+ICLE+ICNALE	44.5	55.8	44.9	53.1
Lang-8+FCE+ICLE+ICNALE+Indian news	45.2	*56.5*	45.5	54.9
Lang-8+FCE+ICLE+ICNALE+Indian tweets	44.9	56.4	45.1	53.4
Lang-8+FCE+ICLE+ICNALE+Indian translated blog	45.4	50.1	45.7	49.9
Lang-8+FCE+ICLE+ICNALE+News+Tweets	45.2	57.5	45.5	55.2
Lang-8+FCE+ICLE+ICNALE+News+Tweets $r = 0.1$	44.9	**58.2**	45.0	**58.2**

Table 10: Indian corpus testing for Open-training task 1; best result is in bold.

Training Set	Accuracy (%)	
	no BA	with BA
Indian news	50.0	54.0
Indian tweets	54.0	**56.0**
Indian blogs	51.5	**56.0**

adaption, would have been enough to take first place in this task. Adding other corpora, including the Indian corpora but not the ICCI, did consistently improve performance, as suggested by our testing in other corpora. Although the translated blog data was useful in distinguishing Hindi from Telugu alone, it had an unpredictable effect in the main task, lowering bias-adapted performance. Training set selection does seem to have a small positive effect, though we did not see this consistently in our original testing.

7 Conclusion

Our efforts in the 2013 NLI shared task focused on the potential benefits of external corpora. We have shown here that including training data from multiple corpora is effective at creating good cross-corpus NLI systems, particularly when domain adaptation, i.e. bias adaption or training set selection, is also applied; we were the highest-performing group in open-training task 1 by a large margin. This approach can also be applied to improve performance even when training data from the same corpus is available, as in open-training task 2. However, in the closed-training task, despite testing a number of new features, we did not see much improvement on our simple model based on earlier work. Other teams clearly did find some ways to improve on this straightforward approach, and we hope to see to what extent those improvements are generalizable across different NLI corpora.

Acknowledgements

This work was financially supported by the Natural Sciences and Engineering Research Council of Canada.

References

Daniel Blanchard, Joel Tetreault, Derrick Higgins, Aoife Cahill, and Martin Chodorow. 2013. TOEFL11: A corpus of non-native English. Technical report, Educational Testing Service.

Julian Brooke and Graeme Hirst. 2011. Native language detection with 'cheap' learner corpora. Presented at the 2011 Learner Corpus Research Conference. Published in Sylviane Granger, Gaëtanelle Gilquin and Fanny Meunier, editors, (2013) *Twenty Years of Learner Corpus Research: Looking back, Moving ahead*. Corpora and Language in Use - Proceedings 1, Louvain-la-Neuve: Presses universitaires de Louvain.

Julian Brooke and Graeme Hirst. 2012a. Measuring interlanguage: Native language identification with L1-influence metrics. In *Proceedings of the Eighth International Conference on Language Resources and Evaluation (LREC '12)*, pages 779–784, Istanbul, Turkey.

Julian Brooke and Graeme Hirst. 2012b. Robust, lexicalized native language identification. In *Proceedings of the 24th International Conference on Computational Linguistics (COLING '12)*.

Kevin Burton, Akshay Java, and Ian Soboroff. 2009. The ICWSM 2009 Spinn3r Dataset. In *Proceedings of the Third Annual Conference on Weblogs and Social Media (ICWSM 2009)*, San Jose, CA.

Serhiy Bykh and Detmar Meurers. 2012. Native language identification using recurring *n*-grams – investigating abstraction and domain dependence. In *Proceedings of the 24th International Conference on Computational Linguistics (COLING '12)*.

Max Coltheart. 1980. *MRC Psycholinguistic Database User Manual: Version 1*. Birkbeck College.

Scott A. Crossley and Danielle S. McNamara. 2012. Detecting the first language of second language writers using automated indicies of cohesion, lexical sophistication, syntactic complexity and conceptual knowledge. In Scott Jarvis and Scott A. Crossley, editors, *Approaching Language Transfer through Text Classification: Explorations in the Detection-based Approach*. Multilingual Matters.

Rong-En Fan, Kai-Wei Chang, Cho-Jui Hsieh, Xiang-Rui Wang, and Chih-Jen Lin. 2008. LIBLINEAR: A library for large linear classification. *Journal of Machine Learning Research*, 9:1871–1874.

Sylviane Granger, Estelle Dagneaux, Fanny Meunier, and Magali Paquot. 2009. *International Corpus of Learner English (Version 2)*. Presses Universitaires de Louvain, Louvain-la-Neuve.

Bo Han, Paul Cook, and Timothy Baldwin. 2012. Geolocation prediction in social media data by finding location indicative words. In *Proceedings of the 24th International Conference on Computational Linguistics (COLING '12)*.

Shin'ichiro Ishikawa, 2011. *A new horizon in learner corpus studies: The aim of the ICNALE project*, pages 3–11. University of Strathclyde Press, Glasgow, UK.

Dan Klein and Christopher D. Manning. 2003. Accurate unlexicalized parsing. In *Proceedings of the 41st Meeting of the Association for Computational Linguistics*, pages 423–430.

Moshe Koppel, Jonathan Schler, and Kfir Zigdon. 2005. Determining an author's native language by mining a text for errors. In *Proceedings of the 11th ACM SIGKDD International Conference on Knowledge Discovery in Data Mining (KDD '05)*, pages 624–628, Chicago, Illinois, USA.

Barbara Plank and Gertjan van Noord. 2011. In *Proceedings of the 49th Annual Meeting of the Association for Computational Linguistics: Human Language Technologies*, pages 1566–1576, Portland, Oregon, USA, June.

Ben Swanson and Eugene Charniak. 2012. Native language detection with tree substitution grammars. In *Proceedings of the 50th Annual Meeting of the Association for Computational Linguistics (ACL '12)*, pages 193–197, Jeju, Korea.

Ben Swanson and Eugene Charniak. 2013. Extracting the native language signal for second language acquisition. In *Proceedings of the 2013 Conference of the North American Chapter of the Association for Computational Linguistics: Human Language Technologies (NAACL HLT '13)*.

Joel Tetreault, Daniel Blanchard, Aoife Cahill, and Martin Chodorow. 2012. Native tongues, lost and found: Resources and empirical evaluations in native language identification. In *Proceedings of the 24th International Conference on Computational Linguistics (COLING '12)*.

Joel Tetreault, Daniel Blanchard, and Aoife Cahill. 2013. Summary report on the first shared task on native language identification. In *Proceedings of the Eighth Workshop on Building Educational Applications Using NLP*, Atlanta, GA, USA, June. Association for Computational Linguistics.

Yukio Tono, Yuji Kawaguchi, and Makoto Minegishi, editors. 2012. *Developmental and Cross-linguistic Perspectives in Learner Corpus Research*. John Benjamins, Amsterdam/Philadelphia.

Ian H. Witten and Eibe Frank. 2005. *Data Mining: Practical Machine Learning Tools and Techniques*. Morgan Kaufmann, San Francisco.

Sze-Meng Jojo Wong and Mark Dras. 2011. Exploiting parse structures for native language identification. In *Proceedings of the 2011 Conference on Empirical Methods in Natural Language Processing (EMNLP '11)*, pages 1600–1610, Edinburgh, Scotland, UK.

Sze-Meng Jojo Wong, Mark Dras, and Mark Johnson. 2012. Exploring adaptor grammars for native language identification. In *Proceedings of the 2012 Joint Conference on Empirical Methods in Natural Language Processing and Computational Natural Language Learning (EMNLP-CoNLL '12)*, Jeju, Korea.

Helen Yannakoudakis, Ted Briscoe, and Ben Medlock. 2011. A new dataset and method for automatically grading ESOL texts. In *Proceedings of the 49th Annual Meeting of the Association for Computational Linguistics*, pages 180–189, Portland, Oregon.

Combining Shallow and Linguistically Motivated Features in Native Language Identification

Serhiy Bykh Sowmya Vajjala Julia Krivanek Detmar Meurers
Seminar für Sprachwissenschaft, Universität Tübingen
{sbykh, sowmya, krivanek, dm}@sfs.uni-tuebingen.de

Abstract

We explore a range of features and ensembles for the task of *Native Language Identification* as part of the *NLI Shared Task* (Tetreault et al., 2013). Starting with recurring word-based n-grams (Bykh and Meurers, 2012), we tested different linguistic abstractions such as part-of-speech, dependencies, and syntactic trees as features for NLI. We also experimented with features encoding morphological properties, the nature of the realizations of particular lemmas, and several measures of complexity developed for proficiency and readability classification (Vajjala and Meurers, 2012). Employing an ensemble classifier incorporating all of our features we achieved an accuracy of 82.2% (rank 5) in the *closed* task and 83.5% (rank 1) in the *open-2* task. In the *open-1* task, the word-based recurring n-grams outperformed the ensemble, yielding 38.5% (rank 2). Overall, across all three tasks, our best accuracy of 83.5% for the standard TOEFL11 test set came in second place.

1 Introduction

Native Language Identification (NLI) tackles the problem of determining the native language of an author based on a text the author has written in a second language. With Tomokiyo and Jones (2001), Jarvis et al. (2004), and Koppel et al. (2005) as first publications on NLI, the research focus in computational linguistics is relatively young. But with over a dozen new publications in the last two years, it is gaining significant momentum.

In Bykh and Meurers (2012), we explored a data-driven approach using recurring n-grams with three levels of abstraction using parts-of-speech (POS). In the present work, we continue exploring the contribution and usefulness of more linguistically motivated features in the context of the NLI Shared Task (Tetreault et al., 2013), where our approach is included under the team name "Tübingen".

2 Corpora used

T11: TOEFL11 (Blanchard et al., 2013) This is the main corpus of the NLI Shared Task 2013. It consists of essays written by English learners with 11 native language (L1) backgrounds (Arabic, Chinese, French, German, Hindi, Italian, Japanese, Korean, Spanish, Telugu, Turkish), and from three different proficiency levels (low, medium, high). Each L1 is represented by a set of 1100 essays (*train*: 900, *dev*: 100, *test*: 100). The labels for the *train* and *dev* sets were given from the start, the labels for the *test* set were provided after the results were submitted.

ICLE: International Corpus of Learner English (Granger et al., 2009) The ICLEv2 corpus consists of 6085 essays written by English learners of 16 different L1 backgrounds. They are at a similar level of English proficiency, namely higher intermediate to advanced and of about the same age. For the cross-corpus tasks we used the essays for the seven L1s in the intersection with T11, i.e., Chinese (982 essays), French (311), German (431), Italian (391), Japanese (366), Spanish (248), and Turkish (276).

FCE: First Certificate in English Corpus (Yannakoudakis et al., 2011) The FCE dataset consists of 1238 scripts produced by learners taking the First Certificate in English exam, assessing English at an upper-intermediate level. For the cross-corpus tasks, we used the essays by learners of the eight L1s in the intersection with T11, i.e., Chinese (66 essays), French (145), German (69), Italian (76), Japanese (81), Korean (84), Spanish (198), and Turkish (73).

BALC: BUiD (British University in Dubai) Arab Learner Corpus (Randall and Groom, 2009) The BALC corpus consists of 1865 English learner texts written by students with an Arabic L1 background from the last year of secondary school and the first year of university. The texts were scored and assigned to six proficiency levels. For the cross-corpus NLI tasks, we used the data from the levels 3–5 amounting to overall 846 texts. We excluded the two lowest and the highest, sixth level based on pretests with the full BALC data.

ICNALE: International Corpus Network of Asian Learners of English (Ishikawa, 2011) The version of the ICNALE corpus we used consists of 5600 essays written by college students in ten countries and areas in Asia as well as by English native speakers. The learner essays are assigned to four proficiency levels following the CEFR guidelines (A2, B1, B2, B2+). For the cross-corpus tasks, we used the essays written by learners from Korea (600 essays) and from Pakistan (400).[1] Without access to a corpus with Hindi as L1, we decided to label the essays written by Pakistani students as Hindi. Most of the languages spoken in Pakistan, including the official language Urdu, belong to the same Indo-Aryan/-Iranian language family as Hindi. Our main focus here was on avoiding overlap with Telugu, the other Indian language in this shared task, which belongs to the Dravidian language family.

TÜTEL-NLI: Tübingen Telugu NLI Corpus We collected 200 English texts written by Telugu native speakers from bilingual (English-Telugu) blogs, literary articles, news and movie review websites.

NT11: NON-TOEFL11 We combined the ICLE, FCE, ICNALE, BALC and TÜTEL-NLI sources discussed above in the NT11 corpus consisting of overall 5843 essays for 11 L1s, as shown in Table 1.

[1]We did not include ICNALE data for more L1s to avoid overrepresentation of already well-represented Asian L1s.

	Corpora					
L1	ICLE	FCE	BALC	ICNALE	TÜTEL	#
ARA	-	-	846	-	-	846
CHI	982	66	-	-	-	1048
FRE	311	145	-	-	-	456
GER	431	69	-	-	-	500
HIN	-	-	-	400	-	400
ITA	391	76	-	-	-	467
JPN	366	81	-	-	-	447
KOR	-	84	-	600	-	684
SPA	248	198	-	-	-	446
TEL	-	-	-	-	200	200
TUR	276	73	-	-	-	349
#	3005	792	846	1000	200	**5843**

Table 1: Distribution of essays for the 11 L1s in NT11

3 Features

Recurring word-based n-grams (rc. word ng.) Following, Bykh and Meurers (2012), we used all word-based n-grams occurring in at least two texts of the training set. We focused on recurring unigrams and bigrams, which in our previous work and in T11 testing with the *dev* set worked best. For the larger T11 *train* ∪ NT11 set, recurring n-grams up to length five were best, but for uniformity we only used word-based unigrams and bigrams for all tasks. As in our previous work, we used a binary feature representation encoding the presence or absence of the n-gram in a given essay.

Recurring OCPOS-based n-grams (rc. OCPOS ng.) All OCPOS n-grams occurring in at least two texts of the training set were obtained as described in Bykh and Meurers (2012). OCPOS means that the open class words (nouns, verbs, adjectives and cardinal numbers) are replaced by the corresponding POS tags. For POS tagging we used the OpenNLP toolkit (`http://opennlp.apache.org`).

In Bykh and Meurers (2012), recurring OCPOS n-grams up to length three performed best. However, for T11 we found that including four- and five-grams was beneficial. This confirms our assumption that longer n-grams can be sufficiently common to be useful (Bykh and Meurers, 2012, p. 433). Thus we used the recurring OCPOS n-grams up to length five for the experiments in this paper. We again used a binary feature representation.

Recurring word-based dependencies (rc. word dep.) Extending the perspective on recurring pieces of data to other data types, we explored a new feature: recurring word-based dependencies. A feature of this type consists of a head and all its immediate dependents. The dependencies were obtained using the MATE parser (Bohnet, 2010). The words in each n-tuple are recorded in lowercase and listed in the order in which they occur in the text; heads thus are not singled out in this encoding. For example, the sentence *John gave Mary an interesting book* yields the following two potential features *(john, gave, mary, book)* and *(an, interesting, book)*. As with recurring n-grams we utilized only features occurring in at least two texts of the training set, and we used a binary feature representation.

Recurring function-based dependencies (rc. func. dep.) The recurring function-based dependencies are a variant of the recurring word-based dependencies described above, where each dependent is represented by its grammatical function. The above example sentence thus yields the two features *(sbj, gave, obj, obj)* and *(nmod, nmod, book)*.

Complexity Given that the proficiency level of a learner was shown to play a role in NLI (Tetreault et al., 2012), we implemented all the text complexity features from Vajjala and Meurers (2012), who used measures of learner language complexity from SLA research for readability classification. These features consist of lexical richness and syntactic complexity measures from SLA research (Lu, 2010; 2012) as well as other syntactic parse tree properties and traditionally used readability formulae. The parse trees were built using the Berkeley parser (Petrov and Klein, 2007) and the syntactic complexity measures were estimated using the Tregex package (Levy and Andrew, 2006).

In addition, we included morphological and POS features from the CELEX Lexical Database (Baayen et al., 1995). The morphological properties of words in CELEX include information about the derivational, inflectional and compositional features of the words along with information about their morphological origins and complexity. POS properties of the words in CELEX describe the various attributes of a word depending on its parts of speech. We included all the non-frequency based and non-word-string attributes from the English Morphology Lemma (EML) and English Syntax Lemma (ESL) files of the CELEX database. We also defined Age of Acquisition features based on the psycholinguistic database compiled by Kuperman et al. (2012). Finally, we included the ratios of various POS tags to the total number of words as POS density features, using the POS tags from the Berkeley parser output.

Suffix features The use of different derivational and inflectional suffixes may contain information regarding the L1 – either through L1 transfer, or in terms of what suffixes are taught, e.g., for nominalization. In a very basic approximation of morphological analysis, we used the porter stemmer implementation of MorphAdorner (`http://morphadorner.northwestern.edu`). For each word in a learner text, we removed the stem it identified from the word, and if a suffix remained, we matched it against the Wiktionary list of English suffixes (`http://en.wiktionary.org/wiki/Appendix:Suffixes:English`). For each valid suffix thus identified, we defined a binary feature (suffix, bin.) recording the presence/absence and a feature counting the number of occurrences (suffix, cnt.) in a given learner text.

Stem-suffix features We also wondered whether the subset of morphologically complex unigrams may be more indicative than considering all unigrams as features. As a simple approximation of this idea, we used the stemmer plus suffix-list approach mentioned above and used all words for which a suffix was identified as features, both binary (stemsuffix, bin.) and count-based (stemsuffix, cnt.).

Local trees Based on the syntactic trees assigned by the Berkeley Parser (Petrov and Klein, 2007), we extracted all local trees, i.e., trees of depth one. For example, for the sentence *I have a tree*, the parser output is: *(ROOT (S (NP (PRP I)) (VP (VBP have) (NP (DT a) (NN tree))) (. .)))* for which the local trees are *(S NP VP .), (NP PRP), (NP DT NN), (VP VBP NP), (ROOT S)*. Count-based features are used.

Stanford dependencies Tetreault et al. (2012) explored the utility of basic dependencies as features for NLI. In our approach, we extracted all Stanford dependencies (de Marneffe et al., 2006) using the trees assigned by the Berkeley Parser. We considered lemmatized typed dependencies (type dep. lm.) such as *nsubj(work,human)* and POS tagged ones (type dep. POS) such as *nsubj(VB,NN)* for our features. We used count-based features for those typed dependencies.

Dependency number (dep. num.) We encoded the number of dependents realized by a verb lemma, normalized by this lemma's count. For example, if the lemma *take* occurred ten times in a document, three times with two dependents and seven times with three dependents, we get the features *take:2-dependents = 3/10* and *take:3-dependents = 7/10.*

Dependency variability (dep. var.) These features count possible dependent-POS combinations for a verb lemma, normalized by this verb lemma's count. If in the example above, the lemma *take* occurred three times with two dependents JJ-NN, two times with three dependents JJ-NN-VB, and five times with three dependents NN-NN-VB, we obtain *take:JJ-NN = 3/10*, *take:JJ-NN-VB = 2/10*, and *take:NN-NN-VB = 5/10.*

Dependency POS (dep. POS) These features are derived from the dep. var. features and encode how frequent which kind of category was a dependent for a given verb lemma. Continuing the example above, *take* takes dependents of three different categories: JJ, NN and VB. For each category, we create a feature, the value of which is the category count divided by the number of dependents of the given lemma, normalized by the lemma's count in the document. In the example, we obtain *take:JJ = (1/2 + 1/3)/10*, *take:NN = (1/2 + 1/3 + 2/3)/10*, and *take:VB = (1/3 + 1/3)/10.*

Lemma realization matrix (lm. realiz.) We specified a set of features that is calculated for each distinct lemma and three feature sets generalizing over all lemmas of the same category:

1. Distinct lemma counts of a specific category normalized by the total count of this category in a document. For example, if the lemma *can* is found in a document two times as a verb and five times as a noun, and the document contains 30 verbs and 50 nouns, we obtain the two features *can:VB = 2/30* and *can:NN = 5/50.*
2. Type-Lemma ratio: lemmas of same category normalized by total lemma count
3. Type-Token ratio: tokens of same category normalized by total token count
4. Lemma-Token Ratio: lemmas of same category normalized by tokens of same category

Proficiency and prompt features Finally, for some settings in the *closed* task we also included two nominal features to encode the *proficiency* (low, medium, high) and the *prompt* (P1–P8) features provided as meta-data along with the T11 corpus.

4 Results

4.1 Evaluation Setup

We developed our approach with a focus on the *closed* task, training the models on the T11 *train* set and testing them on the T11 *dev* set. For the *closed* task, we report the accuracies on the *dev* set for all models (single feature type models and ensembles as introduced in sections 4.2 and 4.3), before presenting the accuracies on the submitted *test* set models, which were trained on the T11 *train* ∪ *dev* set. In addition, for the submitted models we report the accuracies obtained via 10-fold cross-validation on the T11 *train* ∪ *dev* set using the folds specification provided by the organizers of the NLI Shared Task 2013.

The results for the *open-1* task are obtained by training the models on the NT11 set, and the results for the *open-2* task are obtained by training the models on the T11 *train* ∪ *dev* set ∪ NT11 set. For the *open-1* and *open-2* tasks, we report the basic single feature type results on the T11 *dev* set and two sets of results on the T11 *test* set: the results for the actual *submitted* systems and the results for the *complete* systems, i.e., including the features used in the *closed* task submissions that for the open tasks were only computed after the submission deadline (given our focus on the *closed* task and finite computational infrastructure). We include the figures for the complete systems to allow a proper comparison of the performance of our models across the tasks.

Below we provide a description of the various accuracies (%) we report for the different tasks:

- Acc_{test}: Accuracy on the T11 <u>test</u> set after training the model on:
  - *closed*: T11 *train* ∪ *dev* set
  - *open-1*: NT11 set
  - *open-2*: T11 *train* ∪ *dev* set ∪ NT11 set
- Acc_{dev}: Accuracy on the T11 <u>dev</u> set after training the model on:
  - *closed*: T11 *train* set
  - *open-1*: NT11 set
  - *open-2*: T11 *train* set ∪ NT11 set
- $Acc^{10}_{train \cup dev}$: Accuracy on the T11 <u>train ∪ dev</u> set obtained via 10-fold cross-validation using the data split information provided by the organizers, applicable only for the *closed* task.

In terms of the tools used for classification, we employed LIBLINEAR (Fan et al., 2008) using L2-regularized logistic regression, LIBSVM (Chang and Lin, 2011) using C-SVC with the RBF kernel and WEKA SMO (Platt, 1998; Hall et al., 2009) fitting logistic models to SVM outputs (the -M option). Which classifier was used where is discussed below.

4.2 Single Feature Type Classifier Results

First we evaluated the performance of each feature separately for the *closed* task by computing the Acc_{dev} values. These results constituted the basis for the ensembles discussed in section 4.3. We also report the corresponding results for the *open-1* and *open-2* tasks, which were partly obtained after the system submission and thus were not used for developing the approach. As classifier, we generally used LIBLINEAR, except for complexity and lm. realiz., where SMO performed consistently better. The summary of the single feature type performance is shown in Table 2.

	Acc_{dev}		
Feature type	**closed**	**open-1**	**open-2**
1. rc. word ng.	***81.3***	***42.0***	***80.3***
2. rc. OCPOS ng.	67.6	26.6	64.8
3. rc. word dep.	67.7	30.9	69.4
4. rc. func. dep.	62.4	28.2	61.3
5. complexity	37.6	19.7	36.5
6. stemsuffix, bin.	50.3	21.4	48.8
7. stemsuffix, cnt.	48.2	19.3	47.1
8. suffix, bin.	20.4	9.1	17.5
9. suffix, cnt.	19.0	13.0	17.7
10. type dep. lm.	67.3	25.7	67.5
11. type dep. POS	46.6	27.8	27.6
12. local trees	49.1	26.2	25.7
13. dep. num.	39.7	19.6	41.8
14. dep. var.	41.5	18.6	40.1
15. dep. POS	47.8	21.5	47.4
16. lm. realiz.	70.3	30.3	66.9

Table 2: Single feature type results on T11 *dev* set

The results reveal some first interesting insights into the employed feature sets. The figures show that the recurring word-based n-grams (rc. word ng.) taken from Bykh and Meurers (2012) are the best performing single feature type in our set yielding an Acc_{dev} value of 81.3%. This finding is in line with the previous research on different data sets showing that lexical information seems to be highly relevant for the task of NLI (Brooke and Hirst, 2011; Bykh and Meurers, 2012; Jarvis et al., 2012; Jarvis and Paquot, 2012; Tetreault et al., 2012). But also the more abstract linguistic features, such as complexity measures, local trees, or dependency variation measures seem to contribute relevant information, considering the random baseline of 9% for this task.

Having explored the performance of the single feature type models, the interesting question was, whether it is possible to obtain a higher accuracy than yielded by the recurring word-based n-grams by combining multiple feature types into a single model. We thus investigated different combinations, with a primary focus on the *closed* task.

4.3 Combining Feature Types

We followed Tetreault et al. (2012) in exploring two options: On the one hand, we combined the different feature types directly in a *single vector*. On the other hand, we used an *ensemble* classifier. The ensemble setup used combines the probability distributions provided by the individual classifier for each of the incorporated feature type models. The individual classifiers were trained as discussed above, and ensembles were trained and tested using LIBSVM, which in our tests performed better for this purpose than LIBLINEAR. To obtain the ensemble *training files*, we performed 10-fold cross-validation for each feature model on the T11 *train* set (for internal evaluation) and on the T11 *train* ∪ *dev* set (for submission) and took the corresponding probability estimate distributions. For the ensemble *test files*, we took the probability estimate distribution yielded by each feature model trained on the T11 *train* set and tested on the T11 *dev* set (for internal evaluation), as well as by each feature model trained on the T11 *train* ∪ *dev* set and tested on the T11 *test* set (for submission).

In our tests, the ensemble classifier always outperformed the single vector combination, which is in line with the findings of Tetreault et al. (2012). We thus focused on ensemble classification for combining the different feature types.

4.4 *Closed* Task (Main) Results

We submitted the predictions for the systems listed in Table 3, which we chose in order to test all feature types together, the best performing single feature type, everything except for the best single feature type, and two subsets, with the latter primarily including more abstract linguistic features.

id	system description	system type
1	overall system	ensemble
2	rc. word ng.	single model
3	#1 minus rc. word ng.	ensemble
4	well performing subset	ensemble
5	"linguistic subset"	ensemble

Table 3: Submitted systems for all three tasks

The results for the submitted systems are shown in Table 4. Here and in the following result tables, the system ids in the table headers correspond to the ids in Table 3, the best result on the *test* set is shown in bold, and the symbols have the following meaning:

- x = feature type used
- - = feature type not used
- -* = feature type ready after submission

We report the Acc_{test}, Acc_{dev} and $Acc^{10}_{train \cup dev}$ accuracies introduced in section 4.1. The Acc_{dev} results are consistently better than the Acc_{test} results, highlighting that relying on a single development set can be problematic. The cross-validation results are more closely aligned with the ultimate test set performance.

	systems				
Feature type	**1**	**2**	**3**	**4**	**5**
1. rc. word ng.	x	x	-	x	-
2. rc. OCPOS ng.	x	-	x	x	-
3. rc. word dep.	x	-	x	x	-
4. rc. func. dep.	x	-	x	x	-
5. complexity	x	-	x	x	x
6. stemsuffix, bin.	x	-	x	x	x
7. stemsuffix, cnt.	x	-	x	-	x
8. suffix, bin.	x	-	x	x	x
9. suffix, cnt.	x	-	x	-	x
10. type dep. lm.	x	-	x	-	x
11. type dep. POS	x	-	x	-	x
12. local trees	x	-	x	-	x
13. dep. num.	x	-	x	x	-
14. dep. var.	x	-	x	x	-
15. dep. POS	x	-	x	x	-
16. lm. realiz.	x	-	x	x	-
proficiency	x	-	x	x	-
prompt	x	-	x	x	-
Acc_{test}	**82.2**	79.6	81.0	81.5	74.7
Acc_{dev}	85.4	81.3	83.5	84.9	76.3
$Acc^{10}_{train \cup dev}$	82.4	78.9	80.7	81.7	74.1

Table 4: Results for the ***closed*** task

Overall, comparing the results for the different systems shows the following main points (with the system ids in the discussion shown in parentheses):

- The overall system performed better than any single feature type alone (cf. Tables 2 and 4). The ensemble thus is successful in combining the strengths of the different feature types.
- The rc. word ng. feature type alone (2) performed very well, but the overall system without that feature type (3) still outperformed it. Thus apparently the different properties accessed by more elaborate linguistic modelling contribute some information not provided by the surface-based n-gram feature.
- A system incorporating a subset of the different feature types (4) performed still reasonably well. Hence, it is conceivable that a subsystem consisting of some selected feature types would perform equally well (eliminating only information present in multiple feature types) or even outperform the overall system (by removing some noise). This point will be investigated in detail in our future work.

- System 5, combining a subset of feature types, where each one incorporates some degree of linguistic abstraction (in contrast to pure surface-based feature types such as word-based n-grams), performed at a reasonably high level, supporting the assumption that incorporating more linguistic knowledge into the system design has something to contribute.

Putting our results into the context of the NLI Shared Task 2013, with our best Acc_{test} value of 82.2% for *closed* as the main task, we ranked fifth out of 29 participating teams. The best result in the competition, obtained by the team "Jarvis", is 83.6%. According to the significance test results provided by the shared task organizers, the difference of 1.4% is not statistically significant (0.124 for pairwise comparison using McNemar's test).

4.5 *Open-1* Task Results

The Acc_{dev} values for the single feature type models for the *open-1* task were included in Table 2. The results for the *test* set are presented in Table 5. We report two different Acc_{test} values: the accuracy for the actual *submitted* systems (Acc_{test}) and for the corresponding *complete* systems (Acc_{test} with $*$) as discussed in section 4.1.

	systems				
Feature type	1	2	3	4	5
1. rc. word ng.	x	x	-	x	-
2. rc. OCPOS ng.	x	-	x	x	-
3. rc. word dep.	x	-	x	x	-
4. rc. func. dep.	x	-	x	x	-
5. complexity	x	-	x	x	x
6. stemsuffix, bin.	x	-	x	x	x
7. stemsuffix, cnt.	x	-	x	-	x
8. suffix, bin.	x	-	x	x	x
9. suffix, cnt.	x	-	x	-	x
10. type dep. lm.	-*	-	-*	-	-*
11. type dep. POS	-*	-	-*	-	-*
12. local trees	-*	-	-*	-	-*
13. dep. num.	x	-	x	x	-
14. dep. var.	x	-	x	x	-
15. dep. POS	x	-	x	x	-
16. lm. realiz.	x	-	x	x	-
Acc_{test}	36.4	**38.5**	33.2	37.8	21.2
Acc_{test} with $*$	37.0	n/a	35.4	n/a	29.9

Table 5: Results for the ***open-1*** task

Conceptually, the *open-1* task is a cross-corpus task, where we used the NT11 data for training and T11 data for testing. It is more challenging for several reasons. First, the models are trained on data that is likely to be different from the one of the *test* set in a number of respects, including possible differences in genre, task and topic, or proficiency level. Second, the amount of data we were able to obtain to train our model is far below what was provided for the *closed* task. Thus a drop in accuracy is to be expected.

Particularly interesting is the fact that our best result for the *open-1* task (38.5%) was obtained using the rc. word ng. feature type alone. Thus adding the more abstract features did not improve the accuracy. The reason for that may be the smaller training corpus size, the uneven distribution of the texts among the different L1s in the NT11 corpus, or the mentioned potential differences between NT11 and T11 in genre, task and topic, and learner proficiency. Also interesting is the fact that the system combining a subset of feature types outperformed the overall system. This finding supports the assumption mentioned in section 4.4 that the ensemble classifier can be optimized by informed, selective model combination instead of combining all available information.

To put our results into the context of the NLI Shared Task 2013, our best Acc_{test} value of 38.5% for the *open-1* task achieved rank two out of three participating teams. The best accuracy of 56.5% was obtained by the team "Toronto". While the *open-1* task results in general are much lower than the *closed* task results, highlighting an important challenge for future NLI work, they nevertheless are meaningful steps forward considering the random baseline of 9%.

4.6 *Open-2* Task Results

For the *open-2* task we provide the same information as for *open-1*. The Acc_{dev} values for the single feature type models are shown in Table 2, and the two Acc_{test} values, i.e., the accuracy for the actual *submitted* systems (Acc_{test}) and for the *complete* systems (Acc_{test} with $*$) can be found in Table 6.

For the *open-2* task, we put the T11 *train* $\cup$ *dev* and NT11 sets together to train our models. The interesting question behind this task is, whether it is possible to improve the accuracy of NLI by adding

Feature type	systems 1	2	3	4	5
1. rc. word ng.	x	x	-	x	-
2. rc. OCPOS ng.	x	-	x	x	-
3. rc. word dep.	-*	-	-*	-*	-
4. rc. func. dep.	x	-	x	x	-
5. complexity	x	-	x	x	x
6. stemsuffix, bin.	x	-	x	x	x
7. stemsuffix, cnt.	x	-	x	-	x
8. suffix, bin.	x	-	x	x	x
9. suffix, cnt.	x	-	x	-	x
10. type dep. lm.	-*	-	-*	-	-*
11. type dep. POS	x	-	x	-	x
12. local trees	x	-	x	-	x
13. dep. num.	x	-	x	x	-
14. dep. var.	x	-	x	x	-
15. dep. POS	x	-	x	x	-
16. lm. realiz.	x	-	x	x	-
Acc_{test}	83.5	81.0	79.3	82.5	64.8
Acc_{test} with $*$	**84.5**	n/a	83.3	82.9	79.8

Table 6: Results for the ***open-2*** task

data from corpora other than the one used for testing. This is far from obvious, especially considering the low results obtained for the *open-1* task pointing to significant differences between the T11 and the NT11 corpora.

Overall, when using all feature types, our results for the *open-2* task (84.5%) are better than those we obtained for the *closed* task (82.2%). So adding data from a different domain improves the results, which is encouraging since it indicates that something general about the language used is being learned, not (just) something specific to the T11 corpus. Essentially, the *open-2* task also is closest to the real-world scenario of using whatever resources are available to obtain the best result possible.

Putting the results into the context of the NLI Shared Task 2013, our best Acc_{test} value of 83.5% (84.5%) is the highest accuracy for the *open-2* task, i.e, first rank out of four participating teams.

5 Conclusions

We explored the task of Native Language Identification using a range of different feature types in the context of the NLI Shared Task 2013. We considered surface features such as recurring word-based n-grams system as our basis. We then explored the contribution and usefulness of some more elaborate, linguistically motivated feature types for the given task. Using an ensemble model combining features based on POS, dependency, parse trees as well as lemma realization, complexity and suffix information features, we were able to outperform the high accuracy achieved by the surface-based recurring n-grams features alone. The exploration of linguistically-informed features thus is not just of analytic interest but can also make a quantitative difference for obtaining state-of-the-art performance.

In terms of future work, we have started exploring the various feature types in depth to better understand the causalities and correlations behind the results obtained. We also intend to explore more complex linguistically motivated features further, such as features based on syntactic alternations as used in Krivanek (2012). Studying such variation of linguistic properties, instead of recording their presence as we mostly did in this exploration, also stands to provide a more directly interpretable perspective on the feature space identified as effective for NLI.

Acknowledgments

We thank Dr. Shin'ichiro Ishikawa and Dr. Mick Randall for providing access to the ICNALE corpus and the BALC corpus respectively. We also thank the shared task organizers for organizing this interesting competition and sharing the TOEFL11 corpus. Our research is partially funded through the European Commission's 7th Framework Program under grant agreement number 238405 (CLARA).

References

R. H. Baayen, R. Piepenbrock, and L. Gulikers. 1995. The CELEX lexical database (cd-rom). CDROM, http://www.ldc.upenn.edu/Catalog/readme_files/celex.readme.html.

Daniel Blanchard, Joel Tetreault, Derrick Higgins, Aoife Cahill, and Martin Chodorow. 2013. TOEFL11: A corpus of non-native english. Technical report, Educational Testing Service.

Bernd Bohnet. 2010. Top accuracy and fast dependency parsing is not a contradiction. In *Proceedings of the 24th International Conference on Computational Linguistics (COLING)*, pages 89–97.

Julian Brooke and Graeme Hirst. 2011. Native language detection with 'cheap' learner corpora. In

Learner Corpus Research 2011 (LCR 2011), Louvain-la-Neuve.

Serhiy Bykh and Detmar Meurers. 2012. Native language identification using recurring n-grams – investigating abstraction and domain dependence. In *Proceedings of the 24th International Conference on Computational Linguistics (COLING)*, pages 425–440, Mumbay, India.

Chih-Chung Chang and Chih-Jen Lin. 2011. LIBSVM: A library for support vector machines. *ACM Transactions on Intelligent Systems and Technology*, 2:27:1–27:27. Software available at `http://www.csie.ntu.edu.tw/~cjlin/libsvm`.

Marie-Catherine de Marneffe, Bill MacCartney, and Christopher Manning. 2006. Generating typed dependency parses from phrase structure parses. In *Proceedings of the 5th International Conference on Language Resources and Evaluation (LREC-2006)*, Genoa, Italy, May 24-26.

R.E. Fan, K.W. Chang, C.J. Hsieh, X.R. Wang, and C.J. Lin. 2008. Liblinear: A library for large linear classification. *The Journal of Machine Learning Research*, 9:1871–1874. Software available at `http://www.csie.ntu.edu.tw/~cjlin/liblinear`.

Sylviane Granger, Estelle Dagneaux, Fanny Meunier, and Magali Paquot, 2009. *International Corpus of Learner English, Version 2*. Presses Universitaires de Louvain, Louvain-la-Neuve.

Mark Hall, Eibe Frank, Geoffrey Holmes, Bernhard Pfahringer, Peter Reutemann, and Ian H. Witten. 2009. The weka data mining software: An update. In *The SIGKDD Explorations*, volume 11, pages 10–18.

Shin'ichiro Ishikawa. 2011. A new horizon in learner corpus studies: The aim of the ICNALE projects. In G. Weir, S. Ishikawa, and K. Poonpon, editors, *Corpora and language technologies in teaching, learning and research*, pages 3–11. University of Strathclyde Publishing, Glasgow, UK. `http://language.sakura.ne.jp/icnale/index.html`.

Scott Jarvis and Magali Paquot. 2012. Exploring the role of n-grams in L1-identification. In Scott Jarvis and Scott A. Crossley, editors, *Approaching Language Transfer through Text Classification: Explorations in the Detection-based Approach*, pages 71–105. Multilingual Matters.

Scott Jarvis, Gabriela Castañeda-Jiménez, and Rasmus Nielsen. 2004. Investigating L1 lexical transfer through learners' wordprints. Presented at the 2004 Second Language Research Forum. State College, Pennsylvania, USA.

Scott Jarvis, Gabriela Castañeda-Jiménez, and Rasmus Nielsen. 2012. Detecting L2 writers' L1s on the basis of their lexical styles. In Scott Jarvis and Scott A. Crossley, editors, *Approaching Language Transfer through Text Classification: Explorations in the Detection-based Approach*, pages 34–70. Multilingual Matters.

Moshe Koppel, Jonathan Schler, and Kfir Zigdon. 2005. Determining an author's native language by mining a text for errors. In *Proceedings of the eleventh ACM SIGKDD international conference on Knowledge discovery in data mining (KDD '05)*, pages 624–628, New York.

Julia Krivanek. 2012. Investigating syntactic alternations as characteristic features of learner language. Master's thesis, University of Tübingen, April.

Victor Kuperman, Hans Stadthagen-Gonzalez, and Marc Brysbaert. 2012. Age-of-acquisition ratings for 30,000 english words. *Behavior Research Methods*, 44(4):978–990.

Roger Levy and Galen Andrew. 2006. Tregex and tsurgeon: tools for querying and manipulating tree data structures. In *5th International Conference on Language Resources and Evaluation*, Genoa, Italy.

Xiaofei Lu. 2010. Automatic analysis of syntactic complexity in second language writing. *International Journal of Corpus Linguistics*, 15(4):474–496.

Xiaofei Lu. 2012. The relationship of lexical richness to the quality of ESL learners' oral narratives. *The Modern Languages Journal.*

Slav Petrov and Dan Klein. 2007. Improved inference for unlexicalized parsing. In *Human Language Technologies 2007: The Conference of the North American Chapter of the Association for Computational Linguistics; Proceedings of the Main Conference*, pages 404–411, Rochester, New York, April.

John C. Platt. 1998. Sequential minimal optimization: A fast algorithm for training support vector machines. Technical Report MSR-TR-98-14, Microsoft Research.

Mick Randall and Nicholas Groom. 2009. The BUiD Arab learner corpus: a resource for studying the acquisition of L2 english spelling. In *Proceedings of the Corpus Linguistics Conference (CL)*, Liverpool, UK.

Joel Tetreault, Daniel Blanchard, Aoife Cahill, and Martin Chodorow. 2012. Native tongues, lost and found: Resources and empirical evaluations in native language identification. In *Proceedings of the 24th International Conference on Computational Linguistics (COLING)*, pages 2585–2602, Mumbai, India.

Joel Tetreault, Daniel Blanchard, and Aoife Cahill. 2013. A report on the first native language identification shared task. In *Proceedings of the Eighth Workshop on Building Educational Applications Using NLP*, Atlanta, GA, USA, June. Association for Computational Linguistics.

Laura Mayfield Tomokiyo and Rosie Jones. 2001. You're not from round here, are you? naive bayes detection of non-native utterance text. In *Proceedings of the 2nd Meeting of the North American Chapter of the Association for Computational Linguistics (NAACL)*, pages 239–246.

Sowmya Vajjala and Detmar Meurers. 2012. On improving the accuracy of readability classification using insights from second language acquisition. In Joel Tetreault, Jill Burstein, and Claudial Leacock, editors, *Proceedings of the 7th Workshop on Innovative Use of NLP for Building Educational Applications (BEA7) at NAACL-HLT*, pages 163—-173, Montréal, Canada, June. Association for Computational Linguistics.

Helen Yannakoudakis, Ted Briscoe, and Ben Medlock. 2011. A new dataset and method for automatically grading ESOL texts. In *Proceedings of the 49th Annual Meeting of the Association for Computational Linguistics: Human Language Technologies - Volume 1*, HLT '11, pages 180–189, Stroudsburg, PA, USA. Association for Computational Linguistics. Corpus available from `http://ilexir.co.uk/applications/clc-fce-dataset`.

Linguistic Profiling based on General–purpose Features and Native Language Identification

Andrea Cimino, Felice Dell'Orletta, Giulia Venturi and Simonetta Montemagni
Istituto di Linguistica Computazionale "Antonio Zampolli" (ILC–CNR)
ItaliaNLP Lab - *www.italianlp.it*
via G. Moruzzi, 1 – Pisa (Italy)
{name.surname}@ilc.cnr.it

Abstract

In this paper, we describe our approach to native language identification and discuss the results we submitted as participants to the First NLI Shared Task. By resorting to a wide set of general–purpose features qualifying the lexical and grammatical structure of a text, rather than to ad hoc features specifically selected for the NLI task, we achieved encouraging results, which show that the proposed approach is general–purpose and portable across different tasks, domains and languages.

1 Introduction

Since the seminal work by Koppel et al. (2005), within the Computational Linguistics community there has been a growing interest in the NLP–based Native Language Identification (henceforth, NLI) task. However, so far, due to the unavailability of balanced and wide–coverage benchmark corpora and the lack of evaluation standards it has been difficult to compare the results achieved for this task with different methods and techniques (Tetreault et al., 2013). The First Shared Task on Native Language Identification (Tetreault et al., 2013) can be seen as an answer to the above mentioned problems.

In this paper, we describe our approach to native language identification and discuss the results we submitted as participants to the First NLI Shared Task. Following the guidelines by the Shared Task Organizers based on the previous literature on this topic, Native Language Identification is tackled as a text classification task combining NLP–enabled feature extraction and machine learning: see e.g. Tetreault et al. (2013) and Brooke and Hirst (2012). Interestingly, the same methodological paradigm is shared by other tasks like e.g. author recognition and verification (see e.g. van Halteren (2004), authorship attribution (see Juola (2008) for a survey), genre identification (Mehler et al., 2011) as well as readability assessment (see Dell'Orletta et al. (2011a) for an updated survey), all relying on feature extraction from automatically parsed texts and state–of–the–art machine learning algorithms. Besides obvious differences at the level of the typology of selected linguistic features and of learning techniques, these different tasks share a common approach to the problems they tackle: i.e. they succeed in determining the language variety, the author, the text genre or the level of readability of a text by exploiting the distribution of different types of linguistic features automatically extracted from texts.

Our approach to NLI relies on multi–level linguistic analysis, covering morpho–syntactic tagging and dependency parsing. In the NLI literature, the range of features used is wide and includes characteristics of the linguistic structure underlying the L2 text, encoded in terms of sequences of characters, words, grammatical categories or of syntactic constructions, as well as of the document structure: note however that, in most part of the cases, the exploited features are task–specific. In our approach, we decided to resort to a wide set of features ranging across different levels of linguistic description (i.e. lexical, morpho–syntactic and syntactic) without any a priori selection: the same set of features was successfully exploited in NLI–related tasks, i.e. focusing on the linguistic form rather than the content of texts, such as readability assessment (Dell'Orletta et al., 2011a) or the classification of textual genres (Dell'Orletta et al., 2012).

The exploitation of general features qualifying the lexical and grammatical structure of a text, rather than ad hoc features specifically selected for the task at hand, is not the only peculiarity of our approach to NLI. Following Biber (1993), we start from the assumption that "linguistic features from all levels function together as underlying dimensions of variation". This choice stems from studies on linguistic variation, in particular from Biber and Conrad (2009) who claim that linguistic varieties – called "registers" from a functional perspective – differ "in their characteristic distributions of pervasive linguistic features, not the single occurrence of an individual feature". This is to say that by carrying out the linguistic analysis of collections of essays each written by different L1 native speakers, we need to quantify the extent to which a given feature occurs in each collection, in order to reconstruct the linguistic profile underlying each L1 collection: differences lie at the level of the distribution of linguistic features, which can be common and pervasive in some L1 collections but comparatively rare in others. This approach is the basis of so–called "linguistic profiling" of texts, within which "the occurrences of a large number of linguistic features in a text, either individual items or combinations of items, are counted" (van Halteren, 2004) with the final aim of reconstructing the profile of a text.

We carried out native language identification in two steps. The first step consisted of the identification of the set of linguistic features characterizing the essays written by different L1 native speakers, i.e. the linguistic profiling of the different sections of TOEFL11 corpus (Blanchard et al., 2013) distributed as training and development data. In the second step, the features which turned out to have highly discriminative power were used for the classification of essays written by different L1 native speakers. Essay classification has been carried out by experimenting with different approaches: i.e. a single–classifier method and two different multi–model ensemble approaches.

The paper is organised as follows: after introducing the set of used linguistic features (Section 2), Section 3 illustrates a selection of the linguistic profiling results obtained with respect to the training section of the TOEFL11 corpus; Section 4 describes the different classification approaches we followed and the feature selection process; in Section 5 achieved results are reported and discussed.

2 Features

In this study, we focused on a wide set of features ranging across different levels of linguistic description. Differing from previous work on NLI, no a priori selection of features was carried out. Instead of focusing on particular classes of errors or on different types of stylistic idiosyncrasies, we took into account a wide range of features which are typically used in studies focusing on the "form" of a text, e.g. on issues of genre, style, authorship or readability. As previously pointed out, this represents a peculiarity of our approach. This choice makes the selected features language–independent, domain–independent and reusable across different types of tasks, as empirically demonstrated in Dell'Orletta et al. (2011a) where the same set of features has been successfully exploited for readability assessment, and in Dell'Orletta et al. (2012) where the features have been used for the classification of different types of textual genre. Note that in both cases the language dealt with was Italian: for the NLI Shared Task we had to specialize the feature extraction process with respect to the English language as well as to the annotation scheme used to represent the underlying linguistic structure.

The whole set of features we started with is described below, organised into four main categories: namely, raw text and lexical features as well as morpho-syntactic and syntactic features. This proposed four–fold partition closely follows the different levels of linguistic analysis automatically carried out on the text being evaluated, i.e. tokenization, lemmatization, morpho-syntactic tagging and dependency parsing.

2.1 Raw and Lexical Text Features

Sentence Length, calculated as the average number of words per sentence.
Word Length, calculated as the average number of characters per word.
Document Length, calculated as the total number

of words per document.
Character bigrams.
Word n-grams, including both unigrams and bigrams.
Type/Token Ratio: the Type/Token Ratio (TTR) is a measure of vocabulary variation which has shown to be a helpful measure of lexical variety within a text as well as style marker in an authorship attribution scenario: a text characterized by a low type/token ratio will contain a great deal of repetition whereas a high type/token ratio reflects vocabulary richness and variation. Due to its sensitivity to sample size, TTR has been computed for text samples of equivalent length (the first 50 tokens).

2.2 Morpho–syntactic Features

Coarse grained Part-Of-Speech n-grams: distribution of unigrams and bigrams of coarse–grained PoS, corresponding to the main grammatical categories (e.g. noun, verb, adjective, etc.).
Fine grained Part-Of-Speech n-grams: distribution of unigrams and bigrams of fine–grained PoS, which represent subdivisions of the coarse–grained tags (e.g. the class of nouns is subdivided into proper vs common nouns, verbs into main verbs, gerund forms, past particles, etc.).
Verbal chunks: distribution of sequences of verbal PoS (also including adverbs). This feature can be seen as a proxy to capture different aspects of verbal predication, with particular attention to idiosyncratic usages of verbal mood, tense, person and adverbial modification.
Lexical density: ratio of content words (verbs, nouns, adjectives and adverbs) to the total number of lexical tokens in a text.

2.3 Syntactic Features

Dependency types n-grams: distribution of unigrams and bigrams of dependency types calculated with respect to *i)* the hierarchical parse tree structure and *ii)* the surface linear ordering of words.
Dependency triples: distribution of triplets representing a dependency relation consisting of a syntactic head (h), the dependency relation type (t) and the dependent (d). Two different variants of this feature are distinguished, based on the fact that either the coarse–grained PoS or the word–form of h and d is considered: we will refer to the former as *Coarse grained Part-Of-Speech dependency triples* and to the latter as *Lexical dependency triples*. In both cases, the relative ordering of h and d, i.e. whether h precedes or follows d at the level of the linear ordering of words within the sentence, is also considered.
Dependency Subtrees: distribution of dependency subtrees consisting of a dependency relation (represented as the dependency triple $\{h, t, d\}$), the head father and the dependency relation linking the two. As in the previous case, two different variants of this feature are distinguished, based on the fact that either the coarse grained PoS or the word–forms of the nodes in the dependency subtree are considered.
Parse tree depth features: this set of features is meant to capture different aspects of the parse tree depth and includes: *a)* the depth of the whole parse tree, calculated in terms of the longest path from the root of the dependency tree to some leaf; *b)* the average depth of embedded complement 'chains' governed by a nominal head and including either prepositional complements or nominal and adjectival modifiers; *c)* the probability distribution of embedded complement 'chains' by depth. These features represent reliable indicators of sentence complexity, as stated by, among others, Yngve (1960), Frazier (1985) and Gibson (1998), and they can thus allow capturing specific difficulties of L2 learners.
Coarse grained Part-Of-Speech of sentence root: this feature refers to coarse grained POS of the syntactic root of a sentence.
Arity of verbal predicates: this feature refers to the number of dependencies (corresponding to either subcategorized arguments or modifiers) governed by the same verbal head. In the NLI context, it can allow capturing improper verbal usage by L2 learners due to language transfer (e.g. with pro–drop languages as L1).
Subordination features: this set of features is meant to capture different aspects of the use of subordination and includes: *a)* the distribution of subordinate vs main clauses; *b)* the average depth of 'chains' of embedded subordinate clauses and *c)* the probability distribution of embedded subordinate clauses 'chains' by depth. Similarly to parse tree depth, this set of features can be taken to reflect the structural complexity of sentences and can thus be indicative of specific difficulties of L2 learners.
Length of dependency links: measured in terms

of the words occurring between the syntactic head and the dependent. This is another feature which reflects the syntactic complexity of sentences (Lin, 1996; Gibson, 1998) and which can be successfully exploited to capture syntactic idiosyncracies of L2 learners due to L1 interferences.

2.4 Other features

Two further features have been considered for NLI purposes, which were included in the distributed datasets. For each document, we have also considered i) the English language proficiency level (high, medium, or low) based on human assessment by language specialists, and ii) the topic of the essays.

3 Linguistic Profiling of TOEFL11 Corpus

In this section, we illustrate the results of linguistic profiling carried out on the training and development sets extracted from the TOEFL11 corpus. This corpus, described in Blanchard et al. (2013), contains 1,100 essays per 11 languages (for a total of 12,100 essays) sampled as evenly as possible from 8 prompts (i.e., topics) along with score levels (low/medium/high) for each essay. The considered L1s are: Arabic, Chinese, French, German, Hindi, Italian, Japanese, Korean, Spanish, Telugu, and Turkish. For the specific purposes of the NLI Shared Task, a total of 9,900 essays has been distributed as training data (900 essays per L1), 1,100 as development data (100 per L1) and the remaining 1,100 essays have been used as test data.

We started from the automatic linguistic annotation of training and development data whose output has been searched for with respect to the features illustrated in Section 2.

3.1 Linguistic Pre–processing

Both training and development data were automatically morpho-syntactically tagged by the POS tagger described in Dell'Orletta (2009) and dependency–parsed by the DeSR parser using Multi–Layer Perceptron as learning algorithm (Attardi et al., 2009), a state–of–the–art linear–time Shift–Reduce dependency parser. Feature extraction is carried out against the output of the multi–level automatic linguistic analysis carried out during the pre–processing stage: lexical and grammatical patterns corresponding to the wide typology of selected features are looked for within each annotation layer and quantified.

3.2 Linguistic Profiling

Generally speaking, linguistic profiling makes it possible to identify (groups of) texts which are similar, at least with respect to the "profiled" features (van Halteren, 2004). In what follows we report the results of linguistic profiling obtained with respect to the 11 L1 sub–corpora considered in this study. Figure 1 shows the results obtained with respect to a selection of the features described in Section 2. These results refer to the combined training and development data sets: note, however, that we also calculated the values of these features in the two datasets separately and it turned out that they do not vary significantly between the two sets. This fact can be taken as a proof both of the reliability of our approach to linguistic profiling and of the relevance of these features for NLI purposes.

Starting from raw textual features (Figures 1(a) and 1(b)), both average sentence length and average word length vary significantly across L1s. In particular, if on the one hand the essays written by Arabic and Spanish L1 speakers contain the shortest words and the longest sentences, on the other hand the Hindi and Telugu L1 essays are characterized by the longest words; the L1 Japanese and Korean corpora contain the shortest sentences.

Let us focus now on the distribution of unigrams of coarse grained Parts–Of–Speech. If we consider the distributions of determiners and nouns, two features typically used for NLI purposes (Wong and Dras, 2009) which also represent stylistic markers associated with different linguistic varieties (Biber and Conrad, 2009), it can be noticed (see Figures 1(c) and 1(d)) that for Japanese and Korean the essays show the lowest percentage of determiners, while for Hindi and Telugu they are characterized by the highest percentage of nouns.

For what concerns syntactic features, we observe that essays by Japanese and Korean speakers are characterized by quite a different distribution with respect to the other L1 corpora. In particular, they show the shallowest parse trees, the shortest dependency links as well as the shortest 'chains' of embedded complements governed by a nominal head. On the other hand, the essays by Spanish and Ara-

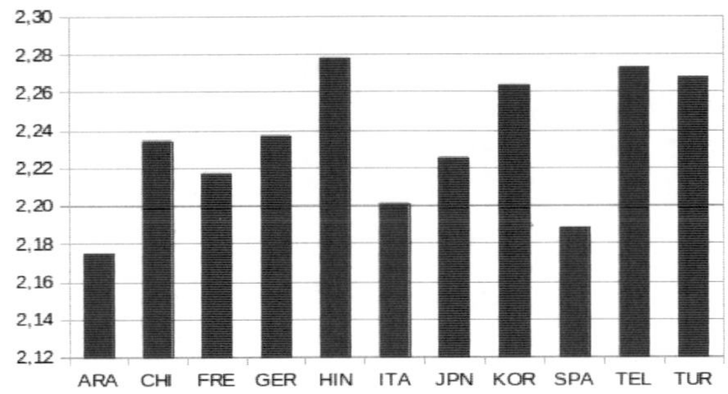

(a) Average word length

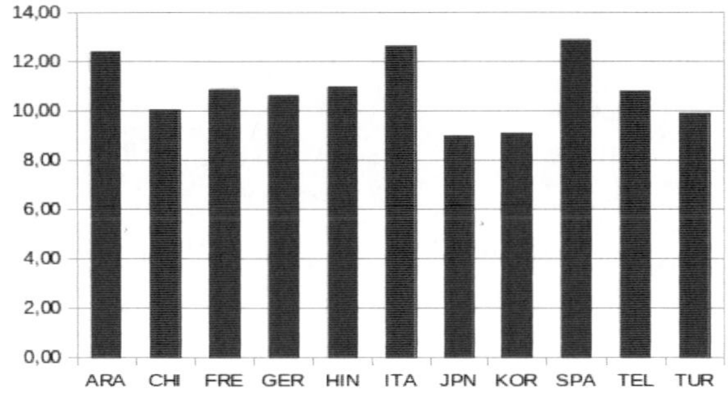

(b) Average sentence length

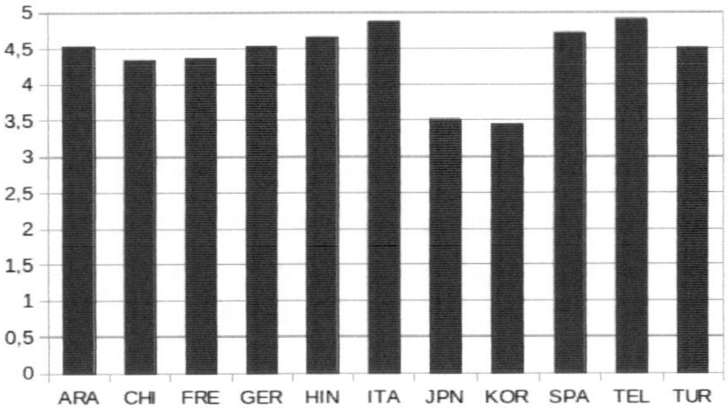

(c) Distribution of Determiners

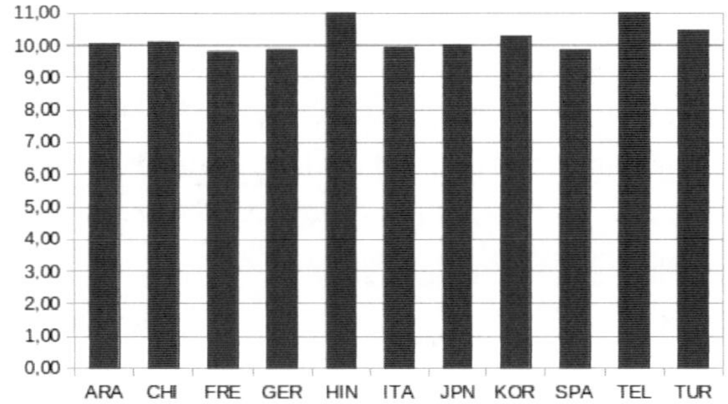

(d) Distribution of Nouns

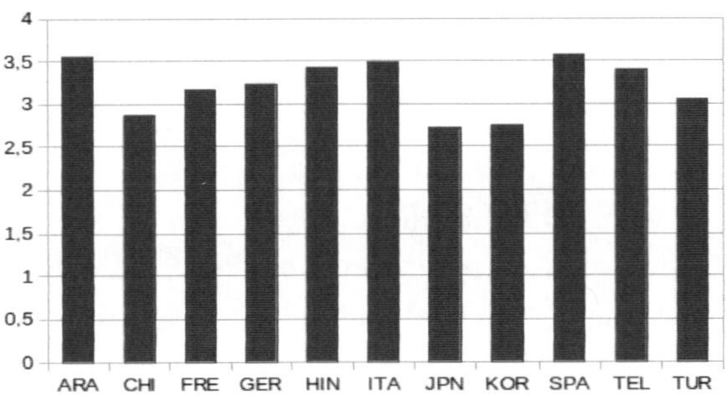

(e) Average parse tree depth

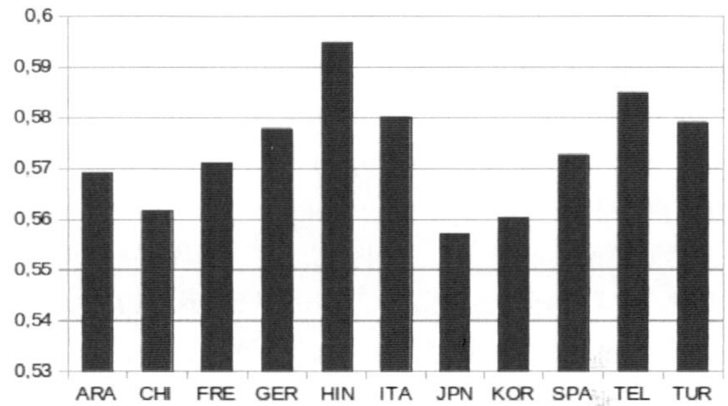

(f) Average depth of embedded complement 'chains'

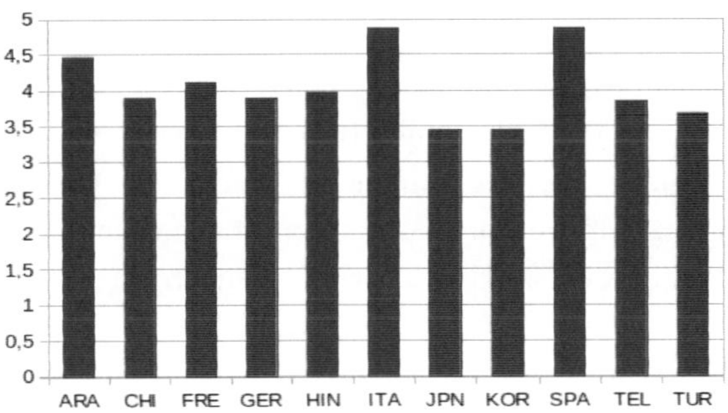

(g) Average length of the longest dependency link

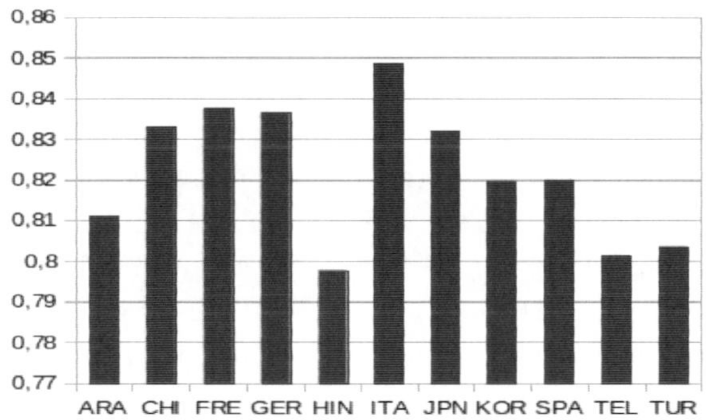

(h) Arity of verbal predicates

Figure 1: Results of linguistic profiling carried out on the combined training and development sections of the TOEFL11 corpus.

bic speakers contain the deepest parse trees, for Italian and Spanish we observe the longest dependency links and for Hindi and Telugu the longest sequences of embedded complements. Moreover, while the essays by Italians are characterised by the highest value of arity of verbal predicates, for Hindi, Telugu and Korean essays much lower values are recorded.

Interestingly, these linguistic profiling results show similar trends across the 11 languages at different levels of linguistic analysis. For instance, it can be noted that Japanese and Korean or Italian and Spanish, which belong to two different language families, show similar distributions of features. Similarities have also been recorded in the sub–corpora by Hindi and Telugu speakers, even if these languages do not belong to the same family; we can hypothesize that this might originate from language contact phenomena.

4 System Description

4.1 Machine Learning Classifier

Our approach to Native Language Identification has been implemented in a software prototype, i.e. a classifier operating on mopho–syntactically tagged and dependency parsed texts which assigns to each document a score expressing its probability of belonging to a given L1 class. The highest score represents to the most probable class. Given a set of features and a training corpus, the classifier creates a statistical model using the feature statistics extracted from the training corpus. This model is used in the classification of unseen documents. The set of features and the machine learning algorithm can be parameterized through a configuration file.

For each feature, we have implemented three different variants, depending on whether the feature value is encoded in terms of: *i*) presence/absence of the feature (*binary* variant), *ii*) the normalized frequency (*normalized frequency* variant), and *iii*) the normalized *tf*idf* value (*normalized tf*idf* variant). Since the binary feature variant outperformed the other two, in all the experiments carried out on the development set reported in Section 5 we illustrate the results obtained using this variant only. This is in line with the results obtained by Brooke and Hirst (2012) and Tetreault et al. (2013). According to (Brooke and Hirst, 2012), a possible explanation is that "in these relatively short texts, there is high variability in normalized frequencies, and a simpler metric, by having less variability, is easier for the classifier to leverage". Support Vector Machines (SVM) using LIBSVM (Chang and Lin, 2001) and Maximum Entropy (ME) using MaxEnt[1] have been used as machine learning algorithms.

We experimented two classification approaches: a single classifier method and two ensemble systems, combining the output of several classifiers.

The single classifier uses the set of features resulting from the feature selection process described in Section 4.2 and the SVM using linear kernel as machine learning algorithm. This choice is due to the fact that in all the experiments the linear SVM outperformed the SVM using polynomial kernel. There are two possible explanations for this fact, namely: a) the number of features is much higher than the number of training instances, accordingly it might not be necessary to map data to a higher dimensional space, therefore the nonlinear mapping does not improve the performance; b) Weston et al. (2000) showed that SVMs can indeed suffer in high dimensional spaces where many features are irrelevant. Note that in Section 5, we report the results of this classifier using different sets of features corresponding to the lexical, morpho–syntactic and syntactic levels of linguistic analysis.

The two ensemble systems combine the outputs of the component classifiers following two different strategies. The first one is based on the majority voting method (henceforth, *VoteComb*): the combination strategy is seen as a classical voting problem where for each essay is assigned the L1 class that has been selected from the majority of classifiers. In case of ties, the L1 class predicted from the best individual model (as resulting from the experiments carried out on the development set) is selected. The second strategy combines the outputs of the component classifiers via another classifier (henceforth referred to as *meta–classifier*): we will refer to this second strategy as *ClassComb*. The meta–classifier uses as a feature the probability score predicted from each component classifier for each L1 class. Differently from the component classifiers, the meta–classifier is based on polynomial kernel SVM. In both en-

[1]https://github.com/lzhang10/maxent#readme

semble systems, the component classifiers use linear SVM and ME as machine learning algorithms and exploit different sets of features among the ones resulting from the feature selection process described below.

4.2 Features Selection Process

Since our approach to NLI relies on a wide number of general–purpose features, a feature selection process was necessary in order to prune irrelevant and redundant features which could negatively affect the classification results. The selection process starts taking into account all the n features described in Section 2. In each iteration, for each feature f_i we generate a configuration c_i such that f_i is disabled and all the other features are enabled. When an iteration finishes, we obtain for each c_i a corresponding accuracy score $score(c_i)$ which is computed as the average of the accuracy obtained by the classifier on the development set (a_d) and on an internal development set (a_i), corresponding to the 10% of the training set, used in order to reduce the overfitting risk. Being c_b the best configuration among all the c_i configurations, if $score(c_b) \leq$ of the accuracy scores resulting from the previous iterations the process stops. Otherwise:

1. store in F the pair $\langle f_b, disabled \rangle$;
2. for each configuration c_i, if $score(c_i) \leq$ of the accuracy scores resulting from the previous iterations, we store in F the pair $\langle f_i, enabled \rangle$;
3. set $C = \langle c_b, score(c_b) \rangle$

where F is a map containing elements $feature \rightarrow \{disabled, enabled\}$ and C is a pair that contains the current best configuration c_b and the corresponding score $score(c_b)$. In each iteration, we consider only the features which do not occur in F. At the initialization step F is empty and C contains the configuration where all the considered features are enabled.

In spite of the fact that the described selection process does not guarantee to obtain the global optimum, it however permitted us to obtain an improvement of about 8% with respect to the starting model indiscriminately using all features.

Table 1 lists the features resulting from the feature selection process. It can be noted that some

Lexical features:
Word n-grams
Morpho–syntactic features:
Coarse grained Part-Of-Speech unigrams
Fine grained Part-Of-Speech bigrams
Syntactic features:
Dependency types unigrams
Lexical dependency triples
Parse tree depth features
Coarse grained Part-Of-Speech of sentence root
Arity of verbal predicates
Subordination features
Length of dependency links

Table 1: Features resulting from the feature selection process.

of them coincide with those typically used for NLI purposes: this is the case of n–grams of words, Parts-Of-Speech and syntactic dependencies. Interestingly, to our knowledge, other features such as arity of verbal predicates, length of dependency links as well as subordination and parse tree depth features have not been used for NLI so far, in spite of their being widely exploited in the syntactic complexity literature (as discussed in Section 2).

5 Results

Table 2 reports the overall Accuracy achieved with the different classifier models in the NLI classification task on the official test set as well as the F-measure score recorded for each L1 class. The first two lines show the accuracies of the two combination models, while the last three report the results obtained by the single classifier using i) the set of features resulting by the features selection process (*Best_Single*), ii) the selected lexical features only (see Table 1) (*Lexical*) and iii) the lexical and morpho–syntactic features (*Lex+Morph*).

The two combination models outperform all the single model classifiers: note that *ClassComb* achieved much better results with respect to *VoteComb*. By comparing these results with the F-measure scores obtained on the distributed development data (see Table 3), it can be seen that the ranking of the scores achieved by the different classifiers remains the same even if on the test data we obtained a performance of -2,2% with respect to the develop-

	Accuracy	ARA	CHI	FRE	GER	HIN	ITA	JAP	KOR	SPA	TEL	TUR
ClassComb	**77,9**	73,8	77,5	**83,2**	87,3	71,1	**86,0**	78,8	**74,2**	**70,8**	76,2	**78,0**
VoteComb	77,2	74,3	77,0	80,0	87,0	72,8	81,6	79,6	73,8	67,7	77,6	77,6
Best_Single	76,6	71,9	**77,6**	75,8	85,7	73,2	82,0	**80,0**	74,0	69,0	76,9	76,5
Lex+Morph	76,4	**77,2**	76,2	78,6	85,9	72,1	80,4	76,8	71,9	68,0	76,4	76,4
Lexical	76,2	71,1	76,5	79,0	**87,6**	**74,5**	80,8	77,7	70,8	66,7	**79,2**	73,4

Table 2: Classification results of different classifiers on official test data.

ment test set.

Let us consider now the results obtained by the single model classifiers. In all cases the *Best_Single* outperforms the other two models demonstrating the reliability of the features selection process and that a combination of lexical, morpho–syntactic and syntactic features leads to better results.

Although the best performing model is the *ClassComb*, this is not true for all the 11 languages. In Table 2, the best results for each L1 are bolded. Interestingly, even though *Lexical* is the worst model, it is the best performing one for three L1s while the best model, i.e. *ClassComb*, for five only.

It can be noted that with respect to the development data set the syntactic features used by the *Best_Single* model allow an increment of +1% as opposed to the *Lexical* model: this represents a much higher increase if compared with the result obtained on the test data, which is +0,4%. This is an unexpected result since the feature selection described in Section 4.2 was carried out on an internal development set in order to prevent the risk of overfitting on the distributed development data.

Classifier	Accuracy
ClassComb	**80,1**
VoteComb	79,3
Best_Single	78,8
Lex+Morph	78,2
Lexical	77,8

Table 3: Classification results of different classifiers on distributed development data.

6 Conclusion

In this paper, we reported our participation results to the First Native Language Identification Shared Task. By resorting to a wide set of general–purpose features qualifying the lexical and grammatical structure of a text, rather than to ad hoc features specifically selected for the task at hand, we achieved encouraging results. After a feature selection process, new features which to our knowledge have never been exploited so far for NLI purposes turned out to contribute significantly to the task. Interestingly, the same set of features we started from has been previously successfully exploited in other related tasks, such as readability assessment and genre classification, operating on the Italian language. The obtained results suggest that our approach is general–purpose and portable across different domains and languages. Further directions of research currently include: i) comparison of results obtained with general purpose features and with NLI–specific features (e.g. typical errors or different types of stylistic idiosyncrasies specific to L2 learners), with a view to combining them to achieve better results; ii) design and development of new ensemble classification methods as well as new feature selection methods considering not only classes of features but also individual features; iii) testing our approach to NLI on different L2s (e.g. Italian) .

References

Giuseppe Attardi, Felice Dell'Orletta, Maria Simi and Joseph Turian. 2009. Accurate dependency parsing with a stacked multilayer perceptron. In *Proceedings of EVALITA, Evaluation of NLP and Speech Tools for Italian*, Reggio Emilia, Italy.

Douglas Biber. 1993. Using Register–diversified Corpora for General Language Studies. *Computational Linguistics Journal*, 19(2): 219–241.

Douglas Biber and Susan Conrad. 2009. Genre, Register, Style. Cambridge: CUP.

Daniel Blanchard, Joel Tetreault, Derrick Higgins, Aoife Cahill and Martin Chodorow. 2013. TOEFL11: A Corpus of Non-Native English. Educational Testing Service.

Julian Brooke and Graeme Hirst. 2012. Robust, Lexicalized Native Language Identification. In *Proceedings of COLING 2012*, Mumbai, India, 391–408.

Chih-Chung Chang and Chih-Jen Lin. 2001. LIBSVM: a library for support vector machines. *Software available at http://www.csie.ntu.edu.tw/ cjlin/libsvm*

Walter Daelemans. 2012. Explanation in Computational Stylometry. In A. Gelbukh (ed.) *CICLing 2012, Part II*, LNCS 7817, Springer–Verlag, 451–462.

Felice Dell'Orletta. 2009. Ensemble system for Part-of-Speech tagging. In *Proceedings of Evalita'09, Evaluation of NLP and Speech Tools for Italian*, Reggio Emilia, December.

Felice Dell'Orletta, Simonetta Montemagni and Giulia Venturi. 2011a. READ-IT: Assessing Readability of Italian Texts with a View to Text Simplification. In *Proceedings of the Workshop on "Speech and Language Processing for Assistive Technologies" (SLPAT 2011)*, Edinburgh, July 30, 73–83.

Felice Dell'Orletta, Simonetta Montemagni and Giulia Venturi. 2012. Genre–oriented Readability Assessment: a Case Study. In *Proceedings of the Workshop on Speech and Language Processing Tools in Education (SLP-TED)*, 91–98.

Lyn Frazier. 1985. Syntactic complexity. In D.R. Dowty, L. Karttunen and A.M. Zwicky (eds.), *Natural Language Parsing*, Cambridge University Press, Cambridge, UK.

Edward Gibson. 1998. Linguistic complexity: Locality of syntactic dependencies. In *Cognition*, 68(1), pp. 1–76.

Patrick Juola. 2008. *Authorship Attribution*. Now Publishers Inc.

Moshe Koppel, Jonathan Schler and Kfir Zigdon. 2005. Automatically determining an anonymous author's native language. In *Intelligence and Security Informatics*, vol. 3495, LNCS, Springer–Verlag, 209–217.

Dekan Lin. 1996. On the structural complexity of natural language sentences. In *Proceedings of COLING 1996*, pp. 729–733.

Ryan McDonald and Joakim Nivre. 2007. Characterizing the Errors of Data-Driven Dependency Parsing Models. In *Proceedings of EMNLP-CoNLL, 2007*, 122–131.

Alexander Mehler, Serge Sharoff and Marina Santini (Eds.). 2011. *Genres on the Web. Computational Models and Empirical Studies*. Springer Series: Text, Speech and Language Technology.

Sze–Meng Jojo Wong and Mark Dras. 2009. Contrastive Analysis and Native Language Identification. In *Proceedings of the Australasian Language Technology Association Workshop*.

Hans van Halteren. 2004. Linguistic profiling for author recognition and verification. In *Proceedings of the Association for Computational Linguistics (ACL04)*, 200–207.

Joel Tetreault, Daniel Blanchard, Aoife Cahill and Martin Chodorow. 2012. Native Tongues, Lost and Found: Resources and Empirical Evaluations in Native Language Identification. In *Proceedings of COLING 2012*, Mumbai, India, 2585–2602.

Joel Tetreault, Daniel Blanchard and Aoife Cahill. 2013. Summary Report on the First Shared Task on Native Language Identification. In *Proceedings of the Eighth Workshop on Building Educational Applications Using NL*, Atlanta, GA, USA.

Victor H.A. Yngve. 1960. A model and an hypothesis for language structure. In *Proceedings of the American Philosophical Society*, 444–466.

Jason Weston, Sayan Mukherjee, Oliver Chapelle, Massimiliano Pontil, Tomaso Poggio and Vladimir Naumovich Vapnik. 2000. Feature selection for SVMs. In *Advances in Neural Information Processing Systems 13*, MIT Press, 668–674.

Improving Native Language Identification with TF-IDF Weighting

Binyam Gebrekidan Gebre[1], Marcos Zampieri[2], Peter Wittenburg[1], Tom Heskes[3]
[1]Max Planck Institute for Psycholinguistics
[2]University of Cologne
[3]Radboud University
bingeb@mpi.nl,mzampier@uni-koeln.de,
peter.wittenburg@mpi.nl,t.heskes@science.ru.nl

Abstract

This paper presents a Native Language Identification (NLI) system based on TF-IDF weighting schemes and using linear classifiers - support vector machines, logistic regressions and perceptrons. The system was one of the participants of the 2013 NLI Shared Task in the closed-training track, achieving 0.814 overall accuracy for a set of 11 native languages. This accuracy was only 2.2 percentage points lower than the winner's performance. Furthermore, with subsequent evaluations using 10-fold cross-validation (as given by the organizers) on the combined training and development data, the best average accuracy obtained is 0.8455 and the features that contributed to this accuracy are the TF-IDF of the combined unigrams and bigrams of words.

1 Introduction

Native Language Identification (NLI) is the task of automatically identifying the native language of a writer based on the writer's foreign language production. The task is modeled as a classification task in which automatic methods have to assign class labels (native languages) to objects (texts). NLI is by no means trivial and it is based on the assumption that the mother tongue influences Second Language Acquisition (SLA) and production (Lado, 1957).

When an English native speaker hears someone speaking English, it is not difficult for him/her to identify if this person is a native speaker or not. Moreover, it is, to some extent, possible to assert the mother tongue of non-native speakers by his/hers pronunciation patterns, regardless of their language proficiency. In NLI, the same principle that seems intuitive for spoken language, is applied to text. If it is true that the mother tongue of an individual influences speech production, it should be possible to identify these traits in written language as well.

NLI methods are particularly relevant for languages with a significant number of foreign speakers, most notably, English. It is estimated that the number of non-native speakers of English outnumbers the number of native speakers by two to one (Lewis et al., 2013). The written production of non-native speakers is abundant on the Internet, academia, and other contexts where English is used as *lingua franca*.

This study presents the system that participated in the 2013 NLI Shared Task (Tetreault et al., 2013) under the name *Cologne-Nijmegen*. The novel aspect of the system is the use of TF-IDF weighting schemes. For this study, we experimented with a number of algorithms and features. Linear SVM and logistic regression achieved the best accuracies on the combined features of unigrams and bigrams of words. The rest of the paper will explain in detail the features, methods and results achieved.

2 Motivation

There are two main reasons to study NLI. On one hand, there is a strong linguistic motivation, particularly in the field of SLA and on the other hand, there is the practical relevance of the task and its integration to a number of computational applications.

The linguistic motivation of NLI is the possibility of using classification methods to study the interplay between native and foreign language acquisition and performance (Wong and Dras, 2009). One of the SLA theories that investigate these phenomena is contrastive analysis, which is used to explain why some structures of L2 are more difficult to acquire than others (Lado, 1957).

Contrastive analysis postulates that the difficulty in mastering L2 depends on the differences between L1 and L2. In the process of acquiring L2, *language transfer* (also known as L1 interference) occurs and speakers apply knowledge from their native language to a second language, taking advantage of their similarities. Computational methods applied to L2 written production can function as a corpus-driven method to level out these differences and serve as a source of information for SLA researchers. It can also be used to provide more targeted feedback to language learners about their errors.

NLI is also a relevant task in computational linguistics and researchers have turned their attention to it in the last few years. The task is often regarded as a part of a broader task of authorship profiling, which consists of the application of automatic methods to assert information about the writer of a given text, such as age, gender as well native language. Authorship profiling is particularly useful for forensic linguistics.

Automatic methods of NLI may be integrated in NLP applications such as spam detection or machine translation. NLP tasks such as POS tagging and parsing might also benefit from NLI, as these resources are trained on standard language written by native speakers. These tools can be more accurate to tag non-native speaker's text if trained with L2 corpora.

3 Related Work

In the last years, a couple of attempts at identifying native language have been described in the literature. Tomokiyo and Jones (2001) uses a Naive Bayes algorithm to classify transcribed data from three native languages: Chinese, Japanese and English. The algorithm reached 96% accuracy when distinguishing native from non-native texts and 100% when distinguishing English native speakers from Chinese native speakers.

Koppel et al. (2005) used machine learning to identify the native languages of non-native English speakers with five different mother tongues (Bulgarian, Czech, French, Russian, and Spanish), using data retrieved from the International Corpus of Learner English (ICLE) (Granger et al., 2009). The features used in this study were function words, character n-grams, and part-of-speech (POS) bigrams.

Tsur and Rappoport (2007) investigated the influence of the phonology of a writer's mother tongue through native language syllables modelled by character bigrams. Estival et al. (2007) addressed NLI as part of authorship profiling. Authors aim to attribute 10 different characteristics of writers by analysing a set of English e-mails. The study reports around 84% accuracy in distinguishing e-mails written by English Arabic and Spanish L1 speakers.

SVM, the algorithm that achieved the best results in our experiments, was also previously used in NLI (Kochmar, 2011). In this study, the author identified error types that are typical for speakers of different native languages. She compiled a set of features based on these error types to improve the classification's performance.

Recently, the TOEFL11 corpus was compiled to serve as an alternative to the ICLE corpus (Tetreault et al., 2012). Authors argue that TOEFL11 is more suitable to NLI than ICLE. This study also experimented with different features to increase results in NLI and reports best accuracy results of 90.1% on ICLE and 80.9% on TOEFL11.

4 Methods

We approach the task of native language identification as a kind of text classification. In text classification, decisions and choices have to be made at three levels. First, how do we use the training and development data? Second, what features do we extract and how do we select the most informative ones? Third, which machine learning algorithms perform best and which parameters can we tune under the constraints of memory and time? In the following subsections, we answer these questions.

4.1 Dataset: TOEFL11

The dataset used for the shared task is called TOEFL11 (Blanchard et al., 2013). It consists of 12,100 English essays (about 300 to 400 words long) from the Test of English as a Foreign Language (TOEFL). The essays are written by 11 native language speakers (L1). Table 1 shows the 11 native languages. Each essay is labelled with an English language proficiency level (high, medium, or low) based on the judgments of human assessment specialists. We used 9,900 essays for training data and 1,100 for development (parameter tuning). The shared task organizers kept 1,100 essays for testing.

Table 1: TOEFL11

L1 languages	Arabic, Chinese, French, German, Hindi, Italian, Japanese, Korean, Spanish, Telugu, Turkish
# of essays per L1	900 for training 100 for validating 100 for testing

4.2 Features

We explored different kinds and combinations of features that we assumed to be different for different L1 speakers and that are also commonly used in the NLI literature (Koppel et al., 2005; Tetreault et al., 2012). Table 2 shows the sources of the features we considered. Unigrams and bigrams of words are explored separately and in combination. One through four grams of part of speech tags have also been explored. For POS tagging of the essays, we applied the default POS tagger from NLTK (Bird, 2006).

Spelling errors have also been treated as features. We used the collection of words in Peter Norvig's website[1] as a reference dictionary. The collection consists of about a million words. It is a concatenation of several public domain books from Project Gutenberg and lists of most frequent words from Wiktionary and the British National Corpus.

Character n-grams have also been explored for both the words in the essays and for words with spelling errors. The maximum n-gram size considered is six.

All features, consisting of either characters or words or part-of-speech tags or their combinations, are mapped into normalized numbers (norm L2). For the mapping, we use TF-IDF, a weighting technique popular in information retrieval but which is also finding its use in text classification. Features that occurred in less than 5 of the essays or those that occurred in more than 50% of the essays are removed (all characters are in lower case). These cut-off values are experimentally selected.

Table 2: A summary of features used in our experiments

Word n-grams	Unigrams and bigrams of words present in the essays.
POS n-grams	One up to four grams of POS tags present in the essays; tagging is done using default NLTK tagger (Bird, 2006).
Character n-grams	One up to six grams of characters in each essay.
Spelling errors	All words that are not found in the dictionary of Peter Norvig's spelling corrector.

4.2.1 Term Frequency (TF)

Term Frequency refers to the number of times a particular term appears in an essay. In our experiments, terms are n-grams of characters, words, part-of-speech tags or any combination of them. The intuition is that a term that occurs more frequently identifies/specifies the essay better than another term that occurs less frequently. This seems a useful heuristic but what is the relationship between the frequency of a term and its importance to the essay? From among many relationships, we selected a logarithmic relationship (sublinear TF scaling) (Manning et al., 2008):

$$wf_{t,e} = \begin{cases} 1 + \log(tf_{t,e}) & \text{if } tf_{t,e} > 0 \\ 0 & \text{otherwise} \end{cases} \quad (1)$$

[1] http://norvig.com/spell-correct.html

where $wf_{t,e}$ refers to weight and $tf_{t,e}$ refers to the frequency of term t in essay e.

The $wf_{t,e}$ weight tells us the importance of a term in an essay based on its frequency. But not all terms that occur more frequently in an essay are equally important. The effective importance of a term also depends on how infrequent the term is in other essays and this intuition is handled by Inverse Document Frequency(IDF).

4.2.2 Inverse Document Frequency(IDF)

Inverse Document Frequency (IDF) quantifies the intuition that a term which occurs in many essays is not a good discriminator, and should be given less weight than one which occurs in fewer essays. In mathematical terms, IDF is the log of the inverse probability of a term being found in any essay (Salton and McGill, 1984):

$$idf(t_i) = \log \frac{N}{n_i}, \quad (2)$$

where N is the number of essays in the corpus, and term t_i occurs in n_i of them. IDF gives a new weight when combined with TF to form TF-IDF.

4.2.3 TF–IDF

TF–IDF combines the weights of TF and IDF by multiplying them. TF gives more weight to a frequent term in an essay and IDF downscales the weight if the term occurs in many essays. Equation 3 shows the final weight that each term of an essay gets before normalization.

$$w_{i,e} = (1 + \log(tf_{t,e})) \times \log(N/n_i) \quad (3)$$

Essay lengths are usually different and this has an impact on term weights. To abstract from different essay lengths, each essay feature vector is normalized to unit length. After normalization, the resulting essay feature vectors are fed into classifiers.

4.3 Classifiers

We experimented with three linear classifiers - linear support vector machines, logistic regression and perceptrons - all from scikit-learn (Pedregosa et al., 2011). These algorithms are suitable for high dimensional and sparse data (text data is high dimensional and sparse). In the following paragraphs, we briefly describe the algorithms and the parameter values we selected.

SVMs have been explored systematically for text categorization (Joachims, 1998). An SVM classifier finds a hyperplane that separates examples into two classes with maximal margin (Cortes and Vapnik, 1995) (Multi-classes are handled by multi one-versus-rest classifiers). Examples that are not linearly separable in the feature space are mapped to a higher dimension using kernels. In our experiments, we used a linear kernel and a penalty parameter of value 1.0.

In its various forms, logistic regression is also used for text classification (Zhang et al., 2003; Genkin et al., 2007; Yu et al., 2011) and native language identification (Tetreault et al., 2012). Logistic regression classifies data by using a decision boundary, determined by a linear function of the features. For the implementation of the algorithm, we used the LIBLINEAR open source library (Fan et al., 2008) from scikit-learn (Pedregosa et al., 2011) and we fixed the regularization parameter to 100.0.

For baseline, we used a perceptron classifier (Rosenblatt, 1957). Perceptron (or single layer network) is the simplest form of neural network. It is designed for linear separation of data and works well for text classification. The number of iterations of the training algorithm is fixed to 70 and the rest of parameters are left with their default values.

5 Results and Discussion

For each classifier, we ran ten-fold cross-validation experiments. We divided the training and development data into ten folds using the same fold splitting ids as requested by the shared task organizers and also as used in (Tetreault et al., 2012). Nine of the folds were used for training and the tenth for testing the trained model. This was repeated ten times with each fold being held out for testing. The performance of the classifiers on different features are presented in terms of average accuracy.

Table 3 gives the average accuracies based on the TF-IDF of word and character n-grams. Linear SVM gives the highest accuracy of 84.55% using features extracted from unigrams and bigrams of words. Logistic regression also gives comparable accuracy of 84.45% on the same features.

Table 3: Cross-validation results; accuracy in %

N-gram	Linear SVM	Logistic Regression	Perceptron
Words			
1	74.73	74.18	65.45
2	80.91	80.27	75.45
1 and 2	**84.55**	84.45	78.82
(1 and 2)*	83.36	83.27	78.73
* minus country and language names			
Characters			
1	18.45	19.27	9.09
2	43.27	40.82	10.36
3	71.36	68.00	36.91
4	80.36	79.91	59.64
5	83.09	82.64	73.91
6	**84.09**	84.00	76.45

The size of the feature vector of unigrams and bigrams of words is 73,626[2]. For each essay, only a few of the features have non-zero values. Which features are active and most discriminating in the classifiers? Table 4 shows the ten most informative features for the 10th run in the cross-validation (as picked up linear SVM).

Table 4: Ten most informative features for each L1

ARA	many reasons / from / self / advertisment / , and / statment / any / thier / alot of / alot
CHI	in china / hold / china / time on / may / taiwan / just / still / , the / . take
FRE	french / conclude , / even if / in france / france / to conclude / indeed , / ... / . indeed / indeed
GER	special / furthermore / might / germany / , because / have to / . but / - / often / , that
HIN	which / and concept / various / hence / generation / & / towards / then / its / as compared
ITA	in italy / , for / infact / that a / italy / i think / in fact / italian / think that / :
JPN	, and / i disagree / is because / . it / . if / i think / japan , / japanese / in japan / japan
KOR	. however / however , / even though / however / these days / various / korea , / korean / in korea / korea
SPA	an specific / because is / moment / , etc / going to / , is / necesary / , and / diferent / , but
TEL	may not / the statement / every one / days / the above / where as / with out / when compared / i conclude / and also
TUR	ages / istanbul / addition to / conditions / enough / in turkey / the life / ; / . because / turkey

The ten most informative features include country and language names. For example, for Japanese and Korean L1s, four of the ten top features include Korea or Korean in the unigrams or bigrams. How would the classification accuracy decrease if we removed mentions of country or language names?

We made a list of the 11 L1 language names and the countries where they are mainly spoken (for example, German, Germany, French, France, etc.). We considered this list as stop words (i.e. removed them from corpus) and ran the whole classification experiments. The new best accuracy is 83.36% (a loss of just 1.2%). Table 3 shows the new accuracies for all classifiers. The new top ten features mostly consist of function words and some spelling errors. Table 5 shows all of the new top ten features.

The spelling errors seem to have been influenced by the L1 languages, especially for French and Spanish languages. The English words *example* and *developed* have similar sounding/looking equivalents in French (*exemple* and *développé*) . Similarly, the English words *necessary* and *different* have similar sounding/looking words in Spanish (*necesario* and *diferente*). These spelling errors made it to the top ten features. But how discriminating are they on their own?

Table 5: Ten most informative features (minus country and language names) for each L1

ARA	many reasons / from / self / advertisment / , and / statment / any / thier / alot of / alot
CHI	and more / hold / more and / time on / taiwan / may / just / still / . take / , the
FRE	conclude / exemple / developped / conclude , / even if / to conclude / indeed , / ... / . indeed / indeed
GER	has to / special / furthermore / might / , because / have to / . but / - / often / , that
HIN	and concept / which / various / hence / generation / & / towards / then / its / as compared
ITA	possibility / probably / particular / , for / infact / that a / i think / in fact / think that / &
JPN	i agree / the opinion / tokyo / two reasons / is because / , and / i disagree / . it / . if / i think
KOR	creative / , many / 's / . also / . however / even though / however , / various / however / these days
SPA	activities / an specific / moment / , etc / going to / , is / necesary / , and / diferent / , but
TEL	may not / the statement / every one / days / the above / where as / when compared / with out / i conclude / and also
TUR	enjoyable / being / ages / addition to / istanbul / enough / conditions / the life / ; / . because

We ran experiments with features extracted from

[2]features that occur less than 5 times or that occur in more than 50% of the essays are removed from the vocabulary

Table 6: Confusion matrix: Best accuracy is for German (95%) and the worst is for Hindi (72%)

	ARA	CHI	FRE	GER	HIN	ITA	JPN	KOR	SPA	TEL	TUR
ARA	**83**	1	4	1	1	3	1	2	3	1	0
CHI	0	**88**	2	0	2	0	2	5	1	0	0
FRE	3	0	**88**	2	1	2	0	1	2	0	1
GER	2	0	1	**95**	0	0	0	0	1	0	1
HIN	2	1	1	1	**72**	0	0	0	2	***18***	3
ITA	0	0	6	3	0	**84**	0	0	6	0	1
JPN	1	2	0	1	1	0	**84**	***10***	0	0	1
KOR	0	3	0	2	3	0	***8***	**81**	1	1	1
SPA	6	2	5	2	0	4	0	0	**79**	0	2
TEL	0	0	0	0	***16***	0	1	0	0	**83**	0
TUR	1	1	0	1	3	0	0	0	1	0	**93**

only spelling errors. For comparison, we also ran experiments with POS tags with and without their words. None of these experiments beat the best accuracy obtained using unigram and bigram of words - not even the unigram and bigram of POS tagged words. See table 7 for the obtained results.

Table 7: Cross-validation results; accuracy in %

N-gram	Linear SVM	Logistic Regression	Perceptron
POS			
1	17.00	17.09	9.09
2	43.45	40.00	11.18
3	55.27	53.55	35.36
4	56.09	56.18	48.64
POS + Word			
1	75.09	74.18	64.09
2	80.45	80.64	76.18
1 and 2	83.00	83.36	79.09
Spelling errors - characters			
1	20.36	21.00	9.09
2	34.09	32.64	9.73
3	47.00	44.64	26.82
4	50.82	48.09	41.64
1–4	51.82	48.27	34.18
words	42.73	39.45	28.73

All our reported results so far have been global classification results. Table 6 shows the confusion matrix for each L1. The best accuracy is 95% for German and the worst is for Hindi (72%). Hindi is classified as Telugu (18%) of the times and Telugu is classified as Hindi 16% of the times and only one Telugu essay is classified as any other than Hindi. More generally, the confusion matrix seems to suggest that geographically closer countries are more confused with each other: Hindi and Telugu, Japanese and Korean, Chinese and Korean.

The best accuracy (84.55%) obtained in our experiments is higher than the state-of-the-art accuracy reported in (Tetreault et al., 2012) (80.9%). But the features we used are not different from those commonly used in the literature (Koppel et al., 2005; Tetreault et al., 2012) (n-grams of characters or words). The novel aspect of our system is the use of TF-IDF weighting on all of the features including on unigrams and bigrams of words.

TF-IDF weighting has already been used in native language identification (Kochmar, 2011; Ahn, 2011). But its importance has not been fully explored. Experiments in Kochmar (2011) were limited to character grams and in a binary classification scenario. Experiments in Ahn (2011) applied TF-IDF weighting to identify content words and showed how their removal decreased performance (Ahn, 2011). By contrast, in this paper, we applied TF-IDF weighting consistently to all features - same type features (e.g. unigrams) or combined features (e.g. unigram and bigrams).

How would the best accuracy change if TF-IDF weighting is not applied? Table 8 shows the changes to the best average accuracies with and without TF/IDF weighting for the three classifiers.

Table 8: The importance of TF-IDF weighting

TF	IDF	SVM	LR	Perceptron
Yes	Yes	84.55	84.45	78.82
Yes	No	80.82	80.73	63.18
No	Yes	82.36	82.27	78.82
No	No	79.18	78.55	56.36

6 Conclusions

This paper has presented the system that participated in the 2013 NLI Shared Task in the closed-training track. Cross-validation testing on the TOEFL11 corpus showed that the system could achieve an accuracy of about 84.55% in categorizing unseen essays into one of the eleven L1 languages.

The novel aspect of the system is the use of TF-IDF weighting schemes on features – which could be any or combination of n-gram words/characters/POS tags. The feature combination that gave the best accuracy is the TF-IDF of unigrams and bigrams of words. The next best feature class is the TF-IDF of 6-gram characters , which achieved 84.09%, very close to 84.55%. Both linear support vector machines and logistic regression classifiers have performed almost equally.

To improve performance in NLI, future work should examine new features that can classify geographically or typologically related languages such as Hindi and Telugu. Future work should also analyze the information obtained in NLI experiments to quantify and investigate differences in the usage of foreign language lexicon or grammar according to the individual's mother tongue.

Acknowledgments

The research leading to these results has received funding from the European Commissions 7th Framework Program under grant agreement no 238405 (CLARA). The authors would like to thank the organizers of the NLI Shared Task 2013 for providing prompt reply to all our inquiries and for coordinating a very interesting and fruitful shared task.

References

Charles S. Ahn. 2011. *Automatically detecting authors' native language*. Ph.D. thesis, Monterey, California. Naval Postgraduate School.

Steven Bird. 2006. NLTK: the natural language toolkit. In *Proceedings of the COLING/ACL on Interactive presentation sessions*, pages 69–72. Association for Computational Linguistics.

Daniel Blanchard, Joel Tetreault, Derrick Higgins, Aoife Cahill, and Martin Chodorow. 2013. TOEFL11: A Corpus of Non-Native English. Technical report, Educational Testing Service.

Corinna Cortes and Vladimir Vapnik. 1995. Support-vector networks. *Machine learning*, 20(3):273–297.

Dominique Estival, Tanja Gaustad, Son Bao Pham, Will Radford, and Ben Hutchinson. 2007. Author Profiling for English Emails. In *Proceedings of the 10th Conference of the Pacific Association for Computational Linguistics (PACLING)*, pages 263–272.

Rong-En Fan, Kai-Wei Chang, Cho-Jui Hsieh, Xiang-Rui Wang, and Chih-Jen Lin. 2008. Liblinear: A library for large linear classification. *The Journal of Machine Learning Research*, 9:1871–1874.

Alexander Genkin, David D Lewis, and David Madigan. 2007. Large-scale bayesian logistic regression for text categorization. *Technometrics*, 49(3):291–304.

Sylviane Granger, Estelle Dagneaux, and Fanny Meunier. 2009. *International Corpus of Learner English*. Presses Universitaires de Louvain, Louvain-la-Neuve.

Thorsten Joachims. 1998. *Text categorization with support vector machines: Learning with many relevant features*. Springer.

Ekaterina Kochmar. 2011. Identification of a writer's native language by error analysis. Master's thesis, University of Cambridge, United Kingdom.

Moshe Koppel, Jonathan Schler, and Kfir Zigon. 2005. Automatically determining an anonymous author's native language. *Lecture Notes in Computer Science*, 3495:209—217.

Robert Lado. 1957. *Applied Linguistics for Language Teachers*. University of Michigan Press.

Paul Lewis, Gary Simons, and Charles Fennig. 2013. *Ethnologue: Languages of the World, Seventeeth Edition*. SIL International.

Christopher D. Manning, Prabhakar Raghavan, and Hinrich Schütze. 2008. *Introduction to information retrieval*, volume 1. Cambridge University Press Cambridge.

Fabian Pedregosa, Gaël Varoquaux, Alexandre Gramfort, Vincent Michel, Bertrand Thirion, Olivier Grisel, Mathieu Blondel, Peter Prettenhofer, Ron Weiss, Vincent Dubourg, Jake Vanderplas, Alexandre Passos, David Cournapeau, Matthieu Brucher, Matthieu Perrot, and Édouard Duchesnay. 2011. Scikit-learn: Machine learning in Python. *Journal of Machine Learning Research*, 12:2825–2830.

Frank Rosenblatt. 1957. *The perceptron, a perceiving and recognizing automaton Project Para*. Cornell Aeronautical Laboratory.

Gerard Salton and Michael McGill. 1984. *Introduction to Modern Information Retrieval*. McGraw-Hill Book Company.

Joel Tetreault, Daniel Blanchard, Aoife Cahill, and Martin Chodorow. 2012. Native tongues, lost and found: Resources and empirical evaluations in native language identification. In *Proceedings of COLING 2012*, pages 2585–2602, Mumbai, India, December. The COLING 2012 Organizing Committee.

Joel Tetreault, Daniel Blanchard, and Aoife Cahill. 2013. Summary report on the first shared task on native language identification. In *Proceedings of the Eighth Workshop on Building Educational Applications Using NLP*, Atlanta, GA, USA, June. Association for Computational Linguistics.

Laura Mayfield Tomokiyo and Rosie Jones. 2001. You're not from 'round here, are you?: Naive bayes detection of non-native utterance text. In *Proceedings of the second meeting of the North American Chapter of the Association for Computational Linguistics on Language technologies (NAACL '01)*.

Oren Tsur and Ari Rappoport. 2007. Using classifier features for studying the effect of native language on the choice of written second language words. In *Proceedings of the Workshop on Cognitive Aspects of Computational Language Acquisition*, pages 9–16.

Sze-Meng Jojo Wong and Mark Dras. 2009. Contrastive analysis and native language identification. In *Proceedings of the Australasian Language Technology Association Workshop*, pages 53–61. Citeseer.

Hsiang-Fu Yu, Fang-Lan Huang, and Chih-Jen Lin. 2011. Dual coordinate descent methods for logistic regression and maximum entropy models. *Machine Learning*, 85(1-2):41–75.

Jian Zhang, Rong Jin, Yiming Yang, and Alexander G. Hauptmann. 2003. Modified logistic regression: An approximation to svm and its applications in large-scale text categorization. In *ICML*, pages 888–895.

Native Language Identification: a Simple n-gram Based Approach

Binod Gyawali and **Gabriela Ramirez** and **Thamar Solorio**
CoRAL Lab
Department of Computer and Information Sciences
University of Alabama at Birmingham
Birmingham, Alabama, USA
{bgyawali,gabyrr,solorio}@cis.uab.edu

Abstract

This paper describes our approaches to Native Language Identification (NLI) for the NLI shared task 2013. NLI as a sub area of author profiling focuses on identifying the first language of an author given a text in his second language. Researchers have reported several sets of features that have achieved relatively good performance in this task. The type of features used in such works are: lexical, syntactic and stylistic features, dependency parsers, psycholinguistic features and grammatical errors. In our approaches, we selected lexical and syntactic features based on n-grams of characters, words, Penn TreeBank (PTB) and Universal Parts Of Speech (POS) tagsets, and perplexity values of character of n-grams to build four different models. We also combine all the four models using an ensemble based approach to get the final result. We evaluated our approach over a set of 11 native languages reaching 75% accuracy.

1 Introduction

Recently, a growing number of applications are taking advantage of author profiling to improve their services. For instance, in security applications (Abbasi and Chen, 2005; Estival et al., 2007) to help limit the search space of, for example, the author of an email threat, or in marketing where the demography information about customers is important to predict behaviors or to develop new products.

Particularly, author profiling is a task of identifying several demographic characteristics of an author from a written text. Demographic groups can be identified by age, gender, geographic origin, level of education and native language. The idea of identifying the native language based on the manner of speaking and writing a second language is borrowed from Second Language Acquisition (SLA), where this is known as *language transfer*. The theory of language transfer says that the first language (L1) influences the way that a second language (L2) is learned (Ahn, 2011; Tsur and Rappoport, 2007). According to this theory, if we learn to identify what is being transfered from one language to another, then it is possible to identify the native language of an author given a text written in L2. For instance, a Korean native speaker can be identified by the errors in the use of articles *a* and *the* in his English writings due to the lack of similar function words in Korean. As we see, error identification is very common in automatic approaches, however, a previous analysis and understanding of linguistic markers are often required in such approaches.

In this paper we investigate if it is possible to build native language classifiers that are not based on the analysis of common grammatical errors or in deeper semantic analysis. On the contrary, we want to find a simple set of features related to n-grams of words, characters, and POS tags that can be used in an effective way. To the best of our knowledge, almost all the works related to L1 identification use fine grained POS tags, but do not look into whether a coarse grained POS tagset could help in their work. Here, we explore the use of coarse grained Universal POS tags with 12 POS categories in the NLI task and compare the result with the fine grained Penn TreeBank (PTB) POS tags with 36 POS categories.

Moreover, we also investigate how the system works when perplexity values are used as features in identifying native languages. Using an ensemble based approach that combines four different models built by various combinations of feature sets of n-grams of words, characters, and POS tags, and perplexity values, we identify the native language of the author, over 11 different languages, with an accuracy close to 80% and 75% in development and test dataset respectively.

2 Related Work

The first known work about native language identification appears in 2005 (Koppel et al., 2005). In their study, the authors experimented with three types of features, i.e. function words, letter n-grams, errors and idiosyncrasies. But their analysis was focused on the identification of common errors. They found that using a combination of all the features in a Support Vector Machine (SVM), they can obtain an accuracy of 80% in the classification of 5 different native languages. As in this first study, analyzing errors is common in native language identification methods, since it is a straightforward adaptation of how this task is performed in SLA. For instance, Wong and Dras (2009) investigate the use of error types such as disagreement on subject-verb and noun-number, as well as misuse of determiners to show that error analysis is helpful in this task. But their results could not outperform the results obtained by Koppel et al. (2005). They also suggested that analyzing other types of errors might help to improve their approach. In the same path, Jarvis et al. (2012) investigate a larger variety of errors, for example lexical words and phrase errors, determiner errors, spelling errors, adjective order errors and errors in the use of punctuation marks, among others. But they also could not achieve results comparable to the previous results in this task.

Since language transfer occurs when grammatical structures from a first language determine the grammatical structures of a second language, the inclusion of function words and dependency parsers as features seem to be helpful to find such transfers as well as error types (Tetreault et al., 2012; Brooke and Hirst, 2011; Wong et al., 2012). It is common that the analysis of the structure of certain grammatical patterns is also informative to find the use or misuse of well-established grammatical structures (e.g. to distinguish between the use of verb-subject-object, subject-verb-object, and subject-object-verb), in such cases n-grams of POS tags can be used. Finally, according to Tsur and Rappoport (2007), the transfer of phonemes is useful in identifying the native language. Even though the phonemes are usually speech features, the authors suggest that this transfer can be captured by the use of character n-grams in the text. Character n-grams have been proved to be a good feature in author profiling as well since they also capture hints of style, lexical information, use of punctuation and capitalization.

In sum, there are varieties of feature types used in native language identification, most of them combine three to nine types. Each type aims to capture specific information such as lexical and syntactic information, structural information, idiosyncrasies, or errors.

3 Shared Task Description

The Native Language Identification (NLI) shared task focuses on identifying the L1 of an author based on his writing in a second language. In this case, the second language is English. The shared task had three sub-tasks: one closed training and two open training. The details about the tasks are described by Tetreault et al. (2013). For each subtask, the participants were allowed to submit up to five runs. We participated in the closed training sub-task and submitted five runs.

The data sets provided for the shared task were generated from the TOEFL corpus (Blanchard et al., 2013) that contains $12,100$ English essays. The corpus comprised 11 native languages (L1s): Arabic (ARA), Chinese (CHI), French (FRE), German (GER), Hindi (HIN), Italian (ITA), Japanese (JPN), Korean (KOR), Spanish (SPA), Telugu (TEL), and Turkish (TUR), each containing 1100 essays. The corpus was divided into training, development, and test datasets with 9900, 1100, and 1100 essays respectively. Each L1 contained an equal number of essays in each dataset.

Feature Sets	N-grams	Error rates for top k features				
		500	**800**	**1000**	**3000**	**6000**
Character n-grams	2 grams	78.27	77.64	77.18	**75.82**	-
	3 grams	78.55	60.55	64.27	**43.73**	44.36
Word n-grams	2 grams	66.55	58.36	55.64	44.91	**38.73**
	3 grams	75.55	69.18	76.36	67.09	**54.18**
PTB POS n-grams	2 grams	69.73	76.73	69.55	**72.09**	-
	3 grams	72.82	72.45	67.27	**56.18**	62.27
Universal POS n-grams	2 grams	**85.36**	-	-	-	-
	3 grams	78.1818	79.55	**72.36**	85.27	-

Table 1: Error rates in L1 identification using various feature sets with different number of features

4 General System Description

In this paper we describe two sets of experiments. We performed a first set of experiments to evaluate the accuracy of different sets of features in order to find the best selection. This set was also intended to determine the threshold of the number of top features in each set needed to obtain a good performance in the classification task. These experiments are described in Section 5.

In the second set, we performed five different experiments for five runs. Four of the five models used different combinations of feature sets to train the classifier. The major goal of these experiments was to find out how good the results achieved can be by using lower level lexical and shallow syntactic features. We also compared the accuracy obtained by using the fine grained POS tags and the coarse grained POS tags. In one of these experiments, we used perplexity values as features to see how effective these features can be in NLI tasks. Finally, the fifth experiment was an ensemble based approach where we applied a voting scheme to the predictions of the four approaches to get the final result. The details of these experiments are described in Section 6.

In our experiments, we trained the classifier using the training dataset, and using the model we tested the accuracy on the development and test dataset. We used an SVM multiclass classifier (Crammer and Singer, 2002) with default parameter settings for the machine learning tasks. We used character n-grams, word n-grams, Parts of Speech (POS) tag n-grams, and perplexity of character trigrams as features. For all the features except perplexity, we used a TF-IDF weighting scheme. To reduce the number of features, we selected only the top k features based on the document frequency in the training data.

The provided dataset contained all the sentences in the essays tokenized by using ETS's proprietary tokenizers. For the POS tags based features, we used two tagsets: Penn TreeBank (PTB) and Universal POS tags. For PTB POS tags, we tagged the text with the Stanford parser (Klein and Manning, 2003). In order to tag the sentences with Universal POS tags, we mapped the PTB POS tags to universal POS tags using the mapping described by Petrov et al. (2011).

We also used perplexity values from language models in our experiments. To generate the language models and compute perplexity, we used the SRILM toolkit (Stolcke et al., 2011). We used training data to generate the language models and train the classifier. Finally, all the sentences were converted into lower case before finding the word and character n-grams.

5 Feature Sets Evaluation

We performed a series of experiments using a single feature set per experiment in order to find the best combinations of features to use in classification models. All of the feature sets were based on n-grams. We ranked the n-grams by their frequencies on the training set and then used the development set to find out the best top k features in the training set. We used the values of k as 500, 800, 1000, 3000, and 6000 for this set of experiments. The error rates of these experiments are shown in Table 1. Since the total number of features in character bigrams, PTB

	Exp-$W_{2,3}PTB_3C_3$			Exp-$W_{2,3}Univ_3C_3$			Exp_ClassBased			Exp_Perplexity			Exp_Ensemble		
L1	**P**	**R**	**F1**	**P**	**R**	**F1**	**P**	**R**	**F1**	**P**	**R**	**F1**	**P**	**R**	**F1**
ARA	90.7	68.0	77.7	87.1	54.0	66.7	72.2	70.0	71.1	70.8	51.0	59.3	90.9	70.0	**79.1**
CHI	79.0	83.0	81.0	57.9	84.0	68.6	75.0	78.0	76.5	71.7	66.0	68.8	78.4	87.0	**82.5**
FRE	91.5	75.0	82.4	75.7	81.0	78.3	92.8	64.0	75.7	71.2	74.0	72.5	90.8	79.0	**84.5**
GRE	86.0	92.0	88.9	77.5	86.0	81.5	84.2	85.0	84.6	63.8	83.0	72.2	88.3	91.0	**89.7**
HIN	67.3	66.0	66.7	70.0	63.0	66.3	66.3	63.0	64.6	52.3	45.0	48.4	70.2	66.0	**68.0**
ITA	72.3	94.0	81.7	76.9	83.0	79.8	66.4	89.0	76.1	65.3	77.0	70.6	74.6	94.0	**83.2**
JPN	86.6	71.0	78.0	76.0	76.0	76.0	64.3	81.0	71.7	51.7	60.0	55.6	85.2	75.0	**79.8**
KOR	78.3	83.0	**80.6**	65.0	80.0	71.7	68.1	64.0	66.0	55.1	49.0	51.9	78.8	82.0	80.4
SPA	72.3	68.0	70.1	90.9	50.0	64.5	65.4	68.0	66.7	58.5	38.0	46.1	74.5	70.0	**72.2**
TEL	68.4	80.0	73.7	66.9	83.0	74.1	68.2	75.0	71.4	53.4	71.0	60.9	69.2	81.0	**74.7**
TUR	77.9	81.0	79.4	84.0	63.0	72.0	83.3	55.0	66.3	69.5	66.0	67.7	81.8	81.0	**81.4**
Overall	78.3			73.0			72.0			61.8			79.6		

Table 2: L1 identification accuracy in development data

POS bigrams, Universal POS bigrams, and Universal POS trigrams were 1275, 1386, 144, and 1602 respectively, some fields in the table are blank.

A trivial baseline for this task is to classify all the instances to a single class, which gives 9.09% accuracy. The table above shows that the results obtained in all cases is better than the baseline. In five cases, better results were obtained when using the top 3000 or 6000 features compared to other feature counts. In the case of the character trigram feature set, though the result using top 3000 features is better than the others, the difference is very small compared to the experiment using top 6000 features. The accuracy obtained by using top 3000 features in PTB POS tags is 6% higher than that with top 6000 features. In case of Universal POS tags trigrams, better results were obtained with top 1000 features.

Results show that bigram and trigram feature sets of words give higher accuracy compared to bigrams and trigrams of characters and POS tags. Comparing the results of n-grams of two different POS tagsets, the results obtained when using the PTB tagset are better than those when using the Universal tagsets. In the case of character, PTB POS tag, and Universal POS tag bigram feature sets, the overall accuracy is less than 30%. Based on these results, we decided to use the following sets of features: trigrams of characters and POS tags (PTB and Universal) and bigrams of words in our experiments below.

6 Final Evaluation

We submitted five runs for the task based on five classifiers. We named the experiments based on the features used and the approaches used for feature selection. Details about the experiments and their results are described below.

1. **Exp-$W_{2,3}PTB_3C_3$**: In this experiment, we used bigrams at the word level, and trigrams at the word, character level, as well as PTB POS tag trigrams as feature sets. We selected these feature sets based on the accuracies obtained in the experiments described in Section 5. We tried to use a consistent number of features in each feature set. As seen in Table 1, though the results obtained by using top 3000 and 6000 features are better in equal number of cases (2 and 2), the difference in accuracies when using 6000 features is higher than that when using 3000 features. Thus, we decided to use the top 6000 features in all the four feature sets.

2. **Exp-$W_{2,3}Univ_3C_3$**: The PTB POS tagset contains 36 fine grained POS categories while the Universal POS tagset contains only 12 coarse POS categories. In the second experiment, we tried to see how the performance changes when using coarse grained Universal POS categories instead of fine grained PTB POS tags. Thus, we performed the second experiment with the same settings as the first experiment except we used Universal POS tags instead of PTB POS tags. Since the total number of Universal POS

	Exp-$W_{2,3}PTB_3C_3$			Exp-$W_{2,3}Univ_3C_3$			Exp_ClassBased			Exp_Perplexity			Exp_Ensemble		
L1	**P**	**R**	**F1**	**P**	**R**	**F1**	**P**	**R**	**F1**	**P**	**R**	**F1**	**P**	**R**	**F1**
ARA	74.3	55.0	63.2	90.9	50.0	64.5	67.9	74.0	**70.8**	54.3	44.0	48.6	79.7	63.0	70.4
CHI	76.2	80.0	78.0	65.9	81.0	72.6	74.5	73.0	73.7	69.3	61.0	64.9	80.2	81.0	**80.6**
FRE	86.4	70.0	77.3	75.8	75.0	75.4	90.6	58.0	70.7	54.5	54.0	54.3	85.7	72.0	**78.3**
GRE	83.2	89.0	86.0	79.1	91.0	84.7	82.7	86.0	84.3	65.2	86.0	74.1	87.6	92.0	**89.8**
HIN	63.7	65.0	64.4	64.5	69.0	66.7	59.6	56.0	57.7	60.0	54.0	56.8	67.0	67.0	**67.0**
ITA	62.5	90.0	73.8	70.0	84.0	**76.4**	61.4	86.0	71.7	52.5	64.0	57.7	62.5	90.0	73.8
JPN	85.7	72.0	78.3	67.2	78.0	72.2	62.1	87.0	72.5	52.6	50.0	51.3	81.9	77.0	**79.4**
KOR	75.0	75.0	**75.0**	60.3	73.0	66.1	68.1	62.0	64.9	52.6	50.0	51.3	72.8	75.0	73.9
SPA	60.0	57.0	58.5	81.1	43.0	56.2	57.6	57.0	57.3	55.6	45.0	49.7	67.1	57.0	**61.6**
TEL	75.3	67.0	70.9	70.0	77.0	**73.3**	71.7	71.0	71.4	66.1	74.0	69.8	73.0	73.0	73.0
TUR	66.4	79.0	72.1	79.0	64.0	70.7	80.6	50.0	61.7	61.4	51.0	55.7	72.4	76.0	**74.1**
Accuracy	72.6			71.4			69.1			58.6			74.8		

Table 3: L1 identification accuracy in test data

trigrams was only 1602, we replaced 6000 PTB POS trigrams with 1602 Universal POS trigrams.

3. **Exp_ClassBased**: The difference in this experiment from the first one lies in the process of feature selection. Instead of selecting the top k features from the whole training data, the selection was done considering the top m features for each L1 class present in the training dataset, i.e., we first selected the top m features from each L1 class and combined them for a total of p where p is greater than or equal to m and k. After a number of experiments performed with different combinations of features to train the classifier and testing on the development dataset, we obtained the best result using character trigrams, PTB POS tag bigrams and trigrams, and word bigrams feature sets with 3000, 1000, 1000, and 6000 features from each L1 respectively. This makes the total number of features in character trigrams, POS tag bigrams, POS tag trigrams, and word bigrams as 3781, 1278, 1475, and 15592 respectively.

4. **Exp_Perplexity:** In this experiment, we used the perplexity values as the features that were computed from character trigram language models. Language models define the probability distribution of a sequence of tokens in a given text. We used perplexity values since these have been successfully used in some authorship attribution tasks (Sapkota et al., 2013).

5. **Exp_Ensemble**: In the fifth experiment, we used an ensemble based approach with our above mentioned four different models. We allowed each of the four models to have two votes. The first vote is a weighted voting schema in which the models were ranked according to their results in the development dataset and the weight for each model was given by $w_c = 1/rank(c)$, where $rank(c)$ is the position of c in the ranked list. The final output was based on the second vote that used a majority voting schema. In the second vote, the output of the first voting schema was also used along with the output of four models.

The results obtained by the above mentioned five experiments on the development and test datasets are shown in Tables 2 and 3 respectively. The tables show that the results obtained in the development dataset are better than those in the test dataset for all the approaches. In both datasets, we achieved the best results using the ensemble based approach, i.e. 79.2% and 74.8% accuracies in the development and test dataset respectively. Considering the accuracies of individual L1s, this approach achieved the highest accuracy in 10 L1s in the development dataset and in 7 L1s in the test dataset. Our system has the best accuracy for German in both development and test dataset. The other classes with higher accuracies in both datasets are French and Chinese. In both datasets, our system had the lowest accuracy for the Hindi and Spanish classes. Arabic and Telugu have

	ARA	**CHI**	**FRE**	**GER**	**HIN**	**ITA**	**JPN**	**KOR**	**SPA**	**TEL**	**TUR**
ARA	**63**	2	1	0	6	8	1	5	6	4	4
CHI	2	**81**	0	1	2	1	5	4	0	0	4
FRE	2	0	**72**	7	1	11	0	0	4	0	3
GER	0	2	2	**92**	1	1	0	0	1	0	1
HIN	2	2	0	0	**67**	2	0	2	3	19	3
ITA	0	0	2	2	0	**90**	0	0	3	0	3
JPN	3	3	1	1	0	3	**77**	9	1	1	1
KOR	1	7	1	0	0	0	8	**75**	4	1	3
SPA	1	1	3	0	2	25	1	4	**57**	0	6
TEL	1	0	0	0	21	0	1	0	3	**73**	1
TUR	4	3	2	2	0	3	1	4	3	2	**76**

Table 4: Confusion Matrix

3rd and 4th lowest accuracies.

Besides the ensemble based approach, the second best result was obtained by the first experiment (Exp_$W_{2,3}PTB_3C_3$). Comparing the overall accuracies of the first and second (Exp-$W_{2,3}Univ_3C_3$) experiments, though the difference between them does not seem very high in the test dataset, there is a difference of more than 5% in the development dataset. In the test dataset, the second experiment has the best results among all the approaches for classes Italian and Telugu, and has better results than the first experiment for classes Arabic and Hindi. The difference in the approaches used in the first and second experiments was the use of n-grams of different POS tagsets. The use of coarse grained Universal POS tagset features generalizes the information and loses the discriminating features that the fine grained PTB POS tagset features captures. For instance, the PTB POS tagset differentiates verbs into six categories while the Universal POS tagset has only one category for that grammatical class. Because of this, the fine grained POS tagset seems better for identifying the native languages than using a coarse grained POS tagset in most of the cases. More studies are needed to analyze the cases where Universal POS tagset works better than the fine grained PTB POS tagset.

The difference in accuracies obtained between the first experiment (Exp_$W_{2,3}PTB_3C_3$) and the third experiment (Exp_ClassBased) is more than 6% in the development dataset and more than 3% in the test dataset. In the test dataset, the third experiment has the highest accuracy for Arabic class and has better accuracy than the first experiment for Telugu class. The difference between these approaches was the feature selection approach used to create the feature vector. The results show that in most of the cases selecting the features from the whole dataset achieves better accuracy in identifying native languages compared to using the stratified approach of selecting the features from individual classes. The main reason behind using the class based feature selection was that we tried to capture some features that are specifically present in one class and not in others. Since all the texts in our dataset were about one of the eight prompts, and we have a balanced dataset, there was no benefit of doing the class based feature selection approach.

The fourth experiment (Exp_Perplexity) using perplexity values as features did not achieve accuracy comparable to the first three experiments. Because of the time constraint, we calculated perplexity based on only character trigram language models. Though the result we achieved is not promising, this approach could be an interesting work in future experiments where we could use other language models or the combination of various language models to compute the perplexity.

7 Error Analysis

The confusion matrix of the results obtained in the test dataset by using the ensemble based approach is shown in Table 4. The table shows the German class has the best accuracy with only a small number of texts of German mispredicted to other languages, while 7 texts of French class are mispredicted as German. The German language is rich in morphology and shares a common ancestor with English. It also has a different grammatical structure from the other languages in the task. The features we used in our experiments are shallow syntactic and lexical features, which could discriminate the writing styles and the structure of the German class texts, thus having a higher prediction accuracy.

The table shows that French, Italian, and Spanish classes seem to be confused with each other. Though the misclassification rate of texts in the Italian class is considerably low, a good number of texts in the French and Spanish classes are misclassified as Italian. The highest number of documents mispredicted is from Spanish to Italian, i.e. 25 texts of Spanish class are mispredicted as Italian. These three languages fall under the same language family i.e. Indo-European/Romance and have a similar grammatical features. The grammatical structure is a particular example of the high rate of misclassification among these classes. While English language is very strict in the order of words (Subject-Verb-Object), Spanish, Italian and French allow more flexibility. For instance, in Spanish, the phrases 'the car red' (*el auto rojo*) and 'the red car' (*el rojo auto*) are both correct although the later is a much less common construction. In this scenario, it is easy to see that the n-grams of words and POS tags are beneficial to distinguish them from English, but these n-grams might be confusing to identify the differences among these three languages since the patterns of language transfer might be similar.

Though Hindi and Telugu languages do not fall under the same language family, they are highly confused with each other. After Spanish to Italian, the second highest number of misclassified texts is from Telugu to Hindi. Similarly, 19 texts from the class Hindi are mispredicted as Telugu. Both of these languages are spoken in India. Hindi is the National and official language of India, while Telugu is an official language in some states of India. Moreover, English is also one of the official languages. So, it is very likely that the speakers are exposed to the same English dialect and therefore their language transfer patterns might be very similar. This might have caused our approach of lexical and syntactic features to be unable to capture enough information to identify the differences between the texts of these classes.

Texts from Arabic class are equally misclassified to almost all the other classes, while misclassification to Arabic do not seem that high. Texts of the Japanese, Korean, Chinese classes seem to be confused with each other, but the confusion does not seem very high thus having a good accuracy rate.

8 Conclusion and Future Work

In this paper, we describe our approaches to Native Language identification for the NLI Shared Task 2013. We present four different models for L1 identification, three of them using various combinations of n-gram features at the word, character and POS tag levels and a fourth one using perplexity values as features. Results show that all these approaches give a good accuracy in L1 identification. We achieved the best result among these by using the combination of character, words, and PTB POS tags. Finally, we applied an ensemble based approach over the results of the four different models that gave the highest overall accuracy of 79.6% and 74.8% in the development and test dataset respectively.

In our approaches, we use simple n-grams and do not consider grammatical errors in L1 identification. We would like to expand our approach by using the errors such as misspelled words and subject-verb, and noun-number disagreements as features. Moreover, in our current work of using perplexity values, the result seems good but is not promising. In this approach, we used the perplexity values based on only character trigram language models. We would like to incorporate other word and character n-gram language models to calculate perplexity values in our future work.

Acknowledgements

We would like to thank the organizers of NLI shared task 2013. We would also like to thank CONACyT for its partial support of this work under scholarship 310473.

References

Ahmed Abbasi and Hsinchun Chen. 2005. Applying authorship analysis to Arabic web content. In *Proceedings of the 2005 IEEE international conference on Intelligence and Security Informatics*, ISI'05, pages 183–197, Berlin, Heidelberg. Springer-Verlag.

Charles S. Ahn. 2011. Automatically Detecting Authors'

Native Language. Master's thesis, Naval Postgraduate School, Monterey, CA.

Daniel Blanchard, Joel Tetreault, Derrick Higgins, Aoife Cahill, and Martin Chodorow. 2013. TOEFL11: A Corpus of Non-Native English. Technical report, Educational Testing Service.

Julian Brooke and Graeme Hirst. 2011. Native language detection with 'cheap' learner corpora. In *Conference of Learner Corpus Research (LCR2011)*, Louvain-la-Neuve, Belgium. Presses universitaires de Louvain.

Koby Crammer and Yoram Singer. 2002. On the algorithmic implementation of multiclass kernel-based vector machines. *The Journal of Machine Learning Research*, 2:265–292.

Dominique Estival, Tanja Gaustad, Son Bao Pham, Will Radford, and Ben Hutchinson. 2007. Author profiling for English emails. In *Proceedings of the 10th Conference of the Pacific Association for Computational Linguistics*, pages 263–272, Melbourne, Australia.

Scott Jarvis, Yves Bestgen, Scott A. Crossley, Sylviane Granger, Magali Paquot, Jennifer Thewissen, and Danielle McNamara. 2012. The Comparative and Combined Contributions of n-Grams, Coh-Metrix Indices and Error Types in the L1 Classification of Learner Texts. In Scott Jarvis and Scott A. Crosley, editors, *Approaching Language Transfer through Text Classification*, pages 154–177. Multilingual Matters.

Dan Klein and Christopher D Manning. 2003. Accurate unlexicalized parsing. In *Proceedings of the 41st Annual Meeting on Association for Computational Linguistics-Volume 1*, pages 423–430. Association for Computational Linguistics.

Moshe Koppel, Jonathan Schler, and Kfir Zigdon. 2005. Determining an author's native language by mining a text for errors. In *Proceedings of the eleventh ACM SIGKDD international conference on Knowledge discovery in data mining*, pages 624–628, Chicago, IL. ACM.

Slav Petrov, Dipanjan Das, and Ryan McDonald. 2011. A universal part-of-speech tagset. *arXiv preprint arXiv:1104.2086*.

Upendra Sapkota, Thamar Solorio, Manuel Montes-y Gómez, and Paolo Rosso. 2013. The use of orthogonal similarity relations in the prediction of authorship. In *Computational Linguistics and Intelligent Text Processing*, pages 463–475. Springer.

Andreas Stolcke, Jing Zheng, Wen Wang, and Victor Abrash. 2011. SRILM at sixteen: Update and outlook. In *Proceedings of IEEE Automatic Speech Recognition and Understanding Workshop*.

Joel Tetreault, Daniel Blanchard, Aoife Cahill, and Martin Chodorow. 2012. Native tongues, lost and found: Resources and empirical evaluations in native language identification. In *Proceedings of COLING 2012*, pages 2585–2602, Mumbai, India, December. The COLING 2012 Organizing Committee.

Joel Tetreault, Daniel Blanchard, and Aoife Cahill. 2013. A report on the first native language identification shared task. In *Proceedings of the Eighth Workshop on Building Educational Applications Using NLP*, Atlanta, GA, USA, June. Association for Computational Linguistics.

Oren Tsur and Ari Rappoport. 2007. Using classifier features for studying the effect of native language on the choice of written second language words. In *Proceedings of the Workshop on Cognitive Aspects of Computational Language Acquisition*, pages 9–16, Prague, Czech Republic, June. Association for Computational Linguistics.

Sze-Meng Jojo Wong and Mark Dras. 2009. Contrastive Analysis and Native Language Identification. In *Proceedings of the Australasian Language Technology Association Workshop 2009*, pages 53–61, Sydney, Australia, December.

Sze-Meng Jojo Wong, Mark Dras, and Mark Johnson. 2012. Exploring Adaptor Grammars for Native Language Identification. In *Proceedings of the 2012 Joint Conference on Empirical Methods in Natural Language Processing and Computational Natural Language Learning*, pages 699–709, Jeju Island, Korea, July. Association for Computational Linguistics.

Feature Engineering in the NLI Shared Task 2013: Charles University Submission Report

Barbora Hladká, Martin Holub and **Vincent Kríž**
Charles University in Prague
Faculty of Mathematics and Physics
Institute of Formal and Applied Linguistics
Prague, Czech Republic
{hladka, holub,kriz}@ufal.mff.cuni.cz

Abstract

Our goal is to predict the first language (L1) of English essays's authors with the help of the TOEFL11 corpus where L1, prompts (topics) and proficiency levels are provided. Thus we approach this task as a classification task employing machine learning methods. Out of key concepts of machine learning, we focus on feature engineering. We design features across all the L1 languages not making use of knowledge of prompt and proficiency level. During system development, we experimented with various techniques for feature filtering and combination optimized with respect to the notion of mutual information and information gain. We trained four different SVM models and combined them through majority voting achieving accuracy 72.5%.

1 Introduction

Learner corpora are collections of texts written by second language (L2) learners, e.g. English as L2 – ICLE (Granger et al., 2009), Lang-8 (Tajiri et al., 2012), Cambridge Learner Corpus,[1] German as L2 – FALKO (Reznicek et al., 2012), Czech as L2 – CzeSL (Hana et al., 2010). They are a valuable resource for second language acquisition research, identifying typical difficulties of learners of a certain proficiency level (e.g. low/medium/high) or learners of a certain native language (L1 learners of L2). Research on the learner corpora does not concentrate on text collections only. Studying the errors in learner language is undertaken in the form of error annotation like in the projects (Hana et al., 2012), (Boyd et al., 2012), (Rozovskaya and Roth, 2010), (Tetreault and Chodorow, 2008). Once the errors and other relevant data are recognized in the learner corpora, automatic procedures for e.g. error correction, author profiling, native language identification etc. can be designed.

Our attention is focused on the task of automatic Native Language Identification (NLI), namely with English as L2.

In this report, we summarize the involment of the Charles University team in the first shared task in NLI co-located with the 8th Workshop on Innovative Use of NLP for Building Educational Applications in June 2013 in Atlanta, USA. The report is organized as follows: we briefly review related works in Section 2. The data sets to experiment with are characterized in Section 3. Section 4 lists the main concepts we pursue during the system development. Our approach is entirely focused on feature engineering and thus Section 5 is the most important one. We present there our main motivation for making such a decision, describe patterns according to which the features are generated and techniques that manipulate the features. We revise our ideas experimentally as documented in Section 6. In total, we submitted five systems to the sub-task of closed-training. In Sections 7 and 8, we describe these systems and discuss their results in detail. We summarize our two month effort in the shared task in Section 9.

[1] http://www.cambridge.org/gb/elt

2 Related work

We understand the task of native language identification as a subtask of natural language processing and we consider it as still a young task since the very first attempt to address it occurred eight years ago in 2005, as evident from the literature, namely (Koppel et al., 2005b), (Koppel et al., 2005a).

We appreciate all the previous work concerned with the given topic but we focus on the latest three papers only, all of them published at the 24th International Conference on Computational Linguistics held in December 2012 in Bombay, India, namely (Brooke and Hirst, 2012), (Bykh and Meurers, 2012), and (Tetreault et al., 2012). They provide a comprehensive review of everything done since the very first attempts. We do not want to replicate their chapters. Rather, we summarize them from the aspects we consider the most important ones in any machine learning system, namely the data, the feature design, the feature manipulation, and the machine learning methods - see Table 1.

3 Data sets

A new publicly available corpus of non-native English writing called TOEFL11[2] consists of essays on eight different topics written by non-native speakers of three proficiency levels (low/medium/high); the essays' authors have 11 different native languages. The corpus contains 1,100 essays per language with an average of 348 word tokens per essay. A corpus description and motivation to build such corpus can be found in (Blanchard et al., 2013).

The texts from TOEFL11 were released for the purpose of the shared task as three subsets, namely $Train$ for training, $DevTest$ for testing while system development, and $EvalTest$ for final testing. The texts were already tokenized and we processed them with the Standford POS tagger (Toutanova et al., 2003).

4 System settings

1. **Task:** Having a collection of English essays written by non-native speakers, the goal is to predict a native language of the essays' authors. Languages L1 are known in advance. Since we have a collection of English essays for which L1 is known (TOEFL11) at our disposal, we formulate this task as a classification task addressed by using supervised machine learning methods.

2. **Feature set**: A set $A = \{A_1, A_2, ..., A_m\}$ of m features where m changes as we perform various feature combinations and filtering steps. We prefer to work with binary features. We do not include two extra features, proficiency level and prompt, provided with the data. In addition, we design features across all 11 languages, i.e. we do not design features separately for a particular L1. Doing so, we address the task of predicting L1 from the text only, without any additional knowledge.

3. **Input data**: A set X of instances being texts from TOEFL11 corpus represented as feature vectors, $\mathbf{x} = \langle x_1, x_2, ..., x_m \rangle \in X, x_i \in A_i$.

4. **Output classes**: A set C of L1 languages, C = {ARA, CHIN, FRE, GER, HIN, ITA, JPN, KOR, SPA, TEL, TUR}, $|C| = 11$.

5. **True prediction**: A set $D = \{< \mathbf{x}, y >: \mathbf{x} \in X, y \in C\}$, $|D| = 12,100$ and its pairwise disjoint subsets $Train$, $DevTest$, $EvalTest$ where $Train \cup DevTest \cup EvalTest = D$, $|Train| = 9,900$, $|DevTest| = 1,100$, $|EvalTest| = 1,100$.

6. **Training data**: $Train \cup DevTest$. No other type of training data is used.

7. **Learning mechanism**: Since we focus on feature engineering, we do not study appropriateness of particular machine learning methods to our task in details. Instead, reviewing the related works, we selected the Support Vector Machine algorithm to experiment with.

8. **Evaluation**: 10-fold cross-validation with the sample $Train \cup DevTest$. Accuracy, Precision, Recall. Proficiency-based evaluation. Topic-based evaluation.

[2]**Source:** Derived from data provided by ETS. Copyright © 2013 ETS. www.ets.org.

PAPER	DATA	FEATURE DESIGN	FEATURE MANIPULATION	ML METHOD
[1]	Lang-8, ICLE, Cambridge Learner Corpus	function words, character n-grams, POS n-grams, POS/function n-grams, context-free-grammar productions, dependencies, word n-grams	frequency-based feature selection	SVM, MaxEnt
[2]	ICLE	binary features spanning word-based recurring n-grams, function words, recurring POS based n-grams and combination of them	no special feature treatment	logistic regression
[3]	ICLE, TOEFL11	character n-grams, function words, POS, spelling errors, writing quality	no special feature treatment	logistic regression

Table 1: A summary of latest related works [1](Brooke and Hirst, 2012), [2](Bykh and Meurers, 2012), [3](Tetreault at al., 2012)

5 Feature engineering

We split the process of feature engineering into two mutually interlinked steps. The first step aims at an understanding of the task projected into features describing properties of entities we experiment with. These experiments represent the second step where we find out how the features interact with each other and how they interact with a chosen machine learning algorithm.

We compose a *feature family* as a group of patterns that are relevant for a particular task. The features are then extracted from the data according to them. Since we experiment with English texts written by non-native speakers, we have to search for specific and identifiable text properties, i.e. tendencies of certain first language writers, based on the errors caused by the difference between L1 and L2. In addition, we look for phenomena that are not necessarily incorrect in written English but they provide clear evidence of characteristics typical for L1. Our feature family is built from chunks of various length in the texts, formally lexically and part-of-speech based *n*-grams. In total, the feature family contains eight patterns described in Table 2 - six for binary features *l,n,p,s1,s2,sp* and two for continuous features *a,r*. Outside the feature family, its patterns can be combined into joint patterns, like $l{+}sp$, $n{+}sp{+}r$.

Considering the key issues of machine learning, we mainly pay attention to overfitting. We are aware of many aspects that may cause overfitting, like complexity of the model trained, noise in training data, a small amount of training data. Features can lead to overfitting as well, thus we address it using elaborated feature engineering visualised in Figure 1. We can see there the data components and the process components having the features in common. The scheme can be traced either with individual patterns from the feature family or with joint patterns.

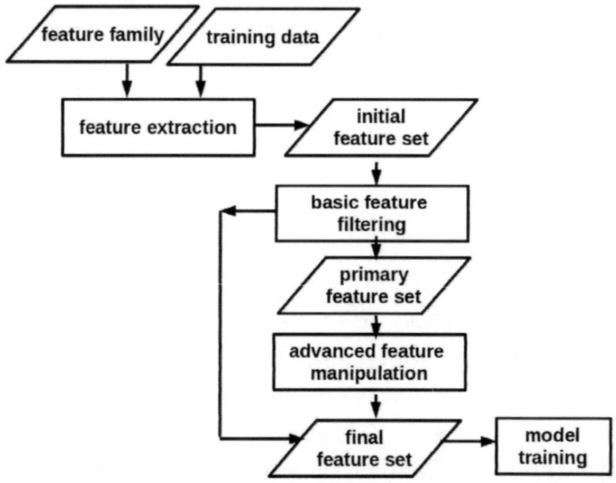

Figure 1: Feature engineering

Both basic feature filtering and advanced feature manipulation apply selected concepts from informa-

FEATURE FAMILY PATTERN	DESCRIPTION *n=1,2,3*	EXAMPLES
l	n-grams of lemmas	*picture; to see; you, be, not*
n	n-grams of words	*picture; to see; you, are, not*
p	n-grams of function words and POS tags of content words, i.e. nouns, verbs, adjectives, cardinal numbers	*not*; PRP; *you*, VBP; JJ, *to*, VB
s1	skipgrams of words: bigram w_{i-2}, w_i and trigrams w_{i-3}, w_{i-1}, w_i, w_{i-3}, w_{i-2}, w_i extracted from a sequence of words $w_{i-3}\ w_{i-2}\ w_{i-1}\ w_i$	*you,not; able, see; to, see,in; to things, in*
s2	skipgrams of words: bigrams w_{i-3}, w_i, w_{i-4}, w_i and trigrams w_{i-4}, w_{i-3}, w_i, w_{i-4}, w_{i-2}, w_i, w_{i-4}, w_{i-1}, w_i extracted from a sequence of words $w_{i-4}\ w_{i-3}\ w_{i-2}\ w_{i-1}\ w_i$	*are,see; you,see; you,are,see; you,able,see; you,to,see;*
sp	n-grams of function words and shrunken POS tags of content words: POS tags N* are shrunken into a tag N, V* into V, J* into J	*not*; PRP; *you* V; J *to* V
a	relative frequency of POS tags and function words	
r	relative frequency of POS tags	

Table 2: A feature family. Examples are taken from the file 498.txt, namely from the sentence *You are not able to see things in a big picture.* tagged as follows: (You/you/PRP are/be/VBP not/not/RB able/able/JJ to/to/TO see/see/VB things/thing/NNS in/in/IN a/a/DT big/big/JJ picture/picture/NN ./././)

tion theory.

5.1 Concepts from information theory

Consider a random variable A having two possible values 0 and 1 where the probability of 1 is p and 0 is $1 - p$. A degree of uncertainty we deal with when predicting the value of the variable depends on p. If p is close to zero or one, then we are almost confident about the value and our uncertainty is low. If the values are equally likely (i.e. $p = 0.5$), our uncertainty is maximal.

The **entropy** $H(A)$ measures the uncertainty. In other words, it quantifies the amount of information needed to predict the value of the variable. The formula 1 for the entropy treats variables with $N \geq 1$ possible values.

$$H(A) = -\sum_{i=1}^{N} p(A = a_i) \log_2 p(A = a_i) \quad (1)$$

The **conditional entropy** $H(A|B)$ quantifies the amount of information needed to predict the value of the random variable A given that the value of another random variable B is known, see Formula 2. Then $H(A|B) \leq H(A)$ holds.

$$H(A|B) = \sum_{b \in B} p(B = b) H(A|B = b) \quad (2)$$

The amount $H(A) - H(A|B)$ by which $H(A)$ decreases reflects additional information about A provided by B and is called **mutual information** $I(A; B)$ - see Formula 3. In other words, $I(A; B)$ quantifies the mutual dependence of two random variables A and B.

$$I(A; B) = H(A) - H(A|B) \quad (3)$$

Proceeding from statistics to machine learning, independent random variables correspond to features. Thus we can directly speak about the entropy of a feature, the conditional entropy of a feature given another feature and the mutual information of two features.

Information gain of feature A_k - $IG(A_k)$ - measures the expected reduction in entropy caused by partitioning the data set $Data$ according to the values of the feature A_k (Quinlan, 1987):

$$IG(A_k) = H(Data) - \sum_{i=j}^{c} \frac{|D_{v_j}|}{|Data|} H(D_{v_j}), \quad (4)$$

where $A_k^v = \{v_1, v_2, ..., v_c\}$ is a set of possible values of feature A_k and D_{v_i} is a subset of $Data$ containig instances with the feature value $x_k = v_j$.

C being a target feature, $H(Data) = H(C)$. Thus the mutual information between C and A_k - $I(C; A_k)$ - is the information gain of the feature A_k, i.e.

$$I(C; A_k) = IG(A_k). \quad (5)$$

All mentioned concepts are visualized in Figure 2 for our settings:

- Our target feature C has eleven possible values (i.e. L1 languages). These values are uniformly distributed in the data D, thus $H(C) = -\sum_{i=1}^{11} \frac{1}{11} \log_2 \frac{1}{11} = \log_2 11 \doteq 3.46$. Sample features (only for illustration) $A_1, A_2, A_3, A_4 \in A$ are binary features so $H(A_i) \leq 1 < H(C) = 3.46$, $i = 1, ..., 4$. The circle areas correspond to the entropy of features.
- The black areas correspond to mutual information $I(A_i; A_k)$.
- The striped areas correspond to the mutual information $I(C; A_k)$ between C and A_k.
- Features A_1 and A_3 are independent, so $I(A_1; A_3) = 0$.
- A_2 has the highest mutual dependence with C,
- $H(A_2) = H(A_3)$ and $IG(A_2) > IG(A_3)$

In addition to the concepts from information theory, we introduce another measure to quantify features: the **document frequency** of feature A_k – $df(A_k)$ is the number of texts in which A_k occurs, i.e. $df(A_k) \geq 0$.

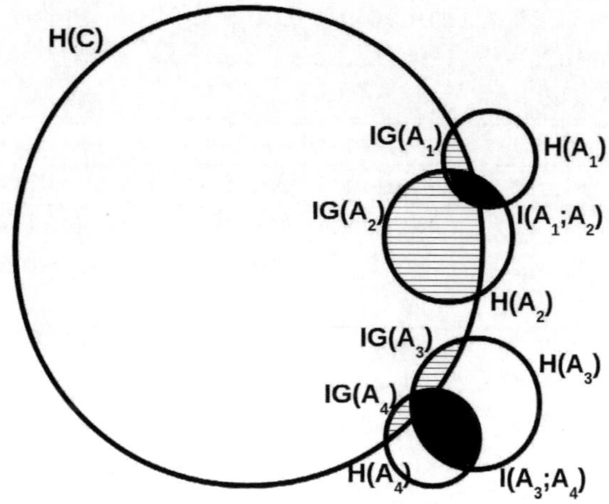

Figure 2: Information gain and mutual information visualization

5.2 Discussion on features

We impose a fundamental requirement on features: they should be both **informative** (i.e. useful for the classification task) and **robust** (i.e. not sensitive to training data). We control the criterion of *being informative* by information gain maximization. The criterion of *being robust* is quantified by document frequency. If $df(A_k)$ is high enough, then we can expect that A_k will occur in test data frequently. We propose two techniques to increase df: (i) filtering out features with low df; (ii) feature combination driven by IG.

The fulfillment of both criteria is always dependent on training data, i.e. the final feature set tends to fit training data and our goal is to weaken this tendency in order to get a more robust feature set. Both basic feature filtering and advanced feature combination help us to address this issue.

5.3 Basic feature filtering

We obtained the feature set A^0 by extracting features according to the feature family patterns) from the training data. Basic feature filtering removes features from A^0 in two steps that result in a primary feature set A^1:

1. Remove binary feature A_k if $df(A_k) < \delta_{df}$. Remove continous feature A_k if $relative\_frequency(A_k) < \delta_{rf}$ or $df(relative\_frequency(A_k) \geq \delta_{rf}) < \delta_{df}$.
2. Remove binary feature A_k if $IG(A_k) \leq \delta_{IG}$.

5.4 Advanced feature manipulation

The process of advanced feature manipulation handles m input features from the primary feature set A^1 in two different ways, filter them and combine them, in order to generate a final feature set A^f ready to train the model:

- **Filter them**. We use Fast Correlation-Based Filter (FCBF; (Fleuret, 2004), (Yu and Liu, 2003)) that addresses the correlation between features. It first ranks the features according to their information gain, i.e. $IG(A_1) \geq IG(A_2) \geq ... \geq IG(A_m)$. In the second step, it iteratively removes any feature A_k if there exists a feature A_j such that $IG(A_j) \geq IG(A_k)$ and $I(A_k; A_j) \geq IG(A_k)$, i.e. A_j is better as a predictor of C and A_k is more similar to A_j than to C. In the situation visualized in Figure 2, the feature A_4 will be filtered out because there is a feature A_3 such that $IG(A_3) \geq IG(A_4)$ and $I(A_3; A_4) \geq IG(A_4)$

- **Combine them**. We combine (COMB) binary features using logical operations (AND, OR, XOR, AND NOT, etc.) getting a new binary feature.

  For example, if we combine two features A_1 and A_2 using the OR operator, we get a new binary feature $Y = A_1$ OR A_2 for which the inequalities $df(Y) > df(A_1)$ and $df(Y) > df(A_2)$ hold. Thus we get a feature that is more robust than the two input features. To know whether it is more informative, we need to know how high $IG(Y)$ is with respect to $IG(A_1)$ and $IG(A_2)$. Without loss of generality, assume that $IG(A_1) > IG(A_2)$. If $IG(Y) > IG(A_1) > IG(A_2)$, then Y is more informative than A_1 and A_2, but both of these features could be informative enough as well. It depends on the threshold we set up for *being informative*. We can easily iterate this process - let $Y_1 = A_1$ OR A_2 and $Y_2 = A_3$ OR A_4. Then we can combine $Y_3 = Y_1$ OR A_5 or $Y_4 = Y_1$ OR Y_2, etc.

Then, advanced feature manupilation runs according to scenarios formed as a series of FCBF and COMB, for example $A^1 \rightarrow$ FCBF $\rightarrow$ COMB $\rightarrow$ FCBF $\rightarrow A^f$ or $A^1 \rightarrow$ COMB $\rightarrow$ FCBF $\rightarrow A^f$.

6 System development

During system development, we formulated hypotheses how to avoid overfitting and get features robust and informative enough. In parallel, we run the experiments with parameters using which we controlled this requirement.

Basic feature filtering We set the thresholds δ_{df}, δ_{IG}, δ_{rf} empirically to the values 4, 0 and 0.02, respectively. Table 3 shows the changes in the size of the initial feature set after the basic feature filtering. It is evident that even such trivial filtering reduces the number of features substantially.

FEATURE FAMILY PATTERN	INITIAL FEATURE SET (i.e. $\|A^0\|$)	AFTER *df* FILTERING	AFTER *IG* FILTERING (i.e. $\|A^1\|$)
l	2,078,105	156,722	2,827
n	2,411,516	163,939	2,840
p	1,116,986	161,681	2,467
s1	4,794,702	242,969	1,877
s2	7,632,011	382,881	4,566
sp	781,018	123,431	933
a	181	111	111
r	48	48	48

Table 3: Volumes of initial feature sets extracted from $Train \cup DevTest$ (1st column). Volumes of primary feature sets after basic filtering of A^0 (3rd column)

Learning mechanisms Originally, we started with two learning algorithms, Random Forests (RF) and Support Vector Machines (SVM), running them in the R system.[3]

The **Random forests**[4] algorithm joins randomness with classification decision trees. They iterate the process of two random selections and training a decision tree k-times on a subset of m features. Each of them classifies a new input instance $\mathbf{x}$ and the class with the most votes becomes the output class of $\mathbf{x}$.

Support Vector Machines (Vapnik, 1995) efficiently perform both linear and non-linear classification employing different *Kernel* functions and

[3] `http://www.r-project.org`

[4] `http://www.stat.berkeley.edu/~breiman/`

avoiding the overfitting by two parameters, *cost* and *gamma*.

We run a number of initial experiments with the following settings: the feature family pattern n; the basic feature filtering, RF with different values of parameters k and m, SVM with different values of parameters *kernel*, *gamma* and *cost*

Cross-validation on the data set $Train$ performed with SVM showed significantly better results than those obtained with RF. We were quite suprised that RF ran with low performance so that we decided to stop experimenting with this algorithm. Step by step, we added patterns into the feature family and carried out experiments with SVM only on the data set $Train \cup DevTest$. We fixed the values of the SVM parameters *kernel, degree, gamma, cost* after several experiments as follows *kernel = polynomial, degree = 1, gamma = 0.0004, cost = 1*. Then we included the advanced feature manipulation into the experiments according to the scenarios $A^1 \rightarrow$ FCBF $\rightarrow$ COMB $\rightarrow$ FCBF $\rightarrow A^f$ and $A^1 \rightarrow$ COMB $\rightarrow$ FCBF $\rightarrow A^f$. COMB was composed using the OR operator only. Unfortunately, none of them outperformed the initial experiments with the basic filtering only.

Table 4 contains candidates for the final submission. The highlighted candidates were finally selected for the submission.

FEATURE PATTERNS	CROSS-VALIDATION on $Train$	Acc (%) on $DevTest$
l + a	**72.97 ± 0.76**	**71.09**
n + a	72.45 ± 0.98	63.00
l + sp + a	**72.00 ± 0.72**	**70.64**
l+sp	**71.09 ± 0.72**	**71.45**
n+sp	70.38 ± 0.69	52.27
l	71.67 ± 0.57	70.18
n	71.27 ± 0.84	68.72
l+p	**71.17 ± 2.41**	**71.27**
n+s1	69.90 ± 1.04	66.72
n+s2	68.75 ± 1.50	67.63
n+s1+s2	67.97 ± 0.96	66.81

Table 4: Candidates for the final submission. Candidates in bold were submitted.

MODEL	FEATURE FAMILY PATTERN	Acc (%)
CUNI-closed-1	majority voting of CUNI-closed-[2-5]	72.5
CUNI-closed-2	l+a	71.6
CUNI-closed-3	l+p	71.6
CUNI-closed-5	l+sp+a	71.1
CUNI-closed-4	l+sp	69.7

Table 5: An overview of models submitted.

MODEL	Acc (%)
CUNI-closed-1	74.2
CUNI-closed-2	73.4
CUNI-closed-3	73.9
CUNI-closed-4	73.1
CUNI-closed-5	72.9

Table 6: Cross-validation results for all submitted CUNI-closed systems.

7 Submission to the shared task

In total, we submitted five systems to the closed-training sub-task - see their overview in Table 5. The results correspond to our expectations that we made based on the results of cross-validation presented in Table 4. The best system, CUNI-closed-1, was the outcome of majority voting of the remaining four systems. The performance of this system per language is presented in Table 7.

Table 6 reports accuracy results when doing 10-fold cross-validation on $Train \cup DevTest$. The folds for this experiment were provided by the organizers to get more reliable comparison of the NLI systems.

It is interesting to analyse the complementarity of the CUNI-closed-[2-5] systems that affects the performance of CUNI-closed-1. In Table 8, we list the numerical characteristics of five possible situations that can occur when comparing the outputs of two systems i and j. Situations **2** and **3** capture how complementary the systems are. The numbers for our systems are presented in Table 9.

We grouped languages according to the thresholds of F-measure. First we did it across the data, no matter what the proficiency level and prompt are - see the first row of Table 10. Second we did grouping

	Acc(%)	P(%)	R(%)	F(%)
ARA	72	67	72	69,6
CHI	78	71	78	74,3
FRE	73	74	73	73,7
GER	83	83	83	83,0
HIN	75	68	75	71,4
ITA	83	85	83	83,8
JPN	70	65	70	67,6
KOR	64	70	64	67,0
SPA	66	70	66	68,0
TEL	68	72	68	69,7
TUR	65	72	65	68,4

Table 7: CUNI-closed-1 on *EvalTest*: Acc, P, R, F

1. the number of instances both systems predicted correctly;
2. the number of instances both systems predicted incorrectly;
3. the number of instances the systems predicted differently: i system correctly and j system incorrectly;
4. the number of instance the systems predicted differently: i system incorrectly and j system correctly;
5. the number of instances the systems predicted differently and both incorrectly.

Table 8: Pair of two systems i and j and their predictions.

	pair of CUNI-closed-i and CUNI-closed-j systems					
	2-3	2-4	2-5	3-4	3-5	4-5
1	707	717	745	701	710	732
2	161	215	242	183	181	250
3	81	71	43	87	78	35
4	81	50	37	66	72	50
5	70	47	33	63	59	33

Table 9: CUNI-closed-[2-5]: complementary rates.

	≥ 90%	≥ 80%	≥ 70%	< 70%
overall		GER, ITA	CHI, FRE, HIN	TEL, ARA, TUR, SPA, JPN, KOR
high		GER, ITA	CHI, HIN, FRE	KOR, TUR, SPA, TEL, ARA, JPN
medium		ITA, GER, FRE, TEL	CHI, ARA, SPA, TUR	JPN, KOR, HIN
low	GER	ITA, FRE, JPN	ARA	KOR, TEL, HIN, TUR, SPA, CHI, FRE

Table 10: CUNI-closed-1 on *EvalTest*: Groups of languages sorted according to F-measure w.r.t. proficiency level.

for a particular proficiency level - see the remaining rows in Table 10. We can see that both GER and ITA are languages with the highest F-measure on all levels. Third we grouped by a particular prompt - see Table 11. We can see there diversed numbers for L1 languages despite the fact that prompts are formulated generally. Even more, we observe a topic similarity between prompts P2, P3, and P8, between P4 and P5, and between P1 and P7.

8 Future plans

In our future research, w want to elaborate ideas that concern the feature engineering. We plan to work with the feature family that we designed in our initial experiments. However, we will think about more specific patterns in the essays, like the average count of tokens/punctuation/capitalized nouns/articles per sentence. As Table 12 shows, there is only one candidate, namely the number of tokens in sentence, to be taken into considerations since there is the largest difference between minimum and maximum.

We confronted Ken Lackman,[5] an English teacher, with the task of *manual* native language identification by English teachers. He says: "*I think*

[5] `http://kenlackman.com`

	$\geq 90\%$	$\geq 80\%$	$\geq 70\%$	$< 70\%$
P1	GER, ITA	FRE, HIN, ARA, TEL	CHI, KOR, TUR	SPA, JPN
P2	GER, FRE, ITA, TEL	ARA, HIN, JPN	SPA, KOR, CHI	TUR
P3	GER	CHI, KOR	HIN, ITA	FRE, JPN, TUR, ARA, SPA, TEL
P4		ITA	CHI, TUR, HIN, FRE	TEL, SPA, GER, JPN, ARA, KOR
P5	ITA	TUR, JPN, GER	FRE, TEL, KOR	HIN, CHI, SPA, ARA
P6		ITA, CHI, SPA	KOR, ARA, JPN	HIN, FRE, TEL, GER, TUR
P7		ITA, CHI, TUR	SPA, GER, HIN, FRE	ARA, JPN, KOR, TEL
P8		ARA	GER, TEL, SPA, ITA	FRE HIN, KOR, JPN, TUR, CHI

Table 11: CUNI-closed-1 on *EvalTest*: Groups of languages sorted according to F-measure w.r.t. prompt.

AVG COUNT PER SENTENCE	*Train* MIN (L1) - MAX (L1)
TOKEN	18 (JPN) -25.8 (SPA)
PUNCTUATION	1.5 (HIN, TEL) - 2.1 (SPA)
CAPITALIZED NOUN	0.1 (CHI) - 0.3 (HIN)
the	0.6 (KOR) - 1.2 (ITA, SPA, TEL)
a/an	0.3 (JPN, KOR) - 0.7 (ITA, SPA)

Table 12: Data counts on *Train*.

it's quite possible to do but you would need a set of guidelines to supply teachers with. The guidelines would list tendancies of certain first language writers, based on errors caused by difference between L1 and L2. For example, Germans tend to capitalize too many nouns, since there are far more nouns capitalized in their language, Asians tend to leave out articles and Arab students tend to use the verb "to be" inappropriately before other verbs." Looking into the data, we observe the phenomena Ken is speaking about, but the quantity of them is not statistically significant to distinguish L1s.

We formulate an idea of a *bootstrapped feature extraction* that has not been published yet, at least to our knowledge. Let us assume a set of operations that can be performed over a feature set (so far, we have proposed two possible operations with the features, filtering them out and their combinations). Determining whether a condition to perform a given operation holds is done on the *high* number of random samples. If the condition holds on the *majority* of them, then the operation is performed. The only parameter that must be set up is the *majority*. Instead of setting a threshold that is adjusted for all the features, bootstrapped feature extraction deals with fitting the data individually for each feature.

9 Conclusion

It was the very first experience for our team to address the task of NLI. We assess it as very stimulating and we understand our participation as setting the baseline for applying other ideas. An overall table of results (Tetreault et al., 2013) for all the teams involved in the NLI 2013 Shared Task shows that there is still space for improvement of our baseline.

We really appreciate all the work done by the organizers. They've made an effort to prepare the high-quality data and set up the framework by which the use of various NLI systems can be reliably compared.

Acknowledgments

The authors would like to thank Eva Hajičová and Jirka Hana for their valuable comments. We also thank Ken Lackman and Leslie Ryan[6] for sharing

[6] http://lesliestreet.cz

their teaching experience. This research was supported by the Czech Science Foundation, grant no. P103/12/G084 and the Technology Agency of the Czech Republic, grant no. TA02010182.

References

Daniel Blanchard, Joel Tetreault, Derrick Higgins, Aoife Cahill, and Martin Chodorow. 2013. TOEFL11: A Corpus of Non-Native English. Technical report, Educational Testing Service.

Adriane Boyd, Marion Zepf, and Detmar Meurers. 2012. Informing Determiner and Preposition Error Correction with Hierarchical Word Clustering. In *Proceedings of the 7th Workshop on Innovative Use of NLP for Building Educational Applications (BEA7)*, pages 208–215, Montreal, Canada. Association for Computational Linguistics.

Julian Brooke and Graeme Hirst. 2012. Robust, Lexicalized Native Language Identification. In *Proceedings of COLING 2012*, pages 391–408, Mumbai, India, December.

Serhiy Bykh and Detmar Meurers. 2012. Native Language Identification using Recurring n-grams – Investigating Abstraction and Domain Dependence. In *Proceedings of COLING 2012*, pages 425–440, Mumbai, India, December.

F. Fleuret. 2004. Fast Binary Feature Selection with Conditional Mutual Information. *Journal of Machine Learning Research (JMLR)*, 5:1531–1555.

Sylviane Granger, Estelle Dagneaux, Fanny Meunier, and Magali Paquot. 2009. *International Corpus of Learner English v2 (Handbook + CD-ROM)*. Presses universitaires de Louvain, Louvain-la-Neuve.

Jirka Hana, Alexandr Rosen, Svatava Škodová, and Barbora Štindlová. 2010. Error-tagged Learner Corpus of Czech. In *Proceedings of the Fourth Linguistic Annotation Workshop (LAW IV)*, pages 11–19, Stroudsburg, USA. Association for Computational Linguistics.

Jirka Hana, Alexandr Rosen, Barbora Štindlová, and Petr Jäger. 2012. Building a learner corpus. In *Proceedings of the 8th International Conference on Language Resources and Evaluation (LREC 2012)*, İstanbul, Turkey. European Language Resources Association.

Moshe Koppel, Jonathan Schler, and Kfir Zigdon. 2005a. Automatically determining an anonymous author's native language. *Intelligence and Security Informatics*, pages 41–76.

Moshe Koppel, Jonathan Schler, and Kfir Zigdon. 2005b. Determining an author's native language by mining a text for errors. In *Proceedings of the 11th ACM SIGKDD*, pages 624–628, Chicago, IL. ACM.

John Ross Quinlan. 1987. Simplifying decision trees. *International Journal of ManMachine Studies, 27, 221-234*.

Marc Reznicek, Anke Ludeling, Cedric Krummes, Franziska Schwantuschke, Maik Walter, Karin Schmidt, Hagen Hirschmann, and Torsten Andreas. 2012. Das Falko-Handbuch. Korpusaufbau und Annotationen Version 2.01. Technical report, Department of German Studies and Linguistics, Humboldt University, Berlin, Germany.

Alla Rozovskaya and Dan Roth. 2010. Annotating ESL Errors: Challenges and Rewards. In *Proceedings of the NAACL HLT 2010 Fifth Workshop on Innovative Use of NLP for Building Educational Applications*, pages 28–36, Los Angeles, California, June. Association for Computational Linguistics.

Toshikazu Tajiri, Mamoru Komachi, and Yuji Matsumoto. 2012. Tense and Aspect Error Correction for ESL Learners Using Global Context. In *In Proceedings of the 50th ACL: Short Papers*, pages 192–202.

Joel R. Tetreault and Martin Chodorow. 2008. Native judgments of non-native usage: experiments in preposition error detection. In *Proceedings of the Workshop on Human Judgements in Computational Linguistics*, HumanJudge '08, pages 24–32, Stroudsburg, PA, USA. Association for Computational Linguistics.

Joel Tetreault, Daniel Blanchard, Aoife Cahill, and Martin Chodorow. 2012. Native Tongues, Lost and Found: Resources and Empirical Evaluations in Native Language Identification. In *Proceedings of COLING 2012*, pages 2585–2602, Mumbai, India, December. The COLING 2012 Organizing Committee.

Joel Tetreault, Daniel Blanchard, and Aoife Cahill. 2013. A Report on the First Native Language Identification Shared Task. In *Proceedings of the Eighth Workshop on Innovative Use of NLP for Building Educational Applications*, Atlanta, GA, USA, June. Association for Computational Linguistics.

Kristina Toutanova, Dan Klein, Christopher Manning, and Yoram Singer. 2003. Feature-Rich Part-of-Speech Tagging with a Cyclic Dependency Network. In *Proceedings of HLT-NAACL 2003*, pages 252–259.

Vladimir N. Vapnik. 1995. *The Nature of Statistical Learning Theory*. Springer-Verlag, New York.

L. Yu and H. Liu. 2003. Feature Selection for High-Dimensional Data: A Fast Correlation-Based Filter Solution. In *Proceedings of The Twentieth International Conference on Machine Leaning (ICML-03)*, pages 856–863, Washington, D.C., USA. Association for Computational Linguistics.

Native Language Identification: A Key N-gram Category Approach

Kristopher Kyle, Scott Crossley
Georgia State University
34 Peachtree Ave, Ste 1200
Atlanta, GA 30303
kkyle3@student.gsu.edu,
scrossley@gsu.edu

Jianmin Dai, Danielle S. McNamara
Arizona State University
PO Box 872111
Tempe, AZ 85287
Jianmin.Dai@asu.edu,
dsmcnamara1@gmail.com

Abstract

This study explores the efficacy of an approach to native language identification that utilizes grammatical, rhetorical, semantic, syntactic, and cohesive function categories comprised of key n-grams. The study found that a model based on these categories of key n-grams was able to successfully predict the L1 of essays written in English by L2 learners from 11 different L1 backgrounds with an accuracy of 59%. Preliminary findings concerning instances of crosslinguistic influence are discussed, along with evidence of language similarities based on patterns of language misclassification.

1. Introduction

Native language identification (NLI) is generally an automated task that can be used in authorship profiling (Wong & Dras, 2009) and in assisting automatic writing evaluation systems provide focused feedback (e.g., Rozovskaya & Roth, 2011). NLI is achieved by identifying patterns of language use that are common to a group of users of a particular second language (L2; e.g., English) that share a native language (L1). Useful to the discussion of these patterns is the concept of crosslinguistic influence (CLI), which references 'the consequences - both direct and indirect - that being a speaker of a particular native language (L1) has on the person's use of a later learned language (Jarvis, 2012, p.1). Beyond its theoretical applications, CLI can also be used to inform L2 classroom pedagogy (Granger, 2009; Laufer & Girsai, 2008). NLI studies, then, are informed by and can inform CLI, and have diverse applications.

The current study seeks to add to the discussions of NLI and CLI by testing the efficacy of a new approach – the use of grammatical, rhetorical, semantic, syntactic, and cohesive function categories of key n-grams.

2. Background

In this section we outline two approaches to CLI, provide a selected review of relevant literature, and address gaps in the current body of NLI research.

2.1 Approaches to CLI

Jarvis (2000, 2010, 2012) has outlined two approaches to the investigation of CLI: a comparison-based and a detection-based approach. The comparison-based approach is generally constructed based on specific observed difference between language systems (e.g., article usage in English as compared to article usage in Korean). Whether or not these L1 differences affect L2 production is then analyzed by examining example texts (e.g., inappropriate use of articles by native speakers of Korean writing in English as an L2). The detection-based argument, on the other hand, is built with the opposite trajectory. Instead of beginning with hypotheses based on differences in language systems, researchers begin by identifying patterns of language use (e.g., inappropriate article use) that occur regularly by members of an L1 that use a particular L2 (intragroup homogeneity) but do not occur regularly by other L1 users of the same L2 (intergroup heterogeneity). These patterns of use are then verified through statistical and machine learning techniques that use these patterns to predict the L1 group membership of L2 texts (i.e., NLI).

Recent advances in corpus development and natural language processing allow for larger numbers of texts to be searched using a greater number of linguistic features. These features can then be used to create an NLI predictor model. A successful model not only fulfills the NLI task, but provides further evidence that the observed patterns of language use can be attributable to CLI. While Type I errors are certainly a potential issue in this argument, Jarvis (2012) explains that false positives can be mitigated by balancing or controlling for potentially confounding variables (e.g., proficiency levels and essay prompts) during the construction of the target corpus.

2.2 Selected literature review

A limited but growing number of studies have investigated CLI using the detection-based approach, many of which are included in a volume edited by Jarvis and Crossley (2012). Researchers have explored the topic of CLI in the areas of lexical style (Jarvis et al., 2012a), lexical n-grams (Jarvis & Paquot, 2012), character n-grams (Tsur & Rappoprot, 2007), using variables related to cohesion, lexical sophistication, syntactic complexity and conceptual knowledge (Crossley & McNamara, 2012), error patterns (Bestgen, et al., 2012; Wong & Dras, 2009), and a combination of these approaches (Jarvis et al., 2012b; Koppel et al., 2005; Mayfield Tomokiyo & Jones, 2001, Wong & Dras, 2009).

Such studies have demonstrated relatively strong success rates for classifying an L2 writing sample based on the L1 of the writer. For instance, Jarvis and Paquot (2012), using 1-4-grams as predictor variables on a subset of argumentative essays included in the International Corpus of Learner English (ICLE) (Granger et al., 2009) achieved a 53.6% classification accuracy for 12 groups of L1s. Crossley and McNamara (2012) used features related to cohesion, lexical sophistication, syntactic complexity, and conceptual knowledge taken from the computational tool Coh-Metrix (Graesser et al., 2004) to classify essays written in English by Czech, Finnish, German, and Spanish participants and achieved an L1 classification accuracy of 65-67.6%. Using error types, Bestgen et al. (2012), on 223 ICLE essays written by French, German, and Spanish L1 participants, achieved a classification accuracy of 65%. In a follow-up study, Jarvis et al. (2012b) explored the relative efficacy of these three CLI methods (n-grams, Coh-Metrix indices, and error types) using the corpus found in Bestgen et al. (2012). When all three approaches were used in the classification task, the accuracy increased to 79%.

2.3 Weakness of extant research in CLI

Although the studies discussed so far have produced statistical models that can predict the L1 group of a text written in L2 English with accuracies well above chance, the degree to which these studies have demonstrated instances of CLI may be questionable as they draw on the ICLE corpus, which is arguably imbalanced (Jarvis et al., 2012a, and Mayfield Tomokiyo, & Jones, 2001 being the exceptions). While ICLE was designed with an attempt to control for a number of variables, the proficiency levels vary across language groups (as suggested by Koppel et al., 2005, and empirically confirmed by Bestgen et al., 2012) and though the argumentative texts are limited to a particular set of prompts within the corpus, these prompts are not equally distributed across language groups, raising the question of the degree to which the observed differences in texts were due to CLI, proficiency level, or essay prompt.

In addition, many of the linguistic features previously investigated did not lend themselves to providing strong links between observed differences and CLI (e.g., the word concreteness and word frequency variables investigated in Crossley & McNamara, 2012). A potentially promising method that has not been applied to detection-based CLI studies that may address these limitations is the use of rhetorical, syntactic, grammatical and cohesive categories comprised of key n-grams. Such features have recently been investigated by Crossley, Defore, Kyle, Dai, and McNamara (submitted for publication), in which they explored their usefulness for assessing the efficacy of an automatic writing evaluation (AWE) system. In this study, Crossley et al. separated a corpus of essays into introduction, body, and conclusion paragraphs, and then further separated these into high and low proficiency categories based on overall essay score. They then identified n-grams that occurred significantly more often (positive keyness values) in paragraphs of a certain type (e.g., introduction) from high scoring essays than the same type of paragraphs from low-scoring essays. Additionally, they identified n-grams that occurred significantly less often (negative keyness values) in high-scoring paragraphs of a certain type than low-scoring paragraphs of the same type. Positively and negatively key n-grams for each paragraph type were then separated into categories based on their rhetorical, syntactic, grammatical, and cohesive features. These categories were then successfully used as variables in a multiple regression to create a model that accounted for between 24%-33% of the variance in essay scores. This study demonstrates the efficacy of using grammatical, rhetorical, syntactic, and cohesive function categories of key n-grams to identify instances of linguistic variation that successfully predict essay quality. These findings hold promise for the use of similar methods to contribute to the study of CLI by identifying linguistic variation across different L1 groups writing in the same L2.

2.4 Goals of the current study

The current study, while drawing on previous research (notably Jarvis & Paquot, 2012 and Crossley et al., submitted for publication), contributes to the detection-based CLI discussion by: a) examining a prompt and proficiency-controlled corpus and, b) using n-gram indices related to grammatical, rhetorical, semantic, syntactic, and cohesive functions to assess difference in L2 essays based on the L1 of the writers. This study is guided by the following research questions:

1. Can a model consisting of functional categorical n-grams predict the native language of an L2 writer of English?

2. Does the resulting model inform theories of CLI?

3. Method

In this section, we describe the corpus used for our training and test set, the methods used for key n-gram identification, and the grouping of these n-grams into grammatical, rhetorical, semantic, syntactic, and cohesive categories.

3.1 Corpus

For this project we used an 11,000 essay subset of the 12,100 essay TOEFL11 corpus (Blanchard, Tetreault, Higgins, Cahill, & Chodorow, 2013). The TOEFL11 corpus is comprised of independent task essays written during administrations of the Test of English as a Foreign Language (TOEFL) between 2006-2007 (Blanchard et al., 2013). The corpus is balanced across 11 native language (L1) groups, includes responses to eight different independent-task prompts, and includes essays written by low, medium, and high proficiency writers. The languages represented include Arabic, Chinese, French, German, Hindi, Italian, Japanese, Korean, Spanish, Telugu, and Turkish. Following the procedures of the NLI shared task (Tetreault, Blanchard, & Cahill, 2013), 1,100 of the original 11,000 essays were set aside as the test set, leaving a training corpus of 9,900 essays.

3.2 Identifying key n-grams

In this study, we considered n-grams from 1-10 words in length. N-grams were considered to be *key* if they occur in a corpus significantly more or less frequently than in a reference corpus. We identified key n-grams using the KeyWords function of Wordsmith Tools 6 (Scott, 2013) and the default log likelihood method of identifying key n-grams (McEnery & Hardie, 2012). To ensure that the keyness of a particular n-gram was representative of use across a particular L1 group and not due to prolific use by a small number of individuals, we set the minimum threshold for inclusion at a range of 10 percent (n-grams had to occur in at least 10 percent of the texts written by a particular L1 group). Using these parameters, we conducted keyness tests for each language group. To create the key n-gram list for the Arabic group, for example, we compared the frequency of n-grams in the Arabic group to the frequency of n-grams in all of the other language groups combined. This process was completed for each language group until a key n-gram list existed for each.

Because one of the goals of our study was to generalize instances of CLI to essays written on prompts other than those included in the TOEFL11 Corpus, it was important to remove all prompt-based words from our key n-gram lists. Removing *all* words occurring in the prompts from the n-grams list would remove a number of high frequency words that may not be prompt-based (e.g., *the*, *to*), so prompt-based words were operationally defined as content words and their lemmas included in the prompt that had a Kucera and Francis (1967) written frequency value of 715 or less. N-grams were removed from potential predictor sets if they contained any of these prompt-based words. The remaining key n-grams for each language group were then sorted by absolute keyness in each group and filtered for redundancy. For example, prior to this stage, the Chinese key n-gram list included both *more* and *have more*. Because *more* had a higher absolute keyness value than *have more*, *have more* was removed from the Chinese key n-gram list.

Table 1 provides a summary of the length of key n-grams identified in each stage of the selection process. Although n-grams from 1-10 words in length were initially considered, no n-grams longer than 5-grams were identified as being key. Additionally, all 5-grams, such as the key Chinese n-gram 'group led by a tour', and the Telugu n-gram 'agree with the statement that' contained prompt-based words and were removed from further consideration. After the final n-gram refining step, the longest n-gram was a single 4-gram, the Turkish n-gram 'on the other hand'.

N-gram Length	Original	No Prompt Words	After Final Sort
5	5	0	0
4	19	3	1
3	110	54	8
2	699	512	147
1	1100	877	770
Total	1933	1446	926

Table 1: Length of key n-grams.

3.3 Grouping of key n-grams into indices

The last stage in our variable selection process was to group the key n-grams in each language group into categories. First, two indices for each language group were created. The first included all n-grams with positive keyness values that remained after the filtering process described above. The second included all of the n-grams with negative keyness values after filtering. Next, positive and negative n-grams were sorted into grammatical, rhetorical, semantic, syntactic, and cohesive function categories by two trained linguists with experience in the area of second language writing. The purpose of sorting n-grams in this manner was to identify patterns of relative over/underuse by each language group. See Table 2 for a list of all of the indices created during this process.

3.4 Evaluation of model

In CLI studies and other studies that attempt to predict the group membership of a text, discriminant function analysis (DFA) is often used (Jarvis & Paquot, 2012; Crossley & McNamara, 2012). Although other methods can be used, such as support vector machine decision trees (e.g., Koppel et al., 2005) or Naïve Bayes (e.g., Mayfield Tomokiyo & Jones, 2001), DFA has the advantage of being the most transparent of these with regard to interpreting results (Jarvis, 2012). DFA was therefore chosen as the method of analysis for this study, using L1 as the dependent variable and n-gram indices as independent variables.

The first step in the analysis was to check the independent variables for multicollinearity using a Pearson correlation matrix. Any two variables above a threshold of $p>.899$ were flagged for further analysis. A MANOVA was then conducted using the languages from one proficiency group as independent variables and the predictor indices/n-grams as dependent variables. The effect sizes produced by the MANOVA were used to select which variables flagged in the correlation matrix would be retained, and which would be eliminated. Within each highly correlated pair, the variable with the largest effect size was kept. Finally, a DFA was conducted on the training set. The predictor model sets identified in the DFA were then

Variable	Category	L1 Index Coverage -	+	Total	Examples
ALL		11	11	22	see below
Adjectives	Syntactic	0	1	1	little, kind, real
Adverbs	Syntactic	0	2	4	always, easily just, still
Articles	Cohesion	8	8	16	a, an, the
Auxilliary Verbs	Syntactic	2	0	2	has, have, will
Certainty	Semantic	0	1	1	necessary, sure, true
Cognition	Semantic	0	1	1	experience, thought
Comparatives	Rhetorical	0	1	1	easier, much more
Conjunctions	Cohesion	6	5	11	and, because, or
Connectives	Cohesion	1	2	3	and to, and that, also
Determiners	Cohesion	1	0	1	that, this
Evaluation	Semantic	0	1	1	good, fun, like to
Examples	Semantic	0	1	1	particular, etc
Explanation	Semantic	0	4	4	explain, in order to, that is
Go	Semantic	0	1	1	are going, go, going to
Irrealis	Grammatical	0	1	1	what, will
Modality	Rhetorical	9	9	18	we can, could, can be
Negation	Syntactic	3	8	11	but not, no
Nouns	Syntactic	3	7	10	country, person, places
Options	Rhetorical	0	1	1	consider, different, instead
People	Semantic	1	4	5	people, society, friends
Place	Semantic	0	1	1	city, place, places
Possession	Semantic	1	1	2	his, having, your
Possibility	Rhetorical	0	3	3	probably, maybe, possible
Pre-infinitive	Syntactic	0	1	1	how to, time to, way to
Prepositions	Grammatical	10	9	19	from, about, with a
Problems	Semantic	1	1	2	problem, problems
Pronouns	Cohesion	10	11	21	he, his, your
Quantity	Semantic	11	11	22	every, more than, some
Questions	Syntactic	7	6	13	where, who, why, question
Science/ Technology	Semantic	0	2	2	computer, internet
Signifying	Rhetorical	0	1	1	see, mean
Specificity	Rhetorical	0	3	3	certain, especially, special
Stance	Rhetorical	2	6	8	feel that, in my, opinion
Temporality	Semantic	6	7	13	during, more and more, often
To Be	Syntactic	6	8	14	are, been, it is
Transitions	Cohesion	4	9	13	but, however, therefore
Vagueness	Semantic	0	1	1	general, someone, something
Verbs	Syntactic	5	8	13	choose, make, play
Work/Study	Semantic	2	7	9	money, study, parents
Total		110	167	277	

Table 2: Negative and positive key n-gram variables.

	ARA	CHI	FRE	GER	HIN	ITA	JPN	KOR	SPA	TEL	TUR	Precision	Recall	F-measure
ARA	66	0	5	3	1	3	2	4	8	1	7	53.2%	66.0%	58.9%
CHI	3	63	5	3	2	0	6	9	0	3	6	57.8%	63.0%	60.3%
FRE	3	4	64	7	3	6	2	1	6	0	4	64.6%	64.0%	64.3%
GER	2	5	5	64	3	5	2	4	6	0	4	62.7%	64.0%	63.4%
HIN	4	5	0	7	54	1	0	1	6	17	5	56.8%	54.0%	55.4%
ITA	4	1	9	10	1	64	2	1	6	0	2	68.8%	64.0%	66.3%
JPN	6	7	1	1	0	1	64	9	2	1	8	61.5%	64.0%	62.7%
KOR	5	9	2	1	2	0	19	56	2	0	4	57.7%	56.0%	56.9%
SPA	14	6	6	3	4	9	2	3	43	2	8	47.3%	43.0%	45.0%
TEL	5	3	0	1	22	1	1	1	4	60	2	70.6%	60.0%	64.9%
TUR	12	6	2	2	3	3	4	8	8	1	51	50.5%	51.0%	50.7%

Table 3: Test set confusion matrix.

used on the essays in the test set to determine whether the model sets could generalize to a new population.

4. Results

The training set DFA predicted L1 group membership of TOEFL independent essays with an accuracy of 60% using 184 indices (df= 100, n= 9900, χ^2= 32997.259, p< .001), which is significantly higher than the baseline chance of 9%. The reported Kappa = .560, indicates a moderate relationship between actual and predicted L1.

The predictive accuracy of the model was verified on the test set, in which L1 group membership was predicted with an accuracy of 59% (df= 100, n= 1100, χ^2= 3550.791, p< .001). The reported Kappa = .549, indicates a moderate agreement between the actual and predicted L1. Table 3 includes the test set confusion matrix.

5. Discussion

The results of this study suggest the usefulness of key n-grams grouped into categories based on their grammatical, rhetorical, semantic, syntactic, and cohesive features for NLI. The results demonstrate that such indices can correctly classify 59% of essays written in English as belonging to 1 of 11 L1 populations.

In addition, with regard to n-gram length, we found that although n-grams 1-10 words in length were initially considered, no n-grams longer than 5-grams were identified as key, and the longest n-gram that remained after removing prompt-based and redundancy was a single 4-gram. This suggests that 4-grams (or possibly even 3-grams) may be a useful threshold for future investigations.

5.1 Preliminary CLI findings

As Jarvis (2012) notes, CLI studies that use the detection-based argument to CLI are exploratory in nature, while studies that use the comparison-based argument are confirmatory in nature. The present study is, thus, exploratory in nature, and without substantial further investigation, we cannot definitively posit whether observed differences and similarities in English use can be attributed to the influence of the L1 itself or to cultural or educational norms.

Nonetheless, a few preliminary observations are worthy of discussion. First, we identified a number of patterns of language use that may be attributable to CLI. Although a full discussion of these is beyond the scope of this paper, Table 4 includes examples of potential CLI features in reference to the German writers represented in the corpus. The table demonstrates the particular n-grams that German writers are likely to use more or less often than writers of the other 10 languages. German writers, for example, are more likely to use the phrasal modals *able to*, *have to*, *has to*, and singular modals *might* and *would* more often than writers of the other language groups, but are less likely to use the modals *can* and *may*. These findings are preliminary, and further research that links these English n-grams with patterns of use in German is needed.

Additionally, our findings provide some evidence for close relationships between languages. For example, when checking for multicollinearity, we found that the All Negative Japanese and All Negative Korean categories were very strongly correlated (r =.946, p< .001). Upon further examination, 8 of the 19 n-grams (42%) in the All Negative Japanese category occurred in the corresponding Korean category. The overlapping n-grams were the n-grams *all*, *any*, *but*, *different*, *or*, *person*, *this*, and *your*, which may indicate similarities between these language systems in that speakers from both language avoid the use of these words.

Variable	Positive	Negative
Adverbs	just, only, there, necessary	
Comparatives	easier, much more	
Conjunctions	or, but, as well	
Modals	able to, have to, has to, might, would	can, may
Nouns	development, job, topic, something	person, place
Prepositions	at, on	about, by
Pronouns	everybody, this, you, your	she, its, I his, us, he, we, they, our
Quantity (and example)	another, amount of, both, less, lot, whole	any, many, some, such
Specific	certain, especially, special	
Stance	in my, of course, opinion, point	
Temporality	often, still	day, now, second, then, time to, second
To Be	be able, it is, to be	was
Transitions	furthermore, one hand, other hand	
Verbs	look, to get, work	go, going, study

Table 4: German predictor variables.

Patterns of essay categorization also provide preliminary insights into language similarities. Based on the test set confusion matrix (see Table 3), a few conflicting patterns emerged. Among the Indo-European languages represented, the Romance (French, Italian, and Spanish) and Germanic (German) languages were regularly miscategorized as one another. Italian essays, for example, were predicted to be French, German, and Spanish 9%, 10%, and 6% of the time, respectively, but were predicted to be other languages only 0%-4% of the time. This seems to confirm generally accepted language taxonomies, though Spanish was predicted to be Arabic (14%) and Turkish (8%) more often than Italian (6%) or French (6%) (as compared to 3% for German, and no more than 4% for other languages).

While similarities between language families seem to support extant language taxonomies (see Blanchard et al., 2013) and lend credence to claims of CLI, other observations may cast doubt on these. Hindi (an Indo-Iranian member of the Indo-European family) essays were predicted to be Telugu (Dravidian) essays 17% of the time, and Telugu essays were predicted to be Hindi essays 22% of the time. This may indicate instances of cultural proximity or educational similarities as opposed to linguistic transfer (and/or borrowing) because these languages are both spoken within India. Further investigations of these issues are clearly needed.

5.2 Limitations

While we have confidence in our findings, there are limitations to the analysis that need to be discussed. The TOEFL11 corpus was designed to be comparable across languages. While it largely accomplishes this goal, it is not well balanced across proficiency levels (which may reflect the relative proficiency levels of TOEFL test-takers). Although medium and high proficiency levels are well (though not equally) represented, the low proficiency group represents only 11% of the number of texts and an estimated 7.2% of total words (based on mean lengths of essays from each proficiency level given in Blanchard et al., 2013). The medium proficiency group represented 54.4% of the texts and an estimated 52.8% of words in the corpus, and the high proficiency group comprised the remaining 34.7% of the texts and an estimated 40% of the words. This indicates that caution should be used when generalizing any CLI findings from this study to low proficiency language users. Furthermore, any CLI findings will be biased towards medium proficiency language users.

Another limitation that may have affected the accuracy of the model was the way in which potential predictor variables were refined. For each language, the absolute keyness values were used when refining the lists of potential n-gram predictors (as discussed in Section 3.2). After the data had been processed, we discovered that this process removed some n-grams that should have remained. In a very few instances redundant n-grams (e.g., *have; have more)* had a positive keyness value for one n-gram *(have)* and a negative keyness value for the other (*have more*). Because all n-grams were later grouped into categories based on positive and negative keyness values, both *have* and *have more* should have been retained (as they would not have occurred in any of the same categories). In future studies, positive and negative n-grams will be kept separate during the elimination of redundant n-grams.

Another limitation that was discovered after the data analysis was that a data input error caused All Negative Chinese n-gram category to be combined with two n-grams included in the Positive Chinese School and Home category. A similar error retained two positive German adverb categories (with one overlapping n-gram, *just*). The models described in this study retained these variables, as they were not highly correlated with each other or any other variable (based on the $r > .899$ threshold), so any CLI findings based solely on these variables should be considered with caution.

5.3 Future research

Although it is clear that categorical n-grams can be used as successful NLI predictor variables, it is unclear whether this approach is more or less effective than the use of raw counts of frequent words or n-grams (e.g., Jarvis et al., 2012a; Jarvis & Paquot, 2012). Future research should explore the relative effectiveness of these methods using the TOEFL11 corpus to determine whether the time involved to create key n-gram lists and then sort those lists into categories is warranted.

Finally, another remaining question is whether the key n-grams identified in this study are due to linguistic factors or, alternatively, other influences such as culture and educational materials.

Acknowledgements

We thank ETS for compiling and providing the TOEFL11 corpus, and we also thank the organizers of the NLI Shared Task 2013.

References

Bestgen, Y., Granger, S., & Thewissen, J. (2012). Error patterns and automatic l1 identification. In S. Jarvis and S. A. Crossley (Eds.), *Approaching Language Transfer through Text Classification: Explorations in the Detection-Based Approach*. (pp. 127-153). Bristol, UK: Multilingual Matters.

Blanchard, D., Tetreault, J., Higgins, D., Cahill, A., & Chodorow, M. (2013). *TOEFL11: A Corpus of Non-Native English*. Princeton, NJ: Educational Testing Service.

Crossley, S. A., & McNamara, D. S. (2012). Detecting the first language of second language writers using automated indices of cohesion, lexical sophistication, syntactic complexity, and conceptual knowledge. In S. Jarvis and S. A. Crossley (Eds.), *Approaching Language Transfer through Text Classification: Explorations in the Detection-Based Approach*. (pp. 106-126). Bristol, UK: Multilingual Matters.

Crossley, S. A., Defore, C., Kyle, K., Dai, J., & McNamara, D. S. (under review). *Paragraph specific n-gram approaches to automatically assessing essay quality*. Sixth International Conference on Educational Data Mining, Memphis, TN.

Graesser, A. C., McNamara, D. S., Louwerse, M. M., & Cai, Z. (2004). Coh-metrix: Analysis of text on cohesion and language. *Behavior Research Methods, Instruments, & Computers, 36*(2), 193-202.

Granger, S., Dagneaux, E.., Meunier, F., Paquot, M. (Eds.) (2009). *International corpus of learner english. version 2.* Belgium: Presses universitaires de Louvain.

Granger, S. (2009) The contribution of learner corpora to second language acquisition and foreign language teaching: A critical evaluation. In: Aijmer, K., *Corpora and Language Teaching*, Benjamins: Amsterdam and Philadelphia, 2009, p. 13-32.

Jarvis, S. (2000). Methodological rigor in the study of transfer: Identifying L1 influence in the interlanguage lexicon. *Language Learning, 50*, 245-309.

Jarvis, S. (2010). Comparison-based and detection-based approaches to transfer research. In L. Roberts,

M. Howard, M. Ó Laoire, & D. Singleton (Eds.), *EUROSLA Yearbook 10* (pp. 169-192). Amsterdam: Benjamins.

Jarvis, S. (2012). The detection-based approach: An overview. In S. Jarvis & S.A. Crossley (Eds.), *Approaching language transfer through text classification: Explorations in the detection-based approach* (pp. 1-33). Bristol, UK: Multilingual Matters.

Jarvis, S., & Crossley, S. A. (2012). *Approaching language transfer through text classification: Explorations in the detection-based approach.* Bristol, UK: Multilingual Matters.

Jarvis, S., Bestgen, Y., Crossley, S. A., Granger, S., Paquot, M., Thewissen, J., & McNamara, D. S. (2012). The comparative and combined contributions of n-grams, Coh-Metrix indices, and error types in the L1 classification of learner texts. In S. Jarvis & S.A. Crossley (Eds.), *Approaching language transfer through text classification: Explorations in the detection-based approach* (pp. 154-177). Bristol, UK: Multilingual Matters.

Jarvis, S., & Paquot, M. (2012). Exploring the role of n-grams in L1 identification. In S. Jarvis & S.A. Crossley (Eds.), *Approaching language transfer through text classification: Explorations in the detection-based approach* (pp. 71-105). Bristol, UK: Multilingual Matters.

Jarvis, S., Castañeda-Jiménez, G., & Nielsen, R. (2012). Detecting L2 writers' L1s on the basis of their lexical styles. In S. Jarvis & S.A. Crossley (Eds.), *Approaching language transfer through text classification: Explorations in the detection-based approach* (pp. 34-70). Bristol, UK: Multilingual Matters.

Koppel, M., Schler, J. & Zigdon, K. (2005). Determining an author's native language by mining for text errors. In *Proceedings of the Eleventh ACM SIGKDD International Conference on Knowledge Discovery in Data Mining* (pp. 624-628). Chicago: Association for Computing Machinery.

Kucera, H. and Francis, W. N. (1967). *Computational Analysis of Present-Day American English* Providence, RI: Brown University Press.

Laufer, B., & Girsai, N. (2008). Form-focused instruction in second language vocabulary learning: A case for contrastive analysis and translation. *Applied Linguistics, 29*(4), 694-716.

Mayfield Tomokiyo, L. & Jones, R. (2001). You're not from 'round here, are you? Naïve Bayes detection of non-native utterance text. In *Proceedings of the Second Meeting of the North American Chapter of the Association for Computational Linguistics* (NAACL '01), unpaginated electronic document. Cambridge, MA: The Association for Computational Linguistics.

McEnery, T., & Hardie, A. (2012). *Corpus linguistics: method, theory and practice*. Cambridge, New York: Cambridge University Press, 2012.

Rozovskaya, A. & Roth, D. (2011). Algorithm selection and model adaptation for ESL correction tasks. In *Proceedings of the 49th Annual Meeting of the Association for Computational Linguistics* (ACL '11).

Scott, M., (2013). *WordSmith Tools*. Liverpool: Lexical Analysis Software.

Tetreault, J., Blanchard, D., & Cahill, A. (2013). Summary report on the first shared task on native language identification. In *Proceedings of the Eighth Workshop on Building Educational Applications Using NLP*, unpaginated electronic document. Atlanta, GA: Association for Computational Linguistics.

Tsur, O. & Rappoport, A. (2007). Using classifier features for studying the effect of native language on the choice of written second language words. In *Proceedings of the Workshop on Cognitive Aspects of Computational Language Acquisition.* (pp. 9-16). Cambridge, MA: The Association for Computational Linguistics.

Wong, S.-M.J. & Dras, M. (2009). Contrastive analysis and native language identification. In *Proceedings of the Australasion Language Technology Association* (pp. 53-61). Cambridge, MA: The Association for Computational Linguistics.

Using N-gram and Word Network Features for Native Language Identification

Shibamouli Lahiri **Rada Mihalcea**
Computer Science and Engineering
University of North Texas
Denton, TX 76207, USA
shibamoulilahiri@my.unt.edu, rada@cs.unt.edu

Abstract

We report on the performance of two different feature sets in the Native Language Identification Shared Task (Tetreault et al., 2013). Our feature sets were inspired by existing literature on native language identification and word networks. Experiments show that word networks have competitive performance against the baseline feature set, which is a promising result. We also present a discussion of feature analysis based on information gain, and an overview on the performance of different word network features in the Native Language Identification task.

1 Introduction

Native Language Identification (NLI) is a well-established problem in NLP, where the goal is to identify a writer's native language (L1) from his/her writing in a second language (L2), usually English. NLI is generally framed as a multi-class classification problem (Koppel et al., 2005; Brooke and Hirst, 2011; Wong and Dras, 2011), where native languages (L1) are considered class labels, and writing samples in L2 are used as training and test data. The NLI problem has recently seen a big surge in interest, sparked in part by three influential early papers on this problem (Tomokiyo and Jones, 2001; van Halteren and Oostdijk, 2004; Koppel et al., 2005). Apart from shedding light on the way non-native learners (also called "L2 learners") learn a new language, the NLI task allows constrastive analysis (Wong and Dras, 2009), study of different types of errors that people make while learning a new language (Kochmar, 2011; Bestgen et al., 2012; Jarvis et al., 2012), and identification of language transfer patterns (Brooke and Hirst, 2012a; Jarvis and Crossley, 2012), thereby helping L2-students improve their writing styles and expediting the learning process. It also helps L2 educators to concentrate their efforts on particular areas of a language that cause the most learning difficulty for different L1s.

The NLI task is closely related to traditional NLP problems of authorship attribution (Juola, 2006; Stamatatos, 2009; Koppel et al., 2009) and author profiling (Kešelj et al., 2003; Estival et al., 2007a; Estival et al., 2007b; Bergsma et al., 2012), and shares many of the same features. Like authorship attribution, NLI is greatly benefitted by having function words and character n-grams as features (Brooke and Hirst, 2011; Brooke and Hirst, 2012b). Native languages form a part of an author's socio-cultural and psychological profiles, thereby being related to author profiling (van Halteren and Oostdijk, 2004; Torney et al., 2012).

Researchers have used different types of features for the NLI problem, including but not limited to function words (Brooke and Hirst, 2012b); character, word and POS n-grams (Brooke and Hirst, 2012b); spelling and syntactic errors (Koppel et al., 2005); CFG productions (Brooke and Hirst, 2012b); Tree Substitution Grammar productions (Swanson and Charniak, 2012); dependencies (Brooke and Hirst, 2012b); Adaptor Grammar features (Wong et al., 2012); L1-influence (Brooke and Hirst, 2012a); stylometric features (Golcher and Reznicek, 2011;

Crossley and McNamara, 2012; Jarvis et al., 2012); recurrent n-grams on words and POS (Bykh and Meurers, 2012); and features derived from topic models (Wong et al., 2011). State-of-the-art results are typically in the 80%-90% range, with results above 90% reported in some cases (Brooke and Hirst, 2012b). Note, however, that results vary greatly across different datasets, depending on the number of languages being considered, size and difficulty of data, etc.

2 Our Approach

The NLI 2013 Shared Task (Tetreault et al., 2013) marks an effort in bringing together the NLI research community to share and compare their results and evaluations on a common dataset - TOEFL11 (Blanchard et al., 2013) - consisting of 12,100 unique English essays written by non-native learners of eleven different languages.[1] The dataset has 9,900 essays for training, 1,100 essays for test, and 1,100 essays for development. Each of the three sets is balanced across different L1s.

Inspired by previous work in NLI, in our different NLI systems submissions we used several different types of character, word, and POS n-gram features (cf. Section 2.1). Although not included in the systems submitted, we also experimented with a family of new features derived from a word network representation of natural language text (cf. Section 2.2). We used Weka (Hall et al., 2009) for all our classification experiments. The systems that were submitted gave best 10-fold cross-validation accuracy on training data among different feature-classifier combinations (Section 3). Word network features - although competitive against the baseline n-gram features - were not able to beat the baseline features on the training set, so we did not submit that system for evaluation. Section 2.1 discusses our n-gram features, followed by a discussion of word network features in Section 2.2.

2.1 N-gram Features

We used several baseline n-gram features based on words, characters, and POS. We experimented with the raw frequency, normalized frequency, and binary presence/absence indicator on top 100, 200, 500 and 1000 n-grams:[2]

1. word n-grams (n = 1, 2, 3), with and without punctuation.

2. character n-grams (n = 1, 2, 3), with and without space characters.

3. POS n-grams (n = 1, 2, 3), with and without punctuation.[3]

We experimented with punctuation because previous research indicates that punctuation is helpful (Wong and Dras, 2009; Kochmar, 2011). In total, there are 216 types of n-gram feature vectors (with dimensions 100, 200, 500 and 1000) for a particular document. Because of size restrictions (e.g., some n-gram dictionaries are smaller than the specified feature vector dimensions), we ended up with 168 types of feature vectors per document (cf. Tables 2 to 4).

2.2 Word Networks

A "word network" of a particular document is a network (graph) of unique words found in that document. Each node (vertex) in this network is a word. Edges between two nodes (unique words) can be constructed in several different ways. The simplest type of edge connects word A to word B, if word A is followed by word B in the document at least once. In our work, we have assumed a directed edge with direction from word A to word B. Note that we could have used undirected edges as well (cf. (Mihalcea and Tarau, 2004)). Moreover, edges can be weighted/unweighted. We assumed unweighted edges.

A deeper issue with this network construction process concerns what we should do with stopwords. Should we keep them, or should we remove them? Since stopwords and function words have proved to be of special importance in previous native language identification studies (Wong and Dras, 2009; Brooke and Hirst, 2012b), we chose to keep them in our word networks.

Two other choices we made in the construction of our word networks concern sentence boundaries

[1]Arabic, Chinese, French, German, Hindi, Italian, Japanese, Korean, Spanish, Telugu and Turkish.

[2]Note that these most frequent n-grams were extracted from the training+development set.

[3]We used CRFTagger (Phan, 2006) for POS tagging.

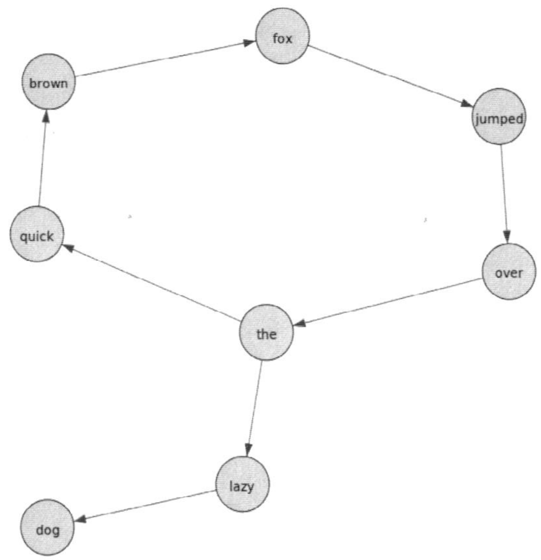

Figure 1: Word network of the sentence *"the quick brown fox jumped over the lazy dog"*.

and word co-occurrence. Word networks can be constructed either by respecting sentence boundaries (where the last word of sentence 1 does *not* link to the first word of sentence 2), or by disregarding them. In our case, we disregarded all sentence boundaries. Moreover, a network edge can either link two words that appeared side-by-side in the original document, or it can link two words that appeared within a window of n words in the document (cf. (Mihalcea and Tarau, 2004)). In our case, we chose the first option - linking unique words that appeared side-by-side at least once. Finally, we did not perform any stemming/morphological analysis to retain subtle cues that might be revealed from inflected/derived words.

The word network of an example sentence ("the quick brown fox jumped over the lazy dog") is shown in Figure 1. Note that the word "the" appeared twice in this sentence, so the corresponding network contains a cycle that starts at "the" and ends at "the". In a realistic word network of a large document, there can be many such cycles. In addition, it is observed that such word networks show power-law degree distribution and a small-world structure (i Cancho and Solé, 2001; Matsuo et al., 2001).

Once the word networks have been constructed, we extract a set of simple features from these networks[4] that represent local properties of individual nodes. We have extracted ten local features for each node in a word network:

1. in-degree, out-degree and degree
2. in-coreness, out-coreness and coreness[5]
3. in-neighborhood size (order 1), out-neighborhood size (order 1) and neighborhood size (order 1)
4. local clustering coefficient

We take a set of *representative words*, and convert a document into a local feature vector - each local feature pertaining to one word in the set of representative words. For example, when we use the top 200 most frequent words as the representative set, a document can be represented as the degree vector of these 200 words in the document's word network, or as the local clustering coefficient vector of these words in the word network, or as the coreness vector of the words (and so on). A document can also be represented as a concatenation (*mixture*) of these vectors. For example, it can be represented as $concat(degree\_vector, coreness\_vector)$ of top 200 most frequent words. We are yet to explore how such mixed feature sets perform in the NLI task, and this constitutes a part of our future work (Section 4). We experimented with top k most frequent words (with k = 100, 200, 500, 1000) on training+development data as our representative wordset.

3 Results

Table 1 describes the three systems we submitted. The first two systems (*UNT-closed-1.csv* and *UNT-closed-2.csv*) were based on a bag of words model using all the words from the training set. The systems used a home-grown implementation of the Naïve Bayes classifier, and achieved 10-fold cross-validation accuracy of 64.5% and 65.1% respectively, on the training set. The first system used raw

[4]We used the igraph (Csardi and Nepusz, 2006) software package for graph feature extraction.

[5]Coreness is an index given to a particular vertex based on its position in the k-core decomposition of the word network (Batagelj and Zaversnik, 2003).

Submitted System	10-fold CV Accuracy on Training Set (%)	Accuracy on Test Set (%)	Description
UNT-closed-1.csv	64.50	63.20	Raw frequency of all words in the training set including stopwords. Naïve Bayes classifier.
UNT-closed-2.csv	65.10	63.70	Raw frequency of all words in the training set except stopwords. Naïve Bayes classifier.
UNT-closed-3.csv	62.46	64.50	Raw frequency of 1000 most frequent words in the training+development set including punctuation. SVM (SMO) classifier.

Table 1: Performance summary and description of the systems we submitted.

term frequency of all words including stopwords as features, and the second system used raw term frequency of all words except stopwords. These two systems achieved test set accuracy of 63.2% and 63.7%, respectively.

The third system we submitted (*UNT-closed-3.csv*) was based on n-gram features (cf. Section 2.1). We used the raw frequency of top 1000 word unigrams, including punctuation, as features. The Weka SMO implementation of SVM (Hall et al., 2009) was used as classifier with default parameter settings. This system gave us the best 10-fold cross-validation accuracy of 62.46% in the training set, among all n-gram features. Note that this system was also the top performer among the systems we submitted in NLI evaluation, with a test set accuracy of 64.5%, and a 10-fold CV accuracy of 63.77% on the training+development set folds specified by the organizers.

We will now describe in the following two subsections how our n-gram features and word network features performed on the training set. All results reported here reflect best 10-fold cross-validation accuracy in the training set among different classifiers (SVM, Naïve Bayes, 1-nearest-neighbor (1NN), J48 decision tree, and AdaBoost). SVM and Naïve Bayes gave best results in our experiments, so only these two are shown in Tables 2 to 5.

3.1 Performance of N-gram Features

Recall from Section 2.1 that we extracted 168 different n-gram feature vectors corresponding to the raw frequency, normalized frequency, and binary presence/absence indicator of top k n-grams (with k = 100, 200, 500, 1000) in the training+development set. Performance of these n-gram features is given in Tables 2 to 4. A general observation with Tables 2 to 4 is that cross-validation performance improves as k increases, although there are a few exceptions. We marked those exceptions with an asterisk ("*").

It is interesting to note that top k word unigrams with punctuation were the top performers in most of the cases. Also interesting is the fact that SVM mostly gave best performance on n-gram features among different classifiers. Note that Naïve Bayes was best performer in a few cases (Table 4). Performance of raw and normalized frequency features were mostly comparable (Tables 2 and 3), whereas binary presence/absence indicator achieved worse accuracy values in general than raw and normalized frequency features (Table 4).

Among different n-grams, word unigrams performed better than bigrams and trigrams, POS bigrams performed better than POS trigrams, and character bigrams and character trigrams performed comparably well (Tables 2 and 3). Exceptions to this observation are seen in Table 4, where character trigrams performed better than character bigrams, and word bigrams sometimes performed better than word unigrams. In general, word n-grams performed the best, followed by POS and character n-grams.

3.2 Performance of Word Network Features

Word networks and word network features were described in Section 2.2. We extracted ten local features on four different *representative sets* of words - the top k most frequent words (k = 100, 200, 500, 1000) on the training+development set, respectively. Performance of these features is given in Table 5. Note that in general, word network features per-

N-gram Feature		Best Cross-validation Accuracy (%) on Top k Most Frequent N-grams			
		$k = 100$	$k = 200$	$k = 500$	$k = 1000$
Word unigram	w/ punctuation	**45.07 (SVM)**	**52.85 (SVM)**	**60.14 (SVM)**	**62.46 (SVM)**
	w/o punctuation	41.63 (SVM)	50.15 (SVM)	58.33 (SVM)	60.85 (SVM)
Word bigram	w/ punctuation	39.54 (SVM)	44.75 (SVM)	51.70 (SVM)	56.06 (SVM)
	w/o punctuation	33.40 (SVM)	39.34 (SVM)	47.54 (SVM)	51.86 (SVM)
Word trigram	w/ punctuation	30.62 (SVM)	35.26 (SVM)	41.56 (SVM)	44.97 (SVM)
	w/o punctuation	26.67 (SVM)	30.14 (SVM)	36.68 (SVM)	41.22 (SVM)
POS unigram	w/ punctuation	N/A	N/A	N/A	N/A
	w/o punctuation	N/A	N/A	N/A	N/A
POS bigram	w/ punctuation	41.79 (SVM)	45.87 (SVM)	48.11 (SVM)	47.49 (SVM)*
	w/o punctuation	35.95 (SVM)	39.23 (SVM)	41.23 (SVM)	39.58 (SVM)*
POS trigram	w/ punctuation	34.97 (SVM)	38.78 (SVM)	43.17 (SVM)	44.52 (SVM)
	w/o punctuation	29.73 (SVM)	34.31 (SVM)	37.58 (SVM)	38.40 (SVM)
Character unigram	w/ space	N/A	N/A	N/A	N/A
	w/o space	N/A	N/A	N/A	N/A
Character bigram	w/ space	42.48 (SVM)	48.43 (SVM)	55.87 (SVM)	56.12 (SVM)
	w/o space	36.84 (SVM)	45.93 (SVM)	51.11 (SVM)	53.41 (SVM)
Character trigram	w/ space	41.65 (SVM)	48.68 (SVM)	54.54 (SVM)	57.77 (SVM)
	w/o space	36.64 (SVM)	43.44 (SVM)	51.46 (SVM)	55.52 (SVM)

Table 2: Performance of raw frequency of n-gram features. Stratified ten-fold cross-validation accuracy values on TOEFL11 training set are shown, along with the classifiers that achieved these accuracy values. Best results in different columns are boldfaced. Table cells marked "N/A" are the ones that correspond to an n-gram dictionary size $< k$.

N-gram Feature		Best Cross-validation Accuracy (%) on Top k Most Frequent N-grams			
		$k = 100$	$k = 200$	$k = 500$	$k = 1000$
Word unigram	w/ punctuation	**44.65 (SVM)**	**52.21 (SVM)**	**59.81 (SVM)**	**62.35 (SVM)**
	w/o punctuation	41.15 (SVM)	50.41 (SVM)	58.18 (SVM)	60.61 (SVM)
Word bigram	w/ punctuation	39.63 (SVM)	44.69 (SVM)	52.31 (SVM)	56.08 (SVM)
	w/o punctuation	33.44 (SVM)	39.11 (SVM)	47.61 (SVM)	52.56 (SVM)
Word trigram	w/ punctuation	30.42 (SVM)	34.97 (SVM)	41.89 (SVM)	45.68 (SVM)
	w/o punctuation	26.08 (SVM)	30.03 (SVM)	37.16 (SVM)	42.39 (SVM)
POS unigram	w/ punctuation	N/A	N/A	N/A	N/A
	w/o punctuation	N/A	N/A	N/A	N/A
POS bigram	w/ punctuation	41.08 (SVM)	45.04 (SVM)	48.23 (SVM)	47.78 (SVM)*
	w/o punctuation	34.85 (SVM)	38.95 (SVM)	41.16 (SVM)	40.84 (SVM)*
POS trigram	w/ punctuation	34.74 (SVM)	38.38 (SVM)	42.89 (SVM)	44.86 (SVM)
	w/o punctuation	28.74 (SVM)	33.67 (SVM)	36.93 (SVM)	38.64 (SVM)
Character unigram	w/ space	N/A	N/A	N/A	N/A
	w/o space	N/A	N/A	N/A	N/A
Character bigram	w/ space	41.93 (SVM)	47.79 (SVM)	56.31 (SVM)	56.22 (SVM)*
	w/o space	36.21 (SVM)	45.18 (SVM)	51.58 (SVM)	53.63 (SVM)
Character trigram	w/ space	40.70 (SVM)	47.90 (SVM)	54.40 (SVM)	57.36 (SVM)
	w/o space	35.84 (SVM)	42.79 (SVM)	50.94 (SVM)	55.71 (SVM)

Table 3: Performance of normalized frequency of n-gram features. Stratified ten-fold cross-validation accuracy values on TOEFL11 training set are shown, along with the classifiers that achieved these accuracy values. Best results in different columns are boldfaced. Table cells marked "N/A" are the ones that correspond to an n-gram dictionary size $< k$.

N-gram Feature		Best Cross-validation Accuracy (%) on Top k Most Frequent N-grams			
		k = 100	k = 200	k = 500	k = 1000
Word unigram	w/ punctuation	33.42 (SVM)	42.49 (SVM)	**50.63 (Naïve Bayes)**	**56.95 (SVM)**
	w/o punctuation	33.05 (SVM)	**42.82 (SVM)**	50.13 (SVM)	55.91 (SVM)
Word bigram	w/ punctuation	**37.74 (SVM)**	40.99 (SVM)	46.16 (SVM)	52.66 (SVM)
	w/o punctuation	32.02 (SVM)	37.24 (SVM)	42.29 (SVM)	48.36 (SVM)
Word trigram	w/ punctuation	29.87 (SVM)	33.79 (SVM)	38.48 (SVM)	42.00 (SVM)
	w/o punctuation	25.75 (SVM)	28.79 (SVM)	34.14 (SVM)	37.80 (SVM)
POS unigram	w/ punctuation	N/A	N/A	N/A	N/A
	w/o punctuation	N/A	N/A	N/A	N/A
POS bigram	w/ punctuation	29.75 (SVM)	35.50 (SVM)	40.39 (Naïve Bayes)	41.11 (Naïve Bayes)
	w/o punctuation	25.47 (SVM)	31.41 (SVM)	33.33 (Naïve Bayes)	33.78 (Naïve Bayes)
POS trigram	w/ punctuation	29.20 (SVM)	33.28 (SVM)	38.98 (Naïve Bayes)	43.74 (Naïve Bayes)
	w/o punctuation	23.71 (SVM)	28.98 (SVM)	32.21 (SVM)	37.49 (Naïve Bayes)
Character unigram	w/ space	N/A	N/A	N/A	N/A
	w/o space	N/A	N/A	N/A	N/A
Character bigram	w/ space	15.26 (SVM)	23.69 (SVM)	40.07 (SVM)	41.76 (SVM)
	w/o space	15.73 (SVM)	25.27 (SVM)	37.05 (SVM)	41.52 (SVM)
Character trigram	w/ space	20.42 (SVM)	28.17 (SVM)	37.61 (SVM)	47.93 (SVM)
	w/o space	23.85 (SVM)	30.38 (SVM)	37.39 (SVM)	45.60 (SVM)

Table 4: Performance of binary presence/absence indicator on n-gram features. Stratified ten-fold cross-validation accuracy values on TOEFL11 training set are shown, along with the classifiers that achieved these accuracy values. Best results in different columns are boldfaced. Table cells marked "N/A" are the ones that correspond to an n-gram dictionary size $< k$.

Word Network Feature	Best Cross-validation Accuracy (%) on Top k Most Frequent Words			
	k = 100	k = 200	k = 500	k = 1000
Clustering Coefficient	15.31 (SVM)	17.73 (SVM)	19.96 (SVM)	20.71 (SVM)
In-degree	39.89 (SVM)	49.28 (SVM)	56.83 (SVM)	59.47 (SVM)
Out-degree	40.66 (SVM)	49.67 (SVM)	57.16 (SVM)	59.62 (SVM)
Degree	41.05 (SVM)	**50.74 (SVM)**	**58.17 (SVM)**	60.21 (SVM)
In-coreness	32.52 (SVM)	42.44 (SVM)	51.09 (SVM)	55.50 (SVM)
Out-coreness	32.41 (SVM)	43.15 (SVM)	51.34 (SVM)	55.39 (SVM)
Coreness	35.32 (SVM)	45.84 (SVM)	53.54 (SVM)	57.18 (SVM)
In-neighborhood Size (order 1)	40.54 (SVM)	50.08 (SVM)	56.92 (SVM)	59.69 (SVM)
Out-neighborhood Size (order 1)	41.09 (SVM)	50.09 (SVM)	57.71 (SVM)	59.73 (SVM)
Neighborhood Size (order 1)	**41.83 (SVM)**	50.68 (SVM)	57.40 (SVM)	**60.41 (SVM)**

Table 5: Performance of word network features. Stratified ten-fold cross-validation accuracy values on TOEFL11 training set are shown, along with the classifiers that achieved these accuracy values. Best results in different columns are boldfaced.

Rank	Word Network Feature	Information Gain
1	Degree of the word *a*	0.1058
2	Neighborhood size of the word *a*	0.1054
3	Out-neighborhood size of the word *a*	0.1050
4	Outdegree of the word *a*	0.1049
5	In-neighborhood size of the word *a*	0.1017
6	Indegree of the word *a*	0.1016
7	Neighborhood size of the word *however*	0.0928
8	Degree of the word *however*	0.0928
9	Indegree of the word *however*	0.0928
10	In-neighborhood size of the word *however*	0.0928
11	Outdegree of the word *however*	0.0916
12	Out-neighborhood size of the word *however*	0.0916
13	Out-coreness of the word *however*	0.0851
14	Coreness of the word *however*	0.0851
15	In-coreness of the word *however*	0.0850
16	Outdegree of the word *the*	0.0793
17	Out-neighborhood size of the word *the*	0.0790
18	Degree of the word *the*	0.0740
19	Neighborhood size of the word *the*	0.0740
20	Coreness of the word *a*	0.0710

Table 6: Ranking of word network features based on Information Gain, on TOEFL11 training set. We took 1000 most frequent words on the training+development set, and collected all their word network features in a single file. This ranking reflects the top 20 features in that file, along with their information gain values.

formed quite well, with the best result (60.41% CV accuracy on the train set) being competitive against (but slightly worse than) the baseline n-gram features (62.46% CV accuracy on the train set). Performance improved with increasing k, thereby corroborating our general observation from Tables 2 to 4. Clustering coefficient performed poorly, and seems rather unsuitable for the NLI task. But degree, coreness, and neighborhood size performed good. Here also, SVM turned out to be the best classifier, giving best CV accuracy in all cases.

We experimented with the *in-*, *out-*, and *overall* versions of degree, coreness and neighborhood size. Their performance was mostly comparable with each other (Table 5). To investigate which word network features are the most discriminatory in this task, we collected all ten word network features of the top 1000 words in a single file, and then ranked those features on the training set based on Information Gain (IG). The 20 top-ranking features are shown in Table 6, along with their corresponding IG values. Note that the words *a*, *the*, and *however* were among the most discriminatory, and different versions of degree, neighborhood size and coreness appeared among the top, which is in line with our earlier observation that clustering coefficients were not very discriminatory at the native language classification task.

4 Conclusions and Future Work

In this paper, we described experiments with the NLI task using a baseline set of n-gram features, and a set of novel features derived from a word network representation of text documents. Useful and less useful n-gram features were identified, along with the fact that SVM was the best classifier in most of the cases. We learned that when using raw or normalized frequency, lower-order n-grams perform at least as good as higher-order n-grams; moreover, Naïve Bayes sometimes give good results when binary presence/absence indicator variables are used as features.

We described the construction of our word networks in detail, and discussed experiments with word network features. These features are competitive against the baseline n-gram features, and we need to fine-tune our classifiers to see if they can exceed the performance of the baseline. Clustering coefficients were found to be less useful for the NLI task, and feature ranking based on information gain helped us identify the most important word network features in a collection of top 1000 words in the training+development set.

Future work consists of experimenting with combined word network features; mixed word network features and baseline n-gram features; and the one-vs-all classification scheme instead of the multiclass classification scheme.

References

Vladimir Batagelj and Matjaz Zaversnik. 2003. An O(m) Algorithm for Cores Decomposition of Networks. *CoRR*, cs.DS/0310049.

Shane Bergsma, Matt Post, and David Yarowsky. 2012. Stylometric Analysis of Scientific Articles. In *Proceedings of the 2012 Conference of the North American Chapter of the Association for Computational Linguistics: Human Language Technologies*, pages 327–337, Montréal, Canada, June. Association for Computational Linguistics.

Yves Bestgen, Sylviane Granger, and Jennifer Thewissen. 2012. Error Patterns and Automatic L1 Identification. In Scott Jarvis and Scott A. Crossley, editors, *Approaching Language Transfer through Text Classification*, pages 127–153. Multilingual Matters.

Daniel Blanchard, Joel Tetreault, Derrick Higgins, Aoife Cahill, and Martin Chodorow. 2013. TOEFL11: A Corpus of Non-Native English. Technical report, Educational Testing Service.

Julian Brooke and Graeme Hirst. 2011. Native language detection with 'cheap' learner corpora. In *Conference of Learner Corpus Research (LCR2011)*, Louvain-la-Neuve, Belgium. Presses universitaires de Louvain.

Julian Brooke and Graeme Hirst. 2012a. Measuring Interlanguage: Native Language Identification with L1-influence Metrics. In Nicoletta Calzolari, Khalid Choukri, Thierry Declerck, Mehmet Uğur Doğan, Bente Maegaard, Joseph Mariani, Jan Odijk, and Stelios Piperidis, editors, *Proceedings of the Eighth International Conference on Language Resources and Evaluation (LREC-2012)*, pages 779–784, Istanbul, Turkey, May. European Language Resources Association (ELRA). ACL Anthology Identifier: L12-1016.

Julian Brooke and Graeme Hirst. 2012b. Robust, Lexicalized Native Language Identification. In *Proceedings of COLING 2012*, pages 391–408, Mumbai, India, December. The COLING 2012 Organizing Committee.

Serhiy Bykh and Detmar Meurers. 2012. Native Language Identification using Recurring n-grams – Investigating Abstraction and Domain Dependence. In *Proceedings of COLING 2012*, pages 425–440, Mumbai, India, December. The COLING 2012 Organizing Committee.

Scott A. Crossley and Danielle McNamara. 2012. Detecting the First Language of Second Language Writers Using Automated Indices of Cohesion, Lexical Sophistication, Syntactic Complexity and Conceptual Knowledge. In Scott Jarvis and Scott A. Crossley, editors, *Approaching Language Transfer through Text Classification*, pages 106–126. Multilingual Matters.

Gabor Csardi and Tamas Nepusz. 2006. The igraph software package for complex network research. *InterJournal*, Complex Systems:1695.

Dominique Estival, Tanja Gaustad, Son Bao Pham, Will Radford, and Ben Hutchinson. 2007a. Author profiling for English emails. In *Proceedings of the 10th Conference of the Pacific Association for Computational Linguistics*, pages 263–272, Melbourne, Australia.

Dominique Estival, Tanja Gaustad, Son Bao Pham, Will Radford, and Ben Hutchinson. 2007b. TAT: An Author Profiling Tool with Application to Arabic Emails. In *Proceedings of the Australasian Language Technology Workshop 2007*, pages 21–30, Melbourne, Australia, December.

Felix Golcher and Marc Reznicek. 2011. Stylometry and the interplay of topic and L1 in the different annotation layers in the FALKO corpus. *QITL-4–Proceedings of Quantitative Investigations in Theoretical Linguistics*, 4:29–34.

Mark Hall, Eibe Frank, Geoffrey Holmes, Bernhard Pfahringer, Peter Reutemann, and Ian H. Witten. 2009. The WEKA data mining software: an update. *SIGKDD Explor. Newsl.*, 11(1):10–18, November.

Ramon Ferrer i Cancho and Ricard V. Solé. 2001. The Small World of Human Language. *Proceedings: Biological Sciences*, 268(1482):pp. 2261–2265.

Scott Jarvis and Scott A. Crossley, editors. 2012. *Approaching Language Transfer Through Text Classification: Explorations in the Detection-based Approach*, volume 64. Multilingual Matters Limited, Bristol, UK.

Scott Jarvis, Yves Bestgen, Scott A. Crossley, Sylviane Granger, Magali Paquot, Jennifer Thewissen, and Danielle McNamara. 2012. The Comparative and Combined Contributions of n-Grams, Coh-Metrix Indices and Error Types in the L1 Classification of Learner Texts. In Scott Jarvis and Scott A. Crossley, editors, *Approaching Language Transfer through Text Classification*, pages 154–177. Multilingual Matters.

Patrick Juola. 2006. Authorship Attribution. *Found. Trends Inf. Retr.*, 1(3):233–334, December.

Vlado Kešelj, Fuchun Peng, Nick Cercone, and Calvin Thomas. 2003. N-gram-based author profiles for authorship attribution. In *Proceedings of the Conference Pacific Association for Computational Linguistics, PACLING*, volume 3, pages 255–264.

Ekaterina Kochmar. 2011. Identification of a writer's native language by error analysis. Master's thesis, University of Cambridge.

Moshe Koppel, Jonathan Schler, and Kfir Zigdon. 2005. Determining an author's native language by mining a text for errors. In *Proceedings of the eleventh ACM SIGKDD international conference on Knowledge discovery in data mining*, pages 624–628, Chicago, IL. ACM.

Moshe Koppel, Jonathan Schler, and Shlomo Argamon. 2009. Computational methods in authorship attribution. *J. Am. Soc. Inf. Sci. Technol.*, 60(1):9–26, January.

Yutaka Matsuo, Yukio Ohsawa, and Mitsuru Ishizuka. 2001. A Document as a Small World. In *Proceedings of the Joint JSAI 2001 Workshop on New Frontiers in Artificial Intelligence*, pages 444–448, London, UK, UK. Springer-Verlag.

Rada Mihalcea and Paul Tarau. 2004. TextRank: Bringing Order into Texts. In Dekang Lin and Dekai Wu, editors, *Proceedings of EMNLP 2004*, pages 404–411, Barcelona, Spain, July. Association for Computational Linguistics.

Xuan-Hieu Phan. 2006. CRFTagger: CRF English POS Tagger.

Efstathios Stamatatos. 2009. A survey of modern authorship attribution methods. *J. Am. Soc. Inf. Sci. Technol.*, 60(3):538–556, March.

Benjamin Swanson and Eugene Charniak. 2012. Native Language Detection with Tree Substitution Grammars. In *Proceedings of the 50th Annual Meeting of the Association for Computational Linguistics (Volume 2: Short Papers)*, pages 193–197, Jeju Island, Korea, July. Association for Computational Linguistics.

Joel Tetreault, Daniel Blanchard, and Aoife Cahill. 2013. A Report on the First Native Language Identification Shared Task. In *Proceedings of the Eighth Workshop on Innovative Use of NLP for Building Educational Applications*, Atlanta, GA, USA, June. Association for Computational Linguistics.

Laura Mayfield Tomokiyo and Rosie Jones. 2001. You're not from'round here, are you?: naive Bayes detection of non-native utterance text. In *Proceedings of the second meeting of the North American Chapter of the Association for Computational Linguistics on Language technologies*, pages 1–8, Pittsburgh, PA. Association for Computational Linguistics.

Rosemary Torney, Peter Vamplew, and John Yearwood. 2012. Using psycholinguistic features for profiling first language of authors. *Journal of the American Society for Information Science and Technology*, 63(6):1256–1269.

Hans van Halteren and Nelleke Oostdijk. 2004. Linguistic profiling of texts for the purpose of language verification. In *Proceedings of Coling 2004*, pages 966–972, Geneva, Switzerland, Aug 23–Aug 27. COLING.

Sze-Meng Jojo Wong and Mark Dras. 2009. Contrastive Analysis and Native Language Identification. In *Proceedings of the Australasian Language Technology Association Workshop 2009*, pages 53–61, Sydney, Australia, December.

Sze-Meng Jojo Wong and Mark Dras. 2011. Exploiting Parse Structures for Native Language Identification. In *Proceedings of the 2011 Conference on Empirical Methods in Natural Language Processing*, pages 1600–1610, Edinburgh, Scotland, UK., July. Association for Computational Linguistics.

Sze-Meng Jojo Wong, Mark Dras, and Mark Johnson. 2011. Topic Modeling for Native Language Identification. In *Proceedings of the Australasian Language Technology Association Workshop 2011*, pages 115–124, Canberra, Australia, December.

Sze-Meng Jojo Wong, Mark Dras, and Mark Johnson. 2012. Exploring Adaptor Grammars for Native Language Identification. In *Proceedings of the 2012 Joint Conference on Empirical Methods in Natural Language Processing and Computational Natural Language Learning*, pages 699–709, Jeju Island, Korea, July. Association for Computational Linguistics.

LIMSI's Participation in the 2013 Shared Task on Native Language Identification

Thomas Lavergne, Gabriel Illouz, Aurélien Max
LIMSI-CNRS
Univ. Paris Sud
Orsay, France
{firstname.lastname}@limsi.fr

Ryo Nagata
LIMSI-CNRS & Konan University
8-9-1 Okamoto
Kobe 658-0072 Japan
rnagata@konan-u.ac.jp

Abstract

This paper describes LIMSI's participation to the first shared task on Native Language Identification. Our submission uses a Maximum Entropy classifier, using as features character and chunk n-grams, spelling and grammatical mistakes, and lexical preferences. Performance was slightly improved by using a two-step classifier to better distinguish otherwise easily confused native languages.

1 Introduction

This paper describes the submission from LIMSI to the 2013 shared task on Native Language Identification (Tetreault et al., 2013). The creation of this new challenge provided us with a dataset (12,100 TOEFL essays by learners of English of eleven native languages (Blanchard et al., 2013)) that was necessary to us to develop an initial framework for studying Native Language Identification in text. We expect that this challenge will draw conclusions that will provide the community with new insights into the impact of native language in foreign language writing. We believe that such a research domain is crucial, not only for improving our understanding of language learning and language production processes, but also for developing Natural Language Processing applications to support text improvement.

This article is organized as follows. We first describe in Section 2 our maximum entropy system used for the classification of a given text in English into the native languages of the shared task. We then introduce the various sets of features that we have included in our submission, comprising basic n-gram features (3.1) and features to capture spelling mistakes (3.2), grammatical mistakes (3.3), and lexical preference (3.4). We next report the performance of each of our sets of features (4.1) and our attempt to perform a two-step classification to reduce frequent misclassifications (4.2). We finally conclude with a short discussion (section 5).

2 A Maximum Entropy model

Our system is based on a classical maximum entropy model (Berger et al., 1996):

$$p_\theta(y|x) = \frac{1}{Z_\theta(x)} \exp(\theta^\top F(x,y))$$

where F is a vector of feature functions, θ a vector of associated parameter values, and $Z_\theta(x)$ the partition function.

Given N independent samples (x^i, y^i), the model is trained by minimizing, with respect to θ, the negative conditional log-likelihood of the observations:

$$\mathcal{L}(\theta) = -\sum_{i=1}^{N} \log p(y^i|x^i).$$

This term is complemented with an additional regularization term so as to avoid overfitting. In our case, an ℓ_1 regularization is used, with the additional effect to produce a sparse model.

The model is trained with a gradient descent algorithm (L-BFGS) using the Wapiti toolkit (Lavergne et al., 2010). Convergence is determined either by error rate stability on an held-out dataset or when limits of numerical precision are reached.

3 Features

Our submission makes use of basic features, including n-grams of characters and part-of-speech tags. We further experimented with several sets of features that will be described and compared in the following sections.

3.1 Basic features

We used n-grams of characters up to length 4 as features. In order to reduce the size of the feature space and the sparsity of these features, we used a hash kernel (Shi et al., 2009) of size 2^{16} with a hash family of size 4. This allowed us to significantly reduce the training time with no noticeable impact on the model's performance.

Our set of basic features also includes n-grams of part-of-speech (POS) tags and chunks up to length 3. Both were computed using an in-house CRF-based tagger trained on PennTreeBank (Marcus et al., 1993). The POS tags sequences were post-processed so that word tokens were used in lieu of their corresponding POS tags for the following: coordinating conjunctions, determiners, prepositions, modals, predeterminers, possessives, pronouns, and question adverbs (Nagata, 2013).

For instance, from this sentence excerpt:

```
[NP Some/DT people/NNS] [VP
might/MD think/VB] [SBAR that/IN]
[VP traveling/VBG] [PP in/IN]...
```

we extract n-grams from the pseudo POS-tag sequence:

```
Some NNS MD VB that VBG in...
```

and n-grams from the chunk sequence:

```
NP VP SBAR VP PP...
```

The length of chunks is encoded as separate features that correspond to mean length of each type of chunks. As shown in (Nagata, 2013), length of noun sequences is also informative and thus was encoded as a feature.

3.2 Capturing spelling mistakes

We added a set of features to capture information about spelling mistakes in the model, following the intuition that some spelling mistakes may be attributed to the influence of the writer's native language.

To extract these features, each document is processed using the `ispell`[1] spell checker. This results in a list of incorrectly written word forms and a set of potential corrections. For each word, the best correction is next selected using a set of rules, which were built manually after a careful study of the training dataset.

When a corrected word is found, the incorrect fragment of the word is isolated by striping from the original and corrected words common prefix and suffix, keeping only the inner-most substring difference. For example, given the following mistake and correction:

$$appartment \rightarrow apartment$$

this procedure generates the following feature:

$$pp \rightarrow p$$

Such a feature may for instance help to identify native languages (using latin scripts) where doubling of letters is frequent.

3.3 Capturing grammatical mistakes

Errors at the grammatical level are captured using the "language tool" toolkit (Milkowski, 2010), a rule-based grammar and style checker. Each rule firing in a document is mapped to an individual feature. This triggers features such as BEEN_PART_AGREEMENT, corresponding to cases where the auxiliary *be* is not followed by a past participle, or EN_A_VS_AN, corresponding to confusions between the correct form the articles *a* and *an*.

3.4 Capturing lexical preferences

Learners of a foreign language may have some preference for lexical choice given some semantic content that they want to convey[2]. We made the following assumption: the lexical variant chosen for each word may correspond to the less ambiguous choice if mapping from the native language to English[3].

[1] `http://www.gnu.org/software/ispell/`

[2] We assumed that we should not expect thematic differences in the contents of the essays across original languages, as the prompts for the essays were evenly distributed.

[3] This assumption of course could not hold for advanced learners of English, who should make their lexical choices independently of their native language.

Thus, for each word in an English essay, if we knew a corresponding word (or *sense*) that a writer may have thought of in her native language, we would like to consider the most likely translation into English, according to some reliable probabilistic model of lexical translation into English, as the lexical choice most likely to be made by a learner of this native language.

As we obviously do not have access to the word in the native language of the writer, we approximate this information by searching for the word that maximizes the translation probability of translating back from the native language after translating from the original English word. This in fact corresponds to a widely used way of computing paraphrase probabilities from bilingual translation distributions (Bannard and Callison-Burch, 2005):

$$\hat{e}_l \approx \operatorname*{argmax}_{e} \sum_{f} p_l(f|e).p_l(e|f)$$

where f ranges over all possible translations of English word e in a given native language l.

Preferably, we would like to obtain candidate translations into the native language in context, that is, by translating complete sentences and using *a posteriori* translation probabilities. We could not do this for a number of reasons, the main one being that we did not have the possibility of using or building Statistical Machine Translation systems for all the language pairs involving English and the native languages of the shared task. We therefore resorted to simply finding, for each English word, the most likely back-translation into English *via* a given native language. Using the Google Translation online Statistical Machine Translation service[4], which proposed translations from and to English and all the native languages of the shared task, a further approximation had to be made as, in practice, we were only able to access the most likely translations for words in isolation: we considered only the best translation of the original English word in the native language, and then kept its best back-translation into English. We here note some common intuitions with the use of roundtrip translation as a Machine Translation evaluation metrics (Rapp, 2009).

[4]http://translate.google.com

Table 1 provides various examples of back-translations for English adjectives obtained *via* each native language. The samples from the Table show that our procedure produces a significant number of non identical back-translations. They also illustrate some types of undesirable results obtained, which led us to only consider as features for our classifier the proportion of words in essays for which the above-defined back-translation yielded the same word, considering all possible native languages. We only considered content words, as out-of-context back-translation for function words would be too unreliable. Table 2 shows values for some documents of the training set. As can be seen, there are important differences across languages, some languages obtaining high scores on average (e.g. French and Japanese) and others obtaining low scores on average (e.g. Korean, Turkish). Furthermore, the highest score is only rarely obtained for the actual native language of each document, showing that keeping the most probable language according to this value alone would not allow to obtain a good classification performance.

4 Experiments

4.1 Results per set of features

For all our experiments reported here, we used the full training data provided using cross-validation to tune the regularization parameter. Our results are presented in the top part of Table 3. Using our complete set of features yields our best performance on accuracy, corresponding to a 0.75% absolute improvement over using our basic n-gram features only. No type of features allows a significant improvement over the n-gram features when added individually.

4.2 Two-step classification

Table 4 contains the confusion matrix for our system across languages. It clearly stands out that two language pairs were harder to distinguish: Hindi (hin) and Telugu (tel) on the one hand, and Korean (kor) and Japanese (jpn) on the other.

In order to improve the performance of our model, we performed a two-step classification focused on these difficult pairs. For this, we built additional classifiers for each difficult pairs. Both are built

eng	abrupt	affirmative	amazing	ambiguous	anarchic	atrocious	attentive	awkward
ara	**sudden**	**positive**	amazing	**mysterious**	**messy**	**terrible**	**heedful**	**inappropriate**
chi	**sudden**	**sure**	amazing	ambiguous	anarchic	atrocious	**careful**	awkward
fre	**sudden**	affirmative	amazing	ambiguous	anarchic	atrocious	**careful**	awkward
ger	abrupt	affirmative	**incredible**	ambiguous	**anarchical**	**gruesome**	**attentively**	awkward
hin	**suddenly**	**positive**	amazing	**vague**	**chaotic**	**brutal**	**observant**	**clumsy**
ita	abrupt	affirmative	amazing	ambiguous	**anarchist**	atrocious	**careful**	**uncomfortable**
jap	**sudden**	**positive**	**surprising**	ambiguous	**anarchy**	**heinous**	**cautious**	awkward
kor	**fortuitous**	**positive**	amazing	ambiguous	anarchic	**severe**	**kind**	awkward
spa	abrupt	affirmative	**surprising**	ambiguous	anarchic	atrocious	attentive	**clumsy**
tel	abrupt	affirmative	amazing	ambiguous	anarchic	**formidable**	attentive	awkward
tur	**sudden**	**positive**	amazing	**uncertain**	anarchic	**brutal**	attentive	**strange**

Table 1: Examples of back translations for English adjectives from the training set *via* each of the eleven native languages of the shared task. Back-translations that differ from the original word are indicated using a bold face.

Doc id.	Native l.	ARA	CHI	FRE	GER	HIN	ITA	JPN	KOR	SPA	TEL	TUR
976	ARA	0.80	0.88	0.91	0.95	0.75	0.91	0.87	0.73	0.89	0.79	0.71
29905	CHI	0.84	0.81	0.93	0.87	0.79	0.89	0.89	0.56	0.93	0.62	0.75
61765	FRE	0.73	0.84	0.90	0.71	0.73	0.83	0.86	0.50	0.91	0.58	0.66
100416	GER	0.78	0.80	0.86	0.83	0.72	0.89	0.86	0.70	0.90	0.67	0.67
26649	HIN	0.68	0.75	0.88	0.89	0.67	0.85	0.86	0.69	0.86	0.75	0.77
39189	ITA	0.68	0.85	0.92	0.94	0.74	0.93	0.89	0.69	0.92	0.72	0.72
3044	JPN	0.83	0.81	0.89	0.83	0.68	0.94	0.91	0.71	0.94	0.83	0.70
3150	KOR	0.75	0.86	0.91	0.84	0.76	0.88	0.87	0.55	0.88	0.67	0.73
6614	SPA	0.79	0.90	0.86	0.85	0.78	0.85	0.92	0.67	0.90	0.70	0.68
12600	TEL	0.65	0.74	0.84	0.73	0.71	0.92	0.90	0.76	0.95	0.82	0.58
5565	TUR	0.70	0.77	0.88	0.78	0.70	0.84	0.86	0.72	0.84	0.74	0.71

Table 2: Values corresponding to the proportion of content words in a random essay for each native language for which back-translation yielded the same word.

	FRE	GER	ITA	SPA	TUR	ARA	HIN	TEL	KOR	JPN	CHI
FRE	79	4	4	3	2	3	0	0	2	2	1
GER	0	89	2	4	1	0	1	0	2	1	0
ITA	6	1	83	6	1	1	0	0	0	1	1
SPA	4	4	5	72	2	3	3	2	1	1	3
TUR	3	2	1	3	81	1	3	2	0	3	1
ARA	3	0	1	3	3	81	5	2	1	0	1
HIN	1	1	1	3	2	1	64	26	1	0	0
TEL	0	0	1	0	0	1	17	81	0	0	0
KOR	1	1	0	0	3	1	0	0	80	12	2
JPN	1	0	2	2	0	3	0	1	13	73	5
CHI	0	1	0	0	2	2	0	2	3	3	87

Table 4: Confusion matrix on the Test set.

Features	X-Val	Test
ngm	74.83%	75.27%
ngm+ort	74.98%	75.29%
ngm+grm	75.18%	75.63%
ngm+lex	74.85%	75.47%
all	75.57%	75.81%
2-step (a)	75.46%	75.69%
2-step (b)	75.89%	75.98%

Table 3: Accuracy results obtained by cross-validation and using the provided Test set for various combinations of features and our two 2-step strategies. The feature sets are: character and part-of-speech n-grams features (ngm), spelling features (ort), grammatical features (grm), and lexical preference features (lex).

from the same feature sets as for the first-step model but with only three labels: one for each language of the pair and one for any other language.

The training data used for these new models include all documents from both languages as well as document misclassified as one of them by the first-step classifier (using cross-validation to label the full training set). The formers keep their original labels while the later are relabeled as *other*.

Document classified in one of the difficult pairs by the first-step classifier were post-processed with these new models. When the new label predicted is *other*, the second best choice of the first step is used.

We investigated two setups for the first classifier: (a) using the original 11 native languages classifier, and (b) using a new classifier with languages of the difficult pairs merged, resulting in 9 native "languages".

Our results, shown in Figure 3 for easy comparison, improve over our system using all features only when the first-pass classifier uses the set of 9 merged pseudo-languages (b). We obtain a moderate 0.32% absolute improvement in accuracy over one-step classification on cross-validation, and 0.17% improvement on the Test set.

5 Discussion and conclusion

We have submitted on maximum entropy system to the shared task on Native Language Identification, for which our basic set of n-gram features already obtained a level of performance, around 75% in accuracy, close to the best performance reported in our submission. The additional feature sets that we have included in our system, while improving the model, did not allow us to capture a deeper influence of the native language.

A first analysis reveals that the model fails to fully use the additional feature sets due to lack of context. Future experiments will need to link more closely these features to the documents for which they provide useful information.

Due to time constraints and engineering issues, the two-pass system was not ready by the time of submission. The results that we have included in this report show that it is a promising approach that we should continue to explore. We also plan to conduct experiments that exploit the information about the level of English available in the essays, something that we did not consider for this submission. While this information is not directly available, it may be infered from the data as a first-step classification. We believe that studying its influence on the mistakes make learners of different native language is a promising direction.

The approach that we have described in this submission, as most of previously published approaches for this task, attempts to find mistakes in the text of the documents. The most typical mistakes are then used by the classifier to detect the native language. This does not take into consideration the fact that native English writers also make errors. It would be interesting to explore the divergence between various sets of writers/learners, not from the mean of non-native writers, but from the mean of native writers.

References

Colin Bannard and Chris Callison-Burch. 2005. Paraphrasing with bilingual parallel corpora. In *Proceedings of the 43rd Annual Meeting of the Association for Computational Linguistics (ACL'05)*, pages 597–604, Ann Arbor, Michigan.

Adam Berger, Stephen Della Pietra, and Vincent Della Pietra. 1996. A maximum entropy approach to natural language processing. *Computational Linguistics*, 22(1), March.

Daniel Blanchard, Joel Tetreault, Derrick Higgins, Aoife Cahill, and Martin Chodorow. 2013. TOEFL11: A Corpus of Non-Native English. Technical report, Educational Testing Service.

Thomas Lavergne, Olivier Cappé, and François Yvon.

2010. Practical very large scale CRFs. In *Proceedings the 48th Annual Meeting of the Association for Computational Linguistics (ACL)*, pages 504–513. Association for Computational Linguistics, July.

Mitchell P. Marcus, Mary Ann Marcinkiewicz, and Beatrice Santorini. 1993. Building a large annotated corpus of English: The Penn treebank. *Computational Linguistics*, 19(2):313–330.

Marcin Milkowski. 2010. Developing an open-source, rule-based proofreading tool. *Software - Practice and Experience*, 40(7):543–566.

Ryo Nagata. 2013. Generating a language family tree from indo-european non-native english texts (to appear). In *Proceedings the 51th Annual Meeting of the Association for Computational Linguistics (ACL)*. Association for Computational Linguistics.

Reinhard Rapp. 2009. The backtranslation score: Automatic mt evalution at the sentence level without reference translations. In *Proceedings of the ACL-IJCNLP 2009 Conference Short Papers*, pages 133–136, Suntec, Singapore.

Qinfeng Shi, James Petterson, Gideon Dror, John Langford, Alex Smola, and S.V.N. Vishwanathan. 2009. Hash kernels for structured data. *Journal of Machine Learning Research*, 10:2615–2637, December.

Joel Tetreault, Daniel Blanchard, and Aoife Cahill. 2013. A Report on the First Native Language Identification Shared Task. In *Proceedings of the Eighth Workshop on Building Educational Applications Using NLP*, Atlanta, GA, USA, June. Association for Computational Linguistics.

Native Language Identification using large scale lexical features

André Lynum
Norwegian University of Science and Technology
Department of Computer and Information and Science
Sem Sælands vei 7-9
NO-7491 Trondheim, Norway
andrely@idi.ntnu.no

Abstract

This paper describes an effort to perform Native Language Identification (NLI) using machine learning on a large amount of lexical features. The features were collected from sequences and collocations of bare word forms, suffixes and character n-grams amounting to a feature set of several hundred thousand features. These features were used to train a linear Support Vector Machine (SVM) classifier for predicting the native language category.

1 Introduction

Much effort in Native Language Identification (NLI) has focused on identifying specific characteristics of the errors in texts produced by English Second Language (ESL) learners, like the work presented in (Bestgen et al., 2012) and (Koppel et al., 2005). This might be specific spelling errors, syntactic or morphological mistakes. One motivation for this approach has been the notion that aspects of the L1 language influences which errors and mistakes are produced by L2 learners, which has guided the model building towards a smaller number of features and models which lend themselves to interpretation in terms of linguistic knowledge.

Research so far has shown mixed support that this notion of *language transfer* is the best indicator of L1 language. While many such features are highly predictive, features that are usually indicative of the text topic has shown strong performance when applied to the NLI task as demonstrated in (Ahn, 2011) and (Koppel et al., 2005). This is largely lexical features such as frequency measures of token, lemma or character n-grams. There has been some effort in identifying if this is an artifact of biases in the available corpora or if it is indeed an indication of a substantial phenomenon in ESL language use by different L1 learners (Ahn, 2011).

The approach in this paper extends the use of lexicalized features and shows that such lexicalized features can by themselves form the basis of a competitive and robust NLI system. This approach entails possibly abondoning interpretability and other linguistic considerations in order to build an as efficient as possible system on the NLI classification tasks itself. It is also motivated by the possibility that simple lexicalized features can be applied efficiently in a task that on the face of it requires the system to on some level learn differences syntactic relations in addition to the differences in morphology found in text produced by the ESL learners.

The experiments presented in this paper are a result of exploring a range of features and machine learning approaches. The best systems found used a combination of bareword features, character n-grams, suffix and bareword collocations with TF-IDF weighting. The resulting feature space contains several hundred thousand features which were used to train a linear Support Vector Machine (SVM) classifier. I will first present the features an how they were extracted in section 2, details of the SVM model is presented in section 3, the different systems submitted to the shared task are described in section 4, along with the results in section 5. I have also included som discussion of issues encountered during the development of features and models in section 6.

2 Model features

This section describes the features used in the submitted systems. All the different text features are derived from the surface form of the training and development corpora without any additional processing or annotation. The provided tokenization was used and no steming, lemmatization or syntactic parsing was performed on the data.

2.1 Bareword features

The frequency of each token by itself was used as a feature, without any processing or normalization. I.e. no stemming was used, and any capitalization was kept.

2.2 Character n-gram features

These features consists of n-grams of length n. Character n-grams includes single spaces between tokens and newlines between lines. The systems presented in this paper uses n-gram orders 3-6 or 1-7.

2.3 Bareword directed collocation features

These are frequencies of the collocations of the bare tokens. The features includes the direction of the collocation, such that a different feature is generated if a token is collocated to the left or right of another token. The collocations are restricted to a window around the target token, and all the systems in this paper uses a window of one token making this feature identical to token bigrams.

2.4 Suffix directed collocation features

These features are constructed in the same manner as the directed bareword collocation features described in 2.3 except that they are based on the 4-character long suffix of each token.

2.5 Feature filtering and TF-IDF weighting

Features that are presumed to be uninformative are filtered out before classifier training and prediction. Features with a document count less than a certain limit varying between the systems were ignored, along with features which appears in more than 50% of the documents, i.e. with a Document Frequency (DF) over 0.5.

All the features based on character n-gram or word counts from the corpus was scaled using sublinear Term Frequency (TF) scaling as described in for exeample (Manning et al., 2008). In addition the IDF was adjusted using add-one smoothing, i.e. one was added to all DF counts[1].

2.6 Proficiency and prompt features

Both proficiency value and prompt value for the document are used as features in the form of $0-1$ indicators for the possible values.[2]

3 SVM classification

The system uses an SVM multiclass classifier. The SVM classifier was trained without a kernel, i.e. linear, and with the cost parameter optimized through cross validation. SVM was used since it can train models with a large number of features efficiently, and has been successsfully used to construct high-dimensional models in many NLP tasks (Joachims, 1998), including NLI (Tsur and Rappoport, 2007; Koppel et al., 2005).

The cost hyperparameter of the SVM models was optimized over 5-fold cross validation on the training set.

4 Systems submitted

Four systems were submitted to the shared task. Of these three share the same feature types and differ in the DF cutoff used to prune individual features. The fourth system adds additional character n-grams to the features found in the other three systems.

The first three systems are based on the following features:

- Weighted token counts.
- Weighted character n-grams of orders 3 through 6.
- Prompt and proficiency values.

[1]The documentation of the software used for feature extraction notes that this smoothing is mainly for numerical considerations, i.e. avoiding division by zero errors (http://scikit-learn.org/stable/modules/generated/sklearn.feature_extraction.text.TfidfTransformer.html)

[2]While the prompt value is included in the submitted systems it was not found to be an effective feature and did not have any effect on the performance of the systems. Its inclusion in the feature set is an oversight.

- Weighted directed token collocation counts with a window size of one, i.e. token bigrams.
- Weighted directed 4 character suffix collocation counts with a window size of 1, i.e. 4 character suffix bigrams.

The three systems vary in the DF cutoff with no cutoff in systmem 1, a cutoff of 5 in system 2 and a cutoff of 10 in system 3.

System 4 uses different cutoffs for different features; 10 for token and character n-gram frequencies and 5 for the token and suffix collocation features. It also uses character n-grams of order 1 through 7 instead of 3 through 6.

Table 1 show the performance of the four systems on the development data set in addition to the feature count for each of the systems. The table shows both classification accuracy on the development data set in addition to average and standard deviation for 10-fold cross validation scores over the combined training and development data sets.

The software used to generate the systems is available at https://github.com/andrely/NLI2013-submission.

5 Results

The final results shows competitive performance from all the submitted systems with little variation in performance between them. Both test set accuracies and average 10-fold cross validation scores with standard deviation for the shared tasks fixed folds are given in table 2.

6 Some impressions

Performance stability: When developing the various systems the performance was always robust for the features described in this paper and variations on them. There were little variation in 5-fold cross validation scores, or difference between cross validation and held out scores. This was taken as an indication that the system was not being overfitted despite the amount of and specificity of the features.

Feature comparison: All the lexical features used were highly predictive also in isolation, and could be used for a competetive system by themselves.

POS tags and lemmatization: Similar features based on POS tags or lemmatized tokens turned out to be much less predictive than the lexical features. This could be caused by low quality of such annotation on data with many spelling or other errors.

Acknowledgments

The Python software package Scikit-learn[3] (Pedregosa et al., 2011) and libSVM[4] (Chang and Lin, 2011) was used to implement the systems described in this paper.

References

Charles S. Ahn. 2011. Automatically Detecting Authors' Native Language. Master's thesis, Naval Postgraduate School, Monterey, CA.

Yves Bestgen, Sylviane Granger, and Jennifer Thewissen. 2012. Error Patterns and Automatic L1 Identification. In Scott Jarvis and Scott A. Crosley, editors, *Approaching Language Transfer through Text Classification*, pages 127–153. Multilingual Matters.

Chih-Chung Chang and Chih-Jen Lin. 2011. LIBSVM: A library for support vector machines. *ACM Transactions on Intelligent Systems and Technology*, 2:27:1–27:27. Software available at http://www.csie.ntu.edu.tw/ cjlin/libsvm.

Thorsten Joachims. 1998. Text categorization with suport vector machines: Learning with many relevant features. In *Proceedings of the 10th European Conference on Machine Learning*, ECML '98, pages 137–142, London, UK, UK. Springer-Verlag.

Moshe Koppel, Jonathan Schler, and Kfir Zigdon. 2005. Automatically determining an anonymous author's native language. *Intelligence and Security Informatics*, pages 41–76.

Christopher D. Manning, Prabhakar Raghavan, and Hinrich Schütze. 2008. *Introduction to Information Retrieval.* Cambridge University Press, New York, NY, USA.

F. Pedregosa, G. Varoquaux, A. Gramfort, V. Michel, B. Thirion, O. Grisel, M. Blondel, P. Prettenhofer, R. Weiss, V. Dubourg, J. Vanderplas, A. Passos, D. Cournapeau, M. Brucher, M. Perrot, and E. Duchesnay. 2011. Scikit-learn: Machine learning in Python. *Journal of Machine Learning Research*, 12:2825–2830.

Oren Tsur and Ari Rappoport. 2007. Using Classifier Features for Studying the Effect of Native Language

[3] http://scikit-learn.org/

[4] http://www.csie.ntu.edu.tw/ cjlin/libsvm/

System	# of features	Dev. 10-fold accuracy	Dev. accuracy
1	867479	0.841 ± 0.010	0.827
2	439063	0.839 ± 0.012	0.824
3	282797	0.838 ± 0.012	0.823
4	510191	0.836 ± 0.011	0.824

Table 1: Performance and number of features for the submitted systems. Performance is shown as accuracy on the development data set and 10-fold cross validation on the training and test set. The feature counts shown are for the final systems trained on the training and development data sets. The systems are described in section 4.

System	Accuracy	10-fold accuracy
1	0.833	0.839 ± 0.013
2	0.834	0.837 ± 0.011
3	0.833	0.835 ± 0.012
4	0.830	0.835 ± 0.012

Table 2: Final accuracy scores on the test set and 10-fold cross validation for the submitted systems. The systems are described in section 4.

on the Choice of Written Second Language Words. In *Proceedings of the Workshop on Cognitive Aspects of Computational Language Acquisition*, pages 9–16, Prague, Czech Republic, June. Association for Computational Linguistics.

The Story of the Characters, the DNA and the Native Language

Marius Popescu
University of Bucharest
Department of Computer Science
Academiei 14, Bucharest, Romania
popescunmarius@gmail.com

Radu Tudor Ionescu
University of Bucharest
Department of Computer Science
Academiei 14, Bucharest, Romania
raducu.ionescu@gmail.com

Abstract

This paper presents our approach to the 2013 Native Language Identification shared task, which is based on machine learning methods that work at the character level. More precisely, we used several string kernels and a kernel based on Local Rank Distance (LRD). Actually, our best system was a kernel combination of string kernel and LRD. While string kernels have been used before in text analysis tasks, LRD is a distance measure designed to work on DNA sequences. In this work, LRD is applied with success in native language identification.

Finally, the Unibuc team ranked third in the closed NLI Shared Task. This result is more impressive if we consider that our approach is language independent and linguistic theory neutral.

1 Introduction

This paper presents our approach to the shared task on Native Language Identification, NLI 2013. We approached this task with machine learning methods that work at the character level. More precisely, we treated texts just as sequences of symbols (strings) and used different string kernels in conjunction with different kernel-based learning methods in a series of experiments to assess the best performance level that can be achieved. Our aim was to investigate if identifying native language is possible with machine learning methods that work at the character level. By disregarding features of natural language such as words, phrases, or meaning, our approach has an important advantage in that it is language independent.

Using words is natural in text analysis tasks like text categorization (by topic), authorship identification and plagiarism detection. Perhaps surprisingly, recent results have proved that methods handling the text at character level can also be very effective in text analysis tasks (Lodhi et al., 2002; Sanderson and Guenter, 2006; Popescu and Dinu, 2007; Grozea et al., 2009; Popescu, 2011; Popescu and Grozea, 2012). In (Lodhi et al., 2002) string kernels were used for document categorization with very good results. Trying to explain why treating documents as symbol sequences and using string kernels led to such good results the authors suppose that: "the [string] kernel is performing something similar to stemming, hence providing semantic links between words that the word kernel must view as distinct". String kernels were also successfully used in authorship identification (Sanderson and Guenter, 2006; Popescu and Dinu, 2007; Popescu and Grozea, 2012). For example, the system described in (Popescu and Grozea, 2012) ranked first in most problems and overall in the PAN 2012 Traditional Authorship Attribution tasks. A possible reason for the success of string kernels in authorship identification is given in (Popescu and Dinu, 2007): "the similarity of two strings as it is measured by string kernels reflects the similarity of the two texts as it is given by the short words (2-5 characters) which usually are function words, but also takes into account other morphemes like suffixes ('ing' for example) which also can be good indicators of the author's style".

Even more interesting is the fact that two methods, that are essentially the same, obtained very good results for text categorization (by topic) (Lodhi et al., 2002) and authorship identification (Popescu and Dinu, 2007). Both are based on SVM and a string kernel of length 5. How is this possible? Traditionally, the two tasks, text categorization (by topic) and authorship identification are viewed as opposite. When words are considered as features, for text categorization the (stemmed) content words are used (the stop words being eliminated), while for authorship identification the function words (stop words) are used as features, the others words (content words) being eliminated. Then, why did the same string kernel (of length 5) work well in both cases? In our opinion the key factor is the kernel-based learning algorithm. The string kernel implicitly embeds the texts in a high dimensional feature space, in our case the space of all (sub)strings of length 5. The kernel-based learning algorithm (SVM or another kernel method), aided by regularization, implicitly assigns a weight to each feature, thus selecting the features that are important for the discrimination task. In this way, in the case of text categorization the learning algorithm (SVM) enhances the features (substrings) representing stems of content words, while in the case of authorship identification the same learning algorithm enhances the features (substrings) representing function words.

Using string kernels will make the corresponding learning method completely language independent, because the texts will be treated as sequences of symbols (strings). Methods working at the word level or above very often restrict their feature space according to theoretical or empirical principles. For example, they select only features that reflect various types of spelling errors or only some type of words, such as function words, for example. These features prove to be very effective for specific tasks, but other, possibly good features, depending on the particular task, may exist. String kernels embed the texts in a very large feature space (all substrings of length k) and leave it to the learning algorithm (SVM or others) to select important features for the specific task, by highly weighting these features.

A method that considers words as features can not be language independent. Even a method that uses only function words as features is not completely language independent because it needs a list of function words (specific to a language) and a way to segment a text into words which is not an easy task for some languages, like Chinese.

Character n-grams were already used in native language identification (Brooke and Hirst, 2012; Tetreault et al., 2012). The reported performance when only character n-grams were used as features was modest compared with other type of features. But, in the above mentioned works, the authors investigated only the bigrams and trigrams and not longer n-grams. Particularly, we have obtained similar results with (Tetreault et al., 2012) when using character bigrams, but we have achieved the best performance using a range of 5 to 8 n-grams (see section 4.3). We have used with success a similar approach for the related task of identifying translationese (Popescu, 2011).

The first application of string kernel ideas came in the field of text categorization, with the paper (Lodhi et al., 2002), followed by applications in bioinformatics (Leslie et al., 2002). Computer science researchers have developed a wide variety of methods that can be applied with success in computational biology. Such methods range from clustering techniques used to analyze the phylogenetic trees of different organisms (Dinu and Sgarro, 2006; Dinu and Ionescu, 2012b), to genetic algorithms used to find motifs or common patterns in a set of given DNA sequences (Dinu and Ionescu, 2012a). Most of these methods are based on a distance measure for strings, such as Hamming (Chimani et al., 2011; Vezzi et al., 2012), edit (Shapira and Storer, 2003), Kendall-tau (Popov, 2007), or rank distance (Dinu, 2003). A similar idea to character n-grams was introduced in the early years of bioinformatics, where k-mers are used instead of single characters [1]. There are recent studies that use k-mers for the phylogenetic analysis of organisms (Li et al., 2004), or for sequence alignment (Melsted and Pritchard, 2011). Analyzing DNA at substring level is also more suited from a biological point of view, because DNA substrings may contain meaningful information. For example, genes are encoded by a number close to 100 base pairs, or codons that encode the twenty standard amino acids are formed of 3-mers. Local Rank Dis-

[1] In biology, single DNA characters are also referred to as nucleotides or monomers. Polymers are also known as k-mers.

tance (LRD) (Ionescu, 2013) has been recently proposed as an extension of rank distance. LRD drops the annotation step of rank distance, and uses k-mers instead of single characters. The work (Ionescu, 2013) shows that LRD is a distance function and that it has very good results in phylogenetic analysis and DNA sequence comparison. But, LRD can be applied to any kind of string sequences, not only to DNA. Thus, LRD was transformed into a kernel and used for native language identification. Despite the fact it has no linguistic motivation, LRD gives surprisingly good results for this task. Its performance level is lower than string kernel, but LRD can contribute to the improvement of string kernel when the two methods are combined.

The paper is organized as follows. In the next section, the kernel methods we used are briefly described. Section 3 presents the string kernels and the LRD, and shows how to transform LRD into a kernel. Section 4 presents details about the experiments. It gives details about choosing the learning method, parameter tuning, combining kernels and results of submitted systems. Finally, conclusions are given in section 5.

2 Kernel Methods and String Kernels

Kernel-based learning algorithms work by embedding the data into a feature space (a Hilbert space), and searching for linear relations in that space. The embedding is performed implicitly, that is by specifying the inner product between each pair of points rather than by giving their coordinates explicitly.

Given an input set $\mathcal{X}$ (the space of examples), and an embedding vector space $\mathcal{F}$ (feature space), let $\phi : \mathcal{X} \rightarrow \mathcal{F}$ be an embedding map called feature map.

A *kernel* is a function k, such that for all $x, z \in \mathcal{X}$, $k(x, z) =< \phi(x), \phi(z) >$, where $< \cdot, \cdot >$ denotes the inner product in $\mathcal{F}$.

In the case of binary classification problems, kernel-based learning algorithms look for a discriminant function, a function that assigns $+1$ to examples belonging to one class and -1 to examples belonging to the other class. This function will be a linear function in the space $\mathcal{F}$, that means it will have the form:

$$f(x) = \text{sign}(< w, \phi(x) > +b),$$

for some weight vector w. The kernel can be exploited whenever the weight vector can be expressed as a linear combination of the training points, $\sum_{i=1}^{n} \alpha_i \phi(x_i)$, implying that f can be expressed as follows:

$$f(x) = \text{sign}(\sum_{i=1}^{n} \alpha_i k(x_i, x) + b).$$

Various kernel methods differ by the way in which they find the vector w (or equivalently the vector α). Support Vector Machines (SVM) try to find the vector w that defines the hyperplane that maximally separates the images in $\mathcal{F}$ of the training examples belonging to the two classes. Mathematically, SVMs choose the w and the b that satisfy the following optimization criterion:

$$\min_{w,b} \frac{1}{n} \sum_{i=1}^{n} [1 - y_i(< w, \phi(x_i) > +b)]_+ + \nu ||w||^2$$

where y_i is the label ($+1/-1$) of the training example x_i, ν a regularization parameter and $[x]_+ = \max(x, 0)$.

Kernel Ridge Regression (KRR) selects the vector w that simultaneously has small empirical error and small norm in Reproducing Kernel Hilbert Space generated by kernel k. The resulting minimization problem is:

$$\min_{w} \frac{1}{n} \sum_{i=1}^{n} (y_i - < w, \phi(x_i) >)^2 + \lambda ||w||^2$$

where again y_i is the label ($+1/-1$) of the training example x_i, and λ a regularization parameter.

Details about SVM and KRR can be found in (Taylor and Cristianini, 2004). The important fact is that the above optimization problems are solved in such a way that the coordinates of the embedded points are not needed, only their pairwise inner products which in turn are given by the kernel function k.

3 String Kernels and Local Rank Distance

The kernel function offers to the kernel methods the power to naturally handle input data that are not in the form of numerical vectors, for example strings. The kernel function captures the intuitive notion of similarity between objects in a specific domain and can be any function defined on the respective domain that is symmetric and positive definite. For strings, many such kernel functions exist with various applications in computational biology and computational linguistics (Taylor and Cristianini, 2004).

3.1 String Kernels

Perhaps one of the most natural ways to measure the similarity of two strings is to count how many substrings of length p the two strings have in common. This gives rise to the p-spectrum kernel. Formally, for two strings over an alphabet Σ, $s, t \in \Sigma^*$, the p-spectrum kernel is defined as:

$$k_p(s,t) = \sum_{v \in \Sigma^p} \text{num}_v(s) \cdot \text{num}_v(t)$$

where $\text{num}_v(s)$ is the number of occurrences of string v as a substring in s [2]. The feature map defined by this kernel associates to each string a vector of dimension $|\Sigma|^p$ containing the histogram of frequencies of all its substrings of length p (p-grams).

A variant of this kernel can be obtained if the embedding feature map is modified to associate to each string a vector of dimension $|\Sigma|^p$ containing the presence bits (instead of frequencies) of all its substrings of length p. Thus the character p-grams presence bits kernel is obtained:

$$k_p^{0/1}(s,t) = \sum_{v \in \Sigma^p} \text{in}_v(s) \cdot \text{in}_v(t)$$

where $\text{in}_v(s)$ is 1 if string v occurs as a substring in s and 0 otherwise.

Normalized versions of these kernels ensure a fair comparison of strings of different lengths:

$$\hat{k}_p(s,t) = \frac{k_p(s,t)}{\sqrt{k_p(s,s) \cdot k_p(t,t)}}$$

$$\hat{k}_p^{0/1}(s,t) = \frac{k_p^{0/1}(s,t)}{\sqrt{k_p^{0/1}(s,s) \cdot k_p^{0/1}(t,t)}}.$$

Taking into account p-grams of different length and summing up the corresponding kernels, new kernels (called *blended spectrum kernels*) can be obtained.

[2]Note that the notion of substring requires contiguity. See (Taylor and Cristianini, 2004) for a discussion about the ambiguity between the terms *substring* and *subsequence* across different traditions: biology, computer science.

3.2 Local Rank Distance

Local Rank Distance is an extension of rank distance that drops the annotation step and uses n-grams instead of single characters. Thus, characters in one string are simply matched with the nearest similar characters in the other string. To compute the LRD between two strings, the idea is to sum up all the offsets of similar n-grams between the two strings. For every n-gram in one string, we search for a similar n-gram in the other string. First, look for similar n-grams in the same position in both strings. If those n-grams are similar, sum up 0 since there is no offset between them. If the n-grams are not similar, start looking around the initial n-gram position in the second string to find an n-gram similar to the one in the first string. If a similar n-gram is found during this process, sum up the offset between the two n-grams. The search goes on until a similar n-gram is found or until a maximum offset is reached. LRD is formally defined next.

Definition 1 *Let $S_1, S_2 \in \Sigma^*$ be two strings with symbols (n-grams) from the alphabet Σ. Local Rank Distance between S_1 and S_2 is defined as:*

$$\begin{aligned}\Delta_{LRD}(S_1,S_2) &= \Delta_{left} + \Delta_{right} \\ &= \sum_{x_s \in S_1} \min_{x_s \in S_2} \{|pos_{S_1}(x_s) - pos_{S_2}(x_s)|, m\} + \\ &+ \sum_{y_s \in S_2} \min_{y_s \in S_1} \{|pos_{S_1}(y_s) - pos_{S_2}(y_s)|, m\},\end{aligned}$$

where x_s and y_s are occurrences of symbol $s \in \Sigma$ in strings S_1 and S_2, $pos_S(x_s)$ represents the position (or the index) of the occurrence x_s of symbol $s \in \Sigma$ in string S, and $m \geq 1$ is the maximum offset.

A string may contain multiple occurrences of a symbol $s \in \Sigma$. LRD matches each occurrence x_s of symbol $s \in \Sigma$ from a string, with the nearest occurrence of symbol s in the other string. A symbol can be defined either as a single character, or as a sequence of characters (n-grams). Overlapping n-grams are also permitted in the computation of LRD. Notice that in order to be a symmetric distance measure, LRD must consider every n-gram in both strings. The complexity of an algorithm to compute LRD can be reduced to $O(l \times m)$ using advanced string searching algorithms, where l is the maximum length of the two strings involved in the computation of LRD, and m is the maximum offset.

To understand how LRD actually works, consider example 1 where LRD is computed between strings s_1 and s_2 using 1-grams (single characters).

Example 1 *Let* $s_1 = CCBAADACB$, $s_2 = DBACDCA$, *and* $m = 10$ *be the maximum offset. The LRD between* s_1 *and* s_2 *is given by:*

$$\Delta_{LRD}(s_1, s_2) = \Delta_{left} + \Delta_{right}$$

where the two sums Δ_{left} *and* Δ_{right} *are computed as follows:*

$$\Delta_{left} = \sum_{x_s \in s_1} \min_{x_s \in s_2} \{|pos_{s_1}(x_s) - pos_{s_2}(x_s)|, 10\}$$
$$= |1-4| + |2-4| + |3-2| + |4-3| + |5-3| +$$
$$+ |6-5| + |7-7| + |8-6| + |9-2| = 19$$

$$\Delta_{right} = \sum_{y_s \in s_2} \min_{y_s \in s_1} \{|pos_{s_1}(y_s) - pos_{s_2}(y_s)|, 10\}$$
$$= |1-6| + |2-3| + |3-4| + |4-2| + |5-6| +$$
$$+ |6-8| + |7-7| = 12.$$

In other words, Δ_{left} *considers every symbol from* s_1*, while* Δ_{right} *considers every symbol from* s_2*. Observe that* $\Delta_{LRD}(s_1, s_2) = \Delta_{LRD}(s_2, s_1)$*.*

LRD measures the distance between two strings. Knowing the maximum offset (used to stop similar n-gram searching), the maximum LRD value between two strings can be computed as the product between the maximum offset and the number of pairs of compared n-grams. Thus, LRD can be normalized to a value in the $[0, 1]$ interval. By normalizing, LRD is transformed into a dissimilarity measure. LRD can be also used as a kernel, since kernel methods are based on similarity. The classical way to transform a distance or dissimilarity measure into a similarity measure is by using the Gaussian-like kernel (Taylor and Cristianini, 2004):

$$k(s_1, s_2) = e^{-\frac{LRD(s_1, s_2)}{2\sigma^2}}$$

where s_1 and s_2 are two strings. The parameter σ is usually chosen to match the number of features (characters) so that values of $k(s_1, s_2)$ are well scaled.

4 Experiments

4.1 Dataset

The dataset for the NLI shared task is the TOEFL11 corpus (Blanchard et al., 2013). This corpus contains 9900 examples for training, 1100 examples for development (or validation) and another 1100 examples for testing. Each example is an essay written in English by a person that is a non-native English speaker. The people that produced the essays have one of the following native languages: German, French, Spanish, Italian, Chinese, Korean, Japanese, Turkish, Arabic, Telugu, Hindi. For more details see (Blanchard et al., 2013).

We participated only in the closed NLI shared task, where the goal of the task is to predict the native language of testing examples, only by using the training and development data. In our approach, documents or essays from this corpus are treated as strings. Thus, when we refer to *strings* throughout this paper, we really mean *documents* or *essays*. Because we work at the character level, we didn't need to split the texts into words, or to do any NLP-specific preprocessing. The only editing done to the texts was the replacing of sequences of consecutive space characters (space, tab, new line, etc.) with a single space character. This normalization was needed in order to not artificially increase or decrease the similarity between texts as a result of different spacing. Also all uppercase letters were converted to the corresponding lowercase ones. We didn't use the additional information from *prompts* and English language proficiency level.

4.2 Choosing the Learning Method

SVM and KRR produce binary classifiers and native language identification is a multi-class classification problem. There are a lot of approaches for combining binary classifiers to solve multi-class problems. Typically, the multiclass problem is broken down into multiple binary classification problems using common decomposing schemes such as: one-versus-all (OVA) and one-versus-one (OVO). There are also kernel methods that directly take into account the multiclass nature of the problem such as the kernel partial least squares regression (KPLS).

We conducted a series of preliminary experiments in order to select the learning method. In these ex-

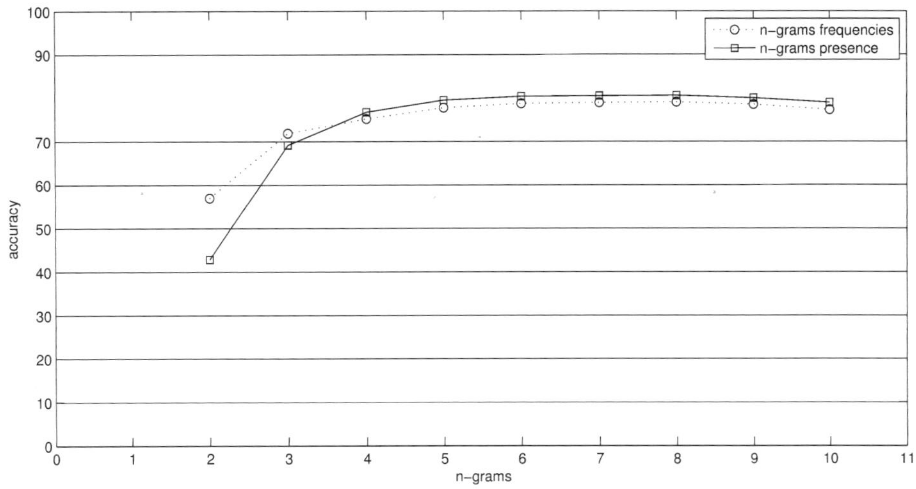

Figure 1: 10-fold cross-validation accuracy on the train set for different n-grams.

Method	Accuracy
OVO SVM	72.72%
OVA SVM	74.94%
OVO KRR	73.99%
OVA KRR	$\mathbf{77.74\%}$
KPLS	74.99%

Table 1: Accuracy rates using 10-fold cross-validation on the train set for different kernel methods with $\hat{k}_5$ kernel.

periments we fixed the kernel to the p-spectrum normalized kernel of length 5 ($\hat{k}_5$) and plugged it in the following learning methods: OVO SVM, OVA SVM, OVO KRR, OVA KRR and KPLS. Note that in this stage we were interested only in selecting the learning method and not in finding the best kernel. We chose the $\hat{k}_5$ because it was reported to work well in the case of the related task of identifying translationese (Popescu, 2011).

We carried out a 10-fold cross-validation on the training set and the result obtained (with the best parameters setting) are shown in Table 1.

The results show that for native language identification the one-vs-all scheme performs better than the one-versus-one scheme. The same fact was reported in (Brooke and Hirst, 2012). See also (Rifkin and Klautau, 2004) for arguments in favor of one-vs-all. The best result was obtained by one-vs-all Kernel Ridge Regression and we selected it as our learning method.

4.3 Parameter Tuning for String Kernel

To establish the type of kernel, (blended) p-spectrum kernel or (blended) p-grams presence bits kernel, and the length(s) of of n-grams that must be used, we performed another set of experiments. For both p-spectrum normalized kernel and p-grams presence bits normalized kernel, and for each value of p from 2 to 10, we carried out a 10-fold cross-validation on the train set. The results are summarized in Figure 1. As can be seen, both curves have similar shapes, both achieve their maximum at 8, but the accuracy of the p-grams presence bits normalized kernel is generally better than the accuracy of the p-spectrum normalized kernel. It seem that in native language identification the information provided by the presence of an n-gram is more important than the the information provided by the frequency of occurrence of the respective n-gram. This phenomenon was also noticed in the context of sexual predator identification (Popescu and Grozea, 2012).

We also experimented with different blended kernels to see if combining n-grams of different lengths can improve the accuracy. The best result was obtained when all the n-grams with the length in the range 5-8 were used, that is the 5-8-grams presence bits normalized kernel ($\hat{k}^{0/1}_{5-8}$). The 10-fold cross-validation accuracy on the train set for this kernel

Method	Accuracy
KRR + K_{LRD_6}	42.1%
KRR + K_{nLRD_4}	70.8%
KRR + K_{nLRD_6}	74.4%
KRR + K_{nLRD_8}	**74.8%**

Table 2: Accuracy rates, using 10-fold cross-validation on the training set, of LRD with different n-grams, with and without normalization. Normalized LRD is much better.

was 80.94% and was obtained for the KRR parameter λ set to 10^{-5}. The authors of (Bykh and Meurers, 2012) also obtained better results using n-grams with the length in a range than using n-grams of a fixed length.

4.4 Parameter Tuning for LRD Kernel

Parameter tuning for LRD kernel (K_{LRD}) was also done by using 10-fold cross validation on the training data. First, we observed that the KRR based on LRD works much better with the normalized version of LRD (K_{nLRD}). Another concern was to choose the right length of n-grams. We tested with several n-grams such as 4-grams, 6-grams and 8-grams that are near the mean English word length of 5-6 letters. The tests show that the LRD kernels based on 6-grams (K_{nLRD_6}) and 8-grams (K_{nLRD_8}) give the best results. In the end, the LRD kernels based on 6-grams and 8-grams are combined to obtain even better results (see section 4.5). Finally, the maximum offset parameter m involved in the computation of LRD was chosen so that it generates search window size close to the average number of letters per document from the TOEFL 11 set. There are 1802 characters per document on average, and m was chosen to be 700. This parameter was also chosen with respect to the computational time of LRD, which is proportional to the parameter value. Table 2 shows the results of the LRD kernel with different parameters cross validated on the training set. For K_{nLRD}, the σ parameter of the Gaussian-like kernel was set to 1. The reported accuracy rates were obtained with the KRR parameter λ set to 10^{-5}.

Regarding the length of strings, we observed that LRD is affected by the variation of string lengths. When comparing two documents with LRD, we tried to cut the longer one to match the length of the shorter. This made the accuracy even worse. It seems that the parts cut out from longer documents contain valuable information for LRD. We decided to use the entire strings for LRD, despite the noise brought by the variation of string lengths.

Method	Accuracy
KRR + $K_{nLRD_{6+8}}$	75.4%
KRR + $\hat{k}^{0/1}_{5-8}$ + $K_{nLRD_{6+8}}$	**81.6%**
KRR + $(\hat{k}^{0/1} + K_{nLRD})_{6+8}$	80.9%

Table 3: Accuracy rates of different kernel combinations using 10-fold cross-validation on the training set.

4.5 Combining Kernels

To improve results, we thought of combining the kernels in different ways. First, notice that the blended string kernels presented in section 4.3 are essentially a sum of the string kernels with different n-grams. This combination improves the accuracy, being more stable and robust. In the same manner, the LRD kernels based on 6-grams and 8-grams, respectively, were summed up to obtain the kernel denoted by $K_{nLRD_{6+8}}$. Indeed, the $K_{nLRD_{6+8}}$ kernel works better (see Table 3).

There are other options to combine the string kernels with LRD kernels, besides summing them up. One option is by kernel alignment (Cristianini et al., 2001). Instead of simply summing kernels, kernel alignment assigns weights for each to the two kernels based on how well they are aligned with the ideal kernel YY' obtained from labels. Thus, the 5-8-grams presence bits normalized kernel ($\hat{k}^{0/1}_{5-8}$) was combined with the LRD kernel based on sum of 6,8-grams ($K_{nLRD_{6+8}}$), by kernel alignment. From our experiments, kernel alignment worked slightly better than the sum of the two kernels. This also suggests that kernels can be combined only by kernel alignment. The string kernel of length 6 was aligned with the LRD kernel based on 6-grams. In the same way, the string kernel of length 8 was aligned with the LRD kernel based on 8-grams. The two kernels obtained by alignment are combined together, again by kernel alignment, to obtain the kernel denoted by $(\hat{k}^{0/1} + K_{nLRD})_{6+8}$. The results of all kernel combinations are presented in Table 3. The reported accuracy rates were obtained with the KRR parameter

Method	Submission	CV Tr.	Dev.	CV Tr.+Dev.	Test
KRR + $\hat{k}^{0/1}_{5-8}$	Unibuc-1	80.9%	85.4%	82.5%	82.0%
KRR + $K_{nLRD_{6+8}}$	Unibuc-2	75.4%	76.3%	75.7%	75.8%
KRR + $\hat{k}^{0/1}_{5-8}$ + $K_{nLRD_{6+8}}$	Unibuc-3	**81.6%**	**85.7%**	**82.6%**	82.5%
KRR + $(\hat{k}^{0/1} + K_{nLRD})_{6+8}$	Unibuc-4	80.9%	85.6%	82.0%	81.4%
KRR + $\hat{k}^{0/1}_{5-8}$ + $K_{nLRD_{6+8}}$ + heuristic	Unibuc-5	-	-	-	**82.7%**

Table 4: Accuracy rates of submitted systems on different evaluation sets. The Unibuc team ranked third in the closed NLI Shared Task with the kernel combination improved by the heuristic to level the predicted class distribution.

λ set to 10^{-5}.

4.6 Results and Discussion

For the closed NLI Shared Task we submitted the two main systems, namely the 5-8-grams presence bits normalized kernel and the LRD kernel based on sum of 6,8-grams, separately. Another two submissions are the kernel combinations discussed in section 4.5. These four systems were tested using several evaluation procedures, with results shown in Table 4. First, they were tested using 10-fold cross validation on the training set. Next, the systems were tested on the development set. In this case, the systems were trained on the entire training corpus. Another 10-fold cross validation procedure was done on the corpus obtained by combining the training and the development sets. The folds were provided by the organizers. Finally, the results of our systems on the NLI Shared Task test set are given in the last column of Table 4. For testing, the systems were trained on the entire training and development set, with the KRR parameter λ set to $2 \cdot 10^{-5}$.

We didn't expect $K_{nLRD_{6+8}}$ kernel to perform very well on the test set. This system was submitted just to be compared with systems submitted by other participants. Considering that LRD is inspired from biology and that it has no ground in computational linguistics, it performed very well, by standing in the top half of the ranking of all submitted systems.

The kernel obtained by aligning the $\hat{k}^{0/1}_{5-8}$ and $K_{nLRD_{6+8}}$ kernels gives the best results, no matter the evaluation procedure. It is followed closely by the other two submitted systems.

We thought of exploiting the distribution of the testing set in our last submitted system. We knew that there should be exactly 100 examples per class for testing. We took the kernel obtained by combining the $\hat{k}^{0/1}_{5-8}$ and $K_{nLRD_{6+8}}$ kernels, and tried to adjust its output to level the predicted class distribution. We took all the classes with more than 100 examples and ranked the examples by their confidence score (returned by regression) to be part of the predicted class. The examples ranked below 100 were chosen to be redistributed to the classes that had less than 100 examples per class. Examples were redistributed only if their second most confident class had less than 100 examples. This heuristic improved the results on the test set by 0.2%, enough to put us on third place in the closed NLI Shared Task.

5 Conclusion

In this paper, we have presented our approach to the 2013 NLI Shared Task. What makes our system stand out is that it works at the character level, making the approach completely language independent and linguistic theory neutral. The results obtained were very good. A standard approach based on string kernels, that proved to work well in many text analysis tasks, obtained an accuracy of 82% on test data with a difference of only 1.6% between it and the top performing system. A second system based on a new kernel K_{LRD}, inspired from biology with no ground in computational linguistics, performed also unexpectedly well, by standing in the top half of the ranking of all submitted systems. The combination of the two kernels obtained an accuracy of 82.5% making it to the top ten, while an heuristic improvement of this combination ranked third with an accuracy of 82.7%. Obviously, an explanation for these results was needed. It will be adressed in future work.

References

Daniel Blanchard, Joel Tetreault, Derrick Higgins, Aoife Cahill, and Martin Chodorow. 2013. TOEFL11: A Corpus of Non-Native English. Technical report, Educational Testing Service.

Julian Brooke and Graeme Hirst. 2012. Robust, Lexicalized Native Language Identification. In *Proceedings of COLING 2012*, pages 391–408, Mumbai, India, December. The COLING 2012 Organizing Committee.

Serhiy Bykh and Detmar Meurers. 2012. Native Language Identification using Recurring n-grams – Investigating Abstraction and Domain Dependence. In *Proceedings of COLING 2012*, pages 425–440, Mumbai, India, December. The COLING 2012 Organizing Committee.

Markus Chimani, Matthias Woste, and Sebastian Bocker. 2011. A Closer Look at the Closest String and Closest Substring Problem. *Proceedings of ALENEX*, pages 13–24.

Nello Cristianini, John Shawe-Taylor, André Elisseeff, and Jaz S. Kandola. 2001. On kernel-target alignment. In Thomas G. Dietterich, Suzanna Becker, and Zoubin Ghahramani, editors, *NIPS*, pages 367–373. MIT Press.

Liviu P. Dinu and Radu Tudor Ionescu. 2012a. An Efficient Rank Based Approach for Closest String and Closest Substring. *PLoS ONE*, 7(6):e37576, 06.

Liviu P. Dinu and Radu Tudor Ionescu. 2012b. Clustering based on Rank Distance with Applications on DNA. *Proceedings of ICONIP*, 7667:722–729.

Liviu P. Dinu and Andrea Sgarro. 2006. A Low-complexity Distance for DNA Strings. *Fundamenta Informaticae*, 73(3):361–372.

Liviu P. Dinu. 2003. On the classification and aggregation of hierarchies with different constitutive elements. *Fundamenta Informaticae*, 55(1):39–50.

C. Grozea, C. Gehl, and M. Popescu. 2009. ENCOPLOT: Pairwise Sequence Matching in Linear Time Applied to Plagiarism Detection. In *3rd PAN WORKSHOP. UNCOVERING PLAGIARISM, AUTHORSHIP AND SOCIAL SOFTWARE MISUSE*, page 10.

Radu Tudor Ionescu. 2013. Local Rank Distance and its Applications on DNA. Submitted to PKDD.

Christina S. Leslie, Eleazar Eskin, and William Stafford Noble. 2002. The spectrum kernel: A string kernel for svm protein classification. In *Pacific Symposium on Biocomputing*, pages 566–575.

Ming Li, Xin Chen, Xin Li, Bin Ma, and Paul M. B. Vitanyi. 2004. The similarity metric. *IEEE Transactions on Information Theory*, 50(12):3250–3264.

Huma Lodhi, Craig Saunders, John Shawe-Taylor, Nello Cristianini, and Christopher J. C. H. Watkins. 2002. Text classification using string kernels. *Journal of Machine Learning Research*, 2:419–444.

Pall Melsted and Jonathan Pritchard. 2011. Efficient counting of k-mers in DNA sequences using a bloom filter. *BMC Bioinformatics*, 12(1):333.

Marius Popescu and Liviu P. Dinu. 2007. Kernel methods and string kernels for authorship identification: The federalist papers case. In *Proceedings of the International Conference on Recent Advances in Natural Language Processing (RANLP-07)*, Borovets, Bulgaria, September.

Marius Popescu and Cristian Grozea. 2012. Kernel methods and string kernels for authorship analysis. In Pamela Forner, Jussi Karlgren, and Christa Womser-Hacker, editors, *CLEF (Online Working Notes/Labs/Workshop)*.

Marius Popescu. 2011. Studying translationese at the character level. In *Proceedings of the International Conference Recent Advances in Natural Language Processing 2011*, pages 634–639, Hissar, Bulgaria, September. RANLP 2011 Organising Committee.

V. Yu. Popov. 2007. Multiple genome rearrangement by swaps and by element duplications. *Theoretical Computer Science*, 385(1-3):115–126.

Ryan Rifkin and Aldebaro Klautau. 2004. In defense of one-vs-all classification. *Journal of Machine Learning Research*, 5(January):101–141.

Conrad Sanderson and Simon Guenter. 2006. Short text authorship attribution via sequence kernels, markov chains and author unmasking: An investigation. In *Proceedings of the 2006 Conference on Empirical Methods in Natural Language Processing*, pages 482–491, Sydney, Australia, July. Association for Computational Linguistics.

Dana Shapira and James A. Storer. 2003. Large Edit Distance with Multiple Block Operations. *Proceedings of SPIRE*, 2857:369–377.

J. S. Taylor and N. Cristianini. 2004. *Kernel Methods for Pattern Analysis*. Cambridge University Press, New York, NY, USA.

Joel Tetreault, Daniel Blanchard, Aoife Cahill, and Martin Chodorow. 2012. Native Tongues, Lost and Found: Resources and Empirical Evaluations in Native Language Identification. In *Proceedings of COLING 2012*, pages 2585–2602, Mumbai, India, December. The COLING 2012 Organizing Committee.

Francesco Vezzi, Cristian Del Fabbro, Alexandru I. Tomescu, and Alberto Policriti. 2012. rNA: a fast and accurate short reads numerical aligner. *Bioinformatics*, 28(1):123–124.

Identifying the L1 of non-native writers: the CMU-Haifa system

Yulia Tsvetkov* **Naama Twitto†** **Nathan Schneider*** **Noam Ordan†**
Manaal Faruqui* **Victor Chahuneau*** **Shuly Wintner†** **Chris Dyer***

*Language Technologies Institute
Carnegie Mellon University
Pittsburgh, PA
cdyer@cs.cmu.edu

†Department of Computer Science
University of Haifa
Haifa, Israel
shuly@cs.haifa.ac.il

Abstract

We show that it is possible to learn to identify, with high accuracy, the native language of English test takers from the content of the essays they write. Our method uses standard text classification techniques based on multiclass logistic regression, combining individually weak indicators to predict the most probable native language from a set of 11 possibilities. We describe the various features used for classification, as well as the settings of the classifier that yielded the highest accuracy.

1 Introduction

The task we address in this work is identifying the native language (L1) of non-native English (L2) authors. More specifically, given a dataset of short English essays (Blanchard et al., 2013), composed as part of the *Test of English as a Foreign Language (TOEFL)* by authors whose native language is one out of 11 possible languages—Arabic, Chinese, French, German, Hindi, Italian, Japanese, Korean, Spanish, Telugu, or Turkish—our task is to identify that language.

This task has a clear empirical motivation. Non-native speakers make different errors when they write English, depending on their native language (Lado, 1957; Swan and Smith, 2001); understanding the different types of errors is a prerequisite for correcting them (Leacock et al., 2010), and systems such as the one we describe here can shed interesting light on such errors. Tutoring applications can use our system to identify the native language of students and offer better-targeted advice. Forensic linguistic applications are sometimes required to determine the L1 of authors (Estival et al., 2007b; Estival et al., 2007a). Additionally, we believe that the task is interesting in and of itself, providing a better understanding of non-native language. We are thus equally interested in defining *meaningful* features whose contribution to the task can be linguistically interpreted. Briefly, our features draw heavily on prior work in general text classification and authorship identification, those used in identifying so-called *translationese* (Volansky et al., forthcoming), and a class of features that involves determining what minimal changes would be necessary to transform the essays into "standard" English (as determined by an n-gram language model).

We address the task as a multiway text-classification task; we describe our data in §3 and classification model in §4. As in other author attribution tasks (Juola, 2006), the choice of features for the classifier is crucial; we discuss the features we define in §5. We report our results in §6 and conclude with suggestions for future research.

2 Related work

The task of L1 identification was introduced by Koppel et al. (2005a; 2005b), who work on the International Corpus of Learner English (Granger et al., 2009), which includes texts written by students from 5 countries, Russia, the Czech Republic, Bulgaria, France, and Spain. The texts range from 500 to 850 words in length. Their classification method is a linear SVM, and features include 400 standard function words, 200 letter n-grams, 185 error types and 250 rare part-of-speech (POS) bigrams. Ten-fold cross-validation results on this dataset are 80% accuracy.

The same experimental setup is assumed by Tsur and Rappoport (2007), who are mostly interested in testing the hypothesis that an author's choice of words in a second language is influenced by the *phonology* of his or her L1. They confirm this hypothesis by carefully analyzing the features used by Koppel et al., controlling for potential biases.

Wong and Dras (2009; 2011) are also motivated by a linguistic hypothesis, namely that *syntactic* errors in a text are influenced by the author's L1. Wong and Dras (2009) analyze three error types statistically, and then add them as features in the same experimental setup as above (using LIBSVM with a radial kernel for classification). The error types are subject-verb disagreement, noun-number disagreement and misuse of determiners. Addition of these features does not improve on the results of Koppel et al.. Wong and Dras (2011) further extend this work by adding as features horizontal slices of parse trees, thereby capturing more syntactic structure. This improves the results significantly, yielding 78% accuracy compared with less than 65% using only lexical features.

Kochmar (2011) uses a different corpus, the Cambridge Learner Corpus, in which texts are 200-400 word long, and are authored by native speakers of five Germanic languages (German, Swiss German, Dutch, Swedish and Danish) and five Romance languages (French, Italian, Catalan, Spanish and Portuguese). Again, SVMs are used as the classification device. Features include POS *n*-grams, character *n*-grams, phrase-structure rules (extracted from parse trees), and two measures of error rate. The classifier is evaluated on its ability to distinguish between pairs of closely-related L1s, and the results are usually excellent.

A completely different approach is offered by Brooke and Hirst (2011). Since training corpora for this task are rare, they use mainly L1 (blog) corpora. Given English word bigrams $\langle e_1, e_2 \rangle$, they try to assess, for each L1, how likely it is that an L1 bigram was translated literally by the author, resulting in $\langle e_1, e_2 \rangle$. Working with four L1s (French, Spanish, Chinese, and Japanese), and evaluating on the International Corpus of Learner English, accuracy is below 50%.

3 Data

Our dataset in this work consists of TOEFL essays written by speakers of eleven different L1s (Blanchard et al., 2013), distributed as part of the Native Language Identification Shared Task (Tetreault et al., 2013). The training data consists of 1000 essays from each native language. The essays are short, consisting of 10 to 20 sentences each. We used the provided splits of 900 documents for training and 100 for development. Each document is annotated with the author's English proficiency level (low, medium, high) and an identification (1 to 8) of the essay prompt. All essays are tokenized and split into sentences. In table 1 we provide some statistics on the training corpora, listed by the authors' proficiency level. All essays were tagged with the Stanford part-of-speech tagger (Toutanova et al., 2003). We did not parse the dataset.

	Low	Medium	High
# Documents	1,069	5,366	3,456
# Tokens	245,130	1,819,407	1,388,260
# Types	13,110	37,393	28,329

Table 1: Training set statistics.

4 Model

For our classification model we used the `creg` regression modeling framework to train a 11-class logistic regression classifier.[1] We parameterize the classifier as a multiclass logistic regression:

$$p_\lambda(y \mid \mathbf{x}) = \frac{\exp \sum_j \lambda_j h_j(\mathbf{x}, y)}{Z_\lambda(\mathbf{x})},$$

where $\mathbf{x}$ are documents, $h_j(\cdot)$ are real-valued feature functions of the document being classified, λ_j are the corresponding weights, and y is one of the eleven L1 class labels. To train the parameters of our model, we minimized the following objective,

$$\mathcal{L} = \alpha \overbrace{\sum_j \lambda_j^2}^{\ell_2 \text{ reg.}} - \sum_{\{(\mathbf{x}_i, y_i)\}_{i=1}^{|\mathcal{D}|}} \Big(\overbrace{\log p_\lambda(y_i \mid \mathbf{x}_i)}^{\text{log likelihood}} + \underbrace{\tau\, \mathbb{E}_{p_\lambda(y' \mid \mathbf{x}_i)} \log p_\lambda(y' \mid \mathbf{x}_i)}_{-\text{conditional entropy}} \Big),$$

[1] `https://github.com/redpony/creg`

which combines the negative log likelihood of the training dataset $\mathcal{D}$, an ℓ_2 (quadratic) penalty on the magnitude of λ (weighted by α), and the *negative* entropy of the predictive model (weighted by τ). While an ℓ_2 weight penalty is standard in regression problems like this, we found that the the additional entropy term gave more reliable results. Intuitively, the entropic regularizer encourages the model to remain maximally uncertain about its predictions. In the metaphor of "maximum entropy", the entropic prior finds a solution that has *more* entropy than the "maximum" model that is compatible with the constraints.

The objective cannot be minimized in closed form, but it does have a unique minimum and is straightforwardly differentiable, so we used L-BFGS to find the optimal weight settings (Liu et al., 1989).

5 Feature Overview

We define a large arsenal of features, our motivation being both to improve the accuracy of classification and to be able to interpret the characteristics of the language produced by speakers of different L1s.

While some of the features were used in prior work (§2), we focus on two broad novel categories of features: those inspired by the features used to identify translationese by Volansky et al. (forthcoming) and those extracted by automatic statistical "correction" of the essays. Refer to figure 1 to see the set of features and their values that were extracted from an example sentence.

POS *n*-grams Part-of-speech *n*-grams were used in various text-classification tasks.

Prompt Since the prompt contributes information on the domain, it is likely that some words (and, hence, character sequences) will occur more frequently with some prompts than with others. We therefore use the prompt ID in conjunction with other features.

Document length The number of tokens in the text is highly correlated with the author's level of fluency, which in turn is correlated with the author's L1.

Pronouns The use of pronouns varies greatly among different authors. We use the same list of 25 English pronouns that Volansky et al. (forthcoming) use for identifying translationese.

Punctuation Similarly, different languages use punctuation differently, and we expect this to taint the use of punctuation in non-native texts. Of course, character *n*-grams subsume this feature.

Passives English uses passive voice more frequently than other languages. Again, the use of passives in L2 can be correlated with the author's L1.

Positional token frequency The choice of the first and last few words in a sentence is highly constrained, and may be significantly influenced by the author's L1.

Cohesive markers These are 40 function words (and short phrases) that have a strong discourse function in texts (*however*, *because*, *in fact*, etc.). Translators tend to spell out implicit utterances and render them explicitly in the target text (Blum-Kulka, 1986). We use the list of Volansky et al. (forthcoming).

Cohesive verbs This is a list of manually compiled verbs that are used, like cohesive markers, to spell out implicit utterances (*indicate*, *imply*, *contain*, etc.).

Function words Frequent tokens, which are mostly function words, have been used successfully for various text classification tasks. Koppel and Ordan (2011) define a list of 400 such words, of which we only use 100 (using the entire list was not significantly different). Note that pronouns are included in this list.

Contextual function words To further capitalize on the ability of function words to discriminate, we define pairs consisting of a function word from the list mentioned above, along with the POS tag of its adjacent word. This feature captures patterns such as verbs and the preposition or particle immediately to their right, or nouns and the determiner that precedes them. We also define 3-grams consisting of one or two function words and the POS tag of the third word in the 3-gram.

Lemmas The content of the text is not considered a good indication of the author's L1, but many text categorization tasks use lemmas (more precisely, the stems produced by the tagger) as features approximating the content.

Misspelling features Learning to perceive, produce, and encode non-native phonemic contrasts

Firstly the employers live more savely because they are going to have more money to spend for luxury .

	Presence		Considered alternatives/edits	
Characters	"CHAR_l_y_ ":	log 2 + 1	"DeleteP_p_.":	1.0
	"CharPrompt_P5_g_o_i":	log 1 + 1	"InsertP_p_,":	1.0
	"MFChar_e_ ":	log 1 + 1	"MID:SUBST:v:f":	log 1 + 1
	"Punc_period":	log 1 + 1	"SUBST:v:f":	log 1 + 1
Words	"DocLen_":	log 19 + 1	"MSP:safely":	log 1 + 1
	"MeanWordRank":	422.6	"Match_p_to":	0.5
	"CohMarker_because":	log 1 + 1	"Delete_p_to":	0.5
	"MostFreq_have":	log 1 + 1	"Delete_p_are":	1.0
	"PosToken_last_luxury":	log 1 + 1	"Delete_p_because":	1.0
	"Pronouns_they":	log 1 + 1	"Delete_p_for":	1.0
POS	"POS_VBP_VBG_TO":	log 1 + 1		
	"POS_p_VBP_VBG_TO":	0.059		
Words + POS	"VBP_VBG_to":	log 1 + 1		
	"FW__more RB":	log 1 + 1		

Figure 1: Some of the features extracted for an L1 German sentence.

is extremely difficult for L2 learners (Hayes-Harb and Masuda, 2008). Since English's orthography is largely phonemic—even if it is irregular in many places, we expect leaners whose native phoneme contrasts are different from those of English to make characteristic spelling errors. For example, since Japanese and Korean lack a phonemic /l/-/r/ contrast, we expect native speakers of those languages to be more likely to make spelling errors that confuse *l* and *r* relative to native speakers of languages such as Spanish in which that pair is contrastive. To make this information available to our model, we use a noisy channel spelling corrector (Kernighan, 1990) to identify and correct misspelled words in the training and test data. From these corrections, we extract minimal edit features that show what insertions, deletions, substitutions and joinings (where two separate words are written merged into a single orthographic token) were made by the author of the essay.

Restored tags We focus on three important token classes defined above: punctuation marks, function words and cohesive verbs. We first remove words in these classes from the texts, and then recover the most likely hidden tokens in a sequence of words, according to an *n*-gram language model trained on all essays in the training corpus corrected with a spell checker and containing both words and hidden tokens. This feature should capture specific words or punctuation marks that are consistently omitted (deletions), or misused (insertions, substitutions). To restore hidden tokens we use the `hidden-ngram` utility provided in SRI's language modeling toolkit (Stolcke, 2002).

Brown clusters (Brown et al., 1992) describe an algorithm that induces a hierarchical clustering of a language's vocabulary based on each vocabulary item's tendency to appear in similar left and right contexts in a training corpus. While originally developed to reduce the number of parameters required in *n*-gram language models, Brown clusters have been found to be extremely effective as lexical representations in a variety of regression problems that condition on text (Koo et al., 2008; Turian et al., 2010; Owoputi et al., 2013). Using an open-source implementation of the algorithm,[2] we clustered 8 billion words of English into 600 classes.[3] We included log counts of all 4-grams of Brown clusters that occurred at least 100 times in the NLI training data.

5.1 Main Features

We use the following four feature types as the baseline features in our model. For features that are sensitive to frequency, we use the log of the (frequency-plus-one) as the feature's value. Table 2 reports the accuracy of using each feature type in isolation (with

[2] `https://github.com/percyliang/brown-cluster`
[3] `http://www.ark.cs.cmu.edu/cdyer/en-600/cluster_viewer.html`

Feature	Accuracy (%)
POS	55.18
FreqChar	74.12
CharPrompt	65.09
Brown	72.26
DocLen	11.81
Punct	27.41
Pron	22.81
Position	53.03
PsvRatio	12.26
CxtFxn (bigram)	62.79
CxtFxn (trigram)	62.32
Misspell	37.29
Restore	47.67
CohMark	25.71
CohVerb	22.85
FxnWord	42.47

Table 2: Independent performance of feature types detailed in §5.1, §5.2 and §5.3. Accuracy is averaged over 10 folds of cross-validation on the training set.

10-fold cross-validation on the training set).

POS Part-of-speech *n*-grams. Features were extracted to count every POS 1-, 2-, 3- and 4-gram in each document.

FreqChar Frequent character *n*-grams. We experimented with character *n*-grams: To reduce the number of parameters, we removed features only those character *n*-grams that are observed more than 5 times in the training corpus, and *n* ranges from 1 to 4. High-weight features include: TUR:<Turk>; ITA:<Ital>; JPN:<Japa>.

CharPrompt Conjunction of the character *n*-gram features defined above with the prompt ID.

Brown Substitutions, deletions and insertions counts of Brown cluster unigrams and bigrams in each document.

The accuracy of the classifier on the development set using these four feature types is reported in table 3.[4]

5.2 Additional Features

To the basic set of features we now add more specific, linguistically-motivated features, each adding a small number of parameters to the model. As above, we indicate the accuracy of each feature type in isolation.

[4]For experiments in this paper combining multiple types of features, we used Jonathan Clark's workflow management tool, ducttape (https://github.com/jhclark/ducttape).

Feature Group	# Params	Accuracy (%)	ℓ_2
POS	540,947	55.18	1.0
+ FreqChar	1,036,871	79.55	1.0
+ CharPrompt	2,111,175	79.82	1.0
+ Brown	5,664,461	81.09	1.0

Table 3: Dev set accuracy with feature groups, added cumulatively. The number of parameters is always a multiple of 11 (the number of classes). Only ℓ_2 regularization was used for these experiments; the penalty was tuned on the dev set as well.

DocLen Document length in tokens.

Punct Counts of each punctuation mark.

Pron Counts of each pronoun.

Position Positional token frequency. We use the counts for the first two and last three words before the period in each sentence as features. High-weight features for the *second* word include: ARA:2<,>; CHI:2<is>; HIN:2<can>.

PsvRatio The proportion of passive verbs out of all verbs.

CxtFxn Contextual function words. High-weight features include: CHI:<some JJ>; HIN:<as VBN>.

Misspell Spelling correction edits. Features included substitutions, deletions, insertions, doubling of letters and missing doublings of letters, and splittings (*alot→a lot*), as well as the word position where the error occurred. High-weight features include: ARA:DEL<e>, ARA:INS<e>, ARA:SUBST<e>/<i>; GER:SUBST<z>/<y>; JPN:SUBST<l>/<r>, JPN:SUBST<r>/<l>; SPA:DOUBLE<s>, SPA:MID_INS<s>, SPA:INS<s>.

Restore Counts of substitutions, deletions and insertions of predefined tokens that we restored in the texts. High-weight features include: CHI:DELWORD<do>; GER:DELWORD<on>; ITA:DELWORD<be>

Table 4 reports the empirical improvement that each of these brings independently when added to the main features (§5.1).

5.3 Discarded Features

We also tried several other feature types that did not improve the accuracy of the classifier on the development set.

CohMark Counts of each cohesive marker.

Feature Group	# Params	Accuracy (%)	ℓ_2
+ Position	6,153,015	81.00	1.0
+ PsvRatio	5,664,472	81.00	1.0
	5,664,461	81.09	1.0
+ DocLen	5,664,472	81.09	1.0
+ Pron	5,664,736	81.09	1.0
+ Punct	5,664,604	81.09	1.0
+ Misspell	5,799,860	81.27	5.0
+ Restore	5,682,589	81.36	5.0
+ CxtFxn	7,669,684	81.73	1.0

Table 4: Dev set accuracy with features plus additional feature groups, added independently. ℓ_2 regularization was tuned as in table 3 (two values, 1.0 and 5.0, were tried for each configuration; more careful tuning might produce slightly better accuracy). Results are sorted by accuracy; only three groups exhibited independent improvements over the feature set.

CohVerb Counts of each cohesive verb.

FxnWord Counts of function words. These features are subsumed by the highly discriminative CxtFxn features.

6 Results

The full model that we used to classify the test set combines all features listed in table 4. Using all these features, the accuracy on the development set is 84.55%, and on the test set it is 81.5%. The values for α and τ were tuned to optimize development set performance, and found to be $\alpha = 5, \tau = 2$.

Table 5 lists the confusion matrix on the test set, as well as precision, recall and F_1-score for each L1. The largest error type involved predicting Telugu when the true label was Hindi, which happened 18 times. This error is unsurprising since many Hindi and Telugu speakers are arguably native speakers of Indian English.

Production of L2 texts, not unlike translating from L1 to L2, involves a tension between the imposing models of L1 (and the source text), on the one hand, and a set of cognitive constraints resulting from the efforts to generate the target text, on the other. The former is called *interference* in Translation Studies (Toury, 1995) and *transfer* in second language acquisition (Selinker, 1972). Volansky et al. (forthcoming) designed 32 classifiers to test the validity of the forces acting on translated texts, and found that features sensitive to interference consistently yielded the best performing classifiers. And indeed, in this work too, we find fingerprints of the source language are dominant in the makeup of L2 texts. The main difference, however, between texts translated by professionals and the texts we address here, is that more often than not professional translators translate into their mother tongue, whereas L2 writers write out of their mother tongue by definition. So interference is ever more exaggerated in this case, for example, also phonologically (Tsur and Rappoport, 2007).

We explore the effects of interference by analyzing several patterns we observe in the features. Our classifier finds that the character sequence *alot* is overrepresented in Arabic L2 texts. Arabic has no indefinite article and we speculate that Arabic speakers conceive *a lot* as a single word; the Arabic equivalent for *a lot* is used adverbially like an *-ly* suffix in English. For the same reason, another prominent feature is a missing definite article before nouns and adjectives. Additionally, Arabic, being an Abjad language, rarely indicates vowels, and indeed we find many missing *e*'s and *i*'s in the texts of Arabic speakers. Phonologically, because Arabic conflates /ɪ/ and /ə/ into /i/ (at least in Modern Standard Arabic), we see that many *e*'s are indeed substituted for *i*'s in these texts.

We find that essays that contain hyphens are more likely to be from German authors. We again find evidence of interference from the native language here. First, relative clauses are widely used in German, and we see this pattern in L2 English of L1 German speakers. For example, *any given rational being – let us say Immanual Kant – we find that.* Another source of extra hyphens stems from compounding convention. So, for example, we find *well-known*, *community-help*, *spare-time*, *football-club*, etc. Many of these reflect an effort to both connect and separate connected forms in the original (e.g., *Fussballklub*, which in English would be more naturally rendered as *football club*). Another unexpected feature of essays by native Germans is a frequent substitution of the letter *y* for *z* and vice versa. We suspect this owes to their switched positions on German keyboards.

Lexical item frequency also provides clues to the L1 of the essay writers. The word *that* occurs more frequently in the texts of German L1 speakers. We

true↓	ARA	CHI	FRE	GER	HIN	ITA	JPN	KOR	SPA	TEL	TUR	Precision (%)	Recall (%)	F_1 (%)
ARA	80	0	2	1	3	4	1	0	4	2	3	80.8	80.0	80.4
CHI	3	80	0	1	1	0	6	7	1	0	1	88.9	80.0	84.2
FRE	2	2	81	5	1	2	1	0	3	0	3	86.2	81.0	83.5
GER	1	1	1	93	0	0	0	1	1	0	2	87.7	93.0	90.3
HIN	2	0	0	1	77	1	0	1	5	9	4	74.8	77.0	75.9
ITA	2	0	3	1	1	87	1	0	3	0	2	82.1	87.0	84.5
JPN	2	1	1	2	0	1	87	5	0	0	1	78.4	87.0	82.5
KOR	1	5	2	0	1	0	9	81	1	0	0	80.2	81.0	80.6
SPA	2	0	2	0	1	8	2	1	78	1	5	77.2	78.0	77.6
TEL	0	1	0	0	18	1	2	1	1	73	3	85.9	73.0	78.9
TUR	4	0	2	2	0	2	2	4	4	0	80	76.9	80.0	78.4

Table 5: Official test set confusion matrix with the full model. Accuracy is 81.5%.

hypothesize that in English it is optional in relative clauses whereas in German it is not, so German speakers are less comfortable using the non-obligatory form. Also, *often* is over represented. We hypothesize that since it is cognate of German *oft*, it is not cognitively expensive to retrieve it. We find *many times*—a literal translation of *muchas veces*—in Spanish essays.

Other informative features that reflect L1 features include frequent misspellings involving confusions of *l* and *r* in Japanese essays. More mysteriously, the characters *r* and *s* are misused in Chinese and Spanish, respectively. The word *then* is dominant in the texts of Hindi speakers. Finally, it is clear that authors refer to their native cultures (and, consequently, native languages and countries); the strings *Turkish*, *Korea*, and *Ita* were dominant in the texts of Turkish, Korean and Italian native speakers, respectively.

7 Discussion

We experimented with different classifiers and a large set of features to solve an 11-way classification problem. We hope that studying this problem will improve to facilitate human assessment, grading, and teaching of English as a second language. While the core features used are sparse and sensitive to lexical and even orthographic features of the writing, many of them are linguistically informed and provide insight into how L1 and L2 interact.

Our point of departure was the analogy between translated texts as a genre in its own and L2 writers as pseudo translators, relying heavily on their mother tongue and transferring their native models to a second language. In formulating our features, we assumed that like translators, L2 writers will write in a simplified manner and overuse explicit markers. Although this should be studied vis-à-vis comparable outputs of mother tongue writers in English, we observe that the best features of our classifiers are of the "interference" type, i.e. phonological, morphological and syntactic in nature, mostly in the form of misspelling features, restoration tags, punctuation and lexical and syntactic modeling.

We would like to stress that certain features indicating a particular L1 have no bearing on the quality of the English produced. This has been discussed extensively in Translation Studies (Toury, 1995), where interference is observed by the overuse or underuse of certain features reflecting the typological differences between a specific pair of languages, but which is still within grammatical limits. For example, the fact that Italian native speakers favor the syntactic sequence of determiner + adjective + noun (e.g., *a big risk* or *this new business*) has little prescriptive value for teachers.

A further example of how L2 quality and the ability to predict L1 are uncorrelated, we noted that certain L2 writers often repeat words appearing in their essay prompts, and including information about whether the writer was reusing prompt words improved classification accuracy. We suggest this reflects different educational backgrounds. This feature says nothing about the quality of the text, just as the tendency of Korean and Italian writers to mention their home country more often does not.

Acknowledgments

This research was supported by a grant from the Israeli Ministry of Science and Technology.

References

Daniel Blanchard, Joel Tetreault, Derrick Higgins, Aoife Cahill, and Martin Chodorow. 2013. TOEFL11: A corpus of non-native English. Technical report, Educational Testing Service.

Shoshana Blum-Kulka. 1986. Shifts of cohesion and coherence in translation. In Juliane House and Shoshana Blum-Kulka, editors, *Interlingual and intercultural communication Discourse and cognition in translation and second language acquisition studies*, volume 35, pages 17–35. Gunter Narr Verlag.

Julian Brooke and Graeme Hirst. 2011. Native language detection with 'cheap' learner corpora. In *Conference of Learner Corpus Research (LCR2011)*, Louvain-la-Neuve, Belgium. Presses universitaires de Louvain.

Peter F. Brown, Peter V. de Souza, Robert L. Mercer, Vincent J. Della Pietra, and Jenifer C. Lai. 1992. Class-based *n*-gram models of natural language. *Computational Linguistics*, 18(4).

Dominique Estival, Tanja Gaustad, Son Bao Pham, Will Radford, and Ben Hutchinson. 2007a. Author profiling for English emails. In *Proc. of PACLING*, pages 263–272, Melbourne, Australia.

Dominique Estival, Tanja Gaustad, Son Bao Pham, Will Radford, and Ben Hutchinson. 2007b. TAT: An author profiling tool with application to Arabic emails. In *Proc. of the Australasian Language Technology Workshop*, pages 21–30, Melbourne, Australia, December.

Sylviane Granger, Estelle Dagneaux, Fanny Meunier, and Magali Paquot. 2009. *International Corpus of Learner English*. Presses universitaires de Louvain, Louvain-la-Neuve.

Rachel Hayes-Harb and Kyoko Masuda. 2008. Development of the ability to lexically encode novel second language phonemic contrasts. *Second Language Research*, 24(1):5–33.

Patrick Juola. 2006. Authorship attribution. *Foundations and Trends in Information Retrieval*, 1(3):233–334.

Mark D. Kernighan. 1990. A spelling correction program based on a noisy channel model. In *Proc. of COLING*.

Ekaterina Kochmar. 2011. Identification of a writer's native language by error analysis. Master's thesis, University of Cambridge.

Terry Koo, Xavier Carreras, and Michael Collins. 2008. Simple semi-supervised dependency parsing. In *Proc. of ACL*.

Moshe Koppel and Noam Ordan. 2011. Translationese and its dialects. In *Proc. of ACL-HLT*, pages 1318–1326, Portland, Oregon, USA, June. Association for Computational Linguistics.

Moshe Koppel, Jonathan Schler, and Kfir Zigdon. 2005a. Automatically determining an anonymous author's native language. *Intelligence and Security Informatics*, pages 41–76.

Moshe Koppel, Jonathan Schler, and Kfir Zigdon. 2005b. Determining an author's native language by mining a text for errors. In *Proc. of KDD*, pages 624–628, Chicago, IL. ACM.

Robert Lado. 1957. *Linguistics across cultures: applied linguistics for language teachers*. University of Michigan Press, Ann Arbor, Michigan, June.

Claudia Leacock, Martin Chodorow, Michael Gamon, and Joel Tetreault. 2010. *Automated Grammatical Error Detection for Language Learners*. Morgan and Claypool.

Dong C. Liu, Jorge Nocedal, Dong C. Liu, and Jorge Nocedal. 1989. On the limited memory BFGS method for large scale optimization. *Mathematical Programming B*, 45(3):503–528.

Olutobi Owoputi, Brendan O'Connor, Chris Dyer, Kevin Gimpel, Nathan Schneider, and Noah A. Smith. 2013. Improved part-of-speech tagging for online conversational text with word clusters. In *Proc. of NAACL*.

Larry Selinker. 1972. Interlanguage. *International Review of Applied Linguistics in Language Teaching*, 10(1–4):209–232.

Andreas Stolcke. 2002. SRILM—an extensible language modeling toolkit. In *Procedings of International Conference on Spoken Language Processing*, pages 901–904.

Michael Swan and Bernard Smith. 2001. *Learner English: A Teacher's Guide to Interference and Other Problems*. Cambridge Handbooks for Language Teachers. Cambridge University Press.

Joel Tetreault, Daniel Blanchard, and Aoife Cahill. 2013. A report on the first native language identification shared task. In *Proc. of the Eighth Workshop on Innovative Use of NLP for Building Educational Applications*, Atlanta, GA, USA, June. Association for Computational Linguistics.

Gideon Toury. 1995. *Descriptive Translation Studies and beyond*. John Benjamins, Amsterdam / Philadelphia.

Kristina Toutanova, Dan Klein, Christopher D. Manning, and Yoram Singer. 2003. Feature-rich part-of-speech tagging with a cyclic dependency network. In *Proc. of HLT-NAACL*, pages 173–180, Edmonton, Canada, June. Association for Computational Linguistics.

Oren Tsur and Ari Rappoport. 2007. Using classifier features for studying the effect of native language on the choice of written second language words. In *Proc. of the Workshop on Cognitive Aspects of Computational Language Acquisition*, pages 9–16, Prague, Czech Republic, June. Association for Computational Linguistics.

Joseph Turian, Lev Ratinov, and Yoshua Bengio. 2010. Word representations: A simple and general method for semi-supervised learning. In *Proc. of ACL*.

Vered Volansky, Noam Ordan, and Shuly Wintner. forthcoming. On the features of translationese. *Literary and Linguistic Computing*.

Sze-Meng Jojo Wong and Mark Dras. 2009. Contrastive analysis and native language identification. In *Proc. of the Australasian Language Technology Association Workshop*, pages 53–61, Sydney, Australia, December.

Sze-Meng Jojo Wong and Mark Dras. 2011. Exploiting parse structures for native language identification. In *Proc. of EMNLP*, pages 1600–1610, Edinburgh, Scotland, UK., July. Association for Computational Linguistics.

Evaluating Unsupervised Language Model Adaptation Methods for Speaking Assessment

Shasha Xie
Microsoft
1020 Enterprise Way
Sunnyvale, CA 94089
shxie@microsoft.com

Lei Chen
Educational Testing Service
600 Rosedale Rd
Princeton, NJ
LChen@ets.org

Abstract

In automated speech assessment, adaptation of language models (LMs) to test questions is important to achieve high recognition accuracy However, for large-scale language tests, the ordinary supervised training, which uses an expensive and time-consuming manual transcription process, is hard to utilize for LM adaptation. In this paper, several LM adaptation methods that require either no manual transcription process or just a small amount of transcriptions have been evaluated. Our experiments suggest that these LM adaptation methods can allow us to obtain considerable recognition accuracy gain with no or low human transcription cost.

Index Terms: language model adaptation, unsupervised training, Web as a corpus

1 Introduction

Automated speech assessment, a fast-growing area in the speech research field (Eskenazi, 2009), typically uses an automatic speech recognition (ASR) system to recognize spontaneous speech responses and use the recognition outputs to generate the features for scoring. Since the recognition accuracy directly influences the quality of the speech features, especially for the features related to word entities, such as those measuring grammar accuracy and vocabulary richness, it is important to use ASR systems with high recognition accuracy.

Adaptation of language models (LMs) to test responses is an effective method to improve recognition accuracy. However, it is difficult to only use the ordinary supervised training to adapt LMs to test questions. First, for high-stake tests administered globally, a very large pool of test questions have to be used to strengthen the tests' security and validity. Since a large number of test questions have many possible answers for each question, a large set of audio files needs to be transcribed to cover response content. Second, due to time and cost constraints, it may not be practical to have a pre-test to collect enough speech responses for adaptation purposes. Therefore, it is important to pursue other methods to obtain LM adaptation data in a faster and lower-cost way than the ordinary supervised training.

As we will review in Section 2, some promising technologies, such as *unsupervised training*, *active learning*, and *LM adaptation based on Web data*, have been utilized in broadcast news recognition, dialog system, and so on. In this paper on the LM adaptation task used in automated speech scoring systems, we will report our experiments to obtain LM adaptation data in a faster and more economical way that requires little human involvement. To our knowledge, this is the first such work reported in the automated speech assessment area.

The rest of the paper is organized as follows: Section 2 reviews the related previous research results; Section 3 describes the English test, the data used in our experiments, and the ASR system used; Section 4 reports the experiments of different methods we tried to obtain LM adaptation data; Section 5 discusses our findings and plans for future research.

2 Previous Work

Unsupervised training is the method of using untranscribed audio to adapt a language model (LM). An initial ASR model (seed model) is used to recognize the untranscribed audio, and the obtained ASR outputs are used in the follow-up LM adaptation. (Chen et al., 2003) utilized unsupervised LM adaptation on broadcast news (BN) recognition. The unsupervised adaptation method reduces the word error rate (WER) by 2% relative to using the baseline LM. (Bacchiani and Roark, 2003) reported that unsupervised LM adaptation provided an absolute error rate reduction of 3.9% over the un-adapted baseline performance by using 17 hours of untranscribed adaptation data. This was 51% of the 7.7% adaptation error rate reduction obtained by using an ordinary supervised adaptation method.

Active learning is used to reduce the number of training examples to be annotated by automatically processing the unlabeled examples and then selecting the most informative ones with respect to a given cost function. (Riccardi and Hakkani-Tur, 2003; Tur et al., 2005) proposed using a combination of unsupervised and active learning for ASR training to minimize the workload of human transcription. Their experiments showed that the amount of labeled data needed for a given recognition accuracy can be reduced by 75% when combining these two training approaches.

A recent trend in Natural Language Processing (NLP) and speech recognition research is utilizing Web data to improve the LMs, especially when in-domain training material is limited. (Ng et al., 2005) investigated LM topic adaptation using Web data. Experiments in recognizing Mandarin telephone conversations showed that use of filtered Web data leads to a 7% reduction in the character recognition error rate. (Sarikaya et al., 2005) used Web data to adapt LMs used in a spoken dialog system. From a limited in-domain data set, they generated a series of search queries and retrieved Web pages from Google using these queries. In their recognition experiment done on a dialog system, they achieved a 5.2% word error reduction by using the Web data, compared to a baseline LM trained on 1700 in-domain utterances.

3 Test, Data, and ASR

Our in-domain data was from The Test of English for International Communication, TOEIC®, which tests non-native English speakers' basic speaking ability required in international business communications. In our experiments, we focused on *opinion* testing questions. An example question is: "*Do you agree with the statement that a company should only hire experienced employees? Use specific reasons to support your answer*".

A state-of-the-art HMM LVCSR system, which was provided by a leading ASR vendor, was used in our experiments. It contains a cross-word tri-phone acoustic model (AM) and a combination of bi-gram, tri-gram, and up to four-gram LMs. The AM and LM are trained by supervised training from about 800 hours of audio and manual transcriptions of non-native English speaking data collected from the Test Of English as a Foreign Language (TOEFL®). TOEFL® is targeted to assess test-takers' ability to use English to study in an institution using English as its primary teaching language. Speaking content from TOEFL® data is quite different from the content shown in TOEIC® data. When testing this recognizer on a held-out evaluation set extracted from the TOEFL® test, a word error rate (WER) of 33.0% [1] is observed. This recognizer was used as the *seed* recognizer in our experiments.

4 Experiments

We collected a set of audio responses from the TOEIC® test, focusing on opinion questions. This data set was randomly selected from different first-language (L1) and English speaking proficiency levels. Then, these audio files were manually transcribed. In our experiments, 1470 responses were used for LM adaptation and the remaining 184 responses were used to evaluate speech recognition

[1] ASR on non-native speech is more difficult than on native speech for various reasons (Livescu and Glass, 2000). However, a high WER does not rule out the possibility of using ASR outputs for automated scoring, especially when relying on delivery related features. For example, (Chen et al., 2009) shows that several pronunciation features' contributions for assessment, measured as Pearson correlations between the featuers and human scores, only drop about 10% to 20% when using ASR outputs with a WER as high as 50% compared to using human transcriptions.

accuracy. When using the seed recognizer without any adaptation, the WER on the evaluation set is 42.8%, which is much higher than the accuracy achieved on the TOEFL® data (33.0%). Using the ordinary supervised training, adapting LMs using these 1470 manual transcriptions, the WER is reduced to 34.7%, close to the performance on the in-domain TOEFL® data. Note that a fixed dictionary with a vocabulary size of about 20,000 words, which in general is much larger than the vocabulary mastered by non-native test takers, was used in our experiment.

4.1 Unsupervised LM adaptation

Using the seed recognizer trained on the TOEFL® data, we recognized 1470 adaptation responses and selected varying amounts of ASR outputs for LM adaptation. From ASR outputs of all responses, we selected the responses with high confidence scores estimated by the seed recognizer so that we could use the ASR outputs with higher recognition accuracy on the LM adaptation task. We used two methods to measure the confidence score for each response from word-level confidence scores. First, we took the average of all word confidence scores a response contains, as shown in Equation 1.

$$Conf_{perWord} = \frac{1}{N}\sum_{i=1}^{N} conf(w_i) \quad (1)$$

where $conf(w_i)$ is the confidence score of word, w_i. The other method we used considers each word's duration, as shown in Equation 2.

$$Conf_{perSec} = \frac{\sum_{i=1}^{N} d(w_i) * conf(w_i)}{\sum_{i=1}^{N} d(w_i)} \quad (2)$$

where $d(w_i)$ is the duration of w_i.

In Figure 1, we showed the WER after running unsupervised LM adaptation, where the adaptation responses were selected if they had high word-based ($Conf_{perWord}$) or duration-based ($Conf_{perSec}$) confidence scores. The data sizes used for adaptation vary from 0% (without any adaptation) to 100% (using all adaptation data). We observe continuous reduction of WER when using more and more adaptation data. Selecting responses by the word-based confidence scores performs a little better than the selection method based on the confidence scores normalized by corresponding word durations. However, there is no significant difference between these two selection criteria.

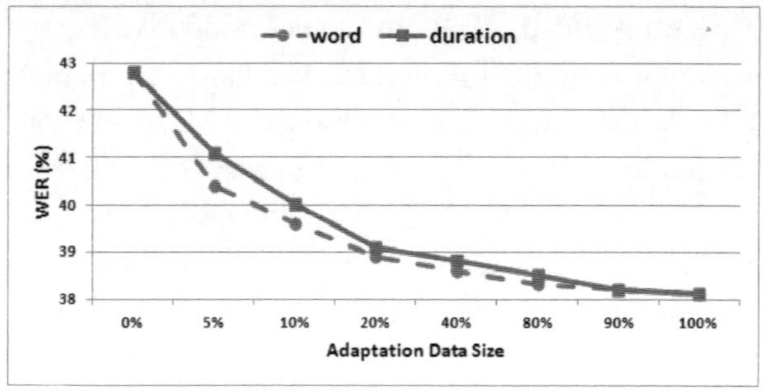

Figure 1: Unsupervised LM adaptation performance using different sizes of development set data.

ASR accuracy may vary within each response. Therefore, instead of using entire responses, we also explored using smaller units for LM adaptation. All of the ASR outputs were split into word sequences with fixed lengths (10-15 words), and the ones with higher per-word confidence scores ($Conf_{perWord}$) were extracted for model adaptation. Our experiment shows that using word-sequence pieces rather than entire responses leads to a faster WER reduction. When only using 5% of the adaptation data, we obtained 3.5% absolute WER reduction compared to the baseline result without adaptation. Note that we only obtained 2.5% absolute WER reduction when using entire responses in adaptation.

4.2 Web data LM adaptation

Given around 40% WER when using our seed ASR, unsupervised learning faces the issue that many recognition errors were included in model adaptation. Can we find another source to obtain LM adaptation inputs with fewer errors? To address this question, we explored building a training corpus from Web data based on test questions. We used BootCat (Baroni and Bernardini, 2004), a corpus building tool designed to collect data from the Web, to collect our LM adaptation data. Based on test prompts in the TOEIC® test, we manually generated search queries. After receiving the search queries, the BootCat tool searched the Web using the Microsoft Bing search engine. Then, top-ranked

Web pages were downloaded and texts on these Web pages were extracted. We examined the Web search results (including URLs and texts) returned by the BootCat tool. The returned Web data has varied matching rates among these prompts and are generally noisy.

By using only the default setup provided by the BootCat tool, we collected 5312 sentences in total. After a simple text normalization, we used the obtained Web data for LM adaptation, and the WER on the evaluation data was 38.5%. This WER result is a little higher than the WER result achieved by unsupervised LM adaptation (38.1%). Without transcribing any response from test-takers, the language model adaptation using Web data already helps to improve recognition accuracy. Then, we tried using both the Web data and the ASR hypotheses for adaptation, and we can further decreased the WER to 37.6%. This is lower than using the two LM adaptation data sets separately.

4.3 Semi-supervised approaches for LM adaptation

For semi-supervised LM adaptation, we replaced the speech responses of lower confidence scores with their corresponding human transcripts. We hoped that by using the responses with high confidence scores together with a small amount of human transcripts, we could get better performance by introducing less noise during adaptation. We set different thresholds for selecting the low confidence responses and replacing them with human transcripts. We find that just manually transcribing a limited amount of audio data gives us further WER reduction, compared to using unsupervised learning. After transcribing just 100 responses, 6.8% of 1470 responses in the adaptation data set, semi-supervised learning can achieve 61.73% of the WER reduction (8.1%) obtained by using the ordinary supervised training that requires transcription of all 1470 responses.

4.4 Discussion

In Table 1, we compared the performance of all the adaptation methods mentioned in this paper, including two unsupervised methods adapted using the ASR hypotheses and "related" Web data, and one semi-supervised method [2], replacing the ASR hypotheses of lower confidence scores with their corresponding human transcripts. For a convenient comparison, we also include the baseline (without LM adaptation) and the result of using the supervised adaptation. All the proposed unsupervised/semi-supervised methods can significantly improve the ASR performance compared to the baseline result. For projects with time limits, we can use these unsupervised/semi-supervised methods to help us get relatively good ASR outputs.

Table 1: The WER on the evaluation set using different LM adaptation methods.

baseline	*unsupervised*			*semi*	*super.*
	ASR	*Web*	*ASR&Web*		
42.8	38.1	38.5	37.6	37.8	34.7

5 Conclusions and Future Work

In this paper, we reported our experiments in applying several LM adaptation methods to automated speech scoring systems that require few, if any, human transcripts, which are expensive and slow to obtain for large-sized adaptation data sets. The unsupervised training (using ASR transcriptions from a seed ASR system) clearly shows higher accuracy than a ASR system without any domain adaptation. We also used test questions to collect related texts from Web. Even though such Web data may be noisy and its relatedness to real test responses is not always guaranteed, text data collected from the Web is helpful to adapt LMs to better fit the responses to test questions. To better cope with recognition errors brought on by using the unsupervised training method, we proposed using human transcriptions on a small amount of poorly recognized responses. Using such little human involvement further helps to obtain a lower WER. Therefore, based on the experiments described in this paper, we conclude that these novel LM adaptation methods provide promising solutions to let us skip the ordinary supervised training for LM adaptation tasks frequently used in automated speech scoring.

[2]The semi-supervised result was from replacing 100 low-confidence responses with human transcripts.

The reported experiments in this paper were conducted on a limited-size data set. We plan to increase the testing data to a larger size and hope to cover more types of test questions and spoken tests. In addition, we plan to investigate how to automatically generate Web search queries based on test questions.

References

M. Bacchiani and B. Roark. 2003. Unsupervised language model adaptation. In *2003 IEEE International Conference on Acoustics, Speech, and Signal Processing, 2003. Proceedings.(ICASSP'03)*.

M. Baroni and S. Bernardini. 2004. BootCaT: bootstrapping corpora and terms from the web. In *Proceedings of LREC*, volume 2004, page 13131316.

L. Chen, J. L Gauvain, L. Lamel, and G. Adda. 2003. Unsupervised language model adaptation for broadcast news. In *2003 IEEE International Conference on Acoustics, Speech, and Signal Processing, 2003. Proceedings.(ICASSP'03)*.

L. Chen, K. Zechner, and X Xi. 2009. Improved pronunciation features for construct-driven assessment of non-native spontaneous speech. In *NAACL-HLT*.

M. Eskenazi. 2009. An overview of spoken language technology for education. *Speech Communication*, 51(10):832–844.

K. Livescu and J. Glass. 2000. Lexical modeling of non-native speech for automatic speech recognition. In *Acoustics, Speech, and Signal Processing, 2000. ICASSP'00. Proceedings. 2000 IEEE International Conference on*, volume 3, pages 1683–1686.

T. Ng, M. Ostendorf, M. Y Hwang, M. Siu, I. Bulyko, and X. Lei. 2005. Web-data augmented language models for mandarin conversational speech recognition. In *Proc. ICASSP*, volume 1.

G. Riccardi and D. Z Hakkani-Tur. 2003. Active and unsupervised learning for automatic speech recognition. In *Proc. 8th European Conference on Speech Communication and Technology*.

R. Sarikaya, A. Gravano, and Y. Gao. 2005. Rapid language model development using external resources for new spoken dialog domains. In *Proc. ICASSP*, volume 1, pages 573–576.

G. Tur, D. Hakkani-Tur, and R. E Schapire. 2005. Combining active and semi-supervised learning for spoken language understanding. *Speech Communication*, 45(2):171–186.

Improving interpretation robustness in a tutorial dialogue system

Myroslava O. Dzikovska and **Elaine Farrow** and **Johanna D. Moore**
School of Informatics, University of Edinburgh
Edinburgh, EH8 9AB, United Kingdom
{m.dzikovska,elaine.farrow,j.moore}@ed.ac.uk

Abstract

We present an experiment aimed at improving interpretation robustness of a tutorial dialogue system that relies on detailed semantic interpretation and dynamic natural language feedback generation. We show that we can improve overall interpretation quality by combining the output of a semantic interpreter with that of a statistical classifier trained on the subset of student utterances where semantic interpretation fails. This improves on a previous result which used a similar approach but trained the classifier on a substantially larger data set containing all student utterances. Finally, we discuss how the labels from the statistical classifier can be integrated effectively with the dialogue system's existing error recovery policies.

1 Introduction

Giving students formative feedback as they interact with educational applications, such as simulated training environments, problem-solving tutors, serious games, and exploratory learning environments, is known to be important for effective learning (Shute, 2008). Suitable feedback can include context-appropriate confirmations, hints, and suggestions to help students refine their answers and increase their understanding of the subject. Providing this type of feedback automatically, in natural language, is the goal of tutorial dialogue systems (Aleven et al., 2002; Dzikovska et al., 2010b; Graesser et al., 1999; Jordan et al., 2006; Litman and Silliman, 2004; Khuwaja et al., 1994; Pon-Barry et al., 2004; VanLehn et al., 2007).

Much work in NLP for educational applications has focused on automated answer grading (Leacock and Chodorow, 2003; Pulman and Sukkarieh, 2005; Mohler et al., 2011). Automated answer assessment systems are commonly trained on large text corpora. They compare the text of a student answer with the text of one or more reference answers supplied by human instructors and calculate a score reflecting the quality of the match. Automated grading methods are integrated into intelligent tutoring systems (ITS) by having system developers anticipate both correct and incorrect responses to each question, with the system choosing the best match (Graesser et al., 1999; Jordan et al., 2006; Litman and Silliman, 2004; VanLehn et al., 2007). Such systems have wide domain coverage and are robust to ill-formed input. However, as matching relies on shallow features and does not provide semantic representations of student answers, this approach is less suitable for dynamically generating adaptive natural language feedback (Dzikovska et al., 2013).

Real-time simulations and serious games are commonly used in STEM learning environments to increase student engagement and support exploratory learning (Rutten et al., 2012; Mayo, 2007). Natural language dialogue can help improve learning in such systems by asking students to explain their reasoning, either directly during interaction, or during post-problem reflection (Aleven et al., 2002; Pon-Barry et al., 2004; Dzikovska et al., 2010b). Interpretation of student answers in such systems needs to be grounded in the current state of a dynamically changing environment, and feedback may also be generated dynamically to reflect the changing system state. This is typically achieved by employing hand-crafted parsers and semantic interpreters to produce structured semantic representations of student input, which are then used to instantiate abstract tutorial strategies with the help of a natural language generation system (Freedman, 2000; Clark et al., 2005; Dzikovska et al., 2010b).

Rule-based semantic interpreters are known to suffer from robustness and coverage problems, failing to interpret out-of-grammar student utterances. In the event of an interpretation failure, most systems have little information on which to base a feedback decision and typically respond by asking the student to rephrase, or simply give away the answer (though more sophisticated strategies are sometimes possible, see Section 4). While statistical scoring approaches are more robust, they may still suffer from coverage issues when system designers fail to anticipate the full range of expected student answers. In one study of a statistical system, a human judge labeled 33% of student utterances as not matching any of the anticipated responses, meaning that the system had no information to use as a basis for choosing the next action and fell back on a single strategy, giving away the answer (Jordan et al., 2009).

Recently, Dzikovska et al. (2012b) developed an annotated corpus of student responses (henceforth, the SRA corpus) with the goal of facilitating dynamic generation of tutorial feedback.[1] Student responses are assigned to one of 5 domain- and task-independent classes that correspond to typical flaws found in student answers. These classes can be used to help a system choose a feedback strategy based only on the student answer and a single reference answer. Dzikovska et al. (2013) showed that a statistical classifier trained on this data set can be used in combination with a semantic interpreter to significantly improve the overall quality of natural language interpretation in a dialogue-based ITS. The best results were obtained by using the classifier to label the utterances that the semantic interpreter failed to process.

In this paper we further extend this result by showing that we can obtain similar results by training the classifier directly on the subset of utterances that cannot be processed by the interpreter. The distribution of labels across the classes is different in this subset compared to the rest of the corpus. Therefore we can train a subset-specific classifier, reducing the amount of annotated training data needed without compromising performance of the combined system.

The rest of the paper is organized as follows. In Section 2 we describe an architecture for combining semantic interpretation and classification in a system with dynamic natural language feedback generation. In Section 3 we describe an experiment to improve combined system performance using a classifier trained only on non-interpretable utterances. We discuss future improvements in Section 4.

2 Background

The SRA corpus is made up of two subsets: (1) the SciEntsBank subset, consisting of written responses to assessment questions (Nielsen et al., 2008b), and (2) the Beetle subset consisting of utterances collected from student interactions with the BEETLE II tutorial dialogue system (Dzikovska et al., 2010b). The SRA corpus annotation scheme defines 5 classes of student answers ("correct", "partially-correct-incomplete", "contradictory", "irrelevant" and "non-domain"). Each utterance is assigned to one of the 5 classes based on pre-existing manual annotations (Dzikovska et al., 2012b).

We focus on the Beetle subset because the Beetle data comes from an implemented system, meaning that we also have access to the semantic interpretations of student utterances produced by the BEETLE II interpretation component. The system uses fine-grained semantic analysis to produce detailed diagnoses of student answers in terms of correct, incorrect, missing and irrelevant parts. We developed a set of rules to map these diagnoses onto the SRA corpus 5-class annotation scheme to support system evaluation (Dzikovska et al., 2012a).

In our previous work (Dzikovska et al., 2013), we used this mapping as the basis for combining the output of the BEETLE II semantic interpreter with the output of a statistical classifier, using a rule-based policy to determine which label to use for each instance. If the label from the semantic interpreter is chosen, then the full range of detailed feedback strategies can be used, based on the corresponding semantic representation. If the classifier's label is chosen, then the system can fall back to using content-free prompts, choosing an appropriate

[1] `http://www.cs.york.ac.uk/semeval-2013/task7/index.php?id=data`

prompt based on the SRA corpus label.

We evaluated 3 rule-based combination policies, chosen to reduce the effects of the errors that the semantic interpreter makes, and taking into account tutoring goals such as reducing student frustration. The best performing policy takes the classifier's output if and only if the semantic interpreter is unable to process the utterance.[2] This allows the system to choose from a wider set of content-free prompts instead of always telling the student that the utterance was not understood.

As discussed earlier, non-interpretable utterances present a problem for both rule-based and statistical approaches. Therefore, we carried out an additional set of experiments, focusing on the performance of system combinations that use policies designed to address non-interpretable utterances. We discuss our results and future directions in the rest of the paper.

3 Improving Interpretation Robustness

3.1 Experimental Setup

The Beetle portion of the SRA corpus contains 3941 unique student answers to 47 different explanation questions. Each question is associated with one or more reference answers provided by expert tutors, and each student answer is manually annotated with the label assigned by the BEETLE II interpreter and a gold-standard correctness label.

In our experiments, we follow the procedure described in (Dzikovska et al., 2013), using 10-fold cross-validation to evaluate the performance of the various stand-alone and combined systems. We report the per-class F_1 scores as evaluation metrics, using the macro-averaged F_1 score as the primary evaluation metric.

Dzikovska et al. (2013) used a statistical classifier based on lexical overlap, taken from (Dzikovska et al., 2012a), and evaluated 3 different rule-based policies for combining its output with that of the semantic interpreter. In two of those policies the interpreter's output is always used if it is available, and the classifier's label is used for a (subset of) non-interpretable utterances:

1. `NoReject`: the classifier's label is used in all cases where semantic interpretation fails, thus creating a system that never rejects student input as non-interpretable
2. `NoRejectCorrect`: the classifier's label is used for non-interpretable utterances which are labeled as "correct" by the classifier. This more conservative policy aims to ensure that correct student answers are always accepted, but incorrect answers may still be rejected with a request to rephrase.

We conducted a new experiment to evaluate these two policies together with an enhanced classifier, discussed in the next section.

3.2 Classifier

For this paper, we extended the classifier from the previous study (Dzikovska et al., 2013), which we will call `Sim8`, with additional features to improve handling of lexical variability and negation.

`Sim8` uses the Weka 3.6.2 implementation of C4.5 pruned decision trees, with default parameters. It uses 8 features based on lexical overlap similarity metrics provided by Perl's `Text::Similarity` package v.0.09: 4 metrics measuring overlap between the student answer and the expected answer, and the same 4 metrics applied to the student's answer and the question text.

In our enhanced classifier, `Sim20`, we extended the baseline feature set with 12 additional features. 8 of these are direct analogs of the baseline features, this time computed on the stemmed text to reduce the impact of syntactic variation, using the Porter stemmer from the `Lingua::Stem` package.[3] In addition, 4 features were added to improve negation handling and thus detection of contradictions. These are:

- `QuestionNeg, AnswerNeg`: features indicating the presence of a negation marker in the question and the student's answer respectively, detected using a regular expression. We distinguish three cases: a negation marker

[2]We will refer to such utterances as "non-interpretable" following (Bohus and Rudnicky, 2005).

[3]We also experimented with features that involve removing stop words before computing similarity scores, and with using SVMs for classification, but failed to obtain better performance. We continue to investigate different SVM kernels and alternative classification algorithms such as random forests for our future work.

	Standalone			Sem. Interp. + Sim20		Sem. Interp. + Sim20NI	
	Sem. Interp.	Sim8	Sim20	no_rej	no_rej_corr	no_rej	no_rej_corr
correct	0.66	0.71	0.71	0.70	0.70	0.70	0.70
pc_inc	0.48	0.38	0.40	0.51	0.48	0.50	0.48
contra	0.27	0.40	0.45	0.47	0.27	0.51	0.27
irrlvnt	0.21	0.05	0.08	0.22	0.21	0.22	0.21
nondom	0.65	0.73	0.78	0.83	0.65	0.83	0.65
macro avg	0.45	0.45	0.48	**0.55**	0.46	**0.55**	0.46

Table 1: F_1 scores for three stand-alone systems, and for combination systems using the Sim20 and Sim20NI classifiers together with the semantic interpreter. Stand-alone performance for Sim20NI is not shown since it was trained only on the non-interpretable data subset and is therefore not applicable for the complete data set.

likely to be associated with domain content (e.g., "not connected"); a negation marker more likely to be associated with general expressions of confusion (such as "don't know"); and no negation marker present.

- BestOverlapNeg: true if the reference answer that has the highest F_1 overlap with the student answer includes a negation marker.
- BestOverlapPolarityMatch: a flag computed from the values of AnswerNeg and BestOverlapNeg. Again, we distinguish three cases: they have the same polarity (both the student answer and the reference answer contain negation markers, or both have no negation markers); they have opposite polarity; or the student answer contains a negation marker associated with an expression of confusion, as described above.

3.3 Evaluation

Evaluation results are shown in Table 1. Unless otherwise specified, all performance differences discussed in the text are significant on an approximate randomization significance test with 10,000 iterations (Yeh, 2000).

Adding the new features to create the Sim20 classifier resulted in a performance improvement compared to the Sim8 classifier, raising macro-averaged F_1 from 0.45 to 0.48, with an improvement in contradiction detection as intended. But these improvements did not translate into improvements in the combined systems. Combinations using Sim20 performed exactly the same as the combinations using Sim8 (not shown due to space limitations, see (Dzikovska et al., 2013)). Clearly, more sophisticated features are needed to obtain further performance gains in the combined systems.

However, we noted that the subset of non-interpretable utterances in the corpus has a different distribution of labels compared to the full data set. In the complete data set, 1665 utterances (42%) are labeled as correct and 1049 (27%) as contradictory. Among the 1416 utterances considered non-interpretable by the semantic interpreter, 371 (26%) belong to the "correct" class, and 598 (42%) to "contradictory" (other classes have similar distributions in both subsets). We therefore hypothesized that a combination system that uses the classifier output only if an utterance is non-interpretable, may benefit from employing a classifier trained specifically on this subset rather than on the whole data set.

If our hypothesis is true, it offers an interesting possibility for combining rule-based and statistical classifiers in similar setups: if the classifier can be trained using only the examples that are problematic for the rule-based system, it can provide improved robustness at a significantly lower annotation cost.

We therefore trained another classifier, Sim20NI, using the same feature set as Sim20, but this time using only the instances rejected as non-interpretable by the semantic interpreter in each cross-validation fold (1416 utterances, 36% of all data instances). We again used the NoReject and NoRejectCorrect policies to combine the output of Sim20NI with that of the semantic interpreter. Evaluation results confirmed our hypothesis. The system combinations that use Sim20 and Sim20NI perform identically on macro-averaged F_1, with `NoReject` being the best combination policy in both cases and significantly outperforming the semantic interpreter alone. However, the `Sim2ONI` classifier has the advantage of needing significantly less annotated data to achieve this performance.

4 Discussion and Future Work

Our research focuses on combining deep and shallow processing by supplementing fine-grained semantic interpretations from a rule-based system with more coarse-grained classification labels. Alternatively, we could try to learn structured semantic representations from annotated text (Zettlemoyer and Collins, 2005; Wong and Mooney, 2007; Kwiatkowski et al., 2010), or to learn more fine-grained assessment labels (Nielsen et al., 2008a). However, such approaches require substantially larger annotation effort. Therefore, we believe it is worth exploring the use of the simpler 5-label annotation scheme from the SRA corpus. We previously showed that it is possible to improve system performance by combining the output of a symbolic interpreter with that of a statistical classifier (Dzikovska et al., 2013). The best combination policy used the statistical classifier to label utterances rejected as non-interpretable by the rule-based interpreter.

In this paper, we showed that similar results can be achieved by training the classifier only on non-interpretable utterances, rather than on the whole labeled corpus. The student answers that the interpreter has difficulty with have a distinct distribution, which is effectively utilized by training a classifier only on this subset. This reduces the amount of annotated training data needed, reducing the amount of manual labor required.

In future, we will further investigate the best combination of parsing and statistical classification in systems that offer sophisticated error recovery policies for non-understandings. Our top-performing policy, `NoReject`, uses deep parsing and semantic interpretation to produce a detailed semantic analysis for the majority of utterances, and falls back on a shallower statistical classifier for utterances that are difficult for the interpreter. This policy assumes that it is always better to use a content-free prompt than to reject a non-interpretable student utterance. However, interpretation problems can arise from incorrect uses of terminology, and learning to speak in the language of the domain has been positively correlated with learning outcomes (Steinhauser et al., 2011). Therefore, rejecting some non-interpretable answers as incorrect could be a valid tutoring strategy (Sagae et al., 2010; Dzikovska et al., 2010a).

The BEETLE II system offers several error recovery strategies intended to help students phrase their answers in more acceptable ways by giving a targeted help message, e.g., "I am sorry, I'm having trouble understanding. Paths cannot be broken, only components can be broken" (Dzikovska et al., 2010a). Therefore, it may be worthwhile to consider other combination policies. We evaluated the `NoRejectCorrect` policy, which uses the statistical classifier to identify correct answers rejected by the semantic interpreter and asks for rephrasings in other cases. Using this policy resulted in only a small improvement in system performance. A different classifier geared towards more accurate identification of correct answers may help, and we are planning to investigate this option in the future.

Alternatively, we could consider a combination policy which looks for rejected answers that the classifier identifies as contradictory and changes the wording of the targeted help message to indicate that the student may have made a mistake, instead of apologizing for the misunderstanding. This has the potential to help students learn correct terminology rather than presenting the issue as strictly an interpretation failure.

Ultimately, all combination policies must be tested with users to ensure that improved robustness translates into improved system effectiveness. We have previously studied the effectiveness of our targeted help strategies with respect to improving learning outcomes (Dzikovska et al., 2010a). A similar study is required to evaluate our combination strategies.

Acknowledgments

We thank Natalie Steinhauser, Gwendolyn Campbell, Charlie Scott, Simon Caine and Sarah Denhe for help with data collection and preparation. The research reported here was supported by the US ONR award N000141010085.

References

Vincent Aleven, Octav Popescu, and Kenneth R. Koedinger. 2002. Pilot-testing a tutorial dialogue system that supports self-explanation. In *Proc. of ITS-02 conference*, pages 344–354.

Dan Bohus and Alexander Rudnicky. 2005. Sorry, I didn't catch that! - An investigation of non-understanding errors and recovery strategies. In *Proceedings of SIGdial-2005*, Lisbon, Portugal.

Brady Clark, Oliver Lemon, Alexander Gruenstein, ElizabethOwen Bratt, John Fry, Stanley Peters, Heather Pon-Barry, Karl Schultz, Zack Thomsen-Gray, and Pucktada Treeratpituk. 2005. A general purpose architecture for intelligent tutoring systems. In JanC.J. Kuppevelt, Laila Dybkjr, and NielsOle Bernsen, editors, *Advances in Natural Multimodal Dialogue Systems*, volume 30 of *Text, Speech and Language Technology*, pages 287–305. Springer Netherlands.

Myroslava O. Dzikovska, Johanna D. Moore, Natalie Steinhauser, and Gwendolyn Campbell. 2010a. The impact of interpretation problems on tutorial dialogue. In *Proc. of ACL 2010 Conference Short Papers*, pages 43–48.

Myroslava O. Dzikovska, Johanna D. Moore, Natalie Steinhauser, Gwendolyn Campbell, Elaine Farrow, and Charles B. Callaway. 2010b. Beetle II: a system for tutoring and computational linguistics experimentation. In *Proc. of ACL 2010 System Demonstrations*, pages 13–18.

Myroslava O. Dzikovska, Peter Bell, Amy Isard, and Johanna D. Moore. 2012a. Evaluating language understanding accuracy with respect to objective outcomes in a dialogue system. In *Proc. of EACL-12 Conference*, pages 471–481.

Myroslava O. Dzikovska, Rodney D. Nielsen, and Chris Brew. 2012b. Towards effective tutorial feedback for explanation questions: A dataset and baselines. In *Proc. of 2012 Conference of NAACL: Human Language Technologies*, pages 200–210.

Myroslava O. Dzikovska, Elaine Farrow, and Johanna D. Moore. 2013. Combining semantic interpretation and statistical classification for improved explanation processing in a tutorial dialogue system. In *In Proceedings of the The 16th International Conference on Artificial Intelligence in Education (AIED 2013)*, Memphis, TN, USA, July.

Reva Freedman. 2000. Using a reactive planner as the basis for a dialogue agent. In *Proceedings of the Thirteenth Florida Artificial Intelligence Research Symposium (FLAIRS 2000)*, pages 203–208.

A. C. Graesser, K. Wiemer-Hastings, P. Wiemer-Hastings, and R. Kreuz. 1999. Autotutor: A simulation of a human tutor. *Cognitive Systems Research*, 1:35–51.

Pamela Jordan, Maxim Makatchev, Umarani Pappuswamy, Kurt VanLehn, and Patricia Albacete. 2006. A natural language tutorial dialogue system for physics. In *Proc. of 19th Intl. FLAIRS conference*, pages 521–527.

Pamela Jordan, Diane Litman, Michael Lipschultz, and Joanna Drummond. 2009. Evidence of misunderstandings in tutorial dialogue and their impact on learning. In *Proc. of 14th International Conference on Artificial Intelligence in Education*, pages 125–132.

Ramzan A. Khuwaja, Martha W. Evens, Joel A. Michael, and Allen A. Rovick. 1994. Architecture of CIRCSIM-tutor (v.3): A smart cardiovascular physiology tutor. In *Proc. of 7th Annual IEEE Computer-Based Medical Systems Symposium*.

Tom Kwiatkowski, Luke Zettlemoyer, Sharon Goldwater, and Mark Steedman. 2010. Inducing probabilistic CCG grammars from logical form with higher-order unification. In *Proc. of EMNLP-2010 Conference*, pages 1223–1233.

Claudia Leacock and Martin Chodorow. 2003. C-rater: Automated scoring of short-answer questions. *Computers and the Humanities*, 37(4):389–405.

Diane J. Litman and Scott Silliman. 2004. ITSPOKE: an intelligent tutoring spoken dialogue system. In *Demonstration Papers at HLT-NAACL 2004*, pages 5–8, Boston, Massachusetts.

Merrilea J. Mayo. 2007. Games for science and engineering education. *Commun. ACM*, 50(7):30–35, July.

Michael Mohler, Razvan Bunescu, and Rada Mihalcea. 2011. Learning to grade short answer questions using semantic similarity measures and dependency graph alignments. In *Proceedings of the 49th Annual Meeting of the Association for Computational Linguistics: Human Language Technologies*, pages 752–762, Portland, Oregon, USA, June. Association for Computational Linguistics.

Rodney D. Nielsen, Wayne Ward, and James H. Martin. 2008a. Learning to assess low-level conceptual understanding. In *Proc. of 21st Intl. FLAIRS Conference*, pages 427–432.

Rodney D. Nielsen, Wayne Ward, James H. Martin, and Martha Palmer. 2008b. Annotating students' understanding of science concepts. In *Proceedings of the Sixth International Language Resources and Evaluation Conference, (LREC08)*, Marrakech, Morocco.

Heather Pon-Barry, Brady Clark, Karl Schultz, Elizabeth Owen Bratt, and Stanley Peters. 2004. Advantages of spoken language interaction in dialogue-based intelligent tutoring systems. In *Proc. of ITS-2004 Conference*, pages 390–400.

Stephen G Pulman and Jana Z Sukkarieh. 2005. Automatic short answer marking. In *Proceedings of the Second Workshop on Building Educational Applications Using NLP*, pages 9–16, Ann Arbor, Michigan, June. Association for Computational Linguistics.

Nico Rutten, Wouter R. van Joolingen, and Jan T. van der Veen. 2012. The learning effects of computer simulations in science education. *Computers and Education*, 58(1):136 – 153.

Alicia Sagae, W. Lewis Johnson, and Stephen Bodnar. 2010. Validation of a dialog system for language learners. In *Proceedings of the 11th Annual Meeting of the Special Interest Group on Discourse and Dialogue*, SIGDIAL '10, pages 241–244, Stroudsburg, PA, USA. Association for Computational Linguistics.

Valerie J Shute. 2008. Focus on formative feedback. *Review of educational research*, 78(1):153–189.

Natalie B. Steinhauser, Gwendolyn E. Campbell, Leanne S. Taylor, Simon Caine, Charlie Scott, Myroslava O. Dzikovska, and Johanna D. Moore. 2011. Talk like an electrician: Student dialogue mimicking behavior in an intelligent tutoring system. In *Proc. of 15th international conference on Artificial Intelligence in Education*, pages 361–368.

Kurt VanLehn, Pamela Jordan, and Diane Litman. 2007. Developing pedagogically effective tutorial dialogue tactics: Experiments and a testbed. In *Proc. of SLaTE Workshop on Speech and Language Technology in Education*, Farmington, PA, October.

Yuk Wah Wong and Raymond J. Mooney. 2007. Learning synchronous grammars for semantic parsing with lambda calculus. In *Proceedings of the 45th Annual Meeting of the Association for Computational Linguistics (ACL-2007)*, Prague, Czech Republic, June.

Alexander Yeh. 2000. More accurate tests for the statistical significance of result differences. In *Proceedings of the 18th International Conference on Computational linguistics (COLING 2000)*, pages 947–953, Stroudsburg, PA, USA. Association for Computational Linguistics.

Luke S. Zettlemoyer and Michael Collins. 2005. Learning to Map Sentences to Logical Form: Structured Classification with Probabilistic Categorial Grammars. In *Proceedings of the 21th Annual Conference on Uncertainty in Artificial Intelligence (UAI-05)*, pages 658–666, Arlington, Virginia. AUAI Press.

Detecting Missing Hyphens in Learner Text

Aoife Cahill*, **Martin Chodorow**†, **Susanne Wolff*** **and Nitin Madnani***

* Educational Testing Service, 660 Rosedale Road, Princeton, NJ 08541, USA
{acahill, swolff, nmadnani}@ets.org
† Hunter College and the Graduate Center, City University of New York, NY 10065, USA
martin.chodorow@hunter.cuny.edu

Abstract

We present a method for automatically detecting missing hyphens in English text. Our method goes beyond a purely dictionary-based approach and also takes context into account. We evaluate our model on artificially generated data as well as naturally occurring learner text. Our best-performing model achieves high precision and reasonable recall, making it suitable for inclusion in a system that gives feedback to language learners.

1 Introduction

While errors of punctuation are not as frequent, nor often as serious, as some of the other typical mistakes that learners make, they are nevertheless an important consideration for students aiming to improve the overall quality of their writing. In this paper we focus on the error of missing hyphens. The following example is a typical mistake made by a student writer:

(1) Schools may have more <u>after school</u> sports.

In this case the tokens *after* and *school* should be hyphenated as they modify the noun *sports*. However, in Example (2) a hyphen between *after* and *school* would be incorrect, since in this instance *after* functions as as the head of a prepositional phrase modifying *went*.

(2) I went to the dentist <u>after school</u> today.

These examples illustrate that purely dictionary-based approaches to detecting missing hyphens are not likely to be sophisticated enough to differentiate the contexts in which a hyphen is required. In addition, learner text frequently contains other grammatical and spelling errors, further complicating automatic error detection. Example (3) contains an error *father like* instead of *father likes to*. This causes difficulty for automated hyphenation systems because *like* is a frequent suffix of hyphenated words and *play* can function as a noun.

(3) My <u>father like</u> play basketball with me.

In this paper, we propose a classifier-based approach to automatically detecting missing hyphen errors. The goal of our system is to detect missing hyphen errors and provide feedback to language learners. Therefore, we place more importance on the precision of the system than recall. We train our model on features that take the context of a pair of words into account, as well as other discriminative features. We present a number of evaluations on both artificially generated errors and naturally occurring learner errors and show that our classifiers achieve high precision and reasonable recall.

2 Related Work

The task of detecting missing hyphens is related to previous work on detecting punctuation errors. One of the classes of errors in the Helping Our Own (HOO) 2011 shared task (Dale and Kilgarriff, 2011) was punctuation. Comma errors are the most frequent kind of punctuation error made by learners. Israel et al. (2012) present a model for detecting these kinds of errors in learner texts. They train CRF models on sentences from unedited essays written by high-level college students and show that they performs well on detecting errors in learner text. As far as we are aware, the HOO 2011 system description of Rozovskaya et al. (2011) is the only work to specifically reference hyphen errors. They use rules derived from frequencies in the training corpus to determine whether a hyphen was required between two words separated by white space.

The task of detecting missing hyphens is related to the task of inserting punctuation into the output of unpunctuated text (for example, the output of speech recognition, automatic generation, machine translation, etc.). Systems that are built on the output of speech recognition can obviously take features like prosody into account. In our case, we are dealing only with written text. Gravano et al. (2009) present an n-gram-based model for automatically adding punctuation and capitalization to the output of an ASR system, *without* taking any of the speech signal information into account. They conclude that more training data, rather than wider n-gram contexts leads to a greater improvement in accuracy.

3 Baselines

We implement three baseline systems which we will later compare to our classification approach. The first baseline is a naïve heuristic that predicts a missing hyphen between bigrams that appear hyphenated in the Collins Dictionary.[1] As a somewhat less-naïve baseline, we implement a heuristic that predicts a missing hyphen between bigrams that occur hyphenated more than 1,000 times in Wikipedia. A third baseline is a heuristic that predicts a missing hyphen between bigrams where the probability of the hyphenated form as estimated from Wikipedia is greater than 0.66, meaning that the hyphenated bigram is twice as likely as the non-hyphenated bigram. This baseline is similar to the approach taken by Rozovskaya et al. (2011), except that the probabilities are estimated from a much larger corpus.

4 System Description

Using the features in Table 1, we build a logistic regression model which assigns a probability to the likelihood of a hyphen occurring between two words, w_i and w_{i+1}. As we are primarily interested in using this system for giving feedback to language learners, we require very high precision. Therefore,

Tokens	$w_{i-1}, w_i, w_{i+1}, w_{i+2}$
Stems	$s_{i-1}, s_i, s_{i+1}, s_{i+2}$
Tags	$t_{i-1}, t_i, t_{i+1}, t_{i+2}$
Bigrams	w_i–w_{i+1}, s_i–s_{i+1}, t_i–t_{i+1}
Dict	Does the hyphenated form appear in the Collins dictionary?
Prob	What is the probability of the word bigram appearing hyphenated in Wikipedia?
Distance	Distance to following and preceding verb, noun
Verb/Noun	Is there a verb/noun preceding/following this bigram

Table 1: Features used in all models. Positive instances are those where there was a hyphen between w_i and w_{i+1} in the data. Stems are generated using NLTK's implementation of the Lancaster Stemmer, and tags are obtained from the Stanford Parser.

we only predict a missing hyphen error when the probability of the prediction is >0.99.

We experiment with two different sources of training data, in addition to their combination. We first train on well-edited text, using almost 1.8 million sentences from the San Jose Mercury News corpus.[2] For training, hyphenated words are automatically split (i.e. *well-known* becomes *well known*). The positive examples for the classifier are all bigrams where a hyphen was removed. Negative examples consist of bigrams where there was no hyphen in the training data. Since this is over 99% of the data, we randomly sample 3% of the negative examples for training. We also restrict the negative examples to only the most likely contexts, where a context is defined as a part-of-speech bigram. A list of possible contexts in which hyphens occur is extracted from the entire training set. Only contexts that occur more than 20 times are selected during training. All contexts are evaluated during testing. Table 2 lists some of the most frequent contexts with examples of when they should be hyphenated and when they should remain unhyphenated.

The second data source for training the model comes from pairs of revisions from Wikipedia articles. Following Cahill et al. (2013), we automatically extract a corpus of error annotations for miss-

[1] LDC catalog number LDC93T1

[2] LDC catalog number LDC93T3A.

Context	Hyphenated	Unhyphenated
NN NN	terrific *truck-stop* waitress	a *quake insurance* surcharge
CD CD	*Twenty-two* thousand	the *126 million* Americans
JJ NN	an *early-morning* blaze	an *entire practice* session
CD NN	a *two-year* contract	about *600 tank* cars
NN VBN	a *court-ordered* program	a *letter delivered* today

Table 2: Some frequent likely POS contexts for hyphenation, with examples from the Brown corpus.

	TP	P	R	F
Baseline				
Collins dict	397	40.5	19.2	26.0
Wiki Counts-1000	359	39.1	17.3	24.0
Wiki Probs-0.66	811	**85.5**	39.1	53.7
Classifier				
SJM-trained	1097	82.0	52.9	**64.3**
Wiki-revision-trained	1061	72.8	51.2	60.1
Combined	1106	80.9	53.4	**64.3**

Table 3: Results of evaluating on the Brown Corpus with hyphens removed

ing hyphens. This is done by extracting the plain text from every revision to every article and comparing adjacent pairs of revisions. For each article, chains of errors are detected, using the surrounding text to identify them. When a chain begins and ends with the same form, it is ignored. Only the first and last points in an error chain are retained for training. An example chain is the following: It has been an ancient {*focal point* → *location* → *focal point* → *focal-point*} of trade and migration., where we would extract the correction *focal point* → *focal-point*. In total, we extract a corpus of 390,298 sentences containing missing hyphen error annotations.

Finally, we combine both data sources.

5 Evaluating on Artificial Data

Since there are large corpora of well-edited text readily available, it is easy to evaluate on artificial data. For testing, we take 24,243 sentences from the Brown corpus and automatically remove hyphens from the 2,072 hyphenated words (but not free-standing dashes). Each system makes a prediction for all bigrams about whether a hyphen should appear between the pair of words. We measure the performance of each system in terms of precision, P, (how many of the missing hyphen errors predicted by the system were true errors), recall, R, (how many of the artificially removed hyphens the system detected as errors) and f-score, F, (the harmonic mean of precision and recall). The results are given in Table 3, and also include the raw number of true positives, TP, detected by each system. The results show that the baseline using Wikipedia probabilities obtains the highest precision, however with low recall. The classifiers trained on newswire text and the combined news and Wikipedia revision text achieve the highest overall f-score. Figure (1a) shows the Precision Recall curves for the Wikipedia baselines and the three classifiers. The curves mirror the results in the table, showing that the classifier trained on the newswire text, and the classifier trained on the combined data perform best. The Wikipedia counts baseline performs worst.

6 Evaluating on Learner Text

We carry out two evaluations of our system on learner text. We first evaluate on the missing hyphen errors contained in the CLC-FCE (Yannakoudakis et al., 2011). This corpus contains 1,244 exam scripts written by learners of English as part of the Cambridge ESOL First Certificate in English. In total, there are 173 instances of missing hyphen errors. The results are given in Table 4, and the precision recall curves are displayed in Figure (1b).

The results show that the classifiers consistently achieve high precision on this data set. This is as expected, given the high threshold set. Looking at the curves, it seems that a slightly lower threshold in this case may lead to better results. The curves show that the combined classifier is performing slightly better than the other two classifiers. The baselines are clearly not performing as well on this dataset.

While the overall size of the CLC-FCE data set is quite large, the low frequency of this kind of error means that the evaluation was carried out on a relatively small number of examples. For this reason, the reliability of the results may be called into question. There is, for instance, a striking difference between the f-scores for the Collins Dictionary base-

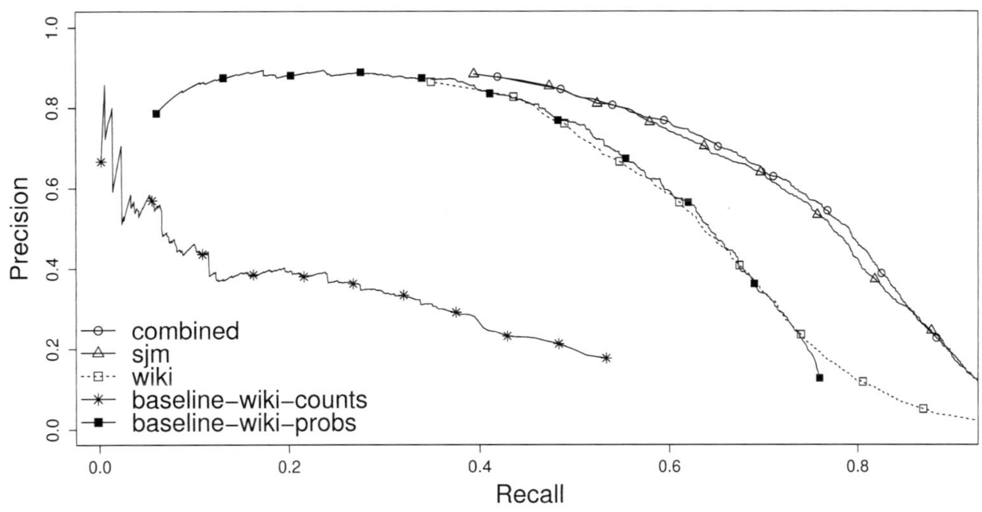

(a) Brown Corpus

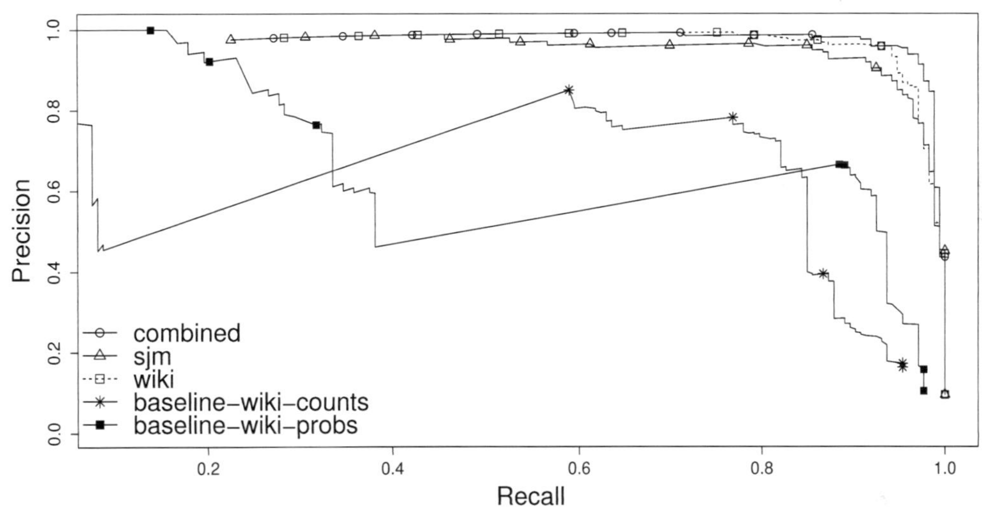

(b) CLC-FCE Corpus

Figure 1: Precision Recall curves for the Wikipedia baselines and the three classifiers.

	TP	P	R	F
Baseline				
Collins dict	131	64.5	75.7	69.7
Wiki Counts-1000	141	73.1	**81.5**	**77.0**
Wiki Probs-0.66	36	92.3	20.8	34.0
Classifier				
SJM-trained	60	84.5	34.7	49.2
Wiki-revision-trained	71	**98.6**	41.0	58.0
Combined	66	98.5	38.2	55.0

Table 4: Results of evaluating on the CLC-FCE dataset

line on the Brown corpus (26.0) and on the learner data (69.7). Inspection of the 131 true positives for the learner data reveal that 87 of these are cases of a single type, the word "make-up", which students often wrote without a hyphen in response to a prompt about a fashion and leisure show. Since the hyphenated form was in the Collins Dictionary, the baseline system was credited with detection of this error. However, when the 87 occurrences of "make up" are removed from the data set, the values of precision, recall and f-score for the Collins Dictionary baseline fall to 37.9, 51.2, and 42.9, respectively. This points to a problem for system evaluation that is more general than the low frequency of an error type, such as missing hyphens. The more general problem is that of non-independence among errors, which occurs when an individual writer contributes multiple times to an error count or when a particular prompt gives rise to many occurrences of the same error, as in the current case of "make-up".

Despite the problem of non-independent errors, a more accurate picture of system performance may nonetheless emerge with more evidence. Therefore, we evaluate system precision on a data set of 1,000 student GRE and TOEFL essays written by both native and nonnative speakers, across a wide range of proficiency levels and prompts. The essays, drawn from 295 prompts, ranged in length from 1 to 50 sentences, with an average of 378 words per essay.

We manually inspect a random sample of 100 instances where each system detected a missing hyphen. Two native-English speakers judged the correctness of the predictions using the Chicago Manual of Style as a guide.[3] Inter-annotator agreement on the binary classification task for 600 items was 0.79κ, showing high agreement. The results are given in Table 5.

	Total Predictions	Judge-1 Precision	Judge 2 Precision
Baseline			
Collins dict	416	11	8
Wiki Counts	2185	20	21
Wiki Probs	224	54	52
Classifier			
SJM-trained	421	62	69
Wiki-revision	577	43	41
Combined	450	60	62

Table 5: Precision results on 1000 student responses, estimated by randomly sampling 100 hyphen predictions of each system and manually evaluating them.

The results show that the first two baseline systems do not perform well on this essay data. This is mainly because they do not take context into account. Many of the errors made by these systems involved verb + preposition bigrams, as in Examples (4) and (5). Restricting the detection by probability clearly improves precision, but at the cost of recall (only 224 total instances of missing hyphen errors detected, the lowest of all 6 systems). In the manual evaluation, the system trained on the SJM corpus achieves the highest precision, though all precision figures are lower than the previous evaluations. Example (6) is a typical example of the kinds of false positives made by the classifier models.

(4) If these men were required to step-down after a limited number of years, the damage would be contained.

(5) These families may even choose to eat at-home than outside.

(6) The wellness program will save money in the long-term.

Future work will explore additional features that may help improve performance. A more thorough study will also be carried out to fully understand the differences in performance of the classifiers across corpora. Another direction to explore in future work is the related task of identifying extraneous hyphens in learner text. These are even less frequent than missing hyphens (87 annotated cases in the CLC-FCE corpus), but we believe a similar classification approach could be successful.

7 Conclusion

In this paper we presented a model for automatically detecting missing hyphen errors in learner text. We experimented with two kinds of training data, one well-edited text, and the other an automatically extracted corpus of error annotations. When evaluating on artificially generated errors in otherwise well-edited text, the classifiers generally performed better than the baseline systems. When evaluating on the small number of missing hyphen errors in the CLC-FCE corpus, the word-based models did well, though the classifiers also achieved consistently high precision. A precision-only evaluation on a sample of learner essays resulted in overall lower scores, but the classifier trained on well-edited text performed best. In general, the classifiers outperform the baseline, especially in terms of precision, showing that taking context into account when detecting these kinds of errors is important.

[3] http://www.chicagomanualofstyle.org

References

Aoife Cahill, Nitin Madnani, Joel Tetreault, and Diane Napolitano. 2013. Robust Systems for Preposition Error Correction Using Wikipedia Revisions. In *Proceedings of the Conference of the North American Chapter of the Association for Computational Linguistics: Human Language Technologies*, Atlanta, GA.

Robert Dale and Adam Kilgarriff. 2011. Helping Our Own: The HOO 2011 Pilot Shared Task. In *Proceedings of the Generation Challenges Session at the 13th European Workshop on Natural Language Generation*, pages 242–249, Nancy, France, September. Association for Computational Linguistics.

Agustin Gravano, Martin Jansche, and Michiel Bacchiani. 2009. Restoring punctuation and capitalization in transcribed speech. In *Acoustics, Speech and Signal Processing, 2009. ICASSP 2009. IEEE International Conference on*, pages 4741–4744. IEEE.

Ross Israel, Joel Tetreault, and Martin Chodorow. 2012. Correcting Comma Errors in Learner Essays, and Restoring Commas in Newswire Text. In *Proceedings of the 2012 Conference of the North American Chapter of the Association for Computational Linguistics: Human Language Technologies*, pages 284–294, Montréal, Canada, June. Association for Computational Linguistics.

Alla Rozovskaya, Mark Sammons, Joshua Gioja, and Dan Roth. 2011. University of Illinois System in HOO Text Correction Shared Task. In *Proceedings of the Generation Challenges Session at the 13th European Workshop on Natural Language Generation*, pages 263–266, Nancy, France, September. Association for Computational Linguistics.

Helen Yannakoudakis, Ted Briscoe, and Ben Medlock. 2011. A New Dataset and Method for Automatically Grading ESOL Texts. In *Proceedings of the 49th Annual Meeting of the Association for Computational Linguistics: Human Language Technologies*, pages 180–189, Portland, Oregon, USA, June. Association for Computational Linguistics.

Applying Machine Translation Metrics to Student-Written Translations

Lisa N. Michaud
Computer Science Department
Merrimack College
North Andover, MA, USA
michaudl@merrimack.edu

Patricia Ann McCoy
Language Department
Universidad de las Americas Puebla
Puebla, Mexico
patricia.mccoy@udlap.mx

Abstract

This paper discusses preliminary work investigating the application of Machine Translation (MT) metrics toward the evaluation of translations written by human novice (student) translators. We describe a study in which we apply the metric TERp (Translation Edit Rate Plus) to a corpus of student-written translations from Spanish to English and compare the judgments of TERp against assessments provided by a translation instructor.

1 Introduction

Extensive work in the field of Computational Linguistics has focused on the development of gold-standard metrics to automatically judge the accuracy of machine-generated translations. We are exploring whether these metrics, or a modified version thereof, may be applied to the translations generated by human novices.

While Machine Translation (MT) metrics have been shown to perform poorly when evaluating human-written translations due to their lack of tolerance for the high level of variation in human-written work, it is our belief that novice student translators keep much closer to the source text, and therefore will be easier to assess using automatic metrics.

Initial motivation for this work comes from developing the King Alfred translation environment (Michaud, 2008) supporting students of Anglo-Saxon English translating sentences into Modern English. Criticisms of the application of computational tools toward language learning have often highlighted the reality that the mainstays of modern language teaching—dialogue and a focus on communicative goals over syntactic perfectionism—parallel the shortcomings of a computational environment. While efforts continue to extend the state of the art toward making the computer a conversational partner, they nevertheless often fall short of providing the language learner with learning assistance in the task of communicative competence that can make a real difference within or without the classroom. The modern learner of ancient or "dead" languages, however, has fundamentally different needs; the focus is on translation from source texts into the learner's L1. An initial goal, therefore, was to provide the King Alfred system with ability to automatically judge and respond to student translations given a single instructor-provided reference.

The potential applications of this work extend beyond the learning of dead languages, however; translation skills in modern languages (until the field of MT reaches its full potential) are still needed for providing readers with access to cross-lingual information. The ability to assist translation instruction via a tutoring system outside of the classroom, or to assess translator skill automatically, is therefore greatly desirable.

The study described in this paper therefore focuses on a corpus of learner-written translations from a Spanish-English translation course; in Section 6 we discuss how these results may compare to those using a corpus of translations from Anglo-Saxon, which is one of our future tasks.

Reference	however	,	under	certain	contexts	a	translator	may	intentionally	strive to	produce	a	literal	translation	.
			S					S		P					
Hyp After Shifts	however	,	in	certain	contexts	a	translator	can	intentionally	try to	produce	a	literal	translation	.

Figure 1: Output from the TERp system.

2 Evaluating Student-Written Translations Using TERp

A primary challenge facing the assessment of translation fitness is the abstract nature of the definition of fitness with respect to the translating task. Most people approach this definition with two major foci: *fluency* (is it well-formed?) and *fidelity* (does it convey original meaning?) (Hovy et al., 2002). There are also stylistic concerns; translation can be defined as "rendering the meaning of a text into another language in the way the author intended the text" (Newmark, 1988)—and intention is difficult to precisely define. None of these viewpoints dictates that there exists only one way to write a translation.

We were drawn to the TERp (Translation Edit Rate Plus) translation metric (Snover et al., 2009) for our initial study because of its particular approach toward capturing this multiplicity of correct translations. Other metrics have addressed this issue; BLEU (Papineni et al., 2002), for example, uses multiple reference translations, in the hopes of capturing diversity through using diverse sources. The creators of TERp, however, create an alignment between reference and hypothesis strings in which direct matches are not required; they acknowledge synonymy by leveraging WordNet synsets (Fellbaum, 1998; Princeton University, 2010), in addition to using a stemmer, and a phrase table to handle probabilistic phrasal substitution. TERp also allows for words or phrases to be shifted into a different position, which nicely accounts for flexibility in terms of prepositional phrase or adverb placement or to handle modifiers that can take multiple forms.

There has been some dismissal of the appropriateness of MT metrics for Computer-Aided Language Learning (CALL) applications (cf. (McCarthy, 2006)) due to the fact that they often provide a holistic score comparing the hypothesis translation to one or more reference translations without identifying the source and nature of the differences. However, the output of TERp also includes more than a holistic score; there is complete documentation of the alignments, with tags identifying the "edits" required to line up the hypothesis with the reference, as seen in Figure 1. This is an excellent resource from the perspective of translation pedagogy. While the METEOR system (Agarwal and Lavie, 2008) also uses WordNet synonymy and a stemmer to similar purpose, we believe that TERp comes the closest to embracing the multiplicity of translation paths while at the same time flagging issues of fundamental concern in a pedagogical application of MT metrics.

3 Related Work

Other environments seeking to support student translations have addressed the issue of automatically determining translation accuracy. A English-Chinese translation environment described by (Wang and Seneff, 2007; Xu and Seneff, 2008) presents students with L1 sentences to translate into L2 speech. Because many of its L1 sentences are automatically generated, there is no possibility of prestored reference translations, so the system uses speech recognition to obtain the L2 sentence, and then parses both the English and Chinese sentences into a common interlingual representation in order to compare for accuracy. The authors report a high level of agreement between the system's judgments on translation acceptability compared to that of a human expert, but unfortunately, the system cannot give a finer-grained judgment on student performance than *accept* or *reject*.

Another English-Chinese system is described by (Shei and Pain, 2002), creators of TMT, the Translation Method Tutor. In this case, students are translating from their L2 (English) into their L1 (Chinese) using source sentences from Jane Austen's *Pride and Prejudice*, each selected to practice a particular linguistic structure. Students' translations are matched against four possible reference translations: word-to-word (MT generated), literal (MT-generated and then post-processed to obey word order rules), semantic (professional translations), and communicative (done by the authors), and the feedback provided to the student includes which translation she matched most closely and a lesson on how to deal with the structure at hand. Comparisons between the student translation and the references look at strict similarity and are heavily influenced by word selection rather than structure.

The Translator Choice Program (McCarthy, 2006) focuses on French-English translation for native English speakers. It presents passages in the L2 (French) and asks students to look at five candidate English translations written by students in previous years. Students either pick the best translation or rank them, and are scored in how similar their judgment is to that of their instructor. This system does not attempt, therefore, to handle novel translations performed by the student.

4 A Corpus of Student-Written Translations

In Spring 2012, we solicited participation from students of a Spanish-English translation course. In this course, students are asked to translate a sequence of articles in both Spanish and English, typically alternating the source language. The articles address varied topics from financial advice to current news. Thirteen students (both native English speakers and native Spanish speakers) opted to have their semester's work collected as part of our study. Reference translations were provided for the entire corpus by the instructor of the course.

For our initial study, we have focused on only the Spanish-to-English translations, as many aspects of the metric we used focus on comparing an English hypothesis sentence against an English reference sentence. This yielded a total of 2,982 sentences. They are described in Table 1.

Table 1: Our Student-Written Translation Corpus.

Number of Subjects	13
Native English Speakers	3
Native Spanish Speakers	10
Number of Articles Translated	11
Average Number of Sentences per Article	28
Total Translated Sentences	2982

5 Comparing Human Judgments to TERp

Before analyzing the translations with the MT metric, we post-processed the corpus to create an alignment between student translations, source sentences, and the instructor reference. One of the challenges we faced in this step is that these students, unlike an MT system, are actively encouraged to recognize the stylistic differences between English and Spanish native writing in terms of sentence brevity. The students therefore sometimes create translations that do not always perfectly match sentence boundaries of the source text; in some cases a single Spanish sentence has been split into multiple English sentences (following a general principle that English native speakers typically use more concise utterances), but sometimes also the opposite occurs, where two source sentences are combined into one translated sentence. While most translations (more than 99%) did obey source sentence boundaries, for alignment purposes whenever a sentence was split both target sentences were concatenated into a single string (including the end-of-sentence punctuation, which is ignored by TERp)[1] for comparison against the reference. Where the student had merged two sentences, the clauses were separated at an appropriate boundary and treated as separate utterances. The instructor-provided references obeyed a 1:1 correspondence between source and target sentences.

Our entire corpus has been graded using the TERp-A variant, with unchanged parameters[2]. The TERp system scores sentences on an interval of [0,100], where a lower score indicates closer agreement to the reference translation, and 100 indicates no agreement; for the ease of our human grader, we normalized the TERp scores to invert the scale and better match a human-intuitive scale of 100 for excellence and 0 for no agreement.

Figure 2 illustrates for those subjects submitting more than three assignments to the study the longitudinal progress of the average TERp score (inverted) across the sentences in each assignment given over

[1]The insertion of a connector, such as 'and,' to form a unified sentence could be penalized by TERp, so it was avoided; the alternative to avoid penalty would be to include whatever connector the original author used, but this would not be available during automated analysis later.

[2]As will be discussed in Section 6, a future goal is to tune the parameters for performance on this data.

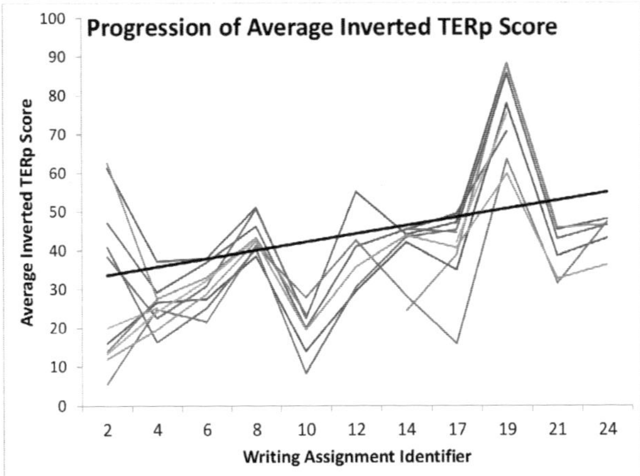

Figure 2: TERp scores across development.

the term. Although there were clearly a couple of assignments that were very challenging to all of the students, the trend line shown indicates that the scores were rising over the course of the semester.

We have also collected instructor-assigned scores on a portion of our corpus in order to compare them against these TERp scores. An example of the rubric used by the instructor as part of her regular grading practices in the course is shown in Table 2. Each of these categories receive a score from 0-10 with 10 being *excellent*, 9 *good*, 8 *satisfactory*, and 0-7 *deficient*.

Table 2: Instructor rubric for assigning sentence grades.

Conveys original meaning	55%
Written in natural language	20%
Uses appropriate vocabulary	10%
Written in accurate language	15%

Our preliminary study has yielded some interesting results. The Pearson correlation between the two sets of scores is r=0.232236, which on a [-1,1] interval indicates weak positive correlation. But if TERp does not have significant agreement with the students' instructor, what is the source of the disagreement? One illustration of this disagreement is the distribution of the grades; Figure 3 shows that the instructor's grades are heavily slanted toward the high end of the scale, with 42% of the sentences scored receiving a grade of 90 or higher; TERp, by contrast, gave very few sentences higher normalized accuracy scores. This is most likely due to the instructor's heavy emphasis placed on communicative rather than syntactic accuracy, as shown in the rubric. We are in the process of rescoring the corpus with a revised rubric that places stronger emphasis on syntactic accuracy.

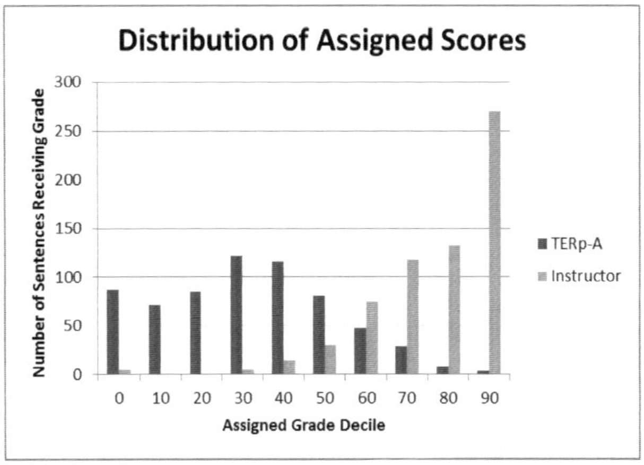

Figure 3: TERp score distribution compared against the human expert.

While TERp has already been evaluated in terms of its correlation to human judgment, this has not been done before with learner-written sentences[3]. We also performed an analysis of a randomized sample of individual sentences with a particular focus on the four edits designed to accommodate divergence but equivalence (or near equivalence): phrase equivalency, stemming, synonymy, and shifts. Our pilot study results indicate that TERp's identified edits have very high precision: 100% for the stemmer, which is to be expected, but also 92% for appropriate shifts, 89% for synonymy, and 83% for phrase equivalency. In recall, the edits performed less well; for example, synonymy achieved a recall of only 65%. This is possibly a limitation of the synset resource.

6 Conclusion and Future Work

We have seen that TERp's identification of the source and nature of divergences between a student

[3]The word *learner* here refers to the fact that the writer is a student of translation, not to whether he or she is writing in an L2.

translation and a teacher's reference translation is reliable; it correctly identifies the nature of the divergence from the reference in a high percentage of cases. This can provide a tutoring environment with sufficient information to address the translation's problems in feedback to the student, and indicates that holistic scores will be much more correlated with human scores that place equal emphasis on syntactic quality. A future version of the King Alfred system will use these error identifications to drive its feedback.

Once the rescoring of the corpus with an emphasis on syntactic accuracy is complete, further work will include tuning the TERp parameters for higher performance on the student corpus, with the aim of greatly improving the correlation of the scores.

We are also looking at post-processing TERp's scores so that certain divergences are not penalized. There is a *cost* associated with the edits that represent mismatches between the reference and hypothesis texts. While the idea of flexible phrase order, and the equality of synonym choice or phrase choice is captured by the metric, the application of such edits worsens the grade of the translation. We believe that stemming and substitution, deletion, or insertion should be penalized, but that synonymy, phrase matches, and shifts should be *free of charge*; those costs will therefore be added back into the final score.

As part of our larger investigation, we will continue to evaluate the applicability of machine translation metrics in general to the learner translation problem. The Mult-Eval suite of metrics (Clark et al., 2011) is a short term target, and iBLEU (Madnani, 2011) may provide useful data for a pedagogical context.

With a recent addition of 14 more subjects, we would also like to do an investigation of whether the performance of an MT metric is affected by whether the novice translator is translating L1→L2, or L2→L1. English native speakers are a minority in our subject pool, but with doubling the size of our corpus, we may be able to explore this more reliably.

One of our other interests going forward is to accommodate the distinct errors made by a very novice human translator. One such error is a tendency to fall prey to false cognates or *faux amis*–false friends, words that look similar (like Spanish *embarazada* and English *embarrassed*) that have significantly different meanings (embarazada, for example, meaning "pregnant"). We have a working hypothesis that student translators are often misled by these similar-looking words. We are currently working to automatically extract potential *faux amis* from parallel Spanish/English dictionaries with the hope of augmenting TERp's ability to align parallel elements between the student and reference translation. We are leveraging the spellcheck algorithm *Hunspell* to identify the similarly-spelled words.

Finally, it is our intention to do a comparative study between evaluating learner translations from modern languages and learner translations from ancient languages such as Anglo-Saxon. One challenge that may arise is that many ancient languages such as Anglo-Saxon are morphologically rich and therefore not strict word order languages; the source text will be fluid with its own order and this may introduce more diversity than in a modern language translation even among novice translators.

Acknowledgments

We wish to sincerely thank the students who have volunteered to share their semester's work with us for the purpose of this study. We would also like to thank the reviewers for their helpful comments and additional references.

References

Abhaya Agarwal and Alon Lavie. 2008. METEOR, M-BLEU and M-TER: Evaluation metrics for high-correlation with human rankings of machine translation output. In *Proceedings of the Third Workshop on Statistical Machine Translation*, pages 115–118, Columbus, Ohio, June. ACL.

Jonathan H. Clark, Chris Dyer, Alon Lavie, and Noah A. Smith. 2011. Better hypothesis testing for statistical machine translation: Controlling for optimizer instability. In *Proceedings of the 49th Annual Meeting of the Association for Computational Linguistics: Human Language Technologies (ACL-HLT)*, pages 176–181. ACL.

Christiane Fellbaum, editor. 1998. *WordNet: An Electronic Lexical Database*. MIT Press.

Eduard Hovy, Margaret Kine, and Andrei Popescu-Belis. 2002. Principles of context-based machine translation evaluation. *Machine Translation*, 17:43–75.

Hunspell: open source spell checking, stemming, morphological analysis and generation under GPL, LGPL or MPL licenses. Website. http://hunspell.sourceforge.net/ Accessed February 2013.

Nitin Madnani. 2011. iBLEU: Interactively debugging and scoring statistical machine translation systems. In *Proceedings of the 2011 IEEE Fifth International Conference on Semantic Computing*, ICSC '11, pages 213–214, Washington, DC, USA. IEEE Computer Society.

Brian McCarthy. 2006. Tutoring translation skills: Reflections on a cmoputer-managed teaching-learning-research triangle. *CALL-EJ Online*, 7(2), January.

Lisa N. Michaud. 2008. King Alfred: A translation environment for learners of anglo-saxon english. In *Proceedings of the 3rd Workshop on Innovative Use of NLP for Building Educational Applications, an ACL-HLT '08 Workshop*, pages 19–26, Columbus, Ohio, June. ACL.

Peter Newmark. 1988. *A Textbook of Translation*. Prentice Hall International, New York.

Kishore Papineni, Salim Roukos, Todd Ward, and Wei-Jing Zhu. 2002. BLEU: a method for automatic evaluation of machine translation. In *Proceedings of the 40th Annual Meeting of the Association for Computational Linguistics*, pages 311–318, Philadelphia, PA, July 6-12. ACL.

Princeton University. 2010. WordNet. Website. http://wordnet.princeton.edu Accessed July 2011.

Chi-Chiang Shei and Helen Pain. 2002. Computer-assisted teaching of translation methods. *Literary & Linguistic Computing*, 17(3):323–343.

Matthew Snover, Nitin Madnani, Bonnie J. Dorr, and Richard Schwartz. 2009. Fluency, adequacy, or HTER? exploring different judgments with a tunable MT metric. In *Proceedings of the EACL 2009 Fourth Workshop on Statistical Machine Translation*, pages 259–268, Athens, Greece, March 30-31. ACL.

Chao Wang and Stephanie Seneff. 2007. Automatic assessment of student translations for foreign language tutoring. In *Proceedings of Human Language Technologies 2007: The Conference of the North American Chapter of the Association for Computational Linguistics (HLT-NAACL)*, pages 468–475, Rochester, NY, April 22-27. ACL.

Yushi Xu and Stephanie Seneff. 2008. Mandarian learning using speech and language technolgies: A translation game in the travel domain. In *Proceedings of the 6th International Symposium on Chinese Spoken Language Processing (ISCSLP08)*, Kunming, China, December.

Author Index

Association for Computational Linguistics
209 N. Eighth Street
Stroudsburg, Pennsylvania 18360

CURRAN ASSOCIATES INC
proceedings.com

10th Workshop on Asian Language Resources

Held at the 24th International Conference on Computational Linguistics (COLING 2012)

Mumbai, India
9 December 2012

ISBN: 978-1-62748-353-7